3D
Computer
Graphics

PEARSON
Education

We work with leading authors to develop the strongest educational materials in computer science, bringing cutting-edge thinking and best learning practice to a global market.

Under a range of well-known imprints, including Addison-Wesley, we craft high quality print and electronic publications which help readers to understand and apply their content whether studying or at work.

To find out about the complete range of our publishing please visit us on the World Wide Web at:

http://www.pearsoned.co.uk

3D Computer Graphics

THIRD EDITION

ALAN WATT

PEARSON

Addison
Wesley

Harlow, England • London • New York • Boston • San Francisco • Toronto • Sydney • Singapore • Hong Kong
Tokyo • Seoul • Taipei • New Delhi • Cape Town • Madrid • Mexico City • Amsterdam • Munich • Paris • Milan

Pearson Education Limited
Edinburgh Gate
Harlow
Essex CM20 2JE
England

and Associated Companies throughout the world

Visit us on the World Wide Web at:
www.pearsoned.co.uk

First published 1989
Second edition 1993
This edition first published 2000

© 1989, 1993 Addison-Wesley Publishing Ltd, Addison-Wesley Publishing Company Inc.
© Pearson Education Limited 2000

ISBN-10: 0-201-39855-9
ISBN-13: 978-0-201-39855-7

British Library Cataloguing-in-Publication Data
A catalogue record for this book can be obtained from the British Library.

Library of Congress Cataloguing-in-Publication Data
Available from the publisher.

Typeset by 42
Printed and bound in The United States of America

10 9 8
07 06 05

Para Dionéa
a garota de Copacabana

Contents

Preface

This is the third edition of a book that deals with the processes involved in converting a mathematical or geometric description of an object – a computer graphics model – into a visualization – a two-dimensional projection – that simulates the appearance of a real object. The analogy of a synthetic camera is often used and this is a good allusion provided we bear in mind certain important limitations that are not usually available in a computer graphics camera (depth of field and motion blur are two examples) and certain computer graphics facilities that do not appear in a camera (near and far clipping planes).

Algorithms in computer graphics mostly function in a three-dimensional domain and the creations in this space are then mapped into a two-dimensional display or image plane at a late stage in the overall process. Traditionally computer graphics has created pictures by starting with a very detailed geometric description, subjecting this to a series of transformations that orient a viewer and objects in three-dimensional space, then imitating reality by making the objects look solid and real – a process known as rendering. In the early 1980s there was a coming together of research – carried out in the 1970s into reflection models, hidden surface removal and the like – that resulted in the emergence of a *de facto* approach to image synthesis of solid objects. But now this is proving insufficient for the new demands of moving computer imagery and virtual reality and much research is being carried out into how to model complex objects, where the nature and shape of the object changes dynamically and into capturing the richness of the world without having to explicitly model every detail. Such efforts are resulting in diverse synthesis methods and modelling methods but at the moment there has been no emergence of new image generation techniques that rival the pseudo-standard way of modelling and rendering solid objects – a method that has been established since the mid-1970s.

So where did it all begin? Most of the development in computer graphics as we know it today was motivated by hardware evolution and the availability of new devices. Software rapidly developed to use the image producing hardware. In this respect the most important development is the so-called raster display, a device that proliferated in the mass market shortly after the development of the PC. In this device the complete image is stored in a memory variously called a

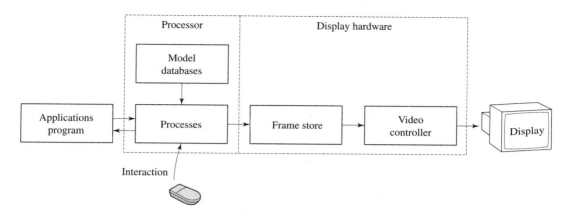

Figure P.1
The main elements of a graphics system.

frame store, a screen buffer or a refresh memory. This information – the discretized computer image – is continually converted by a video controller into a set of horizontal scan lines (a raster) which is then fed to a TV-type monitor. The image is generated by an application program which usually accesses a model or geometric description of an object or objects. The main elements in such a system are shown in Figure P.1. The display hardware to the right of the dotted line can be separate to the processor, but nowadays is usually integrated as in the case of an enhanced PC or a graphics workstation. The raster graphics device overshadows all other hardware developments in the sense that it made possible the display of shaded three-dimensional objects – the single most important theoretical development. The interaction of three-dimensional objects with a light source could be calculated and the effect projected into two-dimensional space and displayed by the device. Such shaded imagery is the foundation of modern computer graphics.

The two early landmark achievements that made shaded imagery possible are the algorithms developed by Gouraud in 1971 and Phong in 1975 enabling easy and fast calculation of the intensities of pixels when shading an object. The Phong technique is still in mainstream use and is undoubtedly responsible for most of the shaded images in computer graphics.

A brief history of shaded imagery

When we look at computer graphics from the viewpoint of its practitioners, we see that since the mid-1970s the developmental motivation has been photorealism or the pursuit of techniques that make a graphics image of an object or scene indistinguishable from a TV image or photograph. A more recent strand of the application of these techniques is to display information in, for example, medicine, science and engineering.

The foundation of photo-realism is the calculation of light–object interaction and this splits neatly into two fields – the development of local reflection models and the development of global models. Local or direct reflection models only consider the interaction of an object with a light source as if the object and light were floating in dark space. That is, only the first reflection of light from the object is considered. Global reflection models consider how light reflects from one object and travels onto another. In other words the light impinging on a point on the surface can come either from a light source (direct light) or indirect light that has first hit another object. Global interaction is for the most part an unsolved problem, although two partial solutions, ray tracing and radiosity, are now widely implemented.

Computer graphics research has gone the way of much modern scientific research – early major advances are created and consolidated into a practical technology. Later significant advances seem to be more difficult to achieve. We can say that most images are produced using the Phong local reflection model (first reported in 1975), fewer using ray tracing (first popularized in 1980) and fewer still using radiosity (first reported in 1984). Although there is still much research being carried out in light–scene interaction methodologies much of the current research in computer graphics is concerned more with applications, for example, with such general applications as animation, visualization and virtual reality. In the most important computer graphics publication (the annual SIGGRAPH conference proceedings) there was in 1985 a total of 22 papers concerned with the production techniques of images (rendering, modelling and hardware) compared with 13 on what could loosely be called applications. A decade later in 1995 there were 37 papers on applications and 19 on image production techniques.

Modelling surface reflection with local interaction

Two early advances which went hand-in-hand were the development of hidden surface removal algorithms and shaded imagery – simulating the interaction of an object with a light source. Most of the hidden surface removal research was carried out in the 1970s and nowadays, for general-purpose use, the most common algorithm is the Z-buffer – an approach that is very easy to implement and combine with shading or rendering algorithms.

In shaded imagery the major prop is the Phong reflection model. This is an elegant but completely empirical model that usually ends up with an object reflecting more light than it receives. Its parameters are based on the grossest aspects of reflection of light from a surface. Despite this, it is the most widely used model in computer graphics – responsible for the vast majority of created images. Why is this so? Probably because users find it adequate and it is easy to implement.

Theoretically based reflection models attempt to model reflection more accurately and their parameters have physical meaning – that is they can be measured for a real surface. For example, light reflects differently from an isotropic surface, such as plastic, compared to its behaviour with a non-isotropic surface such as brushed aluminium and such an effect can be imitated by explicitly modelling the surface characteristics. Such models attempt to imitate the behaviour of light at a 'milliscale' level (where the roughness or surface geometry is still much greater than the wavelength of light). Their purpose is to imitate the material signature – why different materials in reality look different. Alternatively, parameters of a model can be measured on a real surface and used in a simulation. The work into more elaborate or theoretical local reflection models does not seem to have gained any widespread acceptance as far as its implementation in rendering systems is concerned. This may be due to the fact that users do not perceive that the extra processing costs are worth the somewhat marginal improvement in the appearance of the shaded object.

All these models, while attending to the accurate modelling of light from a surface, are local models which means that they only consider the interaction of light with the object as if the object was floating in free space. No object–object interaction is considered and one of the main problems that immediately arises is that shadows – a phenomenon due to global interaction – are not incorporated into the model and have to be calculated by a separate 'add-on' algorithm.

The development of the Phong reflection model spawned research into add-on shadow algorithms and texture mapping, both of which enhanced the appearance of the shaded object and tempered the otherwise 'floating in free space' plastic look of the basic Phong model.

Modelling global interaction

The 1980s saw the development of two significant global models – light reflection models that attempt to evaluate the interaction between objects. Global interaction gives rise to such phenomena as the determination of the intensity of light within a shadow area, the reflection of objects in each other (specular interaction) and a subtle effect known as colour bleeding where the colour from a diffuse surface is transported to another nearby surface (diffuse interaction). The light intensity within a shadow area can only be determined from global interaction. An area in shadow, by definition, cannot receive light directly from a light source but only indirectly from light reflecting from another object. When you see shiny objects in a scene you expect to see in them reflections of other objects. A very shiny surface, such as chromium plate, behaves almost as a mirror taking all its surface detail from its surroundings and distorting this geometrically according to surface curvature.

The successful global models are ray tracing and radiosity. However, in their basic implementation both models only cater for one aspect of global illumination. Ray tracing attends to perfect specular reflection – very shiny objects reflecting in each other, and radiosity models diffuse interaction which is light reflecting off matte surfaces to illuminate other surfaces. Diffuse interaction is common in man-made interiors which tend to have carpets on the floor and matte finishes on the walls. Areas in a room that cannot see the light source are illuminated by diffuse interaction. Mutually exclusive in the phenomena they model, images created by both methods tend to have identifying 'signatures'. Ray-traced images are notable for perfect recursive reflections and super sharp refraction. Radiosity images are usually of softly-lit interiors and do not contain specular or shiny objects.

Computer graphics is not an exact science. Much research in light–surface interaction in computer graphics proceeds by taking existing physical models and simulating then with a computer graphics algorithm. This may involve much simplification in the original mathematical model so that it can be implemented as a computer graphics algorithm. Ray tracing and radiosity are classic examples of this tendency. Simplifications, which may appear gross to a mathematician, are made by computer graphicists for practical reasons. The reason this process 'works' is that when we look at a synthesized scene we do not generally perceive the simplifications in the mathematics unless they result in visible degeneracies known as aliases. However, most people can easily distinguish a computer graphics image from a photograph. Thus computer graphics have a 'realism' of their own that is a function of the model, and the nearness of the computer graphics image to a photograph of a real scene varies widely according to the method. Photo-realism in computer graphics means the image *looks* real not that it approaches, on a pixel by pixel basis, a photograph. This subjective judgement of computer graphics images somewhat devalues the widely used adjective 'photo-realistic', but there you are. With one or two exceptions very little work has been done on comparing a human's perception of a computer graphics image with, say, a TV image of the equivalent real scene.

Acknowledgements

The author would like to thank the following:

- Lightwork Design Ltd (Sheffield, UK) and Dave Cauldron for providing the facilities to produce the front cover image (model of the Tate Gallery, St Ives, UK) and the renderer, RadioRay.

- Daniel Teece for the images on the back cover which he produced as part of his PhD thesis and which comprise three-dimensional paint strokes interactively applied to a standard polygon model.

- Lee Cooper for producing Figures 6.12, 7.8, 8.7, 8.10, 10.4, 18.1, 18.3, 18.5, 18.6, 18.7, 18.8, 18.9, 18.10, 18.11, 18.12, 18.13, 18.14, 18.16, 18.17 and 18.19 together with the majority of images on the CD-ROM. These were produced using Lightworks Application Development System kindly supplied by Lightwork Design Ltd.

- Mark Puller for Figure 13.1.

- Steve Maddock for Figures 1.5, 4.9, 8.8, 8.26.

- Agata Opalach for Figure 2.20.

- Klaus de Geuss for Figures 13.10 and 13.11.

- Guy Brown for Figure 16.19.

- Fabio Policarpo for Figure 8.14.

- IMDM University, Hamburg, for Figure 13.3.

In addition the author would like to thank Keith Mansfield, the production staff at Addison-Wesley, Robert Chaundry of Bookstyle for his care with the manuscript and Dionea Watt for the cover design.

The publishers are grateful to the following for permission to reproduce copyright material:

Figure 2.1 reproduced with the permission of Viewpoint Digital, Inc; Figure 2.4 from *Tutorial: Computer Graphics*, Ze (Beatty and Booth, 1982), © 1982 IEEE, The Institute of Electrical and Electronics Engineers, Inc., New York; Figures 2.7 and 2.8 from *Generative Modelling for Computer Graphics and CAD* (Snyder, 1992), Academic

Press, London; Figure 2.20 reproduced with the permission of Agata Opalach; Figure 13.3 from *VOXEL-MAN, Part 1: Brain and Skull*, CD-ROM for UNIX workstations and LINUX PCs, Version 1.1 © Karl-Heinz Höhne and Springer-Verlag GmbH & Co. KG 1996, reproduced with kind permission; Figure 16.14 reproduced with the permission of Steven Seitz; Figure 17.28 from *ACM Transactions on Graphics*, 15:3, July 1996 (Hubbard, 1996), ACM Publications, New York.

Whilst every effort has been made to trace the owners of copyright material, in a few cases this has proved impossible and we take this opportunity to offer our apologies to any copyright holders whose rights we may have unwittingly infringed.

Trademark notice

Apple™ and QuickTime™ are trademarks of Apple Computer, Inc.
Luxo™ is a trademark of Jac Jacobson Industries.
Kodak™ is a trademark of Eastman Kodak Company.
RenderMan™ is a trademark of Pixar Corporation.
VAX™ is a trademark of Digital Equipment Corporation.
3D Dataset™ is a trademark of Viewpoint Digital, Inc.

1 Mathematical fundamentals of computer graphics

1.1 Manipulating three-dimensional structures

1.2 Structure-deforming transformations

1.3 Vectors and computer graphics

1.4 Rays and computer graphics

1.5 Interpolating properties in the image plane

1.1 Manipulating three-dimensional structures

Transformations are important tools in generating three-dimensional scenes. They are used to move objects around in an environment, and also to construct a two-dimensional view of the environment for a display surface. This chapter deals with basic three-dimensional transformations, and introduces some useful shape-changing transformations and basic three-dimensional geometry that we will be using later in the text.

In computer graphics the most popular method for representing an object is the polygon mesh model. This representation is fully described in Chapter 2. We do this by representing the surface of an object as a set of connected planar polygons and each polygon is a list of (connected) points. This form of representation is either exact or an approximation depending on the nature of the object. A cube, for example, can be represented exactly by six squares. A cylinder, on the other hand can only be approximated by polygons; say six rectangles for the curved surface and two hexagons for the end faces. The number of polygons used in the approximation determines how accurately the object is represented and this has repercussions in modelling cost, storage and rendering cost and quality. The popularity of the polygon mesh modelling technique in computer graphics is undoubtedly due to its inherent simplicity and the development of inexpensive shading algorithms that work with such models.

A polygon mesh model consists of a structure of vertices, each vertex being a three-dimensional point in so-called world coordinate space. Later we will be concerned with how vertices are connected to form polygons and how polygons are structured into complete objects. But to start with we shall consider objects just as a set of three-dimensional vertices and look at how these are transformed in three-dimensional space using linear transformations.

1.1.1

Three-dimensional geometry in computer graphics – affine transformations

In this section we look at three-dimensional affine transformations. These are the transformations that effect rotation, scaling, shear and translation. Affine transformations can be represented by a matrix, and a set of affine transformations can be combined into a single overall affine transformation. Technically we say that an affine transformation is made up of any combination of linear transformations (rotation, scaling and shear) followed by translation.

Objects are defined in a world coordinate system which is conventionally a right-handed system. A right-handed and left-handed three-dimensional coordinate system is shown in Figure 1.1. Right-handed systems are the standard mathematical convention, although left-handed systems have, and still are, used in the special context of viewing systems in computer graphics. The difference between the two systems is the sense of the z axis as shown in the figure. Rotating your fingers around the z axis, from the positive x axis to the positive y axis, gives a different z direction for your thumb depending on which system is used.

It is sometimes convenient to define objects in their own local coordinate system. There are three reasons for this. When a three-dimensional object is modelled it is useful to build up the vertices with respect to some reference point in the object. In fact a complex object may have a number of local coordinate systems, one for each sub-part. It may be that the same object is to appear many times in a scene and a definition with a local origin is the only sensible way to

Figure 1.1
(a) Right-handed and
(b) left-handed coordinate
systems.

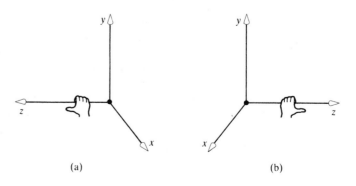

(a)   (b)

set this up. Instancing an object by applying a mix of translations, rotation and scaling transformations can then be seen as transforming the local coordinate system of each object to the world coordinate system. Finally when an object is to be rotated, it is easier if the rotation is defined with respect to a local reference point such as an axis of symmetry.

A set of vertices or three-dimensional points belonging to an object can be transformed into another set of points by a linear transformation. Both sets of points remain in the same coordinate system. Matrix notation is used in computer graphics to describe the transformations and the convention in computer graphics is to have the point or vector as a column matrix, preceded by the transformation matrix T.

Using matrix notation, a point V is transformed under translation, scaling and rotation as:

$$V' = V + D$$
$$V' = S \ V$$
$$V' = R \ V$$

where D is a translation vector and S and R are scaling and rotation matrices.

These three operations are the most commonly used transformations in computer graphics. In animation a rigid body can undergo only rotation and translation, and scaling is used in object modelling. To enable the above transformations to be treated in the same way and combined, we use a system called homogeneous coordinates which increase the dimensionality of the space. The practical reason for this in computer graphics is to enable us to include translation as matrix multiplication (rather than addition) and thus have a unified scheme for linear transformations. In a homogeneous system a vertex:

$$V(x, y, z)$$

is represented as

$$V(w{\cdot}X, w{\cdot}Y, w{\cdot}Z, w)$$

for any scale factor $w \neq 0$. The three-dimensional Cartesian coordinate representation is then:

$$x = X/w$$
$$y = Y/w$$
$$z = Z/w$$

If we consider w to have the value 1 then the matrix representation of a point is:

$$\begin{bmatrix} x \\ y \\ z \\ 1 \end{bmatrix}$$

Translation can now be treated as matrix multiplication, like the other two transformations and becomes:

$$V' = T\ V$$

$$\begin{bmatrix} x' \\ y' \\ z' \\ 1 \end{bmatrix} = \begin{bmatrix} 1 & 0 & 0 & T_x \\ 0 & 1 & 0 & T_y \\ 0 & 0 & 1 & T_z \\ 0 & 0 & 0 & 1 \end{bmatrix} \begin{bmatrix} x \\ y \\ z \\ 1 \end{bmatrix}$$

This specification implies that the object is translated in three dimensions by applying a displacement T_x, T_y and T_z to each vertex that defines the object. The matrix notation is a convenient and elegant way of writing the transformation as a set of three equations:

$$x' = x + T_x$$
$$y' = y + T_y$$
$$z' = z + T_z$$

The set of transformations is completed by scaling and rotation. First scaling:

$$V' = S\ V$$

$$S = \begin{bmatrix} S_x & 0 & 0 & 0 \\ 0 & S_y & 0 & 0 \\ 0 & 0 & S_z & 0 \\ 0 & 0 & 0 & 1 \end{bmatrix}$$

Here S_x, S_y and S_z are scaling factors. For uniform scaling $S_x = S_y = S_z$, otherwise scaling occurs along these axes for which the scaling factor is non-unity. Again the process can be expressed less succinctly by a set of three equations:

$$x' = x \cdot S_x$$
$$y' = y \cdot S_y$$
$$z' = z \cdot S_z$$

applied to every vertex in the object.

To rotate an object in three-dimensional space we need to specify an axis of rotation. This can have any spatial orientation in three-dimensional space, but it is easiest to consider rotations that are parallel to one of the coordinate axes. The transformation matrices for anti-clockwise (looking along each axis towards the origin) rotation about the x, y and z axes respectively are:

$$R_x = \begin{bmatrix} 1 & 0 & 0 & 0 \\ 0 & \cos\theta & -\sin\theta & 0 \\ 0 & \sin\theta & \cos\theta & 0 \\ 0 & 0 & 0 & 1 \end{bmatrix}$$

$$R_y = \begin{bmatrix} \cos\theta & 0 & \sin\theta & 0 \\ 0 & 1 & 0 & 0 \\ -\sin\theta & 0 & \cos\theta & 0 \\ 0 & 0 & 0 & 1 \end{bmatrix}$$

$$R_z = \begin{bmatrix} \cos\theta & -\sin\theta & 0 & 0 \\ \sin\theta & \cos\theta & 0 & 0 \\ 0 & 0 & 1 & 0 \\ 0 & 0 & 0 & 1 \end{bmatrix}$$

The z axis matrix specification is equivalent to the following set of three equations:

$$x' = x\cos\theta - y\sin\theta$$

$$y' = x\sin\theta + y\cos\theta$$

$$z' = z$$

Figure 1.2 shows examples of these transformations.

The inverse of these transformations is often required. T^{-1} is obtained by negating T_x, T_y and T_z. Replacing S_x, S_y and S_z by their reciprocals gives S^{-1} and negating the angle of rotation gives R^{-1}.

Any set of rotations, scaling and translations can be multiplied or concatenated together to give a net transformation matrix. For example if:

$$\begin{bmatrix} x' \\ y' \\ z' \\ 1 \end{bmatrix} = M_1 \begin{bmatrix} x \\ y \\ z \\ 1 \end{bmatrix}$$

and

$$\begin{bmatrix} x'' \\ y'' \\ z'' \\ 1 \end{bmatrix} = M_2 \begin{bmatrix} x' \\ y' \\ z' \\ 1 \end{bmatrix}$$

then the transformation matrices can be concatenated:

$$M_3 = M_2\, M_1$$

and

$$\begin{bmatrix} x'' \\ y'' \\ z'' \\ 1 \end{bmatrix} = M_3 \begin{bmatrix} x \\ y \\ z \\ 1 \end{bmatrix}$$

Note the order: in the product $M_2\, M_1$ the first transformation to be applied is M_1. Although translations are commutative, rotations are not and

$$R_1\, R_2 \neq R_2\, R_1$$

This is demonstrated in Figure 1.2(e) and 1.2(f).

(a) Identity

$$\begin{bmatrix} 1 & 0 & 0 & 0 \\ 0 & 1 & 0 & 0 \\ 0 & 0 & 1 & 0 \\ 0 & 0 & 0 & 1 \end{bmatrix}$$

(b) Z-axis rotation

$$\begin{bmatrix} 0.866 & 0.5 & 0 & 0 \\ -0.5 & 0.866 & 0 & 0 \\ 0 & 0 & 1 & 0 \\ 0 & 0 & 0 & 1 \end{bmatrix}$$

(c) X-scale

$$\begin{bmatrix} 2 & 0 & 0 & 0 \\ 0 & 1 & 0 & 0 \\ 0 & 0 & 1 & 0 \\ 0 & 0 & 0 & 1 \end{bmatrix}$$

(d) Translation

$$\begin{bmatrix} 1 & 0 & 0 & 2 \\ 0 & 1 & 0 & 2 \\ 0 & 0 & 1 & 0 \\ 0 & 0 & 0 & 1 \end{bmatrix}$$

(e) Rotation followed by translation

$$\begin{bmatrix} 1 & 0 & 0 & 2 \\ 0 & 1 & 0 & 2 \\ 0 & 0 & 1 & 0 \\ 0 & 0 & 0 & 1 \end{bmatrix} \begin{bmatrix} 0.866 & 0.5 & 0 & 0 \\ -0.5 & 0.866 & 0 & 0 \\ 0 & 0 & 1 & 0 \\ 0 & 0 & 0 & 1 \end{bmatrix} = \begin{bmatrix} 0.866 & 0.5 & 0 & 2 \\ -0.5 & 0.866 & 0 & 2 \\ 0 & 0 & 1 & 0 \\ 0 & 0 & 0 & 1 \end{bmatrix}$$

(f) Translation followed by rotation

$$\begin{bmatrix} 0.866 & 0.5 & 0 & 0 \\ -0.5 & 0.866 & 0 & 0 \\ 0 & 0 & 1 & 0 \\ 0 & 0 & 0 & 1 \end{bmatrix} \begin{bmatrix} 1 & 0 & 0 & 2 \\ 0 & 1 & 0 & 2 \\ 0 & 0 & 1 & 0 \\ 0 & 0 & 0 & 1 \end{bmatrix} = \begin{bmatrix} 0.866 & 0.5 & 0 & 2.732 \\ -0.5 & 0.866 & 0 & 0.732 \\ 0 & 0 & 1 & 0 \\ 0 & 0 & 0 & 1 \end{bmatrix}$$

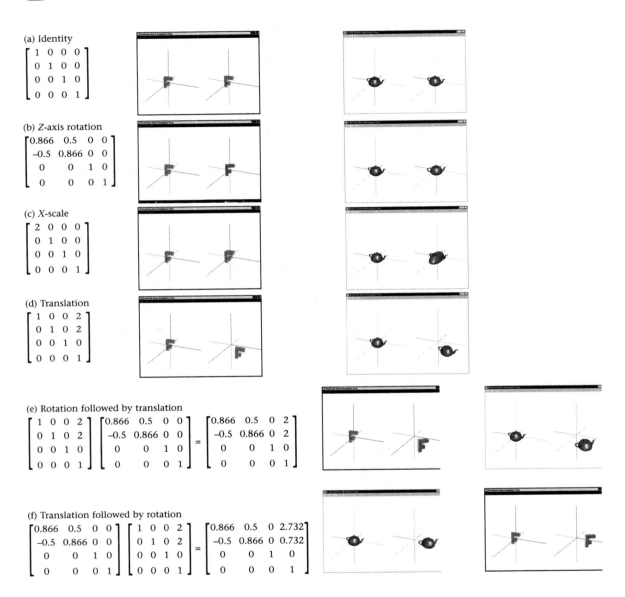

Figure 1.2
Examples of linear
transformations.

A general transformation matrix will be of the form:

$$\begin{bmatrix} A_{11} & A_{12} & A_{13} & T_x \\ A_{21} & A_{22} & A_{23} & T_y \\ A_{31} & A_{32} & A_{33} & T_z \\ 0 & 0 & 0 & 1 \end{bmatrix}$$

The 3×3 upper-left sub-matrix A is the net rotation and scaling while T gives the net translation.

The ability to concatenate transformations to form a net transformation matrix is useful because it gives a single matrix specification for any linear transformation. For example, consider rotating a body about a line parallel to the z axis which passes through the point $(T_x, T_y, 0)$ and also passes through one of the vertices of the object. Here we are implying that the object is not at the origin and we wish to apply rotation about a reference point in the object itself. In other words we want to rotate the object with respect to its own coordinate system known as a local coordinate system (see also Section 1.1.2). We cannot simply apply a rotation matrix because this is defined with respect to the origin and an object not positioned at the origin would rotate and translate – not usually the desired effect. Instead we have to derive a net transformation matrix as follows:

(1) Translate the object to the origin,

(2) Apply the desired rotation, and,

(3) Translate the object back to its original position.

The net transformation matrix is:

$$T_2RT_1 = \begin{bmatrix} 1 & 0 & 0 & -T_x \\ 0 & 1 & 0 & -T_y \\ 0 & 0 & 1 & 0 \\ 0 & 0 & 0 & 1 \end{bmatrix} \begin{bmatrix} \cos\theta & -\sin\theta & 0 & 0 \\ \sin\theta & \cos\theta & 0 & 0 \\ 0 & 0 & 1 & 0 \\ 0 & 0 & 0 & 1 \end{bmatrix} \begin{bmatrix} 1 & 0 & 0 & T_x \\ 0 & 1 & 0 & T_y \\ 0 & 0 & 1 & 0 \\ 0 & 0 & 0 & 1 \end{bmatrix}$$

$$= \begin{bmatrix} \cos\theta & -\sin\theta & 0 & (-T_x\cos\theta + T_y\sin\theta + T_x) \\ \sin\theta & \cos\theta & 0 & (-T_x\sin\theta - T_y\cos\theta + T_y) \\ 0 & 0 & 1 & 0 \\ 0 & 0 & 0 & 1 \end{bmatrix}$$

This process is shown in Figure 1.3 where θ is 30°.

Figure 1.3
Two stages in building up the rotation of an object about one of its own vertices. The rotation is about an axis parallel to the z axis at point $(T_x, T_y, 0)$. A two-dimensional projection (with the z axis coming out of the paper) is shown for clarity. (a) Original object at $(T_x, T_y, 0)$. (b) Translate to the origin. (c) Rotate about the origin. (d) Translate to $p(T_x, T_y, 0)$.

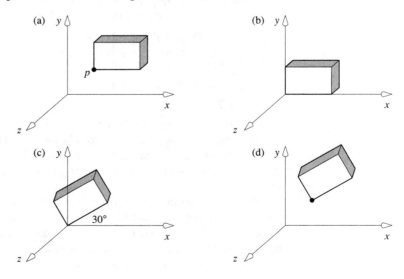

Transformations for changing coordinate systems

Up to now we have discussed transformations that operate on points all of which are expressed relative to one particular coordinate system. This is known as the world coordinate system. In many contexts in computer graphics we need to derive transformations that take points from one coordinate system into another. The commonest context is when we have a number of objects each specified by a set of vertices in a coordinate system embedded in the object itself. This is known as a local coordinate system. Every object will have a convenient local coordinate system; for example, a complex object that is basically cylindrical in shape may have a coordinate axis that coincides with the long axis of the cylinder. If we wish to bring a number of such objects together and position them in a scene then the scene would take the world coordinate system and we would apply translations, rotations and scale transformations to the objects to position them in the scene. Thus we can consider that the transformations operate on the object or equivalently on the local coordinate system of the object. Transformations that emplace an object with a local coordinate system into a position in a world coordinate system are called modelling transformations.

Another important context that involves a change of coordinate system is the transformation from the world coordinate system to the view coordinate system – a viewing transformation. Here we have a new coordinate system – an object if you like – defined with respect to the world coordinate system and we have to transform the vertices in the world coordinate system to this new system.

Consider two coordinate systems with axes parallel, that is the systems which only differ by a translation. If we wish to transform points currently expressed in system 1 into system 2 then we use the inverse of the transformation that takes the origin of system 1 to that of system 2. That is a point $(x, y, z, 1)$ in system 1 transforms to a point $(x', y', z', 1)$ by:

$$\begin{bmatrix} x' \\ y' \\ z' \\ 1 \end{bmatrix} = \begin{bmatrix} 1 & 0 & 0 & -T_x \\ 0 & 1 & 0 & -T_y \\ 0 & 0 & 1 & -T_z \\ 0 & 0 & 0 & 1 \end{bmatrix} \begin{bmatrix} x \\ y \\ z \\ 1 \end{bmatrix}$$

$$= T_{12} = (T_{21})^{-1}$$

which is the transformation that translates the origin of system 1 to that of system 2 (where the point is still expressed relative to system 1). Another way of putting it is to say that the transformation generally required is the inverse of the transformation that takes the old axes to the new axes within the current coordinate system.

This is an important result because we generally find transformations between coordinate systems by considering transformations that operate on origins and axes. In the case of viewing systems a change in coordinate systems involves both translation and rotation and we find the required transformation in this way by considering a combination of rotations and translations.

1.2 Structure-deforming transformations

The above linear transformations either move an object (rotation and translation) or scale the object. Uniform scaling preserves shape. Using different values of S_x, S_y and S_z the object is stretched or squeezed along particular coordinate axes. In this section we introduce a set of transformations that deform the object. These are fully described in Barr (1984) where they are termed global deformations. The particular deformations detailed in this paper are tapering, twisting and bending.

Barr uses a formula definition for the transformations:

$$X = F_x(x)$$
$$Y = F_y(y)$$
$$Z = F_z(z)$$

where (x, y, z) is a vertex in an undeformed solid and (X, Y, Z) is the deformed vertex. Using this notation the scaling transformation above is:

$$X = S_x(x)$$
$$Y = S_y(y)$$
$$Z = S_z(z)$$

Tapering is easily developed from scaling. We choose a tapering axis and differentially scale the other two components setting up a tapering function along this axis. Thus, to taper an object along its Z axis:

$$X = rx$$
$$Y = ry$$
$$Z = z$$

where:

$$r = f(z)$$

is a linear or non-linear tapering profile or function. Thus, the transformation becomes a function of r. That is, we change the transformation depending on where in the space it is applied. In effect we are scaling a scaling tranformation.

Global axial twisting can be developed as a differential rotation just as tapering is a differential scaling. To twist an object about its z axis we apply:

$$X = x \cos\theta - y \sin\theta$$
$$Y = x \sin\theta + y \cos\theta$$
$$Z = z$$

where:

$$\theta = f5(z)$$

and $f'(z)$ specifies the rate of twist per unit length along the z axis.

A global linear bend along an axis is a composite transformation comprising a bent region and a region outside the bent region where the deformation is a rotation and a translation.

Barr defines a bend region along the Y axis as:

$$y_{min} \leq y \leq y_{max}$$

the radius of curvature of the bend is $1/k$ and the centre of the bend is at $y = y_0$. The bending angle is:

$$\theta = k(y' - y_0)$$

where:

$$y' = \begin{cases} y_{min} & y \leq y_{min} \\ y & y_{min} < y < y_{max} \\ y_{max} & y \geq y_{min} \end{cases}$$

The deforming transformation is given by:

$$X = x$$

$$Y = \begin{cases} -\sin\theta(z - \frac{1}{k}) + y_0 & y_{min} \leq y \leq y_{max} \\ -\sin\theta(z - \frac{1}{k}) + y_0 + \cos\theta(y - y_{min}) & y < y_{min} \\ -\sin\theta(z - \frac{1}{k}) + y_0 + \cos\theta(y - y_{max}) & y > y_{max} \end{cases}$$

$$Z = \begin{cases} -\cos\theta(z - \frac{1}{k}) + y_0 & y_{min} \leq y \leq y_{max} \\ -\cos\theta(z - \frac{1}{k}) + \frac{1}{k} + \sin\theta(y - y_{min}) & y < y_{min} \\ -\cos\theta(z - \frac{1}{k}) + \frac{1}{k} + \sin\theta(y - y_{max}) & y > y_{max} \end{cases}$$

Figure 1.4 shows an example of each of these transformations. The deformation on the cube is an intuitive reflection of the effects and the same transformations are applied to the Utah teapot. Figure 1.5 (Colour Plate) shows a rendered version of a polygon mesh object (a corrugated cylinder) that has been twisted and tapered.

Non-constrained, non-linear deformations cannot be applied to polygon meshes in general. One problem is the connectivity constraints between vertices. For example, we cannot twist a cube, represented as six surfaces, without limit and retain a structure suitable for rendering. Another problem is that deformations where vertices move apart have the effect of reducing the polygonal resolution of the original model giving rise to a degradation in silhouette edge aliasing (dealt with in detail in Chapter 4). Thus the polygonal nature of the object model constrains the nature of the deformation and this can only be over-come by subdivision of the original mesh as a function of the 'severity' of the deformation.

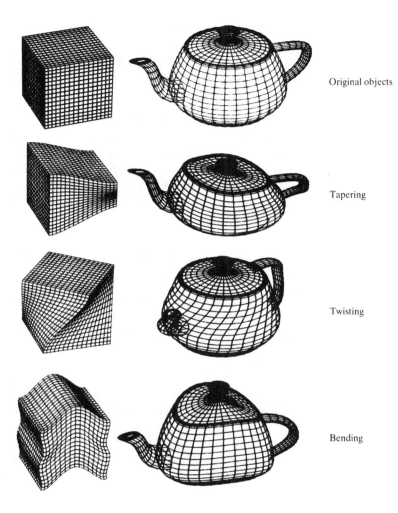

Original objects

Tapering

Twisting

Bending

Figure 1.4
Structure-deforming
transformations.

Vectors and computer graphics

Vectors are used in a variety of contexts in computer graphics. A vector is an entity that possesses magnitude and direction. The common example of a vector is the velocity of a particle moving through space. The velocity possesses both a magnitude and a direction and this distinguishes it from a scalar quantity which only has magnitude. An example of a scalar is the temperature of a point in space. A three-dimensional vector is written as a triple:

$$\boldsymbol{V} = (v_1, \ v_2, \ v_3)$$

where each component v_i is a scalar.

1.3.1 Addition of vectors

Addition of two vectors **V** and **W**, for example, is defined as:

$$X = V + W$$
$$= (x_1, x_2, x_3)$$
$$= (v_1 + w_1, v_2 + w_2, v_3 + w_3)$$

Geometrically this is interpreted as follows. The 'tail' of **W** is placed at the 'head' of **V**, and **X** is the vector formed by joining the tail of **V** to the head of **W**. This is shown in Figure 1.6 for a pair of two-dimensional vectors together with an alternative, but equivalent, interpretation.

1.3.2 Length of vectors

The magnitude or length of a vector is defined as:

$$|V| = (v_1^2 + v_2^2 + v_3^2)^{1/2}$$

and we interpret this geometrically as the distance from its tail to its head.

We normalize a vector to produce a unit vector which is a vector of length equal to one. The normalized version of **V** is:

$$U = \frac{V}{|V|}$$

which is a vector of unit length having the same direction as **U**. We can now refer to **U** as a direction. Note that we can write:

$$V = |V|U$$

which is saying that any vector is given by its magnitude times its direction. Normalization is used frequently in computer graphics because we are interested in calculating and representing the orientation of entities, and comparative orientation requires normalized vectors.

1.3.3 Normal vectors and cross products

In computer graphics considerable processing is carried out using vectors that are normal to a surface. For example, in a polygon mesh model (see Chapter 2) a nor-

Figure 1.6
Two geometric interpretations of the sum of two vectors.

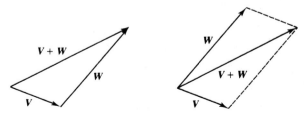

mal vector is used to represent the orientation of a surface when comparing this with the direction of the light. Such a comparison is used in reflection models to compute the intensity of the light reflected from the surface. The smaller the angle between the light vector and the vector that is normal to the surface, the higher is the intensity of the light reflected from the surface (see Chapter 7).

A normal vector to a polygon is calculated from three (non-collinear) vertices of the polygon. Three vertices define two vectors V_1 and V_2 (Figure 1.7) and the normal to the polygon is found by taking the cross product of these:

$$N_p = V_1 \times V_2$$

The cross product of two vectors V and W is a vector X and is defined as:

$$X = V \times W$$
$$= (v_2 w_3 - v_3 w_2)i + (v_3 w_1 - v_1 w_3)j + (v_1 w_2 - v_2 w_1)k$$

where i, j and k are the standard unit vectors:

$$i = (1, 0, 0)$$
$$j = (0, 1, 0)$$
$$k = (0, 0, 1)$$

that is, vectors oriented along the coordinate axes that define the space in which the vectors are embedded.

Geometrically a cross product, as we have implied, is a vector whose orientation is normal to the plane containing the two vectors forming the cross product. When determining the surface normal of a polygon, the cross product must point outwards with respect to the object. In a right-handed coordinate system the sense of the cross product vector is given by the right-hand rule. If the first two fingers of your right hand point in the direction of V and W then the direction of X is given by your thumb.

If the surface is a bi-cubic parametric surface (see Chapter 3), then the orientation of the normal vector varies continuously over the surface. We compute the normal at any point (u, v) on the surface again by using a cross product. This is done by first calculating tangent vectors in the two parametric directions (we outline the procedure here for the sake of completeness and give full details in Chapter 3). For a surface defined as $Q(u, v)$ we find:

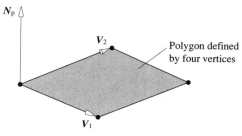

Figure 1.7
Calculating the normal vector to a polygon.

$$\frac{\partial}{\partial u}\,\mathbf{Q}(u,\,v) \quad \text{and} \quad \frac{\partial}{\partial v}\,\mathbf{Q}(u,\,v)$$

We then define:

$$\mathbf{N}_s = \frac{\partial \mathbf{Q}}{\partial u} \times \frac{\partial \mathbf{Q}}{\partial v}$$

This is shown schematically in Figure 1.8.

1.3.4 Normal vectors and dot products

The most common use of a dot product in computer graphics is to provide a measure of the angle between two vectors, where one of the vectors is a normal vector to a surface or group of surfaces. Common applications are shading (the angle between a light direction vector and a surface normal) and visibility testing (the angle between viewing vector and a surface normal).

The dot product of vectors $\mathbf{V}$ and $\mathbf{W}$ is a scalar X which is defined as:

$$X = \mathbf{V}\cdot\mathbf{W}$$
$$= v_1w_1 + v_2w_2 + v_3w_3$$

Figure 1.9(a) shows two vectors. Using the cosine rule we have:

$$|\mathbf{V} - \mathbf{W}|^2 = |\mathbf{V}|^2 + |\mathbf{W}|^2 - 2|\mathbf{V}||\mathbf{W}|\cos\theta$$

where θ is the angle between the vectors. Also it can be shown that:

$$|\mathbf{V} - \mathbf{W}|^2 = |\mathbf{V}|^2 - 2\mathbf{V}\cdot\mathbf{W} + |\mathbf{W}|^2$$

thus:

$$\mathbf{V}\cdot\mathbf{W} = |\mathbf{V}||\mathbf{W}|\cos\theta$$

giving:

$$\cos\theta = \frac{\mathbf{V}\cdot\mathbf{W}}{|\mathbf{V}||\mathbf{W}|}$$

or the angle between two vectors is the dot product of their normalized versions.

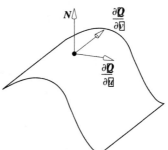

Figure 1.8
Normal **N** to a point on a parametric surface **Q** (u,v)

We can use the dot product to project a vector onto another vector. Consider a unit vector V. If we project any vector W onto V (Figure 1.9(b)) and call the result X, then we have:

$$|X| = |W| \cos \theta$$
$$= |W| \frac{V \cdot W}{|V||W|}$$
$$= V \cdot W \tag{1.1}$$

because V is a unit vector. Thus the dot product of V and W is the length of the projection of W onto V.

A property of the dot product used in computer graphics is its sign. Because of its relationship to $\cos \theta$ the sign of the dot product of V and W (where V and W are of any length) is:

$$V \cdot W > 0 \quad \text{if } \theta < 90°$$
$$V \cdot W = 0 \quad \text{if } \theta = 90°$$
$$V \cdot W < 0 \quad \text{if } \theta > 90°$$

1.3.5 Vectors associated with the normal vector reflection

There are three important vectors that are associated with the surface normal. They are the light direction vector, L, the reflection vector or mirror vector, R, and the viewing vector, V. The light direction vector, L, is a vector whose direction is given by the line from the tail of the surface normal to the light source; which in simple shading contexts is defined as a point on the surface that we are currently considering. This vector is shown in Figure 1.10(a). The reflection vector, R, is given by the direction of the light reflected from the surface due to light incoming along direction L. Sometimes called the mirror direction, geometric optics tells us that the outgoing angle equals the incoming angle as shown in Figure 1.10(b).

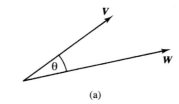

(a)

Figure 1.9
(a) The dot product of the two vectors is related to the cosine of the angle between them:

$$\cos \theta = \frac{V \cdot W}{|V||W|}$$

(b) $|X| = V \cdot W$ is the length of the projection of W onto V.

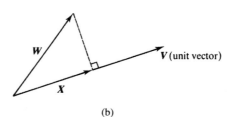

(b)

Figure 1.10
Vectors associated with the
normal vector. (a) **L**, the
light direction vector,
(b) **R**, the reflection vector,
(c) **V**, the view vector, is a
vector of any orientation.

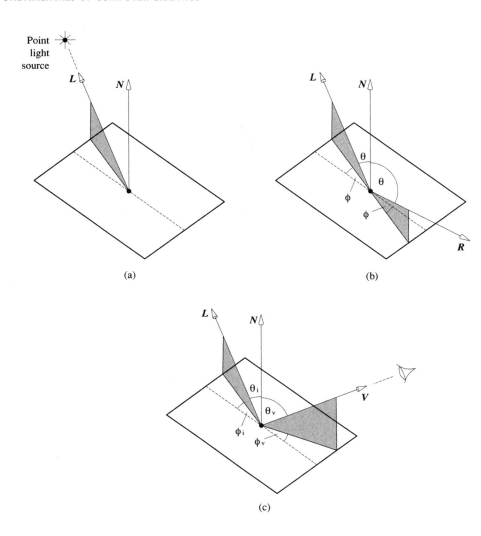

Figure 1.11
Construction of the
reflection vector **R**.

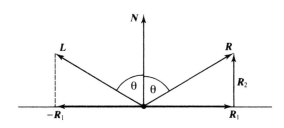

Consider the construction shown in Figure 1.11. This shows:

$$\boldsymbol{R} = \boldsymbol{R}_1 + \boldsymbol{R}_2$$
$$\boldsymbol{R}_1 = -\boldsymbol{L} + \boldsymbol{R}_2$$

Thus:

$$\boldsymbol{R} = 2\boldsymbol{R}_2 - \boldsymbol{L}$$

from Equation 1.1:

$$\boldsymbol{R}_2 = (\boldsymbol{N}{\cdot}\boldsymbol{L})\boldsymbol{N}$$

and

$$\boldsymbol{R} = 2(\boldsymbol{N}{\cdot}\boldsymbol{L})\boldsymbol{N} - \boldsymbol{L} \qquad\qquad (1.2)$$

Figure 1.10(c) shows a view vector $\boldsymbol{V}$. Note that this vector has any arbitrary orientation and we are normally interested in that component of light incoming in direction $\boldsymbol{L}$ that is reflected along $\boldsymbol{V}$. This will depend in general on both the angles ϕ_v and θ_v. We also note that the intensity of outgoing light depends on the incoming angles ϕ_i and θ_i, and this is usually described as a bidirectional dependence because two angles, (ϕ_v, θ_v) and (ϕ_i, θ_i), in three-dimensional space are involved.

1.4 Rays and computer graphics

In computer graphics we are interested in an entity called a ray (mathematically known as a directed line segment) that possesses position, magnitude and direction. We use this mostly to simulate light as an infinitesimally thin beam – a light ray. If we imagine a ray to be a physical line in three space, then its position is the position of the tail of the line, its magnitude the length of the line between its head and tail and its direction the direction of the line. A ray can be specified by two points or by a single point, and a vector. If the end points of the ray are (x_1, y_1, z_1) and (x_2, y_2, z_2) respectively, then the vector is given by:

$$\boldsymbol{V} = (x_2 - x_1, y_2 - y_1, z_2 - z_1)$$

Rays are not only used in ray tracing, but they find uses in volume rendering, rendering constructive solid geometry (CSG) volumes and in calculating form factors in radiosity. We will now look at some of the more important calculations associated with rays.

1.4.1 Ray geometry – intersections

Because ray tracing simulates the path of light through an environment, the most common calculation associated with rays is intersection testing – we see whether a ray has hit an object and if so where. Here we test a ray against all objects in the scene for an intersection. This is potentially a very expensive calculation and the most common technique used to make this more efficient is to enclose objects in the scene in bounding volumes – the most convenient being a sphere – and test first for a ray–sphere intersection. The sphere encloses the object and if the ray does not intersect the sphere it cannot intersect the object. Another common bounding volume is a box.

Sphere and boxes are also used to bound objects for collision detection tests in computer animation (see Chapter 17). Pairs of objects can only collide if their bounding volumes intersect. The motivation here is the same as that for ray tracing – we first cull away pairs that cannot possibly collide before we undertake detailed intersection checking at the individual polygon level. Checking for sphere–sphere intersection is trivial and for boxes – if they are axis aligned – then we only need limit checks in the x, y and z directions.

1.4.2 Intersections – ray–sphere

The intersection between a ray and a sphere is easily calculated. If the end points of the ray are (x_1, y_1, z_1) and (x_2, y_2, z_2) then the first step is to parametrize the ray (Figure 1.12):

$$x = x_1 + (x_2 - x_1)t = x_1 + it$$
$$y = y_1 + (y_2 - y_1)t = y_1 + jt \qquad [1.1]$$
$$z = z_1 + (z_2 - z_1)t = z_1 + kt$$

where:

$$0 \leq t \leq 1$$

A sphere at centre (l, m, n) of radius r is given by:

$$(x - l)^2 + (y - m)^2 + (z - n)^2 = r^2$$

Substituting for x, y and z gives a quadratic equation in t of the form:

$$at^2 + bt + c = 0$$

where:

$$a = i^2 + j^2 + k^2$$
$$b = 2i(x_1 - l) + 2j(y_1 - m) + 2k(z_1 - n)$$
$$c = l^2 + m^2 + n^2 + x_1^2 + y_1^2 + z_1^2 + 2(-lx_1 - my_1 - nz_1) - r^2$$

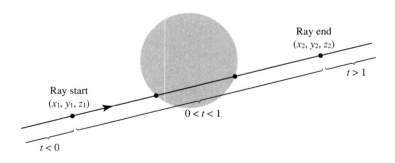

Figure 1.12
Values of parameter t along a ray.

If the determinant of this quadratic is less than 0 then the line does not intersect the sphere. If the determinant equals 0 then the line grazes or is tangential to the sphere. The real roots of the quadratic give the front and back intersections. Substituting the values for t into the original parametric equations yields these points. Figure 1.12 shows that the value of t also gives the position of the points of intersection relative to (x_1, y_1, z_1) and (x_2, y_2, z_2). Only positive values of t are relevant and the smallest value of t corresponds to the intersection nearest to the start of the ray.

Other information that is usually required from an intersection is the surface normal (so that the reflected and refracted rays may be calculated) although, if the sphere is being used as a bounding volume, only the fact that an intersection has occurred, or not, is required.

If the intersection point is (x_i, y_i, z_i) and the centre of the sphere is (l, m, n) then the normal at the intersection point is:

$$N = \left(\frac{x_i - l}{r}, \ \frac{y_i - m}{r}, \ \frac{z_i - n}{r} \right)$$

1.4.3 Intersections – ray–convex polygon

If an object is represented by a set of polygons and is convex then the straight-forward approach is to test the ray individually against each polygon. We do this as follows:

(1) Obtain an equation for the plane containing the polygon.

(2) Check for an intersection between this plane and the ray.

(3) Check that this intersection is contained by the polygon.

A more common application of this operation is clipping a polygon against a view frustum (see Chapter 5). Here the 'ray' is a polygon edge and we need to find the intersection of a polygon edge and a view frustum plane so that the polygon can be split and that part outside the view frustum discarded.

For example, if the plane containing the polygon is:

$$Ax + By + Cz + D = 0$$

and the line is defined parametrically as before, then the intersection is given by:

$$t = \frac{-(Ax_1 + By_1 + Cz_1 + D)}{(Ai + Bj + Ck)} \qquad [1.2]$$

We can exit the test if $t < 0$. This means that the ray is in the half space, defined by the plane that does not contain the polygon (Figure 1.13(a)). We may also be able to exit if the denominator is equal to zero which means that the line and plane are parallel. In this case the ray origin is either inside or outside the poly-hedron. We can check this by examining the sign of the numerator. If the numerator is positive then the ray is in that half space defined by the plane that is outside the object and no further testing is necessary (Figure 1.13(b)).

Figure 1.13
(a) A ray in the half space that does not contain the object ($t < 0$). (b) A possible exit condition. The ray is parallel to the plane containing the polygon currently being tested. It is either inside or outside the object.

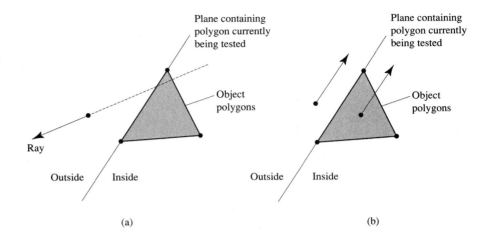

(a)　　　　　　　　　　　　(b)

The straightforward method that tests a point for containment by a polygon is simple but expensive. The sum of the angles between lines drawn from the point to each vertex is 360° if the point is inside the polygon, but not if the point lies outside.

There are three disadvantages or inadequacies in this direct approach. We cannot stop when the first intersection emerges from the test unless we also evaluate whether the polygon is front- or back-facing with respect to the ray direction. The containment test is particularly expensive. It is also possible for errors to occur when a ray and a polygon edge coincide.

All of those disadvantages can be overcome by a single algorithm developed by Haines (1991). Again we use the concept of a plane that contains a polygon defining a half space. All points on one side of the plane are outside the polyhedron. Points on the other side may be contained by the polyhedron. The logical intersection of all inside half spaces is the space enclosed by the polyhedron. A ray that intersects a plane creates a directed line segment (unbounded in the direction of the ray) defined by the intersection point and the ray direction. It is easily seen that the logical intersection of all directed line segments gives the line segment that passes through the polyhedron. Proceeding as before we exit from the test when a parallel ray occurs with an 'outside' origin. Otherwise the algorithm considers every polygon and evaluates the logical intersection of the directed line segments. Consider the example shown in Figure 1.14. For each plane we categorize it as front-facing or back-facing with respect to the ray direction. This is given by the sign of the denominator in Equation 1.2 (positive for back-facing, negative for front-facing). The conditions that form the logical intersection of directed line segments are embedded in the algorithm which is:

{*initialize t_{near} to large negative value*
t_{far} to large positive value}

if {*plane is back-facing*} **and** ($t < t_{far}$)
then $t_{far} = t$

Figure 1.14
Ray–convex polyhedron
intersection testing (after
Haines (1991)).

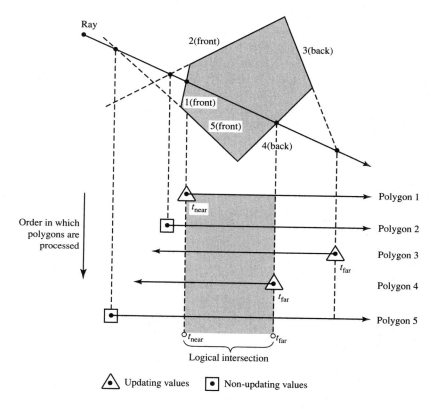

if {plane is front-facing} and ($t > t_{near}$)
then $t_{near} = t$

if ($t_{near} > t_{far}$) then {exit – ray misses}

1.4.4

Intersections – ray–box

Ray–box intersections are important because boxes may be more useful bounding volumes than spheres, particularly in hierarchical schemes. Also generalized boxes can be used as an efficient bounding volume.

Generalized boxes are formed from pairs of parallel planes, but the pairs of planes can be at any angle with respect to each other. In this section we consider the special case of boxes forming rectangular solids, with the normals to each pair of planes aligned in the same direction as the ray tracing axes or the object space axes.

To check if a ray intersects such a box is straightforward. We treat each pair of parallel planes in turn, calculating the distance along the ray to the first plane (t_{near}) and the distance to the second plane (t_{far}). The larger value of t_{near} and the smaller value of t_{far} is retained between comparisons. If the larger value of t_{near} is greater than the smaller value of t_{far}, the ray cannot intersect the box. This is shown, for an example in the xy plane in Figure 1.15. If a hit occurs then the intersection is given by t_{near}.

A more succinct statement of the algorithm comes from considering the distance between the intersection points of a pair of parallel planes as intervals. Then if the intervals intersect, the ray hits the volume. If they do not intersect the ray misses.

Again because our convex polygon is reduced to a rectangular solid, we can define the required distances in terms of the box extent. Distances along the ray are given for the x plane pairs as follows: if the box extent is (x_{b1}, y_{b1}, z_{b1}) and (x_{b2}, y_{b2}, z_{b2}) then:

$$t_{1x} = \frac{x_{b1} - x_1}{x_2 - x_1}$$

is the distance along the ray from its origin to the intersection with the first plane, and:

$$t_{2x} = \frac{x_{b2} - x_1}{x_2 - x_1}$$

The calculations for t_{1y}, t_{2y} and t_{1z}, t_{2z} are similar. The largest value out of the t_1 set gives the required t_{near} and the smallest value of the t_2 set gives the required t_{far}. The algorithm can exit at the y plane calculations.

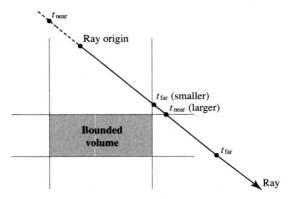

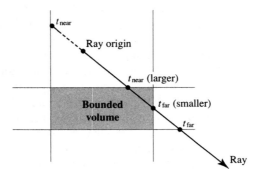

Figure 1.15
Ray–box intersection.

Intersections – ray–quadric

The sphere example given in Section 1.4.2 is a special case of rays intersecting with a general quadric. Ray–quadric intersections can be dealt with by considering the general case, or 'special' objects, such as cylinders, can be treated individually for reasons of efficiency.

The general implicit equation for a quadric is:

$$Ax^2 + Ey^2 + Hz^2 + 2Bxy + 2Fyz + 2Cxz + 2Dx + 2Gy + 2Iz + J = 0$$

Following the same approach as we adopted for the case of the sphere, we substitute Equation 1.1 into the above equation and obtain the coefficients a, b and c for the resulting quadratic as follows:

$$a = Ax_d^2 + Ey_d^2 + Hz_d^2 + 2Bx_dy_d + 2Cx_dz_d + 2Fy_dz_d$$

$$b = d(Ax_1x_d + B(x_1y_d + x_dy_1) + C(x_1z_d + x_dz_1) +$$
$$Dx_d + Ey_1y_d + F(y_1z_d + y_dz_1) + Gy_d + Hz_1z_d + Iz_d$$

$$c = Ax_1^2 + Ey^2 + Hz_1^2 + 2Bx_1y_1 + 2Cx_1z_1 + 2Dx_1 + 2Fy_1z_1 +$$
$$2Gy_1 + 2Iz_1 + J$$

The equations for the quadrics are:

- Sphere
  $$(x - l)^2 + (y - m)^2 + (z - n)^2 = r^2$$
  where (l, m, n) is, as before, the centre of the sphere.

- Infinite cylinder
  $$(x - l)^2 + (y - m)^2 = r^2$$

- Ellipsoid
  $$\frac{(x - l)^2}{\alpha^2} + \frac{(y - m)^2}{\beta^2} + \frac{(z - n)^2}{\gamma^2} - 1 = 0$$
  where α, β and γ are the semi-axes.

- Paraboloid
  $$\frac{(x - l)^2}{\alpha^2} + \frac{(y - m)^2}{\beta^2} - z + n = 0$$

- Hyperboloid
  $$\frac{(x - l)^2}{\alpha^2} + \frac{(y - m)^2}{\beta^2} + \frac{(z - n)^2}{\gamma^2} - 1 = 0$$

Ray tracing geometry – reflection and refraction

The formulae presented in this section are standard formulae in a form that is suitable for incorporation into a simple ray tracer. The source of the formulae is Fresnel's law given in Section 7.1.

Each time a ray intersects a surface it produces, in general, a reflected and refracted ray. The reflection direction, a unit vector, is given (as we saw in Section 1.3.2) by:

$$\boldsymbol{R} = 2\boldsymbol{N}\cos\phi - \boldsymbol{L}$$
$$= 2(\boldsymbol{N}\cdot\boldsymbol{L})\boldsymbol{N} - \boldsymbol{L}$$

where $\boldsymbol{L}$ and $\boldsymbol{N}$ are unit vectors representing the incident ray direction, which is the same as the light vector, and the surface normal respectively. $\boldsymbol{L}$, $\boldsymbol{R}$ and $\boldsymbol{N}$ are co-planar. These vectors are shown in Figure 1.16, where $\boldsymbol{I} = -\boldsymbol{L}$.

A ray striking a partially or wholly transparent object is refracted due to the change in the velocity of light in different media. The angles of incidence and refraction are related by Snell's law:

$$\frac{\sin\phi}{\sin\theta} = \frac{\mu_2}{\mu_1}$$

where the incident and transmitted rays are co-planar with $\boldsymbol{N}$. The transmitted ray is represented by $\boldsymbol{T}$ and this is given by:

$$\boldsymbol{T} = \mu\,\boldsymbol{I} - (\cos\theta + \mu\cos\phi)\,\boldsymbol{N}$$
$$\mu = \mu_1/\mu_2$$
$$\cos\theta = \frac{1}{\mu^2}\,(1 - \mu^2(1 - \cos^2\phi)^{\frac{1}{2}}$$

as shown in Figure 1.16.

If a ray is travelling from a more to a less dense medium then it is possible for the refracted ray to be parallel to the surface (Figure 1.17). ϕ_c is known as the critical angle. If ϕ is increased then total internal reflection occurs.

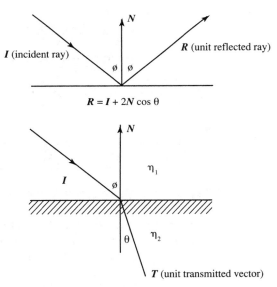

$$R = I + 2N\cos\theta$$

$$T = \mu\,I - (\cos\theta - \mu\cos\phi)N$$

Figure 1.16
Reflection and refraction
geometry.

Figure 1.17
Internal reflection in an
object. (a) ϕ_c = critical
angle. (b) $\phi > \phi_c$.

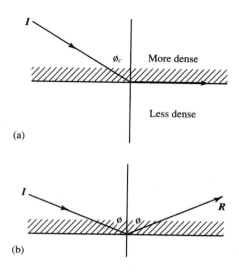

1.5

Interpolating properties in the image plane

In mainstream rendering techniques – that is rendering polygons – various properties required for interior pixels are interpolated from the values of these properties at the vertices of the polygon (that is the pixels onto which the vertices project). Such interpolation is known as bilinear interpolation and it is the foundation of the efficiency of this kind of shading.

Referring to Figure 1.18, the interpolation proceeds by moving a scan line down through the pixel set representing the polygon and obtaining start and end values for a scan line by interpolating between the appropriate pair of vertex properties. Interpolation along a scan line then yields a value for the property at each pixel. The interpolation equations are (for the particular edge pair shown in the illustration):

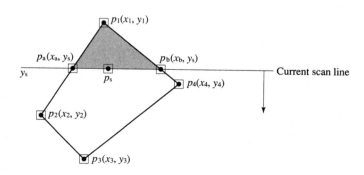

Figure 1.18
Interpolating a property
at a pixel from values at the
vertex pixels.

$$p_a = \frac{1}{y_1 - y_2} \ [p_1(y_s - y_2) + p_2 \ (y_1 - y_s)]$$

$$p_b = \frac{1}{y_1 - y_4} \ [p_1(y_s - y_4) + p_4 \ (y_1 - y_s)]$$

$$p_s = \frac{1}{x_b - x_a} \ [p_a(x_b - x_s) + p_b \ (x_s - x_a)]$$

These would normally be implemented using an incremental form, the final equation, for example, becoming:

$$p_s := p_s + \Delta p$$

with the constant value Δp calculated once per scan line.

Representation and modelling of three-dimensional objects (1)

2.1   Polygonal representation of three-dimensional objects

2.2   Constructive solid geometry (CSG) representation of objects

2.3   Space subdivision techniques for object representation

2.4   Representing objects with implicit functions

2.5   Scene management and object representation

2.6   Summary

Introduction

The primary purpose of three-dimensional computer graphics is to produce a two-dimensional image of a scene or an object from a description or model of the object. The object may be a real or existing object or it may exist only as a computer description. A less common but extremely important usage is where the act of creation of the object model and the visualization are intertwined. This occurs in interactive CAD applications where a designer uses the visualization to assist the act of creating the object. Most object descriptions are approximate in the sense that they describe the geometry or shape of the object only to the extent that inputting this description to a renderer produces an image of acceptable quality. In many CAD applications, however, the description has to be accurate because it is used to drive a manufacturing process. The final output is not a two-dimensional image but a real three-dimensional object.

Modelling and representation is a general phrase which can be applied to any or all of the following aspects of objects:

● Creation of a three-dimensional computer graphics representation.

● The technique or method or data structure used to represent the object.

● Manipulation of the representation – in particular changing the shape of an existing model.

The ways in which we can create computer graphics objects are almost as many and varied as the objects themselves. For example, we might construct an architectural object through a CAD interface. We may take data directly from a device such as a laser ranger or a three-dimensional digitizer. We may use some interface based on a sweeping technique where so-called ducted solids are created by sweeping a cross-section along a spine curve. Creation methods have up to now tended to be manual or semi-manual involving a designer working with an interface. As the demand for the representation of highly complex scenes increases – from such applications as virtual reality (VR) – automatic methods are being investigated. For VR applications of existing realities the creation of computer graphics representations from photographs or video is an attractive proposition.

The representation of an object is very much an unsolved problem in computer graphics. We can distinguish between a representation that is required for a machine or renderer and the representation that is required by a user or user interface. Representing an object using polygonal facets – a polygon mesh representation – is the most popular machine representation. It is, however, an inconvenient representation for a user or creator of an object. Despite this it is used as both a user and a machine representation. Other methods have separate user and machine representations. For example, bi-cubic parametric patches and CSG methods, which constitute user or interface representations may be converted into polygon meshes for rendering.

The polygon mesh form suffers from many disadvantages when the object is complex and detailed. In mainstream computer graphics the number of polygons in an object representation can be anything from a few tens to hundreds of thousands. This has serious ramifications in rendering time and object creation cost and in the feasibility of using such objects in an animation or virtual reality environment. Other problems accrue in animation where a model has both to represent the shape of the object and be controlled by an animation system which may require collisions to be calculated or the object to change shape as a function of time. Despite this the polygon mesh is supreme in mainstream computer graphics. Its inertia is due in part to the development of efficient algorithms and hardware to render this description. This has resulted in a somewhat strange situation where it is more efficient – as far as rendering is concerned – to represent a shape with many simple elements (polygons) than to represent it with far fewer (and more accurate) but more complicated elements such as bi-cubic parametric patches (see Section 3.4.2).

The ability to manipulate the shape of an existing object depends strongly on the representation. Polygon meshes do not admit simple shape manipulation. Moving mesh vertices immediately disrupts the 'polygonal resolution' where a shape has been converted into polygons with some degree of accuracy that is related to the local curvature of the surface being represented. For example, imagine twisting a cube represented by six squares. The twisted object cannot be represented by retaining only six polygons. Another problem with shape manipulation is scale. Sometimes we want to alter a large part of an object which may involve moving many elements at the same time; other times we may require a detailed change.

Different representational methods have their advantages and disadvantages but there is no universal solution to the many problems that still exist. Rather, particular modelling methods have evolved for particular contexts. A good example of this tendency is the development of constructive solid geometry methods (CSG) popular in interactive CAD because they facilitate an intuitive interface for the interactive design of complex industrial objects as well as a representation. CSG is a constrained representation in that we can only use it to model shapes that are made up of allowed combinations of the primitive shapes or elements that are included in the system.

How do we choose a representation? The answer is that it depends on the nature of the object, the particular computer graphics technique that we are going to use to bring the object to life and the application. All these factors are interrelated. We can represent some three-dimensional objects exactly using a mathematical formulation, for example, a cylinder or a sphere; for others we use an approximate representation. For objects that cannot be represented exactly by mathematics there is a trade-off between the accuracy of the representation and the bulk of information used. This is illustrated by the polygon mesh skeletons in Figure 2.1. You can only increase the veracity of the representation by increasing the polygonal resolution which then has high cost implications in rendering time.

The ultimate impossibility of this extrapolation has led to hybrid methods for very complex and unique objects such as a human head. For example, in representing a particular human head we can use a combination of a polygon mesh model and photographic texture maps. The solid form of the head is represented by a generic polygon mesh which is pulled around to match the actual dimensions of the head to be modelled. The detailed likeness is obtained by mapping a photographic texture onto this mesh. The idea here is that the detailed variations in the geometry are suggested by the texture map rather than by detailed excursions in the geometry. Of course, its not perfect because the detail in the photograph depends on the lighting conditions under which it was taken as well as the real geometric detail, but it is a trick that is increasingly being used. Whether we regard the texture mapping as part of the representation or as part of the rendering process is perhaps a matter of opinion; but certainly the use of photographic texture maps in this context enables us to represent a complex object like a human head with a small number of polygons plus a photograph.

This compromise between polygonal resolution and a photographic texture map can be taken to extremes. In the computer games industry the total number of polygons rendered to the screen must be within the limiting number that can be rendered at, say, 15 frames per second on a PC. A recent football game consists of players whose heads are modelled with just a cube onto which a photographic texture is mapped.

Figure 2.1
The art of wireframe – an illustration from Viewpoint Digital's catalogue.
Source: '3D models by Viewpoint Digital, Inc.'
Anatomy, Viewpoint's 3D Dataset™ Catalog, 2nd edn.

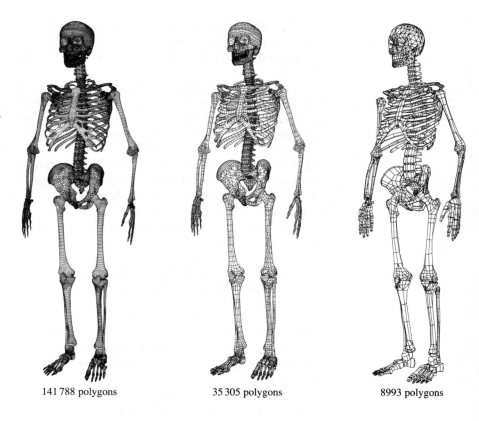

141 788 polygons   35 305 polygons   8993 polygons

We now list, in order of approximate frequency of use, the mainstream models used in computer graphics.

(1) **Polygonal** Objects are approximated by a net or mesh of planar polygonal facets. With this form we can represent, to an accuracy that we choose, an object of any shape. However, the accuracy is somewhat arbitrary in this sense. Consider Figure 2.1 again: are 142 000 polygons really necessary, or can we reduce the polygonal resolution without degrading the rendered image, and if so by how much? The shading algorithms are designed to visually transform the faceted representation in such a way that the piecewise linear representation is not visible in the shaded version (except on the silhouette edge). Connected with the polygonal resolution is the final projected size of the object on the screen. Waste is incurred when a complex object, represented by many thousands of polygons, projects onto a screen area that is made up of only a few pixels.

(2) **Bi-cubic parametric patches** (see Chapter 3) These are 'curved quadrilaterals'. Generally we can say that the representation is similar to the polygon mesh except that the individual polygons are now curved surfaces. Each patch is specified by a mathematical formula that gives the position of

the patch in three-dimensional space and its shape. This formula enables us to generate any or every point on the surface of the patch. We can change the shape or curvature of the patch by editing the mathematical specification. This results in powerful interactive possibilities. The problems are, however, significant. It is very expensive to render or visualize the patches. When we change the shape of individual patches in a net of patches there are problems in maintaining 'smoothness' between the patch and its neighbours. Bi-cubic parametric patches can be either an exact or an approximate representation. They can only be an exact representation of themselves, which means that any object, say, a car body panel, can only be represented exactly if its shape corresponds exactly to the shape of the patch. This somewhat torturous statement is necessary because when the representation is used for real or existing objects, the shape modelled will not necessarily correspond to the surface of the object.

An example of the same object represented by both bi-cubic parametric patches and by polygonal facets is shown in Figure 3.28 (a) and (c). This clearly shows the complexity/number of elements trade-off with the polygon mesh representation requiring 2048 elements against the 32-patch representation.

(3) **Constructive solid geometry (CSG)** This is an exact representation to within certain rigid shape limits. It has arisen out of the realization that very many manufactured objects can be represented by 'combinations' of elementary shapes or geometric primitives. For example, a chunk of metal with a hole in it could be specified as the result of a three-dimensional subtraction between a rectangular solid and a cylinder. Connected with this is the fact that such a representation makes for easy and intuitive shape control – we can specify that a metal plate has to have a hole in it by defining a cylinder of appropriate radius and subtracting it from the rectangular solid, representing the plate. The CSG method is a volumetric representation – shape is represented by elementary volumes or primitives. This contrasts with the previous two methods which represent shape using surfaces. An example of a CSG-represented object is shown in Figure 2.14.

(4) **Spatial subdivision techniques** This simply means dividing the object space into elementary cubes, known as voxels, and labelling each voxel as empty or as containing part of an object. It is the three-dimensional analogue of representing a two-dimensional object as the collection of pixels onto which the object projects. Labelling all of three-dimensional object space in this way is clearly expensive, but it has found applications in computer graphics. In particular, in ray tracing where an efficient algorithm results if the objects are represented in this way. An example of a voxel object is shown in Figure 2.16. We are now representing the three-dimensional space occupied by the object; the other methods we have introduced are representations of the surface of the object.

(5) **Implicit representation** Occasionally in texts implicit functions are mentioned as an object representation form. An implicit function is, for example:

$$x^2 + y^2 + z^2 = r^2$$

which is the definition for a sphere. On their own these are of limited usefulness in computer graphics because there is a limited number of objects that can be represented in this way. Also, it is an inconvenient form as far as rendering is concerned. However, we should mention that such representations do appear quite frequently in three-dimensional computer graphics – in particular in ray tracing where spheres are used frequently – both as objects in their own right and as bounding objects for other polygon mesh representations.

Implicit representations are extended into implicit functions which can loosely be described as objects formed by mathematically defining a surface that is influenced by a collection of underlying primitives such as spheres. Implicit functions find their main use in shape-changing animation – they are of limited usefulness for representing real objects.

We have arranged the categories in order of popularity; another useful comparison is: with voxels and polygon meshes the number of representational elements per object is likely to be high (if accuracy is to be achieved) but the complexity of the representation is low. This contrasts with bi-cubic patches where the number of elements is likely to be much lower in most contexts but the complexity of the representation is higher.

We should not deduce from the above categorization that the choice of a representation is a free one. The representational form is decided by both the rendering technique and the application. Consider, for example, the continuous/discrete representation distinction. A discrete representation – the polygon mesh – is used to represent the arbitrary shapes of existing real world objects – it is difficult to see how else we would deal with such objects. In medical imaging the initial representation is discrete (voxels) because this is what the imaging technology produces. On the other hand in CAD work we need a continuous representation because eventually we are going to produce, say, a machine part from the internal description. The representation has, therefore, to be exact.

The CSG representation does not fit easily into these comparisons. It is both a discrete and a continuous representation, being a discrete combination of interacting primitives, some of which can be described by a continuous function.

Another important distinguishing factor is surface versus volume representation. The polygon mesh is an approximate representation of the surface of an object and the rendering engine is concerned with providing a visualization of that surface. With Gouraud shading the algorithm is only concerned with using geometric properties associated with the surface representation. In ray tracing, because the bulk of the cost is involved in tracking rays through space and finding which objects they intersect, a surface representation implies high rendering cost. Using a volume representation, where the object space is labelled according to object occupancy, greatly reduces the overall cost of rendering.

The relationship between a rendering method and the representation is critically important in the radiosity method and here, to avoid major defects in the final image, there has to be some kind of interaction between the representation and the execution of the algorithm. As the algorithm progresses the representation must adapt so that more accurate consideration is given to areas in the emerging solution that need greater consideration. In other words, because of the expense of the method, it is difficult to decide *a priori* what the level of detail in the representation should be. The unwieldiness of the concept of having a scene representation depend on the progress of the rendering algorithm is at the root of the difficulty of the radiosity method and is responsible for its (current) lack of uptake as a mainstream tool.

2.1 Polygonal representation of three-dimensional objects

This is the classic representational form in three-dimensional graphics. An object is represented by a mesh of polygonal facets. In the general case an object possesses curved surfaces and the facets are an approximation to such a surface (Figure 2.2). Polygons may contain a vertex count that emerges from the technology used to create the model, or we may constrain all polygons to be triangles. It may be necessary to do this, for example, to gain optimal performance from special-purpose hardware or graphics accelerator cards.

Polygonal representations are ubiquitous in computer graphics. There are two reasons for this. Creating polygonal objects is straightforward (although for complex objects the process can be time consuming and costly) and visually effective algorithms exist to produce shaded versions of objects represented in this way. As we have already stated, polygon meshes are strictly a machine representation – rather than a convenient user representation – and they often function in this capacity for other representations which are not directly renderable. Thus bi-cubic parametric patches, CSG and voxel representations are often converted into polygon meshes prior to rendering

There are certain practical difficulties with polygon meshes. Foremost amongst these is accuracy. The accuracy of the model, or the difference between the faceted representation and the curved surface of the object, is usually arbitrary. As far as final image quality is concerned, the size of individual polygons should ideally depend on local spatial curvature. Where the curvature changes

Figure 2.2
Approximating a curved surface using polygonal facets.

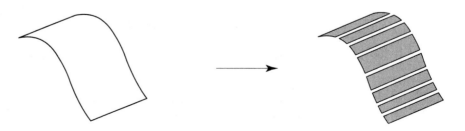

rapidly, more polygons are required per unit area of the surface. These factors tend to be related to the method used for creating the polygons. If, for example, a mesh is being built from an existing object, by using a three-dimensional digitizer to determine the spatial coordinates of polygon vertices, the digitizer operator will decide on the basis of experience how large each polygon should be. Sometimes polygons are extracted algorithmically (as in, for example, the creation of an object as a solid of revolution or in a bi-cubic patch subdivision algorithm) and a more rigorous approach to the rate of polygons per unit area of the surface is possible.

One of the most significant developments in three-dimensional graphics was the emergence in the 1970s of shading algorithms that deal efficiently with polygonal objects, and at the same time, through an interpolation scheme, diminish the visual effect of the piecewise linearities in the representation. This factor, together with recent developments in fixed program rendering hardware, has secured the entrenchment of the polygon mesh structure.

In the simplest case a polygon mesh is a structure that consists of polygons represented by a list of linked (x, y, z) coordinates that are the polygon vertices (edges are represented either explicitly or implicitly as we shall see in a moment). Thus the information we store to describe an object is finally a list of points or vertices. We may also store, as part of the object representation, other geometric information that is used in subsequent processing. These are usually polygon normals and vertex normals. Calculated once only, it is convenient to store these in the object data structure and have them undergo any linear transformations that are applied to the object.

It is convenient to order polygons into a simple hierarchical structure. Figure 2.3(a) shows a decomposition that we have called a conceptual hierarchy for reasons that should be apparent from the illustration. Polygons are grouped into surfaces and surfaces are grouped into objects. For example, a cylinder possesses three surfaces: a planar top and bottom surface together with a curved surface. The reason for this grouping is that we must distinguish between those edges that are part of the approximation – edges between adjacent rectangles in the curved surface approximation to the cylinder, for example – and edges that exist in reality. The way in which these are subsequently treated by the rendering process is different – real edges must remain visible whereas edges that form part of the approximation to a curved surface must be made invisible. Figure 2.3(b) shows a more formal representation of the topology in Figure 2.3(a).

An example of a practical data structure which implements these relationships is shown in Figure 2.3(c). This contains horizontal, as well as vertical, hierarchical links, necessary for programmer access to the next entity in a horizontal sequence. It also includes a vertex reference list which means that actual vertices (referred to by each polygon that shares them) are stored only once. Another difference between the practical structure and the topological diagram is that access is allowed directly to lower-level entities. Wireframe visualizations of an object are used extensively, and to produce a wireframe image requires direct access to the edge level in the hierarchy. Vertical links between the edges' and the polygons' levels can be either backward pointers or forward pointers depending on the type of renderer that is accessing the structure. In a scan line renderer, edges are the topmost entity whereas in a Z-buffer renderer polygons are. A Z-buffer renderer treats polygons as independent entities, rendering one polygon at a time. A scan line renders all those polygons that straddle the scan line being rendered.

The approach just described is more particularly referred to as a vertex-based boundary model. Sometimes it is necessary to use an edge-based boundary

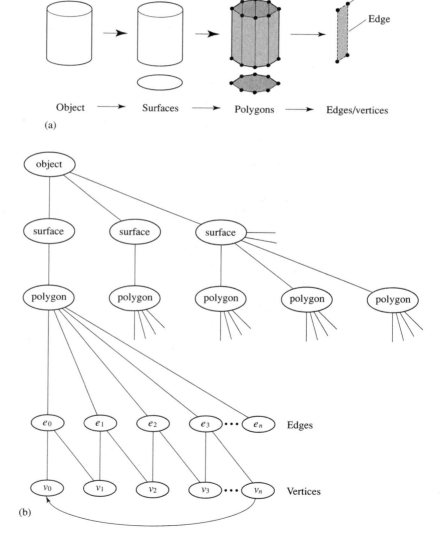

Figure 2.3
Representation of an object as a mesh of polygons.
(a) Conceptual hierarchy.
(b) Topological representation.

Figure 2.3 *continued*
(c) A practical data
structure.

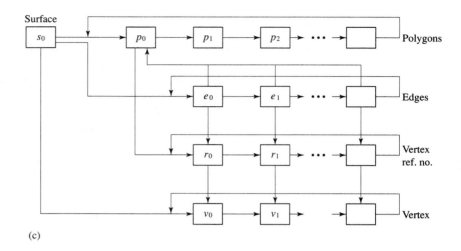

(c)

model, the most common manifestation of which is a winged-edge data structure (Mantyla 1988). An edge-based model represents a face in terms of a closing
sequence of edges.

The data structure just described encapsulates the basic geometry associated
with a polygonal facets of an object. Information required by applications and
renderers is also usually contained in the scene/object database. The following
list details the most common attributes found in polygon mesh structures. They
are either data structure pointers, real numbers or binary flags. It is unlikely that
all of these would appear in a practical application, but a subset is found in most
object representations.

- Polygon attributes
  (1) Triangular or not.
  (2) Area.
  (3) Normal to the plane containing the polygon.
  (4) Coefficients (A, B, C, D) of the plane containing the polygon
      where $Ax + By + Cz + D = 0$.
  (5) Whether convex or not.
  (6) Whether it contains holes or not.
- Edge attributes
  (1) Length.
  (2) Whether an edge is between two polygons or between two surfaces.
  (3) Polygons on each side of the edge.
- Vertex attributes
  (1) Polygons that contribute to the vertex.

(2) Shading or vertex normal – the average of the normals of the polygons that contribute to the vertex.

(3) Texture coordinates (u, v) specifying a mapping into a two-dimensional texture image.

All these are absolute propereties that exist when the object is created. Polygons can aquire attributes as they are passed through the graphics pipeline. For example, an edge can be tagged as a silhouette edge if it is between two polygons with normals facing towards and away from the viewer.

A significant problem that crops up in many guises in computer graphics is the scale problem. With polygonal representation this means that, in many applications, we cannot afford to render all the polygons in a model if the viewing distance and polygonal resolution are such that many polygons project onto a single pixel. This problem bedevils flight simulators (and similarly computer games) and virtual reality applications. An obvious solution is to have a hierarchy of models and use the one appropriate to projected screen area. There are two problems with this; the first is that in animation (and it is animation applications where this problem is most critical) switching between models can cause visual disturbances in the animation sequence – the user can see the switch from one resolution level to another. The other problem is how to generate the hierarchy and to decide how many levels it should contain. Clearly we can start with the highest resolution model and subdivide, but this is not necessarily straightforward. We look at this problem in more detail in Section 2.5.

2.1.1 Creating polygonal objects

Although a polygon mesh is the most common representational form in computer graphics, modelling, although straightforward, is somewhat tedious. The popularity of this representation derives from the ease of modelling, the emergence of rendering strategies (both hardware and software) to process polygonal objects and the important fact that there is no restriction whatever on the shape or complexity of the object being modelled.

Interactive development of a model is possible by 'pulling' vertices around with a three-dimensional locator device but in practice this is not a very useful method. It is difficult to make other than simple shape changes. Once an object has been created, any single polygon cannot be changed without also changing its neighbours. Thus most creation methods use either a device or a program; the only method that admits user interaction is item 4 on the following list.

Four common examples of polygon modelling methods are:

(1) Using a three-dimensional digitizer or adopting an equivalent manual strategy.

(2) Using an automatic device such as a laser ranger.

(3) Generating an object from a mathematical description.

(4) Generating an object by sweeping.

The first two modelling methods convert real objects into polygon meshes, the next two generate models from definitions. We distinguish between models generated by mathematical formulae and those generated by interacting with curves which are defined mathematically.

Manual modelling of polygonal objects

The easiest way to model a real object is manually using a three-dimensional digitizer. The operator uses experience and judgement to emplace points on an object which are to be polygon vertices. The three-dimensional coordinates of these vertices are then input to the system via a three-dimensional digitizer. The association of vertices with polygons is straightforward. A common strategy for ensuring an adequate representation is to draw a net over the surface of the object – like laying a real net over the object. Where curved net lines intersect defines the position of the polygon vertices. A historic photograph of this process is shown in Figure 2.4. This shows students creating a polygon mesh model of a car in 1974. It is taken from a classic paper by early outstanding pioneers in computer graphics – Sutherland *et al.* (1974).

Automatic generation of polygonal objects

A device that is capable of creating very accurate or high resolution polygon mesh objects from real objects is a laser ranger. In one type of device the object is placed on a rotating table in the path of the beam. The table also moves up and down vertically. The laser ranger returns a set of contours – the intersection of the object and a set of closely spaced parallel planes – by measuring the distance to the object surface. A 'skinning' algorithm, operating on pairs of contours, converts the boundary data into a very large number of triangles (Figure 2.5(a)). Figure 2.5(b) is a rendered version of an object polygonized in this way. The skinning algorithm produced, for this object, over 400 000 triangles. Given that only around half of these may be visible on screen and that the object

Figure 2.4
The Utah Beetle – an early example of manual modelling. *Source*: Beatty and Booth *Tutorial: Computer Graphics*, 2nd edn, The Institute of Electrical and Electronics Engineers, Inc.: New York. © 1982 IEEE.

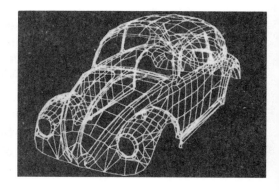

Figure 2.5
A rendered polygonal object scanned by a laser ranger and polygonized by a simple skinning algorithm. (a) A skinning algorithm joins points on consecutive contours to make a three-dimensional polygonal object from the contours. (b) A 400 000 polygonal object produced by a skinning algorithm.

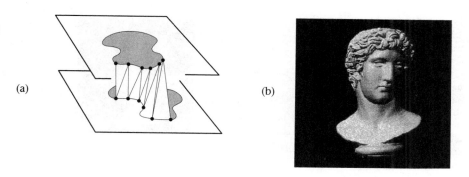

(a)

(b)

projects onto about half the screen surface implies that each triangle projects onto one pixel on average. This clearly illustrates the point mentioned earlier that it is extremely wasteful of rendering resources to use a polygonal resolution where the average screen area onto which a polygon projects approaches a single pixel. For model creation, laser rangers suffer from the significant disadvantage that, in the framework described – fully automatic rotating table device – they can only accurately model convex objects. Objects with concavities will have surfaces which will not necessarily be hit by the incident beam.

2.1.4

Mathematical generation of polygonal objects

Many polygonal objects are generated through an interface into which a user puts a model description in the form of a set of curves that are a function of two-dimensional or two-parameter space. This is particularly the case in CAD applications where the most popular paradigm is that of sweeping a cross-section in a variety of different ways. There are two benefits to this approach. The first is fairly obvious. The user works with some notion of shape which is removed from the low level activity of constructing an object from individual polygonal facets. Instead, shape is specified in terms of notions that are connected with the form of the object – something that Snyder (1992) calls 'the logic of shapes'. A program then takes the user description and transforms it into polygons. The transformation from the user description to a polygon mesh is straightforward. A second advantage of this approach is that it can be used in conjunction with either polygons as primitive elements or with bi-cubic parametric patches (see Section 3.6).

The most familiar manifestation of this approach is a solid of revolution where, say, a vertical cross-section is swept through 180° generating a solid with a circular horizontal cross-section (Figure 2.6(a)). The obvious constraint of solids of revolution is that they can only represent objects possessing rotational symmetry.

A more powerful generative model is arrived at by considering the same solid generated by sweeping a circle, with radius controlled by a profile curve,

Figure 2.6
Straight spine objects – solid of revolution vs cross-sectional sweeping. (a) A solid of revolution generated by sweeping a (vertical) cross-section. (b) The same solid can be generated by sweeping a circle, whose radius is controlled by a profile curve, up a straight vertical spine. (c) Non-circular cross-section.

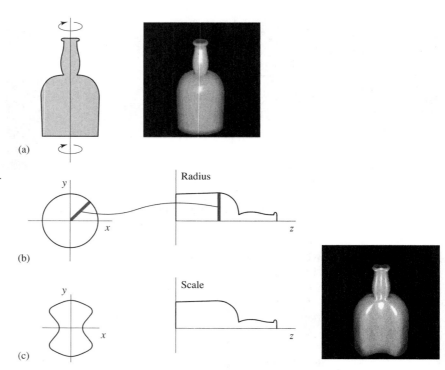

vertically up a straight spine (Figure 2.6(b)). In the event that the profile curve is a constant, we have the familiar notion of extrusion. This immediately removes the constraint of a circular cross-section and we can have cross-sections of arbitrary shape (Figure 2.6(c)).

Now consider controlling the shape of the spine. We can incorporate the notion of a curved spine and generate objects that are controlled by a cross-sectional shape, a profile curve and a spine curve as Figure 2.9 demonstrates.

Other possibilities emerge. Figure 2.7 shows an example of what Snyder calls a rail product surface. Here a briefcase carrying handle is generated by sweeping a cross-section along a path determined by the midpoints of two rail curves. The long axis extent of the elliptical-like cross-section is controlled by the same two curves – hence the name. A more complex example is the turbine blade shown in Figure 2.8. Snyder calls this an affine transformation surface – because the spine is now replaced by affine transformations, controlled by user specified curves. Each blade is generated by extruding a rectangular cross-section along the z axis. The cross-section is specified as a rectangle, and three shape controlling curves, functions of z, supply the values used in the transformations of the cross-section as it is extruded. The cross-section is, for each step in z, scaled separately in x and y, translated in x, rotated around, translated back in x, and extruded along the z axis.

Figure 2.7
Snyder's rail curve product surfaces. *Source:* J.M. Snyder, *Generative Modelling for Computer Graphics and CAD,* Academic Press, 1992.

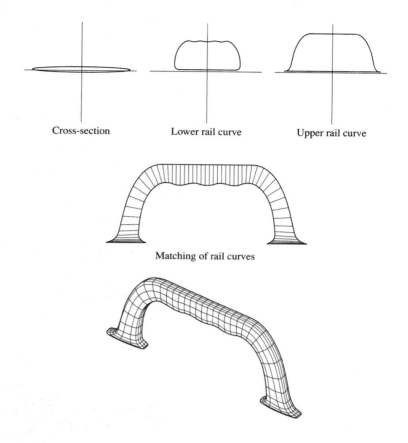

Cross-section   Lower rail curve   Upper rail curve

Matching of rail curves

A complicated shape is thus generated by a general cross-section and three curves. Clearly implicit in this example is a reliance on a user/designer being able to visualize the final required shape in three-dimensions so that he is able to specify the appropriate shape curves. Although for the turbine blade example this may seem a somewhat tall order, we should bear in mind that shapes of such complexity are the domain of professional engineers where the use of such generative models for shape specification will not be unfamiliar.

Certain practical problems emerge when we generalize to curved spines. There are three difficulties in allowing curved spines that immediately emerge. These are illustrated in Figure 2.9. Figure 2.9(a) shows a problem in the curve to polygon procedure. Here it is seen that the size of the polygonal primitives depends on the excursion of the spine curve. The other is how do we orient the cross-section with respect to a varying spine (Figure 2.9(b))? And, finally, how do we prevent cross-sections self-intersecting (Figure 2.9(c))? It is clear that this will occur as soon as the radius of curvature of the path of any points traced out by the cross-sectional curve exceeds the radius of curvature of the spine. We will now look at approaches to these problems.

Figure 2.8
Snyder's affine
transformation surface.
The generating curves are
shown for a single turbine
blade. *Source*: J.M. Snyder,
*Generative Modelling for
Computer Graphics and CAD*,
Academic Press, 1992.

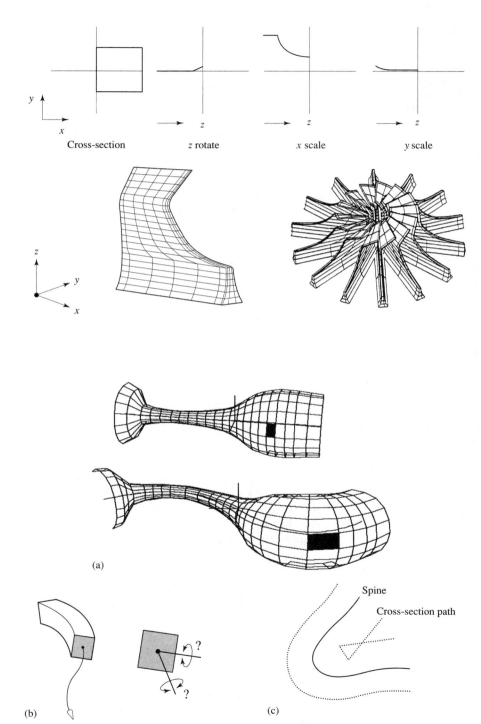

Figure 2.9
Three problems in cross-
sectional sweeping.
(a) Controlling the size of
the polygons can become
problematic. (b) How
should the cross-section be
oriented with resepct to the
spine curve? (c) Self-
intersection of the cross-
section path.

Consider a parametrically defined cubic along which the cross-section is swept. This can be defined (see Section 3.1) as:

$$Q(u) = au^3 + bu^2 + cu + d$$

Now if we consider the simple case of moving a constant cross-section without twisting it along the curve we need to define intervals along the curve at which the cross-section is to be placed and intervals around the cross-section curve. When we have these we can step along the spine intervals and around the cross-section intervals and output the polygons.

Consider the first problem. Dividing u into equal intervals will not necessarily give the best results. In particular the points will not appear at equal intervals along the curve. A procedure known as arc length parametrization divides the curve into equal intervals, but this procedure is not straightforward. Arc length parametrization may also be inappropriate. What is really required is a scheme that divides the curve into intervals that depend on the curvature of the curve. When the curvature is high the rate of polygon generation needs to be increased so that more polygons occur when the curvature twists rapidly. The most direct way to do this is to use the curve subdivision algorithm (see Section 4.2.3) and subdivide the curve until a linearity test is positive.

Now consider the second problem. Having defined a set of sample points we need to define a reference frame or coordinate system at each. The cross-section is then embedded in this coordinate system. This is done by deriving three mutually orthogonal vectors that form the coordinate axes. There are many possibilities.

A common one is the Frenet frame. The Frenet frame is defined by the origin or sample point, P, and three vectors T, N and B (Figure 2.10). T is the unit length tangent vector:

$$T = V/|V|$$

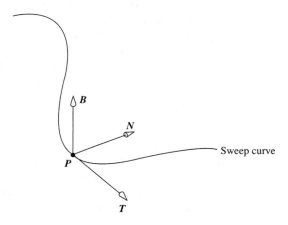

Figure 2.10
The Frenet frame at sample point P on a sweep curve.

where V is the derivative of the curve:

$$V = 3au^2 + 2bu + c$$

The principal normal N is given by:

$$N = K/|K|$$

where:

$$K = V \times A \times V/|V|^4$$

and A is the second derivative of the curve:

$$A = 6au + 2b$$

Finally B is given by:

$$B = T \times N$$

2.1.5   Procedural polygon mesh objects – fractal objects

In this section we will look at a common example of generating polygon mesh objects procedurally. Fractal geometry is a term coined by Benoit Mandelbrot (1977; 1982). The term was used to describe the attributes of certain natural phenomena, for example, coastlines. A coastline viewed at any level of detail – at microscopic level, at a level where individual rocks can be seen or at 'geographical' level, tends to exhibit the same level of jaggedness; a kind of statistical self-similarity. Fractal geometry provides a description for certain aspects of this ubiquitous phenomenon in nature and its tendency towards self-similarity.

In three-dimensional computer graphics, fractal techniques have commonly been used to generate terrain models and the easiest techniques involve subdividing the facets of the objects that consist of triangles or quadrilaterals. A recursive subdivision procedure is applied to each facet, to a required depth or level of detail, and a convincing terrain model results. Subdivision in this context means taking the midpoint along the edge between two vertices and perturbing it along a line normal to the edge. The result of this is to subdivide the original facets into a large number of smaller facets, each having a random orientation in three-dimensional space about the original facet orientation. The initial global shape of the object is retained to an extent that depends on the perturbation at the subdivision and a planar four-sided pyramid might turn into a 'Mont Blanc' shaped object.

Most subdivision algorithms are based on a formulation by Fournier *et al.* (1982) that recursively subdivides a single line segment. This algorithm was developed as an alternative to more mathematically correct but expensive procedures suggested by Mandelbrot. It uses self-similarity and conditional expectation properties of fractional Brownian motion to give an estimate of the increment of the stochastic process. The process is also Gaussian and the only parameters needed to describe a Gaussian distribution are the mean (conditional expectation) and the variance.

A procedure recursively subdivides a line (t_1, f_1), (t_2, f_2) generating a scalar displacement of the midpoint of the line in a direction normal to the line (Figure 2.11(a)).

To extend this procedure to, say, triangles or quadrilaterals in three-dimensional space, we treat each edge in turn generating a displacement along a midpoint vector that is normal to the plane of the original facet (Figure 2.11(b)). Using this technique we can take a smooth pyramid, say, made of large triangular faces and turn it into a rugged mountain.

Fournier categorizes two problems in this method – as internal and external consistency. Internal consistency requires that the shape generated should be the same whatever the orientation in which it is generated, and that coarser

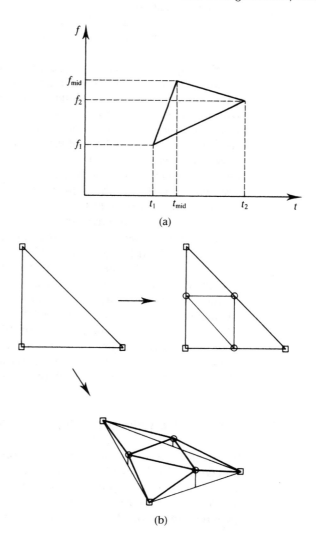

Figure 2.11
An example of procedural generation of polygon mesh objects – fractal terrain. (a) Line segment subdivision. (b) Triangle subdivision.

details should remain the same if the shape is replotted at greater resolution. To satisfy the first requirement, the Gaussian randoms generated must not be a function of the position of the points, but should be unique to the point itself. An invariant point identifier needs to be associated with each point. This problem can be solved in terrain generation by giving each point a key value used to index a Gaussian random number. A hash function can be used to map the two keys of the end points of a line to a key value for the midpoint. Scale requirements of internal consistency means that the same random numbers must always be generated in the same order at a given level of subdivision.

External consistency is harder to maintain. Within the mesh of triangles every triangle shares each of its sides with another; thus the same random displacements must be generated for corresponding points of different connecting triangles. This is already solved by using the key value of each point and the hash function, but another problem still exists, that of the direction of the displacement.

If the displacements are along the surface normal of the polygon under consideration, then adjacent polygons which have different normals (as is, by definition, always the case) will have their midpoints displaced into different positions. This causes gaps to open up. A solution is to displace the midpoint along the average of the normals to all the polygons that contain it but this problem occurs at every level of recursion and is consequently very expensive to implement. Also, this technique would create an unsatisfactory skyline because the displacements are not constrained to one direction. A better skyline is obtained by making all the displacements of points internal to the original polygon in a direction normal to the plane of the original polygon. This cheaper technique solves all problems relating to different surface normals, and the gaps created by them. Now surface normals need not be created at each level of recursion and the algorithm is considerably cheaper because of this.

Another two points are worth mentioning. Firstly, note that polygons should be constant shaded without calculating vertex normals – discontinuities between polygons should not be smoothed out. Secondly, consider colour. The usual global colour scheme uses a height-dependent mapping. In detail, the colour assigned to a midpoint is one of its end point's colours. The colour chosen is determined by a Boolean random which is indexed by the key value of the midpoint. Once again this must be accessed in this way to maintain consistency, which is just as important for colour as it is for position.

2.2

Constructive solid geometry (CSG) representation of objects

We categorized the previous method – polygon mesh – as a machine representation which also frequently functions as a user representation. The CSG approach is very much a user representation and requires special rendering techniques or the conversion to a polygon mesh model prior to representation. It is a high-level representation that functions both as a shape representation and a record of how it was built up. The 'logic of the shape' in this representation is in how the final shape can be made or represented as a combination of primitive shapes. The designer builds up a shape by using the metaphor of three-dimensional building blocks and a selection of ways in which they can be combined. The high-level nature of the representation imposes a certain burden on the designer. Although with hindsight the logic of the parts in Figure 2.14 is apparent; the design of complex machine parts using this methodology is a demanding occupation.

The motivation for this type of representation is to facilitate an interactive mode for solid modelling. The idea is that objects are usually parts that will eventually be manufactured by casting, machining or extruding and they can be built up in a CAD program by using the equivalent (abstract) operations combining simple elementary objects called geometric primitives. These primitives are, for example, spheres, cones, cylinders or rectangular solids and they are combined using (three-dimensional) Boolean set operators and linear transformations. An object representation is stored as an attributed tree. The leaves contain simple primitives and the nodes store operators or linear transformations. The representation defines not only the shape of the object but its modelling history – the creation of the object and its representation become one and the same thing. The object is built up by adding primitives and causing them to combine with existing primitives. Shapes can be added to and subtracted from (to make holes) the current shape. For example, increasing the diameter of a hole through a rectangular solid means a trivial alteration – the radius of the cylinder primitive defining the hole is simply increased. This contrasts with the polygon mesh representation where the same operation is distinctly non-trivial. Even although the constituent polygons of the cylindrical surface are easily accessible in a hierarchical scheme, to generate a new set of polygons means reactivating whatever modelling procedure was used to create the original polygons. Also, account has to be taken of the fact that to maintain the same accuracy more polygons will have to be used.

Boolean set operators are used both as a representational form and as a user interface technique. A user specifies primitive solids and combines these using the Boolean set operators. The representation of the object is a reflection or recording of the user interaction operations. Thus we can say that the modelling information and representation are not separate – as they are in the case of deriving a representation from low-level information from an input device. The low-level information in the case of CSG is already in the form of volumetric primitives. The modelling activity becomes the representation. An example will demonstrate the idea.

Figure 2.12 shows the Boolean operations possible between solids. Figure 2.12(a) shows the union of two solids. If we consider the objects as 'clouds' of points the union operation encloses all points lying within the original two bodies. The second example (Figure 2.12(b)) shows the effect of a difference or subtraction operator. A subtract operator removes all those points in the second body that are contained within the first. In this case a cylinder is defined and

Figure 2.12
Boolean operations between
solids in CSG modelling:
(a) union, (b) subtraction
and (c) intersection.

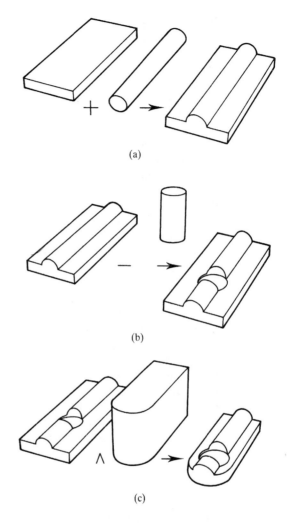

(a)

(b)

(c)

subtracted from the object produced in Figure 2.12(a). Finally, an example is shown of an intersect operation (Figure 2.12(c)). Here a solid is defined that is made from the union of a cylinder and a rectangular solid (the same operation with the same primitives as in Figure 2.12(a)). This solid then intersects with the object produced in Figure 2.12(b). An intersect operation produces a set of points that are contained by both the bodies. An obvious distinguishing feature of this method that follows from this example is that primitives are used not just to build up a model but also to take material away.

Figure 2.13 shows a CSG representation that reflects the construction of a simple object. Three original solids appear at the leaves of the tree: two boxes and a cylinder. The boxes are combined using a union operation and a hole is 'drilled' in one of the boxes by defining a cylinder and subtracting it from the two box

Figure 2.13
A CSG tree reflecting the construction of a simple object made from three primitives.

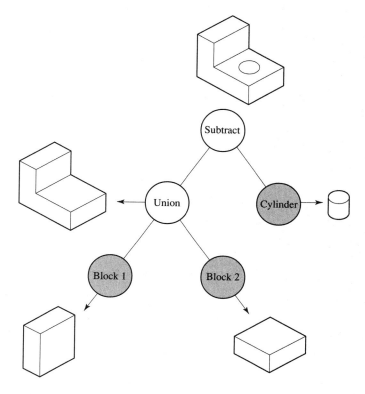

assembly. Thus the only information that has to be stored in the leaves of the tree is the name of the primitive and its dimensions. A node has to contain the name of the operator and the spatial relationship between the child nodes combined by the operator.

The power of Boolean operations is further demonstrated in the following examples. In the first example (Figure 2.14(a)) two parts developed separately are combined to make the desired configuration by using the union operator followed by a difference operator. The second example (Figure 2.14(b)) shows a complex object constructed only from the union of cylinders, which is then used to produce, by subtraction, a complex housing.

Although there are substantial advantages in CSG representation, they do suffer from drawbacks. A practical problem is the computation time required to produce a rendered image of the model. A more serious drawback is that the method imposes limitations on the operations available to create and modify a solid. Boolean operations are global – they affect the whole solid. Local operations, say a detailed modification on one face of a complex object cannot be easily implemented by using set operations. An important local modification required in many objects that are to be designed is blending surfaces. For example, consider the end face of a cylinder joined onto a flat base. Normally for practical manufacturing or aesthetic reasons, instead of the join being a right angle in cross-

Figure 2.14
Examples of geometrically complex objects produced from simple objects and Boolean operations.

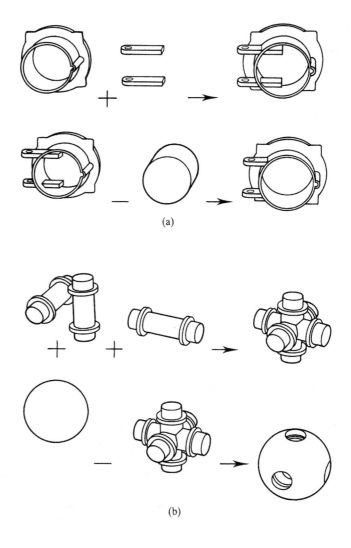

(a)

(b)

section a radius is desired. A radius swept around another curve cannot be represented in a simple CSG system. This fact has led to many solid modellers using an underlying boundary representation. Incidentally there is no reason why Boolean operations cannot be incorporated in boundary representations systems. For example, many systems incorporate Boolean operations but use a boundary representation to represent the object. The trade-off between these two representations has resulted in a debate that has lasted for 15 years. Finally note that a CSG representation is a volumetric representation. The space occupied by the object – its volume – is represented rather than the object surface.

2.3 Space subdivision techniques for object representation

Space subdivision techniques are methods that consider the whole of object space and in some way label each point in the space according to object occupancy. However, unlike CSG, which uses a variety of volumetric elements or geometric primitives, space subdivision techniques are based on a single cubic element known as a voxel. A voxel is a volumetric element or primitive and is the smallest cube used in the representation. We could divide up all of world space into regular or cubic voxels and label each voxel according to whether it is in the object or in empty space. Clearly this is very costly in terms of memory consumption. Because of this voxel representation is not usually a preferred mainstream method but is used either because the raw data are already in this form or it is easiest to convert the data into this representation – the case, for example, in medical imagery; or because of the demands of an algorithm. For example, ray tracing in voxel space has significant advantages over conventional ray tracing. This is an example of an algorithmic technique dictating the nature of the object representation. Here, instead of asking the question: 'does this ray intersect with any objects in the scene?' which implies a very expensive intersection test to be carried out on each object, we pose the question: 'what objects are encountered as we track a ray through voxel space?' This requires no exhaustive search through the primary data structure for possible intersections and is a much faster strategy.

Another example is rendering CSG models (Section 4.3) which is not straightforward if conventional techniques are used. A strategy is to convert the CSG tree into an intermediate data consisting of voxels and render from this. Voxels can be considered as an intermediate representation, most commonly in medical imaging where their use links two-dimensional raw data with the visualization of three-dimensional structures. Alternatively the raw data may themselves be voxels. This is the case with many mathematical modelling schemes of three-dimensional physical phenomena such as fluid dynamics.

The main problem with voxel labelling is the trade-off between the consumption of vast storage costs and accuracy. Consider, for example, labelling square pixels to represent a circle in two-dimensional space. The pixel size /accuracy trade-off is clear here. The same notion extends to using voxels to represent a sphere except that now the cost depends on the accuracy and the cube of the radius. Thus such schemes are only used in contexts where their advantages outweigh their cost. A way to reduce cost is to impose a structural organization on the basic voxel labelling scheme.

The common way of organizing voxel data is to use an octree – a hierarchical data structure that describes how the objects in a scene are distributed throughout the three-dimensional space occupied by the scene. The basic idea is shown in Figure 2.15. In Figure 2.15(a) a cubic space is subject to a recursive subdivision which enables any cubic region of the space to be labelled with a number. This subdivision can proceed to any desired level of accuracy. Figure 2.15(b) shows an object embedded in this space and Figure 2.15(c) shows the subdivision and the

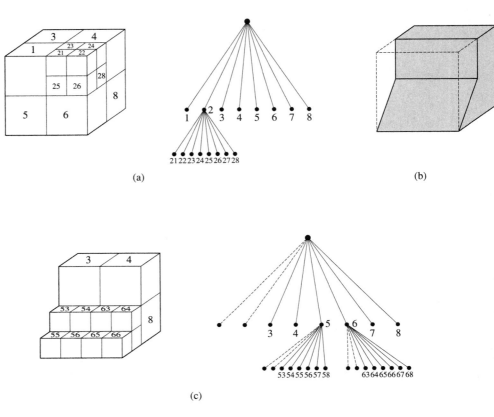

Figure 2.15
Octree representation.
(a) Cubic space and labelling scheme, and the octree for the two levels of subdivision. (b) Object embedded in space. (c) Representation of the object to two levels of subdivision.

related octree that labels cubic regions in the space according to whether they are occupied or empty.

There are actually two ways in which the octree decomposition of a scene can be used to represent the scene. Firstly, an octree as described above can be used in itself as a complete representation of the objects in the scene. The set of cells occupied by an object constitute the representation of the object. However, for a complex scene, high resolution work would require the decomposition of occupied space into an extremely large number of cells and this technique requires enormous amounts of data storage. A common alternative is to use a standard data structure representation of the objects and to use the octree as a representation of the distribution of the objects in the scene. In this case, a terminal node of a tree representing an occupied region would be represented by a pointer to the data structure for any object (or part of an object) contained within that region. Figure 2.16 illustrates this possibility in the two-dimensional case. Here the region subdivision has stopped as soon as a region is encountered that intersects only one object. A region represented by a terminal node is not necessarily completely occupied by the object associated with that region. The shape of the object within the region would be described by its data structure representation. In the case of a surface model representation of a scene, the 'objects' would be polygons or patches. In general, an occupied region represented by a terminal node would intersect with several polygons and would be represented by a list of pointers into the object data structures. Thus unlike the other techniques that we have described octrees are generally not self-contained representational methods. They are instead usually part of a hybrid scheme.

(2.3.1)

Octrees and polygons

As we have already implied, the most common use of octrees in computer graphics is not to impose a data structure, on voxel data, but to organize a scene containing many objects (each of which is made up of many polygons) into a structure of spatial occupancy. We are not representing the objects using voxels, but considering the rectangular space occupied as polygons as entities which are represented by voxel space. As far as rendering is concerned we enclose parts of the scene, at some level of detail, in rectangular regions in the sense of Figure 2.16. For example, we may include groups of objects, single objects, parts of objects or even single polygons in an octree leaf node. This can greatly speed up many aspects of rendering and many rendering methods, particularly ray tracing as we have already suggested.

We will now use ray tracing as a particular example. The high inherent cost in naive ray tracing resides in intersection testing. As we follow a ray through the scene we have to find out if it collides with any object in the scene (and what the position of that point is). In the case that each ray is tested against all objects in the scene, where each object test implies testing against each polygon in the object, the rendering time, for scenes of reasonable complexity, becomes unacceptably high. If the scene is decomposed into an octree representation, then tracing a ray means tracking, using an incremental algorithm from voxel to voxel. Each voxel contains pointers to polygons that it contains and the ray is tested against these. Intersection candidates are reduced from n to m, where:

$$n = \sum_{\text{objects}} \text{polygon count for object}$$

and m is the number of candidate polygons contained by the octree leaf.

However, decomposing a scene into an octree is an expensive operation and has to be judiciously controlled. It involves finding the 'minmax' coordinates of each polygon (the coordinates of its bounding box) and using these as an entity in the decomposition. Two factors that can be used to control the decomposition are:

(1) The minimum number of candidate polygons per node. The smaller this factor, the greater is the decomposition and fewer intersection tests are made by a ray that enters a voxel. The total number of intersection tests per voxel for the entire rendering is approximately given by:

number of rays entering the voxel × (0.5 × number of polygons in voxel)

assuming that on average a ray tests 50% of the candidate polygons before it finds an intersection.

Figure 2.16
Quadtree representation of a two-dimensional scene down to the level of cells containing at most a single object. Terminal nodes for cells containing objects would be represented by a pointer to a data structure representation of the object.

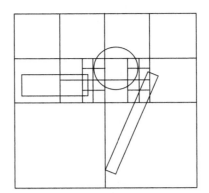

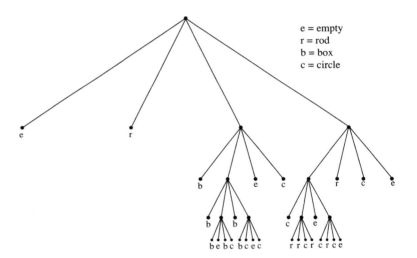

e = empty
r = rod
b = box
c = circle

(2) The maximum octree depth. The greater the depth the greater the decomposition and the fewer the candidate polygons at a leaf node. Also, because the size of a voxel decreases by a factor of 8 at every level, the fewer the rays that will enter the voxel for any given rendering.

In general the degree of decomposition should not be so great that the savings gained on intersection are wiped out by the higher costs of tracking a ray through decomposed space. Experience has shown that a default value of 8 for the above two factors gives good results in general for an object (or objects) distributed evenly throughout the space. Frequently scenes are rendered where this condition does not hold. Figure 2.17 shows an example where a few objects with high polygon count are distributed around a room whose volume is large compared to the space occupied by the objects. In this case octree subdivision will proceed to a high depth subdividing mostly empty space.

Figure 2.17
A scene consisting of a few objects of high polygon count. The objects are small compared with the volume of the room.

2.3.2

BSP trees

An alternative representation to an octree is a BSP or binary space partitioning tree. Each non-terminal node in the BSP tree represents a single partitioning plane that divides the space into two. A two-dimensional analogue illustrating the difference is shown in Figure 2.18. A BSP tree is not a direct object representation (although in certain circumstances it can be). Instead it is a way of partitioning space for a particular purpose – most commonly hidden surface removal. Because of this it is difficult and somewhat pointless to discuss BSP trees without dealing at the same time with HSR (see Chapter 6).

The properties of partitioning planes that can be exploited in computer graphics scenes are:

● Any object on one side of a plane cannot intercept any object on the other side.

● Given a view point in the scene space, objects on the same side as the viewer are nearer than any objects on the other side.

When a BSP tree is used to represent a subdivision of space into cubic cells, it shows no significant advantage over a direct data structure encoding of the octree. It is the same information encoded in a different way. However, nothing said above requires that the subdivision should be into cubic cells. In fact the

Figure 2.18
Quadtree and BSP tree representations of a one-level subdivision of a two-dimensional region.

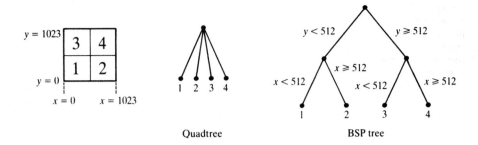

2.3.3 Creating voxel objects

idea of a BSP tree was originally introduced in Fuchs (1980) where the planes used to subdivide space could be at any orientation. We revisit BSP trees in the context of hidden surface removal (Chapter 6).

One of the mainstream uses of voxel objects is in volume rendering in medical imagery. The source data in such applications consist of a set of parallel planes of intensity information collected from consecutive cross-sections from some part of a body, where a pixel in one such plane will represent, say, the X-ray absorption of that part of the body that the pixel physically corresponds to. The problem is how to convert such a stack of planar two-dimensional information into a three-dimensional rendered object. Converting the stack of planes to a set of voxels is the most direct way to solve this problem. Corresponding pixels in two consecutive planes are deemed to form the top and bottom face of a voxel and some operation is performed to arrive at a single voxel value from the two pixel values. The voxel representation is used as an intermediary between the raw collected data, which are two-dimensional, and the required three-dimensional visualization. The overall process from the collection of raw data, through the conversion to a voxel representation and the rendering of the voxel data is the subject of Chapter 13.

Contours collected by a laser ranger can be converted into a voxel representation instead of into a polygon mesh representation. However, this may result in a loss of accuracy compared with using a skinning algorithm.

2.4 Representing objects with implicit functions

As we have already pointed out, representing a whole object by a single implicit formula is restricted to certain objects such as spheres. Nevertheless such a representation does find mainstream use in representing 'algorithmic' objects known as bounding volumes. These are used in many different contexts in computer graphics as a complexity limiting device.

A representation developed from implicit formulae is the representation of objects by using the concept of implicitly defined objects as components. (We use the term component rather than primitive because the object is not simply a set of touching spheres but a surface derived from such a collection.)

Implicit functions are surfaces formed by the effect of primitives that exert a field of influence over a local neighbourhood. For example, consider a pair of point heat sources shown in Figure 2.19. We could define the temperature in their vicinities as a field function where, for each in isolation, we have isothermal contours as spherical shells centred on each source. Bringing the two sources within influence of each other defines a combined global scalar field, the field of each source combining with that of the other to form a composite set of isothermal contours as shown. Such a scalar field, due to the combined effect of a number of primitives is used to define a modelling surface in computer graphics. Usually we consider an isosurface in the field to be the boundary of a volume which is the object that we desire to model. Thus we have the following elements in any implicit function modelling system:

- A generator or primitive for which a distance function $d(\boldsymbol{P})$ can be defined for all points $\boldsymbol{P}$ in the locality of the generator.

- A 'potential' function $f(d(\boldsymbol{P}))$ which returns a scalar value for a point $\boldsymbol{P}$ distance $d(\boldsymbol{P})$ from the generator. Associated with the generator can be an area of influence outside of which the generator has no influence. For a point generator this is usually a sphere. An example of a potential function is:

$$f(\boldsymbol{P}) = (1 - \frac{d^2}{R^2})^2 \qquad d \leq R$$

where d is the distance of the point to the generator and R is its radius of influence.

- A scalar field $F(\boldsymbol{P})$ which determines the combined effect of the individual potential functions of the generators. This implies the existence of a blending method which in the simplest case is addition – we evaluate a scalar field by evaluating the individual contributions of each generator at a point $\boldsymbol{P}$ and adding their effects together.

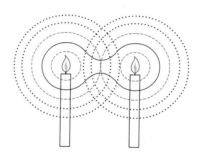

Figure 2.19
An isosurface of equal temperature around two heat sources (solid line).

● An isosurface of the scalar field which is used to represent the physical surface of the object that we are modelling.

An example (Figure 2.20 Colour Plate) illustrates the point. The Salvador Dali imitation on the left is an isosurface formed by point generators disposed in space as shown on the right. The radius of each sphere is proportional to the radius of influence of each generator. The dark spheres represent negative generators which are used to 'carve' concavities in the model. (Although we can form concavities by using only positive generators, it is more convenient to use negative ones as we require far fewer spheres.) The example illustrates the potential of the method for modelling organic shapes.

Deformable object animation can be implemented by displaying or choreographing the points that generate the object. The problem with using implicit functions in animation is that there is not a good intuitive link between moving groups of generators and the deformation that ensues because of this. Of course, this general problem is suffered by all modelling techniques where the geometry definition and the deformation method are one and the same thing.

In addition to this general problem, unwanted blending and unwanted separation can occur when the generators are moved with respect to each other and the same blending method retained.

A significant advantage of implicit functions in an animation context is the ease of collision detection that results from an easy inside–outside function. Irrespective of the complexity of the modelled surface a single scalar value defines the isosurface and a point P is inside the object volume or outside it depending on whether $F(P)$ is less than or greater than this value.

(2.5) Scene management and object representation

As the demand for high quality real time computer graphics continues to grow, from applications like computer games and virtual reality, the issue of efficient scene management has become increasingly important. This means that representational forms have to be extended to collections of objects; in other words the scene has to be considered as an object itself. This has generally meant using hierarchical or tree structures, such as BSP trees to represent the scene down to object and sub-object level. As rendering has increasingly migrated into real time applications, efficiency in culling and hidden surface removal has become as important as efficient rendering for complex scenes. With the advent of 3D graphics boards for the PC we are seeing a trend develop where the basic rendering of individual objects is handled by hardware and the evaluation of which objects are potentially visible is computed by software. (We will look into culling and hidden surface removal in Chapters 5 and 6). An equally important efficiency measure for objects in complex scenes has come to be known as Level of Detail, or LOD, and it is this topic that we will now examine.

Polygon mesh optimization

As we have discussed, polygon mesh models are well established as the *de facto* standard representational form in computer graphics but they suffer from significant disadvantages, notably that the level of detail, or number of polygons, required to synthesize the object for a high quality rendition of a complex object is very large. If the object is to be rendered on screen at different viewing distances the pipeline has to process thousands of polygons that project onto a few pixels on the screen. As the projected polygon size decreases, the polygon overheads become significant and in real time applications this situation is intolerable. High polygon counts per object occur either because of object complexity or because of the nature of the modelling system. Laser scanners and the output from programs like the marching cubes algorithm (which converts voxels into polygons) are notorious for producing very large polygon counts. Using such facilities almost always results in a model that, when rendered, is indistinguishable from a version rendered from a model with far fewer faces.

As early as 1976, one of the pioneers of 3D computer graphics, James H. Clark, wrote:

It makes no sense to use 500 polygons in describing an object if it covers only 20 raster units of the display . . . For example, when we view the human body from a very large distance, we might need to present only specks for the eyes, or perhaps just a block for the head, totally eliminating the eyes from consideration . . . these issues have not been addressed in a unified way.

Did Clark realize that not many years after he had written these words that 500 000 polygon objects would become fairly commonplace and that complex scenes might contain millions of polygons?

Existing systems tend to address this problem in a somewhat ad hoc manner. For example, many cheap virtual reality systems adopt a two- or three-level representation switching in surface detail, such as the numbers on the buttons of a telephone as the viewer moves closer to it. This produces an annoying visual disturbance as the detail blinks on and off. More considered approaches are now being proposed and lately there has been a substantial increase in the number of papers published in this area.

Thus mesh optimization seems necessary and the problem cannot be dismissed by relying on increased polygon throughput of the workstations of the future. The position we are in at the moment is that mainstream virtual reality platforms produce a visually inadequate result even from fairly simple scenes. We have to look forward not only to dealing with the defects in the image synthesis of such scenes, but also to being able to handle scenes of real world complexity implying many millions of polygons. The much vaunted 'immersive' applications of virtual reality will never become acceptable unless we can cope with scenes of such complexity. Current hardware is very far away from being able to deal with a complex scene in real time to the level of quality attainable for single object scenes.

An obvious solution to the problem is to generate a polygon mesh at the final level of detail and then use this representation to spawn a set of coarser descriptions. As the scene is rendered an appropriate level of detail is selected. Certain algorithms have emerged from time to time in computer graphics that use this principle. An example of a method that facilitates a polygon mesh at any level of detail is bi-cubic parametric patches (see Section 4.2.2). Here we take a patch description and turn it into a polygon description. At the same time we can easily control the number of polygons that are generated for each patch and relate this to local surface curvature. This is exactly what is done in patch rendering where a geometric criterion is used to control the extent of the subdivision and produce an image free of geometric aliasing (visible polygon edges in silhouette). The price we pay for this approach is the expense and difficulty of getting the patch description in the first place. But in any case we could build the original patch representation and construct a pyramid of polygon mesh representations off-line.

The idea of storing a 'detail pyramid' and accessing an appropriate level is established in many application areas. Consider the case of mip-mapping, for example (see Chapter 8). Here texture maps are stored in a detail hierarchy and a fine detail map selected when the projection of the map on the screen is large. In the event that the map projects onto just one pixel, then a single pixel texture map – the average of the most detailed map – is selected. Also, in this method the problem of avoiding a jump when going from one level to another is carefully addressed and an approximation to a continuous level of detail is obtained by interpolation between two maps.

The diversity of current approaches underlines the relative newness of the field. A direct and simple approach for triangular meshes derived from voxel sets was reported by Schroeder *et al*. in 1992. Here the algorithm considers each vertex on a surface. By looking at the triangles that contribute to, or share, the vertex, a number of criteria can be enumerated and used to determine whether these triangles can be merged into a single one exclusive of the vertex under consideration. For example, we can invoke the 'reduce the number of triangles where the surface curvature is low' argument by measuring the variance in the surface normals of the triangles that share the vertex. Alternatively we could consider the distance from the vertex to an (average) plane through all the other vertices of the sharing triangles (Figure 2.21). This is a local approach that considers vertices in the geometry of their immediate surroundings.

A more recent approach is the work of Hoppe (1996) which we will now describe. Hoppe gives an excellent categorization of the problems and advantages of mesh optimization, listing these as follows:

- Mesh simplification – reducing the polygons to a level that is adequate for the quality required. (This, of course, depends on the maximum projection size of the object on the screen.)

- Level of detail approximation – a level is used that is appropriate to the viewing distance. In this respect, Hoppe adds: 'Since instantaneous

Figure 2.21
A simple vertex deletion criterion. Delete **V**? Measure d, the distance from **V** to the (average) plane through the triangles that share **V**.

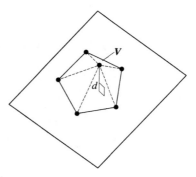

switching between LOD meshes may lead to perceptible "popping", one would like to construct smooth visual transitions, *geomorphs*, between meshes at different resolutions'.

- Progressive transmission – this is a three-dimensional equivalent of the common progressive transmission modes used to transmit two-dimensional imagery over the Internet. Succesive LOD approximations can be transmitted and rendered at the reciever.

- Mesh compression – analagous to two-dimensional image pyramids. We can consider not only reducing the number of polygons but also minimizing the space that any LOD approximation occupies. As in two-dimensional imagery, this is important because an LOD hierarchy occupies much more memory than a single model stored at its highest level of detail.

- Selective refinement – an LOD representation may be used in a context-dependent manner. Hoppe gives the example of a user flying over a terrain where the terrain mesh need only be fully detailed near the viewer.

Addressing mesh compression, Hoppe takes a 'pyramidal' approach and stores the coarsest level of detail approximation together, for each higher level, with the information required to ascend from a lower to a higher level of detail. To make the transition from a lower to a higher level the reverse of the transformation that constructed the hierarchy from the highest to the lowest level is stored and used. This is in the form of a vertex split – an operation that adds an additional vertex to the lower mesh to obtain the next mesh up the detail hierarchy. Although Hoppe originally considered three mesh transformations – an edge collapse, an edge split and an edge swap – he found that an edge collapse is sufficient for simplifying meshes.

The overall scheme is represented in Figure 2.22(a) which shows a detail pyramid which would be constructed off-line by a series of edge collapse transformations that take the original mesh M_n and generate through repeated edge collapse transformations the final or coarsest mesh M_0. The entire pyramid can then be stored as M_0 together with the information required to generate, from M_0 to any finer level M_i in the hierarchy – mesh compression. This inter-level transformation is the reverse of the edge collapse and is the information required

Figure 2.22
Hoppe's (1996) progressive mesh scheme based on edge collapse transformations.

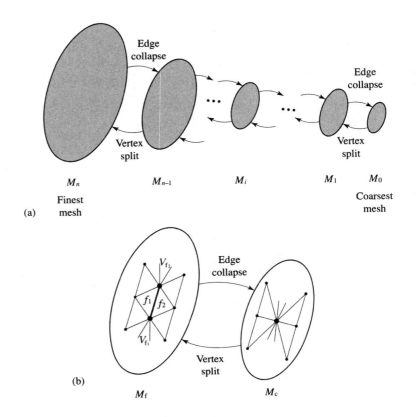

for a vertex split. Hoppe quotes an example of an object with 13 546 faces which was simplified to an M_0 of 150 faces using 6698 edge collapse transformations. The original data are then stored as M_0 together with the 6698 vertex split records. The vertex split records themselves exhibit redundancy and can be compressed using classical data compression techniques.

Figure 2.22(b) shows a single edge collapse between two consecutive levels. The notation is as follows: V_{f1} and V_{f2} are the two vertices in the finer mesh that are collapsed into one vertex V_c in the coarser mesh, where

$$V_c \in \left\{ V_{f1},\ V_{f2},\ \frac{V_{f1} + V_{f2}}{2} \right\}$$

From the diagram it can be seen that this operation implies the collapse of the two faces f_1 and f_2 into new edges.

Hoppe defines a continuum between any two levels of detail by using a blending parameter α. If we define:

$$d = \frac{V_{f1} + V_{f2}}{2}$$

then we can generate a continuum of geomorphs between the two levels by having the edge shrink under control of the blending parameter as:

$$V_{f1} := V_{f1} + \alpha d \quad \text{and} \quad V_{f2} := V_{f2} - \alpha d$$

Texture coordinates can be interpolated in the same way as can scalar attributes associated with a vertex such as colour.

The remaining question is: how are the edges selected for collapse in the reduction from M_i to M_{i-1}? This can be done either by using a simple heuristic approach or by a more rigorous method that measures the difference between a particular approximation and a sample of the original mesh. A simple metric that can be used to order the edges for collapse is:

$$\frac{|V_{f1} - V_{f2}|}{|\mathbf{N}_{f1} \cdot \mathbf{N}_{f2}|}$$

that is, the length of the edge divided by the dot product of the vertex normals. On its own this metric will work quite well, but if it is continually applied the mesh will suddenly begin to 'collapse' and a more considered approach to edge selection is mandatory. Figure 2.23 is an example that uses this technique.

Hoppe casts this as an energy function minimzation problem. A mesh M is optimized with respect to a set of points X which are the vertices of the mesh M_n together (optionally) with points randomly sampled from its faces. (Although this is a lengthy process it is, of course, executed once only as an off-line preprocess.) The energy function to be minimized is:

$$E(M) = E_{dist}(M) + E_{spring}(M)$$

where

$$E_{dist} = \sum_i d^2(x_i, M)$$

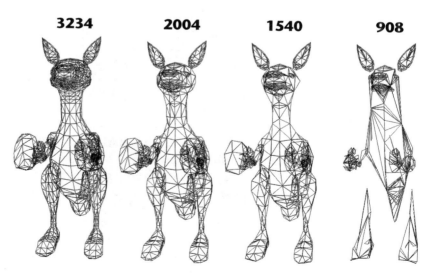

3234   **2004**   **1540**   **908**

Figure 2.23
The result of applying the simple edge elimination criterion described in the text – the model eventually breaks up.

is the sum of the squared distances from the points X to the mesh – when a vertex is removed this term will tend to increase.

$$E_{\text{spring}}(M) = \sum \kappa \|v_j - v_k\|^2$$

is a spring energy term that assists the optimization. It is equivalent to placing on each edge a spring of rest length zero and spring constant κ.

Hoppe orders the optimization by placing all (legal) edge collapse transformations into a priority queue, where the priority of each transformation is its estimated energy cost ΔE. In each iteration, the transformation at the front of the queue (lowest ΔE) is performed and the priorities of the edges in the neighbourhood of this transformation are recomputed. An edge collapse transformation is only legal if it does not change the topology of the mesh. For example, if V_{f1} and V_{f2} are boundary vertices, the edge $\{V_{f1}, V_{f2}\}$ must be a boundary edge – it cannot be an internal edge connecting two boundary points.

2.6 Summary

Object representations have evolved under a variety of influences – ease of rendering, ease of shape editing, suitability for animation, dependence on the attributes of raw data and so on. There is no general solution that is satisfactory for all practical applications and the most popular solution that has served us for so many years – the polygon mesh – has significant disadvantages as soon as we leave the domain of static objects rendered off-line. We complete this chapter by listing the defining attributes of any representation. These allow a (very) general comparison between the methods. (For completeness we have included comments on bi-cubic patches which are dealt with in the next chapter.)

- **Creation of object/representation** A factor that is obviously context dependent. We have the methods which can create representations automatically from physical data (polygon mesh from range data via a skinning algorithm, bi-cubic parametric patches via interpolation of surface data). Other methods map input data directly into a voxel representation. Some methods are suitable for interactive creation (CSG and bi-cubic parametric patches) and some can be created by interacting with a 'mathematically' based interactive facility such as sweeping a cross-section along a spine (polygon mesh and bi-cubic parametric patches).

- **Nature of the primitive elements** The common forms are either methods that represent surfaces – boundary representations (polygon mesh and bi-cubic parametric patches) or volumes (voxels and CSG).

- **Accuracy** Representations are either exact or approximate. Polygon meshes are approximate representations but their accuracy can be increased to any degree at the expense of an expansion in the data. Increasing the accuracy of a polygon mesh representation in an intelligent way is difficult. The easy 'brute force' approach – throwing more polygons at the shape – may result in areas being 'over represented'. Bi-cubic patches can either be exact or approximate depending on the application. Surface interpolation will result in an approximation but designing a car door panel using a single patch results in an exact representation. CSG representations are exact but we need to make two qualifications. They can only describe that subset of shapes that is possible by combining the set of supplied primitives. The representation is abstract in that it is just a formula for the composite object – the geometry has to be derived from the formula to enable a visualization of the object.

- **Accuracy vs data volume** There is always a trade-off between accuracy and data volume – at least as far as the rendering penalty is concerned. To increase the accuracy of a boundary representation or a volume representation we have to increase the number of low-level elements. Although the implicit equation of a sphere is 100% accurate and compact, it has to be converted for rendering using some kind of geometric sampling procedure which generates low-level elements.

- **Data volume vs complexity** There is usually a trade-off also between data volume and the complexity of the representation which has practical ramifications in the algorithms that operate with the representation. This is best exemplified by comparing polygon meshes with their counterpart using bi-cubic parametric patches.

- **Ease of editing/animation** This can mean retrospective editing of an existing model or shape deformation techniques in an animation environment. The best method for editing the shape of static objects is, of course, the CSG representation – it was designed for this. Editing bi-cubic parametric patches is easy or difficult depending on the complexity of the shape and the desired freedom of the editing operations. In this respect editing a single patch is easy, editing a net of patches is difficult. None of the representation methods that we have described is suitable for shape-changing in animated sequences, although bi-cubic parametric patches and implicit functions have been tried. It seems that the needs of accuracy and ease of animating shape change are opposites. Methods that allow a high degree of accuracy are difficult to animate, because they consist of a structure with maybe thousands of low-level primitives as leaves. For example, the common way to control a net of bi-cubic parametric patches representing, say, the face of a character is to organize it into a hierarchy allowing local changes to be made (by descending the hierarchy and operating on a few or even a single patch) and making more global changes by operating at a high level in the structure. This has not resulted in a generally accepted animation technique simply because it does not produce good results (in the case of facial animation anyway). It seems shape-change animation needs a paradigm that is independent of the object model and the most successful techniques involve embedding the object model in *another* structure which is then subject to shape-change animation. Thus we control facial animation by attaching a geometric structure to a muscle control model or immerse a geometric model in the 'field' of an elastic solid and animate the elastic solid. In other words for the representations that we currently use, animation of shape does not seem to be possible by operating directly on the geometry of the object.

3 Representation and modelling of three-dimensional objects (2)

Introduction

In the previous chapter we concentrated mainly on the polygon mesh representation where a polygon was, for example, a (flat) quadrilateral made up of four vertices joined by four straight lines. This chapter is devoted entirely to a representational form where the primitive element – a bi-cubic parametric patch – is a curvilinear quadrilateral. It has four corner points joined by four edges which are themselves cubic curves. The interior of the patch is a curved (cubic) surface where every point on the surface is defined. This contrasts with the polygon mesh approximation where surface points on an object are only defined at the polygon vertices.

Representing surfaces of objects using bi-cubic parametric patches finds two main applications in computer graphics:

(1) As a basis for interactive design in CAD. Here we may obtain the model by an interactive process – a designer building up a model by interacting with a program. In many CAD applications the representational form is transformed *directly* into a real object (or a scaled-down model of the real object). The

computer graphics representation is used to control a device such as a numerical milling machine which sculpts the object in some material. This is exactly the opposite of the 'normal' computer graphics modelling methodology – instead of transforming a real object into a representation we are using the computer graphics model to make the real object.

(2) As an alternative representational form to the polygon mesh – the representation which services the normal computer graphics requirement of transforming a real object into a representational form. In this use we usually wish to exploit the accuracy of the parametric representation over the polygon mesh approximation. Here we may obtain a parametric representation from a real object by some (surface) interpolation technique.

The apparent advantages of this representation over the polygon mesh representation are:

● It is an exact analytical representation.

● It has the potential of three-dimensional shape editing.

● It is a more economical representation.

Given these advantages it is somewhat surprising that this form is not the mainstream representation in computer graphics. It is certainly no more difficult to render an object represented by a net of patches and so we must conclude that its lack of popularity in mainstream computer graphics (it is, of course, used in industrial CAD), is due to the mathematical formalities associated with it.

The exactness of the representation factor needs careful qualification. A real object (or a physical model of a real object) can be represented by a net or mesh of patches (Figure 3.28 and Figure 3.43 are two such objects) but the representation may not be wholly 'exact'. In the first example, the teapot cannot have a perfectly circular cross-section because the representational method, in this case the Bézier form or Bernstein basis, cannot represent a circle exactly. The patches representing the face in the second example may not everywhere be coincident with the real object. We can obtain a suitable set of points that lie in the surface of the object from a three-dimensional digitizer and we could, say, use the same set of points that we would use to build a polygon mesh model. We then use an interpolation technique known as surface fitting, to determine a set of patches that represents the surface. However, the patch surface and the object surface will not necessarily be identical. The exactness of the fit depends on both the nature of the interpolation process and how closely the physical surface conforms to the shape constraints of the bi-cubic patch representation. But we do end up with an object representation that is a smooth surface which has certain advantages over the polygon mesh representation – the silhouette edge problem, which accounts for the most prominent visual defect in rendered polygon mesh objects, is cured.

It is possible to model subtly shaped objects such as the human face with a net of patches. An adequate representation of such an object using a polygon mesh would need an extremely high polygonal resolution. Despite this there is a perceived complexity associated with bi-cubic parametric patches and in many applications we can avoid this by using the polygon mesh representation. When we digitize real objects we are normally working with an application that does not demand exact representation. We may be building a model of a product for an animated TV commercial, for example, in which case a good polygon mesh model will do.

In fact the most common applications of the bi-cubic parametric patch representation are not to build very complex models but as a representation for fairly simple objects in industrial CAD or CAGD applications. The real value of the representation here is that it can be used to transform an abstract design, built up within an interactive program, directly into a physical reality. The description can be made to drive a sculpting device such as a numerically controlled milling machine to produce a prototype object without any human intervention. It is this single factor more than any other that makes bi-cubic parametric patches important in CAD.

Part of their value in CAD comes from the ability to change the shape of an object represented by patches in a way that maintains a smooth surface. Sometimes the allusion to sculpting is made. We can view the representation as a kind of 'abstract clay' model that can be pulled around and deformed into any desirable shape – giving the same freedom to create as a sculptor would have with a real clay model. Here we should be wary of the claims that are made in the computer graphics literature concerning the efficacy of free-form sculpting using bi-cubic parametric patches. We can distinguish between methods that attempt a free-form sculpting model, which places no constraints on the shape complexity of the object formed, and the much more well-established techniques in CAD where the object tends to be fairly simple. A common, early example of this category is the design of car body panels. Bi-cubic parametric patches are manifestly successful in such applications; their success as a metaphor for clay sculpting is more debatable.

We distinguish between objects that are represented by a single patch and objects whose form demands that they are represented by a net of patches. Shape editing a single patch is straightforward but the objects that we can design with a single patch are restricted. Shape editing an object that is represented by a net of patches is much more difficult. One problem is that if we have to alter the shape of one patch in a net, we have to maintain its smoothness relationship with the neighbouring patches in which it is embedded. Another difficulty is yet another manifestation of the scale problem. Say we want to effect a shape change that involves many patches. We have to move these patches together and maintain their continuity with all their neighbouring patches.

Despite these difficulties we should recognize that this representation has a strong potential for shape editing compared with the polygon mesh representation. This is already an approximation and pulling vertices around to change the shape of the represented object results in many difficulties. The accuracy of the polygon mesh representation changes as soon as vertices are moved resulting perhaps in visual defects. It is almost certain that we would always have to move groups of points rather than move a single polygon vertex around in three space. Pulling a single vertex would just result in a local peak.

In this chapter we will mainly confine ourselves to the study of single patches and simple shapes formed from nets of a few patches using rudimentary but powerful CAD techniques, such as generating a solid object by sweeping a profile through 360°.

The analytical representation of patches differs according to the formulation and some have been named after their instigators. One of the most popular formulations is the Bézier patch developed in the 1960s by Pierre Bézier for use in the design of Renault cars. His CAD system called UNISURF was one of the first to be used. In what follows we will concentrate mainly on the Bézier and B-spline formulation.

The usual approach in considering parametric representation is to begin with a description of three-dimensional space curves and then to generalize to surfaces or patches. A three-dimensional space curve is a smooth curve that is a function of the three spatial variables. An example would be the path that a particle traced as it moved through space. Incidentally, curves by themselves also find applications in computer graphics. For example, we can script the path of an object in three-dimensional computer animation by using a space curve. We can model a 'ducted' solid by sweeping a cross-section along a space curve as we saw in the previous chapter.

3.1 Bézier curves

In this section we will look at the pioneering developments of Bézier, who was amongst the first to develop computer tools in industrial design. We will draw on Bézier's own descriptions of the evolution of his method, not just because of their historical interest but also because they give a real insight into the relationship between the representation, the physical reality and the requirements of the designers who were to use his methods.

Bézier's development work was carried out in the Renault car factory in the 1960s and he called his system UNISURF. Car designers are concerned with styling free-form surfaces which are then used to produce master dies which produce the tools that stamp out the manufactured parts. Many other industries use free-form surfaces. Some parts such as ship's hulls, airframes and turbine blades are constrained by aerodynamic and hydrodynamic considerations and shapes evolve through experience and testing in wind tunnels and test tanks, but a designer still needs freedom to produce new shapes albeit within these constraints. Before the advent of this representational form, such free-form surfaces could not be represented analytically and once developed could only be stored for future reproduction and evolution by sampling and storing as coordinates.

Prior to Bézier's innovation the process of going from the abstract design to the prototype was lengthy and involved many people and processes. The following description, abstracted from Bézier's account in Piegl's book (Piegl 1993), is of the process of car design at the time:

(1) Stylists defined a general shape using small-scale sketches and clay mock-ups.

(2) Using offsets (world coordinates in computer graphics terminology) measured on the mock-up, designers traced a full-scale shape of the skin of the car body.

(3) Plasterers built a full-scale model, weighing about eight tons, starting from plywood cross-sections duplicating the curves of the drawing. The clay model was then examined by stylists and sales managers, and modified according to taste.

(4) When at last the model was accepted, offsets were again measured and the final drawings were made. During this period, which could be a year or more, tooling and production specialists often suggested minor changes to avoid difficult and costly operations during production.

(5) The drawings were finalized, and one three-dimensional master was built as the standard for checking the press tools and stamped parts.

(6) The plaster copies of the master were used for milling punches and dies on copy-machine tools.

Bézier's pioneer development completely changed most aspects of these processes by enabling a representation of free-form surfaces. Before, a designer would produce curves using say a device such as a French curve. The designer used his skill and experience to produce a complete curve that was built, step-by-step, using segments along some portion of the French curve. A curve generated in this way could not be stored conveniently except as a set of samples. Bézier's development was a definition that enabled such curves to be represented as four points, known as control points, and an implicit set of basis or blending functions. When the four points are injected into the definition, the curve is generated or reproduced. This has two immediate consequences. The definition can be used directly to drive a numerically controlled milling machine and the part can be produced exactly without the intervention of complications and delays. (Numerically controlled milling machines have been in existence since 1955 and were another motivation for the development of CAGD.) The definition can be used as a basis of a CAD program in which modifications to the curve can be made to a computer visualization.

Bézier describes an intriguing difficulty that he experienced at the time:

When it was suggested that these curves replace sweeps and French curves, most stylists objected that they had invented their own templates and would not change their methods. It was therefore solemnly promised that their secret curves would be translated into secret listings and buried in the most secret part of the computer's memory, and that nobody but them would keep the key of the vaulted cellar. In fact, the standard curves were flexible enough and secret curves were soon forgotten; designers and draughtsmen easily understood the polygons and their relationship with the shape of the corresponding curves.

Many simultaneous developments were occurring in other industries – notably aircraft and ship manufacture, and much of the research was carried out under the auspices of particular manufacturers, who, like Bézier at Renault, developed their own CAD systems and surface representations suited to their own requirements. This has lead to a number of parametric definitions of surfaces and the interested reader is best referred to Piegl's book in which each chapter is written by a pioneer in this field.

Bézier states that one of the most important requirements of his representation was that it should be founded on geometry and that the underlying mathematics should be easily understood. He introduced the concept of a space curve being contained in a cube which when distorted into a parallelepiped distorts the curve (Figure 3.1). The curve is 'fixed' within the parallelepiped as follows:

- The start and end points of the curve are located at opposite vertices of the parallelepiped.
- At its start point the curve is tangential to $0x$.
- At its end point the curve is tangential to $0z$.

This geometric concept uniquely defines any space curve (if it is understood that the curve is a polynomial of a certain degree) and also gives an intuitive feel for how the curve changes shape as the parallelepiped changes. Now the parallelepiped, and thus the curve, can be completely defined by four points – known as control points – P_0, P_1, P_2 and P_3 which are just vertices of the parallelepiped as shown in the figure. Given that the position of the end points of the curve is fixed and its behaviour at the end points is determined, the shape that the curve traces out in space between its extremities needs to be defined. A parametric

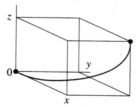

Curve 'contained' by a cube

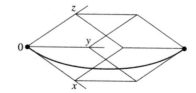

Drawing the cube into a parallelepiped changes the curve

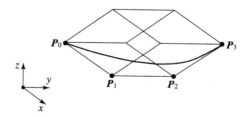

Vertices used as control points

Figure 3.1
Bézier's concept of curve representation.

definition was chosen which means that the space curve $\mathbf{Q}(u)$ is defined in terms of a parameter u $(0 \leq = u \leq = 1)$. As u varies from 0 to 1 we arrive at values for the position of a point on $\mathbf{Q}(u)$ by scaling or blending the control points. That is, each point on the curve is determined by scaling each control point by a cubic polynomial known as a basis or blending function. The curve is then given by:

$$\mathbf{Q}(u) = \sum_{i=0}^{3} \mathbf{P}_i B_i(u) \qquad\qquad [3.1]$$

and in the case of a Bézier curve the basis or blending functions are the Bernstein cubic polynomials:

$$
\begin{aligned}
B_0(u) &= (1-u)^3 \\
B_1(u) &= 3u\,(1-u)^2 \\
B_2(u) &= 3u^2\,(1-u) \\
B_3(u) &= (u)^3
\end{aligned}
$$

Figure 3.2 shows these polynomials and a Bézier curve (projected into the two-dimensional space of the diagram).

A useful intuitive notion is the following. As we move physically along the curve from $u = 0$ to $u = 1$ we simultaneously move a vertical line in the basis function space that defines four values for the basis functions. Weighting each basis function by the control points and summing, we obtain the corresponding point in the space of the curve. We note that for any value of u (except $u = 0$ and $u = 1$) all the functions are non-zero. This means that the position of all the control points contribute to every point on the curve (except at the end points). At $u = 0$ only B_0 is non-zero. Therefore:

$$\mathbf{Q}(0) = \mathbf{P}_0$$

similarly

$$\mathbf{Q}(1) = \mathbf{P}_3$$

Figure 3.2
Moving along the curve by increasing u is equivalent to moving a vertical line through the basis functions. The intercepts of this line with the basis functions give the values of B for the equivalent point.

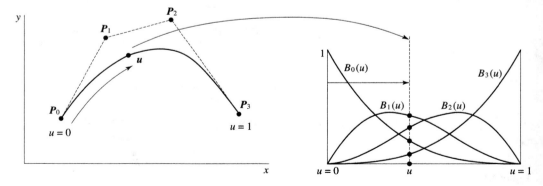

Space of curve   Space of basis functions

We also note that:

$$B_0(u) + B_1(u) + B_2(u) + B_3(u) = 1$$

Joining the four control points together gives the so-called control polygon and moving the control points around produces new curves. Moving a single control point of the curve distorts its shape in an intuitive manner. This is demonstrated in Figure 3.3. The effect of moving the end points is obvious. When we move the inner control points P_1 and P_2 we change the orientation of the tangent vectors to the curves at the end points – again obvious. Less obvious is that the positions of P_1 and P_2 also control the magnitude of the tangent vectors and it can be shown that:

$$Q_u(0) = 3(P_1 - P_0)$$
$$Q_u(1) = 3(P_2 - P_3)$$

where Q_u is the tangent vector to the curve (first derivative) at the end point. It can be seen that the curve is pulled towards the tangent vector with greater magnitude which is controlled by the position of the control points.

Bézier curves find uses not just in highly technical applications but also in popular software. Drawing packages that are found nowadays in word processors and DTP applications almost always include a sketching facility based on Bézier curves. Another well-known application of Bézier curves is shown in Figure 3.4. Here a typeface is in the process of being designed. The outline of the filled character is a set of Bézier curves to which the designer can make subtle alterations by moving the control points that specify curves that describe the outline.

Bézier's original cube concept, encapsulating a curve of three spatial variables, seems to have been lost and most texts simply deal with the curves of two spatial variables enclosed in a control polygon. Applications where three-dimensional space curves have to be designed, three-dimensional computer animation for example, can have interfaces where two-dimensional projections

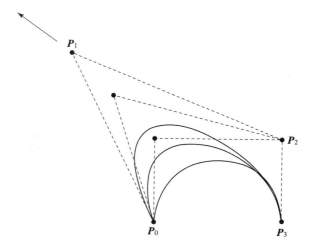

Figure 3.3
Effects of moving control point P_1.

Figure 3.4
Using Bézier curves in font design. Each curve segment control points are symbolized by O + + O.

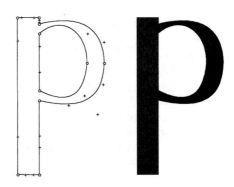

of the curve are used. An example of this application is given in Section 17.2.2. (Note, that for a three-dimensional curve the parallelepiped determines the plane in which the tangents to the curve – the edges of the control polygon – are oriented.)

At this point it is useful to consider all the ramifications of representing a curve with control points. The most important property, as far as interaction is concerned, is that moving the control points gives an intuitive change in curve shape. Another way of putting it is to say that the curve mimics the shape of the control polygon. An important property from the point of view of the algorithms that deal with curves (and surfaces) is that a curve is always enclosed in the convex hull formed by the control polygon. The convex hull of a two-dimensional space curve is illustrated in Figure 3.5 and can be considered to be the polygon formed by placing an elastic band around the control points. This follows from the fact that the basis functions sum to unity for all u.

Now consider transforming curves. Since the curves are defined as linear combinations of the control points, the curve is transformed by any affine transformation (rotation, scaling, translation etc.) in three-dimensional space by

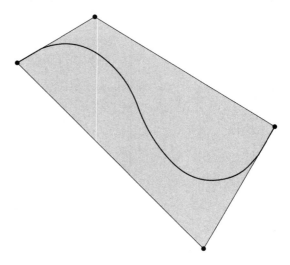

Figure 3.5
Convex hull property for cubic spline. The curve is contained in the shaded area formed from the control points.

applying the appropriate transformations to the set of control points. Thus, to transform a curve we transform the control points then compute the points on the curve. In this context, note that it is not easy to transform a curve by computing the points then transforming (as we might do with an implicit description). For example, it is not clear in scaling, how many points need to ensure smoothness when the curve has been magnified. Note here that perspective transformations are non-affine, so we cannot map control points to screen space and compute the curve there. However, we can overcome this significant disadvantage by using rational curves as we describe later in this chapter.

Finally, a useful alternative notation to the summation form is the following. First, we expand Equation 3.1 to give:

$$Q(u) = P_0 (1-u)^3 + P_1 3u(1-u)^2 + P_2 3u^2 (1-u) + P_3 u^3$$

this can then be written in matrix notation as:

$$Q(u) = UB_zP$$

$$= [u^3 \ u^2 \ u \ 1] \begin{bmatrix} -1 & 3 & -3 & 1 \\ 3 & -6 & 3 & 0 \\ -3 & 3 & 0 & 0 \\ 1 & 0 & 0 & 0 \end{bmatrix} \begin{bmatrix} P_0 \\ P_1 \\ P_2 \\ P_3 \end{bmatrix}$$

3.1.1 Joining Bézier curve segments

Curve segments, defined by a set of four control points, can be joined to make up 'more complex' curves than those obtainable from a single segment. This results in a so-called piecewise polynomial curve. An alternative method of representing more complex curves is to increase the degree of the polynomial, but this has computational and mathematical disadvantages and it is generally considered easier to split the curve into cubic segments. Connecting curve segments implies that constraints must apply at the joins. The default constraint is positional continuity, the next best is first order (or tangential continuity). The difference between positional and first order continuity for a Bézier curve is shown in Figure 3.6. Positional continuity means that the end point of the first segment is coincident with the start point of the second. First order continuity means that the edges of the characteristic polygon are collinear as shown in the figure. This means that the tangent vectors, at the end of one curve and the start of the other, match to within a constant. In shaded surfaces, maintaining only positional continuity would possibly result in the joins being visible in the final rendered object.

If the control points of the two segments are S_i and R_i then first order continuity is maintained if:

$$(S_3 - S_2) = k(R_1 - R_0)$$

Using this condition a composite Bézier curve is easily built up by adding a single segment at a time. However, the advantage of being able to build up

Figure 3.6
Continuity between
Bézier curve segments.
(a) Positional continuity
between Bézier points.
(b) Tangential continuity
between Bézier points.

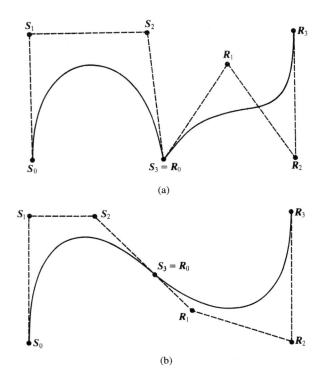

(a)

(b)

Figure 3.7
Examples of possible shape
editing protocols for a two-
segment Bézier curve.
(a) Maintain the orientation
of $R_1 S_2$ and move any of the
three control points R_1,
S_3/R_0, S_2 along this line.
(b) Rotate the line $R_1 S_2$
about S_3/R_0. (c) Move the
three control points R_1,
S_3/R_0, S_2 as a 'locked' unit.

a composite form from segments is somewhat negated by the constraints on
local control that now apply because of the joining conditions.

Figure 3.4 is an example of a multi-segment Bézier curve. In this case a number of curves are joined to represent the outline of the character and first order
continuity is maintained between them. It is useful to consider the ramifications
for an interface through which a user can edit multi-segment curves and maintain continuity. Figure 3.7 shows some possibilities. The illustration assumes that
the user has already constructed a two-segment curve whose shape is to be

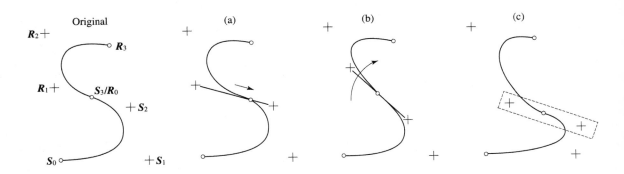

altered around the area of the join point S_3/R_0. To maintain continuity we must operate simultaneously on R_1, R_0/S_3 and S_2. We can do this by:

- Maintaining the orientation of the line R_1,S_2 and moving the join point up and down this line (Figure 3.7(a)).

- Maintaining the position of the join point and rotating the line R_1,S_2 about this point (Figure 3.7(b)).

- Moving all three control points as a locked unit (Figure 3.7(c)).

These three editing possibilities or constraints will enable the user to change the shape of curves made up of any number of segments while at the same time maintaining first order continuity between the curve segments. We will see later that this complication of Bézier curves can be overcome in another way – by using B-spline curves.

3.1.2 Summary of Bézier curve properties

- A Bézier curve is a polynomial. The degree of the polynomial is always one less than the number of control points. In computer graphics we generally use degree 3. Quadratic curves are not flexible enough and going above degree 3 gives rise to complications and so the choice of cubics is the best compromise for most computer graphics applications.

- The curve 'follows' the shape of the control point polygon and is constrained within the convex hull formed by the control points.

- The control points do not exert 'local' control. Moving any control point affects all of the curve to a greater or lesser extent. This can be seen by examining Figure 3.2 which shows that all the basis functions are everywhere non-zero except at the point $u = 0$ and $u = 1$.

- The first and last control points are the end points of the curve segment.

- The tangent vectors to the curve at the end points are coincident with the first and last edges of the control point polygon.

- Moving the control points alters the magnitude and direction of the tangent vectors – the basis of the intuitive 'feel' of a Bézier curve interface.

- The curve does not oscillate about any straight line more often than the control point polygon – this is known as the variation diminishing property. This has implications concerning the nature of the surface that can be represented.

- The curve is transformed by applying any affine transformation (that is, any combination of linear transformations) to its control point representation. The curve is invariant (does not change shape) under such a transformation.

(3.2) B-spline representation

The simplicity and power of the Bézier representation is no doubt responsible for its enduring popularity. It does, however, suffer from limitations and we will address these in this section by looking at how these are overcome by using the B-spline representation. We will as before introduce B-splines by first examining B-spline curves.

Historically, B-splines preceded Bézier curves and their origin relates to industries such as shipbuilding where a designer was required to draw life-size curves representing such entities as the cross-section through the hull of a ship. For small-scale drawing, draughtsmen would use French curves – a set of small, flat pre-formed curve sections. They would draw complete curves by putting together segments formed from different parts of different French curves. For full-scale plans this method was completely impractical and the draughtsmen (called in ship-building loftsmen) would employ long, thin strips of metal. These were pushed into the required curve shape and secured using lead weights called ducks, and the analogue between ducks and control points should be clear. We can push the spline into any desired shape that the system can take up and we can have as many ducks as we require. This is the physical basis of B-splines and we can compare the idea with either a single segment Bézier curve or a multi-segment Bézier curve. If we compare it with a single segment curve we see that adding extra control points or ducks removes the variation diminishing property – the curve can oscillate as we require. Comparing it with a multi-segment Bézier curve we can say that it is equivalent but we do not have to explicitly maintain continuity anywhere. Imagine a loftsmen inserting an extra duck – the physical properties of the metal spline ensures that the new shape that is taken up around the point where the duck was inserted is continuous. The metal takes up a shape that minimizes its internal strain energy. Yet another point that comes out of this real piece of engineering is that the effect of a duck insertion is local. The shape of the curve is only altered in its vicinity. We now deal with these points in a formal manner.

(3.2.1) B-spline curves

Two drawbacks associated with Bézier curves that are overcome by using B-spline curves are their non-localness and the relationship between the degree of the curve and the number of control points. The first property – non-localness – implies that although a control point heavily influences that part of the curve most close to it, it also has some effect on all the curve and this can be seen by examining Figure 3.2. All the basis functions are non-zero over the entire range of u. The second disadvantage means that we cannot use a Bézier cubic curve to approximate or represent n points without the inconvenience of using multiple curve segments (or by increasing the degree of the curve).

Like a Bézier curve a B-spline curve does not pass through its control points. A B-spline is a complete piecewise cubic polynomial consisting of any number of curve segments. (For notational simplicity we will only consider cubic B-splines. We can, however, have B-splines to any degree.) It is a cubic segment over a certain interval, and going from one interval to the next, the coefficients change. For a single segment only, we can compare the B-spline formulation with the Bézier formulation by using the same matrix notation.

The B-spline formulation is:

$$\boldsymbol{Q}_i(u) = \boldsymbol{UB_sP}$$

$$= [u^3\ u^2\ u\ 1]\ \frac{1}{6} \begin{bmatrix} -1 & 3 & -3 & 1 \\ 3 & -6 & 3 & 0 \\ -3 & 0 & 3 & 0 \\ 1 & 4 & 1 & 0 \end{bmatrix} \begin{bmatrix} \boldsymbol{P}_{i-3} \\ \boldsymbol{P}_{i-2} \\ \boldsymbol{P}_{i-1} \\ \boldsymbol{P}_i \end{bmatrix}$$

where $\boldsymbol{Q}_i$ is the ith B-spline segment and $\boldsymbol{P}_j$ is a set of four points in a sequence of control points. Alternatively we can write:

$$\boldsymbol{Q}_i(u) = \sum_{k=0}^{3} \boldsymbol{P}_{i-3+k}B_{i-3+k}(u) \qquad [3.2]$$

where i is the segment number and k is the local control point index – that is the index for the segment i. The value of u over a single curve segment is $0 \leq u \leq 1$. Using this notation we can describe u as a local parameter – locally varying over the parametric range of 0 to 1 – to define a single B-spline curve segment.

Thus in this notation we see that a B-spline curve is a series of $m - 2$ curve segments that we conventionally label $\boldsymbol{Q}_3, \boldsymbol{Q}_4, \ldots, \boldsymbol{Q}_m$ defined or determined by $m+1$ control points $\boldsymbol{P}_0, \boldsymbol{P}_1, \ldots, \boldsymbol{P}_m, m \geq 3$. Each curve segment is defined by four control points and each control point influences four and only four curve segments. This is the local control property of the B-spline curve and its main advantage over the Bézier curve.

Here we must be careful. Barsky (in Bartels *et al.* 1988) points out that comparing Bézier curves and B-spline curves can be misleading because it is not a comparison of like with like but a comparison of a single segment Bézier curve (which may have the control vertex set extended and the degree of the curve raised) with a piecewise or composite B-spline curve. A single segment Bézier curve is subject to global control because moving a control point affects the complete curve. In a composite B-spline curve moving a control point only affects a few segments of the curve. The comparison should be between multi-segment Bézier curves and B-splines. The difference here is that to maintain continuity between Bézier segments the movement of the control points must satisfy constraints, while the control points of a B-spline composite can be moved in any way.

A B-spline exhibits positional, first derivative and second derivative (C^2) continuity and this is achieved because the basis functions are themselves C^2 piecewise polynomials. A linear combination of such basis functions will also be C^2 continuous. We define the entire set of curve segments as one B-spline curve in u:

$$Q(u) = \sum_{i=0}^{m} P_i B_i(u)$$

In this notation i is now a non-local control point number and u is a global parameter discussed in more detail in the next section.

3.2.2 Uniform B-splines

Equation 3.2 shows that each segment in a B-spline curve is defined by four basis functions and four control vertices. Hence there are three more basis functions and three more control vertices than there are curve segments. The join point on the value of u between segments is called the knot value and a uniform B-spline means that knots are spaced at equal intervals of the parameter u. Figure 3.8 shows a B-spline curve that is defined by (the position of) six control vertices or control points $P_0, P_1, \ldots, P_5$. It also shows the effect of varying the degree of the polynomials, and curves are shown for degree 2, 3 and 4. We are generally interested in cubics and this is a curve of three segments with the left-hand end point of Q_3 near P_0 and the right-hand end point of Q_5 near P_5. (Thus we see that a uniform B-spline does not in general interpolate the end control points, unlike a Bézier curve. Also it is the case that a Bézier curve more closely approximates its control point polygon. However, the continuity-maintaining property of the B-spline curve outweighs these disadvantages.)

The notation gives us the following organization (where each curve segment is shown as an alternating full/dotted line):

Q_3 is defined by P_0 P_1 P_2 P_3 which are scaled by B_0 B_1 B_2 B_3

Q_4 is defined by P_1 P_2 P_3 P_4 which are scaled by B_1 B_2 B_3 B_4

Q_5 is defined by P_2 P_3 P_4 P_5 which are scaled by B_2 B_3 B_4 B_5

The fact that each curve segment shares control points is the underlying mechanism whereby C^2 continuity is maintained between curve segments. Figure 3.9

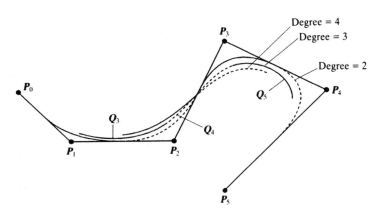

Figure 3.8
A three-segment B-spline cubic curve defined by six control points.

Figure 3.9
Demonstrating the locality property of B-spline curves. Moving P_4 changes Q_5 and Q_4 to a lesser extent. Q_3 is unchanged.

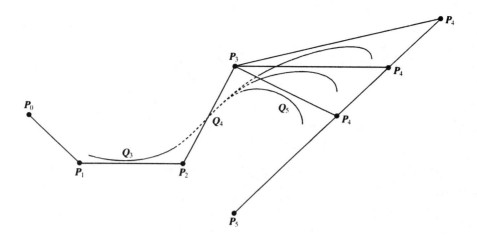

shows the effect of changing the position of control point P_4. This pulls the segment Q_5 in the appropriate direction and also affects, to a lesser extent, segment Q_4 (which is also defined by P_4). However, it does not affect Q_3 and this figure demonstrates the important locality property of B-splines. In general, of course, a single control point influences four curve segments.

We now consider the underlying basis functions that define the curve. Each basis function is non-zero over four successive intervals in u (Figure 3.10). It is, in fact, a cubic composed itself of four segments. The B-spline is non-zero over the intervals $u_i, u_{i+1}, \ldots, u_{i+4}$ and centred on u_{i+2}. Now each control point is scaled by a single basis function and if we assume that our knot values are equally spaced, then each basis function is a copy or translate and the set of basis functions used by the curve in Figure 3.8 is shown in Figure 3.11.

The basis functions sum to unity in the range $u = 3$ to $u = 6$ in this case, the values of the parameter u over which the curve is defined. A consequence of this is that the entire B-spline curve is contained within the convex hull of its control points. If we consider a single segment in the curve, then this defines a parameter range u_i to u_{i+1}. The basis functions that are active in the ith parametric interval, u_i to u_{i+1}, that is the functions that define a single curve segment, are shown highlighted in Figure 3.12. This gives a useful interpretation of the behaviour of the functions as u is varied. In general, for values of u that are not knot values, four basis functions are active and sum to unity. When a knot value $u = u_i$ is

Figure 3.10
The uniform cubic B-spline $B_i(u)$.

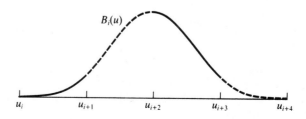

Figure 3.11
The six B-splines used in constructing the curve of Figure 3.8. They are all translates of each other.

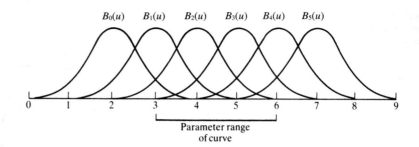

reached one basis function 'switches off' and another 'switches on'. At the knot value there are three basis functions that sum to unity.

At this stage we can summarize and state that a B-spline curve is made up of $m - 2$ segments defined by the position of $m + 1$ basis functions over $m + 5$ knot values. Thus in Figure 3.7 we have three segments, six control points and six basis functions over ten knot values.

Now consider again Figure 3.12. In the parameter range $u_i \leq u \leq u_{i+1}$ we evaluate the four B-splines B_i, B_{i-1}, B_{i-2} and B_{i-3} by substituting $0 \leq u \leq 1$ and computing:

$$B_i = \frac{1}{6} u^3$$

$$B_{i-1} = \frac{1}{6} (-3u^3 + 3u^2 + 3u + 1)$$

$$B_{i-2} = \frac{1}{6} (3u^3 - 6u^2 + 4)$$

$$B_{i-3} = \frac{1}{6} (1 - u)^3$$

[3.3]

It is important to note that this definition gives a single segment from each of the four B-spline basis functions over the range $0 \leq u \leq 1$. It does *not* define a single B-spline basis function which consists of four segments over the range $0 \leq u \leq 4$.

We now come to consider the end control vertices and note again that the curve does not interpolate these points. In general, of course, a B-spline curve does not interpolate any control points. We can make a B-spline curve interpolate control points by introducing multiple vertices. However, this involves a loss of continuity as we shall see. Intuitively we can think of increasing the influence of a control point by repeating it. The curve is attracted to the repeated point. A segment is made by basis functions scaling control points. If a control point is

The Figure 3.12
The four B-splines that are non-zero or active for the first curve segment in Figure 3.8.

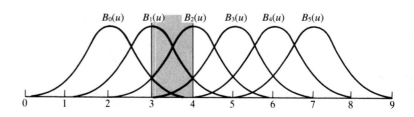

Figure 3.13
Demonstrating the effect of multiple end control points. P_5 is repeated three times forcing the curve to interpolate it.

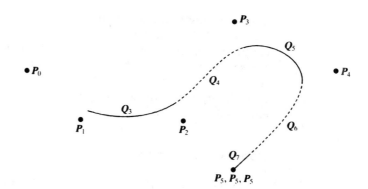

repeated it will be used more than once in the evaluation of a single segment. For example, consider Figure 3.13 and compare it with Figure 3.8. The last control point in the example in Figure 3.8 is now repeated three times. There are now five segments and P_5 is used once in the determination of Q_5, twice in Q_6 and three times in Q_7. The curve now ranges over $3 \leq u \leq 8$. At $u = 8$ the curve is coincident with P_5.

Such a technique can be used to make the curve interpolate both the intermediate control points and the end points. Figure 3.14(a) shows the effect

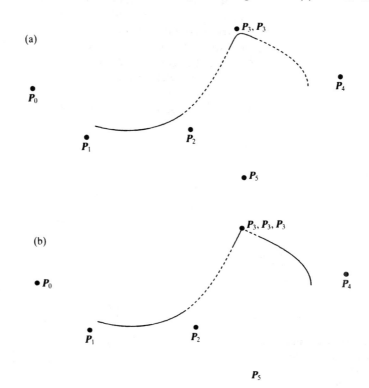

Figure 3.14
Demonstrating the effect of multiple intermediate control points. (a) P_3 is duplicated. (b) P_3 is triplicated.

of introducing multiple intermediate control points. In this figure P_3 has been doubled. P_3 is almost interpolated and an extra segment is introduced. The continuity changes from C^2G^2 to C^2G^1. This means that the continuity across the two segments is reduced by one although the continuity within each segment is still C^2. Figure 3.14(b) shows P_3 made into a triple control point. This time the curve interpolates the control point and the curve becomes a straight line on either side of the control point. The continuity reduces now to C^2G^0.

3.2.3 Non-uniform B-splines

In the previous section we considered a family of curves that we referred to as uniform B-splines because the basis functions were translates of each other. We now look at non-uniform B-splines.

A non-uniform B-spline is a curve where the parametric intervals between successive knot values are not necessarily equal. This implies that the blending functions are no longer translates of each other but vary from interval to interval. The most common form of a non-uniform B-spline is where some of the intervals between successive knot values are reduced to zero by inserting multiple knots. This facility is used to interpolate control points (both end points and intermediate points) and it possesses certain advantages over the method used in the previous section – inserting multiple control points. In particular a control point can be interpolated without the effect that occurred with multiple control vertices – namely straight line curve segments on either side of the control point.

Consider the curve generated in Figure 3.8. The knot values for this curve are $u = 3, 4, 5, 6$. We define a knot vector for this curve as [0,1,2,3,4,5,6,7] and a useful parametric range (within which the basis functions sum to unity) as $3 \leq u \leq 6$. The interval between each knot value is 1. If non-uniform knot values are

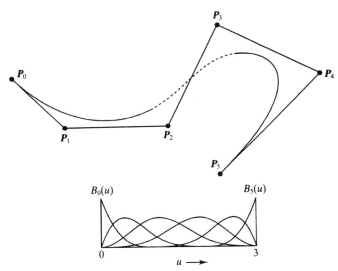

Figure 3.15
A non-uniform B-spline that interpolates the end points by using a knot vector [0,0,0,0,1,2,3,3,3,3].

used, then the basis functions are no longer the same for each parametric interval, but vary over the range of u. Consider Figure 3.15. This uses the same control points as Figure 3.8 and the B-spline curve is still made up of three segments. However, the curve now interpolates the end points because multiple knots have been inserted at each end of the knot vector. The knot vector used is [0,0,0,0,1,2,3,3,3,3]. The basis functions are also shown in the figure. The curve now possesses nine segments Q_0 to Q_8. However, Q_0, Q_1, Q_2 are reduced to a single point. Q_3, Q_4 and Q_5 are defined over the range $0 \leq u \leq 3$. Q_6, Q_7 and Q_8 are reduced to a single point $u = 3$. In practice the knot sequence [0,0,0,0,1,2,...,n–1,n,n,n,n] is often used. That is, interpolation is forced at the end points but uniform knots are used elsewhere. A second example showing the flexibility of a B-spline curve is given in Figure 3.16. Here we have nine control points and thirteen knots. The knot vector is [0,0,0,0,1,2,3,4,5,6,6,6,6].

In general a knot vector is any non-decreasing sequence of knot values u_0 to u_{m+4}. As we have seen, successive knot values can be equal and the number of identical values is called the multiplicity of the knot. Causing a curve to interpolate the end points by using multiple control vertices does not have precisely the same effect as using multiple control vertices and Figure 3.17 shows the final control point P_5 in our standard example interpolated using both a multiple control point and a knot vector with multiplicity 4 on the final knot value.

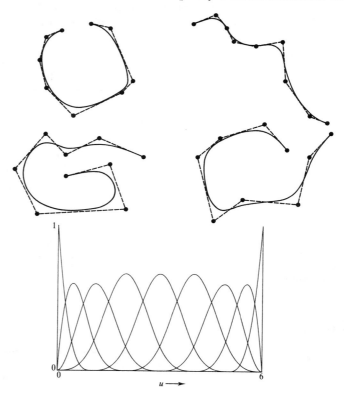

Figure 3.16
Showing the flexibility of B-spline curves. The knot vector is [0,0,0,0,1,2,3,4,5,6,6,6,6].

Figure 3.17
Comparing multiple knots
with multiple control points.
(a) The curve is generated
by a knot vector with
multiplicity 4 on the start
and end values. (b) P_5 is
repeated three times.

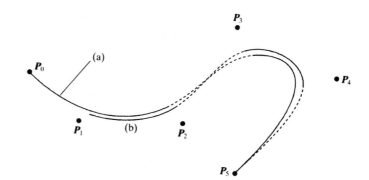

Note that if we use the knot vector [0,0,0,0,1,1,1,1] then we have single segment curve interpolating P_0 and P_3. In this instance the basis functions are the
Bézier basis functions (Figure 3.2) and the resulting curve is a Bézier curve. Thus
we see that a Bézier curve is just a special case of a non-uniform B-spline.

The effect of a multiple knot on the shape of a basis function is easily seen.
Consider Figure 3.18(a) shows the uniform B-spline basis function defined over
the knots 0, 1, 2, 3, 4. As we have explained in the previous section, this is itself
made up of four cubic polynomial segments defined over the given ranges. These
are generated by using Equation 3.3 and translating each cubic segment by
0, 1, 2, 3 and 4 units in u. Alternatively we can use:

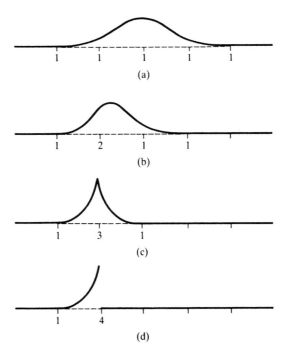

Figure 3.18
The effect of knot
multiplicity on a single cubic
B-spline basis function.
(a) All knot multiplicities
are unity: [0,1,2,3,4].
(b) Second knot has
multiplicity 2: [0,1,1,2,3].
(c) Second knot has
multiplicity 3:
[0,1,1,1,2]. (d) Second
knot has multiplicity 4:
[0,1,1,1,1].

$$B_0(u) = \begin{cases} b_{-0}(u) = \dfrac{1}{6} u^3 & 0 \le u \le 1 \\[2mm] b_{-1}(u) = -\dfrac{1}{6} (3u^3 - 12u^2 + 12u - 4) & 1 \le u \le 2 \\[2mm] b_{-2}(u) = \dfrac{1}{6} (3u^3 - 24u^2 + 60u - 44) & 2 \le u \le 3 \\[2mm] b_{-3}(u) = -\dfrac{1}{6} (u^3 - 12u^2 + 48u - 64) & 3 \le u \le 4 \end{cases}$$

Compared with Equation 3.3 note that this defines a single B-spline basis function over the range $0 \le u \le 4$. If we double the second knot and use [0,1,1,2,3], $b_{-1}(u)$ shrinks to zero length and the function becomes asymmetric as shown in Figure 3.18(b). The double knot eliminates second derivative continuity but first derivative continuity remains. Tripling the second knot by using knot vector [0,1,1,1,2] gives the symmetrical function shown in Figure 3.18(c) which now only has positional continuity. Quadrupling this knot [0,1,1,1,1] produces the function shown in Figure 3.18(d) where even positional continuity is eliminated.

If we now return to the context shown in Figure 3.15. The first basis function is defined over [0,0,0,0,1] and is asymmetric with no positional continuity. The second is defined over a set of knot values that contains a triple knot – [0,0,0,1,2], the third over the sequence [0,0,1,2,3] and is also asymmetric. In this case all functions are asymmetric and summarizing we have:

Knot vector	Basis function
0 0 0 0 1	B_0
0 0 0 1 2	B_1
0 0 1 2 3	B_2
0 1 2 3 3	B_3
1 2 3 3 3	B_4
2 3 3 3 3	B_5

We can further see from this set of basis functions that they sum to unity over the entire range of u and that at $u = 0$ and $u = 3$ the only non-zero basis functions are B_0 and B_5 (both unity) which cause the end points to be interpolated by Q_3 and Q_5 respectively.

We now consider altering the knot multiplicity for interior knots where the issue of continuity changes becomes apparent. Consider the examples given in Figure 3.19. This is the same example as we used in Figure 3.7 except that an extra control point has been added to give us a four segment curve. The knot vector is [0,1,2,3,4,5,6,7,8,9,10] and Figure 3.19(a) shows the curve. Figure 3.19(b) shows the effect of introducing a double knot using vector [0,1,2,3,4,4,5,6,7,8,9]. The number of segments is reduced to three. Q_4 shrinks to zero. The convex hulls containing Q_3 and Q_5 meet on edge P_2P_3 and the join point between Q_3Q_4 and Q_5 is forced to lie on this line. In Figure 3.19(c) a triple knot is introduced – [0,1,2,3,4,4,4,5,6,7,8]. The curve is reduced to two segments. Q_4 and Q_5 shrink to zero at P_3. There is only positional continuity between Q_3 and Q_6 but the segments on either side of the control point P_3 are

Figure 3.19
The effect of interior knot multiplicity on a B-spline curve.
(a) A four-segment B-spline curve. The knot vector is [0,1,2,3,4,5,6,7,8,9,10]. All B-splines are translates of each other.

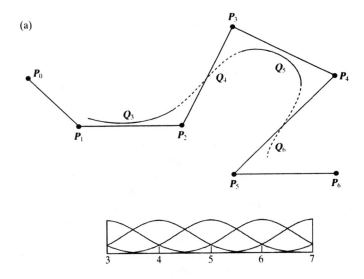

(b) Knot vector is [0,1,2,3,4,4,5,6,7,8,9]. Q_4 shrinks to zero.

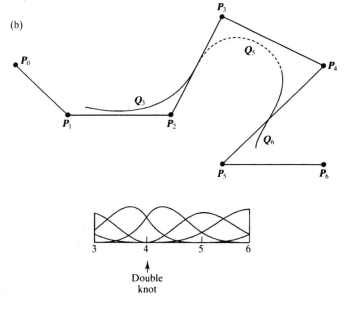

Figure 3.19 *continued*
(c) Knot vector is
[0,1,2,3,4,4,5,6,7,8].
Q₄ and **Q**₅ shrink to zero.
Continuity between **Q**₃ and
Q₆ is positional.

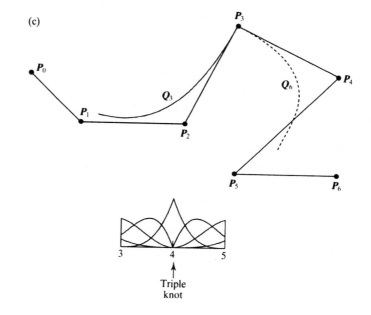

(d) Knot vector is
[0,1,2,3,4,4,4,5,6,7,8].
The curve reduces to a
single segment **Q**₃. Another
control point has been
added to show that the
curve now 'breaks' between
P₃ and **P**₄.

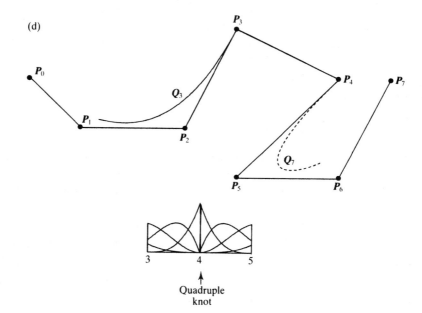

curved. This should be compared with Figure 3.13 produced using a triple control vertex. In Figure 3.19(d) a quadruple knot is introduced – [0,1,2,3,4,4,4,4,5,6,7]. Positional continuity is destroyed. The curve reduces to a single segment. To see what this means we have introduced another control point so that another segment Q_7 now appears. There is now a gap between the end of Q_3 and the start of Q_7. They have no control points in common.

We now consider a recursive method for generating the basis or blending functions for non-uniform B-splines. The method, known as the Cox–de Boor algorithm (Cox 1972; De Boor 1972), remarkably is able to generate uniform or non-uniform B-splines of any degree using a single recursive formula. Because the functions are no longer translates of one another the computation is more expensive. For a cubic (fourth order) curve we can define the recursion in its unwound form. Extending the notation of a B-spline to include order as the second subscript, we define the basis function for weighting control point P_i as $B_{i,j}(u)$ and the recurrence relationships for a cubic B-spline is:

$$B_{i,1}(u) = \begin{cases} 1, & u_i \leq u \leq u_{i+1} \\ 0, & \text{otherwise} \end{cases}$$

$$B_{i,2}(u) = \frac{u - u_i}{u_{i+1} - u_i} B_{i,1}(u) + \frac{u_{i+2} - u}{u_{i+2} - u_{i+1}} B_{i+1,1}(u)$$

$$B_{i,3}(u) = \frac{u - u_i}{u_{i+2} - u_i} B_{i,2}(u) + \frac{u_{i+3} - u}{u_{i+3} - u_{i+1}} B_{i+1,2}(u)$$

$$B_{i,4}(u) = \frac{u - u_i}{u_{i+3} - u_i} B_{i,3}(u) + \frac{u_{i+4} - u}{u_{i+4} - u_{i+1}} B_{i+1,2}(u)$$

When knots are repeated then a quotient of 0/0 can occur in the Cox–de Boor definition and this is deemed to be zero. Computationally the numerator is always checked for zero and the result set to zero irrespective of the denominator value. The choice of a particular knot set in commercial CAD systems that use B-splines is usually a predefined part of the system.

3.2.4 Summary of B-spline curve properties

Some of the properties that we listed for Bézier curves apply to B-spline curves. In particular:

- The curve follows the shape of the control point polygon and is constrained to lie in the convex hull of the control points.
- The curve exhibits the variation diminishing property.
- The curve is transformed by applying any affine transformation to its control point representation.

In addition B-splines possess the following properties:

- A B-spline curve exhibits local control – a control point is connected to four segments (in the case of a cubic) and moving a control point can influence only these segments.

3.3) Rational curves

A rational curve is a curve defined in four-dimensional space – known as projective space – which is then projected into three-dimensional space. We consider first the rational Bézier curve for consistency with our earlier treatment then define the rational form of the non-uniform B-spline, known as the NURBS and is one of the commonest forms used in practice. The advantage of the rational over the non-rational form will become clear in the course of the treatment.

3.3.1) Rational Bézier curves

Let us start by considering the projection of a three-dimensional Bézier curve into two-dimensional space, specifically onto the plane $z = 1$ (Figure 3.20). We do this by dividing by $z(u)$ to define a two-dimensional (rational) curve $\boldsymbol{R}(u)$:

$$\boldsymbol{R}(u) = \left(\frac{x(u)}{z(u)}, \frac{y(u)}{z(u)} \right)$$

The curve is defined in three-dimensional (projective) space as:

$$\boldsymbol{Q}(u) = \sum_{i=0}^{3} \boldsymbol{P}_i B_i(u)$$

where:

$$\boldsymbol{P}_i = (x_i, y_i, z_i)$$

Figure 3.20
Projection of a three-dimensional Bézier curve, $\boldsymbol{Q}(u)$, onto the plane $z=1$ giving the two-dimensional curve $\boldsymbol{R}(u)$.

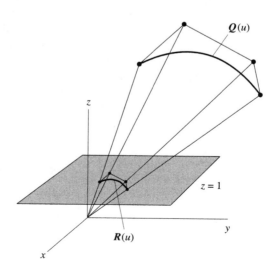

Now, a special notation is used for writing the three-dimensional control points of a rational curve in two-dimensional space which is:

$$\boldsymbol{P}_i = (w_i x_i,\ w_i y_i,\ w_i)$$

and we write our three-dimensional curve as:

$$\boldsymbol{Q}(u) = \sum_{i=0}^{3} \begin{bmatrix} w_i x_i \\ w_i y_i \\ w_i \end{bmatrix} B_i(u)$$

and this is projected into two-dimensional space as:

$$\boldsymbol{R}(u) = \left(\frac{\sum w_i x_i B_i(u)}{\sum w_i B_i(u)},\ \frac{\sum w_i y_i B_i(u)}{\sum w_i B_i(u)} \right)$$

The same formula holds when we project a four-dimensional curve into three-dimensional space where each control point is now:

$$\boldsymbol{P}_i = (w_i x_i,\ w_i y_i,\ w_i z_i,\ w_i)$$

and we have:

$$\boldsymbol{R}(u) = \frac{\sum w_i \boldsymbol{P}_i B_i(u)}{\sum w_i B_i(u)}$$

Rational curves enjoy all the properties of non-rational curves and indeed if the weights are set identically to one the form becomes the standard Bézier curve. Now consider the practical import of this form which allows control points to be weighted in this way. The effect of altering the value of a weight associated with a control point is shown in Figure 3.21. As the name suggests, increasing the weight of a control point gives it more influence. The way in which a weight value affects the curve is subtly different from the movement of a control point as Figure 3.22 demonstrates. Changing the position of a control point moves points on the curve in a direction parallel to that defined by the control point displacement. However, changing the weight of a control point causes points on the curve to move towards that point in the manner shown in the figure. These factors can be used to significant advantage in design programs.

Another important advantage of rational curves is: they can be used to represent conic sections precisely. A circle, or segments of it, is probably one of the most frequently used curves in CAD. A non-rational Bézier curve cannot

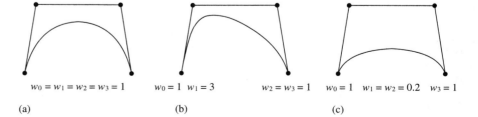

Figure 3.21
Varying the weights of a rational Bézier curve.

(a) $w_0 = w_1 = w_2 = w_3 = 1$

(b) $w_0 = 1$ $w_1 = 3$ $w_2 = w_3 = 1$

(c) $w_0 = 1$ $w_1 = w_2 = 0.2$ $w_3 = 1$

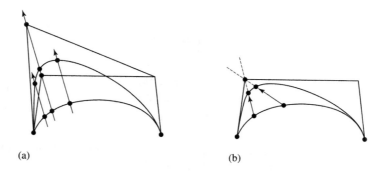

(a)   (b)

represent a circle exactly. Finally, as we have already mentioned, we can only transform the control points of a non-rational curve under an affine transformation. The perspective transformation used in computer graphics is not affine and non-rational curves whose control points are transformed into image space cannot be correctly generated in this space. Rational curves, however, because of the perspective division implicit in the construction of the curves ensures that they are correctly handled in perspective views.

3.3.2   NURBS

NURBS stands for Non-Uniform Rational B-Splines and this representation is probably the most popular in CAD. In design applications it admits the following possibilities:

- Interactive placement and movement of control points.
- Interactive placement and movement of knots.
- Interactive control of control point weights.

Combining the rational curve advantages of the previous section with the properties of non-uniform B-splines, a NURBS curve is defined as a non-uniform B-spline curve on a knot vector where the interior knot spans are not equal. For example, we may have interior knots with multiplicity greater than 1 (that is knot spans of length zero). Some common curves and surfaces, such as, for example, circles and cylinders, require non-uniform knot spacing, and the use of this option generally allows better shape control and the ability to model a larger class of shapes.

A rational B-spline curve is defined by a set of four-dimensional control points:

$$\boldsymbol{P}_i^w = (w_i x_i,\ w_i y_i,\ w_i z_i,\ w_i)$$

The perspective map of such a curve in three-dimensional space is called a rational B-spline curve.

$$\mathbf{R}(u) = H \left[\sum_{i=0}^{n} \mathbf{P}_i{}^w B_{i,k}(u) \right]$$

$$= \frac{\displaystyle\sum_{i=0}^{n} \mathbf{P}_i w_i B_{i,k}(u)}{\displaystyle\sum_{i=0}^{n} w_i B_{i,k}(u)}$$

Rational B-splines have the same analytical and geometric properties as non-rational B-splines and if:

$w_i = 1$ for all i, then:

$R_{i,k}(u) = B_{i,k}(u)$

The w_i associated with each control point are called weights and can be viewed as extra shape parameters. It can be shown that w_i affects the curve only locally. If, for example, w_j is fixed for all $j \neq i$, a change in w_i only affects the curve over k knot spans (just as moving a control point only affects the curve over k spans). w_i can be interpreted geometrically as a coupling factor. The curve is pulled towards a control point $\mathbf{P}_i$ if w_i increases. If w_i is decreased the curve moves away from the control point.

A specialization of rational B-splines is the generalized conic segment important in CAD. Faux and Pratt (1979) show that a rational quadratic form can produce a one parameter (w) family of conic segments.

3.4 From curves to surfaces

The treatment of parametric cubic curve segments given in the foregoing sections is easily generalized to bi-parametric cubic surface patches. A point on the surface patch is given by a bi-parametric function and a set of blending or basis functions is used for each parameter. A cubic Bézier patch is defined as:

$$\mathbf{Q}(u, v) = \sum_{i=0}^{3} \sum_{j=0}^{3} \mathbf{P}_{ij} B_i(u) B_j(v) \qquad [3.4]$$

Mathematically the three-dimensional surfaces are said to be generated from the Cartesian product of two curves. A Bézier patch and its control points are shown in Figure 3.23 where the patches are displayed using iso-parametric lines. The 16 control points form a characteristic polyhedron and this bears a relationship to the shape of the surface, in the same way that the characteristic polygon relates to a curve segment. From Figure 3.23(a) it can be seen intuitively that 12 of the control points are associated with the boundary edges of the patch (four of them specifying the end points). Only the corner vertices lie in the surface. In fact, if we consider the control points to form a matrix of 4×4 points then the four groups of four points forming the edges of the matrix are the control points for

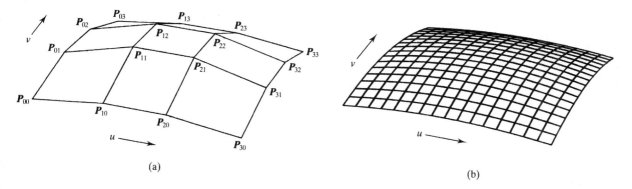

(a)

(b)

Figure 3.23
(a) A control polyhedron and (b) the resulting bi-cubic Bézier patch.

the boundary curves of the patch. Thus the edges of the patch are made up of four Bézier curves. We can now see that the remaining four control points must specify the shape of the surface contained between the boundary edges.

The properties of the Bézier curve formulation are extended into the surface domain. Figure 3.24 shows a patch being deformed by 'pulling out' a single control point. The intuitive feel for the surface through its control points, and the ability to ensure first order continuity are maintained. The surface patch is transformed by applying transformations to each of the control points.

Figure 3.24
The effect of 'lifting' one of the control points of a Bézier patch.

The way in which the control points 'work' can be seen by analogy with the cubic curve. The geometric interpretation is naturally more difficult than that for the curve and, of course, the purpose of the Bézier formulation is to protect the designer against having to manipulate tangent vectors etc., but it is included for completeness.

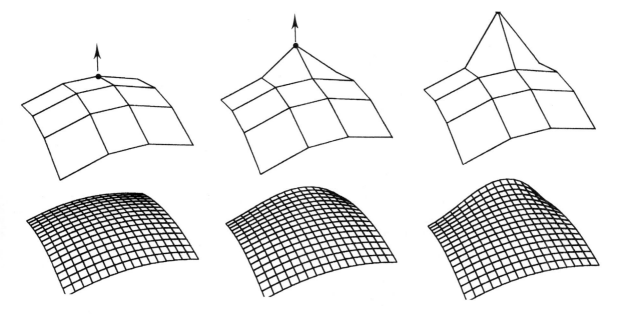

The matrix specification of Equation 3.4 is:

$$\boldsymbol{Q}(u, v) = [u^3 \; u^2 \; u \; 1][B_z \, \boldsymbol{P} \, B_z{}^T] \begin{bmatrix} v^3 \\ v^2 \\ v \\ 1 \end{bmatrix}$$

where:

$$B_z = \begin{bmatrix} -1 & 3 & -3 & 1 \\ 3 & -6 & 3 & 0 \\ -3 & 3 & 0 & 0 \\ 1 & 0 & 0 & 0 \end{bmatrix}$$

$$\boldsymbol{P} = \begin{bmatrix} \boldsymbol{P}_{00} & \boldsymbol{P}_{01} & \boldsymbol{P}_{02} & \boldsymbol{P}_{03} \\ \boldsymbol{P}_{10} & \boldsymbol{P}_{11} & \boldsymbol{P}_{12} & \boldsymbol{P}_{13} \\ \boldsymbol{P}_{20} & \boldsymbol{P}_{21} & \boldsymbol{P}_{22} & \boldsymbol{P}_{23} \\ \boldsymbol{P}_{30} & \boldsymbol{P}_{31} & \boldsymbol{P}_{32} & \boldsymbol{P}_{33} \end{bmatrix}$$

It is instructive to examine the relationship between control points and derivative vectors at the corner of a patch. For example, consider the corner $u = v = 0$. The relationship between the control points and the vectors associated with the vertex $\boldsymbol{P}_{00}$ is as follows:

$$\begin{aligned} \boldsymbol{Q}_u(0,0) &= 3 \, (\boldsymbol{P}_{10} - \boldsymbol{P}_{00}) \\ \boldsymbol{Q}_v(0,0) &= 3 \, (\boldsymbol{P}_{01} - \boldsymbol{P}_{00}) \\ \boldsymbol{Q}_{uv}(0,0) &= 9 \, (\boldsymbol{P}_{00} - \boldsymbol{P}_{01} - \boldsymbol{P}_{10} + \boldsymbol{P}_{11}) \end{aligned} \qquad [3.5]$$

Figure 3.25 shows these vectors at a patch corner. $\boldsymbol{Q}_u(0,0)$ is a constant times the tangent vector at $\boldsymbol{Q}(0,0)$ in the u parameter direction. Similarly $\boldsymbol{Q}_v(0,0)$ relates to the tangent vector in the v parameter direction. The cross derivatives at each end point, sometimes called twist vectors, specify the rate of change of the tangent vectors with respect to u and v. It is a vector normal to the plane containing the tangent vectors.

Analogous to the control points in Bézier curves, patches are specified in terms of four end points, eight tangent vectors (two at each corner) and four twist vectors. Consider Figure 3.25(b) that shows the elements of the control point polyhedron that are involved in the derivatives. Four pairs of points specify the tangent vectors in u at each corner (two rows in the matrix), four pairs specify tangent vectors in v (two columns in the matrix) and all 16 elements specify the twist vectors.

If we set $\boldsymbol{Q}_{uv}(i,j) = 0$ then we have a so-called zero twist surface or a surface with four zero twist vectors. For such a surface the inner control points can be derived from the three adjacent edge points. For example, at the $(0,0)$ corner we have:

$$0 = 9 \, (\boldsymbol{P}_{00} - \boldsymbol{P}_{01} - \boldsymbol{P}_{10} + \boldsymbol{P}_{11})$$

This is important when we wish to derive the 16 control points of a patch and we only have knowledge of the boundary curves. This situation occurs in surface

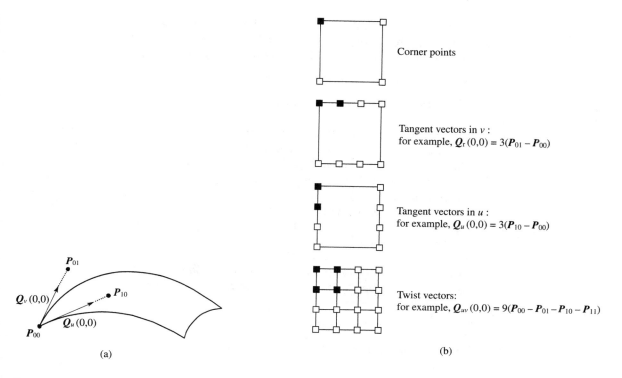

Figure 3.25
Vectors at P_{00}. (a) Tangent vectors at P_{00}. (b) Elements of control point matrix involved in vectors at P_{00}.

fitting or interpolation (see Section 3.6.3) when we wish to fit a patch through a set of points in three space. We do this by first using curve interpolation to define the boundary curves of the patches – giving 12 of the control points for a patch – and estimating in some way the four internal control points. The zero twist solution is a particularly easy way to estimate what the four internal control points should be.

For shading calculations we need to calculate certain surface normals. One of the easiest ways to shade a patch is to subdivide it until the products of the subdivision are approximately planar (this technique is discussed fully later in Chapter 4). The patches can then be treated as planar polygons and Gouraud or Phong shading applied. Vertex normals are calculated from the cross-product of the two tangent vectors at the vertex. For example:

$$\mathbf{a} = (\mathbf{P}_{01} - \mathbf{P}_{00})$$
$$\mathbf{b} = (\mathbf{P}_{10} - \mathbf{P}_{00})$$
$$\mathbf{N} = \mathbf{a} \times \mathbf{b}$$

A normal can be computed at any point on the surface from the cross-product of the two partial derivatives $\partial \mathbf{Q}/\partial u$ and $\partial \mathbf{Q}/\partial v$ but shading a patch by exhaustive calculation of internal points from the parametric description is computationally expensive and is subject to other problems. The advantages of using a parametric patch description of a surface are not contained in the fact that a precise world coordinate is available for every point in the surface – the cost of retrieving this information is generally too high – but in advantages that patch representation has to offer in object modelling.

Continuity and Bézier patches

The Bézier representation is excellent for single segment curves and single patch surfaces. When we want to make a curve (or surface) that is more complex, we have to join Bézier curves together using a continuity constraint. At the end of this chapter we will look at modelling issues in detail. In this section we will look at an issue that is crucial to modelling. This is the way in which we have to join patches together to maintain continuity over a surface and we will do this by developing a similar argument to the one we used for the joining of Bézier curve segments.

Maintaining first order continuity across two patches is a simple extension of the curve joining constraints and is best considered geometrically. Figure 3.26 shows two patches, S and R sharing a common edge. For positional or zero order continuity:

$$S(1, v) = R(0, v) \quad \text{for } 0 < v < 1$$

This condition implies that the two characteristic polygons share a common boundary edge (Figure 3.27) and:

$$S_{33} = R_{03}$$
$$S_{32} = R_{02}$$
$$S_{31} = R_{01}$$
$$S_{30} = R_{00}$$

or:

$$S_{3i} = R_{0i} \quad i = 0, \ldots, 3$$

To satisfy first order (C^1) continuity the tangent vectors at $u = 1$ for the first patch must match these at $u = 0$ for the second patch for all v. This implies that each of the four pairs of polyhedron edges that straddle the boundary must be collinear. That is:

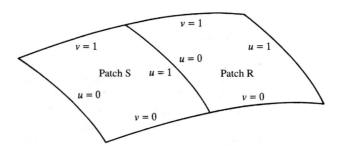

Figure 3.26
Joining two patches.

Figure 3.27
(a) Positional continuity between bi-cubic Bézier patches, and (b) tangential continuity between bi-cubic Bézier patches.

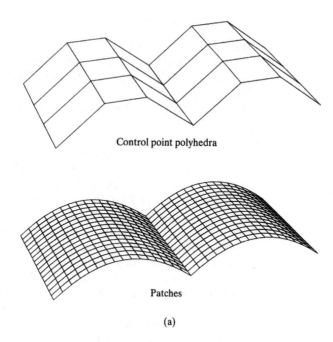

Control point polyhedra

Patches

(a)

Four sets of three control points must be collinear

Boundary

Control point polyhedra

Boundary

Patches

(b)

$$(\boldsymbol{S}_{3i} - \boldsymbol{S}_{2i}) = k(\boldsymbol{R}_{1i} - \boldsymbol{R}_{0i}) \quad i = 0, \ldots, 3$$

Faux, in 1979, pointed out that in CAD contexts, this constraint is severe, if a composite surface is constructed from a set of Bézier patches. For example, a composite surface might be designed by constructing a single patch and working outwards from it. Joining two patches along a common boundary implies that eight of the control points for the second patch are already fixed, and joining a patch to two existing patches implies that 12 of the control points are fixed.

A slightly less restrictive joining condition was developed by Bézier in 1972. In this patch, corners have positional but not gradient continuity. However, tangent vectors of edges meeting at a corner must be co-planar. Even with this marginally greater flexibility, there are still problems with the design of composite surfaces.

It should be mentioned that although the foregoing treatment has dealt with rectangular patches; such patches cannot represent all shapes. Consider, for example, a spherically shaped object. Rectangular patches must degenerate to triangles at the poles. Farin points out that perhaps the main reason for the predominance of rectangular patches in most CAD systems is that the first applications of patches in car design were to the design of the outer body panels. Those parts have a rectangular geometry and it is natural to break them down into smaller rectangles and use rectangularly shaped patches.

(3.4.2)

A Bézier patch object – the Utah teapot

Possibly the most famous object in computer graphics is the so-called Utah teapot – an early example of a Bézier patch mesh. In this section we will describe this much used object and use it to represent an important point concerning this representational form – its economy (compared with the polygon mesh model).

The University of Utah was the centre of research into rendering algorithms in the early 1970s. Various polygon mesh models were set up manually, including a VW Beetle, digitized by Ivan Sutherland's computer graphics class in 1971 (see Figure 2.4).

In 1975, M. Newell developed the Utah teapot, a familiar object that has become a kind of benchmark in computer graphics, and one that has been used frequently in this text. He did this by sketching the profile of the teapot to estimate suitable control points for bi-cubic Bézier patches. The lid, rim and body of the teapot were then treated as solids of revolution and the spout and handle were modelled as ducted solids. This resulted, eventually, in the 32 patches.

The original teapot is now in the Boston Computer Museum, displayed alongside its computer alter ego. A full description of the model and details of the Computer Museum are given in Crow (1987).

A wireframe of lines of constant u and v is shown in Figure 3.28. The object is made up of 32 Bézier patches. A single patch is shown as a heavy line. (Also shown in this figure is a wireframe image made up of the Bézier curves that form

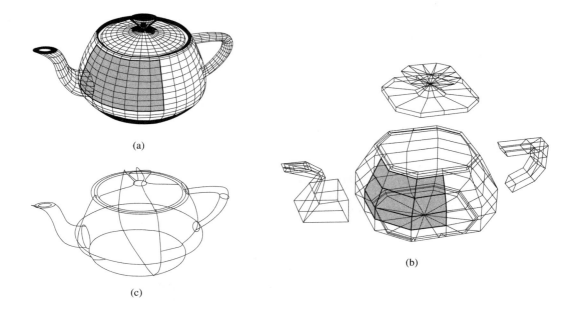

(a)

(b)

(c)

Figure 3.28
The Utah teapot (a) Lines of constant u and v. The teapot is made up of 32 Bézier patches. A single patch is shown shaded. (b) A wireframe of the control points. The shaded region shows the control polyhedron for the shaded patch. (c) A wireframe of the patch edges.

the edges of the constituent patches and a composite control point polyhedron.) This representation consists of:

32 patches × 16 control points/patch

= 288 vertices (approximately, most patches
   share 12 control points)

= 288 × 3 real numbers (say)

On the other hand a 'reasonable' polygon mesh representation would be:

Approximately 2048 × four-sided polygons

= 2048 × 3 real numbers

Thus, the polygon mesh model, an inaccurate representation, uses 2048/32 times as many primitive elements. This is a good demonstration of a point made in Chapter 2 – that throughout the two to three decades that three-dimensional computer graphics has been in existence, we prefer to deal with many simple primitives rather than much more complex ones.

3.5 B-spline surface patches

To form a bi-cubic B-spline surface patch we need to evaluate:

$$Q(u,v) = \sum_{i=0}^{n} \sum_{j=0}^{m} P_{ij}B_{i,j}(u,v)$$

where P_{ij} is an array of control points and $B_{i,j}(u,v)$ is a bivariate basis function. We can generate $B_{i,j}(u,v)$ from:

$$B_{i,j}(u,v) = B_i(u) \ B_j(v)$$

where $B_i(u)$ and $B_j(v)$ are the previously defined univariate cubic B-splines. Thus, we have:

$$Q(u,v) = \sum_{i=0}^{n} \sum_{j=0}^{m} P_{ij}B_i(u)B_j(v)$$

Analogous to B-spline curves we consider a B-spline patch to be made up of several rectangular surface patch segments. We now have two knot sequences in u and v, which taken together form a grid in parameter space.

We consider uniform B-spline patches where the grid of knot values exhibits equal intervals in the u and v parametric directions. First consider a single patch segment. We shall use this phrase to mean the entity in two-parameter space that is analogous to a curve segment in single-parameter space. Thus, we say that a general B-spline surface patch can made up of several patch segments just as a B-spline curve is made up of a number of curve segments. In the case of a single B-spline curve segment we required four control points to define the segment. Extending into two-parameter space we now require a grid, P_{ij}, of 4×4 control points to form a single patch segment. These control points are blended with 4×4 bivariate basis functions. Recall from Section 3.2.2 that a single B-spline segment requires a vector of eight knot values $u_0, \ldots, u_7$. Thus, a single patch segment requires a grid or knot array of 8×8 knot values (Figure 3.29) and the bivariate basis functions peak at the knot values shown with a square.

Consider a simple example. Figure 3.30 shows a single B-spline patch segment determined by 16 control points. Note that the patch is confined to the region nearer the central four control points. Just as with B-spline curves, which do not

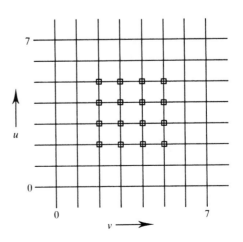

Figure 3.29
The 16 bivariate B-splines peak at the points shown in parametric space.

Figure 3.30
A single B-spline patch
segment.

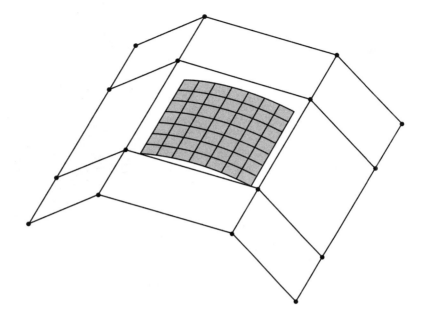

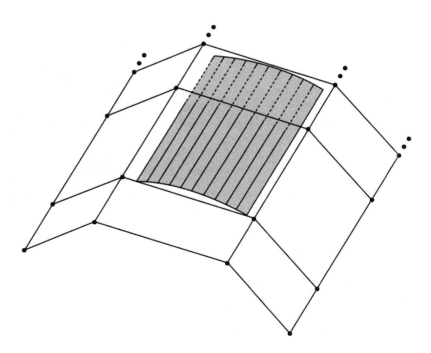

Figure 3.31
Triplicating a row of control
points for the example in
Figure 3.30.

Figure 3.32
A nine-segment B-spline
patch formed by triplicating
a row and a column of
control points.

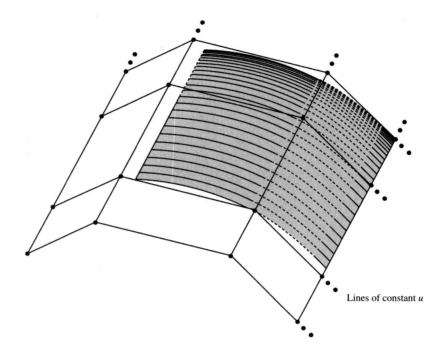

Lines of constant u

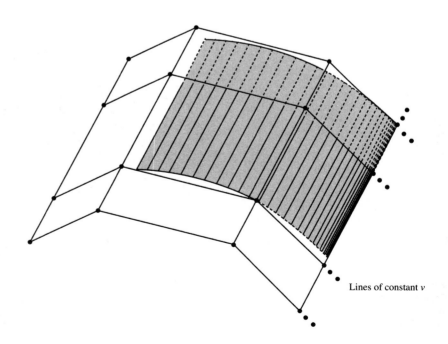

Lines of constant v

Figure 3.33
Triplicating interior control points produces a patch with creases.

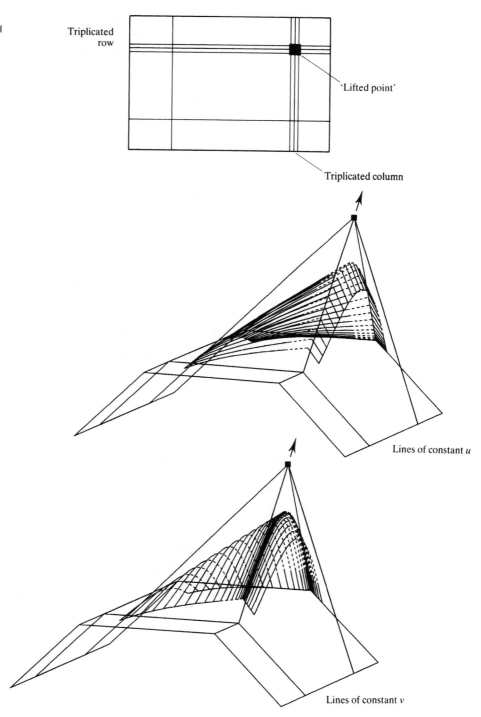

Triplicated row

'Lifted point'

Triplicated column

Lines of constant u

Lines of constant v

interpolate their control points, a B-spline patch segment does not interpolate the inner four control points or any of the outer 12.

We can control the behaviour of patches at the edges of the control point polyhedron by using multiple vertices (just as we controlled curves by using multiple end points). This is easily demonstrated by using a simple example. Consider Figure 3.31. Here we have triplicated a set of boundary vertices forming a control point matrix made up of 24 points as shown in the figure. This causes a three-segment patch to be formed, that is, pulled to the boundary vertices. Note that none of the boundary vertices is actually interpolated.

In the second example (Figure 3.32) we triplicate two sets of boundary vertices one of which forms a collinear set. This results in a nine-segment patch where the collinear vertices are interpolated. If we triple all boundary vertices then we end up with a 25-patch segment surface which in general will only interpolate the corner points.

Duplicating and triplicating interior control points can be used to produce modelling effects that are more powerful than those available with a Bézier patch. Figure 3.33 is an example. The control point polyhedron is as in the previous example except that an inner point has been lifted. A row and a column of control points have been triplicated. In the case of the column, three of the control vertices are collinear and this results in a surface with a crease aligned along the corresponding edge in the control point polyhedron. Now consider the triplicated row. Here the points are not collinear and the creasing effect is less sharp. Clearly these effects can be built into a modelling program where rows and columns are triplicated and the entire edge of the control point polyhedron moved interactively to define or drag a crease in the surface. Surfaces that contain creases are common, for example, in car bodies.

3.6 Modelling or creating patch surfaces

Modelling issues embrace both building up a parametric net description from scratch and editing or changing the shape of an existing description. One of the motivations for using a patch description is the ability to 'sculpt' an existing surface by altering its shape. Whereas modelling with a single patch, for example a Bézier patch, is straightforward, significant difficulties arise when dealing with a mesh of patches. The subject area is still very much a research topic and for that reason much of the material is outside the scope of this text. It is, however, an extremely important area and we will cover it as comprehensively as possible. In this section we will look at the following design or creation methods:

(1) Cross-section design: here we will look at a simplification of the sweeping techniques described in the previous chapter, restricting the objects to linear axis design.

(2) Interactive design by manipulating the control point polyhedron.

(3) Creating a patch net or mesh from a set of three-dimensional points representing a (usually) real object. We could call this surface interpolation, or surface fitting.

Cross-sectional or linear axis design example

We will now look at an example where the design constraints enable us to work and interface with curves to derive an object made up of a net of patches.

Consider using an eight-patch surface to design containers or bowls that in cross-section have four-fold symmetry. That is the final object can be considered to be made by sweeping some kind of cross-section along a linear axis or spine. Many industrial objects fall into this category. We will develop a hierarchy of three manifestations of this design each increasing in complexity in the nature of the variation of the cross-section. This is simply a repeat of the sweeping technique described in the previous chapter. However, this time the result of the modelling operation is a mesh of patches rather than a mesh of polygons. Here we will restrict our consideration to linear spines. Although the general sweeping techniques described for polygon meshes are extendible to patches, there are certain difficulties which are outside the scope of this text.

It may be that a patch model (rather than a polygon mesh representation) is important in this context because we want the ability to make global stylistic changes and also because we want a high quality visualization of the object. Objects such as bottles have most of their shape defined in projection by their silhouette edge and we may not want to encounter the silhouette edge degradation that would come from using a polygon mesh model for the visualization. We decide that to give us a reasonable degree of shape control the minimum number of patches that we can tolerate is eight.

The possibilities and the interactive protocol required are now dealt with. The illustrations show models constructed with eight patches. The formulae given relate in each case to a single patch.

Linear axis design – scaled circular cross-sections

Here we can only have circular cross-sections and the objects that we can design are of the form shown in Figure 3.34. (Actually, Bézier curves can only approximate a perfect circle, but we shall ignore this complication.) To derive the eight patches in this case we need only interact with a two-segment Bézier curve. This is known as a profile curve. This gives the control points for two patches; the control points for the other six patches are obtained by symmetry. Such objects are also well known as solids of revolution.

If we take the z axis as the spine of the object the control points of a bottom patch are given by:

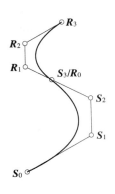

Profile design

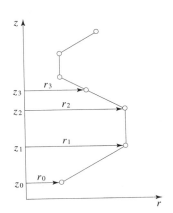

(r, z) coordinates of control points

Object

Figure 3.34
Linear axis design – circular
cross-section, object is
designed by a single profile
curve.

$$
\begin{bmatrix}
\mathbf{P}_{00} & \mathbf{P}_{01} & \mathbf{P}_{02} & \mathbf{P}_{03} \\
\mathbf{P}_{10} & \mathbf{P}_{11} & \mathbf{P}_{12} & \mathbf{P}_{13} \\
\mathbf{P}_{20} & \mathbf{P}_{21} & \mathbf{P}_{22} & \mathbf{P}_{23} \\
\mathbf{P}_{30} & \mathbf{P}_{31} & \mathbf{P}_{32} & \mathbf{P}_{33}
\end{bmatrix}
=
\begin{bmatrix}
\mathbf{T}_{00} \\
\mathbf{T}_{01} \\
\mathbf{T}_{02} \\
\mathbf{T}_{03}
\end{bmatrix}
\begin{bmatrix} r_0 & r_1 & r_2 & r_3 \end{bmatrix}
\begin{bmatrix} k \\ k \\ k \\ k \end{bmatrix}
\begin{bmatrix} z_0 & z_1 & z_2 & z_3 \end{bmatrix}
\qquad [3.6]
$$

where $\mathbf{T}_{00}$, $\mathbf{T}_{10}$, $\mathbf{T}_{20}$ and $\mathbf{T}_{30}$ are the control points for the quarter circle forming a cross-section segment circle:

$\mathbf{T}_{00} = (0, 1, 0)$

$\mathbf{T}_{10} = (c, 1, 0)$

$\mathbf{T}_{20} = (1, c, 0)$

$\mathbf{T}_{30} = (1, 0, 0)$

$c = 0.552$ (approx.)

and the control points for the surface patch lie on circles of radius r_0, r_1, r_2 and r_3 at distances z_0, z_1, z_2 and z_3 along the z axis. The segments $\mathbf{S}_0\mathbf{S}_1$, $\mathbf{S}_2\mathbf{R}_1$ and $\mathbf{R}_2\mathbf{R}_3$ sweep out to form truncated cones. The designed surface is tangential to these conical sections at the top, bottom and join cross-section. We can derive the top patch similarly.

Linear axis design – non-circular scaled cross-sections

This time we allow the quarter cross-section to be any shape and we design now with a profile curve as before and also a curve for the quarter cross-section (Figure 3.35). The cross-section maintains its shape and varies only in scale.

The control points for a bottom patch are again given by Equation 3.6 except that $\mathbf{T}_{00}$, $\mathbf{T}_{10}$, $\mathbf{T}_{20}$ and $\mathbf{T}_{30}$ are obtained from the cross-section design rather than being predefined.

Figure 3.35
Linear axis design – scaled (non-circular) cross-section. Object is designed by one profile curve and one (1/4) cross-section curve.

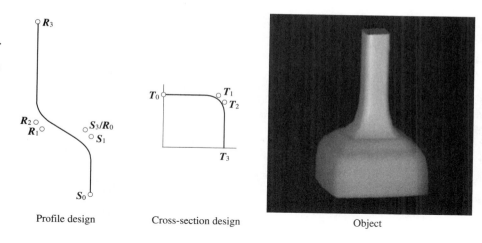

Profile design   Cross-section design   Object

Linear axis design – non-circular varying cross-sections

There are many options for blending different cross-section curves. An easy approach is to confine the blend to a single segment of the profile curve – the upper, say. Thus, in this example the upper four patches will exhibit a varying cross-section while the lower four will have a constant cross-section as before.

Here we allow the cross-section to vary in shape and we design three cross-sections which form the top edge of the top patch, the common bottom/top edge shared by both patches and the bottom edge of the bottom patch (Figure 3.36). Now we need to define intermediate curves form the top and bottom curves of a patch. This can be done simply by defining:

$$\boldsymbol{Q}(u, v) = \boldsymbol{Q}(u, 0)\,(1 - \boldsymbol{r}(v)) + \boldsymbol{Q}(u, 1)\boldsymbol{r}(v)$$

where:

$$\boldsymbol{r}(0) = 0 \quad \text{and} \quad \boldsymbol{r}(1) = 1$$

Figure 3.36
Linear axis design – non-circular varying cross-section. Object is designed by one profile curve and three cross-sections.

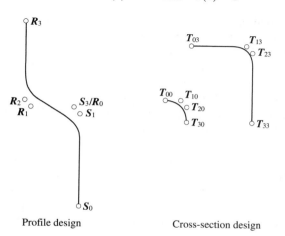

Profile design   Cross-section design   Object

Figure 3.37
Blending two different cross-sections using the profile curve.

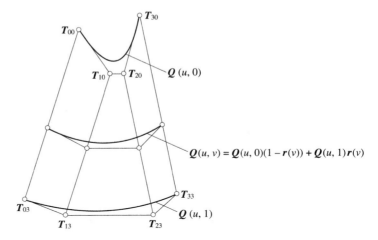

$$Q(u, v) = Q(u, 0)(1 - r(v)) + Q(u, 1)r(v)$$

Figure 3.37 is a representation of this procedure from which it can be seen that the curve $Q(u, v)$ has a characteristic polygon whose control points lie on lines joining the control points of the two cross-sections. The control points of a patch are now given by:

$$\begin{bmatrix} P_{00} & P_{01} & P_{02} & P_{03} \\ P_{10} & P_{11} & P_{12} & P_{13} \\ P_{20} & P_{21} & P_{22} & P_{23} \\ P_{30} & P_{31} & P_{32} & P_{33} \end{bmatrix} = \begin{bmatrix} T_{00} & T_{03} \\ T_{10} & T_{13} \\ T_{20} & T_{23} \\ T_{30} & T_{33} \end{bmatrix} \begin{bmatrix} 1 & 1-r_1 & 1-r_2 & 0 \\ 0 & r_1 & r_2 & 1 \end{bmatrix} \begin{bmatrix} k \\ k \\ k \\ k \end{bmatrix} \begin{bmatrix} z_0 & z_1 & z_2 & z_3 \end{bmatrix}$$

where T_{00}, T_{10}, T_{20} and T_{30} are the control points for the first cross-section (bottom edge) and T_{03}, T_{13}, T_{23} and T_{33} are the control points for the second cross-section (the common edge between the two patches).

3.6.2   Control polyhedron design – basic technique

This approach to modelling with a parametric patch object is the one described in most textbooks. The idea is that given an existing patch model a designer interacts with a loop which enables the control points to be moved and the result of the movement displayed as a new surface. Sometimes it is described as 'free-form sculpting'. The designer can move one or a number of control points at will modelling a surface as if it were some malleable material such as modelling clay. Leaving aside the practical problem of providing a three-dimensional editing system to facilitate control point movement, two fundamental problems arise.

First, what do we do when we are interacting with a mesh of patches rather than a single patch? Although single patch design can cope with a number of practical problems – car body panels, for example – we may need to work with a net of patches. The problem is that we cannot move the control points of a single patch without regard to maintaining continuity with surrounding patches.

Figure 3.38
(a) Four adjoining Bézier patches and their control points. Continuity constraints imply that the central point cannot be moved without considering its eight neighbours. All nine points can be moved together and continuity maintained.
(b) Undeformed two-segment curve.
(c) Deformed curve by moving control points in collinear groups.
(d) Desired deformation.

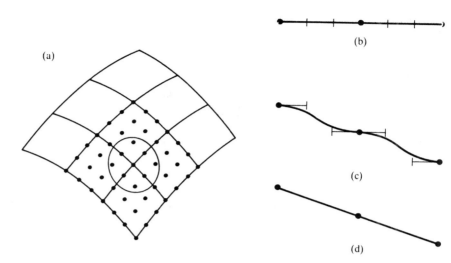

We considered this problem for curves in Section 3.1.1 and directly extending this method to patches we would move groups of nine control points as a single unit, as shown in Figure 3.38(a). This automatically ensures patch continuity but it has the effect of introducing plateaux into the surface. This is clearly seen with curves. Figure 3.38(b) shows a two-segment Bézier curve. If we move control points in collinear groups of three then we get a curved step effect (Figure 3.38(c)). What we may require is a deformation as shown in Figure 3.38(d).

Control polyhedron design – fine control

The other problem that arises is locality of control. We have already discussed this with respect to a Bézier versus B-spline patch and we now consider the B-spline case in more detail. The difficulty centres around the need to be able to vary the *scale* of the deformation. Although moving a control point only changes those patches that share the point, the scale of the deformation in object space is related to the size of the patches. This suggests that we can control the scale by locally subdividing the patches in the region of the deformation if a fine change is required. This is the basis of a technique called hierarchical B-spline deformation (Forsey and Bartels 1988). Figure 3.39 shows a simple example of this technique where the scale of the deformation on the side of a cube is related to the number of patches that make up the face.

Consider the definition of a B-spline patch:

$$Q(u, v) = \sum_{i=0}^{n} \sum_{j=0}^{m} P_{ij} B_i(u) B_j(v)$$

This can be redefined by knot insertion (Farin 1990) to a patch:

$$Q(u, v) = \sum_{i=0}^{N} \sum_{j=0}^{M} R_{ij} B_i(u) B_j(v)$$

Figure 3.39
The scale of a deformation as a function of the number of (initially flat) patches used to represent the side of a cube.

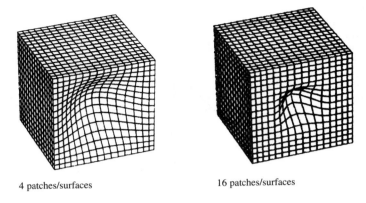

4 patches/surfaces   16 patches/surfaces

where:

$$N > n \quad \text{and} \quad M > m$$

The new control points are derived as described in Forsey and Bartels (1988). The problem is how to apply this strategy to the region of a surface that interests us. Forsey and Bartels do this by defining a minimal surface – the smallest section of the surface that this refinement of control points can be applied to. This minimal surface satisfies two constraints:

(1) Movement of the new control points produces deformations that are localized to this minimal surface.

(2) The derivatives at the boundary of the minimal surface remain unchanged.

This means that deformations within the refined surface will not affect the surface from which it is derived and continuity is everywhere maintained. The motivation for such an elaborate approach is to effect control point refinement only where required. The alternative would be control point refinement over the entire surface. This process can be repeated within the refined surface and so on until a satisfactory level of fine control is achieved – hence the term hierarchical.

A minimal surface is 16 patches defined by a 7×7 control points matrix (Figure 3.40(a)). The control points that are required if the centre four patches are refined to 16 are shown in Figure 3.40(b)). Here we note that 3×3 of the original control points are shared with the refined patches. A dynamic data structure of control points is created with the original surface at the root of a tree of overlays of control points. Editing the surface invokes a tree traversal and one of the important points of the scheme is that traversal can occur in either direction. Coarse refinement will carry previous fine refinements, in the same surface region, due to the representation of control points in terms of offsets relative to a local reference frame.

Figure 3.40
(a) Sixteen patch minimal surface with 49 control points. (b) Central four patches refined to sixteen patches (after Forsey and Bartels (1988)).

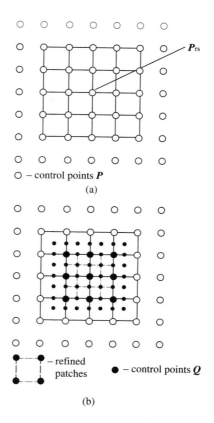

○ – control points P

(a)

● – refined patches

● – control points Q

(b)

Control polyhedron design – coarse control

We now consider the opposite of the previous case – coarse control. Say that we are interested in global shape deformation; for example, taking a cylinder or tubular object and bending it into a toroidal like body. Here we may need to operate, to some degree, on all the control points simultaneously.

Consider the strategy applied to a curve $Q(t)$ defined by four control points P_i. First we enclose the curve in a unit square and divide up this region into a regular grid of points R_{ij}; $i=0, ..., 3$; $j = 0, ..., 3$ as shown in Figure 3.41. If we consider the square to be uv space then we can write:

$$(u, v) = \sum_{i=0}^{3} \sum_{j=0}^{3} R_{ij} B_i(u) B_j(v)$$

Compare this identity with the equation for a bi-cubic parametric Bézier patch. This identity follows from the linear precision property of the polynomials $B_i(u)$ and $B_j(v)$ and it is expressing the fact that a set of coplanar control points will define a planar patch. If the grid of points R_{ij} is now distorted into the grid R'_{ij} (Figure 3.41) then the point (u, v) will be mapped into the point (u', v'):

Figure 3.41
Global distortion of a planar
curve (after Farin (1990)).

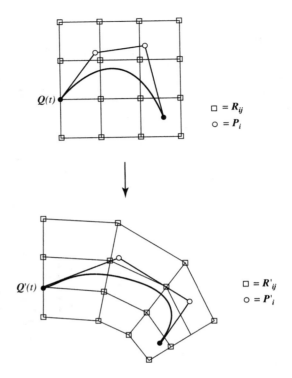

$\square = R_{ij}$

$\circ = P_i$

$\square = R'_{ij}$

$\circ = P'_i$

$$(u', v') = \sum_{i=0}^{3} \sum_{j=0}^{3} \boldsymbol{R'}_{ij} B_i(u) B_j(v)$$

and we can use this equation to derive a new set of control points, $\boldsymbol{P'}_i$, for the new curve $\boldsymbol{Q'}(t)$.

This is a method of changing the shape of the curve globally and indirectly. We are embedding the curve in a planar patch, distorting the patch by moving the control points of the patch, and at the same time changing the shape of the curve.

Now, to extend this principle to operate globally on patches we embed the control points, $\boldsymbol{P}_{ij}$ of the patch that we wish to deform in a *trivariate* Bézier hyperpatch itself specified by a three-dimensional grid of control points, $\boldsymbol{R}_{ijk}$, forming a unit cube. Thus we have:

$$(u', v', w') = \sum_{i=0}^{3} \sum_{j=0}^{3} \sum_{k=0}^{3} \boldsymbol{R'}_{ijk} B_i(u) B_j(v) B_k(w) \tag{3.7}$$

The unit cube grid is distorted globally in any way that we require and the new patch control points, $\boldsymbol{P'}_{ij}$, are calculated.

An important aspect of this technique is that it can be applied to an object with any parametric representation. Thus we can embed B-spline patches in the trivariate Bézier space. We can also embed polygon mesh vertices in the same way. This gives us the concept of any point x embedded in a trivariate hyper-patch volume and then mapped to point x' by globally distorting the control grid of the trivariate patch. To use Equation 3.7 to do this we need to map x into (u, v, w) space and (u',v',w') back into Cartesian space. The conversions are:

$$x = x_0 + u\mathbf{u} + v\mathbf{v} + w\mathbf{w}$$

and

$$u = \mathbf{u}\cdot(x - x_0)$$
$$v = \mathbf{v}\cdot(x - x_0)$$
$$w = \mathbf{w}\cdot(x - x_0)$$

x_0 defines the origin of (u, v, w) space and $\mathbf{u}$, $\mathbf{v}$ and $\mathbf{w}$ define the space. These values are set by the designer who positions the unit cube with respect to the object to be distorted.

The technique was originally developed by Bézier but most graphics-oriented treatments refer to a paper by Sederburg and Parry (1986) wherein the strategy is termed free-form deformation (FFD).

Figure 3.42 (Colour Plate) shows an example of the technique in operation. The semi-transparent rectangular solids surrounding parts of the spoon object are the trivariate patches in which are embedded the vertices of the polygon mesh. The upper patch is specified by a grid of $3 \times 3 \times 7$ control points and note that there are many more polygonal vertices in the equivalent object space. Deforming the grid gives a 'natural' bending of the spoon character for use in animation.

3.6.3 Creating patch objects by surface fitting

In this section we look at taking a set of points in three-dimensional space representing an object and fitting and interpolating a patch surface through them. We will approach the topic by first considering the interpolation of curves then developing an algorithm for surface fitting.

Interpolating curves using B-splines

Fitting a B-spline curve (or surface) through existing data points finds two major applications in computer graphics. First in modelling: a set of sample data points can be produced by a three-dimensional digitizing device, such as a laser ranger. The problem is then to fit a surface through these points so that a complete computer graphics representation is available for manipulation (for say animation or shape change) by a program. Second, in computer animation, we may use a parametric curve to represent the path of an object that is moving through three space. Particular positions of the object (key frame positions) may be defined and we require to fit a curve through these points. A B-spline curve is commonly used for this purpose because of its C^2 continuity property. In animation we are normally interested in smooth motion and a B-spline curve representing the position of an object as a function of time will guarantee this.

We state the problem of B-spline interpolation informally as follows: given a set of data points we require to derive a set of control points for a B-spline curve that will define a 'fair' curve that represents the data points. We may require the curve to interpolate all the points or to interpolate a subset of the points and pass close to the others. For example, in the case where data points are known to be noisy or slightly unreliable we may not require an exact interpolation through all the points. Different methodologies for fitting a B-spline curve to a set of data points are given in Bartels *et al.* (1987).

We can state the problem formally for the case where we require the curve to interpolate all the data points. If we consider the data points to be knot values in u then we have for a cubic:

$$Q(u_p) = \sum_{i=0}^{m} P_i B_i(u_p)$$

$$= D_p \quad \text{for all } p = 3, \ldots, m + 1$$

where:

D_p is a data point

u_p is the knot value corresponding to the data point

The problem we now have is to determine u_p. The easiest solution, and the one we will adopt here, is to set u_p to p. This is called uniform parametrization; it completely ignores the geometric relationship between data points and is usually regarded as giving the poorest interpolant in a hierarchy of possibilities described in detail in Farin (1990). The next best solution, chord length parametrization, sets the knot intervals proportional to the distance between the data points. An advantage of uniform parametrization, however, is that it is invariant under affine transformation of the data points.

Here we are specifying a B-spline curve through the data points. There are $m - 1$ data points to be interpolated and the curve is defined by $m + 1$ control points. If we consider a single component, say, x then we have:

$$x(u_p) = \sum_{i=0}^{m} P_{xi} B_i(u_p)$$

$$= D_{xp}$$

where:

D_{xp} is the x component of the data point

This defines a system of equations that we solve for P_{xi}:

$$\begin{bmatrix} B_0(u_3) & \cdots & B_m(u_3) \\ \vdots & & \vdots \\ B_0(u_{m+1}) & \cdots & B_m(u_{m+1}) \end{bmatrix} \begin{bmatrix} P_{x0} \\ \vdots \\ P_{xm} \end{bmatrix} = \begin{bmatrix} D_{x3} \\ \vdots \\ D_{xm+1} \end{bmatrix}$$

This scheme results in $m - 1$ equations in $m + 1$ unknowns. For example, for $m = 5$ we have six control points to find from four data points. Various possibilities exist. The easiest approach is to select two additional points P_2 and P_7 to be interpolated. Clearly these can be two extra points inserted or be part of the data set, giving:

$$\begin{bmatrix} B_0(u_2) & B_m(u_2) \\ B_0(u_3) & B_m(u_3) \\ \vdots & \vdots \\ B_0(u_{m+1}) & B_m(u_{m+1}) \\ B_0(u_{m+2}) & B_m(u_{m+2}) \end{bmatrix} \begin{bmatrix} P_{x0} \\ \vdots \\ \vdots \\ P_{xm} \end{bmatrix} = \begin{bmatrix} D_{x2} \\ D_{x3} \\ \vdots \\ D_{xm+1} \\ D_{xm+2} \end{bmatrix}$$

In this equation the matrix will have zero entries except in a band $3(k - 1)$ entries wide along the main diagonal, and for uniform cubic B-splines the matrix is:

$$\frac{1}{6} \begin{bmatrix} 4 & 1 & & & & \\ 1 & 4 & 1 & & & \\ & 1 & 4 & 1 & & \\ & & & \ddots & & \\ & & & & 1 & 4 & 1 \\ & & & & & 1 & 4 \end{bmatrix}$$

Interpolating surfaces

Interpolating surfaces means that we wish to interpolate a set of three-dimensional data points with a parametrically defined surface. We do this by first fitting a network of uv curves through the data points. Each data point is interpolated by a curve of constant u and v. These curves are B-splines interpolated through the data points using a standard B-spline curve interpolation technique. In the next stage the B-spline curves are converted to Bézier curves. This curve network is partitioned into individual mesh elements formed from four Bézier curve segments (Figure 3.43). These curve segments are the boundary edge of a Bézier patch and given these we can then derive the control points for the patch. Thus a set of points in three space is converted to a net of Bézier patches using a net of B-spline curves as an intermediary.

Now let us consider the first stage – deriving a net of curves that interpolate the data points. The main problem here is that we may have no knowledge of the topology of the points. (In curve interpolation we know that the points are sequential.) This is a problem that can only be solved in context and one approach is given in Watt and Watt (1992). Consider the case where the points have been obtained from a real object using a manual digitizer and the knowledge of which points to interpolate with curves is known. This is quite a common context and we will proceed with the second stage – that of deriving a net of Bézier patches from a B-spline curve network.

Figure 3.43
A schematic representation of surface fitting. (a) A set of points in three space. (b) Fitting curves through the points in two parametric directions. (c) The grid of curves from the boundaries of the patches. (d) A curve network obtained by interpolation through digitized points. (e) A rendered version of the patch model obtained from (d).

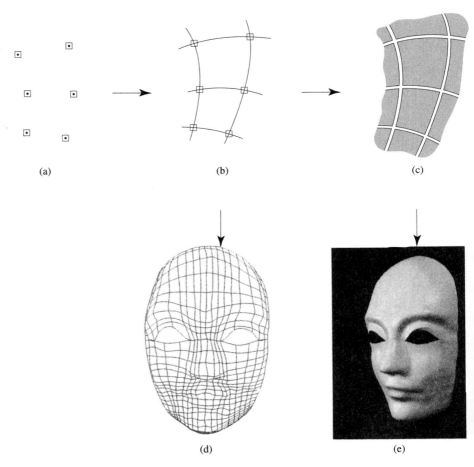

(a) (b) (c)

(d) (e)

First we need to convert the B-spline curves into multi-segment Bézier curves. If we first consider a single B-spline then the conversion to Bézier form is straightforward and is given by:

$$[P_0\ P_1\ P_2\ P_3] = B^{-1}B_s\ [Q_0\ Q_1\ Q_2\ Q_3]$$

$$= \frac{1}{6}\begin{bmatrix} 1 & 4 & 1 & 0 \\ 0 & 4 & 2 & 0 \\ 0 & 2 & 4 & 0 \\ 1 & 4 & 1 & 0 \end{bmatrix}\begin{bmatrix} Q_0 \\ Q_1 \\ Q_2 \\ Q_3 \end{bmatrix}$$

where:

P are the Bézier control points

Q are the B-spline control points

B is the Bézier matrix

B_s is the B-spline matrix

(Note that a change of basis matrix can only be used for uniform B-splines. If the curve network consists of non-uniform B-splines then conversion has to proceed by knot insertion. This more general approach is described in Watt and Watt (1992).)

For a multi-segment B-spline curve we apply this formula repeatedly to the appropriate control points. For example, consider a two-segment B-spline curve defined by five control points $[Q_0\ Q_1\ Q_2\ Q_3\ Q_4]$. The conversion formula is applied twice for the control points sets $[Q_0\ Q_1\ Q_2\ Q_3]$ and $[Q_1\ Q_2\ Q_3\ Q_4]$.

Now consider a net of 5×5 two-segment B-spline curves with control points shown in Figure 3.44(a). Application of the above scheme on a row by row basis yields five two-segment Bézier curves (Figure 3.44(b)). We now interpret these, column by column, and consider each column to be the control points of a B-spline curve. Each column is converted to a two-segment Bézier curve. This yields a net of 7×7 two-segment Bézier curves (Figure 3.44(c)). We know that the boundary edge of a Bézier patch is a Bézier curve and we interpret the unbroken lines in Figure 3.44(c)) as the boundaries of four Bézier patches. Thus we have converted a network of 5×5 two-segment B-spline curves into 2×2 Bézier patches. However, we have only defined the boundaries of each patch – that is we have only determined 12 out of the 16 control points for each patch.

The question that now arises is: how are we to determine the inner four control points? We first consider their significance by reproducing Equation 3.5.

$$Q_{uv}(0,0) = 9(P_{00} - P_{01} - P_{10} + P_{11})$$

This defines the twist of a surface as a mixed partial derivative and can be interpreted as a vector which is the deviation of the corner quadrilateral of the control polyhedron from a parallelogram (Figure 3.45). When the twist is zero this vector reduces to zero and the corner points of the quadrilateral are coplanar. An intuitive grasp of the effect of non-zero twist is difficult. It is easier to look at the geometric significance when a patch has zero twist at all four corners.

Then we have a translational surface where every quadrilateral of the control polygon is a parallelogram. The parallelograms are also translates of each other. Such a patch is called a translational surface because it is generated by two curves $C_1(u)$ and $C_2(v)$. Any iso-parametric line in u is a translate of C_1 and any iso-parametric line in v is a translate of C_2.

Thus the easiest solution to estimating the inner four control points is to assume that the patch is a translational surface, then the inner points are derivable from the boundary points. The implication of this, in terms of surface fitting, is that the boundary curves of the patch should more or less be translates of each other. In any practical situation this will depend on two factors: the shape of the object and the resolution of the uv curve network.

Figure 3.44
Converting a B-spline curve
network to Bézier patches
(after Farin (1990)).
(a) 5 × 5 two-segment
B-spline curve network.
(b) Curve network
converted row-wise to
5 two-segment Bézier
curves. (c) Curve network
converted to 7 × 7 two-
segment Bézier curves
forming the boundaries of
four Bézier patches.

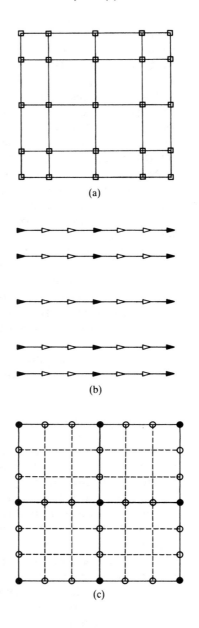

(a)

(b)

(c)

A visualization of the overall process is shown in Figure 3.43. The original surface points were obtained from a real object. You can see in this figure how the validity of zero twist assumption varies across the surface of the object. The method gives us a correct surface with C^1 continuity overall, but it does not guarantee a 'good' shape. Alternative methods for determining the twist of a surface patch are given in Farin (1990).

Figure 3.45
The twist coefficients are proportional to the deviations of the control polygon subquadrilateral from a parallelogram.

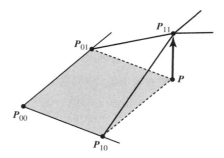

3.7 From patches to objects

We have stressed that one of the main uses of the parametric patch representation is that it can be employed to program a numerically controlled cutting device enabling the abstract design to be converted directly into an object or a model of the object.

In most applications this involves programming a cutting tool to remove material from a stock shape, such as a rectangular prism, to produce the desired object (Figure 3.46 shows an example of such an object). The practical techniques depend on many factors such as the nature of the model, the material and the cutting device. For example, with hard material such as metal it may not be possible to remove all the material in one go. The cutter must be programmed to produce intermediate shapes to arrive eventually at the desired object. There is a minimum radius of curvature that the cutter can cope with due to its physical extent. This is easily imagined in the case of a tool with a hemispherical tip. The actual paths that the cutter must take need to be determined. So we will simply outline the principle here.

In the simplest possible case we can consider a tool tip positioned in a cutting device at a distance d from the reference point of the cutter. That is the three-

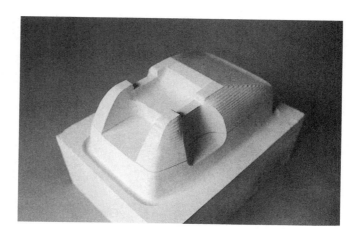

Figure 3.46
Converting a computer graphics model into a real object. Courtesy of H. Chiyokura. *Source*: H. Chiyokura, *Solid Modelling with DESIGNBASE*, Addison-Wesley Longman Singapore Pte Ltd, Singapore, 1988.

dimensional point in the machine that the cutter needs to control. This point, leaving aside the issue of actual paths, generally has to move on a 'parallel' surface to the defined surface. This is known as an offset surface. A simple offset surface for a patch $Q(u, v)$ is given by

$$O(u, v) = Q(u, v) + dN(u, v)$$

This defines a normal surface $O(u, v)$ at a distance d along the normal $N(u, v)$. Having derived this surface cutter, paths could be derived from suitably spaced iso-parametric curves that lie in the offset surface.

Representation and rendering

4.1 Rendering polygon meshes – a brief overview

4.2 Rendering parametric surfaces

4.3 Rendering a CSG description

4.4 Rendering a voxel description

4.5 Rendering implicit functions

Introduction

In this chapter we will examine the different rendering strategies that are used to visualize the representations discussed in Chapters 2 and 3. Rendering methods can either be discussed in terms of particular strategies for particular representations – the theme of this chapter; alternatively they can be methods that implement global illumination models. In the latter category radiosity and ray tracing are notable.

We begin with a short overview that lists the most popular strategies for the representation methods in Chapters 2 and 3. To summarize:

(1) The polygon mesh rendering strategies are of major importance in computer graphics. The methods that are employed have been in constant use since around 1975 and it is the case that most applications use this method. Their other important use comes from the fact that the easiest way to render bi-cubic parametric patches and voxel representations is to convert them into a polygon mesh and use a standard renderer.

(2) Bi-cubic parametric patches: the easiest way to visualize or render a patch is to convert it into polygons. Fast subdivision algorithms lead to a polygon mesh which implies overall a quick rendering time. This, of course, implies approximating the surface but as we shall see this can be done in a way where the visualization does not *look* inaccurate. Approximation is preferable to rendering directly from the mathematical description for reasons that will become clear in this chapter.

(3) CSG objects can be rendered either by using a ray tracing (or ray casting) approach or by converting them into a voxel representation then into polygons. The difficulty inherent in this representation is the evaluation of the Boolean combination operarators.

(4) Voxels: here again we convert into a polygon mesh representation. Usually this involves an inordinate polygon count per object and this is the main disadvantage of the approach.

(5) Implicit representations: these can either be converted into a voxel representation or ray traced.

Because of the importance of polygon mesh rendering we will cover this topic in detail in Chapters 5 and 6. This also applies to the voxel representation which is covered in detail in Chapter 14. We will cover the rendering strategies for the other representations in some detail during the course of this chapter.

4.1 Rendering polygon meshes – a brief overview

As we have already discussed polygonal objects are by far the most common representational form in computer graphics and fixed program hardware is now available on many graphics workstations which renders an object or objects from a polygonal database.

The input to a polygonal renderer is a list of polygons and the output is a colour for each pixel onto which each polygon projects on the screen. The major advantage of polygonal renderers is that algorithms have evolved that treat polygons as single entities or units. Polygons become the lowest level element that a graphics programmer has to consider. This makes for very fast and simple processing. However, we should note that these advantages are eroded as objects become more and more complex. Contexts, where objects are described by hundreds of thousands of polygons, are not uncommon. An example was shown in Figure 2.5(b). As the projected screen area of a polygon approaches a single pixel the advantage of interpolative methods – where work is done at the polygon vertices and pixel colours interpolated – rapidly diminishes.

Rendering engines for polygon mesh objects perform two main tasks. The first is to process the geometry of the object as it is subject to various transformation – modelling transformations, viewing transformations etc., followed by a process that evaluates light–object interaction, loosely called shading.

The most common polygon mesh renderers have two main components for the second process – a shading algorithm that finds the appropriate shade for each pixel within the polygon's projection and a hidden surface removal algorithm that evaluates whether part of a polygon is obscured by another that is closer to the viewer.

Shading algorithms evaluate an intensity at the vertices of the polygon, then interpolate from these values to find an appropriate intensity for the polygon pixels. An equation evaluates the light intensity at the vertices, by comparing the orientation of a normal vector associated with the surface at the vertex, with the position of the light source. An interpolation scheme finds the pixel values and these two operations combine in a way that reduces the visibility of the facet edges and makes a curved surface, that has been approximated by planar polygons, appear to be curved.

Coincident with this operation, a similar interpolation scheme evaluates the depth of each polygon pixel from the depths at the vertices (which are evaluated from the geometry of the scene and the viewer). These depths are stored in an array, known as a Z-buffer, and the stored value for a pixel is compared with the current depth value to ascertain if the current polygon pixel is nearer to the viewer than the nearest previously rendered one.

This approach enables polygons to be fetched from the database in any order and rendered as independent units. It does mean that work is done evaluating the shades of polygons that may finally not be written to the screen buffer (because they are further than previously rendered ones). It is an elegant and straightforward method of visualizing a polygon mesh object. Representational units in the database – polygons – are treated as units by the renderer and the approximate geometric nature of these units is made almost invisible.

This method was contributed to by many people, but those most often named are Gouraud and Phong who developed shading algorithms. The emergence of this approach was possibly the most significant advance in three-dimensional computer graphics and its enduring popularity, in the face of ray tracing and radiosity methods, attests to its elegant simplicity and efficiency.

4.2 Rendering parametric surfaces

Algorithms that render surfaces represented by bi-cubic parametric patches divide naturally into two categories:

(1) Those that render directly from the parametric description, or the equation describing the patch.

(2) Those that approximate the surface by a polygon mesh and use a planar polygon mesh renderer to render this approximation. Thus in this case rendering parametric surfaces reduces to a preprocessing operation or conversion operation.

The second approach appears to be the most popular. It is certainly the easier to implement and is computationally less expensive. Examples of the first are to be found in Blinn (1978), Whitted (1978), Schweitzer and Cobb (1982) and Griffiths (1984). Lane *et al.* (1980) give a comparative description of these methods and describe an implementation of the second approach.

4.2.1 Rendering directly from the patch descriptions

Rendering directly from a patch description implies using a scan line algorithm. As we move along a scan line then for a pixel we evaluate the corresponding point on the patch from the patch equation. Thus we have the problem of imposing a pixel or screen space (x, y) evaluation order on the mathematical description of the patch and this is the source of the difficulties that arise. A rendering order that proceeds in this way is called scan conversion. We can see what the difficulties are by considering a curved patch with a planar or flat one – in other words a polygon or quadrilateral. Those attributes of a polygon that make for simple scan conversion and which are difficult to obtain for a patch are:

(1) The maximum and minimum Y coordinates which are easily obtained from the vertex list.

(2) Incremental equations which can be used to track each of the polygon edges as functions of Y.

(3) Incremental equations which can be used to calculate the screen depth Z as a function of X.

A parametrically defined surface has none of these properties. The maximum and minimum Y coordinates will not necessarily be on the boundary or edges of the surface because a patch will often exhibit a silhouette edge in screen space that results from an internal bulge in the patch. With parametrically defined surfaces both the boundary edge and the silhouette edge need to be tracked. A further complication is that a silhouette edge and a boundary edge may intersect. Finally, in general, neither the boundary nor silhouette edge will be monotonic in X or Y.

First consider that a parametrically defined surface, or surface patch, can be specified by three bivariate functions:

$$x = X(u, v)$$
$$y = Y(u, v)$$
$$z = Z(u, v)$$

where both u and v vary between 0 and 1. The boundaries of a surface patch are defined by the values $u = 0$, $u = 1$, $v = 0$ and $v = 1$. This results in a four-sided patch.

One way of looking at scan conversion in the context of bi-cubic parametric patches is to consider it as an algorithm that finds curves formed by the intersection of the XZ scan plane with the surface (Figure 4.1). Blinn points out that these XZ curves do not have an explicit formulation and the only way to solve for points on the curve is by a numerical method such as Newton iteration. With planar polygons this curve is a straight line and it is only necessary to store the end points. In the case of parametric surfaces all points on the intersection curve need to be determined.

Blinn's algorithm (Blinn 1978) for parametric scan conversion is a straightforward algebraic approach and involves solving equations (using iterative techniques) for the intersection of the boundary curves and the silhouette edge with each scan line. That is the curve may be made up of a number of segments; for example, a segment from a boundary to a silhouette edge, a segment between two silhouette edges and a segment from a silhouette edge to a boundary. The intersection of a scan line Y_s with the boundary of a patch is given by:

Figure 4.1
A scan line algorithm for rendering patches can operate by finding the structure of the patch intersection curve, then using an iterative method to track along it.

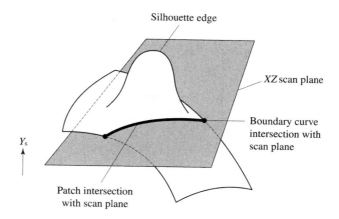

Silhouette edge

XZ scan plane

Boundary curve intersection with scan plane

Y_s

Patch intersection with scan plane

$$Y_s = Y(0, v)$$
$$Y_s = Y(1, v)$$
$$Y_s = Y(u, 0)$$
$$Y_s = Y(u, 1)$$

The silhouette edge intersections are given by:

$$Y_s = Y(u, v)$$
$$0 = \mathbf{N}_z(u, v)$$

where $\mathbf{N}_z$ is the z component of the surface normal to the patch. A silhouette edge is defined by these points on the surface that exhibit a surface normal with zero z component. Local maxima and minima are determined from:

$$Y_u(u, v) = 0$$
$$Y_v(u, v) = 0$$

where Y_u and Y_v are the partial derivatives with respect to u and v.
The points on the curve between these points are given by:

$$Y(u, v) - Y_s = 0$$
$$X(u, v) - X_s = 0$$

Solving these equations yields a set of points (u, v) in parameter space that can be substituted into the X and Z functions to yield the X and Z values of the curve on the current scan plane. This procedure is followed for each patch or surface yielding successive pairs of boundaries representing areas to be shaded. As the scan plane moves down the screen, the boundary and silhouette edges must be tracked and their connectivity maintained. This is not an easy process and Blinn gives an instructive example using saddle points. Detection of a local maximum implies that a new intersection curve is added to an intersection curve list. Curves are deleted at Y minima. The effect of this process is to partition the surface patch into regions that are monotonically decreasing in Y and single valued in Z. It is pointed out in Lane *et al.* (1980) that there are numerous problems with this approach, but that for most shapes the algorithm is robust. Thus, as with planar polygon scan conversion, the outer Y scan loop tracks boundary and silhouette edges and the inner X scan loop 'fills' in points on the intersection curve in the Y scan plane. Blinn further modifies this process by trading off accuracy against speed, approximating the intersection curve by straight line segments.

Whitted's, Schweitzer's and Griffith's methods are all variations of this basic approach.

(4.2.2)

Patch to polygon conversion

Deriving a polygon mesh from a patch mesh is conceptually simple. We simply subdivide the patches and use the corner points of the subdivision products as polygons. Each set of four vertices converts to two triangular facets (Figure 4.2). Thus in converting patches to polygons we go on subdividing until we decide that, to within some limit, the polygonal approximation is sufficiently close to the true (patch) surface. There appears to be a contradiction here. What is the point in going to the expense of a patch representation if we are then going to approximate it with polygonal facets. There are many justifications. The most common is that application requires such a representation – this is mostly the case in CAD. The visualization of the object can be an approximation but the designer needs to work with an accurate representation. We should also bear in mind that the representation allows us to control the accuracy of the polygonal approximation, as we shall see.

This topic splits naturally into categories depending on the criterion used to determine the depth of the subdivision and exactly where it is applied on the patch surface. The main difference is whether the termination criteria operate in object space or screen space. Screen space termination criteria offer the potential of being able to adjust the polygonal resolution of the object to match the projected size of the object on the screen. In object space we compare the approximation against the true surface using object space metrics; in screen space we use pixel units as a metric. Screen space termination is dynamic in the sense that it depends on the view point or viewing distance.

(4.2.3)

Object space subdivision

Dealing with object space first we can list the following simple categories:

(1) Object space – uniform subdivision. This is the simplest case and involves a user specifying a level at which uniform subdivision of all patches is to terminate.

(2) Object space – non-uniform subdivision. This means stopping the subdivision when the subdivision products meet a patch flatness criterion.

Figure 4.2
The patch splitting process.
(a) Continue process until
flat and (b) convert the
vertices into two triangular
facets.

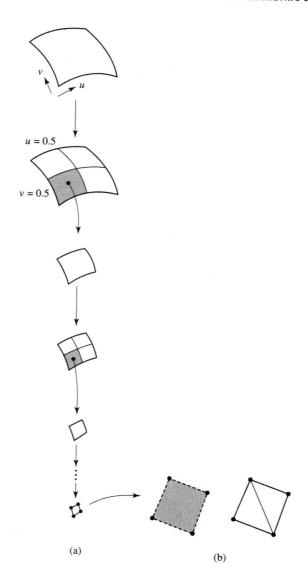

(a)

(b)

The second category is theoretically preferable – here you 'allocate' the degree of subdivision according to where it is required. More subdivision takes place in areas of high surface curvature. However, there is a high cost involved in testing for flatness which may outweigh the cost of unnecessary subdivisions.

Uniform subdivision proceeds as follows. The patch can be divided using iso-parametric curves. (Splitting up a patch into iso-parametric curves is a common method of display in CAD systems, permitting a wireframe visualization of the surface sufficient for the requirements of such systems.) This yields a net or mesh of points at the intersection of these curves with each other and the boundary edges. This net of points can be used to define the vertices for a mesh of planar polygons which can then be rendered using a planar polygon renderer. There are two problems with this rudimentary approach. Visible boundary edges and silhouette edges may exhibit discontinuities. In general, a finer polygon resolution will be necessary to diminish the visibility of piecewise linear discontinuities on edges than is necessary to maintain smooth shading within the patch. Another problem is that internal silhouette edges in the patch will generally be of higher degree than cubic. If special attention is to be devoted to silhouette edges then this is best carried out in screen space as we shall see in the next section.

Now consider non-uniform subdivision. This simply means that areas of the patch that are 'flattish' are subject to few subdivisions. Areas where the local curvature is high are subject to more subdivisions. Effectively the patch is subdivided to a degree that depends on local curvature. This is the approach adopted by Lane and Carpenter in Lane *et al.* (1980). It is demonstrated in Figure 4.3.

Patches are subdivided until the products of the subdivision submit to a flatness criterion. Such patches are now considered to be approximately planar polygons and are scan converted by a normal polygon renderer using the corner points of the patches as vertices for rectangles in the polygon mesh. The set of patches representing the surface can be preprocessed, yielding a set of polygons which are then scan converted as normal. This is the approach adopted in Clark (1979). Lane integrates this patch splitting approach with a scan conversion algorithm.

There are two significant advantages to patch splitting:

(1) It is fast.

(2) The speed can be varied by altering the depth of the subdivision. This is important for interactive systems.

A disadvantage of non-uniform subdivision is that holes can appear between patches due to the approximation of a patch boundary by a straight line. An example of this degenerative process is shown in Figure 4.4.

Subdivision algorithms are best considered for a curve. These are then easily extended or generalized to deal with a patch. The crux of the method is that rather than evaluate points along a curve, the curve is approximated by a piecewise linear version obtained by subdividing the control points recursively. This gives a finer and finer approximation to the curve. The level of subdivision/

Figure 4.3
Uniform and non-uniform subdivison of a Bézier patch.

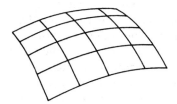
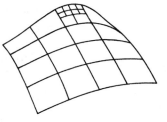

Figure 4.4
Tears produced by non-uniform subdivision of patches.

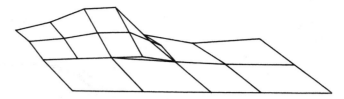

recursion terminates when a linearity criterion is satisfied. Lane and Reisenfeld (1980) show that the piecewise linear approximation to the curve will eventually 'collapse' onto the curve providing enough subdivisions are undertaken.

A subdivision formula for the Bézier basis (or, in general, the Bernstein basis) is given in Lane *et al.* (1980) and derived in Lane and Riesenfeld (1980). (This process can be used for any basis by first converting the representation to the Bézier basis as described in Watt and Watt (1992). A Bézier curve is subdivided into two curves by subdividing the control points, forming two new sets of control points R_i and S_i. The point R_3/S_0 is the end point of the first curve and the start of the second. The formula is:

$$R_0 = Q_0 \qquad\qquad S_0 = R_3$$
$$R_1 = (Q_0 + Q_1)/2 \qquad\qquad S_1 = (Q_1 + Q_2)/4 + S_2/2$$
$$R_2 = R_1/2 + (Q_1 + Q_2)/4 \qquad\qquad S_2 = (Q_2 + Q_3)/2$$
$$R_3 = (R_2 + S_1)/2 \qquad\qquad S_3 = Q_3$$

Figure 4.5 shows how, after a single subdivision, the piecewise linear curve joining the two new sets of control points is a better approximation to the curve than the original. The approximation after three levels of subdivision is shown in Figure 4.6.

The curve splitting process is easily extended to patches as illustrated in Figure 4.7. We consider the patch to be made up of four curves of constant u and four curves of constant v, whose control points are consecutive rows and consecutive

Figure 4.5
Splitting a bi-cubic Bézier curve.

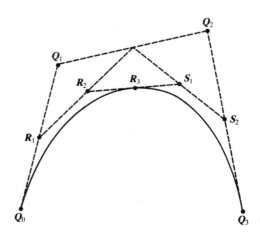

Figure 4.6
Drawing the control points
at each level of subdivision.

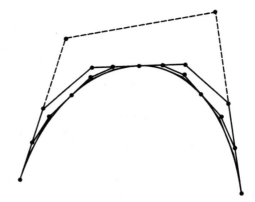

columns of the control point matrix. We apply the curve splitting formula separately to each of the four curves in u yielding two sub-patches of the original patch.
We then repeat the process for each of these two sub-patches this time splitting the
curves in v. Putting these divisions together divides the patch into four.

This efficient formula (that uses only additions and divide by two) makes the
subdivision rapid. The depth of the subdivision is easily controlled using a linearity criterion. The Bézier basis functions sum identically to 1:

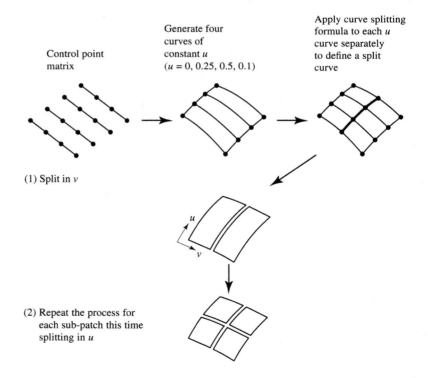

Control point
matrix

Generate four
curves of
constant u
(u = 0, 0.25, 0.5, 0.1)

Apply curve splitting
formula to each u
curve separately
to define a split
curve

(1) Split in v

(2) Repeat the process for
each sub-patch this time
splitting in u

Figure 4.7
Using curve splitting to
subdivide a patch into four.

$$\sum_{i=0}^{3} B_i(u) = 1$$

This means that the curve lies in the convex hull formed by the control points P_i. The piecewise linear subdivision product will coincide with the curve when it 'merges' with the line joining the two end points. The degree to which this is achieved, that is the linearity of the line joining the four control points, can be tested by measuring the distance from the middle two control points to the end point joining line (Figure 4.8).

The philosophy of this test is easily extended to surface patches. A plane is fitted through three non-collinear control points. The distance of each of the other 13 control points from this plane is then calculated. If one of these distances lies outside a prespecified tolerance, then the patch is further subdivided. In effect we are measuring the thickness of a bounding box – a rectangular solid enclosing the patch whose thickness is defined by the largest distance from the plane containing the corner points to the farthest control point. This is sometimes called the convex hull flatness test.

A practical problem that occurs when considering non-uniform subdivision (subdivision until a flatness criterion is satisfied) compared with uniform subdivision to some predetermined level, is the cost of the flatness test. It is debatable if it is a simpler and better, but less elegant approach simply to adopt uniform subdivision and ignore the fact that some areas are going to be unnecessarily subdivided (because they are already flat). For a given image quality, the cost of testing for non-uniform subdivision will be greater than the extra rendering costs of uniform subdivision. The next illustration demonstrates this. Figure 4.9 (Colour Plate) shows a uniform subdivision approach for the Utah teapot at subdivisions of one, two and three. An important aspect of this image is that it shows predictably that the difference in quality between the rendered images is mainly visible along silhouette edges.

If uniform subdivision is adopted then rendering bi-cubic patches can reduce to a pre-processing phase of a normal Z-buffer renderer. This method requires a large database for the subdivision products. If sufficient memory is not available,

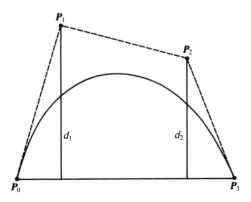

Figure 4.8
A cubic Bézier curve with control points P_0, P_1, P_2, P_3.

and the extra complexity of a scan line algorithm is to be introduced, then it is not a big step to use non-uniform subdivision.

The overall structure of a scan line algorithm, such as the Lane–Carpenter algorithm, is as follows:

(1) Sort the patches by maximum possible Y value. This value, as already stated, may be a corner point, a point on a boundary edge, or a point on a silhouette edge. The only quick way to an estimate of this value is to take the maximum Y value of the convex hull of the control points.

(2) For each scan line an inactive and active list of patches is updated. For each active patch, subdivision is performed until either a flatness criterion is satisfied, or until any one subdivision product no longer straddles a scan line. 'Flat' polygons are added to an active polygon list and scan converted in the normal way. Subdivision products that no longer overlap the scan line can be added to the inactive patch list. Thus we have an active and inactive list of parametric patches together with an active list of flat polygons.

One of the practical points that has to be dealt with is the problem of tears (Figure 4.4). Tears are a natural consequence of recursive or non-uniform subdivision. If one part of a surface patch is subdivided along a boundary shared by another patch that requires no further subdivision, then a gap between the two parts will naturally result. This 'tear' is then an unrepresented area and will appear as a gap or hole in the final rendering phase. The Lane–Carpenter algorithm does not deal with this problem. It can be minimized by making the flatness criterion more rigorous but herein lies the normal computational paradox. The philosophy of the subdivision approach is that areas of a surface are subdivided to a degree that corresponds to local curvature. Large flat areas are minimally subdivided. Areas exhibiting fast curvature changes will be subdivided down to sufficiently small polygons. Tightening the flatness criterion means that many more polygons are generated and the final rendering phase takes much longer.

Clark's method deals with this problem in a more elegant way by adopting a subdivision method that is initially constrained to the boundary curves. There are three steps involved:

(1) The convex curve hull criterion is applied to the boundary edges $u = 1$ and $u = 0$ and the patch is subdivided along the v direction until this is satisfied.

(2) The same method is then applied to the $v = 1$ and $v = 0$ boundaries.

(3) Finally the normal convex hull test is applied to the subdivision products and the process is continued, if necessary, along the u or v direction.

Once a boundary satisfies the convex hull criterion it is assumed to be a straight line. Any further subdivision along this boundary will thus incur no separation.

A possible advantage of subdividing in the direction of the u or v boundaries is that with some objects this will result in fewer patches. Consider, for example, subdividing a 'ducted' solid – a cylinder is a trivial example of such an object.

Subdividing the cylinder along a direction parallel to its long axis will lead this algorithm to converge more quickly and with fewer patches than if the subdivision proceeds in both parametric directions. A disadvantage with this approach is that it is difficult to integrate with a scan line algorithm. A scan line algorithm 'drives' or controls the order of subdivision depending on how the patches lie with respect to the scan lines.

Another aspect that requires consideration is the calculation of surface normals. These are, of course, required for shading. They are easily obtainable from the original parametric description, at any point (u, v) on the surface, by computing the cross-product of the u and v derivatives. However, if a subdivision method is being used to scan convert, then the final polygon rendering is going to utilize a Phong interpolation method and the vertex normals are easily calculated by taking the cross-products of the tangent vectors at the corner points. This will, in general, depending on the level of the subdivision, give non-parallel vertex normals for the 'flat' polygons, but all polygons contributing to a vertex will have the same normal. Two consequences can result from the fact that 'flat' polygons are being sent to a shader with non-parallel vertex normals. Firstly, erroneous shading effects can occur at low levels of subdivision. Secondly, the question of which vertex normal to use for culling arises. Problems occur because not all the polygons surrounding a vertex may be available since subdivision is taking place on the fly and an average vertex normal cannot be calculated as in polygon meshes. Cases can obviously result where one normal subtends an angle of greater than 90° with the view vector and one an angle less than 90°. The only safe course of action is to cull a polygon by testing each of its vertex normals. If any vertex normal is 'visible' the polygon is not culled.

An earlier approach by Catmull (1974) subdivided patches until they approximated the size of a single pixel, writing the results into a Z-buffer. This straightforward but computationally expensive approach side-steps yet another problem – relating the extent of the subdivision to the projected screen size of the patch. Clearly there is no point in subdividing to a greater and greater depth if, when projected into screen space, the patch only covers a few pixels. Clark relates the subdivision test to the depth coordinates of the control points of the patches.

Finally these subdivision methods differ in the basis used. The Lane–Carpenter algorithm uses a cubic Bernstein or Bézier basis. Clark uses a Taylor series expansion and central differences to derive more efficient subdivision formulae and to utilize a flatness test that is available directly from the subdivision components.

4.2.4   Image space subdivision

The methods of the previous section suffice for many applications, particularly in single object CAD work. In applications where the object can form projections of widely varying size in screen space it is better to consider controlling the depth of the subdivision using screen space criteria. We could call this approach view dependent or screen space controlled subdivision.

There are three simple ways in which we can do this. All of these involve projecting sample points from the patch, at its current level of subdivision, into screen space and comparing these against the projection of the polygon that is an approximation to the patch. The comparison is effected using pixel length units as the metric. The measurements are:

(1) Minimum pixel area occupied by a patch.
(2) The screen space flatness of the patch.
(3) The screen space flatness of the silhouette edge.

Minimum pixel area occupied by a patch

Once the patch projects onto a sufficiently small number of pixels, it is deemed to have been subdivided sufficiently. In the limit we can subdivide until the pieces are the size of a single pixel but this is clearly expensive.

Screen space flatness of the patch

For this test we can proceed exactly as in the object space test but use pixel-based metrics instead of object space units. In other words we measure the thickness of the bounding box defined by the convex hull in pixel units. Alternatively we can use a less accurate but faster test. This criterion is illustrated in Figure 4.10

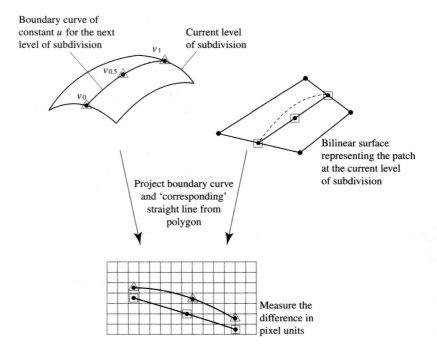

Boundary curve of constant u for the next level of subdivision

Current level of subdivision

v_1

$v_{0.5}$

v_0

Bilinear surface representing the patch at the current level of subdivision

Project boundary curve and 'corresponding' straight line from polygon

Measure the difference in pixel units

Figure 4.10
Screen space subdivision termination increasing the flatness of the patch in screen space at its current level of subdivison.

which shows a single patch at its current level of subdivision. Superimposed on this is are three samples, v_0, $v_{0.5}$ and v_1 that lie in a curve of constant $u_{0.5}$. This curve – the boundary curve at the next level – lies in the true surface of the patch and the three points are the polygon vertices at the next level of subdivision. We can compare these points with points on the bilinear patch formed from the four vertices. (A bilinear patch is a non-planar quadrilateral where all lines of constant u and v are linear.) Comparing these samples of this curve with the straight line bisecting the bilinear patch gives one estimate of the flatness of the patch in screen space. The procedure can be repeated for the curve $v_{0.5}$. As Figure 4.9 (Colour Plate) shows, the interior of an object is not much affected by the level of subdivision because the shading algorithm is specifically designed to diminish the visibility of polygon edges. This observation leads us to deduce that the subdivision needs to be concentrated near the silhouette edge.

Screen space flatness of the silhouette edge

If our goal is to minimize the number of polygons representing the object then, because of the efficacy of the shading algorithms, which means that we can tolerate a fairly coarse polygonal approximation except at the silhouette edge, the best strategy is to have two polygonal resolutions, one for the internal patches and a finer one for the silhouette edges. The trade-offs are illustrated in Figure 4.11. Figure 4.11(a) shows a sphere subdivided with a small screen space flatness criterion. Here the silhouette edge is well defined because of this. In Figure 4.11(b) the rendering quality is retained with far fewer polygons by concentrating the subdivision around the silhouette edge. This strategy does, however, need qualification in this sense. The fact that it is view dependent means that, unless we use some coherence strategy, a new subdivision has to be invoked for every view point change with the attendant cost.

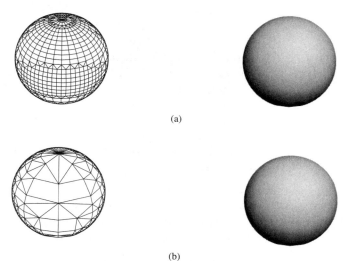

(a)

(b)

Figure 4.11
Screen space flatness of silhouette edges. (a) Subdivision sufficient to eliminate piecewise linearities at the silhouette edge. (b) Maintaining the same image quality with larger 'internal' polygons.

Now consider the problem of silhouette edge detection, or more specifically detecting those patches that contain a silhouette edge curve. Leaving aside the complication of patches that contain folds or cusps, a silhouette edge in view space is defined by those points on the patch that satisfy:

$$\mathbf{N} \cdot \mathbf{L}_{os} = 0$$

where $\mathbf{N}$ is the surface normal and $\mathbf{L}_{os}$ is the line of sight vector.
Alternatively, for a parallel projection with the image plane at $z = 0$, we have:

$$\mathbf{N}_z = 0$$

the z component of the surface normal is zero for points on a silhouette edge. If a patch contains a silhouette edge then it will exhibit a region where $\mathbf{N}_z$ is positive and a region where it is negative. $\mathbf{N}_z$ is given by:

$$\mathbf{N}_z = \frac{\partial x(u, v)}{\partial u} \frac{\partial y(u, v)}{\partial v} - \frac{\partial y(u, v)}{\partial u} \frac{\partial x(u, v)}{\partial v}$$

If the first term is always positive and the second term always negative then $\mathbf{N}_z$ is everywhere positive and cannot contain a silhouette edge. This can be tested by evaluating just 16 differences from the control point matrix.

4.3 Rendering a CSG description

Rendering strategies for CSG models are disparate. The distinguishing feature of CSG representation is that it is not a 'direct' geometric object representation. Rather it is a formula that has to be interpreted. In CSG representation the object database is a tree that relates a set of primitive objects to each other via Boolean operations. You recall that this representation regime facilitates powerful interactivity. The price that we pay for this is an expensive and complex rendering strategy. To illustrate the point, consider, for example, an object formed by intersecting two cylinders as in Figure 2.14. The CSG description consists only of the two geometric primitives and their dimensions, their spatial relationship and the set operator that combines them. This information does not offer a 'constructed' object to a renderer, the composite object, that contains geometric features like the intersection curves which are not in the component parts has to be derived, and it is this derivation or construction of the object that is the root of the difficulty.

The main problem involved in rendering CSG objects is somehow to derive an object representation suitable for rendering from the CSG database. Three techniques have evolved:

(1) CSG ray tracing.

(2) Conversion to a voxel representation followed by volume rendering (see Chapter 14).

(3) Using a version of the Z-buffer algorithm (see Section 6.6.2).

Here we will briefly look at the first of these approaches. This is a fairly straightforward adaptation of standard ray tracing techniques described in Chapter 10.

The evaluation of an object from a CSG description can be achieved by reducing the problem to one dimension. To do this we cast a ray from each pixel in the view plane. In the simplest (parallel projection) case we explore the space of the object with a set of parallel rays. The process divides into two stages. First consider a single ray. Every primitive instance is compared with this ray to see if it intersects the primitive. This means solving a line quadric intersection test as

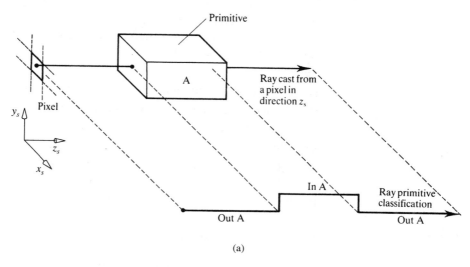

(a)

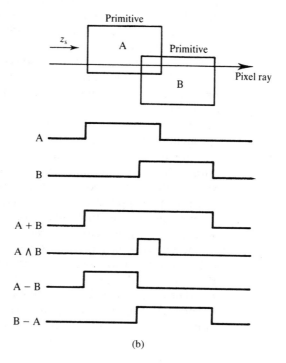

(b)

Figure 4.12
(a) Deriving a ray/primitive classification. (b) Evaluating Boolean operations along a ray.

described in Chapter 1. Any intersections are sorted in Z depth. We then have a ray/primitive classification for each ray (Figure 4.12(a)) and can now look at any Boolean combinations between the first two primitives encountered along the ray. From Figure 4.12(b) it is easily seen that evaluating the Boolean operations between primitives along a ray is straightforward. A shading value can then be allocated to the pixel by a simple reflection model applied at the first intersection along the ray. Note from Figure 4.12(b) that this point varies according to the Boolean operations between the primitives.

Ray tracing in this way is the 'classical' method of rendering the CSG model. It is, however, expensive. Finally we note that the method integrates into a single model:

(1) Evaluation of a boundary representation from a CSG description.

(2) Hidden surface removal – only intersections with the two primitives nearest to the viewer are considered.

(3) Shading.

Note that all operations take place in screen space and we would map directly from the space of the CSG description into screen space. We by-pass the complexities of view space if we use a parallel projection as described above.

4.4   Rendering a voxel description

The choice of rendering objects ultimately represented by voxels is predetermined by the application. As we have already mentioned, a voxel representation may be chosen in a ray tracing algorithms in which case the rendering method is ray tracing. Here the voxels will represent, to an accuracy that depends on their size, solid or conventional objects.

In volume visualization a voxel usually represents a property rather than a physical object, say, the X-ray absorption coefficient of a point inside a body derived from an X-ray CT scanner. Here we have to decide not only how to render but what we want to render. The implication is that the property varies throughout the data space. Each voxel no longer just represents the presence or absence of an object. Instead we have an object that is defined everywhere within the space it occupies – it is no longer just the boundary of a solid object. We are interested in looking at the variation of the information inside the object.

In such an application we may want to render just the boundary information so that the voxel set looks like a solid object; or we may want to volume render which implies the use of transparency. We have the analogy of the visualization of the object – usually an internal organ of the body – as being made up of coloured glass whose colour varies according to the real property of the organ that has been imaged. Say that in a CT data set of a head we wanted to render the skull. Then we would have to locate all those voxels that exhibited the value for bone and render these. Alternatively we may want to render the brain, but also have the skull present in the image as a transparent object.

For rendering the boundary of a voxel set, a crude approach is simply to find these voxels and shade them as if they were individual cubic objects using a standard polygon mesh renderer. Clearly this makes for a 'blocky' appearance and a more usual approach is to fit a polygonally faceted surface to the voxel set using an elegant algorithm known as the marching cubes algorithm. This algorithm was used to extract the surface of the object shown rendered in Figure 2.5(b). Its significant disadvantage is that it generates an extremely large number of polygons. The marching cubes algorithm is covered in detail in Chapter 14.

4.5 Rendering implicit functions

Like the CSG method the implicit function representation is difficult to render. It is similar in principle to the CSG method in that the model is not a direct representation of the geometry but rather a formula from which a geometric form has to be extracted. The problem is simple to describe. We have a definition for an object whereby a point on a surface is defined by a single scalar value and selects a subset of the infinity of points within the collective sphere of influence of all the generators that are used to model the object. There are two common approaches.

The first is an approximation to evaluating the infinity of points associated with each generator. It maps the definition into a voxel set which can then be rendered using a rendering strategy for such an object. The straightforward, but costly, way to do this is as follows. For each generator we evaluate a scalar for every voxel in its field of influence, accumulating within each voxel the sum of all the generators that encompass it. The iso-surface is then extracted and rendered using, say, the marching cubes algorithm.

Another approach uses a simple extension of ray tracing spherical objects (see Chapter 12). For each ray a pair of simultaneous equations, defining the ray and the function $F(P)$ is solved giving the intersection of the ray with the isosurface. This is implemented by:

(1) Finding the generators that contribute to the field of an object along the path of a ray from the intersection of the ray with the spheres of influence of each generator.

(2) Calculating the ray–sphere intersection for each generator.

(3) Finding the nearest and furthest intersection points which gives the intersection point with the object.

The illustration in Figure 2.20 (Colour Plate) was rendered in this way.

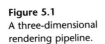

5 The graphics pipeline (1): geometric operations

5.1   Coordinate spaces in the graphics pipeline

5.2   Operations carried out in view space

5.3   Advanced viewing systems (PHIGS and GKS)

Introduction

The purpose of a graphics pipeline is to take a description of a scene in three-dimensional space and map it into a two-dimensional projection on the view surface – the monitor screen. Although various three-dimensional display devices exist, most computer graphics view surfaces are two-dimensional, the most common being the TV-type monitor. In most VR applications a pair of projections is produced and displayed on small monitors encased in a helmet – a head-mounted display, or HMD. The only difference in this case is that we now have a pair of two-dimensional projections instead of one – the operations remain the same.

In what follows we will consider the case of polygon mesh models. We can loosely classify the various processes involved in the graphics pipeline by putting them into one of two categories – geometric (this chapter) and algorithmic (Chapter 6). Geometric processes involve operations on the vertices of polygons – transforming the vertices from one coordinate space to another or discarding

Figure 5.1
A three-dimensional rendering pipeline.

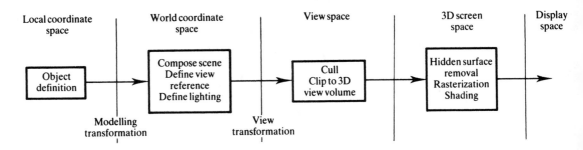

polygons that cannot be seen from the view point, for example. Rendering processes involve operations like shading and texture mapping and are considerably more costly than the geometric operations most of which involve matrix multiplication.

A diagram representing the consecutive process in a graphics pipeline is shown in Figure 5.1. From this it can be seen that the overall process is a progression through various three-dimensional spaces – we transform the object representation from space to space. In the final space, which we have called screen space, the rendering operations take place. This space is also three-dimensional for reasons that we will shortly discover.

5.1 Coordinate spaces in the graphics pipeline

5.1.1 Local or modelling coordinate systems

For ease of modelling it makes sense to store the vertices of a polygon mesh object with respect to some point located in or near the object. For example, we would almost certainly want to locate the origin of a cube at one of the cube vertices, or we would want to make the axis of symmetry of an object generated as a solid of revolution, coincident with the z axis. As well as storing the polygon vertices in a coordinate system that is local to the object, we would also store the polygon normal and the vertex normals. When local transformations are applied to the vertices of an object, the corresponding transformations are applied to the associated normals.

5.1.2 World coordinate systems

Once an object has been modelled the next stage is to place it in the scene that we wish to render. All objects that together constitute a scene have their separate local coordinate systems. The global coordinate system of the scene is known as the 'world coordinate system'. All objects have to be transformed into this common space in order that their relative spatial relationships may be defined. The act of placing an object in a scene defines the transformation required to take the object from local space to world space. If the object is being animated, then the animation system provides a time-varying transformation that takes the object into world space on a frame by frame basis.

The scene is lit in world space. Light sources are specified, and if the shaders within the renderer function are in world space then this is the final transformation that the normals of the object have to undergo. The surface attributes of an object – texture, colour and so on – are specified and tuned in this space.

5.1.3 Camera or eye or view coordinate system

The eye, camera or view coordinate system is a space that is used to establish viewing parameters (view point, viewing direction) and a view volume. (A virtual camera is often used as the analogy in viewing systems, but if such an allusion is made we must be careful to distinguish between external camera parameters – its position and the direction it is pointing in – and internal camera parameters or those that affect the nature and size of the image on the film plane. Most rendering systems imitate a camera which in practice would be a perfect pinhole (or lensless) device with a film plane that can be positioned at any distance with respect to the pinhole. However, there are other facilities in computer graphics that cannot be imitated by a camera and because of this the analogy is of limited utility.)

We will now deal with a basic view coordinate system and the transformation from world space to view coordinate space. The reasons that this space exists, after all we could go directly from world space to screen space, is that certain operations (and specifications) are most conveniently carried out in view space. Standard viewing systems like that defined in the PHIGS graphics standard are more complicated in the sense that they allow the user to specify more facilities and we will deal with these in Section 5.3.

We define a viewing system as being the combination of a view coordinate system together with the specification of certain facilities such as a view volume. The simplest or minimum system would consist of the following:

- A view point which establishes the viewer's position in world space; this can either be the origin of the view coordinate system or the centre of projection together with a view direction N.

- A view coordinate system defined with respect to the view point.

- A view plane onto which the two-dimensional image of the scene is projected.

- A view frustum or volume which defines the field of view.

These entities are shown in Figure 5.2. The view coordinate system, UVN, has N coincident with the viewing direction and V and U lying in a plane parallel to the view plane. We can consider the origin of the system to be the view point C. The view plane containing U and V is of infinite extent and we specify a view volume or frustum which defines a window in the view plane. It is the contents of this window – the projection of that part of the scene that is contained within the view volume – that finally appears on the screen.

Thus, using the virtual camera analogue we have a camera that can be positioned anywhere in world coordinate space, pointed in any direction and rotated about the viewing direction N.

To transform points in world coordinate space we invoke a change of coordinate system transformation and this splits into two components: a translational one and a rotational one (see Chapter 1). Thus:

$$\begin{bmatrix} x_v \\ y_v \\ z_v \\ 1 \end{bmatrix} = T_{view} \begin{bmatrix} x_w \\ y_w \\ z_w \\ 1 \end{bmatrix}$$

Figure 5.2
The minimum entities required in a practical viewing system. (a) View point **C** and viewing direction **N**. (b) A view plane normal to the viewing direction **N** positioned d units from **C**. (c) A view coordinate system with the origin **C** and **UV** axes embedded in plane parallel to the view plane. (d) A view volume defined by the frustum formed by **C** and the view plane window.

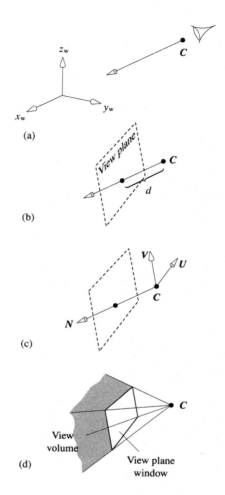

where:

$$\boldsymbol{T}_{\text{view}} = \boldsymbol{RT}$$

and:

$$\boldsymbol{T} = \begin{bmatrix} 1 & 0 & 0 & -C_x \\ 0 & 1 & 0 & -C_y \\ 0 & 0 & 1 & -C_z \\ 0 & 0 & 0 & 1 \end{bmatrix} \qquad \boldsymbol{R} = \begin{bmatrix} U_x & U_y & U_z & 0 \\ V_x & V_y & V_z & 0 \\ N_x & N_y & N_z & 0 \\ 0 & 0 & 0 & 1 \end{bmatrix}$$

The only problem now is specifying a user interface for the system and mapping whatever parameters are used by the interface into **U**, **V** and **N**. A user needs to specify **C**, **N** and **V**. **C** is easy enough. **N**, the viewing direction or view plane normal, can be entered say, using two angles in a spherical coordinate system – this seems reasonably intuitive:

θ   the azimuth angle

φ   the colatitude or elevation angle

where:

$$N_x = \sin \phi \cos \theta$$
$$N_y = \sin \phi \sin \theta$$
$$N_z = \cos \phi$$

V is more problematic. For example, a user may require 'up' to be the same sense as 'up' in the world coordinate system. However, this cannot be achieved by setting:

$$V = (0, 0, 1)$$

because V must be perpendicular to N. A sensible strategy is to allow a user to specify an approximate orientation for V, say V' and have the system calculate V. Figure 5.3 demonstrates this. V' is the user-specified up vector. This is projected onto the view plane:

$$V = V' - (V'.N)N$$

and normalized. U can be specified or not depending on the user's requirements. If U is unspecified, it is obtained from:

$$U = N \times V$$

This results in a left-hand coordinate system, which although somewhat inconsistent, conforms with our intuition of a practical viewing system, which has increasing distances from the view point as increasing values along the view direction axis. Having established the viewing transformation using UVN notation, we will in subsequent sections use (x_v, y_v, z_v) to specify points in the view coordinate system.

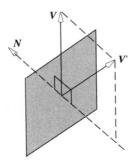

Figure 5.3
The up vector V can be calculated from an 'indication' given by V'.

5.2 Operations carried out in view space

5.2.1 Culling or back-face elimination

Culling or back-face elimination is an operation that compares the orientation of complete polygons with the view point or centre of projection and removes those polygons that cannot be seen. If a scene only contains a single convex object, then culling generalizes to hidden surface removal. A general hidden surface removal algorithm is always required when one polygon partially obscures another (Figure 5.4). On average, half of the polygons in a polyhedron are back-facing and the advantage of this process is that a simple test removes these polygons from consideration by a more expensive hidden surface removal algorithm.

The test for visibility is straightforward and is best carried out in view space. We calculate the outward normal for a polygon (see Section 1.3.3) and examine the sign of the dot product of this and the vector from the centre of projection (Figure 5.5). Thus:

$$\text{visibility} := \boldsymbol{N}_p \cdot \boldsymbol{N} > 0$$

where:

$\boldsymbol{N}_p$ is the polygon normal
$\boldsymbol{N}$ is the 'line of sight' vector

5.2.2 The view volume

In Figure 5.2 the view volume was introduced as a semi-infinite pyramid. In many applications this is further constrained to a general view volume which is defined by a view plane window, a near clip plane and a far clip plane, but to simplify matters we will dispense with the near clip plane, which is of limited practical utility, and reconsider a view volume defined only by a view plane window and a far clip plane (Figure 5.6). Note that the far clip plane is a cut-off plane normal to the viewing direction and any objects beyond this cannot be seen. In effect we have turned a semi-infinite pyramid into an infinite one. Far clip planes are extremely useful and can be used to cut down the number of polygons that need to be processed when rendering a very complex scene. For example, when flying through an environment in a three-dimensional computer

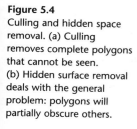

Figure 5.4
Culling and hidden space removal. (a) Culling removes complete polygons that cannot be seen. (b) Hidden surface removal deals with the general problem: polygons will partially obscure others.

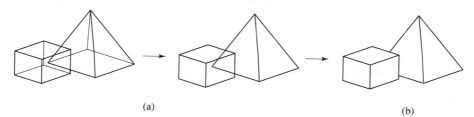

(a)

(b)

Figure 5.5
Culling or back-face
elimination. (a) The desired
view of the object (back
faces shown as dotted lines).
(b) A view of the geometry
of the culling operation.
(c) The culled object.

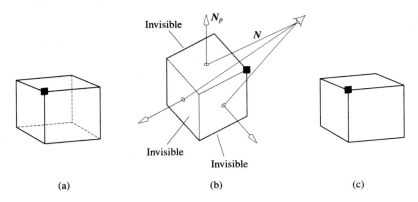

(a) (b) (c)

game we may specify a far clip plane and use depth modulated fog to diminish
the disturbance as objects 'switch-on' when they suddenly intersect the far clip
plane.

If we further simplify the geometry by specifying a square view plane window
of dimension $2h$ arranged symmetrically about the viewing direction, then the
four planes defining the sides of the view volume are given by:

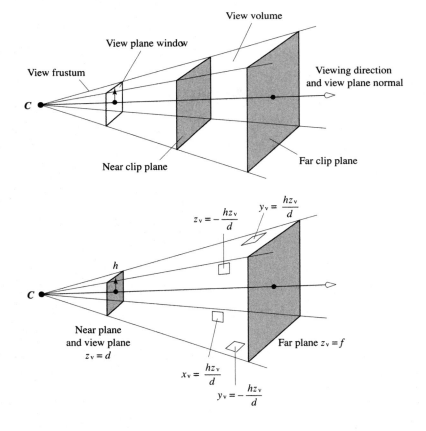

Figure 5.6
A practical view volume:
the near clip plane is made
coincident with the view
plane.

Figure 5.7
Clipping against a view
volume – a routine polygon
operation in the pipeline.
(a) Polygons outside the
view volume are discarded.
(b) Polygons inside the view
volume are retained.
(c) Polygons intersecting
a boundary are clipped.

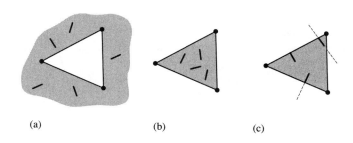

(a)   (b)   (c)

$$x_v = \pm \frac{hz_v}{d}$$

$$y_v = \pm \frac{hz_v}{d}$$

Clipping against the view volume (Figure 5.7) can now be carried out using polygon plane intersection calculations given in Section 1.4.3. This illustrates the principle of clipping, but the calculations involved are more efficiently carried out in three-dimensional screen space as we shall see.

5.2.3 Three-dimensional screen space

The final three-dimensional space in our pipeline we call three-dimensional screen space. In this space we carry out (practical) clipping against the view volume and the rendering processes that we will describe later. Three-dimensional screen space is used because it simplifies both clipping and hidden surface removal – the classic hidden surface removal algorithm being the Z-buffer algorithm which operates by comparing the depth values associated with different objects that project onto the same pixel. Also in this space there is a final transformation to two-dimensional view plane coordinates – sometimes called the perspective divide. (The terms 'screen' and 'view plane' mean slightly different things. Strictly speaking screen coordinates are derived from view plane coordinates by a device-dependent transformation.)

Because the viewing surface in computer graphics is deemed to be flat we consider the class of projections known as planar geometric projections. Two basic projections, perspective and parallel, are now described. These projections and the difference in their nature is illustrated in Figure 5.8.

A perspective projection is the more popular or common choice in computer graphics because it incorporates foreshortening. In a perspective projection relative dimensions are not preserved, and a distant line is displayed smaller than a nearer line of the same length (Figure 5.9). This effect enables human beings to perceive depth in a two-dimensional photograph or a stylization of three-dimensional reality. A perspective projection is characterized by a point known

Figure 5.8
Two points projected onto
a plane using parallel and
perspective projections.

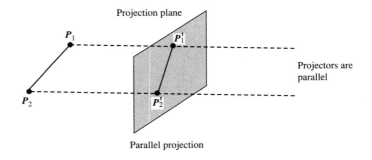

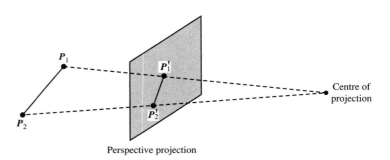

as the centre of projection and the projection of three-dimensional points onto
the view plane is the intersection of the lines from each point to the centre of
projection. These lines are called projectors.

Figure 5.10 shows how a perspective projection is derived. Point P (x_v, y_v, z_v)
is a three-dimensional point in the view coordinate system. This point is to be
projected onto a view plane normal to the z_v axis and positioned at distance d
from the origin of this system. Point P' is the projection of this point in the view
plane and has two-dimensional coordinates (x_s, y_s) in a view plane coordinate
system with the origin at the intersection of the z_v axis and the view plane.

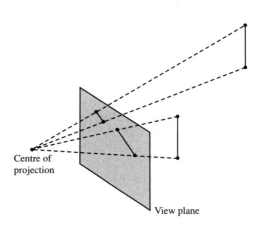

Figure 5.9
In a perspective projection
a distant line is displayed
smaller than a nearer line
the same length.

Figure 5.10
Deriving a perspective
transformation.

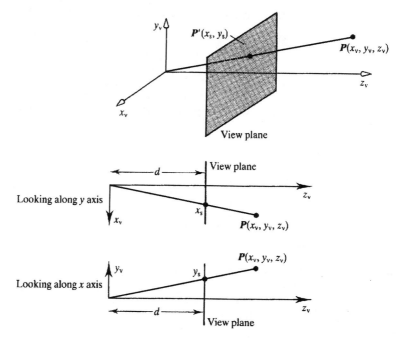

Similar triangles give:

$$\frac{x_s}{d} = \frac{x_v}{z_v} \qquad \frac{y_s}{d} = \frac{y_v}{z_v}$$

To express this non-linear transformation as a 4×4 matrix we can consider it in two parts – a linear part followed by a non-linear part. Using homogeneous coordinates we have:

$$X = x_v$$
$$Y = y_v$$
$$Z = z_v$$
$$w = z_v/d$$

We can now write:

$$\begin{bmatrix} X \\ Y \\ Z \\ w \end{bmatrix} = \boldsymbol{T}_{pers} \begin{bmatrix} x_v \\ y_v \\ z_v \\ 1 \end{bmatrix}$$

where:

$$\boldsymbol{T}_{pers} = \begin{bmatrix} 1 & 0 & 0 & 0 \\ 0 & 1 & 0 & 0 \\ 0 & 0 & 1 & 0 \\ 0 & 0 & 1/d & 0 \end{bmatrix}$$

following this with the perspective divide, we have:

$$x_s = X/w$$
$$y_s = Y/w$$
$$z_s = Z/w$$

In a parallel projection, if the view plane is normal to the direction of projection then the projection is orthographic and we have:

$$x_s = x_v \qquad y_s = y_v \qquad z_v = 0$$

Expressed as a matrix:

$$\mathbf{T}_{ort} = \begin{bmatrix} 1 & 0 & 0 & 0 \\ 0 & 1 & 0 & 0 \\ 0 & 0 & 0 & 0 \\ 0 & 0 & 0 & 1 \end{bmatrix}$$

5.2.4

View volume and depth

We now consider extending the above simple transformations to include the simplified view volume introduced in Figure 5.6. We discuss in more detail the transformation of the third component of screen space, namely z_s – ignored so far because the derivation of this transformation is somewhat subtle. Now, the bulk of the computation involved in rendering an image takes place in screen space. In screen space polygons are clipped against scan lines and pixels, and hidden surface calculations are performed on these clipped fragments. In order to perform hidden surface calculations (in the Z-buffer algorithm) depth information has to be generated on arbitrary points within the polygon. In practical terms this means, given a line and plane in screen space, being able to intersect the line with the plane, and to interpolate the depth of this intersection point, lying on the line, from the depth of the two end points. This is only a meaningful operation in screen space providing that in moving from eye space to screen space, lines transform into lines and planes transform into planes. It can be shown (Newman and Sproull 1973) that these conditions are satisfied provided the transformation of z takes the form:

$$z_s = A + B/z_v$$

where A and B are constants. These constants are determined from the following constraints:

(1) Choosing $B < 0$ so that as z_v increases then so does z_s. This preserves our intuitive Euclidean notion of depth. If one point is behind another, then it will have a larger z_v value, if $B < 0$ it will also have a larger z_s value.

(2) An important practical consideration concerning depth is the accuracy to which we store its value. To ensure this is as high as possible we normalize the range of z_s values so that the range $z_v \in [d, f]$ maps into the range $z_s \in [0, 1]$.

Considering the view volume in Figure 5.6, the full perspective transformation is given by:

$$x_s = d\,\frac{x_e}{hz_v}$$

$$y_s = d\,\frac{y_e}{hz_v}$$

$$z_s = \frac{f(1 - d/z_v)}{(f - d)}$$

where the additional constant, h, appearing in the transformation for x_s and y_s ensures that these values fall in the range [–1, 1] over the square screen. Adopting a similar manipulation to Section 5.2.3, we have:

$$X = \frac{d}{h}\,x_v$$

$$Y = \frac{d}{h}\,y_v$$

$$Z = \frac{fz_v}{f - d} - \frac{df}{f - d}$$

$$w = z_v$$

giving:

$$\begin{bmatrix} X \\ Y \\ Z \\ w \end{bmatrix} = \boldsymbol{T}_{\text{pers}} \begin{bmatrix} x_v \\ y_v \\ z_v \\ 1 \end{bmatrix}$$

where:

$$\boldsymbol{T}_{\text{pers}} = \begin{bmatrix} d/h & 0 & 0 & 0 \\ 0 & d/h & 0 & 0 \\ 0 & 0 & f/(f-d) & -df/(f-d) \\ 0 & 0 & 1 & 0 \end{bmatrix} \qquad [5.1]$$

We can now express the overall transformation from world space to screen space as a single transformation obtained by concatenating the view and perspective transformation giving:

$$\begin{bmatrix} X \\ Y \\ Z \\ w \end{bmatrix} = \boldsymbol{T}_{\text{pers}}\boldsymbol{T}_{\text{view}} \begin{bmatrix} x_w \\ y_w \\ z_w \\ 1 \end{bmatrix}$$

It is instructive to consider the relationship between z_v and z_s a little more closely; although as we have seen by construction, they both provide a measure of the depth of a point, interpolating along a line in eye space is not the same as interpolating this line in screen space. Figure 5.11 illustrates this point. Equal

Figure 5.11
Illustrating the distortion in three-dimensional screen space due to the z_v to z_s transformation.

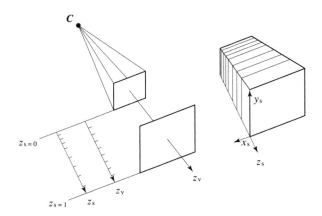

intervals in z_v are compared with the corresponding intervals in z_s. As z_v approaches the far clipping plane, z_s approaches 1 more rapidly. Thus, objects in screen space get pushed and distorted towards the back of the viewing frustum. This difference can lead to errors when interpolating quantities, other than position, in screen space.

In spite of this difficulty, by its very construction screen space is eminently suited to perform the hidden surface calculation. All rays passing through the view point are now parallel to the z_s axis because the centre of projection has been moved to negative infinity along the z_s axis. This can be seen by putting $z_v = 0$ into the above equation giving $z_s = -\infty$. Making those rays that hit the eye parallel, in screen space, means that hidden surface calculation need only be carried out on those points that have the same (x_s, y_s) coordinates. The test reduces to a simple comparison between z_s values to tell if a point is in front of another.

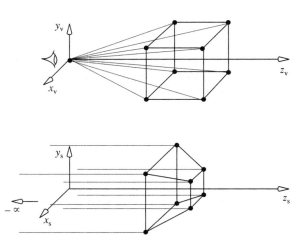

Figure 5.12
Transformation of box and light rays from eye space to screen space.

The transformation of a box with one side parallel to the image plane is shown in Figure 5.12. Here rays from the vertices of the box to the view point become parallel in three-dimensional screen space.

The overall precision required for the screen depth is a function of scene complexity. For most scenes 8 bits is insufficient and 16 bits usually suffices. The effects of insufficient precision is easily seen when, for example, a Z-buffer algorithm is used in conjunction with two intersecting objects. If the objects exhibit a curve where they intersect, this will produce aliasing artefacts of increasing severity as the precision of the screen depth is reduced.

Now return to the problem of clipping. It is easily seen from Figure 5.12 that in the homogeneous coordinate representation of screen space the sides of the view volume are parallel. This means that clipping calculations reduce to limit comparisons – we no longer have to substitute points into plane equations. The clipping operations must be performed on the homogeneous coordinates before the perspective divide, and translating the definition of the viewing frustum into homogeneous coordinates gives us the clipping limits:

$$-w \le x \le w$$

$$-w \le y \le w$$

$$0 \le z \le w$$

It is instructive to also consider the view space to eye space transformation by splitting Equation 5.1 into a product:

$$\mathbf{T}_{pers} = \begin{bmatrix} 1 & 0 & 0 & 0 \\ 0 & 1 & 0 & 0 \\ 0 & 0 & f/(f-d) & -df/(f-d) \\ 0 & 1 & 1 & 0 \end{bmatrix} \begin{bmatrix} d/h & 0 & 0 & 0 \\ 0 & d/h & 0 & 0 \\ 0 & 0 & 1 & 0 \\ 0 & 0 & 0 & 1 \end{bmatrix} = \mathbf{T}_{pers2}\mathbf{T}_{pers1}$$

This enables a useful visualization of the process. The first matrix is a scaling (d/h) in x and y. This effectively converts the view volume from a truncated pyramid with sides sloping at an angle determined by h/d into a regular pyramid with sides sloping at 45° (Figure 5.13). For example, point:

$(0, h, d, 1)$ transforms to $(0, d, d, 1)$

and point:

$(0, -h, d, 1)$ transforms to $(0, -d, d, 1)$

The second transformation maps the regular pyramid into a box. The near plane maps into the (x, y) plane and the far plane is mapped into $z=1$. For example, point:

$(0, d, d, 1)$ transforms to $(0, d, 0, d)$

which is equivalent to $(0, 1, 0, 1)$.

Figure 5.13
Transformation of the view
volume into a canonical
view volume (a box) using
two matrix transformations.

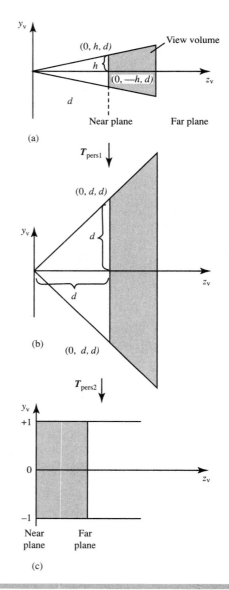

5.3   Advanced viewing systems (PHIGS and GKS)

The viewing systems defined by the graphics standards PHIGS and GKS are far
more general and more difficult to implement and understand than the system
just described and so this section is very much optional reading. An unfortunate
aspect of the standards viewing systems is that because they afford such generality they are hopelessly cumbersome and difficult to interface with. Even if a
subset of parameters is used the default values for the unused parameters have

to be appreciated and understood. Perhaps this is inevitable. The function of a standard, in one sense, is not to reflect common usage but to define a complete set of facilities that a user may require in a general viewing system. That some of these facilities will hardly ever be used is unfortunate. We include the PHIGS viewing system as a topic for study because whatever viewing system you encounter, it will undoubtedly be a subset of this one.

5.3.1   ## Overview of the PHIGS viewing system

We start this section by overviewing the extensions that PHIGS offers over the minimal viewing system described in the previous section. These are:

(1) The notion of a view point or eye point that establishes the origin of the view coordinate system and the centre of projection is now discarded. The equivalent of view space in PHIGS is the view reference coordinate system (VRC) established by defining a view reference point (VRP). A centre of projection is established separately by defining a projection reference point (PRP).

(2) Feature (1) means that a line from the centre of projection to the centre of the view plane window need not be parallel to the view plane normal. The implication of this is that oblique projections are possible. This is equivalent, in the virtual camera analogy, to allowing the film plane to tilt with respect to the direction in which the camera is pointing. This effect is used in certain camera designs to correct for perspective distortion in such contexts as, for example, photographing a tall building from the ground.

(3) Near and far clipping planes are defined as well as a view plane. In the previous viewing system we made the back clipping plane coincident with the view plane.

(4) A view plane window is defined that can have any aspect ratio and can be positioned anywhere in the view plane. In the previous viewing system we defined a square window symmetrically disposed about the 'centre' of the view plane.

(5) Multiple view reference coordinate systems can be defined or many views of a scene can be set up.

Consider the notion of distance in viewing systems. We have previously used the idea of a view point distance to reflect the dominant intuitive notion that the further the view point is from the scene the smaller will be the projection of that scene on the view plane. The problem arises from the fact that in any real system, or a general computer graphics system, there is no such thing as a view point. We can have a centre of projection and a view plane, and in a camera or eye analogy this is fine. In a camera the view plane or film plane is contained in the camera. The scene projection is determined both by the distance of the camera from the subject and the focal length of the lens. However, in computer graphics we are free to move the view plane at will with respect to the centre of projection and the scene. There is no lens as such. How then do we categorize distance? Do we use the distance of the view plane from the world coordinate origin, the distance of the centre of projection from the world coordinate origin or the distance of the view plane from the centre of projection? The general systems such as PHIGS leaves the user to answer that question. It is perhaps this attribute of the PHIGS viewing system that makes it appear cumbersome.

PHIGS categorizes a viewing system into three stages (Figure 5.14). Establishing the position and orientation of the view plane is known as view orientation. This requires the user to supply:

(1) The view reference point (VRP) – a point in world coordinate space.

(2) The viewing direction or view plane normal (VPN) – a vector in world coordinate space.

(3) The view up vector (VUV) – vector in world coordinate space.

The second stage in the process is known as view mapping and determines how points are mapped onto the view plane. This requires:

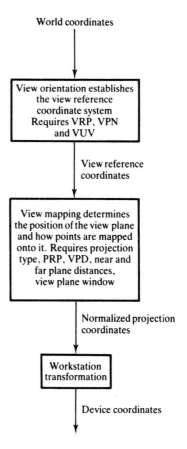

Figure 5.14
Establishing a viewing system PHIGS.

(1) The projection type (parallel or perspective).

(2) The projection reference point (PRP) – a point in VRC space.

(3) A view plane distance (VPD) – a real in VRC space.

(4) A back plane and a front plane distance – reals in VRC space.

(5) View plane window limits – four limits in VRC space.

(6) Projection viewport limits – four limits in normalized projection space (NPC).

This information is used to map information in the VRC or VRCs into normalized projection coordinates (NPC). NPC space is a cube with coordinates in each direction restricted to the range 0 to 1. The rationale for this space is to allow different VRCs to be set up when more than one view of a scene is required (and mapped subsequently into different view ports on the screen). Each view has its own VRC associated with it, and different views are mapped into NPC space.

The final processing stage is the workstation transformation, that is, the normal device dependent transformation.

We now describe these aspects in detail.

5.3.2 The view orientation parameters

In PHIGS we establish a view space coordinate system whose origin is positioned anywhere in world coordinate space by the VRP. Together with the VPN and the VUV this defines a right-handed coordinate system with axes *U*, *V* and *N*. *N* is the viewing direction and *UV* defines a plane that is either coincident or parallel to the view plane. (The VUV has exactly the same function as *V'* in Section 5.1.3). The cross-product of VUV and VPN defines *U* and the cross-product of VPN and *U* defines *V*:

$$U = (\text{VUV}) \times (\text{VPN})$$
$$N = (\text{VPN}) \times U$$

An interface to establish the VPN can easily be set up using the suggestion given in Section 5.1.3. (Note that the VUV must not be parallel to the VPN.) The geometric relationship between the orientation and mapping parameters is shown in Figure 5.15. Thus the view orientation stage establishes the position and orientation of the VRC relative to the world coordinate origin and the view plane specification is defined relative to the VRC.

5.3.3 The view mapping parameters

The view mapping stage defines how the scene, and what part of it, is projected onto the view plane. In the view orientation process the parameters were defined in world coordinate space. In this stage the parameters are defined in view space.

Figure 5.15
PHIGS – view orientation
and view mapping
parameters. Note that this
is a right-handed coordinate
system.

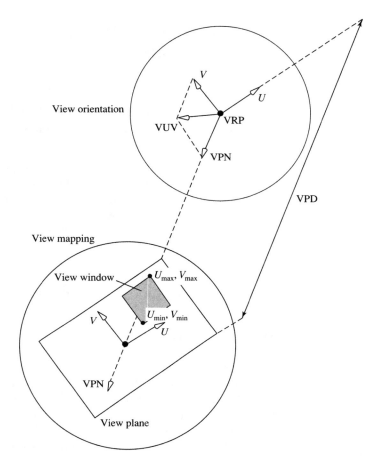

First the view plane is established. This is a plane of (theoretically) infinite extent, parallel to the *UV* plane and at a distance given by the VPD from the VRP. A view volume is established by defining a front and back plane, together with a view window. A view window is any rectangular window in the view plane. It is defined by minimax coordinates in two-dimensional view space. That is the *UV* coordinates transformed along the VPN into the view plane. These are (u_{min}, v_{min}) and (u_{max}, v_{max}). These relationships are shown for a parallel and a perspective projection in Figure 5.16.

A projection type and PRP complete the picture. The PRP as we stated above need not lie on a line, parallel to the VPN, and through the centre of the view plane window. If it lies off this line an oblique projection will be formed.

Two possible relationships between the PRP and the view plane window are shown in Figure 5.17. These are:

Figure 5.16
Geometry of the view
volume for parallel and
perspective projections.

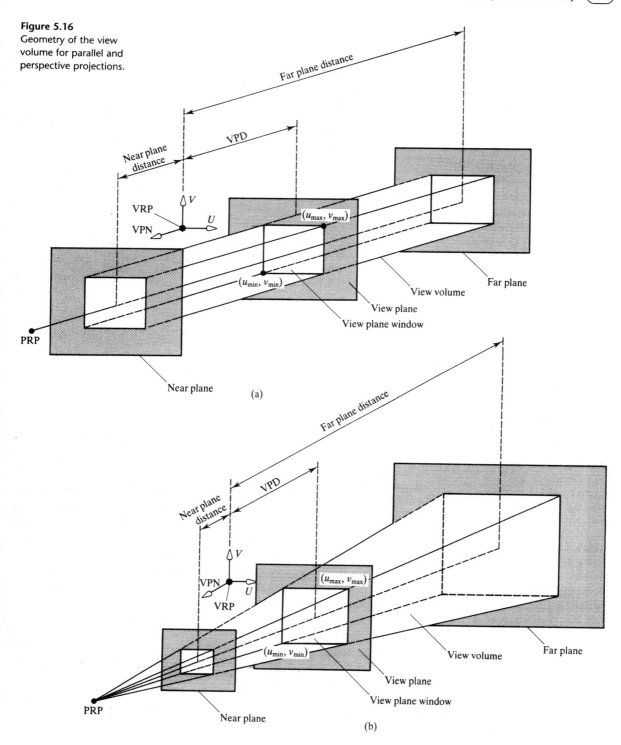

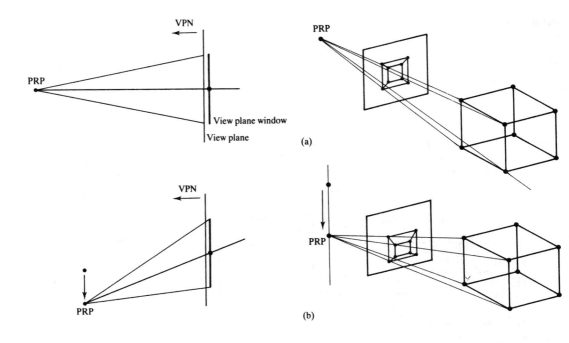

(a)

(b)

Figure 5.17
(a) 'Standard' projection and
(b) oblique projection
obtained by moving the PRP
vertically down in a direction
parallel to the view plane.

(1) A line from the PRP to the view plane window centre is parallel to the VPN.

(2) Moving the PRP results in an oblique projection. The condition in (1) is no longer true.

5.3.4

The view plane in more detail

The position and orientation of a view plane are defined by the view reference point (VRP), the view plane distance (VPD) and the view plane normal (VPN) (see Figure 5.15). The viewing direction is thus set by the VPN. Compared with the previous system, which used the camera and a focus point to establish the VPN and a distance d; we now use two vectors – the VRP and the VPN (plus a distance, the view plane distance (VPD) which displaces the VRP from the view plane). Unlike the previous two systems where the VRP was also used as a centre of projection the PRP or projection reference point has to be separately specified. The VRP is now just a reference point for a coordinate system and can be placed anywhere that is convenient. It can, for example, form the view plane origin, or it can be placed at the world coordinate origin, or at the centre of the object of interest. Placing it other than at the view plane origin has the advantage that the VPD has some meaning as a view distance. If the VRP is located in the view plane the VPD becomes zero and is redundant as a parameter. Also to move further or nearer to an object only the VPD needs changing.

Figure 5.18
A *uv* coordinate system is established in the view plane forming a three-dimensional left-handed (right-handed for GKS-3D and PHIGS) system with the VPN.

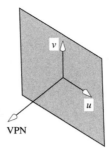

A view plane can be positioned anywhere in world coordinate space. It can be behind, in front of, or cut through objects. Having established the position and orientation of a view plane we set up a *uv* coordinate system in the view plane with the VRP (or its projection with the view plane) as origin (Figure 5.18). The two-dimensional *uv* coordinate system and the VPN form a three-dimensional right-handed coordinate system. This enables the 'twist' of the view plane window about the VPN to be established and a window to be set up (Figure 5.19). This twist is set by the view up vector (VUV) and the general effect of this vector is to determine whether the scene is viewed upright, upside down or whatever. The direction of the *v* axis is determined by the projection of the VUV parallel to the VPN onto the view plane.

With a two-dimensional coordinate system established in the view plane a two-dimensional window can be set (Figure 5.20). This takes care of the mapping from the unconstrained or application-oriented vertex values in world coordinate space to appropriate values in the view plane extent. All other things being equal, this window setting determines the size of the object(s) on the view surface.

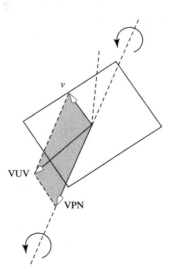

Figure 5.19
The VUV establishes the direction of the *v* axis allowing the view plane to 'twist' about the VPN.

Figure 5.20
Establishing a two-dimensional window in the view plane.

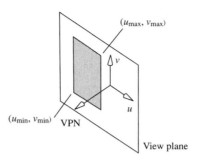

Implementing a PHIGS-type viewing system

Having developed transformations for a simplified viewing system we can deal with a PHIGS-type system by extending these. First consider the PRP. In a PHIGS-type system this is specified as a point in VRC space, that is a point relative to the VRC origin. We can deal with the space disparity between the PRP and the VRC by making the PRP the origin. The view plane and clip plane parameters are distances that need to be expressed relative to the centre of projection and this is accomplished by applying the translation – PRP – to them. We can simplify the PHIGS-type viewing system parameters so that they give us the situation shown in Figure 5.21 which should be compared with Figure 5.13(a). Another feature of the PHIGS-type system is that we now have a view plane, a near plane and a far plane and the view volume has sides of different slope because we have removed the view plane window constraint of the simple system. We adopt the convention shown in Table 5.1.

(Note that although f and d have a similar interpretation to f and d of the simple system they are not the same values. We have retained the same symbols to save a proliferation in the notation.)

T_{pers1} now splits into two components and we have:

Table 5.1

Interface values	After transforming the PRP to the VRC origin
VPD	d
Far plane distance	f
Near plane distance	n
u_{max}, u_{min}	x_{max}, x_{min}
v_{max}, v_{min}	y_{max}, y_{min}

Figure 5.21
(a) The situation after making the PRP the origin.
(b) After transforming to a symmetrical view volume.

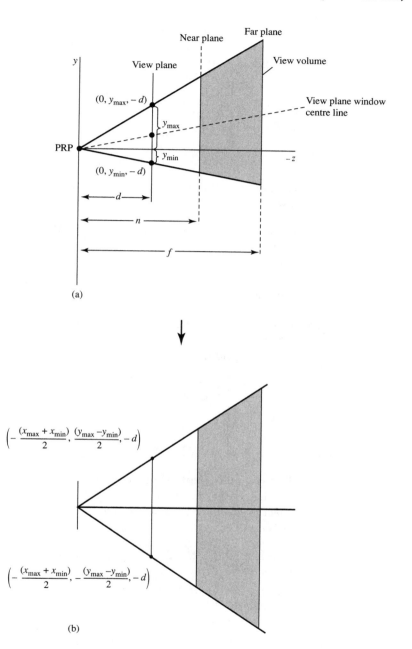

$$\boldsymbol{T}_{pers} = \boldsymbol{T}_{pers2}\boldsymbol{T}_{pers1b}\boldsymbol{T}_{pers1a}$$

where $\boldsymbol{T}_{pers1b}$ and $\boldsymbol{T}_{pers2}$ have the same effect as $\boldsymbol{T}_{pers1}$ and $\boldsymbol{T}_{pers2}$ of the previous viewing system. These are obtained by modifying $\boldsymbol{T}_{pers1}$ and $\boldsymbol{T}_{pers2}$ to include the view plane window parameters and the separation of the near plane from the view plane.

We first need to shear such that the view volume centre line becomes coincident with the z_v axis. This means adjusting x and y values by an amount proportional to z. It is easily seen that:

$$T_{pers1a} = \begin{bmatrix} 1 & 0 & \dfrac{x_{max} + x_{min}}{2d} & 0 \\ 0 & 1 & \dfrac{y_{max} + y_{min}}{2d} & 0 \\ 0 & 0 & 1 & 0 \\ 0 & 0 & 0 & 1 \end{bmatrix}$$

For example, the upper and lower view plane window edges transform as follows:

$(0, y_{max}, -d, 1)$ transforms to $\left(-\dfrac{x_{max} + x_{min}}{2}, \dfrac{y_{max} - y_{min}}{2}, -d, 1 \right)$

and

$(0, y_{min}, -d, 1)$ transforms to $\left(-\dfrac{x_{max} + x_{min}}{2}, -\dfrac{y_{max} - y_{min}}{2}, -d, 1 \right)$

transforming the original view volume into a symmetrical view volume (Figure 5.21(b)).

The second transform is:

$$T_{pers1b} = \begin{bmatrix} \dfrac{2d}{x_{max} - x_{min}} & 0 & 0 & 0 \\ 0 & \dfrac{2d}{y_{max} - y_{min}} & 0 & 0 \\ 0 & 0 & 1 & 0 \\ 0 & 0 & 0 & 1 \end{bmatrix}$$

This scaling is identical in effect to T_{pers1} of the simple viewing system converting the symetrical view volume to a 45° view volume. For example, consider the effect of $T_{pers1} = T_{pers1b}T_{pers1a}$ on the line through the view plane window centre. This transforms the point:

$\left(\dfrac{x_{max} + x_{min}}{2}, \dfrac{y_{max} + y_{min}}{2}, -d, 1 \right)$ to $(0, 0, -d, 1)$

making the line from the origin to this point coincident with the $-z$ axis – the required result.

Finally we have:

$$T_{pers2} = \begin{bmatrix} 1 & 0 & 0 & 0 \\ 0 & 1 & 0 & 0 \\ 0 & 0 & f/(f - n) & -fn/(f - n) \\ 0 & 0 & 1 & 0 \end{bmatrix}$$

which maps the regular pyramid into a box.

The graphics pipeline (2): rendering or algorithmic processes

Introduction

In this chapter we will describe the algorithmic operations that are required to render a polygon mesh object. We will describe a particular, but common, approach which uses a hidden surface algorithm called the Z-buffer algorithm and which utilizes some form of interpolative shading. The advantage of this strategy is that it enables us to fetch individual polygons from the object database in any order. It also means that there is absolutely no upward limit on scene complexity as far as the polygon count is concerned. The enduring success of this approach is due not only to these factors but also to the visual success of interpolative shading techniques in making the piecewise linear nature of the object almost invisible. The disadvantage of this approach, which is not without importance, is its inherent inefficiency. Polygons may be rendered to the screen which are subsequently overwritten by polygons nearer to the viewer.

In this renderer the processes that we need to perform are, rasterization, or finding the set of pixels onto which a polygon projects, hidden surface removal and shading. To this we add clipping against the view volume, a process that we dealt with briefly as a pure geometric operation in the previous chapter. In this chapter we will develop an algorithmic structure that 'encloses' the geometric operation.

As we remarked in the previous chapter, these processes are mostly carried out in three-dimensional screen space, the innermost loop in the algorithm being a 'for each' pixel structure. In other words, the algorithms are known as screen space algorithms. This is certainly not always the case – rendering by ray tracing is mostly a view space algorithm and rendering using the radiosity method is a world space algorithm.

6.1 Clipping polygons against the view volume

We have already considered the principle of clipping in the previous chapter and now we will describe an efficient structure for the task. In that analysis we saw how to determine whether a single point was within the view volume. This is an inefficient approach – we need a fast method for evaluating whether an object is wholly outside, wholly inside or straddles the view volume. Clipping has become an extremely important operation with the growth of polygon counts and the demand for real time rendering. In principle we want to discard as many polygons as possible at an early stage in the rendering pipeline. The two common approaches to avoiding detailed low-level testing are scene management techniques and bounding volumes. (Bounding volumes themselves can be considered a form of scene management.) We will look at using a simple bounding volume.

It is possible to perform a simple test that will reject objects wholly outside the view volume and accept those wholly within the view volume. This can be achieved by calculating a bounding sphere for an object and testing this against the view volume. The radius of the bounding sphere of an object is a fixed value

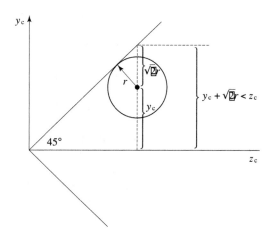

Figure 6.1
Showing one of the conditions for a bounding sphere to lie wholly within the view volume.

and this can be pre-calculated and stored as part of the database. When an object is processed by the 3D viewing pipeline, its local coordinate system origin (the bounding sphere we assume is centred on this origin) is also transformed by the pipeline.

If the object is completely outside the view volume it can be discarded; if it is entirely within the view volume it does not need to be clipped. If neither of these conditions applies then it may need to be clipped. We cannot be certain because although the sphere may intersect the view volume the object that it contains may not. This problem with bounding objects affects their use throughout computer graphics and it is further examined in Chapter 12.

For a sphere the conditions are easily shown (Figure 6.1) to be:

- **Completely inside if all following conditions are true:**

$$z_c > x_c + \sqrt{2}r$$

$$z_c > -x_c + \sqrt{2}r$$

$$z_c > y_c + \sqrt{2}r$$

$$z_c > -y_c + \sqrt{2}r$$

$$z_c > r + n$$

$$z_c > -r + f$$

- **Completely outside if any of the following conditions apply:**

$$z_c > x_c - \sqrt{2}r$$

$$z_c > -x_c - \sqrt{2}r$$

$$z_c > y_c - \sqrt{2}r$$

$$z_c > -y_c - \sqrt{2}r$$

$$z_c > -r + n$$

$$z_c > r + f$$

where:

$$\begin{bmatrix} x_c \\ y_c \\ z_c \\ 1 \end{bmatrix} = \begin{bmatrix} d/h & 0 & 0 & 0 \\ 0 & d/h & 0 & 0 \\ 0 & 0 & 1 & 0 \\ 0 & 0 & 0 & 1 \end{bmatrix} \begin{bmatrix} x_v \\ y_v \\ z_v \\ 1 \end{bmatrix}$$

In other words, this operation takes place in the clipping space shown in Figure 5.13.

Objects that need to be clipped can be dealt with by the Sutherland–Hodgman re-entrant polygon clipper (Sutherland and Hodgman 1974). This is easily extended to three dimensions. A polygon is tested against a clip boundary by testing each polygon edge against a single infinite clip boundary. This structure is shown in Figure 6.2.

We consider the innermost loop of the algorithm, where a single edge is being tested against a single clip boundary. In this step the process outputs zero, one or two vertices to add to the list of vertices defining the clipped polygon. Figure 6.3

Figure 6.2
Sutherland–Hodgman clipper clips each polygon against each edge of each clip rectangle.

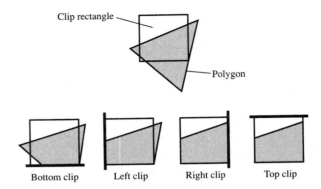

Bottom clip Left clip Right clip Top clip

shows the four possible cases. An edge is defined by vertices **S** and **F**. In the first case the edge is inside the clip boundary and the existing vertex **F** is added to the output list. In the second case the edge crosses the clip boundary and a new vertex **I** is calculated and output. The third case shows an edge that is completely outside the clip boundary. This produces no output. (The intersection for the edge that caused the excursion outside is calculated in the previous iteration and the intersection for the edge that causes the incursion inside is calculated in the next iteration.) The final case again produces a new vertex which is added to the output list.

To calculate whether a point or vertex is inside, outside or on the clip boundary we use a dot product test. Figure 6.4 shows a clip boundary **C** with an outward normal $\mathbf{N}_c$ and a line with end points **S** and **F**. We represent the line parametrically as:

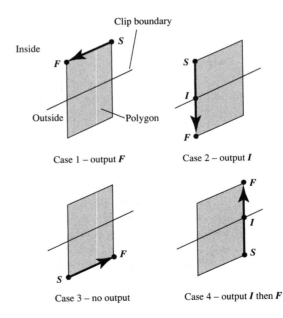

Case 1 – output **F**   Case 2 – output **I**

Case 3 – no output   Case 4 – output **I** then **F**

Figure 6.3
Sutherland–Hodgman clipper – within the polygon loop each edge of a polygon is tested against each clip boundary.

Figure 6.4
Dot product test to determine whether a line is inside or outside a clip boundary.

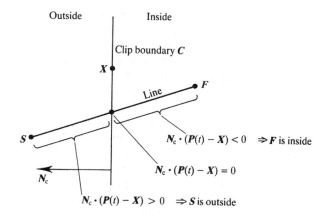

$$\boldsymbol{P}(t) = \boldsymbol{S} + (\boldsymbol{F} - \boldsymbol{S})t \qquad\qquad [6.1]$$

where:

$$0 \le t \le 1$$

We define an arbitrary point on the clip boundary as $\boldsymbol{X}$ and a vector from $\boldsymbol{X}$ to any point on the line. The dot product of this vector and the normal allows us to distinguish whether a point on the line is outside, inside or on the clip boundary. In the case shown in Figure 6.4:

$$\boldsymbol{N}_c \cdot (\boldsymbol{S} - \boldsymbol{X}) > 0 \quad \Rightarrow \boldsymbol{S} \text{ is outside the clip region}$$
$$\boldsymbol{N}_c \cdot (\boldsymbol{F} - \boldsymbol{X}) < 0 \quad \Rightarrow \boldsymbol{F} \text{ is inside the clip region}$$

and:

$$\boldsymbol{N}_c \cdot (\boldsymbol{P}(t) - \boldsymbol{X}) = 0$$

defines the point of intersection of the line and the clip boundary. Solving Equation 6.1 for t enables the intersecting vertex to be calculated and added to the output list.

In practice the algorithm is written recursively. As soon as a vertex is output the procedure calls itself with that vertex and no intermediate storage is required for the partially clipped polygon. This structure makes the algorithm eminently suitable for hardware implementation.

6.2   Shading pixels

The first quality shading in computer graphics was developed by H. Gouraud in 1971 (Gouraud 1971). In 1975 Phong Bui-Tuong (Phong 1975) improved on Gouraud's model and Phong shading, as it is universally known, became the *de facto* standard in mainstream 3D graphics. Despite the subsequent development of 'global' techniques, such as ray tracing and radiosity, Phong shading has remained ubiquitous. This is because it enables reality to be mimicked to an acceptable level at reasonable cost.

There are two separate considerations to shading the pixels onto which a polygon projects. First we consider how to calculate the light reflected at any point on the surface of an object. Given a theoretical framework that enables us to do this, we can then calculate the light intensity at the pixels onto which the polygon projects. The first consideration we call 'local reflection models' and the second 'shading algorithms'. The difference is illustrated conceptually in Figure 6.5. For example, one of the easiest approaches to shading – Gouraud shading – applies a local reflection model at each of the vertices to calculate a vertex intensity, then derives a pixel intensity using the same interpolation equations as we used in the previous section to interpolate depth values.

Basically there is a conflict here. We only want to calculate the shade for each pixel onto which the polygon projects. But the reflected light intensity at every point on the surface of a polygon is by definition a world space calculation. We are basing the calculation on the orientation of the surface with respect to a light source both of which are defined in world space. Thus we use a 2D projection of the polygon as the basis of an interpolation scheme that controls the world space calculations of intensity and this is incorrect. Linear interpolation, using equal increments, in screen space does not correspond to how the reflected intensity should vary across the face of the polygon in world space. One of the reasons for this is that we have already performed a (non-affine) perspective transformation to get into screen space. Like many algorithms in 3D computer graphics it produces an acceptable visual result, even using incorrect mathematics. However, this approach does lead to visible artefacts in certain contexts. The comparative study in Chapter 18 has an illustration of an artefact caused by this.

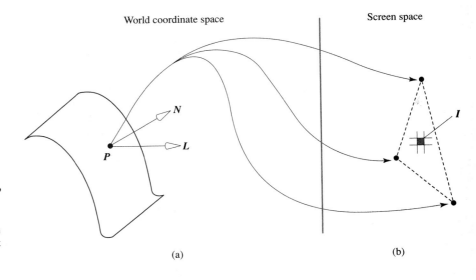

Figure 6.5
Illustrating the difference between local reflection models and shading algorithms. (a) Local reflection models calculate light intensity at any point **P** on the surface of an object. (b) Shading algorithms interpolate pixel values from calculated light intensities at the polygon vertices.

World coordinate space

Screen space

(a)

(b)

Local reflection models

A local reflection model enables the calculation of the reflected light intensity from a point on the surface of an object. The development of a variety of local reflection models is dealt with in Chapter 7, here we will confine ourselves to considering, from a practical view point, the most common model and see how it fits into a renderer.

This model, introduced in 1975, evaluates the intensity of the reflected light as a function of the orientation of the surface at the point of interest with respect to the position of a point light source and surface properties. We refer to such a model as a local reflection model because it only considers direct illumination. It is as if the object under consideration was an isolated object floating in free space. Interaction with other objects that result in shadows and inter-reflection are not taken into account by local reflection models. This point is emphasized in Figure 6.6; in Chapter 10 we deal with global illumination in detail.

The physical reflection phenomena that the model simulates are:

- Perfect specular reflection.
- Imperfect specular reflection.
- Perfect diffuse reflection.

These are illustrated in Figure 6.7 for a point light source that is sending an infinitely thin beam of light to a point on a surface. Perfect specular reflection occurs when incident light is reflected, without diverging, in the 'mirror' direction. Imperfect specular reflection is that which occurs when a thin beam of light strikes an imperfect mirror, that is a surface whose reflecting properties are that of a perfect mirror but only at a microscopic level – because the surface is physically rough. Any area element of such a surface can be considered to be made up of thousands of tiny perfect mirrors all at slightly different orientations.

Figure 6.6
(a) A local reflection model calculates intensity at P_b and P_a considering direct illumination only. (b) Any indirect reflected light from A to B or from B to A is not taken into account.

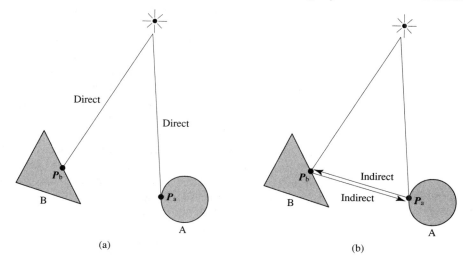

Figure 6.7
The three reflection phenomena used in computer graphics. (a) Perfect specular reflection. (b) Imperfect specular reflection. (c) Perfect diffuse reflection.

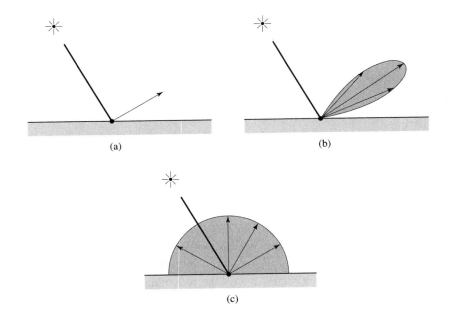

(a)   (b)

(c)

Perfect specular reflection does not occur in practice but we use it in ray tracing models (see Chapter 12) simply because calculating interaction due to imperfect specular reflection is too expensive. A perfect diffuse surface reflects the light equally in all directions and such a surface is usually called matte.

The Phong reflection model considers the reflection from a surface to consist of three components linearly combined:

reflected light = ambient light + diffuse component + specular component

The ambient term is a constant and simulates global or indirect illumination. This term is necessary because parts of a surface that cannot 'see' the light source, but which can be seen by the viewer, need to be lit. Otherwise they would be rendered as black. In reality such lighting comes from global or indirect illumination and simply adding a constant side-steps the complexity of indirect or global illumination calculations.

It is useful to consider what types of surface such a model simulates. Linear combination of a diffuse and specular component occurs in polished surfaces such as varnished wood. Specular reflection results from the transparent layer and diffuse reflection from the underlying surface (Figure 6.8). Many different physical types, although not physically the same as a varnished wood, can be approximately simulated by the same model. The veracity of this can be demonstrated by considering looking at a sample of real varnished wood, shiny plastic and gloss paint. If all contextual clues are removed and the reflected light from each sample exhibited the same spectral distribution, an observer would find it difficult to distinguish between the samples.

Figure 6.8
The 'computer graphics' surface.

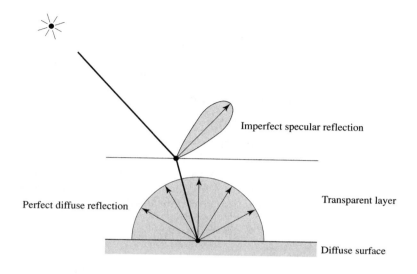

Imperfect specular reflection

Perfect diffuse reflection

Transparent layer

Diffuse surface

As well as possessing the limitation of being a local model, the Phong reflection model is completely empirical or imitative. One of its major defects is that the value of reflected intensity calculated by the model is a function only of the viewing direction and the orientation of the surface with respect to the light source. In practice, reflected light intensity exhibits bi-directional behaviour. It depends also on the direction of the incident light. This defect has led to much research into physically based reflection models, where an attempt is made to model reflected light by simulating real surface properties. However, the subtle improvements possible by using such models – such as the ability to make surfaces look metallic – have not resulted in the demise of the Phong reflection model and the main thrust of current research into rendering methods deals with the limitation of 'localness'. Global methods, such as radiosity, result in much more significant improvements to the apparent reality of a scene.

Leaving aside, for a moment, the issue of colour, the physical nature of a surface is simulated by controlling the proportion of the diffuse to specular reflection and we have the reflected light:

$$I = k_a I_a + k_d I_d + k_s I_s$$

Where the proportions of the three components, ambient, diffuse and specular are controlled by three constants, where:

$$k_a + k_d + k_s = 1$$

Consider I_d. This is evaluated as:

$$I_d = I_i \cos \theta$$

where:

I_i is the intensity of the incident light

θ is the angle between the surface normal at the point of interest and the direction of the light source

In vector notation:

$I_d = I_i \, (\boldsymbol{L} \cdot \boldsymbol{N})$

The geometry is shown in Figure 6.9.

Now physically the specular reflection consists of an image of the light source 'smeared' across an area of the surface resulting in what is commonly known as a highlight. A highlight is only seen by a viewer if the viewing direction is near to the mirror direction. We therefore simulate specular reflection by:

$I_s = I_i \cos^n \Omega$

where:

Ω is the angle between the viewing direction and the mirror direction $\boldsymbol{R}$

n is an index that simulates the degree of imperfection of a surface

When $n = \infty$ the surface is a perfect mirror – all reflected light emerges along the mirror direction. For other values of n an imperfect specular reflector is simulated (Figure 6.7(b)). The geometry of this is shown in Figure 6.10. In vector notation we have:

$I_s = I_i \, (\boldsymbol{R} \cdot \boldsymbol{V})^n$

Bringing these terms together gives:

$I = k_a I_a + I_i(k_d(\boldsymbol{L} \cdot \boldsymbol{N}) + k_s(\boldsymbol{R} \cdot \boldsymbol{V})^n)$

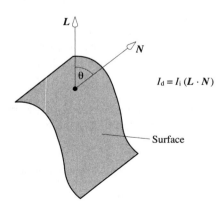

$I_d = I_i \, (\boldsymbol{L} \cdot \boldsymbol{N})$

Surface

Figure 6.9
The Phong diffuse component.

Figure 6.10
The Phong specular
component.

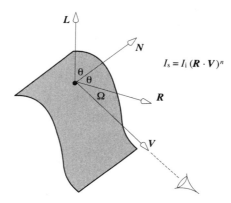

$$I_s = I_i (\mathbf{R} \cdot \mathbf{V})^n$$

The behaviour of this equation is illustrated in Figures 6.11 and 6.12 (Colour Plate). Figure 6.11 shows the light intensity at a single point $\mathbf{P}$ as a function of the orientation of the viewing vector $\mathbf{V}$. The semicircle is the sum of the constant ambient term and the diffuse term – which is constant for a particular value of $\mathbf{N}$. Addition of the specular term gives the profile shown in the figure. As the value of n is increased the specular bump is narrowed. Figure 6.12 (Colour Plate) shows the equation applied to the same object using different values of k_s and k_d and n.

6.2.2

Local reflection models – practical points

A number of practical matters that deal with colour and the simplification of the geometry now need to be explained.

Figure 6.11
The light intensity at point
$\mathbf{P}$ as a function of the
orientation of the viewing
vector $\mathbf{V}$.

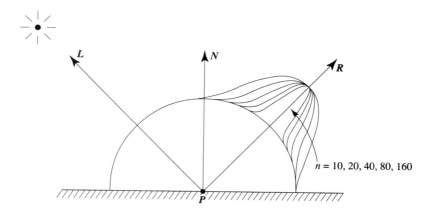

$n = 10, 20, 40, 80, 160$

The expense of the above shading equation, which is applied a number of times at every pixel, can be considerably reduced by making geometric simplifications that reduce the calculation time, but which do not affect the quality of the shading. First if the light source is considered as a point source located at infinity then L is constant over the domain of the scene. Second we can also place the view point at infinity making V constant. Of course, for the view and perspective transformation, the view point needs to be firmly located in world space so we end up using a finite view point for the geometric transformations and an infinite one for the shading equation.

Next the vector R is expensive to calculate and it is easier to define a vector H (halfway) which is the unit normal to a hypothetical surface that is oriented in a direction halfway between the light direction vector L and the viewing vector V (Figure 6.13). It is easily seen that:

$$H = (L + V)/2$$

This is the orientation that a surface would require if it was to reflect light maximally along the V direction. Our shading equation now becomes:

$$I = I_a k_a + I_i(k_d (L \cdot N) + (N \cdot H)^n)$$

because the term $(N \cdot H)$ varies in the same manner as $(R \cdot V)$. These simplifications mean that I is now a function only of N.

For coloured objects we generate three components of the intensity I_r, I_g and I_b controlling the colour of the objects by appropriate setting of the diffuse reflection coefficients k_r, k_b and k_g. In effect the specular highlight is just the reflection of the light source in the surface of the object and we set the proportions of the k_s to match the colour of the light. For a white light, k_s is equal in all three equations. Thus we have:

$$I_r = I_a k_{ar} + I_i((k_{dr}(L \cdot N) + k_s(N \cdot H)^n)$$
$$I_g = I_a k_{ag} + I_i((k_{dg}(L \cdot N) + k_s(N \cdot H)^n)$$
$$I_b = I_a k_{ab} + I_i((k_{db}(L \cdot N) + k_s(N \cdot H)^n)$$

A more detailed treatment of colour in computer graphics is given in Chapter 15.

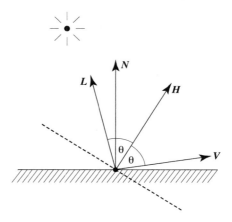

Figure 6.13
H is the normal to a surface orientation that would reflect all the light along V.

Figure 6.14
Light source represented as a specularly reflecting surface.

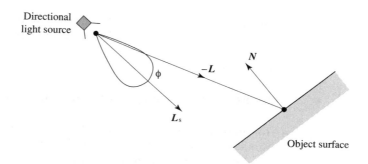

6.2.3

Local reflection models – light source considerations

One of the most limiting approximations in the above model is reducing the light source to a point at infinity. Also we can see in Figure 6.12 (Colour Plate) that there is an unsatisfactory confusion concerning the interpretation of the parameter n that is supposed to give the impression of 'glossiness'. In practice it looks as if we are changing the size of the light source.

A simple directional light (non-point) source is easily modelled and the following was suggested by Warn (1983). In this method a directional light source is modelled in the same way as a specularly reflecting surface, where the light emitted from the source is given by a cosine function raised to a power. Here we assume that for a directional source, the light intensity in a particular direction, given by the angle ϕ is:

$$I_s \cos^m \phi$$

Now ϕ is the angle between $-\mathbf{L}$, the direction of the point on the surface that we are considering, and $\mathbf{L}_s$, the orientation of the light source (Figure 6.14). The value of I_i that we use in the shading equation is then given by:

$$I_i = I_s(-\mathbf{L} \cdot \mathbf{L}_s)^m$$

Note that we can no longer consider the vector $\mathbf{L}$ constant over the scene.

6.3 Interpolative shading techniques

Having dealt with the problem of calculating light intensity at a point, we now consider how to apply such a model to a polygon and calculate the light intensity over its surface. Two classic techniques have emerged – Gouraud and Phong shading. The difference in quality between these two techniques is shown and discussed in the comparitive case study in Chapter 18 and we now deal with each separately. Phong interpolation gives the more accurate highlights – as we shall see – and is generally the preferred model. Gouraud shading on the other hand is considerably cheaper. Both techniques have been developed both to interpolate information efficiently across the face of a polygon and to diminish the visibility of the polygon edges in the final shaded image. Information is interpolated from values at the vertices of a polygon and the situation is exactly analogous to depth interpolation.

6.3.1

Interpolative shading techniques – Gouraud shading

In Gouraud shading we calculate light intensity – using the local reflection model of the previous section – at the vertices of the polygon and then interpolate between these intensities to find values at projected pixels. To do this we use the bilinear interpolation equations given in Section 1.5, the property p being the vertex intensity I. The particular surface normals used at a vertex are special normals called vertex normals. If we consider a polygon in isolation then, of course, the vertex normals are all parallel. However, in Gouraud shading we use special normals called vertex normals and it is this device that reduces the visibility of polygon edges. Consider Figure 6.15. Here the vertex normal $\boldsymbol{N}_A$ is calculated by averaging $\boldsymbol{N}_1$, $\boldsymbol{N}_2$, $\boldsymbol{N}_3$ and $\boldsymbol{N}_4$.

$$\boldsymbol{N}_A = \boldsymbol{N}_1 + \boldsymbol{N}_2 + \boldsymbol{N}_3 + \boldsymbol{N}_4$$

$\boldsymbol{N}_A$ is then used to calculate an intensity at vertex A that is common to all the polygons that share vertex A.

For computational efficiency the interpolation equations are implemented as incremental calculations. This is particularly important in the case of the third equation, which is evaluated for every pixel. If we define Δx to be the incremental distance along a scan line then ΔI, the change in intensity from one pixel to the next, is:

$$\Delta I_s = \frac{\Delta x}{x_b - x_a} (I_b - I_a)$$

$$I_{s,n} = I_{s,\,n-1} + \Delta I_s$$

Because the intensity is only calculated at vertices the method cannot adequately deal with highlights and this is its major disadvantage. The cause of this defect can be understood by examining Figure 6.16(a). We have to bear in mind that the

Figure 6.15
The vertex normal $\boldsymbol{N}_A$ is the average of the normals $\boldsymbol{N}_1$, $\boldsymbol{N}_2$, $\boldsymbol{N}_3$, and $\boldsymbol{N}_4$, the normals of the polygon that meet at the vertex.

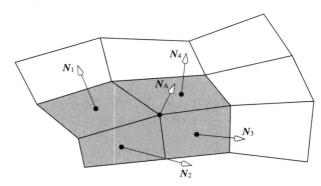

polygon mesh is an approximation to a curved surface. For a particular viewing and light source direction we can have a diffuse component at A and B and a specular highlight confined to some region between them. Clearly if we are deriving the intensity at pixel P from information at A and B we will not calculate a highlight. This situation is neatly taken care of by interpolating vertex normals rather than intensities as shown in Figure 6.16(b). This approach is known as Phong shading.

6.3.2 Interpolative shading techniques – Phong shading

Here we interpolate vertex normals across the polygon interior and calculate for each polygon pixel projection an interpolated normal. This interpolated normal is then used in the shading equation which is applied for every pixel projection. This has the geometric effect (Figure 6.16) of 'restoring' some curvature to polygonally faceted surfaces.

The price that we pay for this improved model is efficiency. Not only is the vector interpolation three times the cost of intensity interpolation, but each vector has to be normalized and a shading equation calculated for each pixel projection.

Incremental computations can be employed as with intensity interpolation, and the interpolation would be implemented as:

$$N_{sx,n} = N_{sx,n-1} + \Delta N_{sx}$$
$$N_{sy,n} = N_{sy,n-1} + \Delta N_{sy}$$
$$N_{sz,n} = N_{sz,n-1} + \Delta N_{sz}$$

Where N_{sx}, N_{sy} and N_{sz} are the components of a general scan line normal vector $\mathbf{N}_s$ and:

$$\Delta N_{sx} = \frac{\Delta x}{x_b - x_a} (N_{bx} - N_{ax})$$

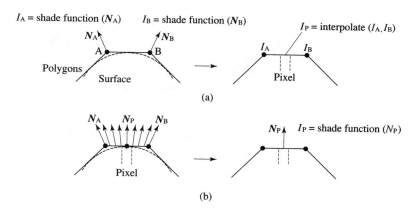

Figure 6.16
Illustrating the difference between Gouraud and Phong shading. (a) Gouraud shading. (b) Phong shading.

$$\Delta N_{sy} = \frac{\Delta x}{x_b - x_a} (N_{by} - N_{ay})$$

$$\Delta N_{sz} = \frac{\Delta x}{x_b - x_a} (N_{bz} - N_{az})$$

6.3.3 Renderer shading options

Most renderers have a hierarchy of shading options where you trade wait time against the quality of the shaded image. This approach also, of course, applies to the addition of shadows and texture. The normal hierarchy is:

- **Wireframe** No rendering or shading at all. A wireframe display may be used to position objects in a scene by interacting with the viewing parameters. It is also commonly used in animation systems where an animator may be creating movement of objects in a scene interactively. He can adjust various aspects of the animation and generate a real time animation sequence in wireframe display mode. In both these applications a full shaded image is obviously not necessary. One practical problem is that using the same overall renderer strategy for wireframe rendering as for shading (that is, independently drawing each polygon) will result in each edge being drawn twice – doubling the draw time for an object.

- **Flat shaded polygons** Again a fast option. The single 'true' polygon normal is used, one shade calculated using the Gouraud equation for each polygon and the shading interpolative process is avoided.

- **Gouraud shading** The basic shading option which produces a variation across the face of polygons. Because it cannot deal properly with specular highlights, a Gouraud shading option normally only calculates diffuse reflection.

- **Phong shading** The 'standard' quality shading method which due to the vector interpolation and the evaluation of a shading equation at every pixel is between four and five times slower than Gouraud shading.

- **Mixing Phong and Gouraud shading** Consider a diffuse object. Although using Gouraud shading for the object produces a slightly different effect from using Phong shading, with the specular reflection coefficient set to zero the difference is not visually important. This suggests that in a scene consisting of specular and diffuse objects we can use Gouraud shading for the diffuse objects and only use Phong shading for the specular ones. The Gouraud–Phong option then becomes part of the object property data.

These options are compared in some detail in the comparative case study in Chapter 18.

Comparison of Gouraud and Phong shading

Gouraud shading is effective for shading surfaces which reflect light diffusely. Specular reflections can be modelled using Gouraud shading, but the shape of the specular highlight produced is dependent on the relative positions of the underlying polygons. The advantage of Gouraud shading is that it is computationally the less expensive of the two models, requiring only the evaluation of the intensity equation at the polygon vertices, and then bilinear interpolation of these values for each pixel.

Phong shading produces highlights which are much less dependent on the underlying polygons. But, more calculations are required involving the interpolation of the surface normal and the evaluation of the intensity function for each pixel. These facts suggest a straightforward approach to speeding up Phong shading by combining Gouraud and Phong shading.

6.4 Rasterization

Having looked at how general points within a polygon can be assigned intensities that are determined from vertex values, we now look at how we determine the actual pixels which we require intensity values for. The process is known as rasterization or scan conversion. We consider this somewhat tricky problem in two parts. First, how do we determine the pixels which the edge of a polygon straddles? Second, how do we organize this information to determine the interior points?

6.4.1 Rasterizing edges

There are two different ways of rasterizing an edge, based on whether line drawing or solid area filling is being used. Line drawing is not covered in this book, since we are interested in solid objects. However, the main feature of line drawing algorithms (for example, Bresenham's algorithm (Bresenham 1965)) is that they must generate a linear sequence of pixels with no gaps (Figure 6.17).

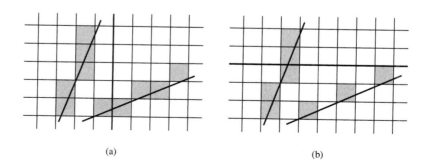

Figure 6.17
Pixel sequences required for (a) line drawing and (b) polygon filling.

(a)　　　　　(b)

For solid area filling, a less rigorous approach suffices. We can fill a polygon using horizontal line segments; these can be thought of as the intersection of the polygon with a particular scan line. Thus, for any given scan line, what is required is the left- and right-hand limits of the segment, that is the intersections of the scan line with the left- and right-hand polygon edges. This means that for each edge, we need to generate a sequence of pixels corresponding to the edge's intersections with the scan lines (Figure 6.17(b)). This sequence may have gaps, when interpreted as a line, as shown by the right-hand edge in the diagram.

The conventional way of calculating these pixel coordinates is by use of what is grandly referred to as a 'digital differential analyzer', or DDA for short. All this really consists of is finding how much the x coordinate increases per scan line, and then repeatedly adding this increment.

Let (x_s, y_s), (x_e, y_e) be the start and end points of the edge (we assume that $y_e > y_s$) The simplest algorithm for rasterizing sufficient for polygon edges is:

$x := x_s$
$m := (x_e - x_s)/(y_e - y_s)$
for $y := y_s$ **to** y_e **do**
   $output(round(x), y)$
   $x := x + m$

The main drawback of this approach is that m and x need to be represented as floating point values, with a floating point addition and real-to-integer version each time round the loop. A method due to Swanson and Thayer (Swanson and Thayer 1986) provides an integer-only version of this algorithm. It can be derived from the above in two logical stages. First we separate out x and m into integer and fractional parts. Then each time round the loop, we separately add the two parts, adding a carry to the integer part should the fractional part overflow. Also, we initially set the fractional part of x to -0.5 to make rounding easy, as well as simplifying the overflow condition. In pseudocode:

$xi := x_s$
$xf := -0.5$
$mi := (x_e - x_s)$ **div** $(y_e - y_s)$
$mf := (x_e - x_s) / (y_e - y_s) - mi$

for $y := y_s$ **to** y_e **do**
   $output(xi, y)$
   $xi := xi + mi$
   $xf := xf + mf$
   if $xf > 0.0$ **then** $\{xi := xi + 1; xf := xf - 1.0\}$

Because the fractional part is now independent of the integer part, it is possible to scale it throughout by $2(y_e - y_s)$, with the effect of converting everything to integer arithmetic:

$$xi := x_s$$
$$xf := -(y_e - y_s)$$
$$mi := (x_e - x_s) \textbf{ div } (y_e - y_s)$$
$$mf := 2*[(x_e - x_s) \textbf{ mod}(y_e - y_s)]$$

for $y := y_s$ **to** y_e **do**
  $output(xi, y)$
  $xi := xi + mi$
  $xf := xf + mf$
  if $xf > 0$ **then** $\{xi := xi + 1; xf := xf - 2(y_e - y_s)\}$

Although this appears now to involve two divisions rather than one, they are both integer rather than floating point. Also, given suitable hardware, they can both be evaluated from the same division, since the second (**mod**) is simply the remainder from the first (**div**). Finally it only remains to point out that the $2(y_e - y_s)$ within the loop is constant and would in practice be evaluated just once outside it.

6.4.2

Rasterizing polygons

Now that we know how to find pixels along the polygon edges, it is necessary to turn our attention to filling the polygons themselves. Since we are concerned with shading, 'filling a polygon' means finding the pixel coordinates of interior points and assigning to these a value calculated using one of the incremental shading schemes described in Section 6.3. We need to generate pairs of segment end points and fill in horizontally between them. This is usually achieved by constructing an 'edge list' for each polygon.

In principle this is done using an array of linked lists, with an element for each scan line. Initially all the elements are set to NIL. Then each edge of the polygon is rasterized in turn, and the x coordinate of each pixel (x, y) thus generated is inserted into the linked list corresponding to that value of y. Each of the linked lists is then sorted in order of increasing x. The result is something like that shown in Figure 6.18. Filling-in of the polygon is then achieved by, for each scan line, taking successive pairs of x values and filling in between them (because

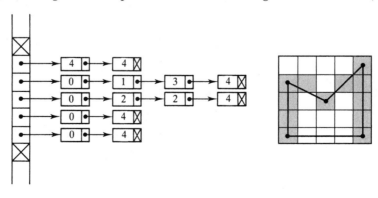

Figure 6.18
An example of a linked list maintained in ploygon rasterization.

a polygon has to be closed, there will always be an even number of elements in the linked list). Note that this method is powerful enough to cope with concave polygons with holes.

In practice, the sorting of the linked lists is achieved by inserting values in the appropriate place initially, rather than by a big sort at the end. Also, as well as calculating the x value and storing it for each pixel on an edge, the appropriate shading values would be calculated and stored at the same time (for example, intensity value for Gouraud shading; x, y and z components of the interpolated normal vector for Phong shading).

If the object contains only convex polygons then the linked x lists will only ever contain two x coordinates; the data structure of the edge list is simplified and there is no sort required. It is not a great restriction in practical computer graphics to constrain an object to convex polygons.

One thing that has been slightly glossed over so far is the consideration of exactly where the borders of a polygon lie. This can manifest itself in adjacent polygons either by gaps appearing between them, or by them overlapping. For example, in Figure 6.19, the width of the polygon is 3 units, so it should have an area of 9 units, whereas it has been rendered with an area of 16 units. The traditional solution to this problem, and the one usually advocated in textbooks, is to consider the sample point of the pixel to lie in its centre, that is, at ($x + 0.5$, $y + 0.5$). (A pixel can be considered to be a rectangle of finite area with dimensions 1.0×1.0, and its sample point is the point within the pixel area where the scene is sampled in order to determine the value of the pixel.) So, for example, the intersection of an edge with a scan line is calculated for $y + 0.5$, rather than for y, as we assumed above. This is messy, and excludes the possibility of using integer-only arithmetic. A simpler solution is to assume that the sample point lies at one of the four corners of the pixel; we have chosen the top right-hand corner of the pixel. This has the consequence that the entire image is displaced half a pixel to the left and down, which in practice is insignificant. The upshot of this is that it provides the following simple rasterization rules:

(1) Horizontal edges are simply discarded.

(2) An edge which goes from scan line y_{bottom} to y_{top} should generate x values for scan lines y_{bottom} through to $y_{top}-1$ (that is missing the top scan line), or if $y_{bottom} = y_{top}$ then it generates no values.

(3) Similarly, horizontal segments should be filled from x_{left} to $x_{right}-1$ (with no pixels generated if $x_{left} = x_{right}$).

Figure 6.19
Problems with polygon boundaries – a 9-pixel polygon fills 16 pixels.

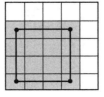

Figure 6.20
Three polygons intersecting a scan line.

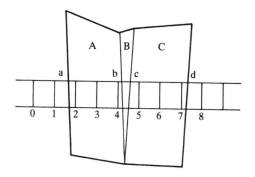

Incidentally, in rules (2) and (3), whether the first or last element is ignored is arbitrary, and the choice is based around programming convenience. The four possible permutations of these two rules define the sample point as one of the four corners of the pixel. The effect of these rules can be demonstrated in Figure 6.20. Here we have three adjacent polygons A, B and C, with edges a, b, c and d. The rounded x values produced by these edges for the scan shown are 2, 4 ,4 and 7 respectively. Rule 3 then gives pixels 2 and 3 for polygon A, none for polygon B, and 4 to 6 for polygon C. Thus, overall, there are no gaps, and no overlapping. The reason why horizontal edges are discarded is because the edges adjacent to them will have already contributed the x values to make up the segment (for example, the base of the polygon in Figure 6.18; note also that, for the sake of simplicity, the scan conversion of this polygon was not done strictly in accordance with the rasterization rules mentioned above).

6.5 Order of rendering

There are two basic ways of ordering the rendering of a scene. These are: on a polygon-by-polygon basis, where each polygon is rendered in turn, in isolation from all the rest; and in scan line order, where the segments of all polygons in that scene which cross a given scan line are rendered, before moving on to the next scan line. In some textbooks, this classification has the habit of becoming hopelessly confused with the classification of hidden surface removal algorithms. In fact, the order of rendering a scene places restrictions upon which hidden surface algorithms can be used, but is of itself independent of the method employed for hidden surface removal. These are the common hidden surface removal algorithms that are compatible with the two methods:

- By polygon: Z-buffer.
- By scan line: Z-buffer; scan line Z-buffer, spanning scan line algorithm.

By-polygon rendering has a number of advantages. It is simple to implement, and it requires little data active at any one time. Because of this, it places no upper limit on scene complexity, unlike scan line rendering, which needs simultaneously to hold in memory rasterization, shading, and perhaps texture information for all polygons which cross a particular scan line. The main drawback of by-polygon rendering is that it does not make use of possible efficiency measures such as sharing information between polygons (for example, most edges in a scene are shared between two polygons). The method can only be used with the Z-buffer hidden surface algorithm, which as we shall see, is rather expensive in terms of memory usage. Also, scan-line-based algorithms possess the property that the completed image is generated in scan line order, which has advantages for hardware implementation and anti-aliasing operations.

An important difference between the two rendering methods is in the construction of the edge list. This has been described in terms of rendering on a polygon-by-polygon basis. If, however, rendering is performed in scan line order, two problems arise. One is that rasterizing all edges of all polygons in advance would consume a vast quantity of memory, setting an even lower bound on the maximum complexity of a scene. Instead, it is usual to maintain a list of 'active edges'. When a new scan line is started, all edges which start on that scan line are added to the list, whilst those which end on it are removed. For each edge in the active list, current values for x, shading information etc. are stored, along with the increments for these values. Each time a new edge is added, these values are initialized; then the increments are added for each new scan line.

The other problem is in determining segments, since there are now multiple polygons active on a given scan line. In general, some extra information will need to be stored with each edge in the active edge list, indicating which polygon it belongs to. The exact details of this depend very much upon the hidden surface removal algorithm in use. Usually an active polygon list is maintained that indicates the polygons intersected by the current scan line, and those therefore that can generate active edges. This list is updated on every scan line, new polygons being added and inactive ones deleted.

The outline of a polygon-by-polygon renderer is thus:

> **for** *each polygon* **do**
>   *construct an edge list from the polygon edges*
>   **for** $y := ymin$ **to** $ymax$ **do**
>   **for** *each pair* (x_i, x_{i+1}) *in EdgeList[y]* **do**
>   *shade the horizontal segment* (x_i, y) *to* (x_{i+1}, y)

whilst that of a scan line renderer is:

> *clear active edge list*
> **for** *each scan line* **do**
>   **for** *each edge starting on that scan line* **do**
>   *add edge to active edge list*
>   *initialize its shading and rasterization values and their increments*
>   *remove edges which end on that scan line*
>   *parse active edge list to obtain and render segments*
>   *add the increments to all active edges*

Finally, it is worth pointing out that it is possible to achieve a hybrid of these two methods. Often it is possible to split a scene up into a number of unconnected objects. If the scene is rendered on an object-by-object basis, using scan line ordering within each object, then the advantage of shared information is realized within each object, and there is no upper limit on scene complexity, only on the complexity of each individual object.

6.6 Hidden surface removal

The major hidden surface removal algorithms are described in most computer graphics textbooks and are classified in an early, but still highly relevant, paper by Sutherland *et al.* (1974) entitled 'A characterization of ten hidden-surface algorithms'. In this paper algorithms are characterized as to whether they operate primarily in object space or image (screen) space and the different uses of 'coherence' that the algorithms employ. Coherence is a term used to describe the process where geometrical units, such as areas or scan line segments, instead of single points, are operated on by the hidden surface removal algorithm.

There are two popular approaches to hidden surface removal. These are scan-line-based systems and Z-buffer-based systems. Other approaches to hidden surface removal such as area subdivision (Warnock 1969), or depth list schemes (Newell *et al.* 1972) are not particularly popular or are reserved for special-purpose applications such as flight simulation.

6.6.1 The Z-buffer algorithm

The Z-buffer algorithm, developed by Catmull (1975), is as ubiquitous in computer graphics as the Phong reflection model and interpolator, and the combination of these represents the most popular rendering option. Using Sutherland's classification scheme (Sutherland *et al.* 1974), it is an algorithm that operates in image, that is, screen space.

Pixels in the interior of a polygon are shaded, using an incremental shading scheme, and their depth is evaluated by interpolation from the z values of the polygon vertices after the viewing transformation has been applied. The equations in Section 1.5 are used to interpolate the depth values.

The Z-buffer algorithm is equivalent, for each point (x_s, y_s) to a search through the associated z values of each interior polygon point, to find that point with the minimum z value. This search is conveniently implemented by using a Z-buffer, that holds for a current point (x, y) the smallest z value so far encountered. During the processing of a polygon we either write the intensity of a point (x, y) into the frame buffer, or not, depending on whether the depth z, of the current point, is less than the depth so far encountered as recorded in the Z-buffer.

One of the major advantages of the Z-buffer is that it is independent of object representation form. Although we see it used most often in the context of polygon mesh rendering, it can be used with any representation – all that is required is the ability to calculate a z value for each point on the surface of an object. It can be used with CSG objects and separately rendered objects can be merged into a multiple object scene using Z-buffer information on each object. These aspects are examined shortly.

The overwhelming advantage of the Z-buffer algorithm is its simplicity of implementation. Its main disadvantage is the amount of memory required for the Z-buffer. The size of the Z-buffer depends on the accuracy to which the depth value of each point (x, y) is to be stored; which is a function of scene complexity. Between 20 and 32 bits is usually deemed sufficient and the scene has to be scaled to this fixed range of z so that accuracy within the scene is maximized. Recall in the previous chapter that we discussed the compression of z_s values. This means that a pair of distinct points with different z_v values can map into identical z_s values. Note that for frame buffers with less than 24 bits per pixel, say, the Z-buffer will in fact be larger than the frame buffer. In the past, Z-buffers have tended to be part of the main memory of the host processor, but now graphics terminals are available with dedicated Z-buffers and this represents the best solution.

The memory problem can be alleviated by dividing the Z-buffer into strips or partitions in screen space. The price paid for this is multiple passes through the geometric part of the renderer. Polygons are fetched from the database and rendered if their projection falls within the Z-buffer partition in screen space.

An interesting use of the Z-buffer is suggested by Foley *et al.* (1989). This involves rendering selected objects but leaving the Z-buffer contents unmodified by such objects. The idea can be applied to interaction where a three-dimensional cursor object can be moved about in a scene. The cursor is the selected object, and when it is rendered in its current position, the Z-buffer is not written to. Nevertheless the Z-buffer is used to perform hidden surface removal on the object and will move about the scene obscuring some objects and being obscured by others.

6.6.2   Z-buffer and CSG representation

The Z-buffer algorithm can be used to advantage in rendering CSG objects. As you will recall from Section 4.3, which describes a ray tracing algorithm for rendering such objects, rendering involves calculating a boundary representation of a complex object that is made up of primitive objects combined with Boolean operators and described or represented by a construction tree.

The problem with the ray tracing method is expense. A normal recursive ray tracer is a method that finds intersections between a ray of arbitrary direction and objects in the scene. This model operates recursively to any depth to evaluate specular interaction. However, with CSG objects, all rays are parallel and we are only interested in the first hit, so in this respect ray tracing is inappropriate and a Z-buffer approach is easier to implement and less expensive (Rossignac and

Requicha 1986). The Z-buffer algorithm is driven from object surfaces rather than pixel-by-pixel rays. Consider the overall structure of both algorithms.

- Ray tracing
  for *each pixel* **do**
  > *generate a ray and find all object surfaces that intersect the ray*
  > *evaluate the CSG tree to determine the boundary of the first surface along the ray*
  > *apply Z-buffer algorithm and shade or not*
- Z-buffer
  for *each primitive object* **do**
  > **for** *primitive surface F* **do**
  > > **for** *each point P in a sufficiently dense grid on F* **do**
  > > > *Project P and apply Z-buffer*
  > > > **if** *currently visible* **then**
  > > > > **if** *by evaluating the CSG tree P is on boundary surface* **then**
  > > > > > *render into frame buffer*

Both algorithms have to apply a test that descends the CSG tree and evaluates the Boolean set operations to find the boundary of the object, but the Z-buffer avoids the intersection tests associated with each pixel ray.

6.6.3

Z-buffer and compositing

An important advantage of Z-buffer-based algorithms is that the z value associated with each pixel can be retained and used to enable the compositing or merging of separately generated scene elements.

Three-dimensional images are often built up from separate sub-images. A system for compositing separate elements in a scene, pixel-by-pixel, was proposed by Porter and Duff (1984) and Duff (1985). This simple system is built round an RGBαZ representation for pixels in a sub-image. The α parameter allows subimages to be built up separately and combined, retaining sub-pixel information that may have been calculated in the rendering of each sub-image.

Composites are built up using a binary operator combining two sub-images:

$c = f \ \mathbf{op} \ b$

For example, consider the operator Z_{min}. We may have two sub-images, say of single objects, that have been rendered separately, the Z values of each pixel in the final rendering contained in the Z channel. Compositing in this context means effecting hidden surface removal between the objects and is defined as:

$$RGB_c = (\mathbf{if} \ Z_f < Z_b \ \mathbf{then} \ RGB_f \ \mathbf{else} \ RGB_b)$$
$$Z_c = \min(Z_f, Z_b)$$

for each pixel.

The α parameter ($0 \leq \alpha \leq 1$) is the fraction of the pixel area that the object covers. It is used as a factor that controls the mixing of the colours in the two images. The use of the α channel effectively extends area anti-aliasing across the compositing of images. Of course, this parameter is not normally calculated by a basic Z-buffer renderer and because of this, the method is only suitable when used in conjunction with the A-buffer hidden surface removal method (Carpenter 1984), an anti-aliased extension to the Z-buffer described in Section 14.6.

The operator **over** is defined as:

$$RGB_c = RGB_f + (1 - \alpha_f)RGB_b$$
$$\alpha_c = \alpha_f + (1 - \alpha_f)\alpha_b$$

This means that as α_f decreases more of RGB_b is present in the pixel.

The compositing operator **comp** combines both the above operators. This evaluates pixel results when Z values at the corners of pixels are different between RGB_f and RGB_b. Z_f is compared with Z_b at each of the four corners. There are 16 possible outcomes to this and if the Z values are not the same at the four corners, then the pixel is said to be confused. Linear interpolation along the edges takes place and a fraction β computed (the area of the pixel where f is in front of b). We then have the **comp** operator:

$$RGB_c = \beta(f \text{ \textbf{over} } b) + (1 - \beta)(b \text{ \textbf{over} } f)$$

Another example of compositing in three-dimensional image synthesis is given in Nakamae *et al.* (1986). This is a montage method, the point of which is to integrate a three-dimensional computer generated image, of say a new building, with a real photograph of a scene. The success of the method is due to the fact that illuminance for the generated object, is calculated from measurements of the background photograph and because atmospheric effects are integrated into the finished image.

With the decreasing cost of memory and the popularity of the OpenGL, the use of accumulation buffers has become common. A powerful and simple use of accumulation buffers is in their support for multi-pass rendering techniques. This approach is described in Section 6.7.

6.6.4 Z-buffer and rendering

The Z-buffer imposes no constraints on database organization (other than those required by the shading interpolation) and in its simplest form can be driven on a polygon-by-polygon basis, with polygons being presented in any convenient order.

In principle, for each polygon we compute:

(1) The (x, y) value of the interior pixels.

(2) The z depth for each point (x, y).

(3) The intensity, I, for each point (x, y).

Thus we have three concurrent bilinear interpolation processes and a triple nested loop. The z values and intensities, I, are available at each vertex and the interpolation scheme for z and I is distributed between the two inner loops of the algorithm.

An extended version of the by-polygon algorithm with Z-buffer hidden surface removal is as follows:

for *all x, y* **do**
    Z-Buffer[x, y] := maximum_depth
for *each polygon* **do**
    construct an edge list from the polygon edges (that is, for each edge, calculate the values of x, z and I for each scan line by interpolation and store them in the edge list)
for $y := y_{min}$ **to** y_{max} **do**
    for *each segment in EdgeList[y]* **do**
        get $X_{left}, X_{right}, Z_{left}, Z_{right}, I_{left}, I_{right}$
        for $x := X_{left}$ **to** X_{right} **do**
        linearly interpolate z and I between Z_{left}, Z_{right} *and* I_{left}, I_{right} *respectively*
        if $z < Z\_Buffer[x,y]$ **then**
            Z_Buffer[x,y] := z
            frame_buffer[x,y] := I

The structure of the algorithm reveals the major inefficiency of the method in that shading calculations are performed on hidden pixels which are then either ignored or subsequently overwritten.

If Phong interpolation is used then the final reflection model calculations, which are a function of the interpolated normal, should also appear within the innermost loop; that is, interpolate N rather than I, and replace the last line with:

frame_buffer[x,y] := ShadingFunction(N)

6.6.5 Scan line Z-buffer

There is a variation of the Z-buffer algorithm for use with scan-line-based renderers, known (not suprisingly) as a scan line Z-buffer. This is simply a Z-buffer which is only one pixel high, and is used to solve the hidden surface problem for a given scan line. It is re-initialized for each new scan line. Its chief advantage lies in the small amount of memory it requires relative to a full-blown Z-buffer; and it is common to see a scan line Z-buffer-based program running on systems which do not have sufficient memory to support a full Z-buffer.

6.6.6 Spanning hidden surface removal

A spanning hidden surface removal algorithm attempts, for each scan line, to find 'spans' across which shading can be performed. The hidden surface removal problem is thus solved by dividing the scan line into lengths over which a single surface is dominant. This means that shading calculations are performed only once per pixel, removing the basic inefficiency inherent in the Z-buffer method. Set against this is the problem that spans do not necessarily correspond to polygon segments, making it harder to perform incremental shading calculations (the start values must be calculated at an arbitary point along a polygon segment, rather than being set to the values at the left-hand edge). The other major drawback is in the increase in complexity of the algorithm itself, as will be seen.

It is generally claimed that spanning algorithms are more efficient than Z-buffer-based algorithms, except for very large numbers of polygons (Foley *et al.* 1989; Sutherland *et al.* 1974). However, since extremely complex scenes are now becoming the norm, it is becoming clear that overall, the Z-buffer is more efficient, unless a very complex shading function is being used.

6.6.7 A spanning scan line algorithm

The basic idea, as has been mentioned, is that rather than solving the hidden surface problem on a pixel-by-pixel basis using incremental z calculation, the spanning scan line algorithm uses spans along the scan line over which there is no depth conflict. The hidden surface removal process uses coherence in x and deals in units of many pixels. The processing implication is that a sort in x is required for each scan line and the spans have to be evaluated.

The easiest way to see how a scan line algorithm works is to consider the situation in three-dimensional screen space (x_s, y_s, z_s). A scan line algorithm effectively moves a scan line plane, that is a plane parallel to the (x_s, z_s) plane, down the y_s axis. This plane intersects objects in the scene and reduces the hidden surface problem to two-dimensional space (x_s, z_s). Here the intersection of the scan line plane with object polygons become lines (Figure 6.21). These line segments are then compared to solve the hidden surface problem by considering 'spans'. A span is that part of a line segment that is contained between the edge intersections of all active polygons. A span can be considered a coherence unit, within the extent of which the hidden surface removal problem is 'constant' and can be solved by depth comparisons at either end of the span. Note that a more complicated approach has to be taken if penetrating polygons are allowed.

It can be seen from this geometric overview that the first stage in a spanning scan line algorithm is to sort the polygon edges by y_s vertex values. This results in an active edge list which is updated as the scan line moves down the y_s axis. If penetrating polygons are not allowed, then each edge intersection with the current scan line specifies a point on the scan line where 'something is changing', and so these collectively define all the span boundary points.

By going through the active edge list in order, it is possible to generate a set of line segments, each of which represents the intersection of the scan line plane with a polygon. These are then sorted in order of increasing x_s.

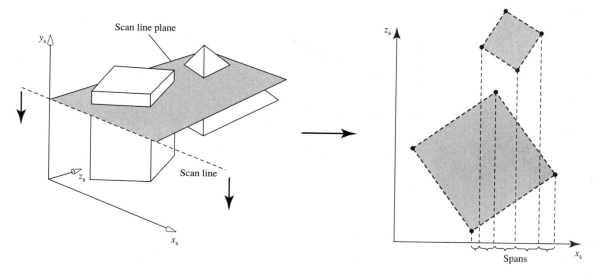

Figure 6.21
A scan line plane is moved down through the scene producing line segments and spans.

The innermost loop then processes each span in the current scan line. Active line segments are clipped against span boundaries and are thus subdivided by these boundaries. The depth of each subdivided segment is then evaluated at one of the span boundaries and hidden surface removal is effected by searching within a span for the closest subdivided segment. This process is shown in Figure 6.22.

In pseudo-code the algorithm is:

> **for** *each polygon* **do**
>   *Generate and bucket sort in y_s the polygon edge information*
>
> **for** *each scan line* **do**
>   **for** *each active polygon* **do**
>   *Determine the segment or intersection of the scan plane and polygon*
>   *Sort these active segments in x_s*
>   *Update the rate of change per scan line of the shading parameters*
>   *Generate the span boundaries*
>   **for** *each span* **do**
>   *Clip active segments to span boundaries*
>   *Evaluate the depth for all clipped segments at one of the span boundaries*
>   *Solve the hidden surface problem for the span with minimum z_s*
>   *Shade the visible clipped line segment*
>   *Update the shading parameters for all other line segments by the rate of change per pixel times the span width*

Note that integrating shading information is far more cumbersome than with the Z-buffer. Records of values at the end of clipped line segments have to be kept and updated. This places another scene complexity overhead (along with the absolute number of polygons overhead) on the efficiency and memory requirements of the process.

Figure 6.22
Processing spans.

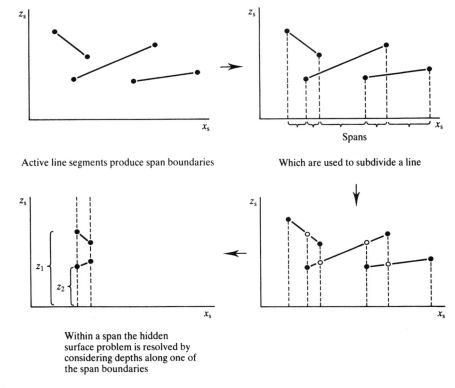

Active line segments produce span boundaries

Which are used to subdivide a line

Within a span the hidden surface problem is resolved by considering depths along one of the span boundaries

(6.6.8)

Z-buffer and complex scenes

Research into hidden surface removal tended to predominate in computer graphics in the 1970s but then with the industry acceptance of the Z-buffer algorithm, hidden surface removal was regarded as solved and the main research effort in rendering moved towards light transport models in the 1980s. (Although research continued into methods of improving the Z-buffer algorithm – dealing with aliasing and image composition methods.) The Z-buffer algorithm suffers from well-known efficiency problems and perhaps the demands of virtual reality image generation will re-emphasize the importance of efficient hidden surface removal.

The disadvantage of the Z-buffer is that it causes unseen polygons to be rendered. If we wish to retain the advantages of the traditional Z-buffer approach then this is a major cost factor that we must avoid in complex scenes. The main advantage of the Z-buffer, apart from its simplicity, is that the computing cost per polygon is low. It exploits image space coherence and adjacent pixels in a polygon projection are handled by a simple incremental calculation. However, this advantage rapidly diminishes as the scene to be rendered becomes more and more complex and the polygons smaller and smaller. The set-up computations at the polygon vertices predominate over the pixel-by-pixel calculations.

Depth complexity of a scene is a function of the number of objects in a scene just as object complexity is, and scenes that we wish to render in virtual reality applications will tend to possess both depth and object complexity.

An approach, reported by Greene *et al.* in 1993 takes the basic Z-buffer algorithm and develops it into a method that is suitable for complex scenes. Compared to a standard Z-buffer, Greene reports a reduction in rendering time from over an hour to 6.45 seconds on a complex scene containing 53 000 000 polygons. (Although an important practical factor that enables this reduction is the fact that the large scene is constructed by replicating a smaller scene of 15 000 polygons.) Another important attribute of the algorithm is that it can be implemented on existing hardware designs with only minor design changes.

The reason for the inefficiency of the Z-buffer algorithm is that it is an image space algorithm. It cannot exploit object space coherence. An algorithm that does exploit object space coherence is the hidden surface element in a ray tracing algorithm that uses a spatial subdivision scheme (an octree, for example) for ray tracking. For each ray cast, the first surface that the ray hits is the visible surface and no surfaces behind the one intersected are considered by the algorithm. (A ray tracing algorithm, on the other hand, does not exploit image space coherence and each pixel calculation is independent of every other.) Greene's development recognizes this and employs spatial subdivision to incorporate object space coherence in the traditional Z-buffer. It also uses a so-called Z-pyramid to further accelerate the traditional Z-buffer image space coherence.

The object space coherence is set up by constructing a conventional octree for the scene and using this to guide the rendering strategy. A node of an octree is hidden if all the faces of the cube associated with that node are hidden with respect to the Z-buffer. If such is the case then, of course, all the polygons or complete objects that the cube contains are hidden. This fact leads to the obvious rendering strategy of starting at the root of the tree and 'rendering' octree cubes, by rendering each face of the cube, to determine whether the whole cube is hidden or not. If it is not hidden we proceed with the geometry inside the cube. Thus a large number of hidden polygons are culled at the cost of rendering cube faces. So we are imposing a rendering order on the normally arbitrary polygon ordering in the Z-buffer. Greene points out that this in itself can be expensive – if the cube being rendered projects onto a large number of pixels – and this consideration leads to further exploiting the normal Z-buffer advantage of image space coherence.

The Z-pyramid is a strategy that attempts to determine complete polygon visibility without pixel-by-pixel elaboration. A Z-pyramid is a detail hierarchy with the original Z-buffer at the lowest level. At each level there is a half resolution Z-buffer, where the z value for a cell is obtained from the largest of the z values of the four cells in the next level down (you might say a depth mip-map). Maintaining the Z-pyramid involves tracking up the hierarchy in the direction of finer resolution until we encounter a depth that is already as far away as the current depth value. Using the Z-pyramid to test the visibility of a cube face involves finding the finest detail level whose corresponding projection in screen space just covers the projection of the face. Then it is simply a matter of comparing the nearest vertex depth of the face against the value in the Z-pyramid. Using the Z-pyramid to test a complete polygon for visibility is the same except that the screen space bounding box of the polygon is used.

In this way the technique tries to make the best of both object and image space coherence. Using spatial subdivision to accelerate hidden surface removal is a old idea and seems to have been first mooted by Schumaker *et al.* (1969). Here the application was flight simulation where the real time constraint was, in 1969, a formidable problem.

Temporal coherence is exploited by retaining the visible cubes from the previous frame. For the current frame the polygons within these cubes are rendered first and the cubes marked as such. The algorithm then proceeds as normal. This strategy plays on the usual event that most of the cubes from the previous frame will still be visible; a few will become invisible in the current frame and a few cubes, invisible in the previous frame, will become visible.

(6.6.9) Z-buffer summary

From an ease of implementation point-of-view the Z-buffer is the best algorithm. It has significant memory requirements particularly for high resolution frame buffers. However, it places no upward limit on the complexity of scenes, an advantage that is now becoming increasingly important. It renders scenes one object at a time and for each object one polygon at a time. This is both a natural and convenient order as far as database considerations are concerned.

An important restriction it places on the type of object that can be rendered by a Z-buffer is that it cannot deal with transparent objects without costly modification. A partially transparent polygon may:

(1) Be completely covered by an opaque nearer polygon, in which case there is no problem; or,

(2) Be the nearest polygon, in which case a list of all polygons behind it must be maintained so that an appropriate combination of the transparent polygon and the next nearest can be computed. (The next nearest polygon is not, of course, known until all polygons are processed.)

Compared with scan line algorithms, anti-aliasing solutions, particularly hardware implementations, are more difficult.

Cook, Carpenter and Catmull (1987) point out that a Z-buffer has an extremely important 'system' advantage. It provides a 'back door' in that it can combine point samples with point samples from other algorithms that have other capabilities such as radiosity or ray tracing.

If memory requirements are too prodigious then a scan line Z-buffer is the next best solution. Unless a renderer is to work efficiently on simple scenes, it is doubtful if it is worth contemplating the large increase in complexity that a spanning scan line algorithm demands.

Historically there has been a shift in research away from hidden surface problems to realistic image synthesis. This has been motivated by the easy availability of high spatial and colour resolution terminals. All of the 'classic' hidden surface removal algorithms were developed prior to the advent of shading complexities and it looks as if the Z-buffer will be the most popular survivor for conventional rendering.

6.6.10 BSP trees and hidden surface removal

Having introduced the idea of BSP trees in Chapter 2, we now return to examine them in more detail; in particular how they can be used to perform hidden surface calculations.

For almost two decades after the introduction of BSP trees into computer graphics applications, their usage seems to have been restricted in the main to flight simulators. With the advent of three-dimensional video games and other animation applications on standard PCs we have seen a renewal of interest in using BSP trees for visibility calculations and we will now look at this method in some detail.

The original BSP hidden surface removal idea depends on having a static scene and a changing view point – the classic flight simulator/computer game application – and works as a two-phase process. In the first phase a BSP tree of the scene is constructed (once only, which in practice would be an off-line process) and in the second phase the view point is compared with this structure to determine visibility. Its attraction for real time graphics is that much visibility processing can take place as a pre-process. We will look first of all at the simpler issue of determining visibility amongst objects then see how the principles can be extended to determine polygon visibility within an object.

If our scene consists of convex objects that can be separated by convex regions made up of planes then we can use a recursive divide and conquer strategy to divide up the space. We assume that we have an appropriate strategy for positioning the planes and that the tree is complete when all regions only contain a single object. Figure 6.23 shows the idea. Each leaf is a label identifying an object and each node is a separating plane. Having constructed a tree (Figure 6.23(a)) we can then determine a visibility ordering for a view point descending the tree from the root node with the view point coordinates to give the object closest to the view point (Figure 6.23(b)). Starting at the root node we descend the subtree on the side of plane A nearest to the view point (in this case the negative side) taking us to the node associated with plane B and thenceforth to object 2. Figure 6.23 (c) indicates the route we take to determine a visibility ordering. Object 3 is the next nearest to the view point and returning to the root node and descending, and the remaining ordering is object 1 followed by object 4. This gives us a near to far visibility ordering which for this scene is objects 2, 3, 1 and 4. Alternatively we can just as easily generate a far to near ordering.

In practice this scheme is not particularly useful because most computer graphics applications are made up of scenes where the object complexity

Figure 6.23
BSP operations for
a four object scene.
(a) Constructing a BSP tree.
(b) Descending the tree
with the view point
coordinates gives
the nearest object.
(c) Evaluating a visibility
order for all objects.

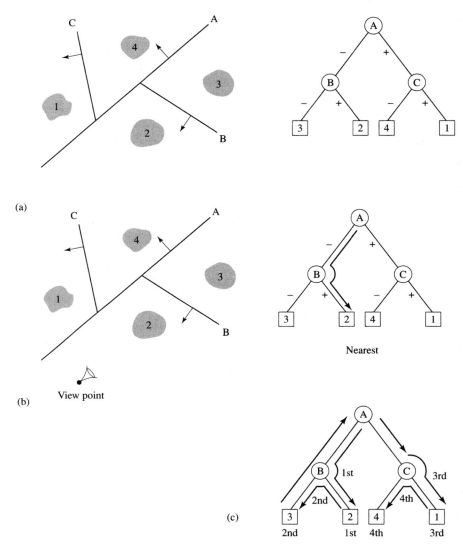

(a)

(b)

Nearest

View point

(c)

2nd 1st 4th 3rd

(number of polygons per object) is much greater than scene complexity (number of objects per scene) and for the approach to be useful we have to deal with polygons within objects rather than entire objects. Also there is the problem of positioning the planes – itself a non-trivial problem. If the number of objects is small then we can have a separating plane for every pair of objects – a total of n^2 for an n object scene.

For polygon visibility ordering we can choose planes that contain the face polygons. A polygon is selected and used as a root node. All other polygons are tested against the plane containing this polygon and placed on the appropriate descendant branch. Any polygon which crosses the plane of the root polygon is split into two constituents. The process continues recursively until all polygons are contained by a plane. Obviously the procedure creates more polygons than were originally in the scene but practice has shown that this is usually less than a factor of two.

The process is shown for a simple example in Figure 6.24. The first plane chosen, plane A, containing a polygon from object 1, splits object 3 into two parts. The tree builds up as before and we now use the convention IN/OUT to say which side of a partition an entity lies since this now has meaning with respect to the polygonal objects.

Far to near ordering was the original scheme used with BSP trees. Rendering polygons into the frame buffer in this order results in the so-called painter's algorithm – near polygons are written 'on top of' farther ones. Near to far ordering can also be used but in this case we have to mark in some way the fact that a pixel has already been visited. Near to far ordering can be advantageous in extremely complicated scenes if some strategy is adopted to avoid rendering completely occluded surfaces, for example, by comparing their image plane extents with the (already rendered) projections of nearer surfaces.

Thus to generate a visibility order for a scene we:

- Descend the tree with view point coordinates.
- At each node, we determine whether the view point is in front of or behind the node plane.
- Descend the far side subtree first and output polygons.
- Descend the near side subtree and output polygons.

This results in a back to front ordering for the polygons with respect to the current view point position and these are rendered into the frame buffer in this order. If this procedure is used then the algorithm suffers from the same efficiency disadvantage as the Z-buffer – rendered polygons may be subsequently obscured. However, one of the disadvantages of the Z-buffer is immediately overcome. Polygon ordering allows the unlimited use of transparency with no additional effort. Transparent polygons are simply composited according to their transparency value.

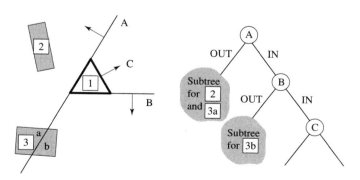

Figure 6.24
A BSP tree for polygons.

6.7 Multi-pass rendering and accumulation buffers

The rendering strategies that we have outlined have all been single pass approaches where a rendered image is composed by one pass through a graphics pipeline. In Section 6.6.3 we looked at a facility that enabled certain operations on separately rendered images with αZ components to be combined. In this section we will look at multi-pass rendering which means composing a single image of a scene from a combination of images of that scene rendered by passing it through the pipeline with different values for the rendering parameters. This approach is possible due to the continuing expansion of hardware and memory dedicated to rendering, manifested in texture mapping hardware which has substantially increased the visual complexity of real time imagery generated on a PC, and the availability of multiple screen resolution buffers such as a stencil buffer and an accumulation buffer (as well as the frame buffer and Z-buffer). The accumulation buffer is a simplified version of the A-buffer and the availability of such a facility has led to an expansion of the algorithms that employ a multi-pass technique.

As the name implies, an accumulation buffer accumulates rendered images and the standard operations are addition and multiplication combined into an 'add with weight' operation. In practice an accumulation buffer may have higher precision than a screen buffer to diminish the effect of rounding errors. The use of an accumulator buffer enables the effect of particular single pass algorithms to be obtained by a number of passes. After the passes are complete the final result in the accumulation buffer is transferred into the screen buffer.

The easiest example is the common anti-aliasing algorithm (see Section 14.7 for full details of this approach) which is to generate a virtual image, at $n \times$ the resolution of the final image, then reduce this to the final image by using a filter. The same effect can be obtained by jittering the view port and generating n images and accumulating these with the appropriate weighting value which is a function of the jitter value. In Figure 6.25, to generate the four images that are required to sample each pixel four times we displace the view window through a $1/2$ pixel distance horizontally and vertically. To find this displacement we only have to calculate the size of the view port in pixel units. (Note that this cannot be implemented using the simple viewing system given in Chapter 5, which assumes that the view window is always centred on the line through the view point.)

In this case we only save on memory. However, in many instances an algorithm implemented as a multi-pass rendering is of lower complexity than the single pass equivalent. Additional examples of motion blur, soft shadows and depth of field are given in Haeberli and Akeley (1990). These effects can be achieved by distributed ray tracing as described in Chapter 10 and the marked difference between the complexity of the two approaches is obvious.

To create a motion blurred image it is only necessary to accumulate a series of images rendered while the moving objects in the scene change their position over

Figure 6.25
Multi-pass super-sampling.
(a) Aliased image
(1 sample/pixel). (b) A one
component/pass of the
anti-aliased image (four
samples/pixel or four
passes). For this pass the
view point is moved up
and to the left by $1/2$ pixel
dimension).

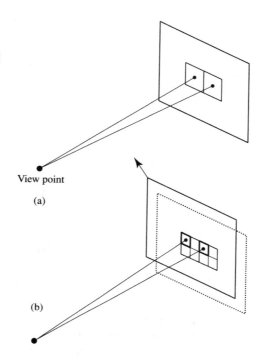

View point

(a)

(b)

time. Exactly analogous to the anti-aliasing example, we are now anti-aliasing in the time domain. There are two approaches to motion blur. We can display a single image by averaging n images built up in the accumulation buffer. Alternatively we can display an image for every calculated image by averaging over a window of n frames moving in time. To do this we accumulate n images initially. At the next step the frame that was accumulated $n-1$ frames ago is re-rendered and subtracted from the accumulation buffer. Then the contents of the accumulation buffer are displayed. Thus, after the initial sequence is generated, each time a frame is displayed two frames have to be rendered – the $(n - 1)$th and the current one.

Simulating depth of field is achieved (approximately) by jittering both the view window as was done for anti-aliasing and the view point. Depth of field is the effect seen in a photograph where, depending on the lens and aperture setting, objects a certain distance from the camera are in focus where others nearer and farther away are out of focus and blurred. Jittering the view window makes all objects out of focus and jittering the view point at the same time ensures objects in the equivalent of the focal plane remain in focus. The idea is shown in Figure 6.26. A plane of perfect focus is decided on. View port jitter values and view point perturbations are chosen so that a common rectangle is maintained in the plane of perfect focus. The overall transformation applied to the view frustum is a shear and translation. Again this facility cannot be implemented using the simple view frustum in Section 5.2 which does not admit shear projections.

Figure 6.26
Simulating depth of field by
shearing the view frustum
and translating the view
point.

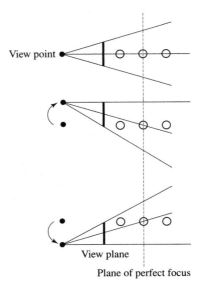

Soft shadows are easily created by accumulating n passes and changing the position of a point light source between passes to simulate sampling of an area source. Clearly this approach will also enable shadows from separate light sources to be rendered.

7 Simulating light–object interaction: local reflection models

Introduction

Local reflection models, and in particular the Phong model (introduced in Chapter 5), have been part of mainstream rendering since the mid-1970s. Combined with interpolative shading of polygons, local reflection models are incorporated in almost every conventional renderer. The obvious constraint of locality is the strongest disadvantage of such models but despite the availability of ray tracers and radiosity renderers the mainstream rendering approach is still some variation of the strategy described earlier – in other words a local reflection model is at the heart of the process. However, nowadays it would be difficult to find a renderer that did not have ad hoc additions such as texture mapping and shadow calculation (see Chapters 8 and 9). Texture mapping adds interest and variety, and geometrical shadow calculations overcome the most significant drawback of local models.

Despite the understandable emphasis on the development of global models, there has been some considerable research effort into improving local reflection models. However, not too much attention has been paid to these, and most renderers still use the Phong model: in one sense a tribute to the efficacy and simplicity of this technique, in another, an unfortunate ignoring of the real advances that have been made in this area.

An important point concerning local models is that they are used in certain global solutions. As will be discovered in Chapter 12, most simple ray tracers are hybrid models that combine a local reflection model with a global ray traced model. A local model is used at every point to evaluate a contribution that is due to any direct illumination that can be seen from that point. To this is added a (ray traced) component that accounts for indirect illumination. (In fact, this is inconsistent because different parameters are used for the local and global contribution, but it is a practice that is widely adopted.)

In this chapter we will look at a representative selection of local models, delving into such questions as: how do we simulate the different light reflection behaviour between, say, shiny plastic and metal that is the same colour? We can usually perceive such subtle differences in real objects and it is appropriate that we should be able to simulate them in computer graphics.

The foundation of most local reflection models involves an empirical or imitative approach in which we devise an easily evaluated function to imitate reflection of light from a surface or the theory of reflection from a perfect surface together with the simulation of an imperfect surface.

7.1 Reflection from a perfect surface

We begin by examining the behaviour of light incident on an optically smooth surface – a perfect mirror. This is determined by the Fresnel formulae – themselves derived from Maxwell's wave equations. This is the source of the ray tracing formulae given in Section 1.4.6. The formula is a coefficient that relates the ratio of reflected and transmitted energy as a function of incident direction, polarization and the properties of the material. Assuming for simplicity that the light is unpolarized (the approach usually taken in computer graphics) and travelling through air (approximated as a vacuum) and assuming that a factor known as the extinction coefficient (see Section 7.6.4) is zero we have:

$$F = \frac{1}{2} \left\{ \frac{\sin^2(\phi - \theta)}{\sin^2(\phi + \theta)} + \frac{\tan^2(\phi - \theta)}{\tan^2(\phi + \theta)} \right\}$$

[7.1]

where:

ϕ is the angle of incidence
θ is the angle of refraction
$\sin\theta = \sin\phi/\mu$ (where μ is the refractive index of the material)

These angles are shown in Figure 7.1. F is minimum, that is most light is absorbed when $\phi = 0$ or normal incidence. No light is absorbed by the surface and F is equal to unity for $\phi = \pi/2$. The wavelength dependent property of F comes from the fact that μ is a function of wavelength.

Figure 7.1
The Fresnel equation.
(a) Angles in the Fresnel
equation. (b) Two examples
showing the behaviours of
the equation.

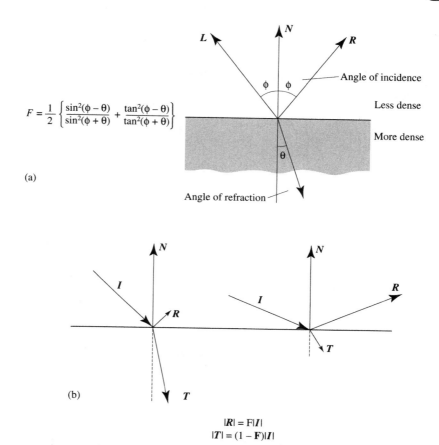

$$F = \frac{1}{2} \left\{ \frac{\sin^2(\phi - \theta)}{\sin^2(\phi + \theta)} + \frac{\tan^2(\phi - \theta)}{\tan^2(\phi + \theta)} \right\}$$

Angle of incidence

Less dense

More dense

Angle of refraction

(a)

(b)

$$|R| = F|I|$$
$$|T| = (1 - F)|I|$$

7.2   Reflection from an imperfect surface

In practice, surfaces are not optically perfect. With the exception of glass or still water, surfaces exhibit a microgeometry. We can, however, still use the Fresnel equation if we incorporate it in a model that simulates the microgeometry. Figure 7.2 shows one way of doing this – we consider the surface to be a collection of microfacets which are for simplicity considered as symmetric V-shaped pits. Over a small region we can describe the reflection of light incident on a representative region of such grooves to form a lobe which we can parametrize.

Of course, surface microgeometry is not the only imperfection that occurs in reality. For example, shiny metal surfaces age and acquire a film of dirt as well as large imperfections like scratches. This kind of 'real' surface is much more difficult to model and it has to be emphasized that a surface whose microgeometry is modelled in the way described is still assumed to be perfectly clean – an unlikely practical event.

Figure 7.2
Simulating a rough surface
with a collection of
microfacets each considered
as a perfect mirror.
(a) Modelling a surface as
a collection of V-shaped
grooves. (b) Reflection lobes
for different values of m in a
Gaussian distribution.

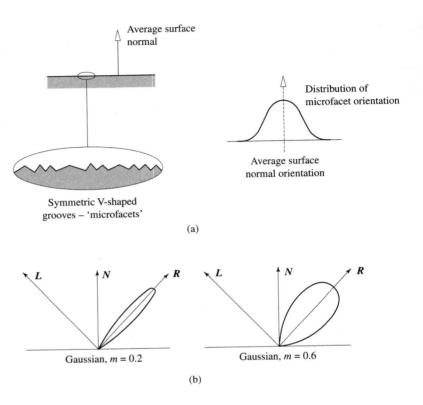

(a)

(b)

7.3   The bi-directional reflectance distribution function

In general, light reflected from a point on the surface of an object is categorized by a bi-directional reflection distribution function, or BRDF. This term emphasizes that the light reflected in any particular direction (in computer graphics we are mostly interested in light reflected along the viewing direction V) is a function not only of this direction but also of the direction of the incoming light. A BRDF can be written as:

$$\text{BRDF} = f(\theta_{in},\ \phi_{in},\ \theta_{ref},\ \phi_{ref}) = f(L, V)$$

and many models used in computer graphics differ amongst themselves according to which of these dependencies are simulated. Figure 7.3 shows these angles together with a BRDF computed for a particular set of angles. The rendered BRDF shows the magnitude of the reflected light (in any outgoing direction) for an infinitely thin beam of light incident in the direction shown. In practice, light may be incident on a surface point from more than one direction and the total reflected light would be obtained by considering a separate BRDF for each incoming light beam and integrating.

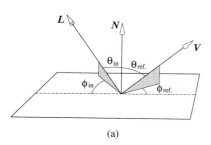

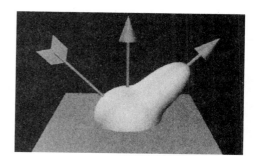

(a)

(b)

Figure 7.3
Bi-directional reflectivity function. (a) A BRDF relates light incident in direction **L** to light reflected along direction **V** as a function of the angles θ_{in}, ϕ_{in}, θ_{ref}, ϕ_{ref}. (b) An example of a BRDF.

For many years computer graphics has worked with simple, highly constrained BRDFs such as that shown in Figure 7.3. Figure 7.4 gives an idea of the difference between such computer graphics models and what actually happens in practice. The illustrations are cross-sections of the BRDF in the plane containing **L** and **R**, the mirror direction for different angles of θ, the angle of incidence (and reflection). In particular, note the great variation in the shape of the reflection lobes as a function of the wavelength of the incident light, the angle of incidence and the material. In the case of aluminium we see that it can behave either like a mirror surface or a directional diffuse surface depending on the wavelength of the incident light. When we also take into account that, in practice, incident light is never monochromatic (and we thus need a separate BRDF for each wavelength of light that we are considering) we see that the behaviour of reflected light is a far more complex phenomenon than we can model by using simple approximations like the Phong model at three wavelengths.

An important distinction that has to be made is between isotropic and anisotropic surfaces. An isotropic surface exhibits a BRDF whose shape is independent of the incoming azimuth angle ϕ_i (Figure 7.3). An anisotropic surface is, for example, brushed aluminium or a surface that retains coherent patterns from a milling machine. In the case of a brushed surface the magnitude of the specular lobe depends on whether the incoming light is aligned with the grain of the surface or not.

Another complication that occurs in reality is the nature of the atmosphere. Most BRDFs used in local reflection models are constrained to apply to light reflected from opaque materials in a vacuum. We mostly do not consider any scattering of reflected light in an atmosphere (in the same way that we do not consider light scattered by an atmosphere before it reaches the object). The reason for this is, of course, simplicity and the subsequent reduction of light intensity calculations to simple comparisons between vectors categorizing surface shapes, light directions and viewing direction.

We might imagine that if we have a BRDF for a material that the light–object interaction is solved. However, a number of problems remain to this day despite a quarter of a century of research. Some of these are:

Figure 7.4
BRDF cross-section for different materials and wavelengths (after an illustration by He *et al.* (1991)).

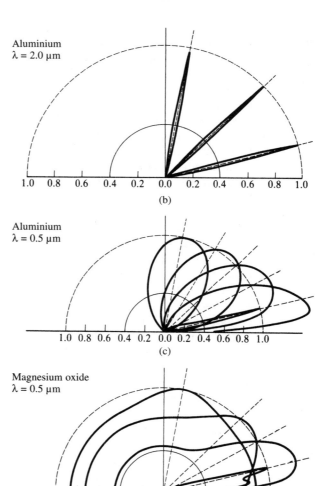

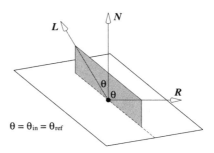

- Where do we get the BRDF from (particularly for real as opposed to perfect materials)? Some data are available for some materials in the metallurgical literature but this is by no means complete.

- At what scale do we attempt to represent a BRDF? What is the area of the region that we should consider receives incident light? Should this be large enough so that the statistical model is consistent over the surface? Should it be large enough to include surface imperfections such as scratches? This is very much an unaddressed problem.

- How do we represent the BRDF? This final point accounts for most variation amongst models. In particular, the distinction between empirical and physically based models is often made. An empirical model is one that imitates light–object interaction. For example, in the Phong model a simple mathematical function is used to represent the specular lobe. In the Cook and Torrance model a statistical ditribution represents the surface geometry and this is termed a physically based model (Cook and Torrance 1982). It is interesting to note that there is no general agreement on the visual efficacy of empirical versus physically based models. Often a better result can be obtained by carefully tuning the parameters of an empirical model than by using a physically based model.

What follows is a review of the early local reflection models and a short selection of more recent advances. In particular we start by looking at the defects inherent in the Phong model and how these can be overcome. The material is by no means a comprehensive review, but is intended as a representation of these departures from the Phong model that have been simulated to provide ever more subtle variations on the way in which light 'paints' an object.

7.4 Diffuse and specular components

Local reflection models used in computer graphics are normally considered as a combination of a diffuse and a specular component. This works well for many cases but it is a simplification. The simpler models of specular reflection consider some imperfect behaviour to be a modification of perfect specular reflection. Perfect specular reflection occurs when light strikes a perfect mirror surface and a thin beam of light incident on such a surface reflects according to the well-known law: the outgoing angle is equal to the angle of incidence. Perfect diffuse reflection occurs when incident light is scattered equally in all directions from a perfect matte surface, which could in practice be a very fine layer of powder. Combining separately calculated specular and diffuse components imitates the behaviour of real surfaces and is an enabling assumption in many computer graphics models. Imitating the subtle visual differences between real surfaces has mostly been achieved by incorporating various effects into the specular component as we shall now examine by looking at a selection of such models. These are:

(1) The Phong model – perfect diffuse reflection combined with empirically spread specular reflection (Phong 1975).

(2) A physically based specular refection model developed by Blinn (1977) and Cook and Torrance (1982).

(3) Pre-calculating BRDFs to be indexed during a rendering process Cabral *et al.* (1987).

(4) A physically based diffuse model developed by Hanrahan and Kreuger (1993).

This selection is both an historical sample and an illustration of the diverse approaches of researchers to local reflection models.

7.5 Perfect diffuse – empirically spread specular reflection (Phong 1975)

This is, in fact, the Phong reflection model. We have already discussed the practicalities of this, in particular, how it is integrated into a rendering system or strategy. Here we will look at it from a more theoretical point of view that enables a comparison with other direct reflection models.

The Phong reflection model accounts for diffuse reflection by Lambert's Cosine Law, where the intensity of the reflected light is a function of the cosine between the surface normal and the incoming light direction.

Phong used an empirically spread specular term. Here the idea is that a practical surface, say, shiny metal, reflects light in a lobe around the perfect mirror direction because it can be considered to be made up of tiny mirrors all oriented in slightly different directions, instead of being made up of a perfectly smooth mirror that takes the shape of the object. Thus the coarseness or roughness of the (shiny) surface can be simulated by the index n – the higher n is, the tighter the lobe and the smoother the surface. All surfaces simulated by this model have a plastic-like appearance.

Geometrically, in three-dimensional space the model produces a cone of rays centred on R whose intensity drops off exponentially as the angle between the ray and R increases.

A more subtle aspect of real behaviour, and one that accounts for the difference in the look of plastic and shiny metal, is missing entirely from this model. This is that the amount of light that is specularly reflected depends on the elevation angle θ_i (Figure 7.3) of the incoming light. Drive a car into the setting sun and you experience a blinding glare from the road surface – a dull surface at midday with little or no specular component. It was to account for this behaviour, which for any object accounts for subtle changes in the shape of a highlight as a function of the incoming light direction, that an early local reflection model, based on a physical microfacet simulation of the surface, emerged.

We can say that, although the direction of the specular bump in the Phong model depends on the incident direction – the specular bump is symmetrically disposed about the mirror direction – its magnitude does not vary and the Phong model implements a BRDF 'reduced' to:

$$BRDF = f(\theta_{ref}, \phi_{ref})$$

The BRDF shown in Figure 7.3 was calculated using the Phong reflection model.

(7.6) Physically based specular reflection (Blinn 1977; Cook and Torrance 1982)

Two years after the appearance of Phong's work in 1975, J. Blinn (1977) published a paper describing how a physically based specular component could be used in computer graphics. In 1982, Cook and Torrance extended this model to account for the spectral composition of highlights – their dependency on material type and the angle of incidence of the light. These advances have a subtle effect on the size and colour of a highlight compared with that obtained from the Phong model. The model still retains the separation of the reflected light into a diffuse and specular component, and the new work concentrates entirely on the specular component, the diffuse component being calculated in the same way as before. The model is most successful in rendering shiny metallic-like surfaces, and through the colour variation in the specular highlight being able to, for example, render similarly coloured metals differently.

The problem of highlight shape is quite subtle. A highlight is just the image of a light source or sources reflected in the object. Unless the object surface is planar, this image is distorted by the object, and as the direction of the incoming light changes, it falls on a different part of the object and its shape changes. Therefore we have a highlight image whose overall shape depends on the curvature of the object surface over the area struck by the incident light and the viewing direction, which determines how much of the highlight is visible from the viewing direction. These are the primary factors that determine the shape of the patches of bright light that we see on the surface of an object and are easily calculated by using the Phong model.

The secondary factors which determine the highlight image are the dependence of its intensity and colour on the angle of incoming light with respect to a tangent plane at the point on the surface under consideration. This identifies the nature of the material to us and enables us to distinguish between metallic and non-metallic objects.

Curiously, despite producing more accurate highlights, these models were not taken up by the graphics community and the cheaper and simpler Phong model remained the more popular, as indeed it does to this day. The possible reason for this is that the differences produced by the more elaborate models are subtle. Objects rendered by the Phong model, although inaccurate and incorrect in highlight rendering, produce objects that look real. In most graphics applications, then and now, this is all that is required. Photo-realism, the much stated goal, of three-dimensional computer graphics, depends on very many factors other than local reflection models. To make objects look more real, only in this manifestly narrow sense, was perhaps not deemed to be worth the cost.

What is meant by a physical simulation in the context of light reflection is that we attempt to model the micro-geometry of the surface that causes the light to reflect, rather than simply imitating the behaviour, as we do in the Phong model, with an empirical term.

This early simulation of specular highlights has four components, and is based on a physical microfacet model consisting of symmetric V-shaped grooves occurring around an average surface (Figure 7.2). We now describe each of these components in turn.

7.6.1 Modelling the micro-geometry of the surface

A statistical distribution is set up for the orientation of the microfacets and this gives a term D for the light emerging in a particular (viewing) direction. A simple Gaussian can be used:

$$D = k \exp[-(\alpha/m)^2)]$$

where α is the angle of the microfacet with respect to the normal of the (mean) surface, that is the angle between N and H, and m is the standard deviation of the distribution. Evaluating the distribution at this angle simply returns the number of microfacets with this orientation, that is the number of microfacets that can contribute to light emerging in the viewing direction. Two reflection lobes for $m = 0.2$ and 0.6 are shown in Figure 7.2(b).

Using microfacets to simulate the dependence of light reflection on surface roughness makes two enabling assumptions:

(1) It is assumed that the microfacets, although physically small, are large with respect to the wavelength of light.

(2) The diameter of the incident beam is large enough to intersect a number of microfacets that is sufficient to result in representative behaviour of the reflected light.

In BRDF terms this factor controls the extent to which the specular role bulges.

7.6.2 Shadowing and masking effects

Where the viewing vector, or the light orientation vector begins to approach the mean surface, interference effects occur. These are called shadowing and masking. Masking occurs when some reflected light is trapped and shadowing when incident light is intercepted, as can be seen from Figure 7.5.

The degree of masking and shadowing is dependent on the ratio l_1/l_2 (Figure 7.5(b)) which describes the proportionate amount of the facets contributing to reflected light that is given by:

$$G = 1 - l_1/l_2$$

Figure 7.5
The interaction of light with a microfacet reflecting surface. (a) Shadowing and masking. (b) Amount of light which escapes depends on $1 - h/l_2$.

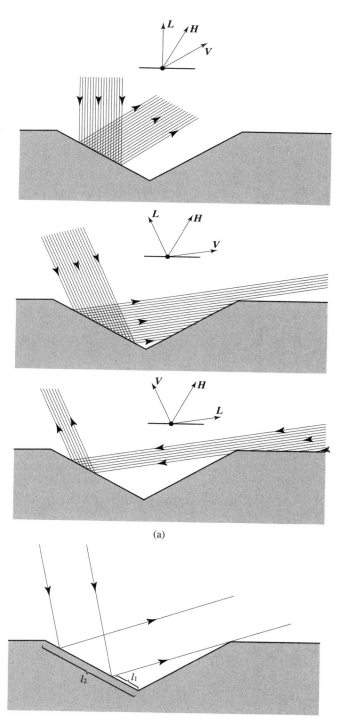

(a)

(b)

In the case where l_1 reduces to zero then all the reflected light escapes and:

$G = 1$

A detailed derivation of the dependence of l_1/l_2 on L, V and H was given by Blinn (1977). For masking:

$G_m = 2(N{\cdot}H)(N{\cdot}V)/V{\cdot}H$

For shadowing the situation is geometrically identical with the role of the vectors L and V interchanged. For masking we have:

$G_s = 2(N{\cdot}H)(N{\cdot}L)/V{\cdot}H$

The value of G that must be used is the minimum of G_s and G_m. Thus:

$G = \min \{1, G_s, G_m\}$

7.6.3 Viewing geometry

Another pure geometric term is implemented to account for the glare effect mentioned in Section 7.5. As the angle between the view vector and the mean surface normal is increased towards 90°, an observer sees more and more microfacets and this is accounted for by a term:

$1/N{\cdot}V$

that is, the increase in area of the microfacets seen by a viewer is inversely proportional to the angle between the viewing direction and the surface normal. If there is incident light at a low angle then more of this light is reflected towards the viewer than if the viewer was intercepting light from an angle of incidence close to normal. This effect is countered by the shadowing effect which comes into play also as the viewing orientation approaches the mean surface orientation.

7.6.4 The Fresnel term

The next term to consider is the Fresnel term, F (see Section 7.1). This term concerns the amount of light that is reflected as opposed to being absorbed – a factor that depends on the material type considered as a perfect mirror surface – which our individual microfacets are. In other words we now consider behaviour for a perfect planar surface having previously modelled the entire surface as a set of such microfacets which individually behave as perfect mirrors. This factor determines the strength of the reflected lobe as a function of incidence angle and wavelength. The wavelength dependence accounts for subtle colour effects in the specular highlight.

The coefficients required to calculate F for any angle of incidence are not usually known and Cook and Torrance (1982) suggest a practical compromise which is to use known (measured) values of F_0 – the value of F at normal incidence – to calculate μ then to use Equation 7.1 to evaluate F for any angle of incidence. At normal incidence, Equation 7.1 reduces to:

$$F_0 = \frac{(\mu - 1)^2}{(\mu + 1)^2}$$

(μ is, in fact, complex and contains an imaginary term – the extinction coefficient. This is zero for dielectrics – plastics, for example – and it is also zero for conductors, for metals at normal incidence; and it can thus be ignored for both categories of materials at normal incidence.)

Another way of calculating F for any incidence angle from F_0 is due to Schlick (1993) and is the formula:

$$F_\phi = F_0 + (1 - \cos \phi)^5 (1 - F_0)$$

The practical effect of this term is to account for subtle changes in colour of the specular highlight as a function of angle of incidence. For any material, when the light is incident at an angle nearly parallel to the surface then the colour of the highlight approaches that of the light source. For other angles the colour depends on both the angle of incidence and the material. An example of this dependency is shown for polished copper in Figure 7.6.

The effect of this term is to cause the reflected intensity to increase as the angle of incidence increases (just as did the previous term $1/\mathbf{N} \cdot \mathbf{V}$) – less light is absorbed by the material and more is reflected. (A more subtle effect is that the peak of the specular lobe shifts away from the perfect mirror direction as the angle of incidence increases – see Figure 7.7.)

Thus putting these together the specular term now becomes:

specular component $= DGF/(\mathbf{N} \cdot \mathbf{V})$

where:

D is the micro-geometry term
G is the shadowing/masking term
F is the Fresnel term
$(\mathbf{N} \cdot \mathbf{V})$ is the glare effect term

Summarizing we have:

(1) A factor that models reflected light intensity as a function of the physical nature of the surface to within the approximations of the geometric simulation.

(2) Two interacting factors that simulate the behaviour of the 'glare' effect which occurs when light is incoming at a high angle (with respect to $\mathbf{N}$, the surface normal) of incidence.

(3) A factor that relates the reflected light intensity at each (perfect mirror) microfacet to the electro-optical properties of the material. This is a function of the direction of the incoming light and controls subtle second order

Figure 7.6
Fresnel equation and
polished copper.
(a) Reflectance F as a
function of wavelength
(λ) and angle of incidence
(polished copper). (b) The
dependence of F on ϕ
for red, green and blue
wavelengths.

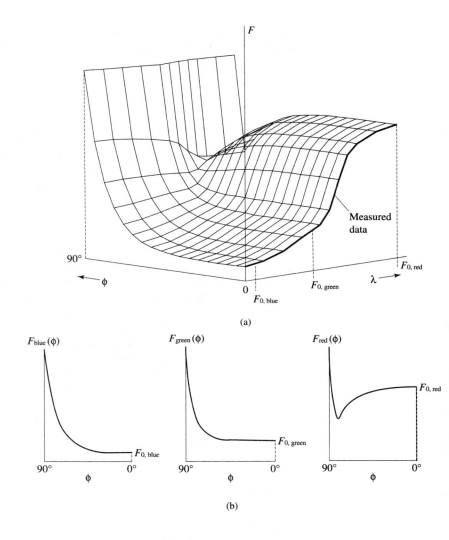

(a)

(b)

effects concerning the shape and the colour of the highlight. This effect is
important when trying to simulate the difference between, say, shiny plastic
and metals. Gold, for example, exhibits yellow highlights when illuminated
with white light and the highlight only tends to white when the light grazes
the surface.

The specular term is separately calculated and combined with a uniform diffuse
term:

$$\text{BRDF} = sR_s + dR_d \quad \text{(where } s + d = 1\text{)}$$

For example, metals are simulated, usually with $d = 0$ and $s = 1$ and shiny plastics with $d = 0.9$ and $s = 0.1$. Note that if d is set to zero for metals the specular

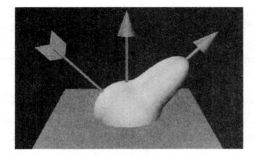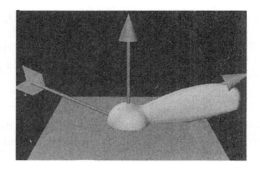

Figure 7.7
BRDFs for different angles of incidence in the Blinn reflection model.

term controls the colour of the object over its entire surface. Compare this with the Phong reflection model where the colour of the object is always controlled by the diffuse component. The Phong model, because of this, is incapable of producing metallic looking surfaces and all surfaces rendered using Phong have a distinct plastic look.

In this model the reflected light intensity depends on the elevation angle of the incoming light but the model is independent of the azimuth angle of the incident light. Whatever the azimuthal direction of the incoming light, it encounters the same statistical distribution of long, parallel, symmetric V-shaped grooves (a somewhat impossible situation in practice). Thus:

$$\text{BRDF} = f(\theta_{in}, \theta_{ref}, \phi_{ref})$$

A pair of BRDFs for a low and high angle of incidence are shown in Figure 7.7. This shows a specular lobe increasing in value (and also moving away from the mirror reflection direction) as the angle of incidence is increased towards the grazing angle. Figure 7.8 (Colour Plate) gives an idea of the variety of object appearances that can be achieved using this model.

7.7 Pre-computing BRDFs

One of the main inadequacies of the previous approach is that it cannot be used to model anisotropic surfaces. Many surfaces exhibit anisotropy reflection characteristics. Cloth and 'brushed' metal used in 'decorative' engineering applications – like car wheels – are two examples. Consider cloth, for example: this exhibits anisotropic reflection because it is made up of parallel threads with circular cross-sections. Each thread scatters light narrowly when the incident light is in a plane parallel to the direction of the thread, and more widely when the incident plane is parallel to the circular cross-section of the thread. The two popular approaches to including anisotropic behaviour in BRDFs have been to set up special surface models – usually based on cylinders – and pre-calculation.

In 1987 a model (Cabral *et al.* 1987) was reported that could deal with the dependence of the azimuth angle of the incoming light. The model pre-calculates a BRDF for each L represented by a hemisphere divided into bins indexed by V. The BRDF is calculated by ray tracing for each incoming direction a bundle of parallel, randomly positioned rays as they strike the surface and reflect to hit the surrounding hemisphere. The dependency of the BRDF on angles is then:

$$BRDF = f(\theta_{in}, \phi_{in}, \theta_{ref}, \phi_{ref})$$

The BRDF is generated by firing rays or beams onto a surface element that encompasses a sufficiently large area of the microsurface. The surface element is modelled by an array or grid of triangular microfacets. The rays that hit the element without being shadowed and emerge without being masked make a contribution to the BRDF, and the complete function is the sum of all such contributions. This information is built up by dividing a hemisphere into a number of cells or bins. A representation of this process is shown in Figure 7.9. The surface microfacets are perturbed out of the mean plane by a bump map as the figure suggests. Note that an advantage of this approach is that there is no restriction on the small-scale geometry – the microfacets do not need to form a Gaussian distribution, for example.

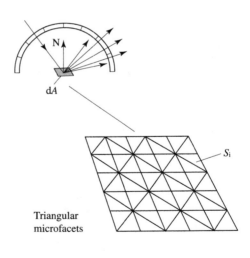

Hemisphere surrounding microsurface element is divided into 24 × 24 cells

Triangular microfacets

Vertex heights perturbed by a bump map

Figure 7.9

Modelling a surface with height-field perturbed triangular microfacets.

The BRDF is then a coarsely sampled version of a continuous BRDF. The pre-calculation is built up by considering each cell to be a source of incoming light and calculating the resulting reflection into the hemisphere. When a surface is being rendered the hemisphere closest to the angle of incident light is selected. The north pole of this distribution then has to be aligned with the surface normal at the point and the pre-calculated BRDF then gives the reflected intensity in the viewing direction.

7.8 Physically based diffuse component (Hanrahan and Kreuger 1993)

Until fairly recently local reflection models in computer graphics have concentrated almost exclusively on the specular component of reflected light and, as we have seen, these have been based on physical microsurface modelling.

Diffuse light is usually modelled on Lambert's Cosine Law which assumes that reflected light is isotropic and proportional in intensity to the cosine of the angle of incidence. Surface simulations of diffuse light are not possible because diffuse reflection originates from light that actually enters the material. This component is absorbed and scattered within the reflecting material. The wavelength-dependent absorption accounts for the colour of the material – incident white light is, in effect, filtered by the material. It is the multiple scattering within the material that causes the emerging light to be (approximately) isotropic. Thus a physical simulation of diffuse reflection would have to be based on subsurface scattering.

We could ask the question: what is wrong with sticking with Lambert's Law? The answer to this would be the same as the motivation for the development of physically based specular models – there are subtle effects produced by diffusely reflecting light that are responsible for the distinctive look of certain materials. Recent work by Hanrahan and Kreuger (1993) develops a physically based model for diffuse reflection that the authors claim is particularly appropriate for layered materials appearing in nature, such as biological tissues (skin, leaves and so on) and inorganic substances like snow and sand. The outcome of the model is, of course, anisotropy – reflecting the fact that very few real materials exhibit isotropic diffuse behaviour.

Hanrahan and Kreuger specify the reflected light from a point on the surface as

$$L_r = L_{rs} + L_{rv}$$

where L_{rs} is the reflected light due to surface scattering – imperfect specular reflection – and L_{rv} is the reflected light that is due to subsurface scattering. The algorithm that determines the subsurface scattering is based on a 1D transport model solved using a Monte Carlo approach. The details are outside the scope of this text; more important for our purposes is a conceptual understanding of the advances made by these researchers and their visual ramifications.

The combination of those two components produces anisotropic behaviour because of a number of factors that we will now describe. First, consider the angle

Figure 7.10
Reflection behaviour due to Hanrahan and Kreuger's model (after Hanrahan and Kreuger (1993)).

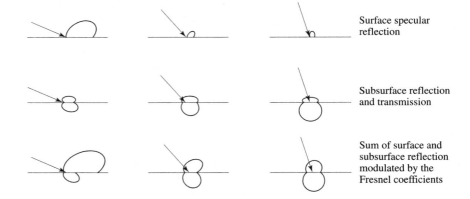

Surface specular reflection

Subsurface reflection and transmission

Sum of surface and subsurface reflection modulated by the Fresnel coefficients

of incidence of the light. For a plane surface the amount of light entering the surface depends on Fresnel's law – the more light that enters the surface, the higher will be the contribution or influence from subsurface events to the total reflected light L_r. So the influence of L_{rv} depends on the angle of incidence. Subsurface scattering depends on the physical properties of the material. A material is modelled by a suspension of scattering sites or particles and parametrized by absorption and scattering cross-sections. These express the probability of occurrence per unit path length of scattering or absorption. The relative size of these parameters determines whether the scattering is forward, backward or isotropic.

The effect of these two factors is shown, for a simple case, in Figure 7.10. The first row shows high/low specular reflection as a function of angle of incidence. The behaviour of reflected light is dominated by surface scattering or specular reflection when the angle of incidence is high and by subsurface scattering when the angle of incidence is low. As we have seen, this behaviour is modelled, to a certain extent, by the Cook and Torrance model of Section 7.6. The second row shows reflection lobes due to subsurface scattering and it can be seen that materials can exhibit backward, isotropic or forward scattering behaviour. (The bottom lobes do not, of course, contribute to L_r but are nevertheless important when considering materials that are made up of multiple layers and thin translucent materials that are backlit.) The third row shows that the combination of L_{rs} and L_{rv} will generally result in non-isotropic behaviour which exhibits the following general attributes:

● Reflection increases as material layer thickness increases due to increased subsurface scattering.

● Subsurface scattering can be backward, isotropic or forward.

● Reflection from subsurface scattering tends to produce functions that are flattened on top of the lobe compared with the (idealized) hemisphere of Lambert's law.

Such factors result in the subtle differences between the model and Lambert's law.

Mapping techniques

Introduction

In this chapter we will look at techniques which store information (usually) in a two-dimensional domain which is used during rendering to simulate textures. The mainstream application is texture mapping but many other applications are described such as reflection mapping to simulate ray tracing. With the advent of texture mapping hardware the use of such facilities to implement real time rendering has seen the development of light maps. These use the texture facilities to enable the pre-calculation of (view independent) lighting which then 'reduces' rendering to a texture mapping operation.

Texture mapping became a highly developed tool in the 1980s and was the technique used to enhance Phong shaded scenes so that they were more visually interesting, looked more realistic or esoteric. Objects that are rendered using only Phong shading look plastic-like and texture mapping is the obvious way to add interest without much expense.

Texture mapping developed in parallel with research into global illumination algorithms – ray tracing and radiosity (see Chapters 10, 11 and 12). It was a device that could be used to enhance the visual interest of a scene, rather than its photo-realism and its main attraction was cheapness – it could be grafted onto a standard rendering method without adding too much to the processing cost. This contrasted to the global illumination methods which used completely different algorithms and were much more expensive than direct reflection models.

Another use of texture mapping that became ubiquitous in the 1980s was to add pseudo-realism to shiny animated objects by causing their surrounding environment to be reflected in them. Thus tumbling logos and titles became chromium and the texture reflected on them moved as the objects moved. This technique – known as environment mapping – can also be used with a real photographed environment and can help to merge a computer animated object with a real environment. Environment mapping does not accomplish anything that could not be achieved by ray tracing – but it is much more efficient. A more recent use of environment mapping techniques is in image-based rendering which is discussed in Chapter 16.

As used in computer graphics, 'texture' is a somewhat confusing term and generally does not mean controlling the small-scale geometry of the surface of a computer graphics object – the normal meaning of the word. It is easy to modulate the colour of a Phong shaded object by controlling the value of the three diffuse coefficients and this became the most common object parameter to be controlled by texture mapping. (Colour variations in the physical world are not, of course, generally regarded as texture.) Thus as the rendering proceeds at pixel-by-pixel level, we pick up values for the Phong diffuse reflection coefficients and the diffuse component (the colour) of the shading changes as a function of the texture map(s). A better term is colour mapping and this appears to be coming into common usage.

This simple pixel-level operation conceals many difficulties and the geometry of texture mapping is not straightforward. As usual we make simplifications that lead to a visually acceptable solution. There are three origins to the difficulties:

(1) We mostly want to use texture mapping with the most popular representation in computer graphics – the polygon mesh representation. This, as we know, is a geometric representation where the object surface is approximated, and this approximation is only defined at the vertices. In a sense we have no surface – only an approximation to one – so how can we physically derive a texture value at a surface point if the surface does not exist?

(2) We want to use, in the main, two-dimensional texture maps because we have an almost endless source of textures that we can derive by frame-grabbing the real world, by using two-dimensional paint software or by generating textures procedurally. Thus the mainstream demand is to map a two-dimensional texture onto a surface that is approximated by a polygon mesh. This situation has become consolidated with the advent of cheap texture mapping hardware facilities.

(3) Aliasing problems in texture mapping are usually highly visible. By definition textures usually manifest some kind of coherence or periodicity.

Aliasing breaks this up and the resulting mess is usually high visible. This effect occurs as the periodicity in the texture approaches the pixel resolution.

We now list the possible ways in which certain properties of a computer graphics model can be modulated with variations under control of a texture map. We have listed these in approximate order of their popularity (which also tends to relate to their ease of use or implementation). These are:

(1) **Colour** As we have already pointed out, this is by far the most common object property that is controlled by a texture map. We simply modulate the diffuse reflection coefficients in the Phong reflection model with the corresponding colour from the texture map. (We could also change the specular coefficients across the surface of an object so that it appears shiny and matte as a function of the texture map. But this is less common, as being able to perceive this effect on the rendered object depends on producing specular highlights on the shiny parts if we are using the basic Phong reflection model.)

(2) **Specular 'colour'** This technique – known as environment mapping or chrome mapping – is a special case of ray tracing where we use texture map techniques to avoid the expense of full ray tracing. The map is designed so that it looks as if the (specular) object is reflecting the environment or background in which it is placed.

(3) **Normal vector perturbation** This elegant technique applies a perturbation to the surface normal according to the corresponding value in the map. The technique is known as bump mapping and was developed by a famous pioneer of three-dimensional computer graphic techniques – J. Blinn. The device works because the intensity that is returned by a Phong shading equation reduces, if the appropriate simplifications are made, to a function of the surface normal at the point currently being shaded. If the surface normal is perturbed then the shading changes and the surface that is rendered looks as if it is textured. We can therefore use a global or general definition for the texture of a surface which is represented in the database as a polygon mesh structure.

(4) **Displacement mapping** Related to the previous technique, this mapping method uses a height field to perturb a surface point along the direction of its surface normal. It is not a convenient technique to implement since the map must perturb the geometry of the model rather than modulate parameters in the shading equation.

(5) **Transparency** A map is used to control the opacity of a transparent object. A good example is etched glass where a shiny surface is roughened (to cause opacity) with some decorative pattern.

There are many ways to perform texture mapping. The choice of a particular method depends mainly on time constraints and the quality of the image required. To start with we will restrict the discussion to two-dimensional texture maps – the most popular and common form – used in conjunction with polygon mesh objects. (Many of the insights detailed in this section are based on descriptions in Heckbert's (1986) defining work in this area.)

Mapping a two-dimensional texture map onto the surface of an object then projecting the object into screen space is a two-dimensional to two-dimensional transformation and can thus be viewed as an image warping operation. The most common way to do this is to inverse map – for each pixel we find its corresponding 'pre-image' in texture space (Figure 8.1(b)). However, for reasons that will shortly become clear, specifying this overall transformation is not straightforward and we consider initially that texture mapping is a two-stage process that takes us from the two-dimensional texture space into the three-dimensional space of the object and then via the projective transform into two-dimensional screen space (Figure 8.1(a)). The first transformation is known as parametrization and the second stage is the normal computer graphics projective transformation. The parametrization associates all points in texture space with points on the object surface.

The use of an anti-aliasing method is mandatory with texture mapping. This is easily seen by considering an object retreating away from a viewer so that its projection in screen space covers fewer and fewer pixels. As the object size decreases, the pre-image of a pixel in texture space will increase covering a larger area. If we simply point sample at the centre of the pixel and take the value of $T(u, v)$ at the corresponding point in texture space, then grossly incorrect results will follow (Figure 8.2(a), (b) and (c)). An example of this effect is shown in Figure 8.3. Here, as the chequerboard pattern recedes into the distance, it begins to break up in a disturbing manner. These problems are highly visible and move when animated. Consider Figure 8.2(b) and (c). Say, for example, that an object projects onto a single pixel and moves in such a way that the pre-image translates across the $T(u, v)$. As the object moves it would switch colour from black to white.

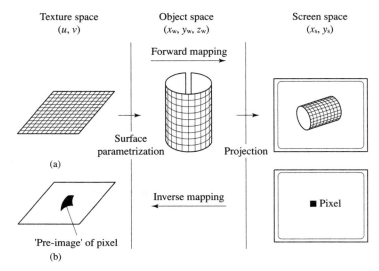

Texture space
(u, v)

Object space
(x_w, y_w, z_w)

Screen space
(x_s, y_s)

Forward mapping

Surface
parametrization

Projection

(a)

Inverse mapping

'Pre-image' of pixel

(b)

■ Pixel

Figure 8.1
Two ways of viewing the process of two-dimensional texture mapping.
(a) Forward mapping.
(b) Inverse mapping.

Figure 8.2
Pixels and pre-images in
$T(u,v)$ space.

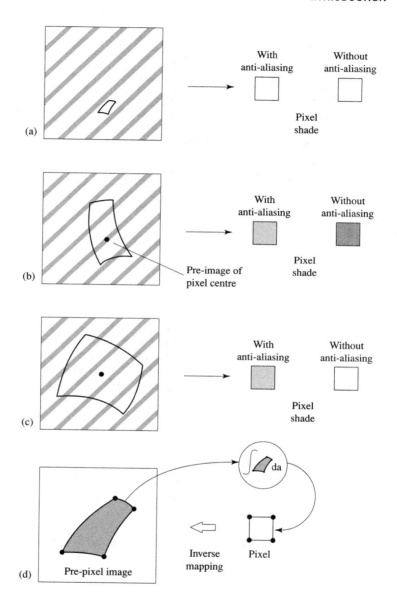

Anti-aliasing in this context then means integrating the information over the pixel pre-image and using this value in the shading calculation for the current pixel (Figure 8.2(d)). At best we can only approximate this integral because we have no knowledge of the shape of the quadrilateral, only its four corner points.

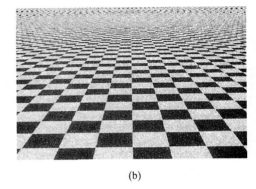

(a)

(b)

Figure 8.3
Aliasing in texture mapping. The pattern in (b) is a super-sampled (anti-aliased) version of that in (a). Aliases still occur but appear at a higher spatial frequency.

8.1 Two-dimensional texture maps to polygon mesh objects

The most popular practical strategy for texture mapping is to associate, during the modelling phase, texture space coordinates (u, v) with polygon vertices. The task of the rendering engine then is to find the appropriate (u, v) coordinate for pixels internal to each polygon. The main problem comes about because the geometry of a polygon mesh is only defined at the vertices – in other words there is no analytical parametrization possible. (If the object has an analytical definition – a cylinder, for example – then we have a parametrization and the mapping of the texture onto the object surface is trivial.)

There are two main algorithm structures possible in texture mapping, inverse mapping (the more common) and forward mapping. (Heckbert refers to these as screen order and texture order algorithms respectively.) Inverse mapping (Figure 8.1(b)) is where the algorithm is driven from screen space and for every pixel we find by an inverse mapping its 'pre-image' in texture space. For each pixel we find its corresponding (u, v) coordinates. A filtering operation integrates the information contained in the pre-image and assigns the resulting colour to the pixel. This algorithm is advantageous if the texture mapping is to be incorporated into a Z-buffer algorithm where the polygon is rasterized and depth and lighting interpolated on a scan line basis. The square pixel produces a curvilinear quadrilateral as a pre-image.

In forward mapping the algorithm is driven from texture space. This time a square texel in texture space produces a curvilinear quadrilateral in screen space and there is a potential problem due to holes and overlaps in the texture image when it is mapped into screen space. Forward mapping is like considering the texture map as a rubber sheet – stretching it in a way (determined by the parametrization) so that it sticks on the object surface thereby performing the normal object space to screen space transform.

Inverse mapping by bilinear interpolation

Although forward mapping is easy to understand, in practical algorithms inverse mapping is preferred and from now on we will only consider this strategy for polygon mesh objects. For inverse mapping it is convenient to consider a single (compound) transformation from two-dimensional screen space (x, y) to two-dimensional texture space (u, v). This is just an image warping operation and it can be modelled as a rational linear projective transform:

$$x = \frac{au + bv + c}{gu + hu + i} \qquad y = \frac{du + ev + f}{gu + hv + i} \tag{8.1}$$

This is, of course, a non-linear transformation as we would expect. Alternatively, we can write this in homogeneous coordinates as:

$$\begin{bmatrix} x' \\ y' \\ w \end{bmatrix} = \begin{bmatrix} a & b & c \\ d & e & f \\ g & h & i \end{bmatrix} \begin{bmatrix} u' \\ v' \\ q \end{bmatrix}$$

where:

$$(x, y) = (x'/w, y'/w) \quad \text{and} \quad (u, v) = (u'/q, v'/q)$$

This is known as a rational linear transformation. The inverse transform – the one of interest to us in practice – is given by:

$$\begin{bmatrix} u' \\ v' \\ q \end{bmatrix} = \begin{bmatrix} A & B & C \\ D & E & F \\ G & H & I \end{bmatrix} \begin{bmatrix} x' \\ y' \\ w \end{bmatrix}$$

$$= \begin{bmatrix} ei - fh & ch - bi & bf - ce \\ fg - di & ai - cg & cd - af \\ dh - eg & bg - ah & ae - bd \end{bmatrix} \begin{bmatrix} x' \\ y' \\ w \end{bmatrix}$$

Now recall that in most practical texture mapping applications we set up, during the modelling phase, an association between polygon mesh vertices and texture map coordinates. So, for example if we have the association for the four vertices of a quadrilateral we can find the nine coefficients $(a, b, c, d, e, f, g, h, i)$. We thus have the required inverse transform for any point within the polygon. This is done as follows. Return to the first half of Equation 8.1, the equation for x. Note that we can multiply top and bottom by an arbitrary non-zero scalar constant without changing the value of y, in effect we only have five degrees of freedom – not six – and because of this we can, without loss of generality set $i = 1$. Thus, in the overall transformation we only have 8 coefficients to determine and our quadrilateral-to-quadrilateral association will give a set of 8 equations in 8 unknowns which can be solved by any standard algorithm for linear equations – Gaussian elimination, for example. Full details of this procedure are given in Heckbert (1986).

A better practical alternative is to achieve the same effect by bilinear interpolation in screen space. So we interpolate the texture coordinates at the same time as interpolating lighting and depth. However, we note from the above that it is the homogeneous coordinates (u', v', q) that we have to interpolate, because the u and v do not change linearly with x and y.

Assuming vertex coordinate/texture coordinate for all polygons we consider each vertex to have homogeneous texture coordinates:

$$(u', v', q)$$

where:

$$u = u'/q$$
$$v = v'/q$$
$$q = 1/z$$

We interpolate using the normal bilinear interpolation scheme within the polygon (see Section 1.5) using these homogeneous coordinates as vertices to give (u', v', q') for each pixel then the required texture coordinates are given by:

$$(u, v) = u'/q, v'/q$$

Note that this costs two divides per pixel. For the standard incremental implementation of this interpolation process we need three gradients down each edge (in the current edge-pair) and three gradients for the current scan line.

Inverse mapping by using an intermediate surface

The previous method for mapping two-dimensional textures is now undoubtedly the most popular approach. The method we now describe can be used in applications where there is no texture coordinate–vertex coordinate correspondence. Alternatively it can be used as a pre-process to determine this correspondence and the first method then used during rendering.

Two-part texture mapping is a technique that overcomes the surface parametrization problem in polygon mesh objects by using an 'easy' intermediate surface onto which the texture is initially projected. Introduced by Bier and Sloan (1986), the method can also be used to implement environment mapping and is thus a method that unifies texture mapping and environment mapping.

The process is known as two-part mapping because the texture is mapped onto an intermediate surface before being mapped onto the object. The intermediate surface is, in general, non-planar but it possesses an analytic mapping function and the two-dimensional texture is mapped onto this surface without difficulty. Finding the correspondence between the object point and the texture point then becomes a three-dimensional to three-dimensional mapping.

The basis of the method is most easily described as a two-stage forward mapping process (Figure 8.4):

Figure 8.4
Two-stage mapping as a
foward process. (a) *S*
mapping. (b) *O* mapping.

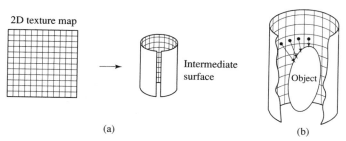

2D texture map

Intermediate
surface

Object

(a)   (b)

(1) The first stage is a mapping from two-dimensional texture space to a simple three-dimensional intermediate surface such as a cylinder.

$$T(u, v) \rightarrow T'(x_i, y_i, z_i)$$

This is known as the *S* mapping.

(2) A second stage maps the three-dimensional texture pattern onto the object surface.

$$T'(x_i, y_i, z_i) \rightarrow O(x_w, y_w, z_w)$$

This is referred to as the *O* mapping.

These combined operations can distort the texture pattern onto the object in a 'natural' way, for example, one variation of the method is a 'shrinkwrap' mapping, where the planar texture pattern shrinks onto the object in the manner suggested by the eponym.

For the *S* mapping, Bier describes four intermediate surfaces: a plane at any orientation, the curved surface of a cylinder, the faces of a cube and the surface of a sphere. Although it makes no difference mathematically, it is useful to consider that $T(u, v)$ is mapped onto the interior surfaces of these objects. For example, consider the cylinder. Given a parametric definition of the curved surface of a cylinder as a set of points (θ, h), we transform the point (u, v) onto the cylinder as follows. We have:

$$S_{cylinder}: (\theta, h) \rightarrow (u, v)$$
$$= \left(\frac{r}{c} (\theta - \theta_0), \frac{1}{d} (h - h_0) \right)$$

where c and d are scaling factors and θ_0 and h_0 position the texture on the cylinder of radius r.

Various possibilities occur for the *O* mapping where the texture values for $O(x_w, y_w, z_w)$ are obtained from $T'(x_i, y_i, z_i)$, and these are best considered from a ray tracing point of view. The four *O* mappings are shown in Figure 8.5 and are:

(1) The intersection of the reflected view ray with the intermediate surface, T'. (This is, in fact, identical to environment mapping described in Section 8.6. The only difference between the general process of using this *O* mapping and environment mapping is that the texture pattern that is mapped onto the intermediate surface is a surrounding environment like a room interior.)

Figure 8.5
The four possible O mappings that map the intermediate surface texture T' onto the object

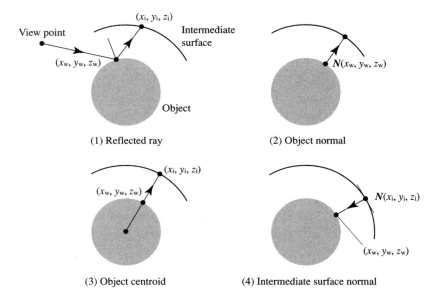

(1) Reflected ray

(2) Object normal

(3) Object centroid

(4) Intermediate surface normal

(2) The intersection of the surface normal at (x_w, y_w, z_w) with T'.

(3) The intersection of a line through (x_w, y_w, z_w) and the object centroid with T'.

(4) The intersection of the line from (x_w, y_w, z_w) to T' whose orientation is given by the surface normal at (x_i, y_i, z_i). If the intermediate surface is simply a plane then this is equivalent to considering the texture map to be a slide in a slide projector. A bundle of parallel rays of light from the slide projector impinges on the object surface. Alternatively it is also equivalent to three-dimensional texture mapping (see Section 8.7) where the field is defined by 'extruding' the two-dimensional texture map along an axis normal to the plane of the pattern.

Let us now consider this procedure as an inverse mapping process for the shrinkwrap case. We break the process into three stages (Figure 8.6).

(1) Inverse map four pixel points to four points (x_w, y_w, z_w) on the surface of the object.

(2) Apply the O mapping to find the point (θ, h) on the surface of the cylinder. In the shrinkwrap case we simply join the object point to the centre of the cylinder and the intersection of this line with the surface of the cylinder gives us (x_i, y_i, z_i).

$$x_w, y_w, z_w \rightarrow (\theta, h)$$

$$= (\tan^{-1}(y_w/x_w), z_w)$$

(3) Apply the S mapping to find the point (u, v) corresponding to (θ, h).

Figure 8.6
Inverse mapping using the
shrinkwrap method.

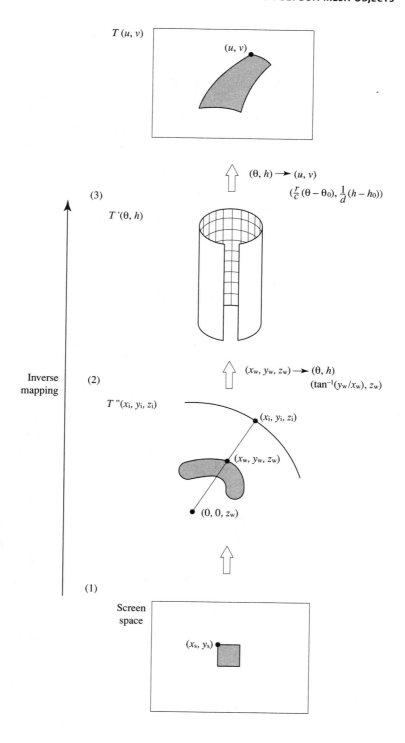

Figure 8.7 (Colour Plate) shows examples of mapping the same texture onto an object using different intermediate surfaces. The intermediate objects are a plane (equivalently no intermediate surface – the texture map is a plane), a cylinder and a sphere. The simple shape of the vase was chosen to illustrate the different distortions that each intermediate object produces. There are two points that can be made from these illustrations. First, you can choose an intermediate mapping that is appropriate to the shape of the object. A solid of revolution may be best suited, for example, to a cylinder. Second, although the method does not place any constraints on the shape of the object, the final visual effect may be deemed unsatisfactory. Usually what we mean by texture does not involve the texture pattern being subject to large geometric distortions. It is for this reason that many practical methods are interactive and involve some strategy like pre-distorting the texture map in two-dimensional space until its produces a good result when it is stuck onto the object.

8.2 Two-dimensional texture domain to bi-cubic parametric patch objects

If an object is a quadric or a cubic then surface parametrization is straightforward. In the previous section we used quadrics as intermediate surfaces exactly for this reason. If the object is a bi-cubic parametric patch, texture mapping is trivial since a parametric patch by definition already possesses (u, v) values everywhere on its surface.

The first use of texture in computer graphics was a method developed by Catmull. This technique applied to bi-cubic parametric patch models; the algorithm subdivides a surface patch in object space, and at the same time executes a corresponding subdivision in texture space. The idea is that the patch subdivision proceeds until it covers a single pixel (a standard patch rendering approach described in detail in Chapter 4). When the patch subdivision process terminates the required texture value(s) for the pixel is obtained from the area enclosed by the current level of subdivision in the texture domain. This is a straightforward technique that is easily implemented as an extension to a bi-cubic patch renderer. A variation of this method was used by Cook where object surfaces are subdivided into 'micropolygons' and flat shaded with values from a corresponding subdivision in texture space.

An example of this technique is shown in Figure 8.8 (Colour Plate). Here each patch on the teapot causes subdivision of a single texture map, which is itself a rendered version of the teapot. For each patch, the u, v values from the parameter space subdivision are used to index the texture map whose u, v values also vary between 0 and 1. This scheme is easily altered to, say, map four patches into the entire texture domain by using a scale factor of two in the u, v mapping.

Billboards

Billboard is the name given to a technique where a texture map is considered as a three-dimensional entity and placed in the scene, rather than as a map that controls the colour over the surface of an object. It is a simple technique that utilizes a two-dimensional image in a three-dimensional scene by rotating the plane of the image so that it is normal to its viewing direction (the line from the view point to its position). The idea is illustrated in Figure 8.9. Probably the most common example of this is the image of a tree which is approximately cylindrically symmetric. Such objects are impossible to render in real time and the visual effect of this trick is quite convincing providing the view vector is close to the horizontal plane in scene space. The original two-dimensional nature of the object is hardly noticeable in the two-dimensional projection, presumably because we do not have an accurate internal notion of what the projection of the tree should look like anyway. The billboard is in effect a two-dimensional object which is rotated about its y axis (for examples like the tree) through an angle which makes it normal to the view direction and translated to the appropriate position in the scene. The background texels in the billboard are set to transparent.

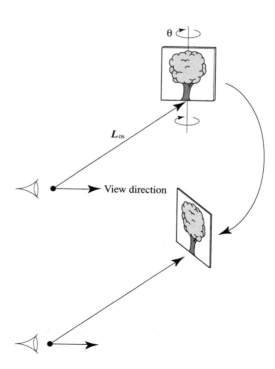

Figure 8.9
Providing the viewing direction is approximately parallel to the ground plane, objects like trees can be represented as a billboard and rotated about their y axis so that they are oriented normal to the L_{os} vector.

The modelling rotation for the billboard is given as:

$$\theta = \pi - \cos^{-1}(\boldsymbol{L}_{os} \cdot \boldsymbol{B}_n)$$

where:

$\boldsymbol{B}_n$ is the normal vector of the billboard, say $(0,0,1)$

$\boldsymbol{L}_{os}$ is the viewing direction vector from the view point to the required position of the billboard in world coordinates

Given θ and the required translation we can then construct a modelling transformation for the geometry of the billboard and transform it. Of course, this simple example will only work if the viewing direction is parallel or approximately parallel to the ground plane. When this is not true the two-dimensional nature of the billboard will be apparent.

Billboards are a special case of impostors or sprites which are essentially precomputed texture maps used to by-pass normal rendering when the view point is only changing slightly. These are described in detail in Chapter 14.

8.4   Bump mapping

Bump mapping, a technique developed by Blinn (1978), is an elegant device that enables a surface to appear as if it were wrinkled or dimpled without the need to model these depressions geometrically. Instead, the surface normal is angularly perturbed according to information given in a two-dimensional bump map and this 'tricks' a local reflection model, wherein intensity is a function mainly of the surface normal, into producing (apparent) local geometric variations on a smooth surface. The only problem with bump mapping is that because the pits or depressions do not exist in the model, a silhouette edge that appears to pass through a depression will not produce the expected cross-section. In other words the silhouette edge will follow the original geometry of the model.

It is an important technique because it appears to texture a surface in the normal sense of the word rather than modulating the colour of a flat surface. Figure 8.10 (Colour Plate) shows examples of this technique.

Texturing the surface in the rendering phase, without perturbing the geometry, by-passes serious modelling problems that would otherwise occur. If the object is polygonal the mesh would have to be fine enough to receive the perturbations from the texture map – a serious imposition on the original modelling phase, particularly if the texture is to be an option. Thus the technique converts a two-dimensional height field $B(u, v)$, called the bump map, and which represents some desired surface displacement, into appropriate perturbations of the local surface normal. When this surface normal is used in the shading equation the reflected light calculations vary as if the surface had been displaced.

Consider a point $\boldsymbol{P}(u, v)$ on a (parameterized) surface corresponding to $B(u, v)$. We define the surface normal at the point to be:

$$N = \frac{\partial P}{\partial u} \times \frac{\partial P}{\partial v}$$

$$= P_u \times P_v$$

where P_u and P_v are the partial derivatives lying in the tangent plane to the surface at point P. What we want to do is to have the same effect as displacing the point P in the direction of the surface normal at that point by an amount $B(u, v)$ – a one-dimensional analogue is shown in Figure 8.11. That is:

$$P'(u, v) = P(u, v) + B(u, v)N$$

Locally the surface would not now be as smooth as it was before because of this displacement and the normal vector N' to the 'new' surface is given by differentiating this equation:

$$N' = P'_u + P'_v$$

$$P'_u = P_u + B_u N + B(u, v)N_u$$

$$P'_v = P_v + B_v N + B(u, v)N_v$$

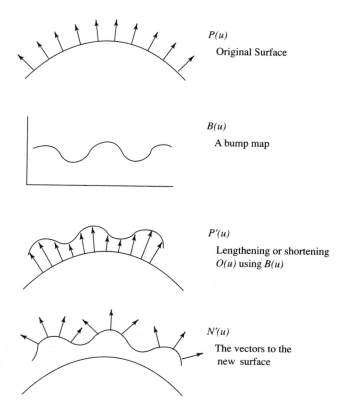

$P(u)$
Original Surface

$B(u)$
A bump map

$P'(u)$
Lengthening or shortening
$O(u)$ using $B(u)$

$N'(u)$
The vectors to the
new surface

Figure 8.11
A one-dimensional example of the stages involved in bump mapping (after Blinn (1978)).

Figure 8.12
Geometric interpretation of
bump mapping.

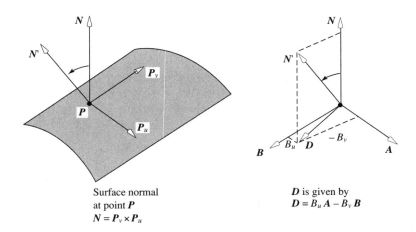

Surface normal
at point P
$N = P_v \times P_u$

D is given by
$D = B_u A - B_v B$

If B is small we can ignore the final term in each equation and we have:

$$N' = N + B_u N \times P_v + B_v P_u \times N$$

or

$$N' = N + B_u N \times P_v - B_v N \times P_u$$

$$= N + (B_u A - B_v B)$$

$$= N + D$$

Then D is a vector lying in the tangent plane that 'pulls' N into the desired orientation and is calculated from the partial derivatives of the bump map and the two vectors in the tangent plane (Figure 8.12).

8.4.1

A multi-pass technique for bump mapping

For polygon mesh objects McReynolds and Blythe (1997) define a multi-pass technique that can exploit standard texture mapping hardware facilities. To do this they split the calculation into two components as follows. The final intensity value is proportional to $N' \cdot L$ where:

$$N' \cdot L = N \cdot L + D \cdot L$$

The first component is the normal Gouraud component and the second component is found from the differential coefficient of two image projections formed by rendering the surface with the height field as a normal texture map. To do this it is necessary to transform the light vector into tangent space at each vertex of the polygon. This space is defined by N, B and T, where:

N is the vertex normal

T is the direction of increasing u (or v) in the object space coordinate system

$B = N \times T$

The normalized components of these vectors defines the matrix that transforms points into tangent space:

$$L_{TS} = \begin{bmatrix} T_X & T_Y & T_Z & 0 \\ B_X & B_Y & B_Z & 0 \\ N_X & N_Y & N_Z & 0 \\ 0 & 0 & 0 & 1 \end{bmatrix} L$$

The algorithm is as follows:

(1) The object is rendered using a normal renderer with texture mapping facilities. The texture map used is the bump map or height field.

(2) T and B are found at each vertex and the light vector transformed into tangent space.

(3) A second image is created in the same way but now the texture/vertex correspondence is shifted by small amounts in the direction of the X, Y components of L_{TS}. We now have two image projections where the height field or the bump map has been mapped onto the object and shifted with respect to the surface. If we subtract these two images we get the differential coefficient which is the required term $D \cdot L$. (Finding the differential coefficient of an image by subtraction is a standard image processing technique – see, for example, Watt and Policarpo (1998)).

(4) The object is rendered in the normal manner *without* any texture and this component is added to the subtrahend calculated in step (3) to give the final bump-mapped image.

Thus we replace the explicit bump mapping calculations with two texture mapped rendering passes, an image subtract, a Gouraud shading pass then an image added to get the final result.

8.4.2

A pre-calculation technique for bump mapping

Tangent space can also be used to facilitate a pre-calculation technique as proposed by Peercy *et al.* (1997). This depends on the fact that the perturbed normal N'_{TS} in tangent space is a function only of the surface itself and the bump map. Peercy *et al.* define this normal at each vertex in terms of three pre-calculated coefficients.

It can be shown (Peercy *et al.* 1997) that the perturbed normal vector on tangent space is given by:

$$N'_{TS} = \frac{a, b, c}{(a^2 + b^2 + c^2)^{1/2}}$$

where:

$$a = - B_u(\boldsymbol{B}.\boldsymbol{P}_v)$$

$$b = - (B_v|\boldsymbol{P}_u| - B_u(\boldsymbol{T}.\boldsymbol{P}_v))$$

$$c = |\boldsymbol{P}_u \times \boldsymbol{P}_v|$$

For each point in the bump map these points can be pre-computed and a map of perturbed normals is stored for use during rendering instead of the bump map.

8.5 Light maps

Light maps are an obvious extension to texture maps that enable lighting to be pre-calculated and stored as a two-dimensional texture map. We sample the reflected light over a surface and store this in a two-dimensional map. Thus shading reduces to indexing into a light map or a light modulated texture map. An advantage of the technique is that there is no restriction on the complexity of the rendering method used in the pre-calculation – we could, for example, use radiosity or any view-independent global illumination method to generate the light maps.

In principle light maps are similar to environment maps (see Section 8.6). In environment mapping we cache, in a two-dimensional map, all the illumination incident at a single point in the scene. With light maps we cache the reflected light from every surface in the scene in a set of two-dimensional maps.

If an accurate pre-calculation method is used then we would expect the technique to produce better quality shading and be faster than Gouraud interpolation. This means that we can incorporate shadows in the final rendering. The obvious disadvantage of the technique is that for moving objects we can only invoke a very simple lighting environment (diffuse shading with the light source at infinity). A compromise is to use dynamic shading for moving objects and assume that they do not interact, as far as shading is concerned, with static objects shaded with a light map.

Light maps can either be stored separately from texture maps, or the object's texture map can be pre-modulated by the light map. If the light map is kept as a separate entity then it can be stored at a lower resolution than the texture map because view-independent lighting, except at shadow edges, changes more slowly than texture detail. It can also be high-pass filtered which will ameliorate effects such as banding in the final image and also has the benefit of blurring shadow edges (in the event that a hard-edged shadow generation procedure has been used).

If an object is to receive a texture then we can modulate the brightness of the texture during the modelling phase so that it has the same effect as if the (unmodulated) texture colours were injected into, say, a Phong shading equation. This is called surface caching because it stores the final value required for the pixel onto which a surface point projects and because texture caching hardware is used to implement it. If this strategy is employed then the texture mapping transform and the transform that maps light samples on the surface of the object into a light map should be the same.

Light maps were first used in two-pass ray tracing (see Section 10.7) and are also used in Ward's (1994) RADIANCE renderer. Their motivation in these applications was to cache diffuse illumination and to enable the implementation of a global illumination model that would work in a reasonable time. Their more recent use in games engines has, of course, been to facilitate shading in real time.

The first problem with light maps is how do we sample and store, in a two-dimensional array, the calculated reflected light across the face of a polygon in three-dimensional space. In effect this is the reverse of texture mapping where we need a mapping from two-dimensional space into three-dimensional object space. Another problem concerns economy. For scenes of any complexity it would clearly be uneconomical to construct a light map for each polygon – rather we require many polygons to share a single light map.

Zhukov *et al.* (1998) approach the three-dimensional sampling problem by organizing polygons into structures called 'polypacks'. Polygons are projected into the world coordinate planes and collected into polypacks if their angle with a coordinate plane does not exceed some threshold (so that the maximal projection plane is selected for a polygon) and if their extent does not overlap in the projection. The world space coordinate planes are subdivided into square cells (the texels or 'lumels') and back projected onto the polygon. The image of a square cell on a polygon is a parallelogram (whose larger angle ≤ 102°). These are called patches and are the subdivided polygon elements for which the reflected light is calculated. This scheme thus samples every polygon with almost square elements storing the result in the light map (Figure 8.13).

These patches form a subdivision of the scene sufficient for the purpose of generating light maps and a single light intensity for each patch can be calculated using whatever algorithm the application demands (for example Phong shading or radiosity). After this phase is complete there exists a set of (parallelogram-shaped) samples for each polygon. These then have to be 'stuffed'

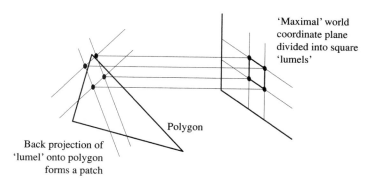

Figure 8.13
Forming a light map in the 'maximal' world coordinate plane.

'Maximal' world coordinate plane divided into square 'lumels'

Polygon

Back projection of 'lumel' onto polygon forms a patch

into the minimum number of two-dimensional light maps in each coordinate plane. Zhukov *et al.* (1998) do this by using a 'first hit decreasing' algorithm which first sorts each polygon group by the number of texels.

Another problem addressed by the authors is that the groups of samples corresponding to a polygon have to be surrounded by 'sand' texels. These are supplementary texels that do not belong to a face group but are used when bilinear interpolation is used in conjunction with a light map and prevent visual lighting artefacts appearing at the edges of polygons. Thus each texture map consists of a mixture of light texels, sand texels and unoccupied texels. Zhukov *et al.* (1998) report that for a scene consisting of 24 000 triangles (700 patches) 14 light maps of 256 × 256 texels were produced which exhibited a breakdown of texels as: 75% light texels, 15% sand texels and 10% unoccupied texels.

A direct scheme for computing light maps for scenes made up of triangles and for which we already have vertex/texture coordinate association is to use this correspondence to derive an affine transformation between texture space and object space and then use this transformation to sample the light across the face of a triangle. The algorithm is then driven from the texture map space (by scan-converting the polygon projection in texture space) and for each texel finding its corresponding point or projection on the object surface from:

$$\begin{bmatrix} x \\ y \\ z \end{bmatrix} = \begin{bmatrix} a & b & c \\ d & e & f \\ g & h & i \end{bmatrix} \begin{bmatrix} u \\ v \\ 1 \end{bmatrix}$$

where (x, y, z) is the point on the object corresponding to the texel (u, v). This transformation can be seen as a linear transformation in three-dimensional space with the texture map embedded in the $z = 1$ plane. The coefficients are found from the vertex/texture coordinate correspondence by inverting the U matrix in:

$$\begin{bmatrix} x_0 & x_1 & x_2 \\ y_0 & y_1 & y_2 \\ z_0 & z_1 & z_2 \end{bmatrix} = \begin{bmatrix} a & b & c \\ d & e & f \\ g & h & i \end{bmatrix} \begin{bmatrix} u_0 & u_1 & u_2 \\ v_0 & v_1 & v_2 \\ 1 & 1 & 1 \end{bmatrix}$$

writing this as:

$$X = AU$$

we have:

$$A = XU^{-1}$$

The inverse U^{-1} is guaranteed to exist providing the three points are non-collinear. Note that in terms of our treatment in Section 8.1 this is a forward mapping from texture space to object space. Examples of a scene lit using this technique are shown in Figure 8.14 (Colour Plate).

8.6 Environment or reflection mapping

Originally called reflection mapping and first suggested by Blinn and Newell (1976), environment mapping was consolidated into mainline rendering techniques in an important paper by Greene (1986). Environment maps are a short-cut to rendering shiny objects that reflect the environment in which they are placed. They can approximate the quality of a ray tracer for specular reflections and do this by reducing the problem of following a reflected view vector to indexing into a two-dimensional map which is no different from a conventional texture map. Thus processing costs that would be incurred in ray tracing programs are regulated to the (off-line) construction of the map(s). In this sense it is a classic partial off-line or pre-calculation technique like pre-sorting for hidden surface removal. An example of a scene and its corresponding (cubic) environment map is shown in Figure 18.8.

The disadvantages of environment mapping are:

- It is (geometrically) correct only when the object becomes small with respect to the environment that contains it. This effect is usually not noticeable in the sense that we are not disturbed by 'wrong' reflections in the curved surface of a shiny object. The extent of the problem is shown in Figure 18.9 which shows the same object ray traced and environment mapped.

- An object can only reflect the environment – not itself – and so the technique is 'wrong' for concave objects. Again this can be seen in Figure 18.9 where the reflection of the spout is apparent in the ray traced image.

- A separate map is required for each object in the scene that is to be environment mapped.

- In one common form of environment mapping (sphere mapping) a new map is required whenever the view point changes.

In this section we will examine three methods of environment mapping which are classified according to the way in which the three-dimensional environment information is mapped into two-dimensions. These are cubic, latitude–longitude and sphere mapping. (Latitude–longitude is also a spherical mapping but the term sphere mapping is now applied to the more recent form.) The general principles are shown in Figure 8.15. Figure 8.15(a) shows the conventional ray tracing paradigm which we replace with the scheme shown in Figure 8.15(b). This involves mapping the reflected view vector into a two-dimensional environment map. We calculate the reflected view vector as (Section 1.3.5):

$$\boldsymbol{R}_v = 2(\boldsymbol{N}\cdot\boldsymbol{V})\boldsymbol{N} - \boldsymbol{V} \qquad [8.2]$$

Figure 8.15(c) shows that, in practice, for a single pixel we should consider the reflection beam, rather than a single vector, and the area subtended by the beam in the map is then filtered for the pixel value. A reflection beam originates either

Figure 8.15
Environment mapping
(a) The ray tracing model –
that part of the environment
reflected at point **P** is
determined by reflecting the
view ray **R**ᵥ. (b) We try to
achieve the same effect as
in (a) by using a function
of **R**ᵥ to index into a two-
dimensional map. (c) A pixel
subtends a reflection beam.

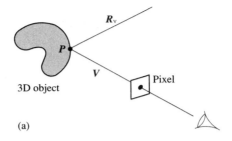

(a)

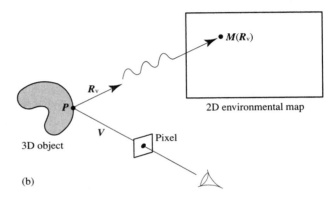

2D environmental map

(b)

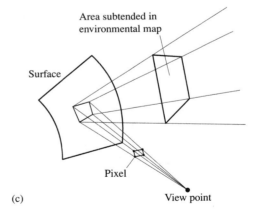

(c)

from four pixel corners if we are indexing the map for each pixel, or from polygon vertices if we are using a fast (approximate) scheme. An important point to
note here is that the area intersected in the environment map is a function of
the curvature of the projected pixel area on the object surface. However, because
we are now using texture mapping techniques we can employ pre-filtering anti-
aliasing methods (see Section 8.8).

In real time polygon mesh rendering, we can calculate reflected view vectors only at the vertices and use linear interpolation as we do in conventional texture mapping. Because we expect to see fine detail in the resulting image, the quality of this approach depends strongly on the polygon size.

In effect an environment map caches the incident illumination from all directions at a single point in the environment with the object that is to receive the mapping removed from the scene. Reflected illumination at the surface of an object is calculated from this incident illumination by employing the aforementioned geometric approximation – that the size of the object itself can be considered to approach the point and a simple BRDF which is a perfect specular term – the reflected view vector. It is thus a view-independent pre-calculation technique.

8.6.1 Cubic mapping

As we have already implied, environment mapping is a two-stage process that involves – as a pre-process – the construction of the map. Cubic mapping is popular because the maps can easily be constructed using a conventional rendering system. The environment map is in practice six maps that form the surfaces of a cube (Figure 8.16). An example of an environment map is shown in Figure 18.8. The view point is fixed at the centre of the object to receive the environment map, and six views are rendered. Consider a view point fixed at the centre of a room. If we consider the room to be empty then these views would contain the

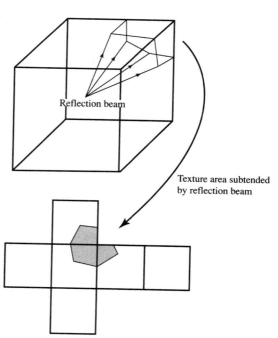

Reflection beam

Texture area subtended
by reflection beam

Figure 8.16
Cubic environment
mapping: the reflection
beam can range over
more than one map.

four walls and the floor and ceiling. One of the problems of a cubic map is that if we are considering a reflection beam formed by pixel corners, or equivalently by the reflected view vectors at a polygon vertex, the beam can index into more than one map (Figure 18.16). In that case the polygon can be subdivided so that each piece is constrained to a single map.

With cubic maps we need an algorithm to determine the mapping from the three-dimensional view vector into one or more two-dimensional maps. (With the techniques described in the next section this mapping algorithm is replaced by a simple calculation.) If we consider that the reflected view vector is in the same coordinate frame as the environment map cube (the case if the view were constructed by pointing the (virtual or real) camera along the world axes in both directions), then the mapping is as follows.

For a single reflection vector:

(1) Find the face it intersects – the map number. This involves a simple comparison of the components of the normalized reflected view vector against the (unit) cube extent which is centred on the origin.

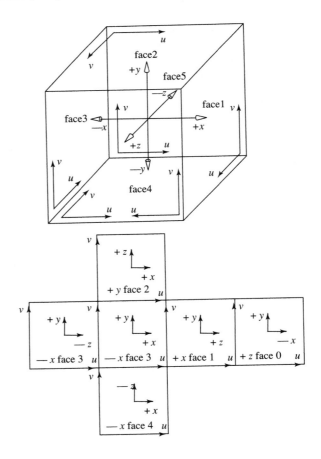

Figure 8.17
Cubic environment map convention.

(2) Map the components into (u, v) coordinates. For example, a point (x, y, z) intersecting the face normal to the negative z axis is given by:

$$u = x + 0.5$$
$$v = -z + 0.5$$

for the convention scheme shown in Figure 8.17.

One of the applications of cubic environment maps (or indeed any environment map method) that became popular in the 1980s is to 'matte' an animated computer graphics object into a real environment. In that case the environment map is constructed from photographs of a real environment and the (specular) computer graphics object can be matted into the scene, and appear to be part of it as it moves and reflects its surroundings.

Sphere mapping

The first use of environment mapping was by Blinn and Newell (1976) wherein a sphere rather than a cube was the basis of the method used. The environment map consisted of a latitude–longitude projection and the reflected view vector, R_v, was mapped into (u, v) coordinates as:

$$u = \frac{1}{2}\left(1 + \frac{1}{\pi} \tan^{-1}\left(\frac{R_{vy}}{R_{vx}}\right)\right) \quad -\pi < \tan^{-1} < \pi$$

$$v = \frac{R_{vz} + 1}{2}$$

The main problem with this simple technique is the singularities at the poles. In the polar area small changes in the direction of the reflection vector produce large changes in (u, v) coordinates. As $R_{vz} \to \pm 1$, both R_{vx} and $R_{vy} \to 0$ and R_{vy}/R_{vx} becomes ill-defined. Equivalently, as $v \to 1$ or 0 the behaviour of u starts to break down causing visual disturbances on the surface. This can be ameliorated by modulating the horizontal resolution of the map with $\sin \theta$ (where θ is the elevation angle in polar coordinates).

An alternative sphere mapping form (Haeberli and Segal 1993; Miller et $al.$ 1998) consists of a circular map which is the orthographic projection of the reflection of the environment as seen in the surface of a perfect mirror sphere (Figure 8.18). Clearly such a map can be generated by ray tracing from the view plane. (Alternatively a photograph can be taken of a shiny sphere.) Although the map caches the incident illumination at the reference point by using an orthographic projection it can be used to generate, to within the accuracy of the process, a normal perspective projection.

To generate the map we proceed as follows. We trace a parallel ray bundle – one ray for each texel (u, v) and reflect each ray from the sphere. The point on the sphere at the point hit by the ray from (u, v) is $\mathbf{P}$, where:

Figure 8.18
Constructing a spherical
map by ray tracing from the
map texels onto a reflective
sphere.

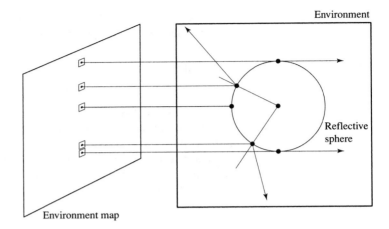

$$P_x = u \qquad P_y = v$$
$$P_z = (1.0 - P_x^2 - P_y^2)^{1/2}$$

This is also the normal to the sphere at the hit point and we can compute the reflected vector using Equation 8.2.

To index into the map we reflect the view vector from the object (either for each pixel or for each polygon vertex) and calculate the map coordinates as:

$$u = \frac{R_x}{m} + \frac{1}{2}$$

$$v = \frac{R_y}{m} + \frac{1}{2}$$

where:

$$m = 2(R_x^2 + R_y^2 + (R_z + 1)^2)^{1/2}$$

8.6.3

Environment mapping: comparative points

Sphere mapping overcomes the main limitation of cubic maps which require, in general, access to a number of the face maps, and is to be preferred when speed is important. However, both types of sphere mapping suffer more from non-uniform sampling than cubic mapping. Refer to Figure 8.19 which attempts to demonstrate this point. In all three cases we consider that the environment map is sampling incoming illumination incident on the surface of the unit sphere. The illustration shows the difference between the areas on the surface of the sphere sampled by a texel in the environment map. Sampling only approaches uniformity when the viewing direction during the rendering phase aligns with the viewing direction from which the map was computed. For this reason this type of spherical mapping is considered to be view dependent and a new map has to be computed when the view direction changes.

Figure 8.19
Sampling the surface
of a sphere. (a) Cubic
perspective: under-sampling
at the centre of the map
(equator and meridian)
compared to the corners.
(b) Mercator or
latitude–longitude: severe
over-sampling at edges of
the map in the *v* direction
(poles). (c) Orthographic:
severe under-sampling at
the edges of the map in the
u direction (equator).

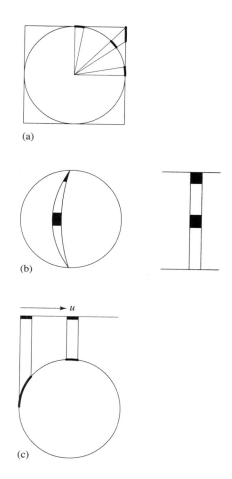

(a)

(b)

(c)

8.6.4

Surface properties and environment mapping

So far we have restricted the discussion to geometry and assumed that the object
which is environment mapped possesses a perfect mirror surface and the map is
indexed by a single reflected view ray. What if we want to use objects with
reflecting properties other than that of a perfect mirror. Using the normal Phong
local reflection model, we can consider two components – a diffuse component
plus a specular component – and construct two maps. The diffuse map is
indexed by the surface normal at the point of interest and the specular map is
indexed by the reflected view vector. The relative contribution from each map is
determined by diffuse and specular reflection coefficients just as in standard
Phong shading. This enables us to render objects as if they were Phong shaded
but with the addition of reflected environment detail which can be blurred to

simulate a non-smooth surface. (Note that this approximates an effect that would otherwise have to be rendered using distributed ray tracing.)

This technique was first reported by Miller and Hoffman (1984). (This reference is to SIGGRAPH course notes. These, particularly the older ones, are generally unavailable and we only refer to them if the material does not, as far as we know, appear in any other publication) and it is their convention that we follow here. Both the diffuse and specular maps are generated by processing the environment map. Thus we can view the procedure as a two-step process where the first step – the environment map – encodes the illumination at a point due to the scene with the object removed and the second step filters the map to encode information about the surface of the object.

Miller and Hoffman (1984) generate the diffuse map from the following definition:

$$D(\mathbf{N}) = \frac{\sum_{\mathbf{L}} I(\mathbf{L}) \times \text{Area}(\mathbf{L}) \times f_d\,(\mathbf{N}\cdot\mathbf{L})}{4\pi}$$

where:

$\mathbf{N}$ is the surface normal at the point of interest

$I(\mathbf{L})$ is the environment map as a function of $\mathbf{L}$ the incident direction to which the entry I in the map corresponds

Area is the area on the surface of the unit sphere associated with $\mathbf{L}$

f_d is the diffuse convolution function:

$f_d(x) = k_d\, x$ for $x > 0$ and $f_d(x) = 0$ for $x \le 0$

k_d is the diffuse reflection coefficient that weights the contribution of $D(\mathbf{N})$ in summing the diffuse and specular contributions

Thus for each value of $\mathbf{N}$ we sum over all values of $\mathbf{L}$ the area-weighted dot product or Lambertian term.

The specular map is defined as:

$$S(\mathbf{R}) = \frac{\sum_{\mathbf{L}} I(\mathbf{L}) \times \text{Area}(\mathbf{L}) \times f_s\,(\mathbf{R}\cdot\mathbf{L})}{4\pi}$$

where:

$\mathbf{R}$ is the reflected view vector

f_s is the specular convolution function;

$f_s(x) = k_s\, x^n$ for $x > 0$ and $f_s(x) = 0$ for $x \le 0$

k_s is the specular reflection coefficient

(Note that if f_s is set to unity the surface is a perfect mirror and the environment map is unaltered.)

The reflected intensity at a surface point is thus:

$D(\mathbf{N}) + S(\mathbf{R})$

8.7   Three-dimensional texture domain techniques

We have seen in preceding sections that there are many difficulties associated with mapping a two-dimensional texture onto the surface of a three-dimensional object. The reasons for this are:

(1) Two-dimensional texture mapping based on a surface coordinate system can produce large variations in the compression of the texture that reflect a corresponding variation in the curvature of the surface.

(2) Attempting to continuously texture map the surface of an object possessing a non-trivial topology can quickly become very awkward. Textural continuity across surface elements that can be of a different type and can connect together in any ad hoc manner is problematic to maintain.

Three-dimensional texture mapping neatly circumvents these problems since the only information required to assign a point a texture value is its position in space. Assigning an object a texture just involves evaluating a three-dimensional texture function at the surface points of the object. A fairly obvious requirement of this technique is that the three-dimensional texture field is procedurally generated. Otherwise the memory requirements, particularly if three-dimensional mip-mapping is used, become exorbitant. Also, it is inherently inefficient to construct an entire cubic field of texture when we only require these values at the surface of the object.

Given a point (x, y, z) on the surface of an object, the colour is defined as $T(x, y, z)$, where T is the value of texture field. That is, we simply use the identity mapping (possibly in conjunction with a scaling):

$$u = x \quad v = y \quad w = z$$

where:

(u, v, w) is a coordinate in the texture field

This can be considered analogous to actually sculpting or carving an object out of a block of material. The colour of the object is determined by the intersection of its surface with the texture field. The method was reported simultaneously by Perlin (1985) and Peachey (1985) wherein the term 'solid texture' was coined.

The disadvantage of the technique is that although it eliminates mapping problems, the texture patterns themselves are limited to whatever definition that you can think up. This contrasts with a two-dimensional texture map; here any texture can be set up by using, say, a frame-grabbed image from a television camera.

8.7.1   Three-dimensional noise

A popular class of procedural texturing techniques all have in common the fact that they use a three-dimensional, or spatial, noise function as a basic modelling primitive. These techniques, the most notable of which is the simulation of turbulence, can produce a surprising variety of realistic, natural-looking texture effects. In this section we will concern ourselves with the issues involved in the algorithmic generation of the basic primitive – solid noise.

Perlin (1985) was the first to suggest this application of noise, defining a function *noise*() that takes a three-dimensional position as its input and returns a single scalar value. This is called model-directed synthesis – we evaluate the noise function only at the point of interest. Ideally the function should possess the following three properties:

(1) Statistical invariance under rotation.

(2) Statistical invariance under translation.

(3) A narrow bandpass limit in frequency.

The first two conditions ensure that the noise function is controllable – that is, no matter how we move or orientate the noise function in space, its general appearance is guaranteed to stay the same. The third condition enables us to sample the noise function without aliasing. Whilst an insufficiently sampled noise function may not produce noticeable defects in static images, if used in animation applications, incorrectly sampled noise will produce a shimmering or bubbling effect.

Perlin's method of generating noise is to define an integer lattice, or a set of points in space, situated at locations (i, j, k) where i, j and k are all integers. Each point of the lattice has a random number associated with it. This can be done either by using a simple look-up table or, as Perlin (1985) suggests, via a hashing function to save space. The value of the noise function, at a point in space coincident with a lattice point, is just this random number. For points in space not on the lattice – in general (u, v, w) – the noise value can be obtained by linear interpolation from the nearby lattice points. If, using this method, we generate a solid noise function $T(u, v, w)$ then it will tend to exhibit directional (axis aligned) coherences. These can be ameliorated by using cubic interpolation but this is far more expensive and the coherences still tend to be visible. Alternative noise generation methods that eliminate this problem are to be found in Lewis (1989); however, it is worth bearing in mind that the entire solid noise function is sampled by the surface and usually undergoes a transformation (it is modulated, for example, to simulate turbulence) and this in itself may be enough to eliminate the coherences.

8.7.2 Simulating turbulence

A single piece of noise can be put to use to simulate a remarkable number of effects. By far the most versatile of its applications is the use of the so-called turbulence function, as defined by Perlin, which takes a position x and returns a turbulent scalar value. It is written in terms of the progression, a one-dimensional version of which would be defined as:

$$\text{turbulence}(x) = \sum_{i=0}^{k} \text{abs}\left(\frac{\text{noise } (2^i x)}{2^i}\right)$$

The summation is truncated at k which is the smallest integer satisfying:

$$\frac{1}{2^{k+1}} < \text{the size of a pixel}$$

The truncation band limits the function ensuring proper anti-aliasing. Consider the difference between the first two terms in the progression, noise (x) and noise $(2x)/2$. The noise function in the latter term will vary twice as fast as the first – it has twice the frequency – and will contain features that are half the size of the first. Moreover, its contribution to the final value for the turbulence is also scaled by one-half. At each scale of detail the amount of noise added into the series is proportional to the scale of detail of the noise and inversely proportional to the frequency of the noise. This is self-similarity and is analogous to the self-similarity obtained through fractal subdivision, except that this time the sub-division drives not displacement, but octaves of noise, producing a function that exhibits the same noisy behaviour over a range of scales. That this function should prove so useful is best seen from the point of view of signal analysis, which tells us that the power spectrum of *turbulence*() obeys a $1/f$ power law, thereby loosely approximating the $1/f^2$ power law of Brownian motion.

The turbulence function in isolation only represents half the story, however. Rendering the turbulence function directly results in a homogeneous pattern that could not be described as naturalistic. This is due to the fact that most textures which occur naturally, contain some non-homogeneous structural features and so cannot be simulated by turbulence alone. Take marble, for example, which has easily distinguished veins of colour running through it that were made turbulent before the marble solidified during an earlier geological era. In the light of this fact we can identify two distinct stages in the process of simulating turbulence, namely:

(1) Representation of the basic, first order, structural features of a texture through some basic functional form. Typically the function is continuous and contains significant variations in its first derivatives.

(2) Addition of second and higher order detail by using turbulence to perturb the parameters of the function.

The classic example, as first described by Perlin, is the turbulation of a sine wave to give the appearance of marble. Unperturbed, the colour veins running through the marble are given by a sine wave passing through a colour map. For a sine wave running along the x axis we write:

$$\text{marble}(x) = \text{marble\_colour } (\sin(x))$$

The colour map *marble_colour*() maps a scalar input to an intensity. Visualizing this expression, Figure 8.20(a) is a two-dimensional slice of marble rendered with the colour spline given in Figure 8.20(b). Next we add turbulence:

(a)

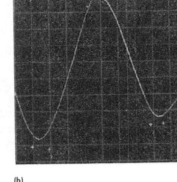

(b)

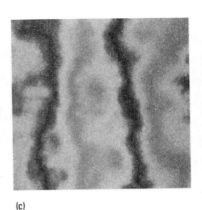

(c)

Figure 8.20
Simulating marble.
(a) Unturbulated slice
obtained by using the spline
shown in (b). (b) Colour
spline used to produce (a).
(c) Marble section obtained
by turbulating the slice
shown in (a).

$$\text{marble}(x) = \text{marble\_colour}(\sin(x + \text{turbulence}(x)))$$

to give us Figure 8.20(c), a convincing simulation of marble texture. Figure 8.21 (Colour Plate) shows the effect in three dimensions.

Of course, use of the turbulence function need not be restricted to modulate just the colour of an object. Any parameter that affects the appearance of an object can be turbulated. Oppenheimer (1986) turbulates a sawtooth function to bump map the ridges of bark on a tree. Turbulence can drive the transparency of objects such as clouds. Clouds can be modelled by texturing an opacity map onto a sphere that is concentric with the earth. The opacity map can be created with a paint program; clouds are represented as white blobs with soft edges that fade into complete transparency. These edges become turbulent after perturbation of the texture coordinates. In an extension to his earlier work, Perlin (1989) uses turbulence to volumetrically render regions of space rather than just evaluating texture at the surface of an object. Solid texture is used to modulate the geometry of an object as well as its appearance. Density modulation functions that specify the soft regions of objects are turbulated and rendered using a ray marching algorithm. A variety of applications are described, including erosion, fire and fur.

Three-dimensional texture and animation

The turbulence function can be defined over time as well as space simply by adding an extra dimension representing time, to the noise integer lattice. So the lattice points will now be specified by the indices (i, j, k, l) enabling us to extend the parameter list to noise (x, t) and similarly for turbulence (x, t). Internal to these procedures the time axis is not treated any differently from the three spatial axes.

For example, if we want to simulate fire, the first thing that we do is to try to represent its basic form functionally, that is, a 'flame shape'. The completely ad hoc nature of this functional sculpting is apparent here. The final form decided on was simply that which after experimentation gave the best results. We shall work in two space due to the expense of the three-dimensional volumetric approach referred to at the end of the last section.

A flame region is defined in the xy plane by the rectangle with minimax co-ordinates $(-b, 0)$, (b, h). Within this region the flame's colour is given by:

$$\text{flame}(x) = (1 - y/h) \, \text{flame\_colour}(\text{abs}(x/b))$$

This is shown schematically in Figure 8.22 (Colour Plate). *Flame_colour* (x) consists of three separate colour splines that map a scalar value x to a colour vector. Each of the R, G, B splines have a maximum intensity at $x = 0$ which corresponds to the centre of the flame and a fade-off to zero intensity at $x = 1$. The green and blue splines go to zero faster than the red. The colour returned by *flame_colour*() is weighted according to its height from the base of the flame to get an appropriate variation along y. The flame is rendered by applying *flame*() to colour a rectangular polygon that covers the region of the flames definition. The opacity of the polygon is also textured by using a similar functional construction. Figure 8.22 also shows the turbulated counterpart obtained by introducing the turbulence function thus:

$$\text{flame}(x, t) = (1 - y/h) \, \text{flame\_colour}(\text{abs}(x/b) + \text{turbulence}(x, t)$$

To animate the flame we simply render successive slices of noise which are per-pendicular to the time axis and equispaced by an amount corresponding to the frame interval. It is as if we are translating the polygon along the time axis. However, mere translation in time is not enough, recognizable detail in the flame, though changing shape with time, remained curiously static in space. This is because there is a general sense of direction associated with a flame, con-vection sends detail upwards. This was simulated, and immediately gave better results, by moving the polygon down in y as well as through time, as shown in Figure 8.23. The final construction is thus:

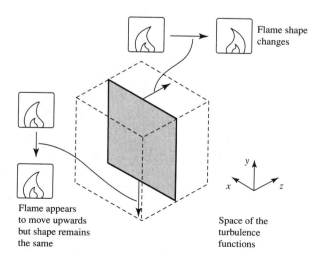

Figure 8.23
Animating turbulence for a two-dimensional object.

Flame shape changes

Flame appears to move upwards but shape remains the same

Space of the turbulence functions

flame$(x, t) = (1 - y/h)$flame_colour(abs(x/b)+turbulence$(x+(0, t\Delta y, 0), t)$)

where Δy is the distance moved in y by the polygon relative to the noise per unit time.

8.7.4 Three-dimensional light maps

In principle there is no reason why we cannot have three-dimensional light maps – the practical restriction is the vast memory resources that would be required. In the event that it is possible we have a method of caching the reflected light at every point in the scene. We use any view-independent rendering method and assign the calculated light intensity at point (x, y, z) in object space to $T(x, y, z)$. It is interesting to now compare our pre-calculation mapping methods.

With environment mapping we cache all the incoming illumination at a *single* point in object space in a two-dimensional map which is labelled by the direction of the incoming light at the point. A reflected view vector is then used to retrieve the reflected light directed towards the user. These are normally used for perfect specular surfaces and give us fast view-dependent effects.

With two-dimensional light maps we cache the reflected light for each surface in the scene in a set of two-dimensional maps. Indexing into these maps during the rendering phase depends on the method that was used to sample three-dimensional object space. We use these to cache view-independent non-dynamic lighting.

With three-dimensional light maps we store reflected light at a point in a three-dimensional structure that represents object space. Three-dimensional light maps are a subset of light fields (see Chapter 16).

8.8 Anti-aliasing and texture mapping

As we have discussed in the introduction to this chapter, artefacts are extremely problematic in texture mapping and most textures produce visible artefacts unless the method is integrated with an anti-aliasing procedure. Defects are highly noticeable, particularly in texture that exhibits coherence or periodicity, as soon as the predominant spatial frequency in the texture pattern approaches the dimension of a pixel. (The classic example of this effect is shown in Figure 8.3.) Artefacts generated by texture mapping are not well handled by the common anti-aliasing method – such as supersampling – and because of this standard two-dimensional texture mapping procedures usually incorporate a specific anti-aliasing technique.

Anti-aliasing in texture mapping is difficult because, to do it properly, we need to find the pre-image of a pixel and sum weighted values of $T(u, v)$ that fall within the extent of the pre-image to get a single texture intensity for the pixel. Unfortunately the shape of the pre-image changes from pixel to pixel and this filtering process consequently becomes expensive. Refer again to Figure 8.2. This shows that when we are considering a pixel its pre-image in texture space is, in general, a curvilinear quadrilateral, because the net effect of the texture mapping and perspective mapping is of a non-linear transformation. The figure also shows, for the diagonal band, texture for which, unless this operation is performed or approximated, erroneous results will occur. In particular, if the texture map is merely sampled at the inverse mapping of the pixel centre then the sampled intensity may be correct if the inverse image size of the pixel is sufficiently small, but in general it will be wrong.

In the context of Figure 8.24(a), anti-aliasing means approximating the integration shown in the figure. An approximate, but visually successful, method ignores the shape but not the size or extent of the pre-image and pre-calculates all the required filtering operations. This is mip-mapping invented by Williams (1983) and probably the most common anti-aliasing method developed specifically for texture mapping. His method is based on pre-calculation and an assumption that the inverse pixel image is reasonably close to a square. Figure 8.24(b) shows the pixel pre-image approximated by a square. It is this approximation that enables the anti-aliasing or filtering operation to be pre-calculated. In fact there are two problems. The first is more common and is known as compression or minification. This occurs when an object becomes small in screen space and consequently a pixel has a large pre-image in texture space. Figure 8.24(c) shows this situation. Many texture elements (sometimes called 'texels') need to be mapped into a single pixel. The other problem is called magnification. Here an object becomes very close to the viewer and only part of the object may occupy the whole of screen space, resulting in pixel pre-images that have less area than one texel (Figure 8.24(d)). Mip-mapping deals with compression and some elaboration to mip-mapping is usually required for the magnification problem.

Figure 8.24
Mip-mapping approximations. (a) The pre-image of a pixel is a curvilinear quadrilateral in texture space.
(b) A pre-image can be approximated by a square.
(c) Compression is required when a pixel maps onto many texels.
(d) Magnification is required when a pixel maps onto less than one texel.

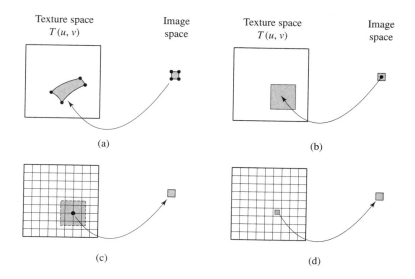

In mip-mapping, instead of a texture domain comprising a single image, Williams uses many images, all derived by averaging down the original image to successively lower resolutions. In other word they form a set of pre-filtered texture maps. Each image in the sequence is exactly half the resolution of the previous. Figure 8.25 shows an approximation to the idea. An object near to the viewer, and large in screen space, selects a single texel from a high-resolution map. The same object further away from the viewer and smaller in screen space selects a single texel from a low-resolution map. An appropriate map is selected by a parameter D. Figure 8.26 (Colour Plate) shows the mip-map used in Figure 8.8.

In a low-resolution version of the image each texel represents the average of a number of texels from the previous map. By a suitable choice of D, an image at appropriate resolution is selected and the filtering cost remains constant – the many texels to one pixel cost problem being avoided. The centre of the pixel is mapped into that map determined by D and this single value is used. In this way the original texture is filtered and, to avoid discontinuities between the images at varying resolutions, different levels are also blended. Blending between levels occurs when D is selected. The images are discontinuous in resolution but D is a continuous parameter. Linear interpolation is carried out from the two nearest levels.

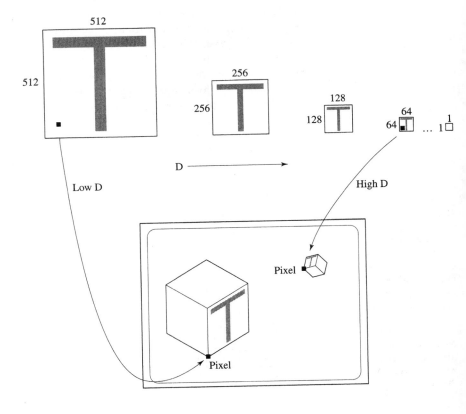

Figure 8.25
Showing the principle of mip-mapping.

Williams selects D from:

$$D = \text{max\_of}\left(\left(\left(\frac{\partial u}{\partial x}\right)^2 + \left(\frac{\partial v}{\partial x}\right)^2\right)^{1/2}, \left(\left(\frac{\partial u}{\partial y}\right)^2 + \left(\frac{\partial v}{\partial y}\right)^2\right)^{1/2}\right)$$

where ∂u and ∂v are the original dimensions of the pre-image in texture space and $\partial x = \partial y = 1$ for a square pixel.

A 'correct' or accurate estimation of D is important. If D is too large then the image will look blurred, too small and aliasing artefacts will still be visible. Detailed practical methods for determining depending on the mapping context are given in Watt and Watt (1992).

In a theoretical sense the magnification problem does not exist. Ideally we would like mip-maps that can be used at any level of detail, but in practice, storage limitations restrict the highest resolution mask to, say, 512×512 texels. This problem does not seem to have been addressed in the literature and the following two approaches are supplied by Silicon Graphics for their workstation family. Silicon Graphics suggest two solutions. First, to simply extrapolate beyond the highest resolution mip-map, and a more elaborate procedure that extracts separate texture information into low and high frequency components.

Extrapolation is defined as:

LOD(+1) = LOD(0) + (LOD(0) − LOD(−1))

where LOD (level of detail) represents mip-maps as follows:

LOD(+1) is the extrapolated mip-map
LOD(0) is the highest resolution stored mip-map
LOD(−1) is the next highest resolution stored mip-map

This operation derives an extrapolated mip-map of blocks of 4×4 pixels over which there is no variation. However, the magnification process preserves edges – hence the name.

Extrapolation works best when high frequency information is correlated with low frequency structural information, that is when the high frequency information represents edges in the texture. For example, consider that texture pattern is made up of block letters. Extrapolation will blur/magnify the interior of the letters, while keeping the edges sharp.

When high frequency information is not correlated with low frequency information, extrapolation causes blurring. This occurs with texture that tends to vary uniformly throughout, for example wood grain. Silicon Graphics suggest separating the low and high frequency information and converting a high resolution (unstorable at, say, $2K \times 2K$) into a 512×512 map that stores low frequency or structural information and a 256×256 map that stores high frequency detail. This separation can be achieved accurately using classical filtering techniques. Alternatively a space domain procedure is as follows:

(1) Make a 512×512 low frequency map by simply re-sampling the original $2K \times 2K$ map.

(2) Make the 256 × 256 detail mask as follows:

(i) Select a 256 × 256 window from the original map that contains representative high frequency texture.

(ii) Re-sample this to 64 × 64 and re-scale to 256 × 256 resulting in a blurred version of the original 256 × 256 map.

(iii) Subtract the blurred map from the original, adding a bias to make the subtrahend image unsigned. This results in a 256 × 256 high frequency.

Now when magnification is required a mix of the 512 × 512 low resolution texture with the high resolution detail is used.

8.9 Interactive techniques in texture mapping

One of the main problems in designing a conventional two-dimensional texture map is the visualization of the result on the rendered object. Say an artist or a designer is creating a texture map by painting directly in the two-dimensional *uv* space of the map. We know that the distortion of the map, when it is 'stuck' on the object is both a function of the shape of the object and the mapping method that is used. To design a texture interactively the artist needs to see the final rendered object and have some intuition of the mapping mechanism so that he can predict the effect of changes made to the texture map.

We will now describe two interactive techniques. In the first the designer paints in *uv* or texture space. The second attempts to make the designer think that he is painting directly on the object in 3D world space.

The first technique is extremely simple and was evolved to texture animals/objects that exhibit a plane of symmetry. It is simply an interactive version of two-part texture mapping with a plane as the intermediate object (see Section 8.1.2). The overall idea is shown in Figure 8.27. The animal model is enclosed in a bounding box. The texture map $T(u, v)$ is then 'stuck' on the two faces of the box using the 'minimax' coordinates of the box and points in $T(u, v)$ are projected onto the object using a parallel projection, with projectors normal to the plane of symmetry.

The second technique is to allow the artist to interact directly with the rendered version on the screen. The artist applies the texture using an interactive device simulating a brush and the effect on the screen is as if the painter was applying paint directly to the 3D object. It is easy to see the advantages of such a method by looking first at how it differs from a normal 2D paint program which basically enables a user to colour selected pixels on the screen.

Say we have a sphere (circle in screen space). With a normal paint program, if we selected, say, the colour green and painted the sphere, then unless we explicitly altered the colour, the sphere's projection would be filled with the selected uniform green colour. However, the idea of using a paint interaction in object space is that as you apply the green paint its colour changes according to the application of the Phong shading equation, and if the paint were gloss a specular highlight would appear. Extending the idea to texture mapping means

Figure 8.27
Interactive texture mapping
– painting in $T(u,v)$ space.
(a) Texture is painted
using an interactive paint
program. (b) Using the
object's bounding box,
the texture map points are
projected onto the object.
All projectors are parallel to
each other and normal to
the bounding box face. (c)
The object is rendered, the
'distortion' visualized and
the artist repeats the cycle if
necessary.

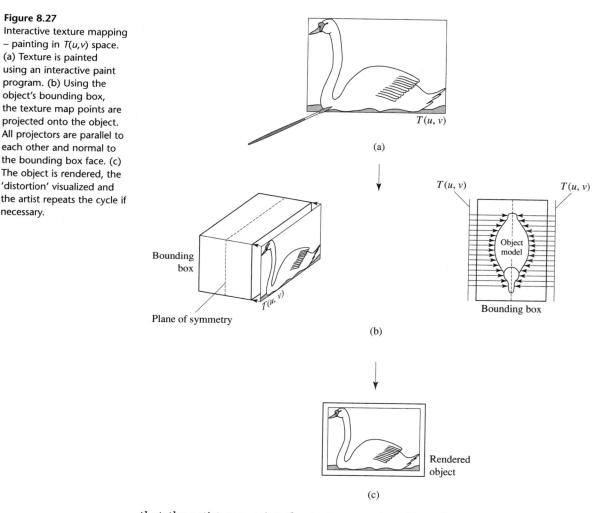

that the artist can paint the texture on the object directly and the program, reversing the normal texture mapping procedure, can derive the texture map from the object. Once the process is complete, new views of the object can be rendered and texture mapped in the normal way.

This approach requires a technique that identifies, from the screen pixel that is being pointed to, the corresponding point on the object surface. In the method described by Hanrahan and Haeberli (1990) an auxiliary frame buffer, known as an item buffer, is used. Accessing this buffer with the coordinates of the screen cursor gives a pointer to the position on the object surface and the corresponding (u, v) coordinate values for the texture map. Clearly we need an object representation where the surface is everywhere parametrized and Hanrahan and Haeberli (1990) divide the object surface into a large number of micropolygons. The overall idea is illustrated in Figure 8.28.

Figure 8.28
Iterative texture mapping –
painting in object space.

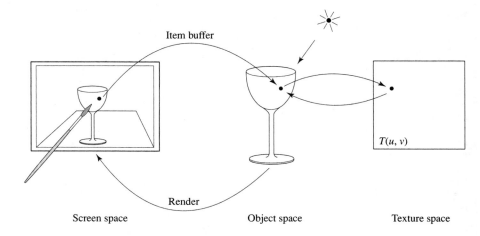

Item buffer

Render

Screen space   Object space   Texture space

$T(u, v)$

Geometric shadows

9.1 **Properties of shadows used in computer graphics**

9.2 **Simple shadows on a ground plane**

9.3 **Shadow algorithms**

Introduction

This chapter deals with the topic of 'geometric' shadows or algorithms that calculate the shape of an area in shadow but only guess at its reflected light intensity. This restriction has long been tolerated in mainstream rendering; the rationale presumably being that it is better to have a shadow with a guessed intensity than to have no shadow at all.

Shadows like texture mapping are commonly handled by using an empirical add-on algorithm. They are pasted into the scene like texture maps. The other parallel with texture maps is that the easiest algorithm to use computes a map for each light source in the scene, known as a shadow map. The map is accessed during rendering just as a texture map is referenced to find out if a pixel is in shadow or not. Like the Z-buffer algorithm in hidden surface removal, this algorithm is easy to implement and has become a pseudo-standard. Also like the Z-buffer algorithm it trades simplicity against high memory cost.

Shadows are important in scenes. A scene without shadows looks artificial. They give clues concerning the scene, consolidate spatial relationships between objects and give information on the position of the light source. To compute shadows completely we need knowledge both of their shape and the light intensity inside them. An area of the scene in shadow is not completely bereft of light. It is simply not subject to direct illumination, but receives indirect illumination from another nearby object. Thus shadow intensity can only be calculated taking this into account and this means using a global illumination model such as radiosity. In this algorithm (see Chapter 11) shadow areas are treated no differently from any other area in the scene and the shadow intensity is a light intensity, reflected from a surface, like any other.

Shadows are a function of the lighting environment. They can be hard edged or soft edged and contain both an umbra and a penumbra area. The relative size of the umbra/penumbra is a function of the size and the shape of the light source and its distance from the object (Figure 9.1). The umbra is that part of a shadow that is completely cut off from the light source, whereas the penumbra is an area that receives some light from the source. A penumbra surrounds an umbra and there is always a gradual change in intensity from a penumbra to an umbra. In computer graphics, if we are not modelling illumination sources, then we usually consider point light sources at large distances, and assume in the simplest case that objects produce umbrae with sharp edges. This is still only an approximation. Even although light from a large distance produces almost parallel rays, there is still light behind the object due to diffraction and the shadow grades off. This effect also varies over the distance a shadow is thrown. These effects, that determine the quality of a shadow, enable us to infer information

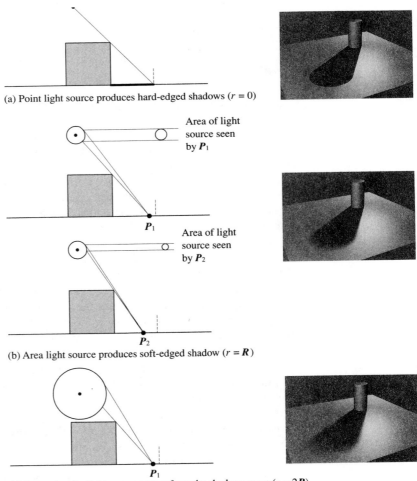

(a) Point light source produces hard-edged shadows ($r = 0$)

Area of light source seen by P_1

P_1

Area of light source seen by P_2

P_2

(b) Area light source produces soft-edged shadow ($r = R$)

P_1

(c) Increasing the light source area softens the shadows more ($r = 2R$)

Figure 9.1
Shadows cast by spherical light sources.

concerning the nature of the light source and they are clearly important to us as human beings perceiving a three-dimensional environment. For example, the shadows that we see outdoors depend on the time of day and whether the sky is overcast or not.

9.1 Properties of shadows used in computer graphics

A number of aspects of shadows are exploited in the computer generation of the phenomenon. These are:

- A shadow from polygon *A* that falls on polygon *B* due to a point light source can be calculated by projecting polygon *A* onto the plane that contains polygon *B*. The position of the point light source is used as the centre of projection.

- No shadows are seen if the view point is coincident with the (single) light source. An equivalent form of this statement is that shadows can be considered to be areas hidden from the light source, implying that modified hidden surface algorithms can be used to solve the shadow problem.

- If the light source, or sources, are point sources then there is no penumbra to calculate and the shadow has a hard edge.

- For static scenes, shadows are fixed and do not change as the view point changes. If the relative position of objects and light sources change, the shadows have to be re-calculated. This places a high overhead on three-dimensional animation where shadows are important for depth and movement perception.

Because of the high computational overheads, shadows have been regarded in much the same way as texture mapping – as a quality add-on. They have not been viewed as a necessity and compared with shading algorithms there has been little consideration of the quality of shadows. Most shadow generation algorithms produce hard edge point light source shadows and most algorithms deal only with polygon mesh models.

9.2 Simple shadows on a ground plane

An extremely simple method of generating shadows is reported by Blinn (1988). It suffices for single object scenes throwing shadows on a flat ground plane. The method simply involves drawing the projection of the object on the ground plane. It is thus restricted to single object scenes, or multi-object scenes where objects are sufficiently isolated so as not to cast shadows on each other. The ground plane projection is easily obtained from a linear transformation and the projected polygon can be scanned into a Z-buffer as part of an initialization procedure at an appropriate (dark) intensity.

If the usual illumination approximation is made – single point source at an infinite distance – then we have parallel light rays in a direction $L = (x_l, y_l, z_l)$ as shown in Figure 9.2. Any point on the object $P = (x_p, y_p, z_p)$ will cast a shadow at $S = (x_{sw}, y_{sw}, 0)$. Considering the geometry in the figure, we have:

$$S = P - \alpha L$$

and given that $z_{sw} = 0$, we have:

$$0 = z_p - \alpha z_l$$
$$\alpha = z_p/z_l$$

and:

$$x_{sw} = x_p - (z_p/z_l)\, x_l$$
$$y_{sw} = y_p - (z_p/z_l)\, y_l$$

As a homogeneous transformation this is

$$\begin{bmatrix} x_{sw} \\ y_{sw} \\ 0 \\ 1 \end{bmatrix} = \begin{bmatrix} 1 & 0 & -x_l/z_l & 0 \\ 0 & 1 & -y_l/z_l & 0 \\ 0 & 0 & 0 & 0 \\ 0 & 0 & 0 & 1 \end{bmatrix} \begin{bmatrix} x_p \\ y_p \\ z_p \\ 1 \end{bmatrix}$$

Note from this that it is just as easy to generate shadows on a vertical back or side plane. Blinn also shows how to extend this idea to handle light sources that are at a finite distance from the object.

This type of approximate shadow (on a flat ground plane) is beloved by traditional animators and its use certainly enhances movement in three-dimensional computer animation.

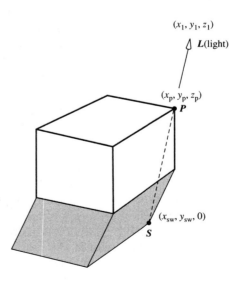

Figure 9.2
Ground plane shadows for single objects.

Shadow algorithms

Unlike hidden surface removal algorithms, where one or two algorithms now predominate and other methods are only used in special cases, no popular candidate has emerged as the top shadow algorithm. In fact, shadow computation is a rather neglected area of computer graphics. What follows, therefore, is a brief description of four major approaches. Shadow generation in ray tracing is separately described in Chapter 12.

9.3.1 Shadow algorithms: projecting polygons/scan line

This approach was developed by Appel (1968) and Bouknight and Kelley (1970). Adding shadows to a scan line algorithm requires a pre-processing stage that builds up a secondary data structure which links all polygons that may shadow a given polygon. Shadow pairs – a polygon together with the polygon that it can possibly shadow – are detected by projecting all polygons onto a sphere centred at the light source. Polygon pairs that cannot interact are detected and discarded. This is an important step because for a scene containing n polygons the number of possible projected shadows is $n(n-1)$.

The algorithm processes the secondary data structure simultaneously with a normal scan conversion process to determine if any shadows fall on the polygon that generated the visible scan line segment under consideration. If no shadow polygon(s) exists then the scan line algorithm proceeds as normal. For a current polygon: if a shadow polygon exists then using the light source as a centre of projection, the shadow is generated by projecting onto the plane that contains the current polygon. Normal scan conversion then proceeds simultaneously with a process that determines whether a current pixel is in shadow or not. Three possibilities now occur:

(1) The shadow polygon does not cover the generated scan line segment and the situation is identical to an algorithm without shadows.

(2) Shadow polygons completely cover the visible scan line segment and the scan conversion process proceeds but the pixel intensity is modulated by an amount that depends on the number of shadows that are covering the segment. For a single light source the segment is either in shadow or is not.

(3) A shadow polygon partially covers the visible scan line segment. In this case the segment is subdivided and the process is applied recursively until a solution is obtained.

A representation of these possibilities is shown in Figure 9.3. These are, in order along the scan line:

(a) Polygon A is visible, therefore it is rendered.

(b) Polygon B is visible and is rendered.

Figure 9.3
Polygons that receive a shadow from another polygon are linked in a secondary data structure. Scan line segments are now delineated by both view point projection boundaries and shadow boundaries.

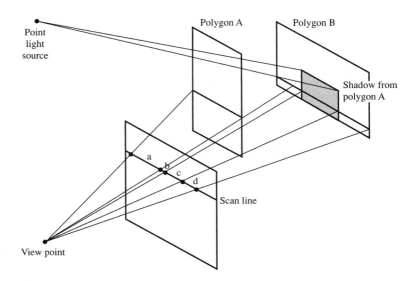

(c) Polygon *B* is shadowed by polygon A and is rendered at an appropriately reduced intensity.

(d) Polygon *B* is visible and is rendered.

9.3.2

Shadow algorithms: shadow volumes

The shadow volume approach was originally developed by Crow (1977) and subsequently extended by others. In particular Brotman and Badler (1984) used the idea as a basis for generating 'soft' shadows – that is, shadows produced by a distributed light source.

A shadow volume is the invisible volume of space swept out by the shadow of an object. It is the infinite volume defined by lines emanating from a point light source through vertices in the object. Figure 9.4 conveys the idea of a shadow volume. A finite shadow volume is obtained by considering the intersection of the infinite volume with the view volume. The shadow volume is computed by first evaluating the contour or silhouette edge of the object, as seen from the light source. The contour edge of a simple object is shown in Figure 9.4(a). A contour edge of an object is the edge made up of one or more connected edges of polygons belonging to the object. A contour edge separates those polygons that can receive light from the light source from those that cannot.

Polygons defined by the light source and the contour edges define the bounding surface of the shadow volume as shown in Figure 9.4(b). Thus each object, considered in conjunction with a point light source, generates a shadow volume object that is made up of a set of shadow polygons. Note that these shadow polygons are 'invisible' and should not be confused with the visible shadow polygons described in the next section. These shadow polygons are themselves used to determine shadows – they are not rendered.

Figure 9.4
Illustrating the formation of a shadow volume. (a) Silhouette edge of an object. (b) Finite shadow volume defined by a silhouette edge polygon, a point light source and a view volume.

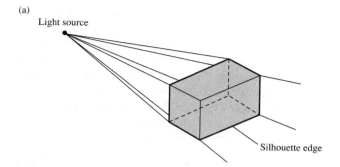

(a)

Light source

Silhouette edge

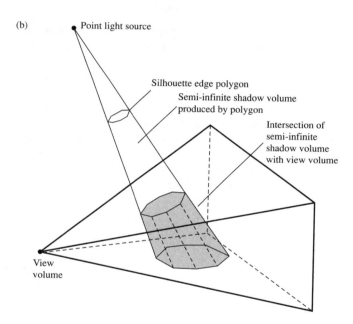

(b)

Point light source

Silhouette edge polygon
Semi-infinite shadow volume produced by polygon

Intersection of semi-infinite shadow volume with view volume

View volume

This scheme can be integrated into a number of hidden surface removal algorithms and the polygons that define the shadow volume are processed along with the object polygons except that they are considered invisible. A distinction is made between 'front-facing' polygons and 'back-facing' polygons and the relationship between shadow polygons labelled in this way and object polygons is examined. A point on an object is deemed to be in shadow if it is behind a front-facing shadow polygon and in front of a back-facing polygon. That is, if it is contained within a shadow volume. Thus a front-facing shadow polygon puts anything behind it in shadow and a back-facing shadow polygon cancels the effect of a front-facing one.

As it stands, the algorithm is most easily integrated with a depth priority hidden surface removal algorithm. Consider the operation of the algorithm for a particular pixel. We consider a vector or ray from the view point through the pixel and look at the relationship between real polygons and shadow polygons along this vector. For a pixel a counter is maintained. This is initialized to 1 if the view point is already in shadow, 0 otherwise. As we descend the depth sorted list of polygons, the counter is incremented when a front-facing polygon is passed and decremented when a back-facing polygon is passed. The value of this counter tells us, when we encounter a real polygon, whether we are inside a shadow volume. This is shown schematically in Figure 9.5.

Brotman and Badler (1984) use an enhanced Z-buffer algorithm and this approach has two significant advantages:

(1) The benefits of the Z-buffer rendering approach are retained.

(2) Their method is able to compute soft shadows or umbra/penumbra effects.

The price to be paid for using a shadow volume approach in conjunction with a Z-buffer is memory cost. The Z-buffer has to be extended such that each pixel location is a record of five fields. As shadow polygons are 'rendered' they modify counters in a pixel record and a decision can be made as to whether a point is in shadow or not.

Soft shadows are computed by modelling distributed light sources as arrays of point sources and linearly combining computations due to each point source.

The original shadow volume approach places heavy constraints on the database environment; the most serious restriction is that objects must be convex polyhedrons. Bergeron (1986) developed a general version of Crow's algorithm that overcomes these restrictions and allows concave objects and penetrating polygons.

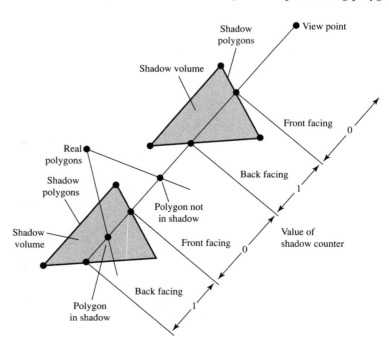

Figure 9.5
Front-facing and back-facing shadow polygons and the shadow counter value.

9.3.3 Shadow algorithms: derivation of shadow polygons from light source transformations

This approach was developed by Atherton *et al.* (1978) and relies on the fact that applying hidden surface removal to a view from the light source produces polygons or parts of polygons that are in shadow. It also relies on the object space polygon clipping algorithm (to produce shadow polygons that are parts of existing polygons) by Weiler and Atherton (1977).

A claimed advantage of this approach is that it operates in object space. This means that it is possible to extract numerical information on shadows from the algorithm. This finds applications, for example, in architectural CAD.

The algorithm enhances the object data structure with shadow polygons to produce a 'complete shadow data file'. This can then be used to produce any view of the object with shadows. It is thus a good approach in generating animated sequences where the virtual camera changes position but the relative position of the object and the light source remain unchanged. The working of the algorithm is shown for a simple example in Figure 9.6. A single shadow polygon is shown for clarity. Referring to Figure 9.6, the first step in the algorithm is to apply a transformation such that the object or scene is viewed from the light source position. Hidden surface removal then produces visible polygons, that is polygons that are visible to the light source and are therefore not in shadow. These are either complete or clipped as the illustration implies. This polygon set can then be combined with the original object polygons, provided both data sets are in the same coordinate system. The process of combining these sets results in a complete shadow data file – the original polygon set enhanced by shadow polygons for a particular light source. Transforming the database to the required view point and applying hidden surface removal will then result in an image with shadows. This algorithm exploits the fact that shadow polygons are view point independent. Essentially the scene is processed twice for hidden surface removal. Once using the light source as a view point, which produces the shadow polygons, and once using normal hidden surface removal (from any view point).

9.3.4 Shadow algorithms: shadow Z-buffer

Possibly the simplest approach to the shadow computation, and one that is easily integrated into a Z-buffer-based renderer is the shadow Z-buffer developed by Williams (1978). This technique requires a separate shadow Z-buffer for each light source and in its basic form is only suitable for a scene illuminated by a single light source. Alternatively a single shadow Z-buffer could be used for many light sources and the algorithm executed for each light source, but this would be somewhat inefficient and slow.

The algorithm is a two-step process. A scene is 'rendered' and depth information stored in the shadow Z-buffer using the light source as a view point. No

Figure 9.6
Derivation of shadow
polygons from
transformations.
(a) Simple polygonal object
in modelling coordinate
system. (b) Plan view
showing the position of the
light source. (c) Hidden
surface removal from the
light source as a view point.
(d) Visible polygons from
(c) transformed back into
modelling coordinate
system. (e) Parts (a) and
(d) merged to produce a
database that contains
shadow polygons. (f) Part
(e) can produce any view of
the object with shadows.

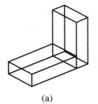

(a)

(b)

(c)

(d)

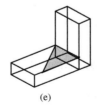

(e)

(f)

intensities are calculated. This computes a 'depth image' from the light source, of these polygons that are visible to the light source.

The second step is to render the scene using a Z-buffer algorithm. This process is enhanced as follows: if a point is visible, a coordinate transformation is used to map (x, y, z), the coordinates of the point in three-dimensional screen space (from the view point) to (x', y', z'), the coordinates of the point in screen space from the light point as a coordinate origin. The (x', y') are used to index the shadow Z-buffer and the corresponding depth value is compared with z'. If z' is greater than the value stored in the shadow Z-buffer for that point, then a surface is nearer to the light source than the point under consideration and the point is in shadow, thus a shadow 'intensity' is used, otherwise the point is rendered as normal. An example of shadow maps is shown in Figure 18.8. Note that in this particular example we have generated six shadow maps. This enables us to render a view of the room from a view point situated anywhere within the scene.

Apart from extending the high memory requirements of the Z-buffer hidden surface removal algorithm, the algorithm also extends its inefficiency. Shadow calculations are performed for surfaces that may subsequently be 'overwritten' – just as shading calculations are.

Anti-aliasing and the shadow Z-buffer

In common with the Z-buffer algorithm, the shadow Z-buffer is susceptible to aliasing artefacts due to point sampling. Two aliasing opportunities occur. First, straightforward point sampling in the creation phase of the shadow Z-buffer produces artefacts. These will be visible along shadow edges – we are considering a hard-edged shadow cast by a point light source. The second aliasing problem is created when accessing the shadow Z-buffer. It is somewhat analogous to the sampling problem created in texture mapping. This problem arises because we are effectively projecting a pixel extent onto the shadow Z-buffer map. This is shown schematically in Figure 9.7. If we consider the so-called pre-image of a square pixel in the shadow Z-buffer map then this will, in general, be a quadrilateral that encloses a number of shadow Z-buffer pixels. It is this many map pixels to one screen pixel problem that we have to deal with. It means that a pixel may be partly in shadow and partly not and if we make a binary decision then aliasing will occur. We thus consider the fraction of the pixel that is in shadow by computing this from the shadow Z-buffer. This fraction can be evaluated by the z' comparisons over the set of shadow Z-buffer pixels that the screen pixel projects onto. The fraction is then used to give an appropriate shadow intensity. The process in summary is:

(1) For each pixel calculate four values of (x', y') corresponding to the four corner points. This defines a quadrilateral in shadow Z-buffer space.

(2) Integrate the information over this quadrilateral by comparing the z value for the screen pixel with each z' value in the shadow Z-buffer quadrilateral. This gives a fraction that reflects the area of the pixel in shadow.

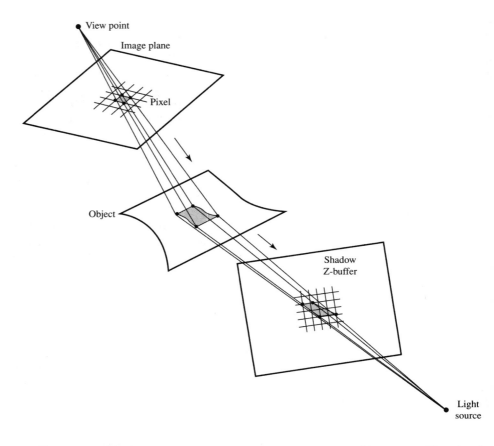

Figure 9.7
'Pre-image' of a pixel in the shadow Z-buffer.

(3) We use this fraction to give an appropriate attenuated intensity. The visual effect of this is that the hard edge of the shadow will be softened for those pixels that straddle a shadow boundary.

Full details of this approach are given in Reeves *et al.* (1987). The price paid for this anti-aliasing is a considerable increase in processing time. Pre-filtering techniques (see Chapter 14) cannot be used and a stochastic sampling scheme for integrating within the pixel pre-image in the shadow Z-buffer map is suggested in Reeves *et al.* (1987).

10 Global illumination

Introduction

In computer graphics, global illumination is the term given to models which render a view of a scene by evaluating the light reflected from a point x taking into account all illumination that arrives at a point. That is we consider not only the light arriving at the point directly from light sources but all indirect illumination that may have originated from a light source via other objects.

It is probably the case that in the general pursuit of photo-realism, most research effort has gone into solving the global illumination problem. Although, as we have seen in Chapter 7, considerable parallel work has been carried out with local reflection models, workers have been attracted to the difficult problem of simulating the interaction of light with an entire environment. Light has to be tracked through the environment from emitter(s) to sensor(s), rather than just from an emitter to a surface then directly to the sensor or eye. Such an approach does not then require add-on algorithms for shadows which are simply areas in which the illumination level is reduced due to the proximity of a nearby object. Other global illumination effects such as reflection of objects in each other and transparency effects can also be correctly modelled.

It is not clear how important global illumination is to photo-realism. Certainly it is the case that we are accustomed to 'closed' man-made environments, where there is much global interaction, but the extent to which this interaction has to be simulated, to achieve a degree of realism acceptable for most computer graphics applications, is still an open question. Rather, the problem has been vigorously pursued as a pure research problem in its own right on the assumption that improvements in the accuracy of global interaction will be valuable.

Two established (partial) global algorithms have now emerged. These are ray tracing and radiosity and, for reasons that will soon become clear, they both, in their most commonly implemented forms, simulate only a subset of global interaction: ray tracing attending to (perfect) specular interaction and radiosity to (perfect) diffuse interaction. In other words, current practical solutions to the problem deal with its inherent intractability by concentrating on particular global interactions, ignoring the remainder and by considering interactions to be perfect. In the case of specular interaction 'perfect' means that an infinitesimally thin beam hitting a surface reflects without spreading – the surface is assumed perfect. In the case of perfect diffuse interaction we assume that an incoming beam of light reflects equally in all directions into the hemisphere centred at the point of reflection.

Ignoring finite computing resources, a solution to the global interaction problem is simply stated. We start at the light source(s) and follow every light path (or ray of light) as it travels through the environment stopping when the light hits the eye point, has its energy reduced below some minimum due to absorption in the objects that it has encountered, or travels out of the environment into space. To see the relevance of global illumination algorithms we need ways of describing the problem – models that capture the essence of the behaviour of light in an environment. In this chapter we will introduce two models of global illumination and give an overview of the many and varied approaches to global illumination. We devote separate chapters to the implementation details of the two well-established methods of ray tracing and radiosity.

We should note that it is difficult to categorize global illumination algorithms because most use a combination of techniques. Is two-pass ray tracing, for example, to be considered as a global illumination method or as an extension to ray tracing? Thus the breakdown by technique that appears in this chapter inevitably contains algorithms that straddle more than one category and the sorting is simply the author's preference.

(10.1) Global illumination models

We start by introducing two 'models' of the global illumination problem. The first is a mathematical formulation and the second is a classification in terms of the nature of the type of interaction that can occur when light travels from one surface to the other. The value of such models is that they enable a comparison between the multitude of global illumination algorithms most of which evaluate a less than complete solution. By their nature the algorithms consist of a wealth of heuristic detail and the global illumination models facilitate a comparison in terms of which aspects are evaluated and which are not.

The rendering equation

The first model that we will look at was introduced into the computer graphics literature in 1986 by Kajiya (Kajiya 1986) and is known as the rendering equation. It encapsulates global illumination by describing what happens at a point x on a surface. It is a completely general mathematical statement of the problem and global illumination algorithms can be categorized in terms of this equation. In fact, Kajiya states that its purpose:

is to provide a unified context for viewing them [rendering algorithms] as more or less accurate approximations to the solution for a single equation.

The integral in Kajiya's original notation is given by:

$$I(x, x') = g(x, x')[\varepsilon(x, x') + \int_s \rho(x, x', x'') \, I(x', x'')dx'']$$

where:

$I(x, x')$ is the transport intensity or the intensity of light passing from point x' to point x. Kajiya terms this the unoccluded two point transport intensity.

$g(x, x')$ is the visibility function between x and x'. If x and x' cannot 'see' each other then this is zero. If they are visible then g varies as the inverse square of the distance between them.

$\varepsilon(x, x')$ is the transfer emittance from x' to x and is related to the intesity of any light self-emitted by point x' in the direction of x.

$\rho(x, x', x'')$ is the scattering term with respect to direction x' and x''. It is the intensity of the energy scattered towards x by a surface point located at x' arriving from point or direction x''. Kajiya calls this the unoccluded three-point transport reflectance. It is related to the BRDF (see Chapter 7) by:

$$\rho(x, x', x'') = \rho(\theta'_{in}, \phi'_{in}, \theta'_{ref}, \phi'_{ref}) \cos \theta \cos \theta'_{ref}$$

where θ' and ϕ' are the azimuth and elevation angles related to point x' (see Section 7.3) and θ is the angle between the surface normal at point x and the line $x'x$.

The integral is over s, all points on all surfaces in the scene, or equivalently over all points on the hemisphere situated at point x'. The equation states that the transport intensity from point x' to point x is equal to (any) light emitted from x' towards x plus the light scattered from x' towards x from all other surfaces in the scene – that is, that originate from direction x''.

Expressed in the above terms the rendering equation implies that we must have:

- A model of the light emitted by a surface $\varepsilon()$.
- A representation of the BRDF $\rho()$ for each surface.
- A method for evaluating the visibility function.

We have already met all these factors; here the formulation gathers them into a single equation. The important general points that come out of considering the rendering equation are:

(1) The complexity of the integral means that it cannot be evaluated analytically and most practical algorithms reduce the complexity in some way. The direct evaluation of the equation can be undertaken by using Monte Carlo methods and many algorithms follow this approach.

(2) It is a view-independent statement of the problem. The point x' is every point in the scene. Global illumination algorithms are either view independent – the common example is the radiosity algorithm – or view dependent where only those points x' visible from the viewing position are evaluated. View dependence can be seen as a way in which the inherent complexity of the rendering equation is reduced. (See Section 10.8 for a more detailed discussion on view dependence/independence.)

(3) It is a recursive equation – to evaluate $I(x, x')$ we need to evaluate $I(x', x'')$ which itself will use the same equation. This gives rise to one of the most popular practical methods for solving the problem which is to trace light from the image plane, in the reverse direction of light propagation, following a path that reflects from object to object. Algorithms that adopt this approach are: path tracing, ray tracing and distributed ray tracing, all of which will be described later.

(10.1.2) Radiance, irradiance and the radiance equation

The original form of the rendering equation is not particularly useful in global illumination methods and in this section we will introduce definitions that enable us to write it in a different form called the radiance equation.

Radiance L is the fundamental radiometric quantity and for a point in three-dimensional space it is the light energy density measured in $W/(sr–m^2)$. The radiance at a point is a function of direction and we can define a radiance distribution function for a point. This will generally be discontinuous as the two-dimensional example in Figure 10.1 demonstrates. Such a distribution function exists at all points in three-dimensional space and radiance is therefore a five-dimensional quantity. Irradiance is the integration of incoming radiance over all directions:

$$E = \int_{\Omega} L_{in} \cos \theta \, d\omega$$

Figure 10.1
Radiance, irradiance and
irradiance distribution
function (after Greger *et al.*
(1998)).

(a) A two-dimensional
radiance distribution for a
point in the centre of a
room where each wall
exhibits a different radiance.

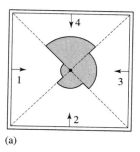

(a)

(b) The field radiance for a
point on a surface element.
Irradiance *E* is the cosine
weighted average of the
radiance – in this case 3.5 π.

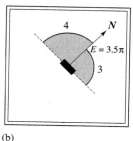

(b)

(c) If the surface element
is rotated an irradiance
distribution function is
defined.

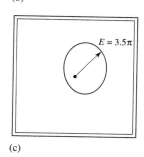

(c)

where:

L_{in} is the incoming or field radiance from direction ω

θ is the angle between the surface normal and ω

If L_{in} is constant, we have for a diffuse surface:

$L_{diffuse} = \rho E / \pi$

The distinction between these two quantities is important in global illumination algorithms as the form of the algorithm can be classified as 'shooting' or 'gathering'. Shooting means distributing radiance from a surface and gathering means integrating the irradiance or accumulating light flux at the surface. (Radiosity B is closely related to irradiance having units W/m².)

An important practical point concerning radiance and irradiance distribution functions is that while the former is generally discontinuous the latter is generally continuous, except for shadow boundaries. This is demonstrated in Figure 10.1 which shows that in this simple example the irradiance distribution function will be continuous because of the averaging effect of the integration.

The rendering equation can be recast as the radiance equation which in its simplest form is:

$$L_{ref} = \int \rho L_{in}$$

Including the directional dependence, we then write:

$$L_{ref} (\mathbf{x}, \omega_{ref}) = L_e (\mathbf{x}, \omega_{ref}) + \int_\Omega \rho(\mathbf{x}, \omega_{in} \to \omega_{out}) L_{in} (\mathbf{x}, \omega_{in}) \cos \theta_{in}\, d\omega_{in}$$

where the symbols are defined in Figure 10.2(b). This can be modified so that the integration is performed over all surfaces – usually more convenient in practical algorithms – rather than all incoming angles and this gives the rendering equation in terms of radiance:

$$L_{ref} (\mathbf{x}, \omega_{ref}) = L_e (\mathbf{x}, \omega_{ref}) + \int_S \rho(\mathbf{x}, \omega_{in} \to \omega_{out}) L_{in} (\mathbf{x}', \omega_{in}) g(\mathbf{x}, \mathbf{x}') \cos \theta_{in} \frac{\cos \theta_0\, dA}{\|\mathbf{x} - \mathbf{x}'\|^2}$$

which now includes the visibility function. This comes about by expressing the solid angle $d\omega_{in}$ in terms of the projected area of the differential surface region visible in the direction of ω_{in} (Figure 10.2(c)):

Figure 10.2
The radiance equation.

(a) The domain of integration is the hemisphere of all incoming directions.

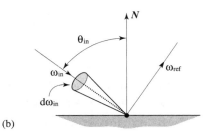

(a)

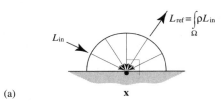

(b) Symbols used to define the directional dependence.

(b)

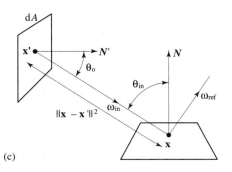

(c) $\cos \theta_0\, dA/\|\mathbf{x} - \mathbf{x}'\|^2$ is the projected area of dA visible in the direction ω_{in}.

(c)

$$d\omega_{in} = \frac{\cos \theta_0 \, dA}{\|\mathbf{x} - \mathbf{x'}\|^2}$$

Path notation

Another way of categorizing the behaviour of global illumination algorithms is to detail which surface-to-surface interactions that they implement or simulate. This is a much simpler non-mathematical categorization and it enables an easy comparison and classification of the common algorithms. We consider which interactions between pairs of interacting surfaces are implemented as light travels from source to sensor. Thus at a point, incoming light may be scattered or reflected diffusely or specularly and may itself have originated from a specular or diffuse reflection at the previous surface in the path. We can then say that for pairs of consecutive surfaces along a light path we have (Figure 10.3):

- Diffuse to diffuse transfer.
- Specular to diffuse transfer.
- Diffuse to specular transfer.
- Specular to specular transfer.

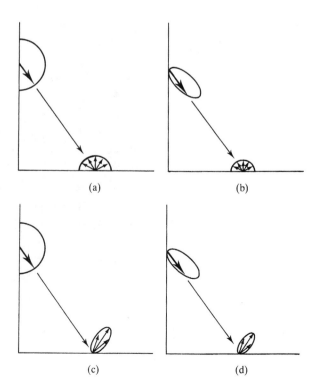

Figure 10.3
The four 'mechanisms' of light transport: (a) diffuse to diffuse; (b) specular to diffuse; (c) diffuse to specular; (d) specular to specular (after Wallace *et al.* (1987)).

In an environment where only diffuse surfaces exist only diffuse–diffuse interaction is possible and such scenes are solved using the radiosity method. Similarly an environment containing only specular surfaces can only exhibit specular interaction and (Whitted) ray tracing deals with these. Basic radiosity does not admit any other transfer mechanism except diffuse–diffuse and it excludes the important specular–specular transfer. Ray tracing, on the other hand can only deal with specular–specular interaction. More recent algorithms, such as 'backwards' ray tracing and enhancements of radiosity for specular interaction require a categorization of all the interactions in a light journey from source to sensor, and this led to Heckbert's string notation (Heckbert 1990) for listing all the interactions that occur along a path of a light ray as it travels from source (L) to the eye (E). Here a light path from the light source to the first hit is termed L, subsequent paths involving transfer mechanisms at a surface point are categorized as DD, SD, DS or SS. Figure 10.4 (also a Colour Plate) shows an example of a simple scene and various paths. The path that finally terminates in the eye is called E. The paths in the example are:

(1) LDDE   For this path the viewer sees the shadow cast by the table. The light reflects diffusely from the right-hand wall onto the floor. Note that any light

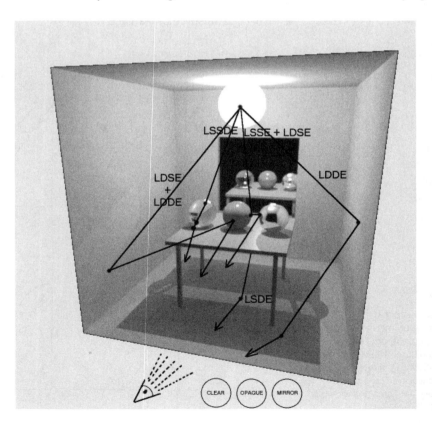

Figure 10.4
A selection of global illuminations paths in a simple environment. See also the Colour Plate version of this figure.

reflected from a shadow area must have a minimum of two interactions between L and E.

(2) LDSE + LDDE   Here the user sees the dark side of the sphere which is not receiving any direct light. The light is modelled as a point source, so any area below the 'equator' of the sphere will be in shadow. The diffuse illumination reflected diffusely from the wall is directed towards the eye and because the sphere is shiny the reflection to the eye is both specular and diffuse.

(3) LSSE + LDSE   Light is reflected from the perfect mirror surface to the eye and the viewer sees a reflection of the opaque or coloured ball in the mirror surface.

(4) LSDE   Here the viewer sees a shadow area that is lighter than the main table shadow. This is due to the extra light reflected from the mirror and directed underneath the table.

(5) LSSDE   This path has three interactions between L and E and the user sees a caustic on the table top which is a diffuse surface. The first specular interaction takes place at the top surface of the sphere and light from the point source is refracted through the sphere. There is a second specular interaction when the light emerges from the sphere and hits the diffuse table surface. The effect of the reflection is to concentrate light rays travelling through the sphere into a smaller area on the table top than they would occupy if the transparent sphere was not present. Thus the user sees a bright area on the diffuse surface.

A complete global illumination algorithm would have to include any light path which can be written as L(D|S)*E, where | means 'or' and * indicates repetition. The application of a local reflection model implies paths of type LD|S (the intensity of each being calculated separately then combined as in the Phong reflection model) and the addition of a hidden surface removal algorithm implies simulation of types LD|SE. Thus local reflection models only simulate strings of length unity (between L and E) and viewing a point in shadow implies a string which is at least of length 2.

10.2 The evolution of global illumination algorithms

We will now look at the development of popular or established global illumination algorithms using as a basis for our discussion the preceding concepts. The order in which the algorithms are discussed is somewhat arbitrary; but goes from incomplete solutions (ray tracing and radiosity) to general solutions. The idea of this section is to give a view of the algorithms in terms of global interaction.

Return to consideration of the brute force solution to the problem. There we considered the notion of starting at a light source and following every ray of light that was emitted through the scene and stated that this was a computationally intractable problem. Approximations to a solution come from constraining the light-object interaction in some way and/or only considering a small subset of the rays that start at the light and bounce around the scene. The main approximations which led to ray tracing and radiosity constrained the scene to contain only specular reflectors or only (perfect) diffuse reflectors respectively.

In what follows we give a review of ray tracing and radiosity sufficient for comparison with the other methods we describe, leaving the implementation details of these important methods for separate chapters.

Established algorithms – ray tracing and radiosity

Whitted ray tracing

Whitted ray tracing (visibility tracing, eye tracing) traces light rays in the reverse direction of propagation from the eye back into the scene towards the light source. To generate a two-dimensional image plane projection of a scene using ray tracing we are only interested in these light rays that end at the sensor or eye point and therefore it makes sense to start at the eye and trace rays out into the scene. It is thus a view-dependent algorithm. A simple representation of the algorithm is shown in Figure 10.5. The process is often visualized as a tree where each node is a surface hit point. At each node we spawn a light ray and a reflected ray or a transmitted (refracted) ray or both.

Whitted ray tracing is a hybrid – a global illumination model onto which is added a local model. Consider the global interaction. The classic algorithm only includes perfect specular interaction. Rays are shot into the scene and when they hit a surface a reflected (and transmitted) ray is spawned at the point of intersection and they themselves are then followed recursively. The process stops when

Figure 10.5
Whitted ray tracing.

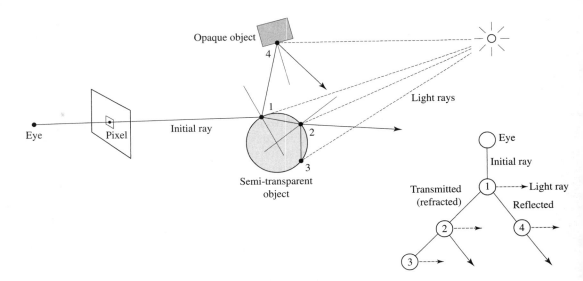

the energy of a ray drops below a predetermined minimum or if it leaves the scene and travels out into empty space or if a ray hits a surface that is perfectly diffuse. Thus the global part of ray tracing only accounts for pure specular–specular interaction. Theoretically there is nothing to stop us calculating diffuse global interaction, it is just that at every hit point an incoming ray would have to spawn reflected rays in every direction into a hemispherical surface centred on the point.

To the global specular component is added a direct contribution calculated by shooting a ray from the point to the light source which is always a point source in this model. The visibility of the point from the light source and its direction can be used to calculate a local or direct diffuse component – the ray is just L in a local reflection model. Thus (direct) diffuse reflection (but not diffuse–diffuse) interaction is considered. This is sometimes called the shadow ray or shadow feeler because if it hits any object between the point under consideration and the light source then we know that the point is shadow. However, a better term is light ray to emphasize that it is used to calculate a direct contribution (using a local reflection model) which is then passed up the tree. The main problem with Whitted ray tracing is its restriction to specular interaction – most practical scenes consist of predominantly diffuse surfaces.

Consider the LSSE + LDSE path in Figure 10.4, reproduced in Figure 10.6 together with the ray tree. The initial ray from the eye hits the perfect mirror

Figure 10.6
Whitted ray tracing: the relationship between light paths and local and global contributions for one of the cases shown in Figure 10.4.

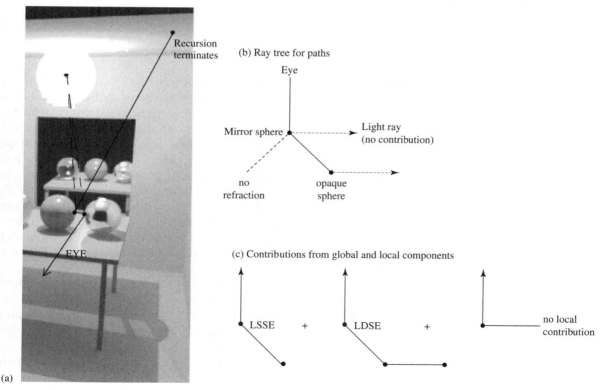

(a)

sphere. For this sphere there is no contribution from a local diffuse model. At the next intersection we hit the opaque sphere and trace a global specular component which hits the ceiling, a perfect diffuse surface, and the recursion is terminated. Also at that point we have a contribution from the local diffuse model for the sphere and the viewer sees in the pixel associated with that ray the colour of the reflected image of the opaque sphere in the mirror sphere.

A little thought will reveal that the paths which can be simulated by Whitted ray tracing are constrained to be LS*E and LDS*E. Ray traced images therefore exhibit reflections in the surfaces of shiny objects of nearby objects. If the objects are transparent any objects that the viewer can see behind the transparent object are refracted. Also, as will be seen in Chapter 12, shadows are calculated as part of the model – but only 'perfect' or hard-edged shadows.

Considering Whitted ray tracing in terms of the rendering equation the following holds. The scattering term ρ is reduced to the law for perfect reflection (and refraction). Thus the integral over all S – the entire scene – reduces to calculating (for reflection) a single outgoing ray plus the light ray which gives the diffuse component and adding these two contributions together. Thus the recursive structure of the rendering equation is reflected perfectly in the algorithm but the integral operation is reduced to a sum of three analytically calculated components – the contributions from the reflected, transmitted and light rays.

(10.3.2)   ## Radiosity

Classic radiosity implements diffuse–diffuse interaction. Instead of following individual rays 'interaction' between patches (or polygons) in the scene are considered. The solution is view independent and consists of a constant radiosity for every patch in the scene. View independence means that a solution is calculated for every point in the scene rather than just those points that can be seen from the eye (view dependent). This implies that a radiosity solution has to be followed by another process or pass that computes a projection, but most work is carried out in the radiosity pass. A problem or contradiction with classical radiosity is that the initial discretization of the scene has to be carried out before the process is started but the best way of performing this depends on the solution. In other words, we do not know the best way to divide up the scene until after we have a solution or a partial solution. This is an outstanding problem with the radiosity method and accounts for most of its difficulty of use.

A way of visualizing the radiosity process is to start by considering the light source as an (array of) emitting patches. We shoot light into the scene from the source(s) and consider the diffuse–diffuse interaction between a light patch and all the receiving patches that are visible from the light patch – the first hit patches. An amount of light is deposited or cached on these patches which are then ordered according to the amount of energy that has fallen onto the patch and has yet to be shot back into the scene. The one with the highest unshot energy is selected and this is considered as the next shooting patch. The process continues iteratively until a (high) percentage of the initial light energy is distributed around the scene. At any stage in the process some of the distributed energy will arrive back on patches that have already been considered and this is why the process is iterative. The process will eventually converge because the reflectivity coefficient associated with each patch is, by definition, less than unity and at each phase in the iteration more and more of the initial light is absorbed. Figure 10.7 (Colour Plate) shows a solution in progress using this algorithm. The stage shown is the state of the solution after 20 iterations. The four illustrations are:

(1) The radiosity solution as output from the iteration process. Each patch is allocated a constant radiosity.

(2) The previous solution after it has been subject to an interpolation process.

(3) The same solution with the addition of an ambient term. The ambient 'lift' is distributed evenly amongst all patches in the scene, to give an early well lit solution (this enhancement is described in detail in Chapter 11).

(4) The difference between the previous two images. This gives a visual indication of the energy that had to be added to account for the unshot radiosity.

The transfer of light between any two patches – the diffuse–diffuse interaction – is calculated by considering the geometric relationship between the patches (expressed as the form factor). Compared to ray tracing we follow light from the light source through the scene as patch-to-patch diffuse interaction, but instead of following individual rays of light, the form factor between two patches averages the effect of the paths that join the patches together. This way of considering the radiosity method is, in fact, implemented as an algorithm structure. It is called the progressive refinement method.

This simple concept has to be modified by a visibility process (not to be confused by the subsequent calculation of a projection which includes, in the normal way, hidden surface removal) that takes into account the fact that in general a patch may be only partially visible to another because of some intervening patch. The end result is the assignment of a constant radiosity to each patch in the scene – a view-independent solution which is then injected into a Gouraud-style renderer to produce a projection. In terms of path classification, conventional radiosity is LD*E.

The obvious problem with radiosity is that although man-made scenes usually consist mostly of diffuse surfaces, specular objects are not unusual and these cannot be handled by a radiosity renderer. A more subtle problem is that the scene has to be discretized into patches or polygons before the radiosities are computed and difficulties occur if this polygonization is too coarse.

We now consider radiosity in terms of the rendering equation. Radiosity is the energy per unit time per unit area and since we are only considering diffuse illumination we can rewrite the rendering equation as:

$$B(x') = \varepsilon(x') + \rho(x') \int_S B(x)F(x, x')\mathrm{d}x$$

where now the only directional dependence is incorporated in the form factor F. The equation now states that the radiosity of a surface element x is equal to the emittance term plus the radiosity radiated by all other elements in the scene onto x. The form factor F is a coefficient that is a function only of the spatial relationship between x and x' and this determines that fraction of $B(x')$ arriving at x. F also includes a visibility calculation.

10.4   Monte Carlo techniques in global illumination

In this section we will give an intuitive introduction to Monte Carlo techniques. The mathematical details are outside the intended scope of this text (see Glassner (1995) for a comprehensive treatment of Monte Carlo theory and its application to global illumination) and it is the case that the methods that use Monte Carlo techniques can be explained in algorithmic terms. However, some intuition concerning the underlying factors is necessary to appreciate the particular strategies employed by the examples which we will describe. Without this intuition it is, for example, difficult to appreciate the difference between Whitted ray tracing and Kajiya's Monte Carlo approach which he termed path tracing (Section 10.5).

Monte Carlo techniques are used to solve integrals like the rendering equation which have no analytical or numerical solution. They do this by computing the average of random samples of the integrand, adding these together and taking the average. The visual effect of this process in the final rendered image is noise. The attraction of Monte Carlo techniques is that they are easy to implement because they are conceptually simple. An equally important advantage is their generality. No a priori simplifications have to be made (like perfect reflectors in Whitted ray tracing and perfect diffusers in radiosity). This comes about because they point sample both the geometry of the scene and the optical properties of the surface. The problem with Monte Carlo methods comes in devising techniques where an accurate or low variance estimate of the integral can be obtained quickly.

The underlying idea of Monte Carlo methods for estimating integrals can be demonstrated using a simple one-dimensional example. Consider estimating the integral:

$$I = \int_0^1 f(x)\ \mathrm{d}x$$

I can be estimated by taking a random number $\xi \in [0,1]$ and evaluating $f(\xi)$. This is called a primary estimator. We can define the variance of the estimate as:

$$\sigma^2_{\mathrm{prim}} = \int_0^1 f^2(x)\mathrm{d}x - f^2(\xi)$$

which for a single sample we would expect to be high. In practice we would take N samples to give a so-called secondary estimate and it is easily shown that:

$$\sigma^2_{sec} = \frac{\sigma^2_{prim}}{N}$$

This observation, that the error in the estimate is inversely proportional to the square root of the number of samples, is extremely important in practice. To halve the error, for example, we must take four times as many samples. Equivalently we can say that each additional sample has less and less effect on the result and this has to be set against the fact that computer graphics implementations tend to involve an equal, and generally high cost, per sample. Thus the main goal in Monte Carlo methods is to get the best result possible with a given number of samples N. This means strategies that result in variance reduction. The two common strategies for selecting samples are stratified sampling and importance sampling.

The simplest form of stratified sampling divides the domain of the integration into equal strata and estimates each partial integral by one or more random samples (Figure 10.8). In this way each sub-domain is allocated the same number of samples. Thus:

$$I = \int_0^1 f(x) \, dx$$

$$= \sum_{i=1}^{N} \int_{S_i} f(x) dx$$

$$= \frac{1}{N} \sum_{i=1}^{N} f(\xi)$$

This estimate results in a variance that is guaranteed to be lower than that obtained by distributing random samples over the integration domain. The most familiar example of stratified sampling in computer graphics is jittering in pixel sampling. Here a pixel represents the domain of the integral which is subdivided into equal strata and a sample point generated by jittering the centre point of each stratum (Figure 10.9).

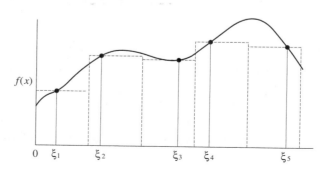

Figure 10.8
Stratified sampling of $f(x)$.

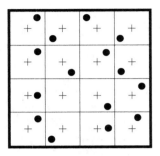

As the name implies, importance sampling tends to select samples in important regions of the integrand. Importance sampling implies prior knowledge of the function that we are going to estimate an integral for, which at first sight appears to be a contradiction. However, most rendering problems involve an integrand which is the product of two functions, one of which is known *a priori* as in the rendering equation. For example, in a Monte Carlo approach to ray tracing a specular surface we would choose reflected rays which tended to cluster around the specular reflection direction thus sampling the (known) BRDF in regions where it is likely to return a high value. Thus, in general, we distribute the samples so that their density is highest in the regions where the function has a high value or where it varies significantly and quickly. Considering again our simple one-dimensional example we can write:

$$I = \int_0^1 p(x) \, \frac{f(x)}{p(x)} \, \mathrm{d}x$$

where the first term $p(x)$ is an importance weighting function. This function $p(x)$ is then the probability density function (PDF) of the samples. That is the samples need to be chosen such that they conform to $p(x)$. To do this we define $P(x)$ to be the cumulative function of the PDF:

$$P(x) = \int_0^x p(t)\mathrm{d}t$$

and choose a uniform random sample τ and evaluate $\xi = P^{-1}(\tau)$. Using this method the variance becomes:

$$\sigma^2{}_{\mathrm{imp}} = \int_0^1 \left[\frac{f(x)}{p(x)} \right]^2 p(x)\mathrm{d}x - I^2$$

$$= \int_0^1 \frac{f^2(x)}{p(x)} \, \mathrm{d}x - I^2$$

The question is how do we choose $p(x)$. This can be a function that satisfies the following conditions:

$$p(x) > 0$$
$$\int p(x)dx = 1$$
$$P^{-1}(x) \text{ is computable}$$

For example, we could choose $p(x)$ to be the normalized absolute value of $f(x)$ or alternatively a smoothed or approximate version of $f(x)$ (Figure 10.10). Any function $f(x)$ that satisfies the above conditions will not necessarily suffice. If we choose an $f(x)$ that is too far from the ideal then the efficiency of this technique will simply drop below that of a naive method that uses random samples. Importance sampling is of critical importance in global illumination algorithms that utilize Monte Carlo approaches for the simple and obvious reason that although the rendering equation describes the global illumination at each and every point in the scene we do not require a solution that is equally accurate. We require, for example, a more accurate result for a brightly illuminated specular surface than for a dimly lit diffuse wall. Importance sampling enables us to build algorithms where the cost is distributed according to the final accuracy that we require as a function of light level and surface type.

An important practical implication of Monte Carlo methods in computer graphics is that they produce stochastic noise. For example, consider Whitted ray tracing and Monte Carlo approaches to ray tracing. In Whitted ray tracing the perfect specular direction is always chosen and in a sense the integration is reduced to a deterministic algorithm which produces a noiseless image. A crude Monte Carlo approach that imitated Whitted ray tracing would produce an image where the final pixels' estimates were, in general, slightly different from the Whitted solution. These differences manifest themselves as noticeable noise. Also note that in Whitted ray tracing if we ignore potential aliasing problems we need only initiate one ray per pixel. With a Monte Carlo approach we are using samples of the rendering equation to compute an estimate of intensity of a pixel and we need to fire many rays/pixels which bounce around the scene. In Kajiya's pioneering algorithm (Kajiya 1986), described in the next section, he used a total of 40 rays per pixel.

Global illumination algorithms that use a Monte Carlo approach are all based on these simple ideas. Their inherent complexity derives from the fact that the integration is now multi-dimensional.

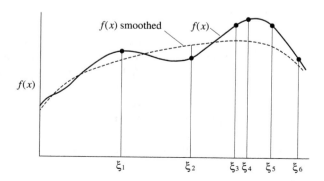

Figure 10.10
Illustrating the idea of importance sample.

Path tracing

In his classic paper that introduced the rendering equation, Kajiya (1986) was the first to recognize that Whitted ray tracing is a deterministic solution to the rendering equation. In the same paper he also suggested a non-deterministic variation of Whitted ray tracing – a Monte Carlo method that he called path tracing.

Kajiya gives a direct mathematical link between the rendering equation and the path tracing algorithm by rewriting the equation as:

$$I = g\varepsilon + gMI$$

where M is the linear operator given by the integral in the rendering equation. This can then be written as an infinite series known as a Neuman series as:

$$I = g\varepsilon + gMg\varepsilon + g(Mg)^2\varepsilon + g(Mg)^3\varepsilon + \ldots$$

where I is now the sum of a direct term, a once scattered term, a twice scattered term, etc. This leads directly to path tracing, which is theoretically known as a random walk. Light rays are traced backwards (as in Whitted ray tracing) from pixels and bounce around the scene from the first hit point, to the second, to the third, etc. The random walk has to terminate after a certain number of steps – equivalent to truncating the above series at some point when we can be sure that no further significant contributions will be encountered.

Like Whitted ray tracing, path tracing is a view-dependent solution. Previously we have said that there is no theoretical bar to extending ray tracing to handle all light–surface interactions including diffuse reflection and transmission from a hit point; just the impossibility of the computation. Path tracing implements diffuse interaction by initiating a large number of rays at each pixel (instead of, usually, one with Whitted ray tracing) and follows a single path for each ray through the scene rather than allowing a ray to spawn multiple reflected children at each hit point. The idea is shown in Figure 10.11 which can be compared with Figure 10.5. All surfaces, whether diffuse or specular can spawn a reflection/transmission ray and this contrasts with Whitted ray tracing where the encounter with a diffuse surface terminates the recursion. The other important difference is that a number of rays (40 in the original example) are initiated for each pixel enabling BRDFs to be sampled. Thus the method simulates full L(D|S)*E interaction.

A basic path tracing algorithm using a single path from source to termination will be expensive. If the random walks do not terminate on a light source then they return zero contribution to the final estimate and unless the light sources are large, paths will tend to terminate before they reach light sources. Kajiya addressed this problem by introducing a light or shadow ray that is shot towards a point on an (area) light source from each hit point in the random walk and accumulating this contribution at each point in the path (if the reflection ray from the same point directly hits the light source then the direct contribution is ignored).

Figure 10.11
Two rays in path tracing
(initiated at the same pixel).

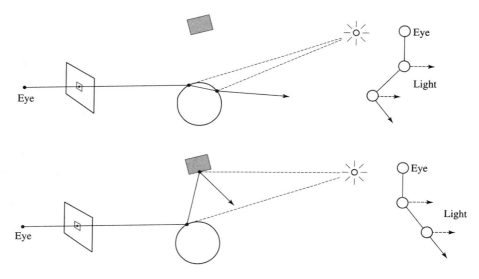

Kajiya points out that Whitted ray tracing is wasteful in the sense that as the algorithm goes deeper into the tree it does more and more work. At the same time the contribution to the pixel intensity from events deep in the tree becomes less and less. In Kajiya's approach the tree has a branching ratio of one, and at each hit point a random variable, from a distribution based on the specular and diffuse BRDFs, is used to shoot a single ray. Kajiya points out that this process has to maintain the correct proportion of reflection, refraction and shadow rays for each pixel.

In terms of Monte Carlo theory the original algorithm reduces the variance for direct illumination but indirect illumination exhibits high variance. This is particularly true for LS*DS* E paths (see Section 10.7 for further consideration of this type of path) where a diffuse surface is receiving light from an emitter via a number of specular paths. Thus the algorithm takes a very long time to produce a good quality image. (Kajiya quotes a time of 20 hours for a 512×512 pixel image with 40 paths per pixel.)

Importance sampling can be introduced into path/ray tracing algorithms by basing it on the BRDF and ensuring that more rays are sent in directions that will return large contributions. However, this can only be done approximately because the associated PDF cannot be integrated and inverted. Another problem is that the BRDF is only one component of the integrand local to the current surface point – we have no knowledge of the light incident on this point from all directions over the hemispherical space – the field radiance (apart from the light due to direct illumination). In conventional path/ray tracing approaches all rays are traced independently of each other, accumulated and averaged into a pixel. No use is made of information gained while the process proceeds. This important observation has led to schemes that cache the information obtained during the ray trace. The most familiar of these is described in Section 10.9.

Distributed ray tracing

Like path tracing, distributed ray tracing can be seen as an extension of Whitted ray tracing or as a Monte Carlo strategy. Distributed ray tracing (distribution ray tracing, stochastic ray tracing), developed by Cook in 1986 (Cook 1986), was presumably motivated by the need to deal with the fact that Whitted ray tracing could only account for perfect specular interaction which would only occur in scenes made up of objects that consisted of perfect mirror surfaces or perfect transmitters. The effect that a Whitted ray tracer produces for (perfect) solid glass is particularly disconcerting or unrealistic. For example, consider a sphere of perfect glass. The viewer sees a circle inside of which perfectly sharp refraction has occurred (Figure 10.12). There is no sense of the sphere as an object as one would experience if scattering due to imperfections had occurred.

As far as light interaction is concerned, distributed ray tracing again only considers specular interaction but this time imperfect specular interaction is simulated by using the ray tracing approach and constructing at every hit point a reflection lobe. The shape of the lobe can depend on the surface properties of the material. Instead of spawning a single transmitted or reflected ray at an intersection a group of rays is spawned which samples the reflection lobe. This produces more realistic ray traced scenes. The images of objects reflected in the surfaces of nearby objects can appeared blurred, transparency effects are more realistic because scattering imperfections can be simulated. Area light sources can be included in the scene to produce shadows. Consider Figure 10.13: if, as would be the case in practice, the mirror surface of the sphere was not physically perfect, then we would expect to see a blurred reflection of the opaque sphere in the mirror sphere.

Thus the path classification scheme is again LDS*E or LS*E but this time all the paths are calculated (or more precisely an estimation of the effects of all the paths is calculated by judicious sampling). In Figure 10.13 three LDSE paths may be discovered by a single eye ray. The points on the wall hit by these rays are combined into a single ray (and eventually a single pixel).

As well as the above effects, Cook *et al.*'s (1984) method considered a finite aperture camera model which produced images that exhibit depth of field, motion blur

Figure 10.12
Perfect refraction through a solid glass sphere is indistinguishable from texture mapping.

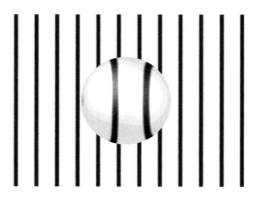

Figure 10.13
Distributed ray tracing for reflection (see Figure 10.4 for the complete geometry of this case).

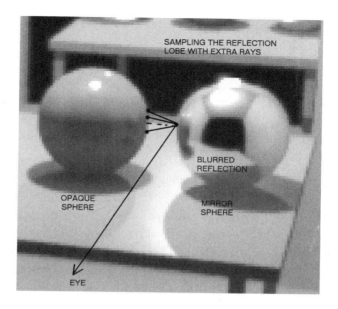

due to moving objects and effective anti-aliasing (see Chapter 14 for the anti-aliasing implications of this algorithm). Figure 10.14 (Colour Plate) is an image rendered with a distributed ray tracer that demonstrates the depth of field phenomenon. The theoretical importance of this work is their realization that all these phenomena could be incorporated into a single multi-dimensional integral which was then evaluated using Monte Carlo techniques. A ray path in this algorithm is similar to a path in Kajiya's method with the addition of the camera lens. The algorithm uses a combination of stratified and importance sampling. A pixel is stratified into 16 sub-pixels and a ray is initiated from a point within a sub-pixel by using uncorrelated jittering. The lens is also stratified and one stratum on the pixel is associated with a single stratum on the lens (Figure 10.15). Reflection and transmission lobes are importance sampled and the sample point similarly jittered. Cook *et al.* (1984) pre-calculate these and store them in look-up tables associated with a surface type. Each ray derives an index as a function of its position in the

Figure 10.15
Distributed ray tracing: four rays per pixel. The pixel, lens and light source are stratified; the reflection lobe is importance sampled.

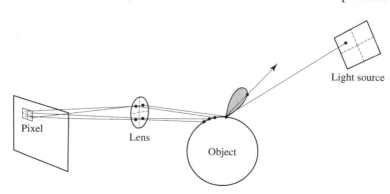

pixel. The primary ray and all its descendants have the same index. This means that a ray emerging from a first hit along a direction relative to R, will emerge from all other hits in the same relative R direction for each object (Figure 10.16). This ensures that each pixel intensity, which is finally determined from 16 samples, is based on samples that are distributed, according to the importance sampling criterion, across the complete range of the specular reflection functions associated with each object. Note that there is nothing to prevent a look-up table being two-dimensional and indexed also by the incoming angle. This enables specular reflection functions that depend on angle of incidence to be implemented. Finally, note that transmission is implemented in exactly the same way using specular transmission functions about the refraction direction.

In summary we have:

(1) The process of distributing rays means that stochastic anti-aliasing becomes an integral part of the method (Chapter 14).

(2) Distributing reflected rays produces blurry reflections.

(3) Distributing transmitted rays produces convincing translucency.

(4) Distributing shadow rays results in penumbrae.

(5) Distributing ray origins over the camera lens area produces depth of field.

(6) Distributing rays in time produces motion blur (temporal anti-aliasing).

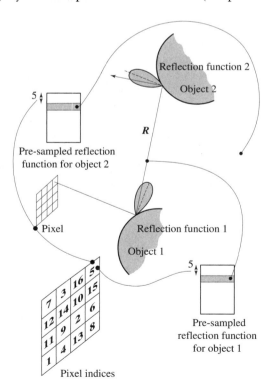

Figure 10.16
Distributed ray tracing and reflected rays.

Two-pass ray tracing

Two-pass ray tracing (or bi-directional ray tracing) was originally developed to incorporate the specular-to-diffuse transfer mechanism into the general ray tracing model. This accounts for caustics which is the pattern formed on a diffuse surface by light rays being reflected through a medium like glass or water. One can usually see on the bottom and sides of a swimming pool beautiful elliptical patterns of bright light which are due to sunlight refracting at the wind-disturbed water surface causing the light energy to vary across the diffuse surface of the pool sides. Figure 10.17 shows a ray from the scene in Figure 10.4 emanating from the light source refracting through the sphere and contributing to a caustic that forms on the (diffuse) table top. This is an LSSDE path.

Two-pass ray tracing was first proposed by Arvo (1986). In Arvo's scheme, rays from the light source were traced through transparent objects and from specular objects. Central to the working of such a strategy is the question of how information derived during the first pass is communicated to the second. Arvo suggests achieving this with a light or illumination map, consisting of a grid of data points, which is pasted onto each object in the scene in much the same way that a conventional texture map would be.

In general, two-pass ray tracing simulates paths of type LS*DS*E. The algorithm 'relies' on there being a single D interaction encountered from both the light source and the eye. The first pass consists of shooting rays from the light source and following them through the specular interactions until they hit a diffuse surface (Figure 10.17). The light energy from each ray is then deposited or cached on the diffuse surface, which has been subdivided in some manner, into elements or

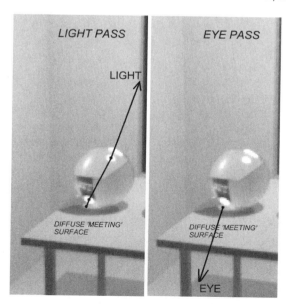

Figure 10.17
Two-pass ray tracing for the LSSDE path in Figure 10.4.

bins. In effect the first pass imposes a texture map or illumination map – the varying brightness of the caustic – on the diffuse surface. The resolution of the illumination map is critical. For a fixed number of shot light rays, too fine a map may result in map elements receiving no rays and too coarse a map results in blurring.

The second pass is the eye trace – conventional Whitted ray tracing – which terminates on the diffuse surface and uses the stored energy in the illumination map as an approximation to the light energy that would be obtained if diffuse reflection was followed in every possible direction from the hit point. In the example shown, the second pass simulates a DE path (or ED path with respect to the trace direction). The 'spreading' of the illumination from rays traced in the first pass over the diffuse surface relies on the fact that the rate of change of diffuse illumination over a surface is slow. It is important to note that there can only be one diffuse surface included in any path. Both the eye trace and the light trace terminate on the diffuse surface – it is the 'meeting point' of both traces.

It is easy to see that we cannot simulate LS*D paths by eye tracing alone. Eye rays do not necessarily hit the light and we have no way of finding out if a surface has received extra illumination due to specular to diffuse transfer. This is illustrated for an easy case of an LSDE path in Figure 10.18.

The detailed process is illustrated in Figure 10.19. A light ray strikes a surface at P after being refracted. It is indexed into the light map associated with the

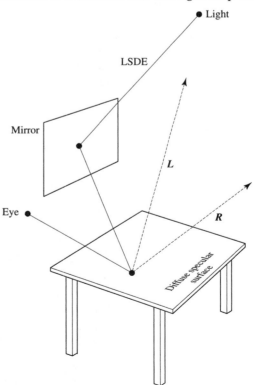

Figure 10.18
An example of an LSDE path (see also Figures 10.4 and 10.17 for examples of SDE paths). An eye ray can 'discover' light ray L and reflected ray R but cannot find the LSDE path.

Figure 10.19
Two-pass ray tracing and
light maps. (a) First pass:
light is deposited in a light
map using a standard
texture mapping T.
(b) Second pass: when
object 2 is conventionally
eye traced extra illumination
at P is obtained by indexing
the light map with T.

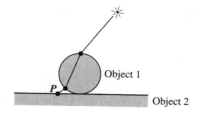

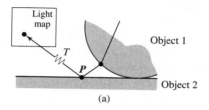

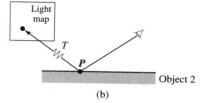

(a)   (b)

object using a standard texture mapping function T. During the second pass an eye ray hits P. The same mapping function is used to pick up any illumination for the point P and this contribution weights the local intensity calculated for that point.

An important point here is that the first pass is view independent – we construct a light map for each object which is analogous in this sense to a texture map – it becomes part of the surface properties of the object. We can use the light maps from any view point after they are completed and they need only be computed once for each scene.

Figure 10.20(a) and (b) (Colour Plate) shows the same scene rendered using a Whitted and two-pass ray tracer. In this scene there are three LSD paths:

(1) Two caustics from the red sphere – one directly from the light and one from the light reflected from the curved mirror.

(2) One (cusp) reflected caustic from the cylindrical mirror.

(3) Secondary illumination from the planar mirror (a non-caustic LSDE path).

Figures 10.20(c)–(e) were produced by shooting an increasing number of light rays and show the effect of the light sprinkled on the diffuse surface. As the number of rays in the light pass increases, these can eventually be merged to form well-defined LSD paths in the image. The number of rays shot in the light pass was 200, 400 and 800 respectively.

Two-pass ray tracing, as introduced by Arvo (1986) was apparently the first algorithm to use the idea of caching illumination. This approach has subsequently been taken up by Ward in his RADIANCE renderer and is the basis of most recent approaches to global illumination (see Section 10.9). We have also introduced the idea of light maps in Chapter 8. The difference between light maps in the context of this chapter and those in Chapter 8 is in their application. In global illumination they are used as part of the rendering process to make a solution more efficient or feasible. Their application in Chapter 8 was as a mechanism for by-passing light calculations in real time rendering. In that context they function as a means of carrying pre-calculated rendering operations into the real time application.

10.8 View dependence/independence and multi-pass methods

In Section 10.5 we introduced path tracing as a method that implemented full L(D|S)* E interaction but pointed out that this is an extremely costly approach to solving the global illumination problem. In this section we will look at approaches which have combined established partial solutions such as ray tracing and radiosity and these are termed multi-pass methods.

A multi-pass method in global illumination most commonly means a combination of a view-independent method (radiosity) with a view-dependent method (ray tracing). (Although we could categorize two-pass ray tracing as a multi-pass method we have chosen to consider it as an extension to ray tracing.) Consider first the implications of the difference between a view-dependent and a view-independent approach. View-independent solutions normally only represent view-independent interactions (pure diffuse–diffuse) because they are mostly solutions where the light levels at every point in the scene are written into a three-dimensional scene data structure. We should bear in mind, however, that in principle there is nothing to stop us computing a view-independent solution that stores specular interactions, we would simply have to increase the dimensionality of the solution to calculate/store the direction of the light on a surface as well as its intensity. We return to this point in Section 10.11.

A pure view-independent algorithm evaluates only sufficient global illumination to determine the final image and if a different view is required the algorithm starts all over again. This is obvious. A more subtle point is that, in general, view-dependent algorithms evaluate an independent solution for each pixel. This is wasteful in the case of diffuse interaction because the illumination on large diffuse surfaces changes only slowly. It was this observation that led to the idea of caching illumination.

View-independent algorithms on the other hand are generally more expensive and do not handle high frequency changes such as specular interaction without significant cost in terms of computation and storage. Multi-pass algorithms exploit the advantages of both approaches by combining them.

A common approach is to post-process a radiosity solution with a ray-tracing pass. A view-independent image with the specular detail added is then obtained. However, this does not account for all path types. By combining radiosity with two-pass ray tracing the path classification, LS*DS*E can be extended to LS*(D*)S*E, the inclusion of radiosity extending the D component to D*. This implies the following ordering for an extended radiosity algorithm. Light ray tracing is employed first and light rays are traced from the source(s) through all specular transports until a diffuse surface is reached and the light energy is

Figure 10.21
The virtual environment method for incorporating DSD paths in the radiosity method.

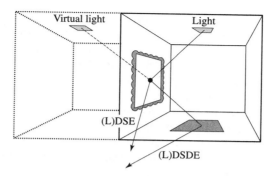

deposited. This accounts for the LS* paths. A radiosity solution is then invoked using these values as emitting patches and the deposited energy is distributed through the D* chain. Finally an eye pass is initiated and this provides the final projection and the ES* or ES*D paths.

Comparing the string LS*(D*)S*E with the complete global solution, we see that the central D* paths should be extended to (D*S*D*)* to make LS*(D*S*D*)*S*E which is equivalent to the complete global solution L(S|D)*E. Conventional or classical radiosity does not include diffuse-to-diffuse transfer that takes place via an intermediate specular surface. In other words once we invoke the radiosity phase we need to include the possibility of transfer via an intermediate specular path DSD.

The first and perhaps the simplest approach to including a specular transfer into the radiosity solution was based on modifying the classical radiosity algorithm for flat specular surfaces, such as mirrors, and is called the virtual window approach. This idea is shown in Figure 10.21. Conventional radiosity calculates the geometric relationship between the light source and the floor and the LDE path is accounted for by the diffuse–diffuse interaction between these two surfaces. (Note that since the light source is itself an emitting diffuse patch we can term the path LDE or DDE). What is missing from this is the contribution of light energy from the LSD or DSD path that would deposit a bright area of light on the floor. The DSD path from the light source via the mirror to the floor can be accounted for by constructing a virtual environment 'seen' through the mirror as a window. The virtual light source then acts as if it was the real light source reflected from the mirror. However, we still need to account for the LSE path which is the detailed reflected image formed in the mirror. This is view dependent and is determined during a second pass ray tracing phase. The fact that this algorithm only deals with what is, in effect, a special case illustrates the inherent difficulty of extending radiosity to include other transfer mechanisms.

(10.9) Caching illumination

Caching illumination is the term we have given to the scheme of storing three- or five-dimensional values for illumination, in a data structure associated with the scene, as a solution progresses. Such a scheme usually relates to view-dependent algorithms. In other words the cached values are used to speed up or increase the accuracy of a solution; they do not comprise a view-dependent solution in their own right. We can compare such an approach with a view-independent solution such as radiosity where final illumination values are effectively cached on the (discretized) surfaces themselves. The difference between such an approach and the caching methods described in this section is that the storage method is independent of the surface. This means that the meshing problems inherent in surface discretization methods (Chapter 11) are avoided. Illumination values on surfaces are stored in a data structure like an octree which represents the entire three-dimensional extent of the scene.

Consider again the simplified form of the radiance equation:

$$L_{surface} = \int \rho L_{in}$$

The BRDF is known but L_{in} is not and this, as we pointed out in Section 10.4, limits the efficacy of importance sampling. An estimate of L_{in} can be obtained as the solution proceeds and this requires that the values are stored. The estimate can be used to improve importance sampling and this is the approach taken by Lafortune and Williams (1995) in a technique that they call adaptive importance sampling. Their method is effectively a path tracing algorithm which uses previously calculated values of radiance to guide the current path. The idea is shown in Figure 10.22 where it is seen that a reflection direction during a path trace is chosen according to both the BRDF for the point and the current value of the field radiance distribution function for that point which has been built up

Figure 10.22
Adaptive importance sampling in path tracing (after Lafortune and Williams (1995)).
(a) Incoming radiance at a point **P** is cached in a 5D tree and builds up into a distribution function.
(b) A future reflected direction from **P** is selected on the basis of both the BRDF and the field radiance distribution function.

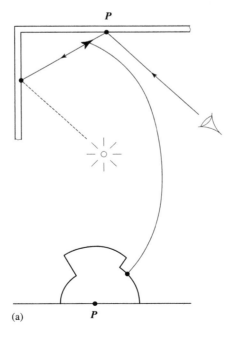

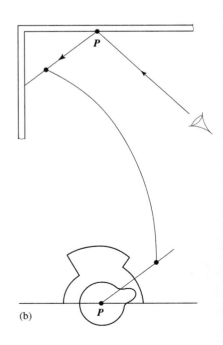

(a)

(b)

from previous values. Lafortune and Williams (1995) cache radiance values in a five-dimensional tree – a two-dimensional extension of a (three-dimensional) octree.

The RADIANCE renderer is probably the most well-known global illumination renderer. Developed by Ward (1994) over a period of nine years, it is a strategy, based on path tracing, that solves a version of the rendering equation under most conditions. The emphasis of this work is firmly on the accuracy required for architectural simulations under a variety of lighting conditions varying from sunlight to complex artificial lighting set-ups. The algorithm is effectively a combination of deterministic and stochastic approaches and Ward (1994) describes the underlying motivations as follows:

The key to fast convergence is in deciding *what* to sample by removing those parts of the integral we can compute deterministically and gauging the importance of the rest so as to maximise the payback from our ray calculations.

Specular calculations are made separately and the core algorithm deals with indirect diffuse interaction. Values resulting from (perfect) diffuse interaction are cached in a (three-dimensional) octree and these cached values are used to interpolate a new value if a current hit point is sufficiently close to a cached point. This basic approach is elaborated by determining the 'irradiance gradient' in the region currently being examined which leads to the use of a higher-order (cubic) interpolation procedure for the interpolation. The RADIANCE renderer is a path tracing algorithm that terminates early if the cached values are 'close enough'.

Finally Ward expresses some strong opinions about the practical efficacy of the radiosity method. It is unusual for such criticisms to appear in a computer graphics paper and Ward is generally concerned that the radiosity method has not migrated from the research laboratories. He says:

For example, most radiosity systems are not well automated, and do not permit general reflectance models or curved surfaces . . .. Acceptance of physically based rendering is bound to improve, but researchers must first demonstrate the real-life applicability of their techniques. There have been few notable successes in applying radiosity to the needs of practising designers. While much research has been done on improving efficiency of the basic radiosity method, problems associated with more realistic complicated geometries, have only recently got the attention they deserve. For whatever reason it appears that radiosity has yet to fulfil its promise, and it is time to re-examine this technique in the light of real-world applications and other alternatives for solving the rendering equation.

An example of the use of the RADIANCE renderer is given in the comparative image study in Chapter 18 (Figure 18.19).

10.10 Light volumes

Light volume is the term given to schemes that cache a view-independent global illumination by storing radiance or irradiance values at sample points over all space (including empty space). Thus they differ from the previous schemes which stored values only at point on surfaces. In Chapter 16 we also encounter light volumes (therein termed light fields). Light fields are the same as light volumes and differ only in their intended application. They are used to efficiently store a pre-calculated view-independent rendering of a scene. In global illumination, however, they are used to facilitate a solution in some way.

An example of the application of light volumes is described by Greger *et al.* (1998). Here the idea is to use a global illumination solution in 'semi-dynamic' environments. Such an environment is defined as one wherein the moving objects are small compared to the static objects, implying that their position in the scene does not affect the global illumination solution to any great extent. A global solution is built up in a light volume and this is used to determine the global illumination received by a moving object – in effect the moving object travels through a static light volume receiving illumination but not contributing to the pre-processed solution.

Particle tracing and density estimation

In this final section we look at a recent approach (Walter *et al.* 1997) whose novelty is to recognize that it is advantageous to separate the global problem into light transport and light representation calculations. In this work rather than caching illumination, particle histories are stored. The reason for this is that light transport – the flow of light between surfaces – has high global or inter-surface complexity. On the other hand the representation of light on the surface of an object has high local or intra-surface complexity. Surfaces may exhibit shadows, specular highlights caustics etc. (A good example of this is the radiosity algorithm where transport and representation are merged into one process. Here the difficulty lies in predicting the meshing required – for example, to define shadow edges – to input into the algorithm. That is, we have to decide on a meshing prior to the light transport solution being available.)

The process is divided into three sequential phases:

- **Particle tracing** In a sense this is a view-independent form of path tracing. Light-carrying particles are emitted from each light source and travel through the environment. Each time a surface is hit this is recorded (surface identifier, point hit and wavelength of the particle) and a reflection/transmission direction computed according to the BRDF of the surface. Each particle generates a list of information for every surface it collides with and a particle process terminates after a minimum of interactions or until it is absorbed. Thus a particle path generates a history of interactions rather than returning a pixel intensity.

- **Density estimation** After the particle tracing process is complete each surface possesses a list of particles and the stored hit points are used to construct the illumination on the surface based on the spatial density of the hit points. The result of this process is a Gouraud shaded mesh of triangles.

- **Mesh optimization** The solution is view independent and the third phase optimizes or decimates the mesh by progressively removing meshes as long as the resulting change due to the removal does not drop below a (perceptually based) threshold. The output from this phase is an irregular mesh whose detail relates to the variation of light over the surface.

Walter *et al.* (1997) point out that a strong advantage of the technique is that its modularity enables optimization for different design goals. For example, the light transport phase can be optimized for the required accuracy of the BRDFs. The density phase can vary its criteria according to perceptual accuracy and the decimation phase can achieve high compression while maintaining perceptual quality.

A current disadvantage of the approach is that it is a three-dimensional view-independent solution which implies that it can only display diffuse–diffuse interaction. However, Walter *et al.* (1997) point out that this restriction comes out of the density estimation phase. The particle tracing module can deal with any type of BRDF.

The radiosity method

Introduction

Ray tracing, the first computer graphics model to embrace global interaction, or at least one aspect of it – suffers from an identifying visual signature: you can usually tell if an image has been synthesized using ray tracing. It only models one aspect of the light interaction – that due to perfect specular reflection and transmission. The interaction between diffusely reflecting surfaces, which tends to be the predominant light transport mechanism in interiors, is still modelled using an ambient constant (in the local reflection component of the model). Consider, for example, a room with walls and ceiling painted with a matte material and carpeted. If there are no specularly reflecting objects in the room, then those parts of the room that cannot see a light source are lit by diffuse interaction. Such a room tends to exhibit slow and subtle changes of intensity across its surfaces.

In 1984, using a method whose theory was based on the principles of radiative heat transfer, researchers at Cornell University, developed the radiosity method (Goral *et al*. 1984). This is now known as classical radiosity and it simulates LD*E paths, that is, it can only be used, in its unextended form, to render scenes that are made up in their entirety of (perfect) diffuse surfaces.

To accomplish this, every surface in a scene is divided up into elements called patches and a set of equations is set up based on the conservation of light energy.

A single patch in such an environment reflects light received from every other patch in the environment. It may also emit light if it is a light source – light sources are treated like any other patch except that they have non-zero self-emission. The interaction between patches depends on their geometric relationship. That is distance and relative orientation. Two parallel patches a short distance apart will have a high interaction. An equilibrium solution is possible if, for each patch in the environment, we calculate its interaction between it and every other patch in the environment.

One of the major contributions of the Cornell group was to invent an efficient way – the hemicube algorithm – for evaluating the geometric relationship between pairs of patches; in fact, in the 1980s most of the innovations in radiosity methods have come out of this group.

The cost of the algorithm is $O(N^2)$ where N is the number of patches into which the environment is divided. To keep processing costs down, the patches are made large and the light intensity is assumed to be constant across a patch. This immediately introduces a quality problem – if illumination discontinuities do not coincide with patch edges artefacts occur. This size restriction is the practical reason why the algorithm can only calculate diffuse interaction, which by its nature changes slowly across a surface. Adding specular interaction to the radiosity method is expensive and is still the subject of much research. Thus we have the strange situation that the two global interaction methods – ray tracing and radiosity – are mutually exclusive as far as the phenomena that they calculate are concerned. Ray tracing cannot calculate diffuse interaction and radiosity cannot incorporate specular interaction. Despite this, the radiosity method has produced some of the most realistic images to date in computer graphics.

The radiosity method deals with shadows without further enhancement. As we have already discussed, the geometry of shadows is more-or-less straightforward to calculate and can be part of a ray tracing algorithm or an algorithm added onto a local reflection model renderer. However, the intensity within a shadow is properly part of diffuse interaction and can only be arbitrarily approximated by other algorithms. The radiosity method takes shadows in its stride. They drop out of the solution as intensities like any other. The only problem is that the patch size may have to be reduced to delineate the shadow boundary to some desired level of accuracy. Shadow boundaries are areas where the rate of change of diffuse light intensity is high and the normal patch size may cause visible aliasing at the shadow edge.

The radiosity method is an object space algorithm, solving for the intensity at discrete points or surface patches within an environment and not for pixels in an image plane projection. The solution is thus independent of viewer position. This complete solution is then injected into a renderer that computes a particular view by removing hidden surfaces and forming a projection. This phase of the method does not require much computation (intensities are already calculated) and different views are easily obtained from the general solution.

11.1 Radiosity theory

Elsewhere in the text we have tried to maintain a separation between the algorithm that implements a method and the underlying mathematics. It is the case, however, that with the radiosity method, the algorithm is so intertwined with the mathematics that it would be difficult to try to deal with this in a separate way. The theory itself consists of nothing more than definitions – there is no manipulation. Readers requiring further theoretical insight are referred to the book by Siegel and Howell (1984).

The radiosity method is a conservation of energy or energy equilibrium approach, providing a solution for the radiosity of all surfaces within an enclosure. The energy input to the system is from those surfaces that act as emitters. In fact, a light source is treated like any other surface in the algorithm except that it possesses an initial (non-zero) radiosity. The method is based on the assumption that all surfaces are perfect diffusers or ideal Lambertian surfaces.

Radiosity, B, is defined as the energy per unit area leaving a surface patch per unit time and is the sum of the emitted and the reflected energy:

$$B_i dA_i = E_i dA_i + R_i \int_j B_j F_{ji} dA_j$$

Expressing this equation in words we have for a single patch i:

radiosity × area = emitted energy + reflected energy

E_i is the energy emitted from a patch. The reflected energy is given by multiplying the incident energy by R_i, the reflectivity of the patch. The incident energy is that energy that arrives at patch i from all other patches in the environment; that is we integrate over the environment, for all j ($j \neq i$), the term $B_j F_{ji} dA_j$. This is the energy leaving each patch j that arrives at patch i. F_{ji} is a constant, called a form factor, that parametrizes the relationship between patches j and i.

We can use a reciprocity relationship to give:

$$F_{ij} A_i = F_{ji} A_j$$

and dividing through by dA_i, gives:

$$B_i = E_i + R_i \int_j B_j F_{ij}$$

For a discrete environment the integral is replaced by a summation and constant radiosity is assumed over small discrete patches, giving:

$$B_i = E_i + R_i \sum_{j=1}^{n} B_j F_{ij}$$

Such an equation exists for each surface patch in the enclosure and the complete environment produces a set of n simultaneous equations of the form:

$$\begin{bmatrix} 1 - R_1F_{11} & -R_1F_{12} & \cdots & -R_1F_{1n} \\ -R_2F_{21} & 1 - R_2F_{22} & \cdots & -R_2F_{2n} \\ \vdots & \vdots & \cdots & \vdots \\ R_nF_{n1} & -R_nF_{n2} & \cdots & 1 - R_nF_{nn} \end{bmatrix} \begin{bmatrix} B_1 \\ B_2 \\ \vdots \\ B_n \end{bmatrix} = \begin{bmatrix} E_1 \\ E_2 \\ \vdots \\ E_n \end{bmatrix} \qquad [11.1]$$

Solving this equation is the radiosity method. Out of this solution comes B_i the radiosity for each patch. However, there are two problems left. We need a way of computing the form factors. And we need to compute a view and display the patches. To do this we need a linear interpolation method – just like Gouraud shading – otherwise the subdivision pattern – the patches themselves – will be visible.

The E_is are non-zero only at those surfaces that provide illumination and these terms represent the input illumination to the system. The R_is are known and the F_{ij}s are a function of the geometry of the environment. The reflectivities are wavelength-dependent terms and the above equation should be regarded as a monochromatic solution; a complete solution being obtained by solving for however many colour bands are being considered. We can note at this stage that $F_{ii} = 0$ for a plane or convex surface – none of the radiation leaving the surface will strike itself. Also from the definition of the form factor the sum of any row of form factors is unity.

Since the form factors are a function only of the geometry of the system they are computed once only. The method is bound by the time taken to calculate the form factors expressing the radiative exchange between two surface patches A_i and A_j. This depends on their relative orientation and the distance between them and is given by:

$$F_{ij} = \frac{\text{Radiative energy leaving surface } A_i \text{ that strikes } A_j \text{ directly}}{\text{Radiative energy leaving surface } A_i \text{ in all directions in the hemispherical space surrounding } A_i}$$

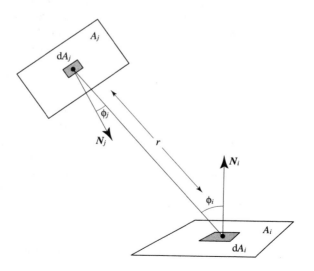

Figure 11.1
Form factor geometry for two patches *i* and *j* (after Goral *et al.* (1984)).

It can be shown that this is given by:

$$F_{ij} = \frac{1}{A_i} \int_{Ai} \int_{Aj} \frac{\cos \phi_i \cos \phi_j}{\pi r^2} \, dA_j dA_i$$

where the geometric conventions are illustrated in Figure 11.1. In any practical environment A_j may be wholly or partially invisible from A_i and the integral needs to be multiplied by an occluding factor which is a binary function that depends on whether the differential area dA_i can see dA_j or not. This double integral is difficult to solve except for specific shapes.

(11.2) Form factor determination

An elegant numerical method of evaluating form factors was developed in 1985 and this is known as the hemicube method. This offered an efficient method of determining form factors and at the same time a solution to the intervening patch problem.

The patch to patch form factor can be approximated by the differential area to finite area equation:

$$F_{dAiAj} = \int_{Aj} \frac{\cos \phi_i \cos \phi_j}{\pi r^2} \, dA_j$$

where we are now considering the form factor between the elemental area dA_i and the finite area A_j. dA_i is positioned at the centre point of patch i. The veracity of this approximation depends on the area of the two patches compared with the distance, r, between them. If r is large the inner integral does not change much over the range of the outer integral and the effect of the outer integral is simply multiplication by unity.

A theorem called the Nusselt analogue tells us that we can consider the projection of a patch j onto the surface of a hemisphere surrounding the elemental patch dA_i and that this is equivalent in effect to considering the patch itself. Also patches that produce the same projection on the hemisphere have the same form factor. This is the justification for the hemicube method as illustrated in Figure 11.2. Patches A, B and C all have the same form factor and we can evaluate the form factor of any patch j by considering not the patch itself, but its projection onto the faces of a hemicube.

A hemicube is used to approximate the hemisphere because flat projection planes are computationally less expensive. The hemicube is constructed around the centre of each patch with the hemicube Z axis and the patch normal coincident (Figure 11.3). The faces of the hemicube are divided into pixels – a somewhat confusing use of the term since we are operating in object space. Every other patch in the environment is projected onto this hemicube. Two patches that project onto the same pixel can have their depths compared and the further patch be rejected, since it cannot be seen from the receiving patch. This approach is analogous to a Z-buffer algorithm except that there is no interest in

Figure 11.2
The justification for using a hemicube. Patches *A, B* and *C* have the same form factor.

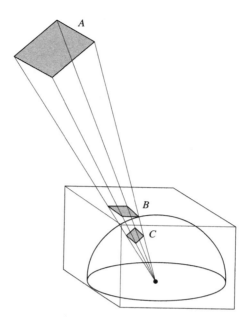

intensities at this stage. The hemicube algorithm only facilitates the calculation of the form factors that are subsequently used in calculating diffuse intensities and a 'label buffer' is maintained indicating which patch is currently nearest to the hemicube pixel.

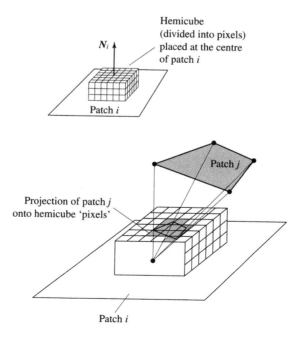

Figure 11.3
Evaluating the form factor F_{ij} by projecting patch *j* onto the faces of a hemicube centred on patch *i*.

Each pixel on the hemicube can be considered as a small patch and a differential to finite area form factor, known as a delta form factor, defined for each pixel. The form factor of a pixel is a fraction of the differential to finite area form factor for the patch and can be defined as:

$$\Delta F_{dAiAj} = \frac{\cos \phi_i \cos \phi_j}{\pi r^2} \Delta A$$

$$= AF_q$$

where ΔA is the area of the pixel.

These form factors are pre-calculated and stored in a look-up table. This is the foundation of the efficiency of the hemicube method. Again, using the fact that areas of equal projection onto the receiving surface surrounding the centre of patch A_i have equal form factors, we can conclude that F_{ij}, for any patch, is obtained by summing the pixel form factors onto which patch A_j projects (Figure 11.4).

Thus form factor evaluation now reduces to projection onto mutually orthogonal planes and a summation operation.

Figure 11.5 (Colour Plate) is an interesting image that shows the state of a hemicube placed on the window (Figure 10.7) after all other patches in the scene have been projected onto it. A colour identifies each patch in the scene (and every partial patch) that can be seen by this hemicube. The algorithm then simply summates all the hemicube element form factors associated with each patch.

The method can be summarized in the following stages:

(1) Computation of the form factors, F_{ij}. Each hemicube emplacement calculates $(n–1)$ form factors or one row in the equation.

(2) Solving the radiosity matrix equation.

(3) Rendering by injecting the results of stage (2) into a bilinear interpolation scheme.

(4) Repeating stages (2) and (3) for the colour bands of interest.

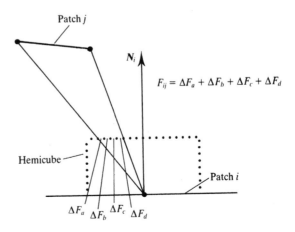

Figure 11.4
F_{ij} is obtained by summing the form factors of the pixels onto which patch i projects.

This process is shown in Figure 11.6. Form factors are a function only of the environment and are calculated once only and can be reused in stage (2) for different reflectivities and light source values. Thus a solution can be obtained for the same environment with, for example, some light sources turned off. The solution produced by stage (2) is a view-independent solution and if a different view is required then only stage (3) is repeated. This approach can be used, for example, when generating an animated walk-through of a building interior. Each frame in the animation is computed by changing the view point and calculating a new view from an unchanging radiosity solution. It is only if we change the geometry of the scene that a re-calculation of the form factors is necessary. If the lighting is changed and the geometry is unaltered, then only the equation needs resolving – we do not have to re-calculate the form factors.

Stage (2) implies the computation of a view-independent rendered version of the solution to the radiosity equation which supplies a single value, a radiosity, for each patch in the environment. From these values vertex radiosities are calculated and these vertex radiosities are used in the bilinear interpolation scheme to provide a final image. A depth buffer algorithm is used at this stage to evaluate the visibility of each patch at each pixel on the screen. (This stage should not be confused with the hemicube operation that has to evaluate inter-patch visibility during the computation of form factors.)

The time taken to complete the form factor calculation depends on the square of the number of patches. A hemicube calculation is performed for every patch (onto which all other patches are projected). The overall calculation time thus depends on the complexity of the environment and the accuracy of the solution,

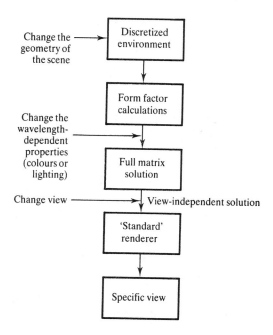

Figure 11.6
Stages in a complete radiosity solution. Also shown are the points in the process where various modifications can be made to the image.

as determined by the hemicube resolution. Although diffuse illumination changes only slowly across a surface, aliasing can be caused by too low a hemicube resolution and accuracy is required at shadow boundaries (see Section 11.7). Storage requirements are also a function of the number of patches required. All these factors mean that there is an upward limit on the complexity of the scenes that can be handled by the radiosity method.

11.3 The Gauss–Siedel method

Cohen and Greenberg (1985) point out that the Gauss–Siedel method is guaranteed to converge rapidly for equation sets such as Equation 11.1. The sum of any row of form factors is by definition less than unity and each form factor is multiplied by a reflectivity of less than one. The summation of the row terms in Equation 11.1 (excluding the main diagonal term) is thus less than unity. The mean diagonal term is always unity ($F_{ii} = 0$ for all i) and these conditions guarantee fast convergence. The Gauss–Siedel method is an extension to the following iterative method. Given a system of linear equations:

$$\mathbf{Ax} = \mathbf{E}$$

such as Equation 11.1, we can rewrite equations for $x_1, x_2, \ldots, x_i$ in the form:

$$x_1 = \frac{E_1 - a_{12}x_2 - a_{13}x_3 - \ldots - a_{1n}x_n}{a_{11}}$$

which leads to the iteration:

$$x_1^{(k+1)} = \frac{E_1 - a_{12}x_2^{(k)} - a_{13}x_3 - \ldots - a_{1n}x_n^{(k)}}{a_{11}}$$

in general:

$$x_i^{(k+1)} = \frac{E_i - a_{i1}x_1^{(k)} - \ldots - a_{i,i-1}x_{i-1}^{(k)} - a_{i,i+1}x_{i+1}^{(k)} - \ldots - a_{in}x_n^{(k)}}{a_{ii}} \qquad [11.2]$$

This formula can be used in an iteration procedure:

(1) Choose an initial approximation, say:

$$x_i^{(0)} = \frac{E_i}{a_{ii}}$$

for $i = 1, 2, \ldots, n$, where E_i is non-zero for emitting surfaces or light sources only.

(2) Determine the next iterate:

$$x_i^{(k+1)} \text{ from } x_i^{(k)}$$

using Equation 11.2.

(3) If $|x_i^{(k+1)} - x_i^{(k)}| < $ a threshold

for $i = 1, 2, \ldots, n$

then stop the iteration, otherwise return to step (2).

This is known as Jacobi iteration. The Gauss–Siedel method improves on the convergence of this method by modifying Equation 11.2 to use the latest available information. When the new iterate $x_i^{(k+1)}$ is being calculated, new values:

$$x_1^{(k+1)}, x_2^{(k+1)}, \ldots, x_{i-1}^{(k+1)}$$

have already been calculated and Equation 11.2 is modified to:

$$x_i^{(k+1)} = \frac{E_i - a_{i1}x_1^{(k+1)} - \ldots - a_{i,i-1}x_{i-1}^{(k+1)} - a_{i,i+1}x_{i+1}^{(k)} - \ldots - a_{in}x_n^{(k)}}{a_{ii}} \qquad [11.3]$$

Note that when $i = 1$ the right-hand side of the equation contains terms with superscript k only, and Equation 11.3 reduces to Equation 11.2. When $i = n$ the right-hand side contains terms with superscript $(k+1)$ only.

Convergence of the Gauss–Siedel method can be improved by the following method. Having produced a new value $x_i^{(k+1)}$, a better value is given by a weighted average of the old and new values:

$$x_i^{(k+1)} = rx_i'^{(k+1)} + (1 - r)x_i^{(k)}$$

where r (>0) is a parameter independent of k and i. Cohen *et al.* (1988) report that a relaxation factor of 1.1 works for most environments.

11.4 Seeing a partial solution – progressive refinement

Using the radiosity method in a practical context, such as in the design of building interiors, means that the designer has to wait a long time to see a completed image. This is disadvantageous since one of the *raisons d'être* of computer-based design is to allow the user free and fast experimentation with the design parameters. A long feedback time discourages experimentation and stultifies the design process.

In 1988 the Cornell team developed an approach, called 'progressive refinement' that enabled a designer to see an early (but approximate) solution. At this stage major errors can be seen and corrected, and another solution executed. As the solution becomes more and more accurate, the designer may see more subtle changes that have to be made. We introduced this method in the previous chapter, we will now look at the details.

The general goal of progressive or adaptive refinement can be taken up by any slow image synthesis technique and it attempts to find a compromise between the competing demands of interactivity and image quality. A synthesis method that provides adaptive refinement would present an initial quickly rendered image to the user. This image is then progressively refined in a 'graceful' way. This is defined as a progression towards higher quality, greater realism etc., in a way that is automatic, continuous and not distracting to the user. Early availability of an approximation can greatly assist in the development of techniques and images, and reducing the feedback loop by approximation is a necessary adjunct to the radiosity method.

The two major cost factors in the radiosity method are the storage costs and the calculation of the form factors. For an environment of 50×10^3 patches, even although the resulting square matrix of form factors may be 90% sparse (many patches cannot see each other) this still requires 10^9 bytes of storage (at four bytes per form factor).

Both the requirements of progressive refinement and the elimination of pre-calculation and storage of the form factors are met by an ingenious restructuring of the basic radiosity algorithm. The stages in the progressive refinement are obtained by displaying the results as the iterative solution progresses. The solution is restructured and the form factor evaluation order is optimized so that the convergence is 'visually graceful'. This restructuring enables the radiosity of all patches to be updated at each step in the solution, rather than a step providing the solution for a single patch. Maximum visual difference between steps in the solution can be achieved by processing patches according to their energy contribution to the environment. The radiosity method is particularly suited to a progressive refinement approach because it computes a view-independent solution. Viewing this solution (by rendering from a particular view point) can proceed independently as the radiosity solution progresses.

In the conventional evaluation of the radiosity matrix (using, for example, the Gauss–Seidel method) a solution for one row provides the radiosity for a single patch i:

$$B_i = E_i + R_i \sum_{j=1}^{n} B_j F_{ij}$$

This is an estimate of the radiosity of patch i based on the current estimate of all other patches. This is called 'gathering'. The equation means that (algorithmically) for patch i we visit every other patch in the scene and transfer the appropriate amount of light from each patch j to patch i according to the form factor. The algorithm proceeds on a row-by-row basis and the entire solution is updated for one step through the matrix (although the Gauss–Seidel method uses the new values as soon as they are computed). If the process is viewed dynamically, as the solution proceeds, each patch intensity is updated according to its row position in the radiosity matrix. Light is gathered from every other patch in the scene and used to update the single patch currently being considered.

The idea of the progressive refinement method is that the entire image of all patches is updated at every iteration. This is termed 'shooting', where the contribution from each patch i is distributed to all other patches. The difference between these two processes is illustrated diagramatically in Figures 11.7(a) and (b). This re-ordering of the algorithm is accomplished in the following way.

A single term determines the contribution to the radiosity of patch j due to that from patch i:

$$B_j \quad \text{due to} \quad B_i = R_j B_i F_{ji}$$

Gathering: a single iteration (k) updates a single patch i by gathering contributions from all other patches.

$$B_i^{(k+1)} = E_i + R_i \sum_{j=1}^{N} F_{ij} B_j^{(k)}$$

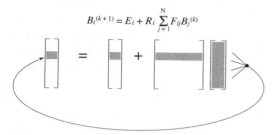

Equivalent to gathering light energy from all the patches in the scene.

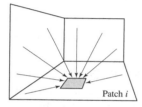

Patch i

(a) Gathering

Shooting: a single step computes form factors from the shooting patch to all receiving patches and distributes (unshot) energy ΔB_i

for all j:
$$B_j^{(k+1)} = B_j^{(k)} + R_j F_{ji} \Delta B_i$$

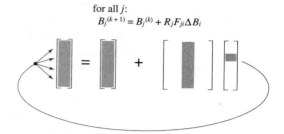

Equivalent to shooting light energy from a patch to all other patches in the scene.

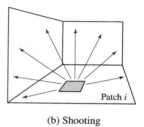

Patch i

(b) Shooting

Figure 11.7
(a) Gathering and
(b) shooting in radiosity
solution strategies
(based on an illustration in
Cohen *et al.* (1988)).

This relationship can be reversed by using the reciprocity relationship:

B_j due to $B_i = R_j B_i F_{ij} A_i / A_j$

and this is true for all patches j. This relationship can be used to determine the contribution to each patch j in the environment from the single patch i. A single radiosity (patch i) shoots light into the environment and the radiosities of all patches j are updated simultaneously. The first complete update (of all the radiosities in the environment) is obtained from 'on the fly' form factor computations. Thus an initial approximation to the complete scene can appear when only the first row of form factors has been calculated. This eliminates high start-up or pre-calculation costs.

This process is repeated until convergence is achieved. All radiosities are initially set either to zero or to their emission values. As this process is repeated for each patch i the solution is displayed and at each step the radiosities for each patch j are updated. As the solution progresses the estimate of the radiosity at a patch i becomes more and more accurate. For an iteration the environment already contains the contribution of the previous estimate of B_j and the so-called 'unshot' radiosity – the difference between the current and previous estimates – is all that is injected into the environment.

If the output from the algorithm is displayed without further elaboration, then a scene, initially dark, gradually gets lighter as the incremental radiosities are added to each patch. The 'visual convergence' of this process can be optimized by sorting the order in which the patches are processed according to the amount of energy that they are likely to radiate. This means, for example, that emitting patches, or light sources, should be treated first. This gives an early well lit solution. The next patches to be processed are those that received most light from the light sources and so on. By using this ordering scheme, the solution proceeds in a way that approximates the propagation of light through an environment. Although this produces a better visual sequence than an unsorted process, the solution still progresses from a dark scene to a fully illuminated scene. To overcome this effect an arbitrary ambient light term is added to the intermediate radiosities. This term is used only to enhance the display and is not part of the solution. The value of the ambient term is based on the current estimate of the radiosities of all patches in the environment, and as the solution proceeds and becomes 'better lit' the ambient contribution is decreased.

Four main stages are completed for each iteration in the algorithm. These are:

(1) Find the patch with the greatest (unshot) radiosity or emitted energy.

(2) Evaluate a column of form factors, that is, the form factors from this patch to every other patch in the environment.

(3) Update the radiosity of each of the receiving patches.

(4) Reduce the temporary ambient term as a function of the sum of the differences between the current values calculated in step (3) and the previous values.

An example of the progressive refinement during execution is shown in Figure 10.7 and Section 10.3.2 contains a full description of this figure.

11.5 Problems with the radiosity method

There are three significant problems associated with radiosity rendering. They are algorithm artefacts that appear in the image, the inability to deal with specular interaction and the inordinate time taken to render a scene of moderate complexity. Curiously, hardly any research effort has been devoted to the time factor, and this is perhaps the reason that radiosity has not generally migrated into applications programs. This contrasts with the situation in ray tracing research in the 1980s, where quite soon after the first ray traced imagery appeared, a large and energetic research effort was devoted to making the method faster. In the remainder of the chapter we will deal exclusively with image quality, noting in passing that it is usually related to execution time – quality can be improved by defining the scene more accurately which in the mainstream method means allowing more iterations in the program.

Developments in the radiosity method beyond the techniques described in the previous chapter have mostly been motivated by defects or artefacts that arise out of the representation of the scene as a set of largish patches. Although other factors, such as taking into account scattering atmospheres and the incorporation of specular reflection are important, addressing the visual defects due to meshing accounts for most research emphasis and it is with this aspect that we will deal.

11.6 Artefacts in radiosity images

The common artefacts in radiosity images that use the classical approach of the previous chapter are due to:

(1) Approximations in the hemicube method for determining the form factors.
(2) Using bilinear interpolation as a reconstruction of the radiosity function from the constant radiosity solution.
(3) Using a meshing or subdivision of the scene that is independent of the nature of the variations in the radiosity function.

The visibility and thus the importance of these depends, of course, on the nature of the scene; but usually the third category is the most noticeable and the most difficult to deal with. In practice the artefacts cannot be treated independently: there is little point in developing a powerful meshing strategy without also dealing with artefacts that emerge from bilinear interpolation. We will now look at these image defects detailing both the cause and the possible cure.

11.6.1 Hemicube artefacts

The serious problem of the hemicube method is aliasing caused by the regular division of the hemicube into uniform pixels. Errors occur as a function of the size of the hemicube pixels due to the assumption that patches will project exactly onto an integer number of pixels, which in general, of course, they do not. This is similar to aliasing in ray tracing. We attempt to gather information from a three-dimensional environment by looking in a fixed number of directions. In ray tracing these directions are given initially by evenly spaced eye-to-pixel rays. In the radiosity method, by projecting the patches onto hemicubes we are effectively sampling with projection rays from the hemicube origin. Figure 11.8 shows a two-dimensional analogue of the problem where a number of identical polygons project onto either one or two pixels depending on the interference between the projection rays and the polygon grid. The polygons are of equal size and equal orientation with respect to patch i. Their form factors should be different – because the number of pixels onto which each polygon projects is different for each polygon. However, as the example shows, neighbouring polygons which should have almost equal form factors will produce values in the ratio 2:1.

The geometry of any practical scene can cause problems with the hemicube method. Its accuracy depends on the distance between the patches involved in the calculation. When distances become small the method falls down. This

Figure 11.8
Interference between
hemicube sampling and a
set of equal polygons (after
Wallace *et al.* (1989)).

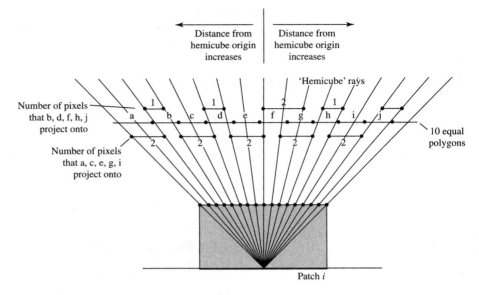

situation occurs in practice, for example, when an object is placed on a support-
ing surface. The errors in form factors occur precisely in those regions from
which we expect the radiosity technique to excel and produce subtle phenomena such as colour bleeding and soft shadows. Baum *et al.* (1989) quantify the
error involved in form factor determination for proximal surfaces, and demonstrate the hemicube method is only accurate in contexts where the inter-patch
distance is at least five patch diameters.

Yet another hemicube problem occurs with light sources. In scenes which the
radiosity method is used to render, we are usually concerned with area sources
such as fluorescent lights. As with any other surface in the environment we divide
the light sources into patches and herein lies the problem. For a standard solution
an environment will be discretized into patches where the subdivision resolution
depends on the area of surface (and the accuracy of the solution required).
However, in the case of light sources the number of hemicubes required or the
number of patches required depends on the distance from the closest surface it
illuminates. A hemicube operation effectively reduces an emitting patch to a
point source. Errors will appear on a close surface as isolated areas of light if the
light source is insufficiently subdivided. With strip lights, where the length to
breadth ratio is great, insufficient subdivision can give rise to banding or aliasing
artefacts that run parallel with the long axis of the light source. An example of
the effect of insufficient light source subdivision is shown in Figure 11.14.

Hemicube aliasing can, of course, be ameliorated by increasing the resolution
of the hemicube, but this is inefficient, increasing the computation required for
all elements in the scene irrespective of whether they are aliased by the
hemicube or not; exactly the same situation which occurs with conventional
(context independent) anti-aliasing measures (Chapter 14).

Problems emerge from the approximation (see the previous chapter):

$$F_{ij} \approx F_{dAiAj}$$

The hemicube evaluates a form factor from a differential area – effectively a point – to a finite area. There are two consequences of this. Figure 11.9 illustrates a problem that can arise with intervening patches. Here the form factor from patch i to patch j is calculated as if the intervening patch did not exist because patch j can be seen in its entirety from the hemicube origin.

Finally, consider the sampling 'efficiency' of the hemicube. Patches that can be 'seen' from the hemicube in the normal direction are more important than patches in the horizon direction. (They project onto hemicube cells that have higher delta form factors.) If we consider distributing the computational effort evenly on the basis of importance sampling then cells nearer the horizon are less important. An investigation reported in Max and Troutman (1993) derives optimal resolution, shapes and grid cell spacings. In this work a top-face resolution 40% higher than that of the sides and a side height of 70% of the width is suggested. Note that this leads also to a reduction in aliasing artefacts caused by uniform hemicube cells.

(11.6.2)

Reconstruction artefacts

Reconstruction artefacts are so called because they originate from the nature of the method used to reconstruct or approximate the continuous radiosity function from the constant radiosity solution. We recall that radiosity methods can only function under the constant radiosity assumption which is that we divide the environment up into patches and solve a system of equations on the basis that the radiosity is constant across each patch.

The commonest approach – bilinear interpolation – is overviewed in Figure 11.10. Here we assume that the curved surface shown in Figure 11.10(a) will exhibit a continuous variation in radiosity value along the dotted line as shown.

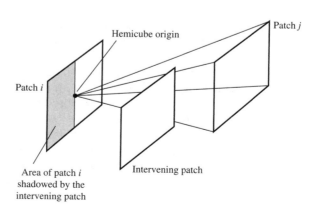

Figure 11.9
All of patch j can be seen from the hemicube origin and the F_{dAiAj} approximation falls down.

Hemicube origin

Patch j

Patch i

Area of patch i shadowed by the intervening patch

Intervening patch

Figure 11.10
Normal reconstruction
approach used in the
radiosity method.
(a) Compute a constant
radiosity solution.
(b) Calculate the vertex
radiosities.
(c) Reconstruction by linear
interpolation.

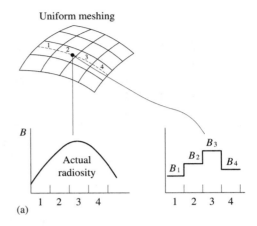

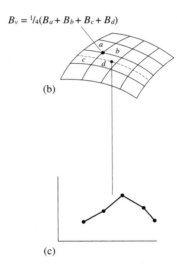

The first step in the radiosity method is to compute a constant radiosity solution which will result in a staircase approximation to the continuous function. The radiosity values at a vertex are calculated by averaging the patch radiosities that share the vertex (Figure 11.10(b)). These are then injected into a bilinear interpolation scheme and the surface is effectively Gouraud shaded resulting in the piecewise linear approximation (Figure 11.10(c)).

The most noticeable defect arising out of this process is Mach bands which, of course, we also experience in normal Gouraud shading, where the same interpolation method is used. The 'visual importance' of these can be reduced by using texture mapping but they tend to be a problem in radiosity applications because many of these exhibit large area textureless surfaces – interior walls in buildings, for example. Subdivision meshing strategies also reduce the visibility of Mach bands because by reducing the size of the elements they reduce the difference between vertex radiosities.

More advanced strategies involve surface interpolation methods (Chapter 3). Here the radiosity values are treated as samples of a continuous radiosity function and quadratic or cubic Bézier/B-spline patch meshes are fitted to these. The obvious difficulties with this approach – its inherent cost and the need to prevent wanted discontinuities being smoothed out – has meant that the most popular reconstruction method is still linear interpolation.

11.6.3 Meshing artefacts

One of the most difficult aspects of the radiosity approach, and one that is still a major research area, is the issue of meshing. In the discussions above we have simply described patches as entities into which the scene is divided with the proviso that these should be large to enable a solution which is not prohibitively expensive. However, the way in which we do this has a strong bearing on the quality of the final image. How should we do this so that the appearance of artefacts is minimized? The reason this is difficult is that we can only do this when we already have a solution, so that we can see where the problems occur. Alternatively we have to predict where the problems will occur and subdivide accordingly. We begin by looking at the nature and origin of meshing artefacts.

First some terminology:

- **Meshing**   This is a general term used in the context of radiosity to describe either the initial scene subdivision or the act of further subdivision that may take place while a program is executing. The 'initial scene subdivision' may be a general scene database not necessarily created for input to a radiosity renderer. However, for reasons that will soon become apparent it is more likely to be a preprocessed version of such a database or a scene that has been specifically created for a radiosity solution.

- **Patches**   These are the entities in the initial representation of the scene. In a standard radiosity solution, where subdivision occurs during the solution, patches form the input to the program.

- **Elements**   These are the portions into which patches are subdivided.

The simplest type of meshing artefact – a so-called D^0 discontinuity – is a discontinuity in the value of the radiosity function. The common sources of such a discontinuity are shadow boundaries caused by a point light source and objects which are in contact. In the former case the light source suddenly becomes visible as we move across a surface and the reconstruction and meshing 'spreads' the shadow edge towards the mesh boundaries. Thus the shadow edge will tend to take the shape of the mesh edges giving it a staircase appearance. However, because we tend to use area light sources in radiosity applications the discontinuities that occur are higher than D^0. Nevertheless these still cause visible

Figure 11.11
Shadow and light leakage.

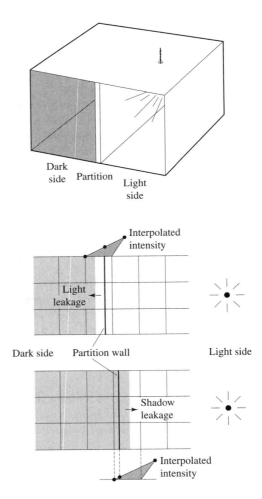

artefacts. Discontinuities in the derivatives of the radiosity function occur at penumbra and umbra boundaries in shadows in scenes illuminated by area light sources. Again there is 'interference' between the boundaries and the mesh, giving a characteristic 'staircase' appearance to the shadow edges. These are more difficult to deal with than D^0 discontinuities.

When objects are in contact, then unless the intersection boundary coincides with a mesh boundary, shadow or light leakage will occur. The idea is shown in Figure 11.11 for a simple scene. Here, the room is divided by a floor-to-ceiling partition, which does not coincide with patch boundaries on the floor. One half of the room contains a light source and the other is completely dark. Depending on the position of the patch boundaries, the reconstruction will produce either light leakage into the dark region or shadow leakage into the lit region. Figure 18.16 shows the effect of shadow and light leakage for a more complex scene. Despite the fact that the representation contains many more patches than we require for a conventional computer graphics rendering (Gouraud shading) the quality is unacceptably low.

It should be apparent that further subdivision of the scene cannot entirely eliminate shadow and light leakage – it can only reduce it to an acceptable level. It can, however, be eliminated entirely by forcing a meshing along the curve of intersection between objects in contact. Figure 18.18 is the result of meshing the area around a wall light by considering the intersection between the lamp and the wall. Now the wall patch boundaries coincide with the lamp patch boundaries eliminating the leakage that occurred before this meshing.

11.7 Meshing strategies

Meshing strategies that attempt to overcome these defects can be categorized in a number of ways. An important distinction can be made on the basis of when the subdivision takes place:

(1) *A priori* – meshing is completed before the radiosity solution is invoked; that is we predict where discontinuities are going to occur and mesh accordingly. This is also called discontinuity meshing.

(2) *A posteriori* – the solution is initiated with a 'start' mesh which is refined as the solution progresses. This is also called adaptive meshing.

As we have seen, when two objects are in contact, we can eliminate shadow and light leakage by ensuring that mesh element boundaries from each object coincide, which is thus an *a priori* meshing.

Another distinction can be made depending on the geometric nature of the meshing. We can, for example, simply subdivide square patches (non-uniformly) reducing the error to an acceptable level. The commonest approach to date, Cohen and Wallace (1993) term this *h*-refinement. Alternatively we could adopt an approach where the discontinuities in the radiosity function are tracked across a surface and the mesh boundaries placed along the discontinuity boundary. A form of this approach is called *r*-refinement by Cohen and Wallace (1993) where the nodes of the initial mesh are moved in a way that equalizes the error in the elements that share the node. These approaches are illustrated conceptually in Figure 11.12.

11.7.1 Adaptive or *a posteriori* meshing

The classic adaptive algorithm, called substructuring, was described by Cohen *et al.* (1986). Reported before the development of the progressive refinement algorithm, this approach was initially incorporated into a full matrix solution. Adaptive subdivision proceeds by considering the radiosity variation at the nodes or vertices of an element and subdividing if the difference exceeds some threshold.

Figure 11.12
Examples of refinement
strategies (*a posteriori*).

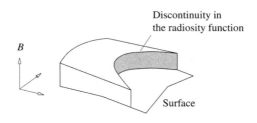

Discontinuity in
the radiosity function

B

Surface

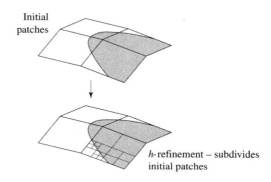

Initial
patches

h-refinement – subdivides
initial patches

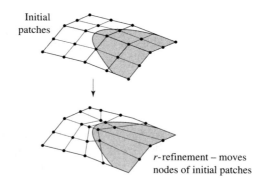

Initial
patches

r-refinement – moves
nodes of initial patches

The idea is to generate an accurate solution for the radiosity of a point from the 'global' radiosities obtained from the initial 'coarse' patch computation. Patches are subdivided into elements. Element-to-patch form factors are calculated where the relationship between element-to-patch and patch-to-patch form factors is given by:

$$F_{ij} = \frac{1}{A_i} \sum_{q=1}^{R} F_{(iq)j} A_{(iq)}$$

where:

F_{ij} is the form factor from patch i to patch j
$F_{(iq)j}$ is the form factor from element q of patch i to patch j
$A_{(iq)}$ is the subdivided area of element q of patch i
R is the number of elements in patch i

Patch form factors obtained in this way are then used in a standard radiosity solution.

This increases the number of form factors from $N \times N$ to $M \times N$, where M is the total number of elements created, and naturally increases the time spent in form factor calculation. Patches that need to be divided into elements are revealed by examining the graduation of the coarse patch solution. The previously calculated (coarse) patch solution is retained and the fine element radiosities are then obtained from this solution using:

$$B_{iq} = E_q + R_q \sum_{j=1}^{N} B_j F_{(iq)j} \qquad [11.4]$$

where:

B_{iq} is the radiosity of element q
B_j is the radiosity of patch j
$F_{(iq)j}$ is the element q to patch j form factor

In other words, as far as the radiosity solution is concerned, the cumulative effect of elements of a subdivided patch is identical to that of the undivided patch; or, subdividing a patch into elements does not affect the amount of light that is reflected by the patch. So after determining a solution for patches, the radiosity within a patch is solved independently among patches. In doing this, Equation 11.4 assumes that only the patch in question has been subdivided into elements – all other patches are undivided. The process is applied iteratively until the desired accuracy is obtained. At any step in the iteration we can identify three stages:

(1) Subdividing selected patches into elements and calculating element-to-patch form factors.

(2) Evaluating a radiosity solution using patch-to-patch form factors.

(3) Determining the element radiosities from the patch radiosities.

Where stage (2) just occurs for the first iteration, the coarse patch radiosities are calculated once only. The method is distinguished from simply subdividing the environment into smaller patches. This strategy would result in $M \times M$ new form factors (rather than $M \times N$) and an $M \times M$ system of equations.

Subdivision of patches into elements is carried out adaptively. The areas that require subdivision are not known prior to a solution being obtained. These areas are obtained from an initial solution and are then subject to a form factor subdivision. The previous form factor matrix is still valid and the radiosity solution is not re-computed.

Only part of the form factor determination is further discretized and this is then used in the third phase (determination of the element radiosities from the coarse patch solution). This process is repeated until it converges to the desired degree of accuracy. Thus image quality is improved in areas that require more accurate treatment. An example of this approach is shown in Figure 11.13. Note the effect on the quality of the shadow boundary. Figure 11.14 shows the same set-up but this time the light source is subdivided to a lower and higher resolution than in Figure 11.13. Although the effect, in this case, of insufficient subdivision of emitting and non-emitting patches is visually similar, the reasons for these discrepancies differ. In the case of non-emitting patches we have changes in reflected light intensity that do not coincide with patch boundaries. We increase the number of patches to capture the discontinuity. With emitting patches the problem is due to the number of hemicube emplacements per light source. Here we increase the number of patches that represent the emitter because each hemicube emplacement reduces a light to a single source and we need a sufficiently dense array of these to represent the spatial extent of the

Figure 11.13
Adaptive subdivision and shadows.

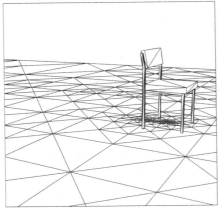

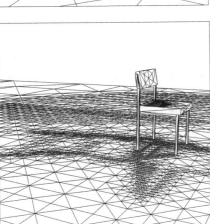

(a) Shape and shadow areas do not correspond to shape of the occluder.

emitter. In this case we are subdividing a patch (the emitter) over whose surface the light intensity will be considered uniform.

Adaptive subdivision can be incorporated in the progressive refinement method. A naive approach would be to compute the radiosity gradient and subdivide based on the contribution of the current shooting patch. However, this approach can lead to unnecessary subdivisions. The sequence, shown in Figure 11.15 shows the difficulties encountered as subdivision, performed after every iteration, proceeds around one of the wall lights. Originally two large patches situated away from the wall provide general illumination of the object. This immediately causes subdivision around the light–wall boundary because the program detects a high difference between vertices belonging to the same patches. These patches have vertices both under the light and on the wall. However, this subdivision is not fine enough and as we start to shoot energy from the light source itself light leakage begins to occur. Light source patches continue to shoot energy in the order in which the model is stored in the data-

Figure 11.13 *continued*

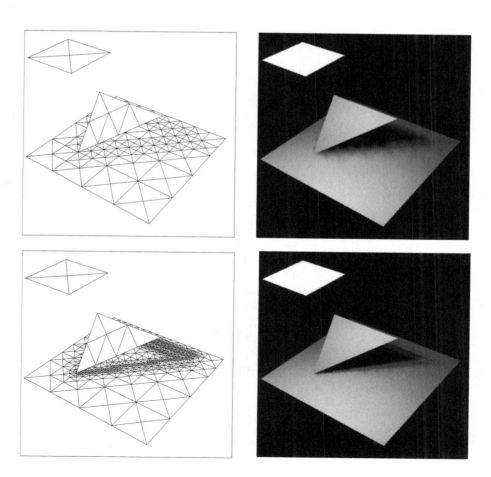

(b) Boundary of shadow is jagged.

Figure 11.14
The effect of insufficient
subdivision of emitters.

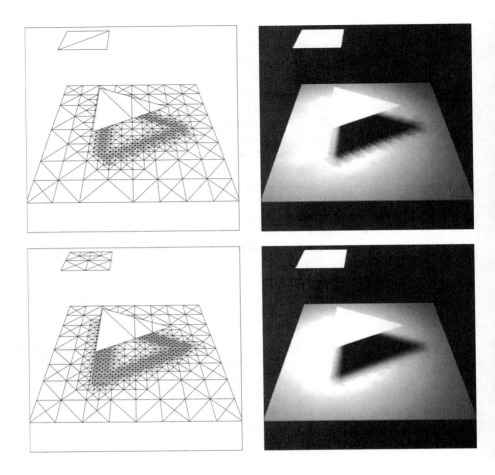

base and we spiral up the sphere, shooting energy onto its inside and causing more and more light leakage. Eventually the light emerges onto the wall and brightens up the appropriate patches. As the fan of light rotates above the light more and more inappropriate subdivision occurs. This is because the subdivision is based on the current intensity gradients which move on as further patches are shot. Note in the final frame this results in a large degree of subdivision in an area of highlight saturation. These redundant patches slow the solution down more and more and we are inadvertently making things worse as far as execution time is concerned.

Possible alternative strategies are:

(1) Limit the subdivision by only initiating it after every n patches instead of after every patch that is shot.

(2) Limit the initiation of subdivision by waiting until the illumination is representative of the expected final distribution.

Figure 11.15
The sequence shows the difficulties encountered as subdivision, performed after every iteration, proceeds around one of the wall lights. As the fan of light rotates above the light more and more inappropriate subdivision occurs. This is because the subdivision is based on the current intensity gradients which move on as further patches are shot. Note in the final frame this results in a large degree of subdivision in an area of high light saturation. These redundant patches slow the solution down more and more and we are inadvertently making things worse as far as execution time is concerned.

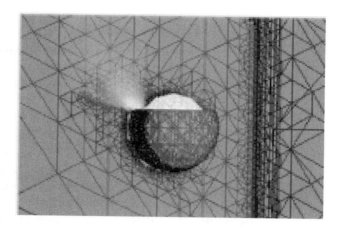

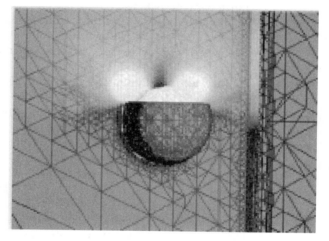

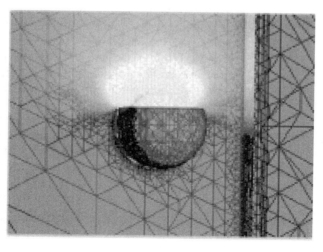

A priori meshing

We will now look at two strategies for *a priori* meshing – processing a scene before it is used in a radiosity solution.

Hierarchical radiosity

Adaptive subdivision is a special case of an approach which is nowadays known as hierarchical radiosity. Hierarchical radiosity is a generalization of adaptive subdivision – a two-level hierarchy – to a subdivision employing a continuum of levels. The interaction between surfaces is then computed using a form factor appropriate to the geometric relationship between the two surfaces. In other words, the hierarchical approach attempts to limit form factor calculation time by limiting the accuracy of the calculation to an amount determined by the distance between patches.

Hierarchical radiosity can be embedded in a progressive refinement approach making an *a posteriori* algorithm; alternatively the hierarchical subdivision can be made on an *a priori* basis and the system then solved. In what follows we will describe the *a priori* framework.

The idea is easily illustrated in principle. Figure 11.16 shows a wall patch *W* and three small objects *A*, *B* and *C* located at varying distances from *W*. The distance from *W* to *A* is comparable to its dimension and we assume that *W* has to be subdivided to calculate the changes in illumination in the vicinity of *A* due to light emitted or reflected from *W*. In the case of *B* we assume that the whole of patch *W* can be used. Detailed variation of the radiosity in the vicinity of *B* due to patch *W* is not unduly affected by subdividing *B*. The distance to *C*, we assume, is sufficiently large to make the form factor between *W* and *C* correspondingly small, and in this case we can consider a larger area on the wall merging *W* into a patch four times its area. Thus for the three interactions we use either a subdivided *W*, the whole of *W* or *W* as part of a larger entity when considering the interaction between the wall and the objects *A*, *B* and *C*. Note that this implies not only subdivision of patches but the opposite process – agglomeration of patches into groups.

The idea, first proposed by Hanrahan *et al.* (1991), proposes that if the form factor between two patches currently under consideration exceeds a threshold, then to use these patches at their current size will introduce an unacceptable error into the solution and the patches should be subdivided. Compared with the strategy in the previous section we are taking our differential threshold one stage further back in the overall process. Instead of comparing the difference between the calculated radiosity of neighbouring patches and subdividing and re-calculating form factors if necessary, we are looking directly at the form factors themselves and subdividing until the form factor falls below a threshold. This idea is easily demonstrated for the simple case of two patches sharing a common border. Figure 11.17 shows the geometric effect of subdivision based on a form factor threshold. The initial form factor estimate is large and the patches

Figure 11.16
Hierarchical radiosity: scene subdivision is determined by energy interchange.

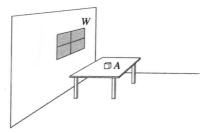

(a) Patch W subdivided into elements for WA interaction

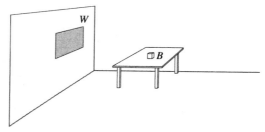

(b) Initial patch used for WB interaction

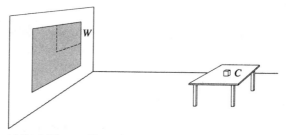

(c) Patch W merged into a larger patch for WC interaction

are subdivided into four elements. At the next level of subdivision only two out of 16 form factor estimates exceed the threshold and they are subdivided. It is easily seen from the illustration that in this example the pattern of subdivision 'homes into' the common edge.

A hierarchical subdivision strategy starts with an (initial) large patch subdivision of n patches. This results in $n(n-1)/2$ form factor calculations. Pairs of patches that cannot be used at this initial level are then subdivided as suggested by the previous figure, the process continuing recursively. Thus each initial patch is represented by a hierarchy and links. The structure contains both the geometric subdivision and links that tie an element to other elements in the scene. A node in the hierarchy represents a group of elements and a leaf node a single element. To make this process as fast as possible a crude estimate of the form factor can be used. For example, the expression inside the integral definition of the form factor:

Figure 11.17
Hierarchical radiosity:
the geometric effect
of subdivision of two
perpendicular patches (after
Hanrahan *et al.* (1991)).

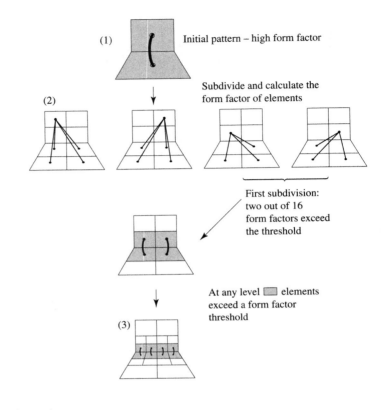

(1)   Initial pattern – high form factor

(2)   Subdivide and calculate the
form factor of elements

First subdivision:
two out of 16
form factors exceed
the threshold

At any level ⬜ elements
exceed a form factor
threshold

(3)

$$\frac{\cos \phi_i \, \cos \phi_j}{\pi r^2}$$

can be used but note that this does not take into account any occluding patches.
Thus the stages in establishing the hierarchy are:

(1) Start with an initial patch subdivision. This would normally use much larger
patches than those required for a conventional solution.

(2) Recursively apply the following:
   (a) Use a quick estimate of the form factor between pairs of linked surfaces.
   (b) If this falls below a threshold or a subdivision limit is reached, record
their interaction at that level.
   (c) Subdivide the surfaces.

It is important to realize that two patches can exhibit an interaction between
any pair of nodes at any level in their respective hierarchies. Thus in Figure 11.18
a link is shown between a leaf node in patch *A* and an internal node in patch *C*.
The tree shown in the figure for *A* represents the subdivisions necessary for its
interaction with patch *B* and that for patch *C* represents its interactions with
some other patch *X*. This means that energy transferred from *A* to the internal
node in *C* is inherited by all the child nodes below the destination in *C*.

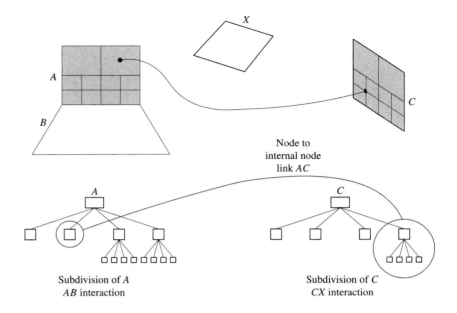

Figure 11.18
Interaction between two patches can consist of energy interchange between any pair of nodes at any level in their respective hierarchy.

Comparing this formulation with the classical full matrix solution we have now replaced the form factor matrix with a hierarchical representation. This implies that a 'gathering' solution proceeds from each node by following all the links from that node and multiplying the radiosity found at the end of the link by the associated form factor. Because links have, in general, been established at any level, the hierarchy needs to be followed in both directions from a node.

The iterative solution proceeds by executing two steps on each root node until a solution has converged. The first step is to gather energy over each incoming link. The second step, known as 'pushpull' pushes a node's reflected radiosity down the tree and pulls it back up again. Pushing involves simply adding the radiosity at each child node. (Note that since radiosity has units of power/unit area the value remains undiminished as the area is subdivided.) The total energy received by an element is the sum of the energy received by it directly plus the sum of the energy received by its parents. When the leaves are reached the process is reversed and the energy is pulled up the tree, the current energy deposited at each node is calculated by averaging the child node contributions.

In effect this is just an elaboration of the Gauss–Siedel relaxation method described in Section 11.3. For a particular patch we are gathering contributions from all other patches in the scene to enable a new estimate of the current patch. The difference now is that the gathering process involves following all links out of the current hierarchy and the hierarchy has to be updated correctly with the bi-directional traversal or pushpull process.

The above algorithm description implies that at each node in the quadtree data structure the following information is available:

gathering and shooting radiosity (B_g and B_s)
emission value (E)
area (A)
reflectivity (ρ)
pointer to four children
pointer to list of (gathering) links (L)

The algorithm itself has a simple elegant structure and following the excellent treatment given in Cohen and Wallace (1993) can be expressed in terms of the following pseudocode:

while not converged
    for *all surfaces (every root node p)*
        GatherRad(*p*)
    for *all surfaces*
        PushPull(*p*,0.0)

The top level procedure is a straightforward iterative process which gathers all the energy from the incoming links, pushes it down the structure then pulls the radiosity values back up the hierarchy.

    GatherRad(*p*) calculates the radiosity absorbed and then reflected at node p. It is as follows:

GatherRad(*p*)
    $p.B_g := 0$
    for *each link L into p*
    $p.B_g := p.B_g + p.\rho\,(L.F_{pq} * L.q.B_s)$
    for *each child r of p*
        GatherRad(*r*)

Here q is the element linked to p by L, F_{pq} is the form factor for this link and ρ is the reflectivity of the element p. The radiosity at the destination/shooter end of the link is B_s. This is converted into the reflected radiosity B_g at the source/gatherer end of the link by multiplying it by the form factor F_{pq} and the reflectivity ρ.

    PushPullRad(*p*,*B*) can be viewed as a procedure that distributes the energy correctly throughout the hierarchy balancing the tree. It is as follows:

PushPullRad(*p*,B_{down})
    if *p is a leaf* **then** $B_{up} := p.E + p.B_g + B_{down}$
    else $B_{up} := 0;$ **for** *each child node r of p*
                    $B_{up} := B_{up} + (r.A/p.A) * $ **PushPullRad**(*r*, $p.B_g + B_{down}$)
    $p.B_s := B_{up}$
    return B_{up}

The procedure is first called at the top of the hierarchy with the gathered radiosity at that level. The recursion has the effect of passing or pushing down this radiosity onto the child nodes. At each internal node the gathered power is added to the inherited power accumulated along the downwards path. When a leaf node is reached any emission is added into the gathered radiosity for that node and the result assigned to the shooting radiosity for that node. The recursion then unwinds pulling the leaf node radiosity up the tree and performing an area weighting at each node.

Although hierarchical radiosity is an efficient method and one that can be finely controlled (the accuracy of the solution depends on the form factor tolerance and the minimum subdivision area) it still suffers from shadow leaks and jagged shadow boundaries because it subdivides the environment regularly (albeit non-uniformly) without regard to the position of shadow boundaries. Reducing the value of the control parameters to give a more accurate solution can still be prohibitively expensive. This is the motivation of the approach described in the next section.

Finally we can do no better than to quote from the original paper, in which the authors give their inspiration for the approach:

The hierarchical subdivision algorithm proposed in this paper is inspired by methods recently developed for solving the N-body problem. In the N-body problem, each of the n particles exerts a force on all the other $n–1$ particles, implying $n(n–1)/2$ pairwise interactions. The fast algorithm computes all the forces on a particle in less than quadratic time, building on two key ideas:

(1) Numerical calculations are subject to error, and therefore, the force acting on a particle need only be calculated to within the given precision.

(2) The force due to a cluster of particles at some distant point can be approximated, within the given precision, with a single term – cutting down on the total number of interactions.

Discontinuity meshing

The commonest, and simplest, type of *a priori* meshing is to take care of the special case of interpenetrating geometry (D^0) as we suggested at the beginning of this section. This is mostly done semi-manually when the scene is constructed and disposes of shadow and light leakage – the most visible radiosity artefact. The more general approaches attend to higher-order discontinuities. D^1 and D^2 discontinuities occur when an object interacts with an area light source – the characteristic penumbra–umbra transition within a shadow area – as described in Chapter 9.

As we have seen, common *a posteriori* methods generally approach the problem by subdividing in the region of discontinuities in the radiosity function and can only eliminate errors by resorting to higher and higher meshing densities. The idea behind discontinuity meshing is to predict where the discontinuities are going to occur and to align the mesh edges exactly with the path of the discontinuity. This approach is by definition an *a priori* method. We predict where the discontinuities will occur and mesh, before invoking the solution phase so that when the solution proceeds there can be no artefacts present due to the non-alignment of discontinuities and mesh edges.

To predict the position of the discontinuities shadow detection algorithms are used and the problem is usually couched in terms of visual events and critical surfaces. Two types of visual events can be considered VE and EEE. VE or vertex–edge events occur when a vertex of a source 'crosses' an edge of an occluding polygon known in this context as a receiver. Figure 11.19 shows the interaction between a vertex of a triangular source and an edge of a rectangular occlude. The edge and vertex together form a critical surface whose intersection with a receiving surface forms part of the outer penumbra boundary. For each edge of the occluder a critical surface can be defined with respect to each vertex in the source. We can also define EV events which occur due to the interaction of a source edge with a receiver polygon.

VE events can cause both D^1 and D^2 discontinuities as Figures 11.20 and 11.21 demonstrate. Figure 11.20 shows the case of a D^1 discontinuity. Here there is the coincidence that the edge of the occluder and the source are parallel. Both vertices V_1 and V_2 contribute to the penumbra. As we travel outwards from the umbra along path xy, the visible area of the source increases linearly and the radiance exhibits piecewise linearity or D^1 discontinuities. A D^2 discontinuity caused by a VE event is shown in Figure 11.21. In this case, a single vertex of the light source is involved along the path xy. As we travel outwards from the umbra the visible area of the source increases quadratically and the radiance exhibits D^2 discontinuities.

EEE or edge–edge–edge events occur when we have multiple occluders. The important difference here is that the boundary of the penumbra – the critical curve – is no longer a straight line as it was in the previous VE examples but a conic. The corresponding discontinuities in the radiance function along the curve are D^2. Also the critical surface is no longer a segment of a plane but is a (ruled) quadric surface.

Visual events can occur for any edges and vertices of any object in the scene. For a scene with n objects there can be $O(n^2)$ VE critical surfaces and $O(n^3)$ EEE critical surfaces. Because of the cost and the higher complexity of EEE events approaches have concentrated on detecting VE events.

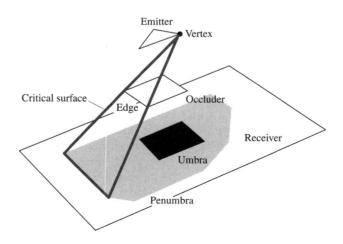

Figure 11.19
VE event: the edge of the occluder and a vertex of the emitter form a critical surface whose intersection with the receiver forms the outer boundary of the penumbra (after Nishita and Nakamae (1985)).

Figure 11.20
VE event causing a D^1 discontinuity (after Lischinski et al. (1992)).

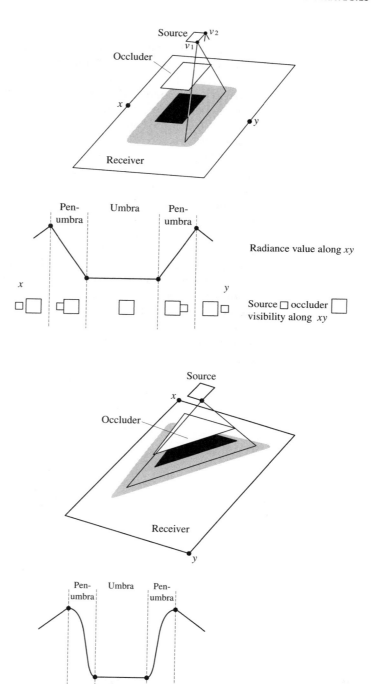

Figure 11.21
VE event causing a D^2 discontinuity (after Lischinski et al. (1992)).

A straightforward approach by Nishita and Nakamae (1985) explicitly determines penumbra and umbra boundaries by using a shadow volume approach. For each object a shadow volume is constructed from each vertex in the light source. Thus, there is a volume associated with each light source vertex just as if it were a point source. The intersection of all volumes on the receiving surface forms the umbra and the penumbra boundary is given by the convex hull containing the shadow volumes. An example is shown in Figure 11.22.

We will now describe in some detail a later and more elaborate approach by Lischinski *et al.* (1992) to discontinuity meshing. This integrates discontinuity meshing into a modified progressive refinement structure and deals only with VE (and EV) events. This particular algorithm is representative in that it deals with most of the factors that must be addressed in a practical discontinuity meshing approach including handling multiple light sources and reconstruction problems.

Lischinski *et al.* build a separate discontinuity mesh for each source, accumulating the results into a final solution. The scene polygons are stored as a BSP tree which means that they can be fetched in front-to-back order from a source vertex. For a source the discontinuities that are due to single VE events are located as follows. Figure 11.23 shows a single VE event generating a wedge defined by the vertex and projectors through the end points of the edge, *E*. The event is processed by fetching the polygons in the order *A*, *B* and *C*. *A* is nearer to the source than *E* and is thus not affected by the event. If a surface (*B* and *C*) faces the source then the intersection of the wedge with the surface adds a

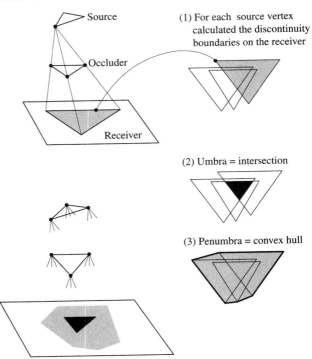

Figure 11.22
Umbra and penumbra from shadow volumes formed by VE events.

Figure 11.23
Processing a VE wedge
(after Lischinski *et al.*
(1992)).

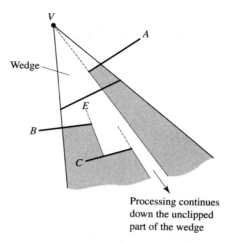

Processing continues
down the unclipped
part of the wedge

discontinuity to that surface. The discontinuity is 'inserted' into the mesh of the surface. As each surface is processed it clips out part of the wedge and the algorithm proceeds 'down' only the unclipped part of the wedge. When the wedge is completely clipped the processing of that particular VE event is complete.

The insertion of the discontinuity into the mesh representing the surface is accomplished by using a DM tree which itself consists of two components – a two-dimensional BSP tree connecting into a winged edge data structure (Mantyla 1988) representing the interconnection of surface nodes. The way in which this works is shown in Figure 11.24 for a single example of a vertex generating three VE events which plant three discontinuity/critical curves on a receiving surface. If the processing order is a, b, c then the line equation for a appears as the root node and splitting it into two regions as shown. b, the next wedge to be processed is checked against region R_1 which splits into R_{11} and R_{12} and so on.

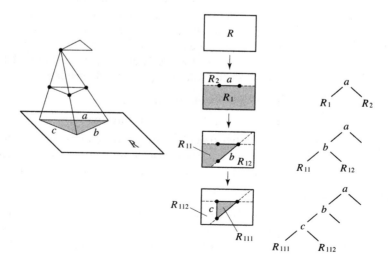

Figure 11.24
Constructing a DM tree for
a single VE event (after
Lischinski *et al.* (1992)).

12 Ray tracing strategies

Introduction – Whitted ray tracing

In Chapter 10 we gave a brief overview of Whitted ray tracing. We will now describe this popular algorithm in detail. Although it was first proposed in by Appel (1968), ray tracing is normally associated with Whitted's classic paper (1980). We use the term 'Whitted ray tracing' to avoid the confusion that has arisen due to the proliferation of adjectives such as 'eye', forward' and 'backward' to describe ray tracing algorithms.

Whitted ray tracing is an elegant partial global illumination algorithm that combines the following in a single model:

● Hidden surface removal.

● Shading due to direct illumination.

● Global specular interaction effects such as the reflection of objects in each other and refraction of light through transparent objects.

● Shadow computation (but only the geometry of hard-edged shadows is calculated).

It usually 'contains' a local reflection model such as the Phong reflection model, and the question arises: why not use ray tracing as the standard approach to rendering, rather than using a Phong approach with extra algorithms for hidden surface removal, shadows and transparency? The immediate answer to this is cost. Ray tracing is expensive, particularly for polygon objects because effectively each polygon is an object to be ray traced. This is the dilemma of ray tracing. It can only function in reasonable time if the scene is made up of 'easy' objects. Quadric objects, such as spheres are easy, and if the object is polygonal the number of facets needs to be low for the ray tracer to function in reasonable time. If the scene is complex (many objects each with many polygons) then the basic algorithm needs to be burdened with efficiency schemes whose own cost tends to be a function of the complexity of the scene. Much of the research into ray tracing in the 1980s concentrated on the efficiency issue. However, we are just about at a point in hardware development where ray tracing is a viable alternative for a practical renderer and the clear advantages of the algorithm are beginning to overtake the cost penalties. In this chapter we will develop a program to ray trace spheres. We will then extend the program to enable polygonal objects to be dealt with.

12.1 The basic algorithm

12.1.1 Tracing rays – initial considerations

We have already seen that we trace infinitesimally thin light rays through the scene, following each ray to discover perfect specular interactions. Tracing implies testing the current ray against objects in the scene – intersection testing – to find if the ray hits any of them. And, of course, this is the source of the cost in ray tracing – in a naive algorithm, for each ray we have to test it against all objects in the scene (and all polygons in each object). At each boundary, between air and an object (or between an object and air) a ray will 'spawn' two more rays. For example, a ray initially striking a partially transparent sphere will generate at least four rays for the object – two emerging rays and two internal rays (Figure 10.5). The fact that we appropriately bend the transmitted ray means that geometric distortion due to refraction is taken into account. That is, when we form a projected image, objects that are behind transparent objects are appropriately distorted. If the sphere is hollow the situation is more complicated – there are now four intersections encountered by a ray travelling through the object.

To perform this tracing we follow light beams in the reverse direction of light propagation – we trace light rays from the eye. We do this eye tracing because tracing rays by starting at the light source(s) would be hopelessly expensive. This is because we are only interested in that small subset of light rays which pass through the image plane window.

At each hit point the same calculations have to be made and this implies that the easiest way to implement a simple ray tracer is as a recursive procedure. The recursion can terminate according to a number of criteria:

- It always terminates if a ray intersects a diffuse surface.
- It can terminate when a pre-set depth of trace has been reached.
- It can terminate when the energy of the ray has dropped below a threshold.

The behaviour of such an approach is demonstrated in Figure 18.11 (Colour Plate). Here the trace is terminated at recursives depths of 2, 3 and 4 and unassigned pixels (pixels which correspond to a ray landing on a pure specular surface with no diffuse contribution) are coloured grey. You can see that the grey region 'shrinks into itself' as a function of recursive depth.

12.1.2 Lighting model components

At each point P that a ray hits an object, we spawn in general, a reflected and a transmitted ray. Also we evaluate a local reflection model by calculating L at that point by shooting a ray to the light source which we consider as a point. Thus at each point the intensity of the light consists of up to three components:

- A local component.
- A contribution from a global reflected ray that we follow.
- A contribution from a global transmitted ray that we follow.

We linearly combine or add these components together to produce an intensity for point P. It is necessary to include a local model because there may be direct illumination at a hit point. However, it does lead to this confusion. The use of a local reflection model does imply empirically blurred reflection (spread highlights); however, the global reflected ray at that point is not blurred but continues to discover any object interaction along an infinitesimally thin path. This is because we cannot afford to blur global reflected rays – we can only follow the 'central' ray. This results in a visual contradiction in ray traced images, which is that the reflection of the light source in an object – the specular highlight – is blurred, but the images of other objects are perfect. The reason for this is that we want objects to look shiny – by having them exhibit a specular highlight – and include images of other objects. Thus most algorithms use a local and a global specular component.

It is also necessary to account for local diffuse reflection, otherwise we could not have coloured objects. We cannot in ray tracing handle diffuse interaction as we did in radiosity. This would mean spawning, for every hit, a set of diffuse rays that sampled the hemispherical set of diffuse rays that occurs at the hit point on the surface of the object, if it happens to be diffuse. Each one of these rays would have to be followed and may end up on a diffuse surface and a combinatorial explosion would develop that no machine could cope with. This problem is the motivation for the development of Monte Carlo methods such as path tracing, as we saw in Chapter 10.

If a ray hits a pure diffuse surface then the trace is terminated. Thus we have the situation where the result of the local model computation at each hit point is passed up the tree along with the specular interaction.

Shadows

Shadows are easily included in the basic ray tracing algorithm. We simply calculate L, the light direction vector, and insert it into the intersection test part of the algorithm. That is, L is considered a ray like any other. If L intersects any objects, then the point from which L emanates is in shadow and the intensity of direct illumination at that point is consequently reduced (Figure 12.1). This generates hard-edged shadows with arbitrary intensity. The approach can also lead to great expense. If there are n light sources, then we have to generate n intersection tests. We are already spawning two rays per hit point plus a shadow ray, and for n light sources this becomes $(n + 2)$ rays. We can see that as the number of light sources increases shadow computations are quickly going to predominate since the major cost at each hit point is the cost of the intersection testing.

In an approach by Haines and Greenberg (1986) a 'light buffer' was used as a shadow testing accelerator. Shadow testing times were reduced, using this procedure, by a factor of between 4 and 30. The method pre-calculates for each light source, a light buffer which is a set of cells or records, geometrically disposed as two-dimensional arrays on the six faces of a cube surrounding a point light source (Figure 12.2). To set up this data structure all polygons in the scene are cast or projected onto each face of the cube, using as a projection centre the position of the light source. Each cell in the light buffer then contains a list of polygons that can be seen from the light source. The depth of each polygon is calculated in a local coordinate system based on the light source, and the records are sorted in ascending order of depth. This means that for a particular ray from the eye, there is immediately available a list of those object faces that may occlude the intersection point under consideration.

Shadow testing reduces to finding the cell through which the shadow feeler ray passes, accessing the list of sorted polygons, and testing the polygons in the list until occlusion is found, or the depth of the potentially occluding polygon is greater than that of the intersection point (which means that there is no occlusion because the polygons are sorted in depth order). Storage requirements are prodigious and depend on the number of light sources and the resolution of the

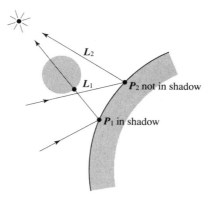

Figure 12.1
Shadow shape is computed by calculating L and inserting it into the intersection tester.

Figure 12.2
Shadow testing accelerator
of Haines and Greenberg
(1986).

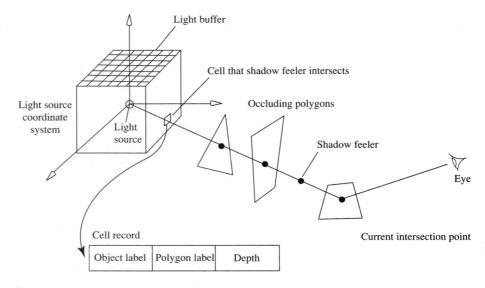

light buffers. (Note the similarity between the light buffer and the radiosity hemicube described in Chapter 11.)

Apart from the efficiency consideration, the main problem with shadows in Whitted ray tracing is that they are hard edged due to the point light source assumption and the light intensity within a shadow area has to be a guess. This is, of course, not inconsistent with the perfect specular interactions that result from tracing a single infinitesimally thin ray from each hit point for each type of interaction. Just as distributed ray tracing (described in Section 10.6) deals with 'blurry' interaction by considering more than one ray per interaction, so it implements soft shadow by firing more than one ray towards a (non-point) light source.

Hidden surface removal

Hidden surface removal is 'automatically' included in the basic ray tracing algorithm. We test each ray against all objects in the scene for intersection. In general this will give us a list of objects which the ray intersects. Usually the intersection test will reveal the distance from the hit point to the intersection and it is simply a matter of looking for the closest hit to find, from all the intersections, the surface that is visible from the ray-initiating view point. A certain subtlety occurs with this model, which is that surfaces hidden, from the point of view of a standard rendering or hidden surface approach, may be visible in ray tracing. This point is illustrated in Figure 12.3 which shows that a surface, hidden when viewed from the eye ray direction, can be reflected in the object hit by the incident ray.

Figure 12.3
A reflected 'hidden' surface.

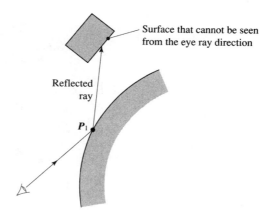

Surface that cannot be seen
from the eye ray direction

Reflected
ray

P_1

12.2 Using recursion to implement ray tracing

We will now examine the working of a ray tracing algorithm using a particular example. The example is based on a famous image, produced by Turner Whitted in 1980, and it is generally acknowledged as the first ray traced image in computer graphics. An imitation is shown in Figure 12.4 (reproduced as a monochrome image here and colour image in the Colour Plate section).

First some symbolics. At every point P that we hit with a ray we consider two major components a local and a global component:

$$I(P) = I_{local}(P) + I_{global}(P)$$
$$= I_{local}(P) + k_{rg} I(P_r) + k_{tg}I(P_t)$$

where:

P is the hit point
P_r is the hit point discovered by tracing the reflected ray from P
P_t is the hit point discovered by tracing the transmitted ray from P
k_{rg} is the global reflection coefficient
k_{tg} is the global transmitted coefficient

This recursive equation emphasizes that the illumination at a point is made up of three components, a local component, which is usually calculated using a Phong local reflection model, and a global component, which is evaluated by finding P_r and P_t and recursively applying the equation at these points. The overall process is sometimes represented as a tree as we indicated in Figure 10.5.

A procedure to implement ray tracing is easily written and has low code complexity. The top-level procedure calls itself to calculate the reflected and transmitted rays. The geometric calculation for the reflected and transmitted ray directions are given in Chapter 1, and details of intersection testing a ray with a sphere will also be found there.

Figure 12.4
The Whitted scene (see also
Colour Plate section).

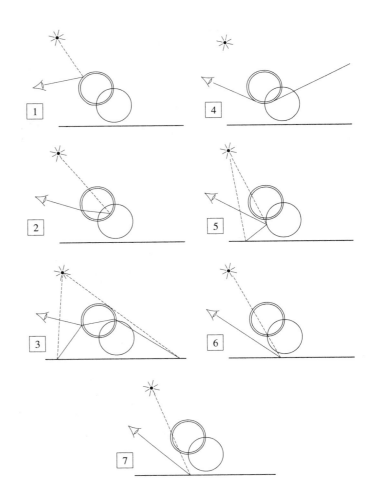

The basic control procedure for a ray tracer consists of a simple recursive procedure that reflects the action at a node where, in general, two rays are spawned. Thus the procedure will contain two calls to itself, one for the transmitted and one for the reflected ray. We can summarize the action as:

ShootRay (*ray structure*)
    intersection test
    if *ray intersects an object*
        get normal at intersection point
        calculate local intensity (I_{local})
        decrement current depth of trace
        if *depth of trace > 0*
            calculate and shoot the reflected ray
            calculate and shoot the refracted ray

where the last two lines imply a recursive call of ShootRay(). This is the basic control procedure. Around the recursive calls there has to be some more detail which is:

Calculate and shoot reflected ray *elaborates as*

    if *object is a reflecting object*
        calculate reflection vector and include in the ray structure
        Ray Origin := intersection point
        Attenuate the ray (multiply the current k_{rg} by its value at the previous invocation)
        ShootRay(*reflected ray structure*)
        if *reflected ray intersects an object*
            combine colours ($k_{rg} I$) with I_{local}

Calculate and shoot refracted ray *elaborates as*

    if *object is a refracting object*
        if *ray is entering object*
            accumulate refractive index
            increment number of objects that the ray is currently inside
            calculate refraction vector and include in refracted ray structure
        else
            de-accumulate refractive index
            decrement number of objects that the ray is currently inside
            calculate refraction vector and include in refracted ray structure
        Ray origin := intersection point
        Attenuate ray (k_{tg})
        if *refracted ray intersects an object*
            combine colours ($k_{tg} I$) with I_{local}

The ray structure needs to contain at least the following information:

- Origin of the ray.
- Its direction.
- Its intersection point.
- Its current colour at the intersection point.
- Its current attenuation.
- The distance of the intersection point from the ray origin.
- The refractive index the ray is currently experiencing.
- Current depth of the trace.
- Number of objects we are currently inside.

Thus the general structure is of a procedure calling itself twice for a reflected and refracted ray. The first part of the procedure finds the object closest to the ray start. Then we find the normal and apply the local shading model, attenuating the light source intensity if there are any objects between the intersection point P and the object. We then call the procedure recursively for the reflected and transmitted ray.

The number of recursive invocations of ShootRay() is controlled by the depth of trace parameter. If this is unity the scene is rendered just with a local reflection model. To discover any reflections of another object at a point P we need a depth of at least two. To deal with transparent objects we need a depth of at least three. (The initial ray, the ray that travels through the object and the emergent ray have to be followed. The emergent ray returns an intensity from any object that it hits.)

12.3 The adventures of seven rays – a ray tracing study

Return to Figure 12.4. We consider the way in which the ray tracing model works in the context of the seven pixels shown highlighted. The scene itself consists of a thin walled or hollow sphere, that is almost perfectly transparent, together with a partially transparent white sphere, both of which are floating above the ubiquitous red and yellow chequerboard. Everywhere else in object space is a blue background. The object properties are summarized in Table 12.1. Note that this model allows us to set k_s to a different value from k_{rg} – the source of the contradiction mentioned in Section 12.1.2; reflected rays are treated differently depending on which component (local or global) is being considered.

Consider the rays associated with the pixels shown in Figure 10.4.

Ray 1

This ray is along a direction where a specular highlight is seen on the highly transparent sphere. Because the ray is near the mirror direction of L, the contribution from the specular component in $I_{local}(P)$ is high and the contributions

Table 12.1

Very transparent hollow sphere

k_d (local)	0.1	0.1	0.1	(low)
k_s (local)	0.8	0.8	0.8	(high)
k_{rg}	0.1	0.1	0.1	(low)
k_{tg}	0.9	0.9	0.9	(high)

Opaque (white) sphere

k_d (local)	0.2	0.2	0.2	(white)
k_s (local)	0.8	0.8	0.8	(white)
k_{rg}	0.4	0.4	0.4	(white)
k_{tg}	0.0	0.0	0.0	

Chequerboard

k_d (local)	1.0	0.0	0.0/1.0	1.0	0.0	(high red or yellow)
k_s (local)	0.2	0.2	0.2			
k_{rg}	0					
k_{tg}	0					

Blue background

k_d (local)	0.1	0.1	1.0	(high blue)

Ambient light	0.3	0.3	0.3
Light	0.7	0.7	0.7

from $k_{rg}I(\mathbf{P}_r)$ is low. For this object k_d, the local diffuse coefficient is low (it is multiplied by 1 – transparency value) and k_s is high with respect to k_{rg}. However, note that the local contribution only dominates over a very small area of the surface of the object. Also note that, as we have already mentioned, the highlight should not be spread. But if we left it as occupying a single pixel it would not be visible.

Ray 2

Almost the same as ray 1 except that the specular highlight appears on the inside wall of the hollow sphere. This particular ray demonstrates another accepted error in ray tracing. Effectively the ray from the light travels through the sphere without refracting (that is, we simply compare $\mathbf{L}$ with the local value of $\mathbf{N}$ and ignore the fact that we are now inside a sphere). This means that the specular highlight is in the *wrong* position but we simply accept this because we have no intuitive expectation of the correct position anyway. We simply accept it to be correct.

Ray 3

Ray 3 also hits the thin-walled sphere. The local contribution at all hits with the hollow sphere are zero and the predominant contribution is the chequerboard.

This is subject to slight distortion due to the refractive effect of the sphere walls. The red (or yellow) colour comes from the high k_d in $I_{local}(\boldsymbol{P})$ where $\boldsymbol{P}$ is a point on the chequerboard. k_{rg} and k_{tg} are zero for this surface. Note, however, that we have a mix of two chequerboards. One is as described and the other is the superimposed reflection on the outside surface of the sphere.

Ray 4

Again this hits the thin-walled sphere, but this time in a direction where the distance travelled through the glass is significant (that is, it only travels through the glass it does not hit the air inside) causing a high refractive effect and making the ray terminate in the blue background.

Ray 5

This ray hits the opaque sphere and returns a significant contribution from the local component due to a white k_d (local). At the first hit the global reflected ray hits the chequerboard. Thus there is a mixture of:

white (from the sphere's diffuse component)
red/yellow (reflected from the chequerboard)

Ray 6

This ray hits the chequerboard initially and the colour comes completely from the local component for that surface. However, the point is in shadow and this is discovered by the intersection of the ray $\boldsymbol{L}$ and the opaque sphere.

Ray 7

The situation with this ray is exactly the same as for ray 6 except that it is the thin walled sphere that intersects $\boldsymbol{L}$. Thus the shadow area intensity is not reduced by as much as the previous case. Again we do not consider the recursive effect that $\boldsymbol{L}$ would in fact experience and so the shadow is in effect in the wrong place.

(12.4) Ray tracing polygon objects – interpolation of a normal at an intersection point in a polygon

Constraining a modelling primitive to be a sphere or at best a quadric solid is hopelessly restrictive in practice and in this section we will look at ray tracing polygonal objects. Extending the above program to cope with general polygon objects requires the development of an intersection test for polygons (see Section 1.4.3) and a method of calculating or interpolating a normal at the hit point $\boldsymbol{P}$. We remind ourselves that the polygonal facets are only approximations to a curved surface and, just as in Phong shading we need to interpolate, from the vertex normals, an approximation to the surface normal of the 'true' surface that

Figure 12.5
A polygon that lies almost in the $x_w y_w$ plane will have a high z_w component. We choose this plane in which to perform interpolation of vertex normals.

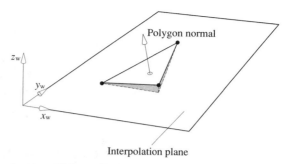

the facet approximates. This entity is required for the local illumination component and to calculate reflection and refraction. Recall that in Phong interpolation (see Section 6.3.2) we used the two-dimensional component of screen space to interpolate, pixel by pixel, scan line by scan line, the normal at each pixel projection on the polygon. We interpolated three of the vertex normals using two-dimensional screen space as the interpolation basis. How do we interpolate from the vertex normals in a ray tracing algorithm, bearing in mind that we are operating in world space? One easy approach is to store the polygon normal for each polygon as well as its vertex normals. We find the largest of its three components x_w, y_w and z_w. The largest component identifies which of the three world coordinate planes the polygon is closest to in orientation, and we can use this plane in which to interpolate using the same interpolation scheme as we employed for Phong interpolation (see Section 1.5). This plane is equivalent to the use of the screen plane in Phong interpolation. The idea is shown in Figure 12.5. This plane is used for the interpolation as follows. We consider the polygon to be represented in a coordinate system where the hit point P is the origin. We then have to search the polygon vertices to find the edges that cross the 'medium' axis. This enables us to interpolate the appropriate vertex normals to find N_a and N_b from which we find the required normal N_p (Figure 12.6). Having found the interpolated normal we can calculate the local illumination component and the reflected and the refracted rays. Note that because we

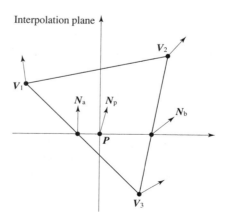

Figure 12.6
Finding an interpolated normal at a hit point P.

are 'randomly' interpolating we lose the efficiency advantages of the Phong interpolation, which was incremental on a pixel by pixel, scan line by scan line basis.

We conclude that in ray tracing polygonal objects we incur two significant costs. First, the more overwhelming cost is that of intersection testing each polygon in an object. Second, we have the cost of finding an interpolated normal on which to base our calculations.

12.5 Efficiency measures in ray tracing

12.5.1 Adaptive depth control

The trace depth required in a ray tracing program depends upon the nature of the scene. A scene containing highly reflective surfaces and transparent objects will require a higher maximum depth than a scene that consists entirely of poorly reflecting surfaces and opaque objects. (Note that if the depth is set equal to unity then the ray tracer functions exactly as a conventional renderer, which removes hidden surfaces and applies a local reflection model.)

It is pointed out in Hall and Greenberg (1983) that the percentage of a scene that consists of highly transparent and reflective surfaces is, in general, small and it is thus inefficient to trace every ray to a maximum depth. Hall and Greenberg suggest using an adaptive depth control that depends on the properties of the materials with which the rays are interacting. The context of the ray being traced now determines the termination depth, which can be any value between unity and the maximum pre-set depth.

Rays are attenuated in various ways as they pass through a scene. When a ray is reflected at a surface, it is attenuated by the global specular reflection coefficient for the surface. When it is refracted at a surface, it is attenuated by the global transmission coefficient for the surface. For the moment, we consider only this attenuation at surface intersections. A ray that is being examined as a result of backward tracing through several intersections will make a contribution to the top level ray that is attenuated by several of these coefficients. Any contribution from a ray at depth n to the colour at the top level is attenuated by the product of the global coefficients encountered at each node:

$$k_1 k_2 \ldots k_{n-1}$$

If this value is below some threshold, there will be no point in tracing further.

In general, of course, there will be three colour contributions (RGB) for each ray and three components to each of the attenuation coefficients. Thus when the recursive procedure is activated it is given a cumulative weight parameter that indicates the final weight that will be given at the top level to the colour returned for the ray represented by that procedure activation. The correct weight for a new procedure activation is easily calculated by taking the cumulative weight for the ray currently being traced and multiplying it by the reflection or transmission coefficient for the surface intersection at which the new ray is being created.

Another way in which a ray can be attenuated is by passing for some distance through an opaque material. This can be dealt with by associating a transmittance coefficient with the material composing an object. Colour values would then be attenuated by an amount determined by this coefficient and the distance a ray travels through the material. A simple addition to the intersection calculation in the ray tracing procedure would allow this feature to be incorporated.

The use of adaptive depth control will prevent, for example, a ray that initially hits an almost opaque object spawning a transmitted ray that is then traced through the object and into the scene. The intensity returned from the scene may then be so attenuated by the initial object that this computation is obviated. Thus, depending on the value to which the threshold is pre-set, the ray will, in this case, be terminated at the first hit.

For a highly reflective scene with a maximum tree depth of 15, Hall and Greenberg report (1983) that this method results in an average depth of 1.71, giving a large potential saving in image generation time. The actual saving achieved will depend on the nature and distribution of the objects in the scene.

12.5.2 First hit speed up

In the previous section it was pointed out that even for highly reflective scenes, the average depth to which rays were traced was between one and two. This fact led Weghorst et al. (1984) to suggest a hybrid ray tracer, where the intersection of the initial ray is evaluated during a preprocessing phase, using a hidden surface algorithm. The implication here is that the hidden surface algorithm will be more efficient than the general ray tracer for the first hit. Weghorst et al. (1984) suggest executing a modified Z-buffer algorithm, using the same viewing parameters. Simple modifications to the Z-buffer algorithm will make it produce, for each pixel in the image plane, a pointer to the object visible at that pixel. Ray tracing, incorporating adaptive depth control then proceeds from that point. Thus the expensive intersection tests associated with the first hit are eliminated.

12.5.3 Bounding objects with simple shapes

Given that the high cost of ray tracing is embedded in intersection testing, we can greatly increase the efficiency of a recursive ray tracer by making this part of the algorithm as efficient as possible. An obvious and much used approach is to enclose the object in a 'simple' volume known as a bounding volume. Initially we test the ray for intersection with a bounding volume and only if the ray enters this volume do we test for intersection with the object. Note that we also used this approach in the operation of culling against a view volume (see Chapter 6) and in collision detection (see Chapter 17).

Two properties are required of a bounding volume. First, it should have a simple intersection test – thus a sphere is an obvious candidate. Second, it should efficiently enclose the object. In this aspect a sphere is deficient. If the object is long and thin the sphere will contain a large void volume and many rays will pass the bounding volume test but will not intersect the object. A rectangular solid, where the relative dimensions are adjustable, is possibly the best simple bounding volume. (Details of intersection testing of both spheres and boxes are given in Chapter 1.)

The dilemma of bounding volumes is that you cannot allow the complexity of the bounding volume scheme to grow too much, or it obviates its own purpose. Usually for any scene, the cost of bounding volume calculations will be related to their enclosing efficiency. This is easily shown conceptually. Figure 12.7 shows a two-dimensional scene containing two rods and a circle representing complex polygonal objects. Figure 12.7(a) shows circles (spheres) as bounding volumes with their low enclosing efficiency for the rods. Not only are the spheres inefficient, but they intersect each other, and the space occupied by other objects. Using boxes aligned with the scene axes (axis aligned bounding boxes, or AABBs) is better (Figure 12.7(b)) but now the volume enclosing the sloping rod is inefficient. For this scene the best bounding volumes are boxes with any orientation (Figure 12.7(c)); the cost of testing the bounding volumes increases from spheres to boxes with any orientation. These are known as OBBs.

Weghorst *et al.* (1984) define a 'void' area, of a bounding volume, to be the difference in area between the orthogonal projections of the object and bounding volume onto a plane perpendicular to the ray and passing through the origin of the ray (see Figure 12.8). They show that the void area is a function of object, bounding volume and ray direction and define a cost function for an intersection test:

$$T = b*B + i*I$$

where:

T is the total cost function
b is the number of times that the bounding volume is tested for intersection
B is the cost of testing the bounding volume for intersection
i is the number of times that the item is tested for intersection (where $i \leq b$)
I is the cost of testing the item for intersection

Figure 12.7
Three different bounding volumes, going from (a) to (c). The complexity cost of the bounding volume increases together with its enclosing efficiency.
(a) Circles (spheres) as bounding volumes;
(b) rectangles (boxes) as bounding volumes;
(c) rectangles (boxes) at any orientation.

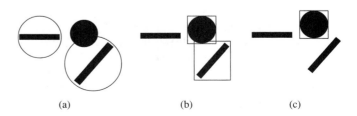

(a)   (b)   (c)

Figure 12.8
The void area of a bounding sphere.

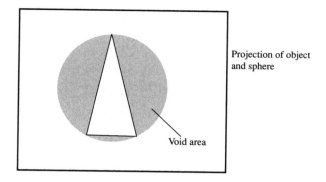

Projection of object and sphere

Void area

It is pointed out by the authors that the two products are generally interdependent. For example, reducing B by reducing the complexity of the bounding volume will almost certainly increase i. A quantitive approach to selecting the optimum of a sphere, a rectangular parallelepiped and a cylinder as bounding volumes is given.

12.5.4 Secondary data structures

Another common approach to efficiency in intersection testing is to set up a secondary data structure to control the intersection testing. The secondary data structure is used as a guide and the primary data structure – the object database – is entered at the most appropriate point.

Bounding volume hierarchies

A common extension to bounding volumes, first suggested by Rubin and Whitted (1980) and discussed in Weghorst *et al.* (1984), is to attempt to impose a hierarchical structure of such volumes on the scene. If it is possible, objects in close spatial proximity are allowed to form clusters, and the clusters are themselves enclosed in bounding volumes. For example, Figure 12.9 shows a container (a) with one large object (b) and four small objects (c_1, c_2, c_3 and c_4) inside it. The tree represents the hierarchical relationship between seven boundary extents: a cylinder enclosing all the objects, a cylinder enclosing (b), a cylinder enclosing (c_1, c_2, c_3, c_4) and the bounding cylinders for each of these objects. A ray traced against bounding volumes means that such a tree is traversed from the topmost level. A ray that happened to intersect c_1 in the above example would, of course, be tested against the bounding volumes for c_1, c_2, c_3 and c_4, but only because it intersects the bounding volume representing that cluster. This example also demonstrates that the nature of the scene should enable reasonable clusters of adjacent objects to be selected, if substantial savings over a non-hierarchical bounding scheme are to be achieved. Now the intersection test is implemented as a recursive process, descending through a hierarchy, only from

Figure 12.9
A simple scene and the associated bounding cylinder tree structure.

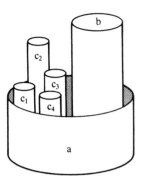

Bounding volume tree structure

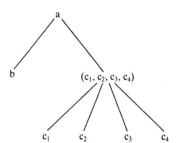

those nodes where intersections occur. Thus a scene is grouped, where possible, into object clusters and each of those clusters may contain other groups of objects that are spatially clustered. Ideally, high-level clusters are enclosed in bounding volumes that contain lower-level clusters and bounding volumes. Clusters can only be created if objects are sufficiently close to each other. Creating clusters of widely separated objects obviates the process. The potential clustering and the depth of the hierarchy will depend on the nature of the scene: the deeper the hierarchy the more the potential savings. The disadvantage of this approach is that it depends critically on the nature of the scene. Also, considerable user investment is required to set up a suitable hierarchy.

Bounding volume hierarchies used in collision detection are discussed in Chapter 17. Although identical in principle, collision detection requires efficient testing for intersection between pairs of bounding volumes, rather than ray/volume testing. OBB hierarchies have proved useful in this and are described in Section 17.5.2.

The use of spatial coherence

Currently, spatial coherence is the only approach that looks like making ray tracing a practical proposition for routine image synthesis. For this reason it is discussed in some detail. Object coherence in ray tracing has generally been ignored. The reason is obvious. By its nature a ray tracing algorithm spawns rays of arbitrary direction anywhere in the scene. It is difficult to use such 'random' rays to access the object data structure and efficiently extract those objects in the path of a ray. Unlike an image space scan conversion algorithm where, for example, active polygons can be listed, there is no *a priori* information on the sequence of rays that will be spawned by an initial or view ray. Naive ray tracing algorithms execute an exhaustive search of all objects after each hit, perhaps modified by a scheme such as bounding volumes, to constrain the search.

The idea behind spatial coherence schemes is simple. The space occupied by the scene is subdivided into regions. Now, rather than check a ray against all objects or sets of bounded objects, we attempt to answer the question: is the region, through which the ray is currently travelling, occupied by any objects? Either there is nothing in this region, or the region contains a small subset of the objects. This group of objects is then tested for intersection with the ray. The size of the subset and the accuracy to which the spatial occupancy of the objects is determined varies, depending on the nature and number of the objects and the method used for subdividing the space.

This approach, variously termed spatial coherence, spatial subdivision or space tracing has been independently developed by several workers, notably Glassner (1984), Kaplan (1985) and Fujimoto *et al.* (1986). All of these approaches involve pre-processing the space to set up an auxiliary data structure that contains information about the object occupancy of the space. Rays are then traced using this auxiliary data structure to enter the object data structure. Note that this philosophy (of pre-processing the object environment to reduce the computational work required to compute a view) was first employed by Schumaker *et al.* (1969) in a hidden surface removal algorithm developed for flight simulators (see Section 6.6.10). In this algorithm, objects in the scene are clustered into groups by subdividing the space with planes. The spatial subdivision is represented by a binary tree. Any view point is located in a region represented by a leaf in the tree. An on-line tree traversal for a particular view point quickly yields a depth priority order for the group clusters. The important point about this algorithm is that the spatial subdivision is computed off-line and an auxiliary structure, the binary tree representing the subdivision, is used to determine an initial priority ordering for the object clusters. The motivation for this work was to speed up the on-line hidden surface removal processing and enable image generation to work in real time.

Dissatisfaction with the bounding volume or extent approach, to reducing the number of ray object intersection tests, appears in part to have motivated the development of spatial coherence methods (Kaplan 1985). One of the major objections to bounding volumes has already been pointed out. Their 'efficiency' is dependent on how well the object fills the space of the bounding volume. A more fundamental objection is that such a scheme may increase the efficiency of the ray–object intersection search, but it does nothing to reduce the dependence on the number of objects in the scene. Each ray must still be tested against the bounding extent of every object and the search time becomes a function of scene complexity. Also, although major savings can be achieved by using a hierarchical structure of bounding volumes, considerable investment is required to set up an appropriate hierarchy, and depending on the nature and disposition of objects in the scene, a hierarchical description may be difficult or impossible. The major innovation of methods described in this section is to make the rendering time constant (for a particular image space resolution) and eliminate its dependence on scene complexity.

The various schemes that use the spatial coherence approach differ mainly in the type of auxiliary data structure used. Kaplan (1985) lists six properties that a practical ray tracing algorithm should exhibit if the technique is to be used in routine rendering applications. Kaplan's requirements are:

(1) Computation time should be relatively independent of scene complexity (number of objects in the environment, or complexity of individual objects), so that scenes having realistic levels of complexity can be rendered.

(2) Per ray time should be relatively constant, and not dependent on the origin or direction of the ray. This property guarantees that overall computation time for a shaded image will be dependent only on overall image resolution (number of first-level rays traced) and shading effects (number of second-level and higher level rays traced). This guarantees predictable performance for a given image resolution and level of realism.

(3) Computation time should be 'rational' and 'interactive' (within a few minutes) on affordable processor systems.

(4) The algorithm should not require the user to supply hierarchical object descriptions or object clustering information. The user should be able to combine data generated at different times, and by different means, into a single scene.

(5) The algorithm should deal with a wide variety of primitive geometric types, and should be easily extensible to new types.

(6) The algorithm's use of coherence should not reduce its applicability to parallel processing or other advanced architectures. Instead, it should be amenable to implementation on such architectures.

Kaplan summarizes these requirements by saying, 'in order to be really usable, it must be possible to trace a large number of rays in a complex environment in a rational, predictable time, for a reasonable cost'.

Two related approaches to an auxiliary data structure have emerged. These involve an octree representation (Fujimoto *et al.* 1986; Glassner 1984) and a data structure called a BSP (binary space partitioning). The BSP tree was originally proposed by Fuchs (1980) and is used in Kaplan (1985).

Use of an octree in ray tracing

An octree (see Chapter 2) is a representation of the objects in a scene that allows us to exploit spatial coherence – objects that are close to each other in space are represented by nodes that are close to each other in the octree.

When tracing a ray, instead of doing intersection calculations between the ray and every object in the scene, we can now trace the ray from subregion to subregion in the subdivision of occupied space. For each subregion that the ray passes through, there will only be a small number of objects (typically one or two) with which it could intersect. Provided that we can rapidly find the node in the octree that corresponds to a subregion that a ray is passing through, we have immediate access to the objects that are on, or close to, the path of the ray. Intersection calculations need only be done for these objects. If space has been subdivided to a level where each subregion contains only one or two objects, then the number of intersection tests required for a region is small and does not tend to increase with the complexity of the scene.

Tracking a ray using an octree

In order to use the space subdivision to determine which objects are close to a ray, we must determine which subregion of space the ray passes through. This involves tracking the ray into and out of each subregion in its path. The main operation required during this process is that of finding the node in the octree, and hence the region in space, that corresponds to a point (x, y, z).

The overall tracking process starts by detecting the region that corresponds to the start point of the ray. The ray is tested for intersection with any objects that lie in this region and if there are any intersections, then the first one encountered is the one required for the ray. If there are no intersections in the initial region, then the ray must be tracked into the next region through which it passes. This is done by calculating the intersection of the ray with the boundaries of the region and thus calculating the point at which the ray leaves the region. A point on the ray a short distance into the next region is then used to find the node in the octree that corresponds to the next region. Any objects in this region are then tested for intersections with the ray. The process is repeated as the ray tracks from region to region until an intersection with an object is found or until the ray leaves occupied space.

The simplest approach to finding the node in the octree that corresponds to a point (x, y, z) is to use a data structure representation of the octree to guide the search for the node. Starting at the top of the tree, a simple comparison of coordinates will determine which child node represents the subregion that contains the point (x, y, z). The subregion, corresponding to the child node, may itself have been subdivided and another coordinate comparison will determine which of its children represents the smaller subregion that contains (x, y, z). The search proceeds down the tree until a terminal node is reached. The maximum number of nodes traversed during this search will be equal to the maximum depth of the tree. Even for a fairly fine subdivision of occupied space, the search length will be short. For example, if the space is subdivided at a resolution of $1024 \times 1024 \times 1024$, then the octree will have depth 10 ($= \log_8(1024 \times 1024 \times 1024)$).

So far we have described a simple approach to the use of an octree representation of space occupancy to speed up the process of tracking a ray. Two variations of this basic approach are described by Glassner (1984) and Fujimoto *et al.* (1986). Glassner describes an alternative method for finding the node in the octree corresponding to a point (x, y, z). In fact, he does not store the structure of the octree explicitly, but accesses information about the voxels via a hash table that contains an entry for each voxel. The hash table is accessed using a code number calculated from the (x, y, z) coordinates of a point. The overall ray tracking process proceeds as described in our basic method.

In Fujimoto *et al.* (1986) another approach to tracking the ray through the voxels in the octree is described. This method eliminates floating point multiplications and divisions. To understand the method it is convenient to start by ignoring the octree representation. We first describe a simple data structure representation of a space subdivision called SEADS (Spatially Enumerated Auxiliary Data Structure). This involves dividing all of occupied space into equally sized voxels regardless of occupancy by objects. The three-dimensional grid obtained in this way is analogous to that obtained by the subdivision of a two-dimensional graphics screen into pixels. Because regions are subdivided regardless of occupancy by objects, a SEADS subdivision generates many more voxels than the octree subdivision described earlier. It thus involves 'unnecessary' demands for storage space. However, the use of a SEADS enables very fast tracking of rays from region to region. The tracking algorithm used is an extension of the DDA (Digital Differential Analyzer) algorithm used in two-dimensional graphics for selecting the sequence of pixels that represent a straight line between two given end points. The DDA algorithm used in two-dimensional graphics selects a subset of the pixels passed through by a line, but the algorithm can easily be modified to find all the pixels touching the line. Fujimoto *et al.* (1986) describe how this algorithm can be extended into three-dimensional space and used to track a ray through a SEADS three-dimensional grid. The advantage of the '3D-DDA' is that it does not involve floating point multiplication and division. The only operations involved are addition, subtraction and comparison, the main operation being integer addition on voxel coordinates.

The heavy space overheads of the complete SEADS structure can be avoided by returning to an octree representation of the space subdivision. The 3D-DDA algorithm can be modified so that a ray is tracked through the voxels by traversing the octree. In the octree, a set of eight nodes with a common parent node represents a block of eight adjacent cubic regions forming a 2 × 2 × 2 grid. When a ray is tracked from one region to another within this set, the 3D-DDA algorithm can be used without alteration. If a ray enters a region that is not represented by a terminal node in the tree, but is further subdivided, then the sub-region that is entered is found by moving down the tree. The child node required at each level of descent can be discovered by adjusting the control variables of the DDA from the level above. If the 3D-DDA algorithm tracks a ray out of the 2 × 2 × 2 region currently being traversed, then the octree must be traversed upwards to the parent node representing the complete region. The 3D-DDA algorithm then continues at this level, tracking the ray within the set of eight regions containing the parent region. The upward and downward traversals of the tree involve multiplication and division of the DDA control variables by 2, but this is a cheap operation.

Finally, we summarize and compare the three spatial coherence methods by listing their most important efficiency attributes:

- Octrees: are good for scenes whose occupancy density varies widely – regions of low density will be sparsely subdivided, high density regions will be finely subdivided. However, it is possible to have small objects in large regions. Stepping from region to region is slower than with the other two methods because the trees tend to be unbalanced.

- SEADS: stepping is faster than an octree but massive memory costs are incurred by the secondary data structure.

- BSP: the depth of the tree is smaller than an octree for most scenes because the tree is balanced. Octree branches can be short, or very long for regions of high spatial occupancy. The memory costs are generally lower than those of an octree. Void areas will tend to be smaller.

12.5.5 Ray space subdivision

In this unique scheme, suggested by Arvo and Kirk (1987), instead of subdividing object space according to occupancy, ray space is subdivided into five-dimensional hypercubic regions. Each hypercube in five-dimensional space is associated with a candidate list of objects for intersection. That stage in object space subdivision schemes where three-space calculations have to be invoked to track a ray through object space is now eliminated. The hypercube that contains the ray is found and this yields a complete list of all the objects that can intersect the ray. The cost of the intersection testing is now traded against higher scene pre-processing complexity.

A ray can be considered as a single point in five-dimensional space. It is a line with a three-dimensional origin together with a direction that can be specified by two angles in a unit sphere. Instead of using a sphere to categorize direction, Arvo and Kirk (1987) use a 'direction cube'. (This is exactly the same tool as the light buffer used by Haines and Greenberg (1986) – see Section 12.1.3.) A ray is thus specified by the 5-tuple (x, y, z, u, v), where x, y, z is the origin of the ray and u, v the direction coordinates; together with a cube face label that indicates which face of the direction cube the ray passes through. Six copies of a five-dimensional hypercube (one for each direction cube face) thus specify a collection of rays having similar origins and similar directions.

This space is subdivided according to object occupancy and candidate lists are constructed for the subdivided regions. A 'hyper-octree' – a five-dimensional analog of an octree – is used for the subdivision.

To construct candidate lists as five-dimensional space is subdivided, the three-dimensional equivalent of the hypercube must be used in three-space. This is a 'beam' or an unbounded three-dimensional volume that can be considered the union of the volume of ray origins and the direction pyramid formed by a ray origin and its associated direction cell (Figure 12.10). Note that the beams in three-space will everywhere intersect each other, whereas their hypercube equivalents in five-space do not intersect. This is the crux of the method – the five-space can be subdivided and that subdivision can be acheived using binary partitioning. However, the construction of the candidate lists is now more difficult than with object space subdivision schemes. The beams must be intersected with the bounding volumes of objects. Arvo and Kirk (1987) report that detecting polyhedral intersections is too costly and suggest the approximation where beams are represented or bounded by cones interacting with spheres as object bounding volumes.

Figure 12.10
A ray (or beam) as a single
point in (*x, y, z, u, v*) space.

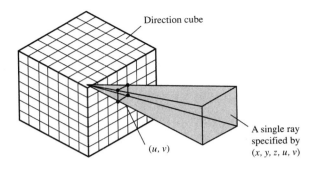

Direction cube

(*u, v*)

A single ray
specified by
(*x, y, z, u, v*)

12.6   The use of ray coherence

Up to now we have considered a ray to be infinitesimally thin and looked at efficiency measures that attempt to speed up the basic algorithm. It is easy to see that a major source of inefficiency that we have not touched on until now is the lack of use of ray coherence. This simply means that if the ray tracing algorithm generates a ray for each pixel and separately traces every such ray we are taking no account whatever of the fact that adjacent initial rays will tend to follow the same path. We will now look at ways in which we can 'broaden' a ray into a geometric entity.

Heckbert and Hanrahan (1984) exploit the coherence that is available from the observation that, for any scene, a particular ray has many neighbours each of which tends to follow the same path. Rather than tracing single rays, then, why not trace groups of parallel rays, sharing the intersection calculations over a bundle of rays? This is accomplished by recursively applying a version of the Weiler–Atherton hidden surface removal algorithm (Weiler and Atherton 1977). The Weiler–Atherton algorithm is a projection space subdivision algorithm involving a preliminary depth sort of polygons followed by a sort of the fragments generated by clipping the sorted polygons against each other. Finally, recursive subdivision is used to sort out any remaining ambiguities. This approach restricts the objects to be polygonal, thus destroying one of the important advantages of a ray tracer which is that different object definitions are easily incorporated due to the separation of the intersection test from the ray tracer.

The initial beam is the viewing frustum. This beam or bundle of rays is traced through the environment and is used to build an intersection tree, different from a single ray tree in that a beam may intersect many surfaces rather than one. Each node in the tree now contains a list of surfaces intersected by the beam.

The procedure is carried out in a transformed coordinate system called the beam coordinate system. Initially this is the view or eye coordinate system. Beams are volumes swept out as a two-dimensional polygon in the *xy* plane is translated along the *z* axis.

Figure 12.11
Reflection in beam tracing.

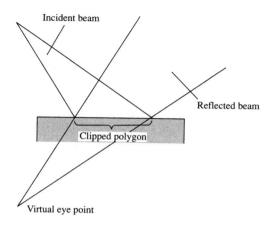

Reflection (and refraction) are modelled by calling the beam tracer recursively. A new beam is generated for each beam–object intersection. The cross-section of any refelected beam is defined by the area of the polygon clipped by the incident beam and a virtual eye point (Figure 12.11).

Apart from the restriction to polygonal objects the approach has other disadvantages. Beams that partially intersect objects change into beams with complex cross-sections. A cross-section can become disconnected or may contain a hole (Figure 12.12). Another disadvantage is that refraction is a non-linear phenomenon and the geometry of a refracted beam will not be preserved. Refraction therefore, has to be approximated using a linear transformation.

Another approach to beam tracing is the pencil technique of Shinya *et al.* (1987). In this method a pencil is formed from rays called 'paraxial rays'. These are rays that are near to a reference ray called an axial ray. A paraxial ray is represented by a four-dimensional vector in a coordinate system associated with the axial ray. Paraxial approximation theory, well known in optical design and electromagnetic analysis, is then used to trace the paraxial rays through the environment. This means that for any rays that are near the axial ray, the pencil transformations are linear and are 4×4 matrices. Error analysis in paraxial theory supplies functions that estimate errors and provide a constraint for the spread angle of the pencil.

Figure 12.12
A beam that partially intersects an object produces a fragmented cross-section.

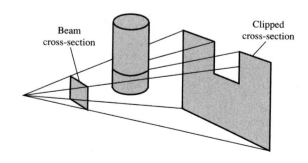

The 4 × 4 system matrices are determined by tracing the axial ray. All the paraxial rays in the pencil can then be traced using these matrices. The paraxial approximation theory depends on surfaces being smooth so that a paraxial ray does not suddenly diverge because a surface discontinuity has been encountered. This is the main disadvantage of the method.

An approach to ray coherence that exploits the similarity between the intersection trees generated by successive rays is suggested by Speer *et al.* (1986). This is a direct approach to beam tracing and its advantage is that it exploits ray coherence without introducing a new geometrical entity to replace the ray. The idea here is to try to use the path (or intersection tree) generated by the previous ray, to construct the tree for the current ray (Figure 12.13). As the construction of the current tree proceeds, information from the corresponding branch of the previous tree can be used to predict the next object hit by the current ray. This means that any 'new' intervening object must be detected as shown in Figure 12.14. To deal with this, cylindrical safety zones are constructed around each ray in a ray set. A safety zone for ray$_{r-2}$ is shown in Figure 12.15. Now if the current ray does not pierce the cylinder of the corresponding previous ray, and this ray intersects the same object, then it cannot intersect any new intervening objects. If a ray does not pierce a cylinder, then new intersection tests are required as in standard ray tracing, and a new tree that is different from the previous tree, is constructed.

In fact, Speer *et al.* (1986) report that this method suffers from the usual computational cost paradox – the increase in complexity necessary to exploit the ray coherence properties costs more than the standard ray tracing as a function of scene complexity. This is despite the fact that two-thirds of the rays behave coherently. The reasons given for this are the cost of maintaining and pierce-checking the safety cylinders, whose average radius and length decrease as a function of scene complexity.

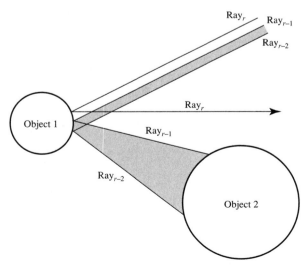

Figure 12.13
Ray coherence: the path of the previous ray can be used to predict the intersections of the current ray.

Figure 12.14
'Intervening' object in the
path of the ray *r*.

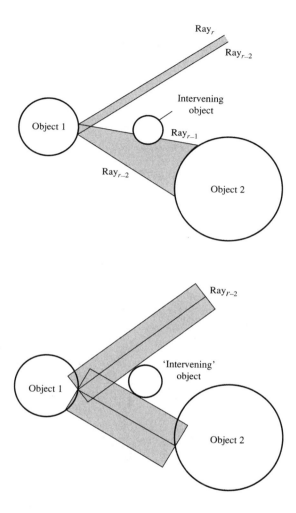

Figure 12.15
Cylindrical safety zones.

12.7   A historical digression – the optics of the rainbow

Many people associate the term 'ray tracing' with a novel technique but, in fact, it has always been part of geometric optics. For example, an early use of ray tracing in geometric optics is found in René Descartes' treatise, published in 1637, explaining the shape of the rainbow. From experimental observations involving a spherical glass flask filled with water, Descartes used ray tracing as a theoretical framework to explain the phenomenon. Descartes used the already known laws of reflection and refraction to trace rays through a spherical drop of water.

Rays entering a spherical water drop are refracted at the first air–water interface, internally reflected at the water–air interface and finally refracted as they emerge from the drop. As shown in Figure 12.16, horizontal rays entering the

Figure 12.16
Tracing rays through a
spherical water drop
(ray 7 is the Descartes ray).

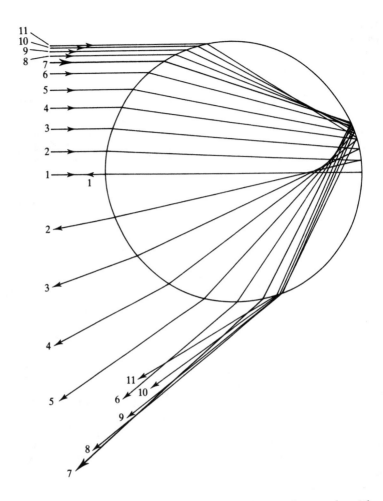

drop above the horizontal diameter emerge at an increasing angle with respect to the incident ray. Up to a certain maximum the angle of the exit ray is a function of the height of the incident ray above the horizontal diameter. This trend continues up to a certain ray, when the behaviour reverses and the angle between the incident and exit ray decreases. This ray is known as the Descartes ray, and at this point the angle between the incident and exit ray is 42°. Incident rays close to the Descartes ray emerge close to it and Figure 12.16 shows a concentration of rays around the exiting Descartes ray. It is this concentration of rays that makes the rainbow visible.

Figure 12.17 demonstrates the formation of the rainbow. An observer looking away from the sun sees a rainbow formed by '42°' rays from the sun. The paths of such rays form a 42° 'hemicone' centred at the observer's eye. (An interesting consequence of this model is that each observer has his own personal rainbow.)

Figure 12.17
Formation of a rainbow.

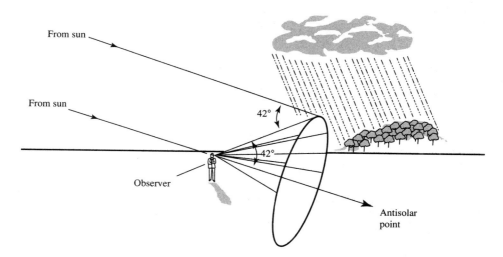

This early, elegant use of ray tracing did not, however, explain that magical attribute of the rainbow – colour. Thirty years would elapse before Newton discovered that white light contained light at all wavelengths. Along with the fact that the refractive index of any material varies for light of different wavelengths, Descartes' original model is easily extended. About 42° is the maximum angle for red light, while violet rays emerge after being reflected and refracted through 40°. The model can then be seen as a set of concentric hemicones, one for each wavelength, centred on the observer's eye.

This simple model is also used to account for the fainter secondary rainbow. This occurs at 51° and is due to two internal reflections inside the water drops.

Volume rendering

Introduction

Volume rendering means rendering or visualizing voxel-based data. In Chapter 2 we introduced data representation techniques that are based on labelling all voxels in a region of object space with object occupancy. We saw that in applications where large homogeneous objects may occupy hundreds or thousands of voxels we may impose a hierarchical structure, such as an octree, on the data. On the other hand, in applications like medical imaging a data structure may be a vast three-dimensional array of voxels that emerges from a scanner. In this chapter we consider visualizing such large unstructured sets of voxels.

In the last decade or so a new discipline, ViSC, or Visualization in Scientific Computing, has emerged. One of the major application areas in this field is the visualization of scalar functions of three-spatial variables. Such data, prior to the availability of hardware and software for volume rendering, was visualized using 'traditional' techniques such as iso-contours in cross-sectional planes. The advent of volume rendering has meant that the data can be considered as a computer graphics object and all three dimensions displayed. Scalar functions of three-spatial variables abound in science and engineering. Engineers are concerned with designing three-dimensional objects and analyzing their potential behaviour. Calculations may produce predictions relating to temperature and stress, for example.

A voxel volume is produced either by a mathematical model, such as in computational fluid dynamics, or the voxels are collected from the real world as in medical imaging. Visualization software generally treats both types in the same way. The major practical distinction between different data sources is the shape of the volume element. In medical imagery the voxels are rectangular or cubic. In other applications this may not be the case. In the example shown in Figure 13.1 (Colour Plate) the volume elements were wedge shaped, that is, a cylinder divided up in a 'slice of cake' manner.

Medical imaging has turned out to be one of the most common applications of volume rendering. It has enabled data, collected from a tomographic system as a set of parallel planes, to be viewed as a three-dimensional computer graphics object. The material in this chapter is mostly based on this particular application. Although certain context-dependent considerations are necessary, the medical imaging problem is quite general and any strategy developed for this will easily adapt to other applications.

In medical imaging three-dimension data are available from stacks of parallel CT (computed tomography) data. These systems reconstruct or collect data in sets of planes according to some particular property, the original modality being the X-ray absorption coefficient at each point in the plane. The basic medical system enables a clinician to view the information in each plane. With visualization the entire stack of planes is considered as volume data and rendered accordingly. A very simplified illustration of a tomographic imaging system is shown in Figure 13.2. From this we should note that information is sampled in many two-dimensional planes of zero thickness. Voxel values are inferred from these data. The data exhibit the characteristic that the resolution within a plane (typically 512×512) is much greater than the resolution between planes. Scans are typically taken at distances of the order of 0.5 cm. These data are then interpreted as a set of voxels where each voxel exhibits an X-ray absorption coefficient and it is this data set that is volume rendered. Currently the systems that reconstruct the tomograms, which are used routinely for diagnosis, and the systems for volume visualization are separate – a point we return to in the next section.

One of the most remarkable projects in medicine is the Visible Human Project (1998). This is a 15 gigabytes voxel data set (male) and 40 gigabytes (female) consisting of MRI, X-ray CT and anatomical images obtained from cadavers. The initial aim of the Visible Human Project was to acquire transverse CT, MRI and cryosection images of a representative male and female cadaver at an average of 1 mm intervals. The corresponding transverse sections in each of the three modalities were to be registered with one another.

The Visible Human Male data set consists of axial MRI images of the head and neck and longitudinal sections of the rest of the body were obtained at 4 mm intervals. The MRI images are 256×256 pixels $\times$ 12 bits resolution. The CT data consist of axial CT scans of the entire body taken at 1 mm intervals at a resolution of 512×512 pixels $\times$ 12 bits. The axial anatomical images are 2048×1216 pixels $\times$ 24 bits. These are also at 1 mm intervals and coincide with the CT axial images. There are 1871 cross-sections for each mode, CT and anatomical.

The Visible Human Female data set has the same characteristics as the male cadaver with one exception. The axial anatomical images were obtained at 0.33

Figure 13.2
X-ray computer tomography and volume rendering.

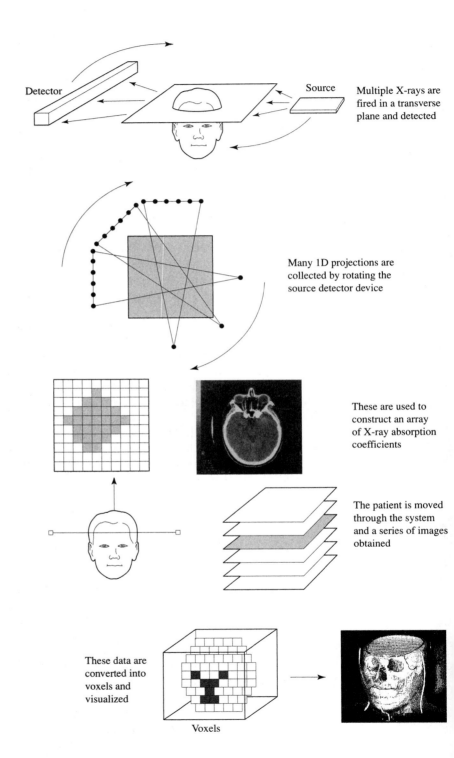

Detector

Source

Multiple X-rays are fired in a transverse plane and detected

Many 1D projections are collected by rotating the source detector device

These are used to construct an array of X-ray absorption coefficients

The patient is moved through the system and a series of images obtained

These data are converted into voxels and visualized

Voxels

mm intervals instead of 1 mm intervals to enable cubic voxels. This resulted in over 5000 anatomical images.

The long-term goal of the project is stated as:

The Visible Human Project data sets are designed to serve as a common reference point for the study of human anatomy, as a set of common public domain data for testing medical imaging algorithms, and as a test bed and model for the construction of image libraries that can be accessed through networks. The data sets are being applied to a wide range of educational, diagnostic, treatment planning, virtual reality, artistic, mathematical and industrial uses by over 1000 licensees in 41 countries. But key issues remain in the development of methods to link such image data to text-based data. Standards do not currently exist for such linkages. Basic research is needed in the description and representation of image-based structures, and to connect image-based structural–anatomical data to text-based functional–physiological data. This is the larger, long-term goal of the Visible Human Project: to transparently link the print library of functional–physiological knowledge with the image library of structural–anatomical knowledge into one unified resource of health information.

13.1 Volume rendering and the visualization of volume data

The basic idea of volume rendering is that a viewer should be able to perceive the data volume from a rendered projection on the view plane. In medical imaging we may want to view a surface, or the volume, or just part of the volume.

Thus we view the extraction and display of 'hard' surfaces that exist in the data as part of the volume rendering problem. In many cases we may have a volume data set from which we have to extract and display surfaces that exist anywhere within the volume. Rather than bounding surfaces of an object, we may be dealing with an object that possesses many 'nested' surfaces – like the skin of an onion. If such surfaces are extractable by some unique property then we can render them visible by making them 100% opaque and all other data in the volume 100% transparent.

We will now extend the medical example and consider techniques for visualizing the stack of CT slices as a three-dimensional volume of data. All of the techniques described in this chapter apply to most volume data. They are more or less completely general. It is simply easier to consider the different possibilities in the context of a particular application area.

As we mentioned previously, our reconstructed CT data consist of a number of infinitely thin slices or two-dimensional arrays, where the inter-slice distance is, in practice, greater than a pixel dimension within the slice. To turn this stack into a regular three-dimensional array of cubic voxels we have to invoke some form of interpolation. We can then consider the various possibilities, or modes of displaying this volume data.

For any application, because we are dealing with volume data, the options available are much greater than with rendering the surface of an object; and the particular mode of display will depend on the applications. The nature of these requirements and also the nature of the data determines the algorithm that is used.

The three basic options available for displaying a volume data set on a two-dimensional display surface are:

(1) To slice the data set with a cross-sectional plane. This is clearly the easiest option and is trivial if the plane is parallel to one of the coordinate planes of the volume data set. It is also the least ambitious as it effectively displays only two dimensions of the data.

(2) To extract an object that is 'known' to exist within the data set and render it in the normal way. Thus an internal organ of a body can be displayed in isolation just as if it had been dissected. This implies, first, that the object can be segmented from the remainder of the data and, second, that the segmented form can be converted into a computer graphics representation.

(3) To assign transparency and colour to voxels within the object then view the entire set from any angle. This is usually known as volume rendering. Alternatively in medical applications it is sometimes called a computed X-ray as it is analogous to a conventional X-ray. In other words it is possible to generate a computed X-ray from any viewing angle, including angles that may be physically impossible with conventional X-ray equipment. As well as having freedom to select any viewing angle we can also change the opacities in any way we require.

Currently, the main application of the visualization of volume data is in medical illustration – in the form of interactive atlases for medical education, medical research, surgical planning and computer graphics research. For diagnostic applications clinicians appear to prefer examining the original tomographic slices side by side. This is due in part to inadequacies in the process that, as we shall see, involve interpolative methods which may interfere with the integrity of the original data. For example, in the second method – extracting an object from the data – small holes in a surface may be filled in.

The connection with medical illustration is reinforced by the fact that many quality issues can be resolved in the original data collection stage – the scanning of the body – but there are usually limits associated with this. In the case of X-ray CT scanning, the X-ray dosage received by the patient is a function of the resolution, both in terms of the spatial resolution within the reconstruction plane and the number of planes collected. To increase the resolution means subjecting the patient to a higher X-ray dosage which is already higher than that for a conventional X-ray. This has meant that the high quality imagery has been generated from data obtained from cadavers.

The development of medical atlases from volume data sets has led to a variety of creative combinations of the above three display options. Examples of common combinations are shown in Figures 13.3 (Colour Plate). The first two examples show an extracted object(s) embedded in a transparent surround of the skull. The extracted structures have been turned into computer graphics objects and rendered normally. They are then effectively re-embedded in the three-dimensional data volume which is displayed with the surrounding voxels set to some semi-transparent value. The semi-transparent voxels can be set to grey scale – to simulate an X-ray – or any desired colour. This can be effected simply by using method 3 and setting the object voxels to be opaque, but a better result is normally obtained, at least for the purposes of medical illustration, by rendering the objects of interest conventionally. The motivation of this type of illustration is obvious – it highlights the object and orients it with respect to the body or skin. Another popular combination (the second two examples) is to cut away a rendered version of the skin to show internal organs as a cross-section positioned within a three-dimensional model. Here, the organs are assigned an appropriate pseudo-colour simply to highlight their shape. Such colours can be 'pure' false colours that identify or label the structure of interest and they can relate to the values associated with the voxels on some understood basis. A standard hue circle set of colours could reflect the value of the absorption coefficient, for example.

The overall idea of volume rendering is shown in Figure 13.4 as a ray casting algorithm which shows a volume data set, represented as a cube, rotated into a desired viewing orientation and intersected by a bundle of parallel rays – one for each pixel. (The term 'ray casting' is used to distinguish the method from ray tracing – in this context the rays continue as a parallel bundle through the volume instead of diverging after a hit.) Such an approach is a useful conceptual starting point; in practice, there are many different ways of implementing this approach. We will now discuss the following general options and considerations with respect to such an algorithm:

- **What properties of the data do we want to see in the image plane?** We may want to see the external boundary surface as a shaded object. In medical imagery this would be the skin surface and this implies that we have to 'find' this surface and shade it. In the ray casting case this would simply involve terminating the ray when it strikes the first non-zero voxel, evaluating a surface normal for the voxel and applying a local shading model. Alternatively we may want to visualize an internal object and shade it. In medical imagery we might want to see bone structure underneath the skin/flesh layer. This implies that we have to extract such a surface for the data set before we can render it as a computer graphics object. We may want to move a cross-sectional cutting plane through the data as shown in Figure 13.4(b) and view the contents of the intersection of the cutting plane with the data as it moves. We may want to see both bones, such as the rib cage, and the organs contained within. This could be accomplished either by rendering the bones as opaque so that the viewer sees the organs through the gaps in the bones, or by rendering the bones as partially transparent. Other possibilities are easily imagined. We could compose a projection that, for each pixel, was the maximum data value encountered along the ray. A less obvious mode is to display the sum along each ray path. This will then give an image analogous to a conventional X-ray, giving us the facility of being able to generate a (virtual) X-ray-type

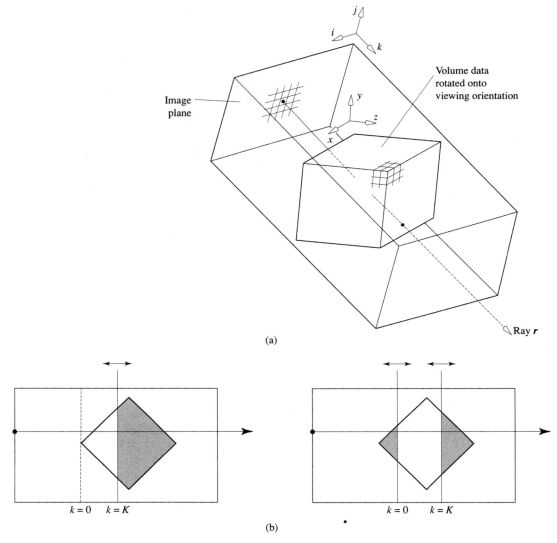

(a)

(b)

Figure 13.4
(a) Volume rendering by casting parallel rays from each pixel (after Levoy (1990)). (b) Using planes parallel to the view plane to construct a view volume of the data set.

image from viewing angles that would be impossible with conventional equipment.

● **What is the relationship between the reality and the data?** Our volume data set will consist, in general, of a three-dimensional array of points, representing a three-dimensional sampling of the reality. This may be a very large data set, say 512^3. We associate the single sample with the entire voxel volume, just as a sample in two-dimensional image processing is associated with a square pixel extent. But what does that single sample represent? Here, the simpler case to consider is binary occupancy. We assume that the voxel resolution is fine enough that any voxel contains only a single material, or it contains nothing. Alternatively, we could consider that a voxel contained a mix of materials. In medical imagery it may be that the physical extent of a voxel corresponds to a region which straddles both bone and tissue. Do we consider the value of a voxel to be constant throughout its extent, or do we consider that the value varies throughout? If the latter, what model do we use to interpolate the variation between neighbouring voxels?

- **What are the implications of voxel size?** Unlike conventional surface rendering, where we have a definition associated with an object for each pixel, it is likely that the projection of a voxel extent onto the image plane will occupy many pixels.

We will now look at these considerations in greater detail.

13.2 'Semi-transparent gel' option

The most general viewing option is somehow to give a viewer the facility to see all the data. No voxel is considered completely opaque and all the data are therefore seen. The physical analogue is an object that is made of different coloured transparent gels. All other options can be considered a particularization of this method. Each voxel is assigned a colour, C, and a transparency, α. The colour associated with the material type can be chosen 'aesthetically'. In the CT example, white could be chosen for bone and the transparency would be made proportional to density so that bone could be made almost completely opaque.

We then cast a ray from each pixel into the data volume which has been rotated into the desired viewing orientation and perform a compositing operation. This accumulates a resultant colour and opacity for that pixel. The process is like considering the volume to be made up of a semi-transparent gel of different colours and opacities. It is as if behind the volume we had diffuse white light and we are looking into it from the front side. The process is analogous to taking a conventional X-ray of the volume in the viewing direction; but now we are transmitting parallel beams of light through a volume whose opacity relates to tissue density and displaying the result.

In clinical application at the Johns Hopkins Medical Institution, Ney *et al.* (1990) state:

The images generated using this unshaded rendering process are reminiscent of a conventional radiographic image. These images are particularly useful for examining bony abnormalities. The bones are semi-transparent and therefore internal detail is visible, as well as surface detail. Unfortunately the unshaded technique does not work well for imaging soft tissue. The high variability of bone density causes the unshaded algorithm to produce the perceived detail. Soft tissue attenuation values are confined to a far narrower spectrum, making it more difficult to separate, for example, a vessel or node from adjacent muscle.

Thus we see that this visualization involves a number of steps:

(1) Classify each voxel in the original data and assign desired colour and opacity values.

(2) Transform the (now classified) volume data into the viewing direction.

(3) For each pixel cast a ray and find, by compositing along the ray, a colour for that pixel.

We now describe each of these steps separately.

(13.2.1) Voxel classification

Considering the more general case of a voxel containing more than one tissue type, a typical classification scheme was introduced by Drebin *et al.* (1988) (for the particular case of X-ray CT data). In this scheme voxels are classified into four types according to the value of the X-ray absorption coefficient. The types are: air, fat, soft tissue and bone. The method is termed 'probabilistic classification' and it assumes that two, but not more than two, materials can exist in a voxel. Thus voxels can consist of seven types: air, air and fat, fat, fat and soft tissue, soft tissue, soft tissue and bone, and bone. Mixtures are only possible between neighbouring materials in the absorption coefficient scale – air, for example, is never adjacent to bone.

The classification scheme uses a piecewise linear 'probability' function (Figure 13.5). Consider a specific material assigned such a function. There will exist a particular CT number that is most likely to represent this material (point A in Figure 13.5(a)). Points B_1 and B_2 represent the maximum deviation in CT number from point A that is still considered this material. Any CT number less than B_1 or greater than B_2 and contained within the limits defined by C_1 and C_2 is classified as a mixture of 'neighbouring' materials. A complete scheme is shown in Figure 13.5(b). Voxels are assigned (R, G, B, α) values according to some

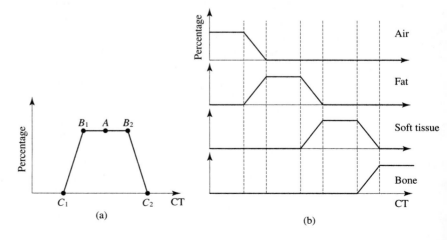

Figure 13.5
Material classification in CT data (due to Drebin *et al.* (1988)). (a) Trapezoid classification function for one material. (b) Classification functions.

scheme and if a mixture of two materials is present in a voxel the two colours are mixed in the same proportion as the materials.

13.2.2 Transforming into the viewing direction

Theoretically a simple process, this step produces difficulties. A simple illustration of the viewing process is shown in Figure 13.6. In general, the data volume can be rotated into any desired orientation and when pixel rays are cast into the rotated volume this involves a resampling operation and aliasing has to be considered. One of the main options in the overall construction of a volume rendering algorithm is the way in which this transformation is performed and its position in the order of the three stages described in Section 13.2.

In the CT example it is only useful to rotate about the z axis (spinal rotation) and about the x axis (somersault rotation). This means that the rotation of the volume can be performed by rotating two-dimensional planes perpendicular to these axes.

13.2.3 Compositing pixels along a ray

The simplest compositing operation (Figure 13.7) is the recursive application of the formula:

$$C_{out} = C_{in} (1 - \alpha) + C \alpha$$

where:

C_{out} is the accumulated colour emerging from a voxel
C_{in} is the accumulated colour into that voxel
α is the opacity of the current voxel
C is the colour of the current voxel

Note that this form is just an extension of the **over** operation defined in Section 6.6.3 for compositing two images. The direction implied by C_{out} and C_{in} is from back to front with respect to the view plane. That is, we start the operation with the voxel furthest from the view plane.

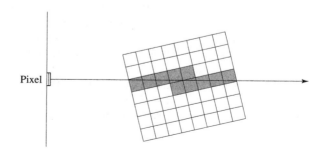

Figure 13.6
Ray casting implies resampling the data. A ray will not, in general, intercept voxel centres.

Pixel

Figure 13.7
The ray compositing
operation.

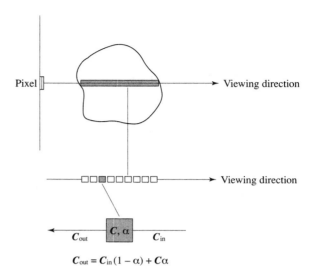

$$C_{out} = C_{in}(1 - \alpha) + C\alpha$$

It does not matter in this model where the light comes from. We simply note that any light exiting from the voxel of interest along the viewing direction has the colour of that voxel plus the product of the incoming light and $(1 - \alpha)$. There are elaborations that can be made on this simple model. For example, α should in reality be a vector quantity since it will differ according to the R, G or B component of the colour of the voxel. The effect of this operation is to make voxels with high α values predominate, obscuring voxels that are behind them and being made visible through voxels in front of them.

13.3 Semi-transparent gel plus surfaces

If we assume that opaque surfaces are present in the data volume then we supplement the previous scheme with a shading scheme, and present the surfaces as part of the display according to the various options that we described in Section 13.1. Assuming that a voxel can contain part of a surface we can evaluate a normal, and a shading component is calculated as a function of this normal and the direction of the illuminating source. This shading component can then replace C in the compositing operation.

The shape of surfaces is now perceived in the normal way as the lighting model enhances the details in the surface. Various options now emerge. We can display just those voxels that contain, say, bone together with its surface shape detail, visible through a fuzzy cloud of soft tissue. Bone can then be made completely opaque or still be given an opacity so that detail behind the bone is still visible.

A surface is detected by evaluating a normal using the volume gradient. The components of this normal are:

$$N_x = R(x+1, y, z) - R(x-1, y, z)$$
$$N_y = R(x, y+1, z) - R(x, y-1, z)$$
$$N_z = R(x, y, z+1) - R(x, y, z-1)$$

where for each voxel, R is evaluated by summing the products of the percentage of each material in the voxel times its assigned density. If a material is homogeneous these differences evaluate to zero and the voxel under consideration is deemed not to contain a surface segment. This scheme is illustrated diagrammatically in Figure 13.8.

The presence of a surface is quantified by the magnitude of the surface normal – the larger this magnitude the more likely it is that a surface exists. The magnitude or 'strength' of the surface ($|N|$) can be used to weight the contribution of the shaded component. No binary decision is taken on the presence or absence of a surface. A normalized version of the surface normal is calculated and can then be used in a shading equation such as the Phong reflection model. We should bear in mind that this technique is purely for the purposes of visualization. It has absolutely no relation to physical reality. We assume that each

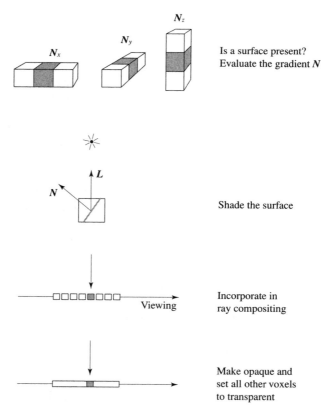

Figure 13.8
Surface detection and shading.

voxel has an uninterrupted view of the light source even though it may be buried in the middle of a volume.

The localness of this operation means that it is sensitive to noise. This can be diminished by reducing the localness. In the above formula the gradient is evaluated by considering six neighbouring voxels. We can extend this to 18 or even 24 voxels.

We have shaded surfaces by calculating the interaction of a normal of the voxel containing the surface with a light source. Then the surface shape detail becomes visible. We can either incorporate the shaded surface in the semi-transparent gel model or we can make the surface opaque and remove all voxels that do not contain a surface. This makes the first surface the ray hits the surface that is seen by the viewer. These options are indicated schematically by Figure 13.8.

It is important to realize that the surface detection is local and is evaluated for single voxels. No decision has to be taken about the existence or otherwise of a surface if the shading component is included in the semi-transparent gel model. This is important in medical applications where clinicians are (rightly) suspicious of methods where binary decisions on the existence of a surface are made. There are, however, applications where such an approach – explicit extraction of an (assumed) continuous surface – is desirable, as we describe in the next section.

13.3.1 Explicit extraction of isosurfaces

If the volume data is such that it is known to contain continuous isosurfaces, then these surfaces can be explicitly extracted and converted into polygon mesh structures and rendered in the normal way. Such an approach finds one or more appropriate polygons for each voxel and produces a continuous set of such polygons from the set of voxels comprising the surface.

So why go to the trouble of finding a polygon mesh surface when we can find and shade surfaces in the volume by using the density gradient? One of the motivations is that conventional rendering techniques can be used if the surface is represented with conventional graphics primitives and volume rendering then reduces to a preprocessing operation of surface extraction.

The technique used is known as the marching cubes algorithm reported by Lorenson and Cline (1987). An actual surface is built up by fitting a polygon or polygons through each voxel that is deemed to contain a surface. A voxel possesses eight vertices and if we assume at the outset that a voxel can sit astride a surface, then we can assign a polygon to the voxel in a way that depends on the configuration of the values at the vertices. By this is meant the distribution of those vertices that are inside and outside the surface over the eight vertices of the cube. If certain assumptions are made, then there happens to be 256 possibilities. From considerations of symmetry these cases can be reduced to 15 and these are shown in Figure 13.9. The final position and orientation of each polygon within each voxel type is determined by the strength of the field values at the vertices. A surface is built up that consists of a normal polygon mesh and the

Figure 13.9
The 15 possibilities in the marching cubes algorithm. Dot (•) used in the figure represents a vertex that is inside a surface.

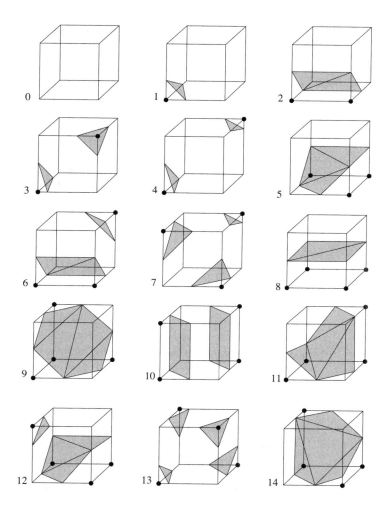

difference in quality between rendering such a surface and effecting surface extraction by appropriate zero–one opacity assignment in volume rendering is due to what is effectively an inferior resolution in the volume rendering method. In the volume rendering method a surface may exist somewhere within the voxel. The opacity of such a voxel is set to one and the information on the position and orientation of the surface fragment is reduced to the surface normal. In the marching cubes algorithm the surface fragment (or fragments) is positioned and oriented accurately within the voxel – at least within the limitations of the interpolation method used. However, explicit surface extraction methods sometimes make errors by making the assumption that a surface exists across neighbouring voxels. They can fit a surface over what in reality are neighbouring surface fragments. In other words, they make a binary decision that may be erroneous. Another problem with the marching cubes algorithm is the sheer volume of primitives that can be generated. This can run into millions where many primitives project onto the same pixel.

Figures 13.10 (Colour Plate) and 13.11 (Colour Plate) compare the two main approaches for rendering an object of interest. The original data are 23 planes of X-ray CT data with a 512 × 512 resolution in each plane. Figure 13.10 shows a skull rendered using the marching cubes algorithms. The second illustration (Figure 13.11) is exactly the same data but this time they are rendered using a volume rendering algorithm with the bone opacity set to unity. Although it may not be too apparent in the reproductions, the marching cube version appears to be of higher quality or resolution – this is an illusory consequence of the algorithm; it is accessing the same data but creating an explicit computer graphics model of one or more polygons per voxel. The volume rendering algorithm is simply assigning normals to each voxel based on local information.

13.4 Structural considerations in volume rendering algorithms

There are many options in setting up a volume rendering algorithm. As we have seen, the process of viewing a volume data is conceptually simple involving as it does the rotation of the volume into the viewing orientation, then ray casting (or an equivalent operation) into the volume to discover a suitable value for each pixel. The main research thrust in volume rendering arises out of the importance of efficient hardware implementation. Interactivity and animation are important in most application areas because of their contribution to the interpretation of the data. Because we are generally dealing with very large data sets – routinely in the order of 512^3 – the relationship between the algorithm design and available hardware (such as parallel processors) becomes of critical importance if interactivity/animation demands are to be met.

The terminology used to describe algorithmic options in volume rendering is somewhat confusing. The confusion seems to arise out of what names to give to the main categories. There are two main categories:

(1) Ray casting methods (with two variants). Also called image or pixel space traversal or back projection.

(2) Voxel projection methods (with two variants). Also called object or voxel space traversal or forward projection.

These options are illustrated diagrammatically in Figure 13.12. In ray casting we can either transform and resample the volume data so that it is oriented with a coordinate axis parallel to the image plane, or we can leave it untransformed. If the data are transformed prior to ray casting then we generate a set of rays parallel to rows (or columns) of the transformed data. For untransformed data the ray set is subject to the inverse viewing transform. Ray casting methods are also categorized as image space methods in that the outermost loop of the algorithm traverses image space.

Figure 13.12
A taxonomy of volume rendering structures.

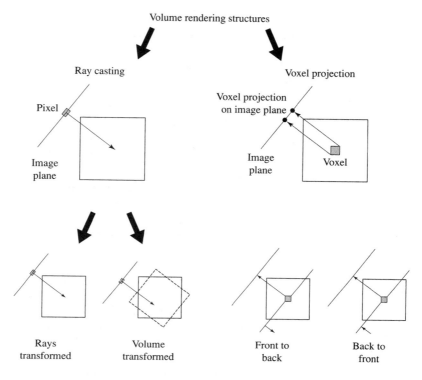

Although at first sight it would seem that ray casting methods can be implemented in parallel, memory bottleneck problems arise. If arbitrary viewing directions are allowed there is no way to distribute voxels in memory to ensure that no contentions occur.

A potential problem with forward projection is that holes may arise in the image plane. For voxel projection methods we have to bear in mind that in most applications a single voxel will form a projection in the image plane that spreads over many pixels. (This has been called a footprint.) If we ignore perspective projections then this footprint is the same for all voxels – for a given view – and such coherence can be used to advantage for fast implementation and efficient anti-aliasing. We will now consider these options in greater detail. The important difference between the methods are manifest in the suitability for parallel implementation and how resampling is accomplished.

13.4.1   Ray casting (untransformed data)

In ray casting we traverse image space and cast a ray from each pixel to find a single colour for that pixel by the compositing operation previously described. (The method bears little or no relationship to ray tracing which traces a pixel ray in any direction through the scene depending on the geometry and nature of the objects that are hit. In volume rendering we cast a set of parallel pixel rays which all remain travelling in the same direction.) To do this two non-trivial tasks have to be performed. First, we have to find these voxels through which the ray passes and, second, we have to find a value for each of the voxels from the classified data set.

Consider the first problem. This in itself breaks down into two parts. Finding the voxels through which a pixel ray passes is a well-worked-out problem – we simply use a 3DDA (three-dimensional differential analyzer) an extension into three-dimensional space of knowledge worked out over the years to deal with the two-dimensional line/pixel problem. However, once we find these voxels, how do we deal with their values? How do we obtain values to insert into our compositing scheme? Using the basic values of each encountered voxel is wrong. One reason is obvious. The path lengths through each voxel will vary from a very small distance, for a ray that just cuts the corner of a voxel, to a large distance for a ray that is close to the diagonal across opposite corners. We are effectively viewing along a ray and a long journey through a voxel should produce a higher contribution to the compositing than a short one. This is, of course, one of the consequences of sampling a practical volume data set with an infinitely thin ray – or more precisely resampling. It is a three-dimensional problem of the equivalent resampling process in image processing. We start with sampled data, rotate them into a new orientation, and resample them. We have to filter when we are resampling to avoid aliasing. The complication in volume rendering is that the data are three-dimensional and the resampling is in three-dimensional space. An appropriate way to proceed therefore, is to measure equal points along the ray and find a resampled value at these points by filtering over a three-dimensional region, using the equally spaced ray sample points as a centre for the three-dimensional filter kernel.

The algorithm is sometimes described as an image space traversal algorithm and the outermost loop is usually defined as 'cast a ray for each pixel'. However, we need to recognize that we can do no better than cast a parallel set of rays into the volume that pass through every voxel in the data. A simple scheme to achieve this is shown in cross-section in Figure 13.13. The ray set is constructed by passing each ray through the centre point of each voxel in the front face of the data set.

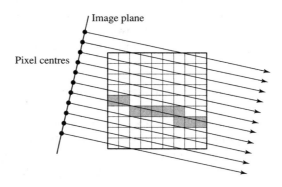

Figure 13.13
An appropriate set of rays in a ray casting algorithm.

Figure 13.14
C_S, the value at a sample point on the ray, is evaluated by bilinear interpolation. C_V is evaluated from C_1 and C_2. C_H is evaluated from C_2 and C_3. C_S is evaluated from C_V and C_H.

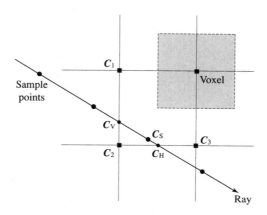

The same concept is used by Yagel *et al.* (1992), who use the idea of a ray 'template'. The ray template method adopts the simple approach of moving the ray one voxel at a time along a line called the base plane. Thus the ray, or ray template, is computed once only and stored in a data structure. All rays are then followed by obtaining the appropriate displacements from this information. The shaded voxels in Figure 13.13 form a ray template. In effect, this approach is exploiting the coherency between rays.

We now consider the question of resampling. If the volume is left undisturbed, then the rendering (or compositing) process and resampling process are merged into one operation. We step along the ray at equal sample points and evaluate, for each sample point, a C to be used in the compositing. We could simply use a value for C that was the value of the voxel that contained the sample point. But normally the more accurate process of trilinear interpolation is used. This is shown in cross-section in Figure 13.14 where it becomes in two dimensions bilinear interpolation. To evaluate C_S we interpolate from the surrounding grid points, evaluating first the horizontal and vertical intersects of the ray with the voxel grid lines. We can then find the value of C_S. The process is a simplified version of bilinear interpolation used in polygon shading (see Chapter 1) where the polygon is a square.

Ray casting (transformed data)

The second variant of ray casting involves pre-transforming the data into the desired orientation. The geometry of the actual ray casting is then trivial (or eliminated) in that we simply composite along rows or columns of the transformed data.

To transform the data a three-pass (all shear) decomposition described in Wolberg (1990) can be used. A viewing transformation then becomes a sequence of pure shears – three for each axis. So a general transformation is a set of nine shears. The importance of a shear-only process lies in its implementation in

Figure 13.15
Resampling is performed
during *each* shear.

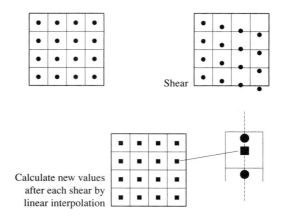

Shear

Calculate new values
after each shear by
linear interpolation

special-purpose hardware. In particular, it possesses the property that every voxel
in a single shear is moved through a constant amount.

The significant difference in the two ray casting variants is involved in the
resampling. Now resampling must be performed during each shear and the
process of resampling is performed *before* the compositing. Resampling during a
shear involves simple linear interpolation (Figure 13.15).

In ray casting methods an important efficiency enhancement is ignoring
empty space in the data volume. A cast ray advances through empty space until
it encounters an object. It penetrates the object until sufficient opacity has accumulated, and for high opacity this may be a short distance compared with the
traversal through empty space. The empty space does not contribute to the final
image and because of the large number of voxels, it is important to implement
some space-skipping procedure. This can be based on a bounding volume, just
as in speed-up schemes in conventional ray tracing, the traversal of the data set
starting from the surface of the bounding volume.

13.4.3 Voxel projection method

This variant of volume rendering possibilities involves traversing the data set
and projecting each voxel onto the image plane, as we indicated in Figure 13.12.
If we move a plane through the data as shown in this figure, then the frame
buffer is used as an accumulator and all pixels are updated simultaneously until
all the data are completely traversed and the pixels have their final values.

We can traverse the data from either front to back or back to front. The significant difference between these two variants is that with back-to-front traversal we only need to accumulate colour, while with front-to-back traversal we
need to accumulate both colour and transparency. (This is exactly equivalent to
saying that with front-to-back traversal we require a Z-buffer.)

Voxel projection algorithms are important because they are more easy to
parallelize. At each point in the process, that is, at each voxel, we only need

knowledge about a small surrounding neighbourhood. This contrasts with ray casting into untransformed data where we generally require the entire data set when we cast a single ray.

Possibly the most well known voxel projection algorithm is due to Westover (1990) and is termed 'splatting'. This strange word is used to describe the effect that one voxel has in the image plane. In effect, the algorithm considers how the contribution of a voxel should be spread or splatted in the image plane. Consider Figure 13.16. A point in the data at the centre of a particular voxel projects onto a single pixel. To determine what the value of the pixel should be we can calculate a contribution by filtering over the three-dimensional region surrounding the sampled voxel. Alternatively, we can take the sample voxel value and spread this over a number of pixels in the image plane. Both approaches are equivalent. If we consider the filter function to be a three-dimensional Gaussian then this projects into the image plane as a circular function. Thus we can project and filter the data by taking the voxel value and splatting it into the image plane by

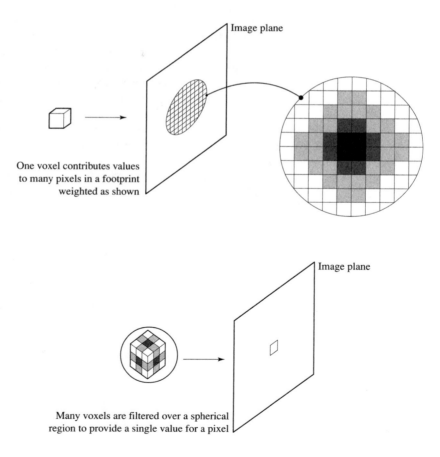

Figure 13.16
Filtering in voxel projection.

One voxel contributes values to many pixels in a footprint weighted as shown

Image plane

Image plane

Many voxels are filtered over a spherical region to provide a single value for a pixel multiplying it with the filter weights and accumulating these values. This set of values is called the footprint of the voxel and for a parallel projection all footprint weights are the same and can be stored in a look-up table.

13.5 Perspective projection in volume rendering

So far we have not mentioned the issue of perspective projection. In the case of medical imaging it may be that a perspective projection is not required. The volume data in medical applications usually has limited spatial extent of some centimetres and we would not expect to perceive significant perspective clues over this distance. Also it is not usually the shape of the overall structure that is important to the viewer, but some detail such as a fracture or a tumour and its relationship to surrounding structures. Some specific applications in medicine do require a perspective projection. An example is the construction of a 'beam's eye view' in radiation therapy planning. Here, the clinician requires a view of the volume looking down a treatment beam. Treatment beams diverge and so a perspective projection is required.

A number of obvious difficulties occur in constructing a perspective projection in a volume renderer. The most serious results from the divergence of rays from the centre of projection (Figure 13.17). If the ray density is such that the nearest plane in the volume data is sampled with one ray per voxel, then in the example shown, this will quickly drop to one ray per two voxels and small detail can be missed. Another problem is anti-aliasing during resampling. If we consider travelling along the four rays that pass through each of the four corners of a pixel and the centre of projection, the geometry of the volume at the centre of the neighbourhood over which we must filter is no longer a cubic voxel but a truncated pyramid.

One of the easiest ways of implementing perspective projection is to augment the voxel projection or footprint algorithm. Full details of this are given by Westover (1990).

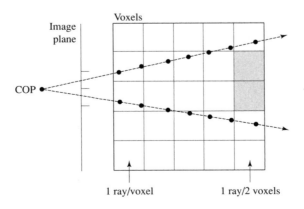

Figure 13.17
Ray density and perspective projection (after Novins *et al.* (1990)). One ray/pixel results in decreasing sampling rate.

13.6

Three-dimensional texture and volume rendering

Since a volume data set can be considered as a three-dimensional texture, then volume rendering can be carried out by a three-dimensional texture mapping facility (Section 8.7). The algorithm (Haeberli and Segal 1993) consists of first calculating the set of parallel polygons that are normal to the viewing direction. This entails finding the intersections between a set of parallel planes and the bounding planes of the data volume. The polygon vertices are then texture mapped and the entire set of polygons is composited in back-to-front order. Since we are now sampling the data with parallel planes, rather than by stepping in equal distances along individual rays, then for a perspective projection the planes will produce unequal sample intervals for rays emanating from the view point. In that case, we need to sample using segments of a sphere rather than planes as shown in Figure 13.18.

Figure 13.18
Volume data 'sampled' using segments of a sphere centred on the eye point.

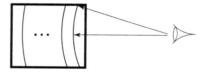

14 Anti-aliasing theory and practice

Note
This chapter discusses the classical approach to anti-aliasing and requires some understanding of Fourier theory. A brief introduction, sufficient for an intuitive appreciation of this is given in Section 14.9 at the end of the chapter.

Introduction

The final quality of computer graphics imagery depends on many varied factors. Artefacts arise out of modelling and other factors that are a consequence of operations in the particular rendering algorithm that was used to generate the image. For example, consider the many image defects in polygon mesh scenes. We have modelling artefacts sometimes called geometric aliasing – the visibility of piecewise linearities on the silhouette edge of a polygon mesh object. There are artefacts that emerge from the shading algorithm such as Mach bands and inadequacies due to the interpolation method (see Chapter 18 for a discussion of these). In the case of the radiosity method the view-independent phase throws up difficult quality problems which are not dealt with by general anti-aliasing approaches as we have already discussed in Chapter 11.

Anti-aliasing is the general term given to methods that deal with discrepancies that arise from undersampling and it is this issue which we deal with in this chapter. Such methods are used in conventional rendering approaches like those discussed in Chapter 6 for polygon mesh objects, ray tracing in Chapter 12 and in the Monte Carlo techniques discussed in Chapter 10. Anti-aliasing in texture mapping is discussed in Chapter 8 for the reason that, although it is a classical approach, the particular implementation – mip-mapping – is used exclusively with texture mapping.

14.1 Aliases and sampling

We first consider the term 'alias'. In theory this refers to a particular image artefact that is mostly visible in texture maps when the periodicity in the texture approaches the dimension of a pixel. This is easily demonstrated and Figure 14.1(a) is the classic example of this effect – an infinite chequerboard. Towards the top of the image the squares reduce, then apparently increase in size, causing a glaring visual disturbance. This is due to undersampling. The notion of sampling in computer graphics comes from the fact that we are calculating a single colour or value for each pixel; we are sampling a solution at discrete points in a solution space. This is a space that is potentially continuous in the sense that, because computer graphics images are generated from abstractions, we can calculate samples anywhere or everywhere in the image plane.

We will now look at a simple one-dimensional example which will relate undersampling, aliases and the notion of spatial frequencies. Consider using a sine wave to represent an information signal (although a sine wave does not contain any information anyway, this does not matter for our purposes). Figure 14.2 shows a sine wave being sampled at different rates (with respect to the frequency of the sine wave). Undersampling the sine wave and reconstructing a

Figure 14.1
The pattern in (b) is a super-sampled version of that in (a). Aliases still occur but appear at a higher spatial frequency.

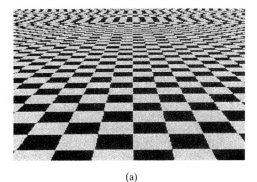

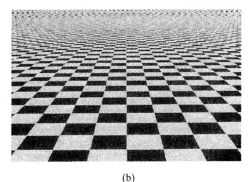

(a)   (b)

continuous signal from the samples (dotted line in the figure) produces an 'alias' of the original signal – another sine wave at a lower frequency than the one being sampled. We can say that this happens because the coherence or regularity of the sampling pattern is interfering with the regularity of the information. To avoid aliasing artefacts we have to sample at an appropriately high frequency with respect to the signal or image information and we normally consider the process of calculating an image function at discrete points in the image plane to be equivalent to sampling.

The defects that arise in computer graphics that are due to insufficient calculations or samples and which are easily modelled by an image plane sampling model are coherent patterns breaking up – the case that we have already discussed – and small fragments that are missed because they fall between two sample points.

Consider the chequerboard example again. The pattern units approach the size of a pixel very quickly and the pattern 'breaks up'. High spatial frequencies are aliasing as lower ones and forming new visually disturbing coherent patterns. Now consider Figure 14.1(b) where we render the same image onto a view plane with double the resolution of the previous one. Aliasing artefacts still appear but at a higher spatial frequency. In theoretical terms we have increased the sampling frequency, but the effect persists except that it happens at a higher spatial frequency. This demonstrates two important facts. Spatial frequencies in a computer graphics image are unlimited because they originate from a mathematical definition. You cannot get rid of aliases by simply increasing the pixel resolution.

Figure 14.2
Space domain representation of the sampling of a sine wave. (a) Sampling interval is less than one-half the period of the sine wave. (b) Sampling interval is equal to one-half the period of the sine wave. (c) Sampling interval is greater than one-half the period of the sine wave. (d) Sampling interval is much greater than one-half the period of the sine wave.

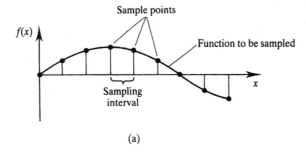

(a)

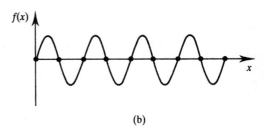

(b)

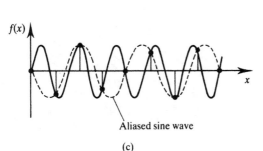

(c)

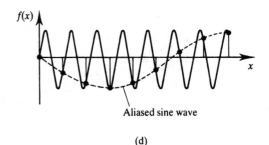

(d)

The artefacts simply occur at a higher spatial frequency. But they are, of course, less noticeable.

Now, the example in Figure 14.2 can be generalized by considering these cases in the frequency domain for an $f(x)$ that contains information, that is not a pure sine wave. We now have an $f(x)$ that is any general variation in x and may, for example, represent the variation in intensity along a segment of a scan line. The frequency spectrum of $f(x)$ will exhibit some 'envelope' (Figure 14.3(a)) whose limit is the highest frequency component in $f(x)$, say, f_{max}. The frequency spectrum of a sampling function (Figure 14.3(b)) is a series of lines, theoretically extending to infinity, separated by the interval f_s (the sampling frequency). Sampling in the space domain involves multiplying $f(x)$ by the sampling function. The equivalent process in the frequency domain is convolution and the frequency spectrum of the sampling function is convolved with $f(x)$ to produce the frequency spectrum shown in Figure 14.3(c) – the spectrum of the sampled version of $f(x)$. This sampled function is then multiplied by a reconstructing filter to reproduce the original function. A good example of this process, in the time domain, is a modern telephone network. In its simplest form this involves sampling a speech waveform, encoding and transmitting

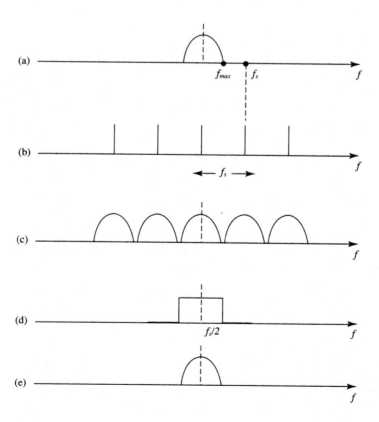

Figure 14.3
Frequency domain representation of the sampling process when $f_s > 2f_{max}$. (a) Frequency spectrum of $f(x)$.
(b) Frequency spectrum of the sampling function.
(c) Frequency spectrum of the sampled function (convolution of (a) and (b)).
(d) Ideal reconstruction filter. (e) Reconstructed $f(x)$.

digital versions of each sample over a communications channel, then reconstructing the original signal from the decoded samples by using a reconstructing filter.

Note that the reconstruction process, which is multiplication in the frequency domain, is convolution in the space domain. In summary, the process in the space domain is multiplication of the original function with the sampled function, followed by convolution of the sampled version of the function with a reconstructing filter.

Now in the above example the condition:

$$f_s > 2f_{max}$$

is true. In the second example (Figure 14.4) we show the same two processes of multiplication and convolution but this time we have:

$$f_s < 2f_{max}$$

Incidentally, $f_s/2$ is known as the Nyquist limit. Here the envelopes, representing the information in $f(x)$, overlap. It is as if the spectrum has 'folded' over a line defined by the Nyquist limit (Figure 14.4(e)). This folding is an information-destroying process; high frequencies (detail in images) are lost and

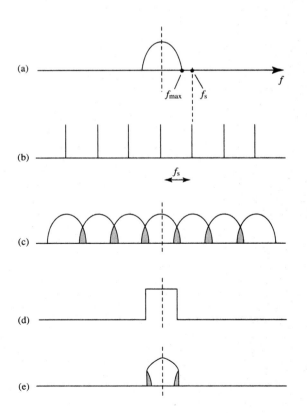

Figure 14.4
Frequency domain representation of the sampling process when $f_s < 2f_{max}$. (a) Frequency spectrum of $f(x)$.
(b) Frequency spectrum of the sampling function.
(c) Frequency spectrum of the sampled function.
(d) Ideal reconstruction filter. (e) Distorted $f(x)$.

appear as interference (aliases) in low frequency regions. This is precisely the effect shown in Figure 14.1 where low spatial frequency structures are emerging in high frequency regions.

The sampling theorem extends to two-dimensional frequencies or spatial frequencies. The two-dimensional frequency spectrum of a graphics image in the continuous generation domain is theoretically infinite. Sampling and reconstructing in computer graphics is the process of calculation of a value at the centre of a pixel and then assigning that value to the entire spatial extent of that pixel.

Aliasing artefacts in computer graphics can be reduced by increasing the frequency of the sampling grid (that is increasing the spatial resolution of the pixel array). There are two drawbacks to this approach: the obvious one that there is both an economic and a technical limit to increasing the spatial resolution of the display (not to mention the computational limits on the cost of the image generation process) and, since the frequency spectrum of computer graphics images can extend to infinity, increasing the sampling frequency does not necessarily solve the problem. When, for example, we applied the increased resolution approach to coherent texture in perspective, we simply shifted the effect up the spatial frequency spectrum.

14.2 Jagged edges

The most familiar defects in computer graphics are called jaggies. These are produced by the finite size of a (usually) square pixel when a high contrast edge appears in the image. These are particularly troublesome in animated images where their movement gives them the appearance of small animated objects and makes them glaringly visible. These defects are easier to get rid of because they do not arise out of the algorithm *per se* – they are simply a consequence of the resolution of the image plane.

Jagged edges are recognized by everyone and described in all computer graphics textbooks; but they are not aliasing defects in the classical sense of an aliased spatial frequency, where a high spatial frequency appears as a disruptive lower one. They are defects produced by the final limiting effect of the display device. We can certainly ameliorate their effect by, for example, calculating an image at a resolution higher than the pixel resolution; in other words increasing the sampling frequency deals with both aliases and jaggies. In the case of jaggies, edge information is 'forced' into the horizontal and vertical edges of the pixels. Consider Figure 14.5 which shows a perfect rectangle and a pixelized version. The Fourier transform for the perfect rectangle maps the edge information into high energy components along directions corresponding to the orientation of the edges in the image. The Fourier version of the pixel version also contains this information together with high energy components along the axes corresponding to the false or pixel edges. Jaggies do not arise because of high spatial frequencies aliasing as lower ones.

Figure 14.5
The effect of jaggies is to rotate high energy components onto the horizontal and vertical axes in the Fourier domain.

(a) Simulation of a perfect line

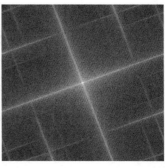

(b) Fourier transform of (a)

(c) Simulation of a jagged line

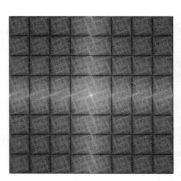

(d) Fourier transform of (c)

14.3 Sampling in computer graphics compared with sampling reality

Let us now return in more detail to the notion of sampling in the image plane. In image synthesis what we are doing is performing, for each pixel, a number of (sometimes very complicated) operations that eventually calculate, for that pixel, a constant value. Usually we calculate a value at the centre of the pixel and 'spread' that value over the pixel extent.

We assume that, in principle, this is no different from having a continuous image in the view plane and sampling this with a discrete two-dimensional array of sample points (one for each pixel). We say that this assumption is valid because we can approach such an image by increasing and increasing the sample resolution and calculating a value for the image at more and more points in the image plane. However, it is important to bear in mind that we do not have access to a continuous image in computer graphics and this limits and conditions our approaches to anti-aliasing measures.

In fact, both the terms 'sampling' and 'reconstruction' – another term borrowed from digital signal processing – are used indiscriminately and, we feel, somewhat confusingly in computer graphics, and we will now emphasize the difference between an image processing system, where their usage is wholly appropriate, and their somewhat artificial use in computer graphics.

Consider Figure 14.6 which shows a schematic diagram for an image processor and a computer graphics system. In the image processor a sampler converts a two-dimensional continuous image into an array of samples. Some operations are then performed on the digital image and a reconstruction filter converts the processed samples back into an analogue signal.

Not so in image synthesis. Sampling does not exist in the same sense – the operations involved in assigning a value to a pixel depend on the rendering algorithm used and we can only ever calculate the value of an image function at these points.

Reconstruction, in image synthesis does not mean generating a continuous image from a digital one but may mean, for example, generating a low (pixel) resolution image from an image stored at a higher (undisplayable) resolution. We are not reconstructing an image since a continuous image never existed in the first place. An appreciation of these differences will avoid confusion. (In reality we do reconstruct a continuous image for display on a computer graphics monitor, but this is done by fixed electronics that operate on the image produced in the framestore by a graphics program. A comprehensive approach to anti-aliasing would need to take the transfer characteristics of the conversion electronics into account but we will not do so in this text.)

To return to the problem of aliasing artefacts. Fourier theory tells us that aliasing occurs because we sample a continuous image (or the equivalent operation in computer graphics) and we do not do this at a high enough resolution to capture the high spatial frequencies or detail in the image. The sampling theorem states that if we wish to sample an image function without loss of information then our (two-dimensional) sampling frequency must be at least twice as high as the highest frequency component in the image.

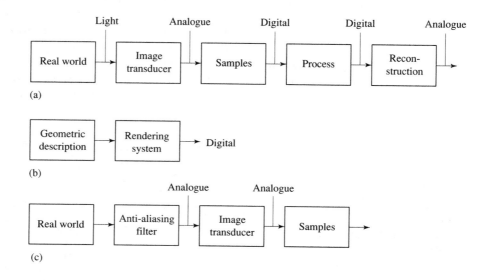

Figure 14.6
Sampling, reconstruction and anti-aliasing in image processing and image synthesis. (a) Image capture and processing. (b) Image synthesis. (c) Anti-aliasing in image capture.

So what does this mean in terms of practical computer graphics? Just this: if we consider we are sampling a continuous image in the view plane with a grid of square pixels, then the highest frequency that can appear along a scan line is:

$$f = 1/2d$$

where d is the distance between pixel centres.

Having fixed these concepts it is easy to see why anti-aliasing is so difficult in computer graphics. The problem stems from two surprising facts. There is no limit to the value of the high frequencies in computer graphics – we have already discussed this using the example of the infinite chequerboard – and there is no direct way to limit (the technical term is band-limit) these spatial frequencies.

This is easily seen by comparing image synthesis with image capture through a device like a TV camera (Figure 14.6c). Prior to sampling a continuous image we can pass it through a band limiting filter (or an anti-aliasing filter). Higher frequencies that cannot be displayed are simply eliminated from the image before it is sampled. We say that the image is pre-filtered. In such systems aliasing problems are simply not allowed to occur.

In image synthesis our scene database exists as a mathematical description or as a set of points connected by edges. Our notion of sampling is inextricably entwined with rendering. We sample by evaluating the projection of the scene at discrete points. We cannot band limit the image because no image exists – we can only define its existence at the chosen points.

14.4 Sampling and reconstruction

In Figure 14.3 we saw that provided the sampling theory is obeyed then reconstruction of the information from the samples is obtained by using a reconstruction filter in the shape of a box. However, this is a Fourier domain representation and in computer graphics all our operations have to take place in the space domain. Therefore the reconstruction process is convolution in the space or image domain. In computer graphics this implies (usually) filtering a rendered image in some way. If the rendered image was continuous then our reconstruction filter would consist of a sinc function $h(x, y)$ – which is the transform of the Fourier domain equivalent of a circular step function (Figure 14.7).

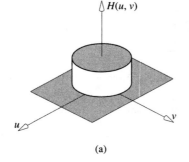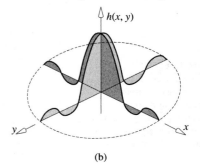

Figure 14.7
Ideal filters in the Fourier and space domains.
(a) An ideal low pass (multiplicative) filter $H(u,v)$.
(b) The equivalent (convolving) filter $h(x,y)$.

(a)   (b)

There are, however, practical difficulties associated with this. The filter cannot have unlimited extent – it has to be truncated at some point and the way in which this is done is an important aspect of the design of the filter.

14.5 A simple comparison

We will now consider the anti-aliasing options in computer graphics briefly in the form of a comparative overview. Figure 14.8 shows four main approaches.

(1) Pre-filtering – 'infinite' samples per pixel

Here we calculate the precise contribution of fragments of projected object structure as it appears in a pixel. This single value is taken as the pixel colour. The practical effect of this approach is simply a reduction of the 'infinite' resolution to the finite resolution of the pixel display. If the physical extent of a pixel is small this is a high quality but totally impractical method. However, note that although this method assumes accurate geometry we assume that the light intensity is constant across any fragment. Effectively what we are doing with this algorithm is pre-filtering – that is, filtering *before* sampling using a box filter.

This is the method which approaches the anti-aliasing filter in Figure 14.6(c). It effectively removes those high frequencies that manifest as sub-pixel detail but because the calculations are continuous it is doing this before sampling.

(2) No filtering – one sample per pixel

In the second case we consider only one sample per pixel. This becomes equivalent to the first case if, and only if, the projection is such that a pixel only ever contains a single geometric structure and all structure boundaries in the projection coincide with pixel edges – impossible constraints in practice. This 'do nothing' approach is extremely common in real-time animation. It is also used as a preview method in off-line production where a final anti-aliased image is generated only when a creator is satisfied with the preview.

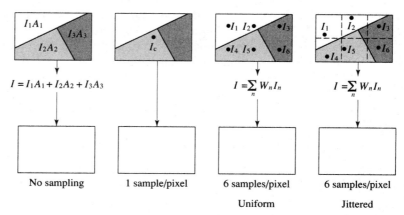

Figure 14.8
A comparison of four approaches to calculating a single value for a pixel.

(3) Post filtering – n *uniform samples per pixel*
This is the commonest approach to anti-aliasing and involves rendering a virtual image at *n* times the resolution of the final screen image. This is an approximation to the notion of a continuous image. The final image is then produced by sampling the virtual image and reconstructing it by a convolution operation. Both operations are combined into a single operation. The effectiveness of this approach depends on the number of supersamples and the relationship between the image structure within a pixel and the sampling grid point. Note that although we can regard this approach as an approximation to the first case, the samples that relate to the same fragment can now have different intensities.

(4) Post-filtering – stochastic samples
This approach can be seen as a simple alteration of the previous – instead of uniformly sampling within a pixel we now jitter the samples according to some scheme. This approach has already been discussed in Chapter 10 (see Figure 10.9) as an integral part of Monte Carlo methods. In this chapter we will look at why it functions as a 'pure' anti-aliasing technique.

14.6 Pre-filtering methods

The originator of this technique was Catmull (Catmull 1978). Although Catmull's original algorithm is prohibitively expensive, it has spawned a number of more practical successors.

The algorithm essentially performs sub-pixel geometry in the continuous image generation domain and returns, for each pixel, an intensity which is computed by using the areas of visible sub-pixel fragments as weights in an intensity sum. This is equivalent to convolving the image with a box filter and using the value of the convolution integral at a single point as the final pixel value. (Note the width of the filter is less than ideal and a wider filter using information from neighbouring regions would give a lower cut-off frequency.) Another way of looking at the method is to say that it is an area sampling method.

We can ask the question: what does performing 'sub-pixel geometry' mean in practical computer graphics terms? To do this we inevitably have to use a practical approximation. (To reiterate an earlier point, we have no access to a continuous image. In computer graphics we can only define an image at certain points.) This means that the distinction between sampling techniques and supersampling is somewhat artificial and indeed the A-buffer approach (described shortly), usually categorized as an area sampling technique, could equally well be seen as supersampling.

Catmull's method is incorporated in a scan line renderer. It proceeds by dividing the continuous image generation domain into square pixel extents. An intensity for each square is computed by clipping polygons against the square pixel boundary. If polygon fragments overlap within a square they are sorted in z and clipped against each other to produce visible fragments. A final intensity is computed by multiplying the shade of a polygon by the area of its visible fragment and summing.

The origin of the severe computational overheads inherent in this method is obvious. The original method was so expensive that it was only used in two-dimensional animation applications involving a few largish polygons. Here, most pixels are completely covered by a polygon and the recursive clipping process of polygon fragment against polygon fragment is not entered.

Recent developments have involved approximating the sub-pixel fragments with bit masks (Carpenter 1984; Fiume *et al.* 1983). Carpenter (1984) uses this approach with a Z-buffer to produce a technique known as the A-buffer (anti-aliased, area averaged, accumulator buffer). The significant advantage of this approach is that floating point geometry calculations are avoided. Coverage and area weighting are accomplished by using bitwise logical operators between the bit patterns or masks representing polygon fragments. It is an efficient area sampling technique, where the processing per pixel square will depend on the number of visible fragments.

Another efficient approach to area sampling, due to Abram *et al.* (1985), pre-computes contributions to the convolution integral and stores these in look-up tables indexed by the polygon fragments. The method is based on the fact that the way in which a polygon covers a pixel can be approximated by a limited number of cases. The algorithm is embedded in a scan line renderer. The convolution is not restricted to one pixel extent but more correctly extends over, say, a 3 × 3 area. A pixel acts as an accumulator whose final value is correct when all fragments that can influence its value have been taken into account.

Consider a 3 × 3 pixel area and a 3 × 3 filter kernel (Figure 14.9). A single visible fragment in the centre pixel will contribute to the convolution integral when the filter is centred on each of the nine squares. The nine contributions that such a fragment makes can be pre-computed and stored in a look-up table. The two main stages in the process are:

(1) Find the visible fragments and identify or categorize their shape.

(2) Index a pre-computed look-up table which gives the nine contributions for each shape. A single multiplication of the fragment's intensity by the pre-computed contribution weighting gives the desired result.

Figure 14.9
A single fragment in the centre pixel will cause contributions to filtering on each of the nine squares.

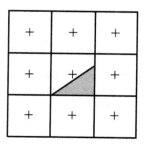

Abram assumes that the shapes fall into one of seven categories:

(1) There is no fragment in the pixel.

(2) The fragment completely covers the pixel.

(3) The fragment is trapezoidal and splits the pixel along opposite edges.

(4) The fragment is triangular and splits the pixel along adjacent edges.

(5) The complement of (4) (a pentagonal fragment).

(6) The fragment is an odd shape that can be described by the difference of two or more of the previous types.

(7) The fragment cannot be easily defined by these simple types.

14.7 Supersampling or post-filtering

Supersampling is the most common form of anti-aliasing and is usually used with polygon mesh rendering. It involves calculating a virtual image at a spatial resolution higher than the pixel resolution and 'averaging down' the high resolution image to a lower (pixel) resolution. In broad terms, subject to the previous reservations about the use of the term 'sampling', we are increasing the sampling frequency. The advantage of the method is trivial implementation which needs to be set against the high disadvantage of cost and increased Z-buffer memory. In terms of Fourier theory we can:

(1) Generate a set of samples of $I(x, y)$ at some resolution (higher than the pixel resolution).

(2) Low pass filter this image which we regard as an approximation to a continuous image.

(3) Re-sample the image at the pixel resolution.

Steps 2 and 3 (often confusingly referred to as reconstruction) are carried out simultaneously by convolving a filter with the virtual image and using as steps in the convolution intervals of pixel width. That is, for a 3 × virtual image, the filter would be positioned on (super) pixels in the virtual image, using a step length of three super-pixels. Figure 14.10 is a representation of the method working and two examples of filters tabulated as weights (note that these are normalized – the filter weights must sum to unity). For an (odd) scaling factor S and a filter h of dimension k:

$$I'(i, j) = \sum_{p=Si-k}^{Si+k} \sum_{q=Sj-k}^{Sj+k} I(p, q)h(Si - p, Sj - q)$$

This method works well with most computer graphics images and is easily integrated into a Z-buffer algorithm. It does not work with images whose spectrum energy does not fall off with increasing frequency. (As we have already mentioned, supersampling is not, in general a theoretically correct method of anti-aliasing.)

Figure 14.10
'Reducing' a virtual image
by convolution.

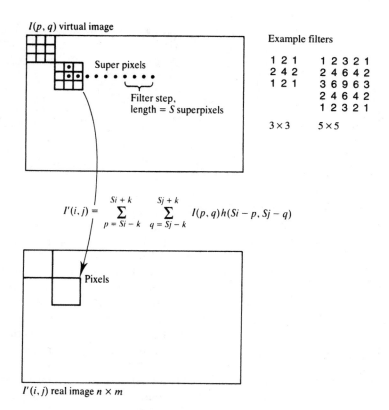

$I(p, q)$ virtual image

Super pixels

Example filters

```
1 2 1        1 2 3 2 1
2 4 2        2 4 6 4 2
1 2 1        3 6 9 6 3
             2 4 6 4 2
             1 2 3 2 1

3 × 3        5 × 5
```

Filter step,
length = S superpixels

$$I'(i, j) = \sum_{p = Si - k}^{Si + k} \sum_{q = Sj - k}^{Sj + k} I(p, q) h(Si - p, Sj - q)$$

Pixels

$I'(i, j)$ real image $n \times m$

Supersampling methods differ trivially in the value of n and the shape of the filter used. For, say, a medium resolution image of 512 × 512 it is usually considered adequate to supersample at 2048 × 2048 ($n = 4$). The high resolution image can be reduced to the final 512 × 512 form by averaging and this is equivalent to convolving with a box filter. Better results can be obtained using a shaped filter, a filter whose values vary over the extent of its kernel. There is a considerable body of knowledge on the optimum shape of filters with respect to the nature of the information that they operate on (see, for example, Oppenheim and Shafer (1975)). Most of this work is in digital signal processing and has been carried out with functions of a single variable $f(t)$. Computer graphics has unique problems that are not addressed by conventional digital signal processing techniques. For example, space variant filters are required in texture mapping. Here, both the weights of the filter kernel and its shape have to change.

To return to supersampling and non-varying filters, Crow (1981) used a Bartlett window, three of which are shown in Table 14.1.

Digital convolution is easy to understand and implement but is computationally expensive. A window is centred on a supersample and a weighted sum of products is obtained by multiplying each supersample by the corresponding

Table 14.1 Bartlett windows used in post-filtering a supersampled image

3 × 3	5 × 5	7 × 7
1 2 1	1 2 3 2 1	1 2 3 4 3 2 1
2 4 2	2 4 6 4 2	2 4 6 8 6 4 2
1 2 1	3 6 9 6 3	3 6 9 12 9 6 3
	2 4 6 4 2	4 8 12 16 12 8 4
	1 2 3 2 1	3 6 9 12 9 6 3
		2 4 6 8 6 4 2
		1 2 3 4 3 2 1

weight in the filter. The weights can be adjusted to implement different filter kernels. The digital convolution proceeds by moving the window through n supersamples and computing the next weighted sum of products. Using a 3 × 3 window means that nine supersamples are involved in the final pixel computation. On the other hand, using the 7 × 7 window means a computation of 49 integer multiplications. The implication of the computation overheads is obvious. For example, reducing a 2048 × 2048 supersampled image to 512 × 512, with a 7 × 7 filter kernel, requires 512 × 512 × 49 multiplications and additions.

An inevitable side-effect of filtering is blurring. In fact, we could say that we trade aliasing artefacts against blurring. This occurs because information is integrated from a number of neighbouring pixels. This means that the choice of the spatial extent of the filter is a compromise. A wide filter has a lower cut-off frequency and will be better at reducing aliasing artefacts. It will, however, blur the image more than a narrower filter which will exhibit a higher cut-off frequency.

Finally, the disadvantages of the technique should be noted. Supersampling is not a suitable method for dealing with very small objects. Also it is a 'global' method – the computation is not context dependent. A scene that exhibited a few large-area polygons would be subject to the same computational overheads as one with a large number of small-area polygons. The memory requirements are large if the method is to be used with a Z-buffer. The supersampled version of the image has to be created and stored before the filtering process can be applied. This increases the storage requirements of the Z-buffer by a factor of n^2, making it essentially a virtual memory technique.

14.8　Non-uniform sampling – some theoretical concepts

Non-uniform sampling has become of great interest in computer graphics because it addresses the high cost problem of conventional anti-aliasing techniques. It does this by getting away from the idea of uniform sampling and allows us to address the issue of context-sensitive anti-aliasing measures, or devoting computing resources to those parts of the image that need attention. The way in which this is done invariably means that we study algorithms where there is no separation between the rendering part and the anti-aliasing part.

We cannot, as we did above with supersampling, render without using the anti-aliasing strategy.

Another benefit of considering non-uniform sampling is that it enables algorithms where we can convert aliases into noise. That is, we can design algorithms in such a way that, for a given pixel resolution, the algorithm produces noise where a conventional algorithm would produce aliases. Approaches that do this are called stochastic sampling methods and they function by making uniform intervals between samples irregular.

Ideally we wish to generate an image using most effort in busy regions and least in regions where the illumination is changing slowly. The crux of the matter in image synthesis is: how do we know which regions to devote most attention to before we have generated the image? This consideration leads us naturally to the most common strategy which is to generate a low resolution image, examine it, and use this to generate a higher resolution image in those areas of the low resolution image that appear to need further attention. We can go on repeating this process recursively until we come up against some pre-specified limit. This is called adaptive refinement (an example of this technique is shown in Figure 18.13).

A simple, but by no means complete, taxonomy of non-uniform sampling would be the two main categories of non-uniform subdivision and stochastic sampling. There are many subdivisions – different ways of effecting the stochastic sampling and ways of combining the two approaches into a single sampling strategy. For example, a stochastic sampling pattern may be generated at different scales (number of samples per unit area) so that it can be incorporated in an adaptive refinement scheme.

The approaches are represented schematically in Figure 14.11. Both these methods are applied after an initial sampling of the image plane has taken place. Most commonly in computer graphics this is uniform sampling, usually but not necessarily at pixel level. The techniques then become non-uniform super-sampling in that the non-uniform strategy operates at sub-pixel level.

Non-uniform subdivision is a general strategy that appears in many algorithms in computer science. It naturally fits into an adaptive refinement scheme in image synthesis which consists of dividing the image plane into a grid of initial (say square) sampling boxes, then recursively subdividing these into squares until a resolution limit is reached. There is another subtle problem with such methods. This is that the output from an algorithm that uses this kind of

Figure 14.11
The two main non-uniform sampling techniques.
(a) Non-uniform subdivision;
(b) stochastic sampling.

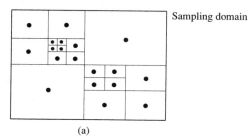

Sampling domain

(a)   (b)

strategy is going to be a set of non-uniform samples. These have to be converted into a uniform set of (pixel) samples prior to display. Alternatively we can say that we have to reconstruct the image from non-uniform samples and then re-sample at a uniform rate. There is no worked out theory that encompasses reconstruction from non-uniform samples and a variety of ad hoc techniques exist. A simple scheme is shown in Figure 14.12.

Stochastic sampling seems at first sight a strange idea but an intuitive explanation of its efficacy is straightforward. Aliases appear in an image as a direct consequence of the regularity of the sampling pattern 'beating' with regularities or coherences in the image. If we make the samples irregular then the higher frequency coherences in the image will appear as noise rather than aliases. This perturbation of regular sampling, and consequent trade-off of aliasing against noise is stochastic sampling.

An easy demonstration of the functioning of this trade-off is to return to our sine wave example. Figure 14.13 shows a sine wave, again being sampled by a regular sampling pattern. Now we can invoke a stochastic sampling technique by 'jittering' each sample by some random amount about the regular sampling instant. Consider the effect of doing this on a sine wave whose frequency is below the Nyquist limit (Figure 14.13(a)). Here our procedure will sample the sine wave inaccurately, introducing amplitude perturbations, or noise, that depends on the extent of the sample instant jitter. For a sine wave whose

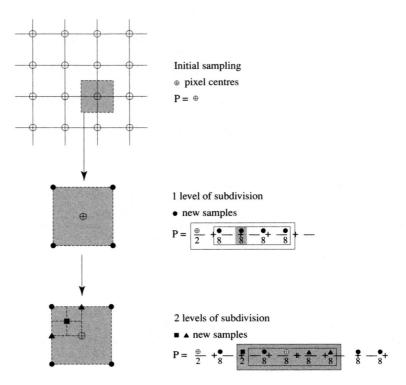

Figure 14.12
Simple reconstruction for non-uniform subdivision.

Figure 14.13
Sampling a sine wave whose frequency is (a) below and (b) above the Nyquist limit (after Cook).

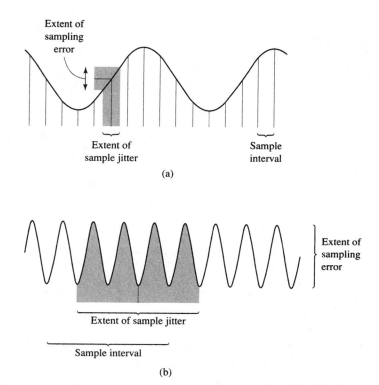

frequency is well above the Nyquist limit (Figure 14.13(b)), the sample jitter extent encompasses many cycles and the effect of sampling successively such packets of waves will simply be to produce a set of random numbers. Thus the aliased sine wave that would be produced by a regular sampling interval is exchanged for noise.

Jittering is easily carried out within a two-dimensional area, such as a pixel, by starting with a uniform grid and applying two component jitters in the x and y directions. This is cheap and easy to do and for this reason it is probably the most common strategy in computer graphics.

Stochastic sampling has an interesting background. In 1982, Yellot (Yellot 1982) pointed out that the human eye contains an array of non-uniformly distributed photoreceptors and he suggested that this is the reason that the human eye does not produce its own aliasing artefacts. Photoreceptor cells in the fovea are tightly packed and the lens acts as an anti-aliasing filter. However, in the region outside the fovea, the spatial density of photoreceptors is much lower and for this reason the cells are non uniformly distributed

These factors are easily demonstrated in the frequency domain by considering the spectrum of a sine wave sampled by this method and again varying the frequency about the Nyquist limit (Figure 14.14). As the sampling frequency is reduced with respect to the sine wave the amplitude of the sine wave spike diminishes and the noise amplitude increases. Eventually the sine wave peak

Figure 14.14
Varying the frequency of a sine wave (*f*) with respect to a perturbed sampling frequency (*f*ₛ).

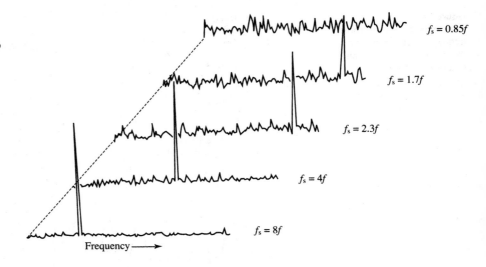

$f_s = 0.85f$

$f_s = 1.7f$

$f_s = 2.3f$

$f_s = 4f$

$f_s = 8f$

Frequency ⟶

disappears. The point of the illustration is that no alias spikes appear. The information represented by the sine wave eventually disappears but instead of aliasing we get noise. The perturbation can range in *x* over a minimum of half a cycle (where the sine wave frequency is at the Nyquist limit) and will in general range over a number of complete cycles. If the range encompasses a number of cycles exactly then, for white noise jitter, the probability of sampling each part of the sine wave tends to be equal and the energy in the samples appears as white noise. A mathematical treatment of the attenuation due to white noise jitter and Gaussian jitter is given in Balakrishnan (1962).

One of the problems of this method is that it is only easily incorporated into methods where independent calculations are made for each sample. This is certainly the case in ray tracing, where rays are spawned in the continuous object space domain, and are, in effect, samples in this space. They can easily be jittered. In 'standard' image synthesis methods, using, say, interpolative shading in the context of a Z-buffer or scan line algorithm, introducing jitter presents much more of a difficulty. The algorithms are founded on uniform incremental methods in screen space and would require substantial modification to have the effect of two-dimensional sampling perturbation. Although such algorithms are equivalent to image generation in a continuous domain succeeded by two-dimensional sampling, in practice the sampling and generation phases are not easily unmeshed.

A major rendering system, called REYES (Cook *et al.* 1987) does, however, integrate a Z-buffer-based method with stochastic sampling. This works by dividing initial primitives, such as bi-cubic parametric patches into (flat) 'micropolygons' (of approximate dimension in screen space of half a pixel). All shading and visibility calculations operate on micropolygons. Shading occurs prior to

Figure 14.15
Graphical primitives
are subdivided into
micropolygons. These
are shaded and visibility
calculations are perfomred
by stochastically sampling
the micropolygons in screen
space (after Cook *et al.*
(1987)).

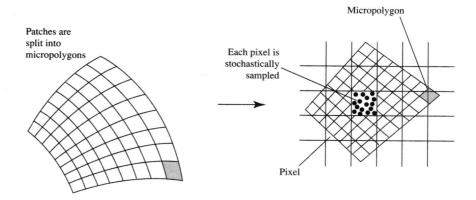

visibility calculations and is constant over a micropolygon. The micropolygons are then stochastically sampled from screen space, the Z value of each sample point calculated by interpolation and the visible sample hits filtered to produce pixel intensities (Figure 14.15). Thus shading is carried out at micropolygon level and visibility calculations at the stochastic sampling level.

This method does away with the coherence of 'classical' rendering methods, by splitting objects into micropolygons. It is most suitable for objects consisting of bi-cubic parametric patches because they can be easily subdivided.

14.9   The Fourier transform of images

Fourier theory is not used to any extent in computer graphics except in specialized applications such as generating terrain height fields using Fourier synthesis. However, an intuitive understanding of it is vital to understanding the effects of and the cure for image defects due to undersampling.

The Fourier transform is one of the fundamental tools of modern science and engineering and it finds applications in both analogue and digital electronics, where information is represented (usually) as a continuous function of time and in work associated with computer imagery where the image $I(x, y)$ is represented as an intensity function of two spatial variables.

Calculating the Fourier transform of an image, $I(x, y)$, means that the image is represented as a weighted set of spatial frequencies (or weighted sinusoidally undulating surfaces) and this confers, as far as certain operations are concerned, particular advantages. The individual spatial frequencies are known as basis functions.

Any process that uses the Fourier domain will usually be made up of three main phases. The image is transformed into the Fourier domain. Some operation is performed on this representation of the image and it is then transformed back into its normal representation – known as the space domain. The transformations are called forward and reverse transforms. Fourier transforms are important, and this is reflected in the fact that the algorithms which perform the transformations are implemented in hardware in image-processing computers.

There is no information lost in transforming an image into the Fourier domain – the visual information in the image is just represented in a different way. For the non-mathematically minded it is, at first sight, a strange beast. One point in the Fourier domain representation of an image contains information about the entire image. The value of the point tells us how much of a spatial frequency is in the image.

We define the Fourier transform of an image $I(x, y)$:

$$F(u, v) = \frac{1}{2\pi} \iint I(x, y)e^{-j(ux+vy)}dxdy$$

and the reverse transform as:

$$I(x, y) = \frac{1}{2\pi} \iint F(u, v)e^{j(ux+vy)}dudv$$

The Fourier transform is a complex quantity and can be expressed as a real and imaginary part:

$$F(u, v) = \text{Real}(u, v) + j\,\text{Imag}(u, v)$$

and we can represent $F(u, v)$ as two functions known as the amplitude and phase spectrum respectively:

$$|F(u, v)| = (\text{Real}^2(u, v) + \text{Imag}^2 (u, v))^{1/2}$$

$$\varphi(u, v) = \tan^{-1}(\text{Imag}(u, v)/\text{Real}(u, v))$$

Now it is important to have an intuitive idea of the nature of the transform and, in particular, the physical meaning of a spatial frequency. We first consider the easier case of a function of a single variable $I(x)$. If we transform this into the Fourier domain then we have the transform $F(u)$. The amplitude spectrum, $|F(u)|$, specifies a set of sinusoids that, when added together, produce the original function $I(x)$ and the phase spectrum specifies the phase relationship of each sinusoid (the value of the sinusoid at $x = 0$). That is each point in $|F(u)|$ specifies the amplitude and frequency of a single sine wave component. Another way of putting it is to say that any function $I(x)$ decomposes into a set of sine wave coefficients. This situation is shown in Figure 14.16. The first part of the figure shows the amplitude spectrum of a single sinusoid which is just a single point (actually a pair of points symetrically disposed about the origin) in the Fourier domain. The second example shows a function that contains information – it could be a speech signal. This exhibits a spectrum that has extent in the Fourier domain. The spread from the minimum to the maximum frequency is called the bandwidth.

A 2D function $I(x, y)$ – an image function – decomposes into a set of spatial frequencies $|F(u, v)|$. A spatial frequency is a surface – a sinusoidal 'corrugation' whose frequency or rate of undulation is given by the distance of the point (u, v) from the origin:

Figure 14.16
One-dimensional Fourier transform. (a) A sine wave maps into a single point. (b) A 'window' of an 'information wave' maps into a frequency spectrum.

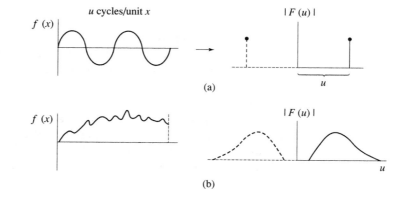

$$\sqrt{u^2 + v^2}$$

and whose orientation – the angle the peaks and troughs of the corrugation make with the x axis is given by:

$$\tan^{-1}(u/v)$$

A single point $F(u, v)$ tells us how much of that spatial frequency is contained by the image. Figure 14.17 is a two-dimensional analogue of Figure 14.16. Here, a sinusoid has spatial extent and maps into a single point (again, actually a pair of points) in the Fourier domain. If we now consider an image $I(x, y)$, this maps into a two-dimensional frequency spectrum that is a function of the two variables u and v. Different categories of images exhibit different categories of Fourier transforms as we shall demonstrate shortly by example. However, most images have Fourier representations with the amplitude characteristic peaking at (0, 0) and decreasing with increasing spatial frequency. Images of natural scenes tend to exhibit Fourier representation that contain no coherent structures. Images of man-made scenes generally exhibit coherences in the Fourier domain reflecting the occurrence of coherent structures (roads, buildings etc.) in the original scene. Computer graphics images often have high energy in high spatial frequency components, reflecting the occurrence of detailed texture in the image.

A property of the Fourier representation that is of importance in image processing is that the circumference of a circle centred on the origin specifies a set of spatial frequencies of identical rate of undulation:

Figure 14.17
An image made up of a single spatial frequency and its Fourier transform.

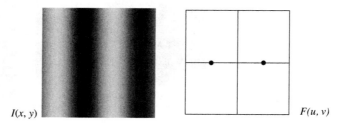

$$r = \sqrt{u^2 + v^2}$$

having every possible orientation.

We will now look at the nature of the transform qualitatively by examining three different examples of amplitude spectra.

Figure 14.18(a)

Figure 14.18(a) is an image from nature. It produces a Fourier transform that exhibits virtually no coherences. Despite the fact that there is much line structure manifested in the edges of the leaves, the lines are at every possible orientation and no coherence is visible in the Fourier domain.

Figure 14.18(b)

Figure 14.18(b) is an image of a man-made scene. There is obvious structure in the Fourier domain that relates to the scene. First, there is the line structure that originates from the tramline discontinuity (top of the arches). Second, there is the discontinuity between the upper and lower arches that manifests as another line in the Fourier domain. There are coherences around the v axis that are due to the horizontal edges of the structure. Because the orientation of these lines varies

(a) Bush

Fourier transform $| F(u, v) |$

(b) Arcos da Lapa
(Rio de Janeiro)

Fourier transform $| F(u, v) |$

Figure 14.18
Fourier transforms of natural and man-made scenes.

about the vertical, due to the camera perspective, they map into non-vertical lines in the Fourier domain. There is a vertical coherence in the Fourier domain that relates to scan lines in the data collection device and also due to horizontal discontinuities manifested by the long shadows. The remainder of the contributions in the Fourier domain originate from the natural components in the image such as the texture on the arch walls.

Figures 14.19(a) and 14.19(b)
Figures 14.19(a) and 14.19(b) are two man-made textures. The relationships between the coherences of the texture and the structures in the Fourier domain should be clear. In both cases the textures have been overlaid with a leaf, which manifests as a blurry 'off-vertical' line in the Fourier domain.

What can we conclude from these examples? A very important observation is that information that is 'spread' throughout the space domain separates out in the Fourier domain. In particular, we see that in the second example the coherences in the image structure are reflected in the Fourier domain as lines or spokes that pass through the origin. In the third example, the texture, produces components that are strictly localized in the Fourier domain at their predomi-

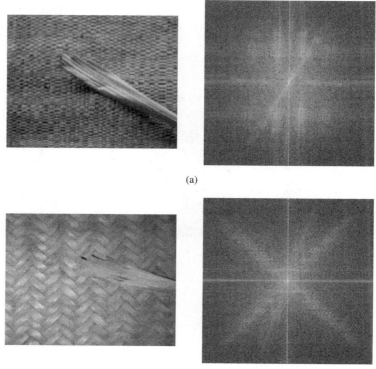

(a)

(b)

Figure 14.19
Fourier transforms of textures.

nant spatial frequencies. This property of the Fourier domain is probably the most commonly used and accounts for spatial filtering, where we may want to enhance some spatial frequencies and diminish others to effect particular changes to the image. It is also used in image compression where we encode or quantize the transform of the image, rather than the image itself. This gives us the opportunity to use less information to encode those components of the transform that we know have less 'importance'. This is a powerful approach and it happens that much less information can be used to encode certain parts of the transform without any significant fall in image quality. The original information in the image is reordered in the transform in a way that enables us to make easy judgements about its relative importance in the image domain.

An extremely important property of the Fourier domain is demonstrated in Figure 14.20. This shows that most of the image power is concentrated in the low frequency components. The figure shows circles superimposed at different radii on the Fourier transform of the image shown in the figure. If we calculate the proportion of the total sum of $|F(u, v)|^2$ over the entire domain contained within each circle, then we find the relationship shown in Figure 14.20(b):

A property of the Fourier transform pair that is fundamental in image processing is known as the convolution theorem. This can be written as:

Figure 14.20
The percentage of image power enclosed in concentric circles of increasing radius.

Pão de Açúcar
(Rio de Janeiro)

(a)

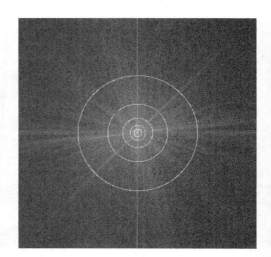

Fourier transform
$|F(u, v)|$

Radius (pixels)	% image power
8	95
16	97
32	98
64	99.4
128	99.8

(b)

$$I(x, y) * h(x, y) = \mathfrak{I}^{-1}(F(u, v)H(u, v))$$

where:

* means convolution

In words: the convolution of the image function $I(x, y)$ with $h(x, y)$ in the space domain is equivalent to (or the inverse transform of) the multiplication of $F(u, v)$ and $H(u, v)$ in the Fourier domain, where:

$$I(x, y) = \mathfrak{I}^{-1}(F(u, v))$$

and:

$$h(x, y) = \mathfrak{I}^{-1}(H(u, v))$$

Analogously we have:

$$I(x, y)h(x, y) = \mathfrak{I}^{-1}(F(u, v) * H(u, v))$$

Both of these results are known as the convolution theorem. Convolution, and its special case – cross-correlation – is the operation that we perform on a computer graphics image when we filter a supersampled image down to screen resolution.

15 Colour and computer graphics

15.1 Colour sets in computer imagery

15.2 Colour and three-dimensional space

15.3 Colour, information and perceptual spaces

15.4 Rendering and colour spaces

15.5 Monitor considerations

Introduction

This chapter is concerned with quantitative aspects of colour. Most treatment of colour in practical computer graphics has been qualitative. In setting up a scene database we tend to choose object colours more or less arbitrarily. However, certain applications are emerging in computer graphics where the accurate simulation of light–object interaction, in terms of colour, is required. Also, in the field of visualization, colour is used to impart numeric information and suitable numeric information to colour mappings must be considered in conjunction with knowledge of the subtle underlying psycho-physical mechanisms of the human colour vision system.

It is curious that an industry which has devoted major research effort to photo-realism has all but ignored a rigorous approach to colour. After all, frame stores whose pixels are capable of displaying any of 16 million colours have been commonplace for many years. We suspect three reasons for this:

(1) The dominance of the RGB or three equation approach in rendering methods such as Phong shading, ray tracing and radiosity, and the high cost of evaluating these models at more than three wavelengths.

(2) The rendering models themselves have obvious shortcomings that are visually far more serious than the unsubtle treatment of colour (spatial domain aliasing is visible, colour domain aliasing is generally invisible).

(3) The lack of demand from applications that require an accurate treatment of colour.

With some exceptions (see, for example, Hall and Greenberg (1983) and Hall (1989) little research into rendering with accurate treatment of colour has been carried out. There are, however, a growing number of applications that would benefit from accurate colour simulation, and a rendering method exists (the radiosity method) that is subtle enough in its treatment of light–object interaction to benefit from such an approach. Clearly this will be one of the major developments in CAAD (computer aided architectural design) in the future. A computer graphics visualization of an architectural design, either interior or exterior, is usually recognizable as such. We know that the image is not a photograph. This appears to be due predominantly to the lack of fine geometric detail. Modelling costs are high and approximations are made. In the radiosity method a coarse detail model is mandatory. So we first notice the inadequate geometry. However, 'second order' effects are no doubt just as important and such aspects as unrealistic shadows and light that 'doesn't look quite right' contribute to the immediate visible signature of a computer graphics image.

Another area where colour is of critical importance is volume rendering in ViSC (Chapter 13). Here colour is used to enable a viewer to perceive variations in data values in three space which may be extremely subtle. In this context it is important that the colours used communicate the information in an optimal way. This topic relies on perceptual colour models.

If we decide that accurate colour simulation is important, this throws up other problems apart from the cost implication in extending from three wavelengths to n wavelengths. These are:

(1) What descriptive colour system or model do we use to categorize colour? Clearly we could simply work with sampled functions of wavelength for the reflectivity characteristics of objects and the intensity of a light source. Although this may be convenient (and necessary) in the calculation domain, it will be useless to an architect, say, who wishes to specify a paint colour in a standard system using a colour label or a triple. What colour space should be used for the storage and the communication of images? It would be extremely impractical to store the results of n wavelength calculations.

(2) A major problem in using accurate colour exists in reproduction and viewing. Two colours specified in a standard system should look the same to a viewer. But this is only true if they are reproduced on carefully calibrated computer graphics monitors that are viewed under identical conditions. Although colour can be measured locally with precision, by using a colourimeter, such perceptual shifts due to, for example, contrast with surrounding colours, will always occur. This practical problem is not easy to overcome and unless it is dealt with it mitigates against the use of accurate colour simulation.

15.1 Colour sets in computer imagery

To deal with colour in computer imagery we need to quantify it in some way and this gives us the notion of a colour space or domain. This is a three-dimensional

Figure 15.1
The hierarchy of colour
sets relevant to computer
imagery. A colour is a two-
dimensional point in this
space.

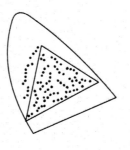

 All perceivable colours
(the human visual system)

 Colours reproducible
on a monitor

 Colours calculated by a program
(normally we would require these
to fall within the monitor gamut)

space in which reside all the colours that we have an interest in. First of all we need to define the hierarchy of colour sets that we will be referring to. These are:

(1) The set of all colours perceivable by human beings with normal colour vision.

(2) The set of colours that can be displayed by a monitor screen or captured by an input device. This is a subset of (1) for reasons that will become clear in the course of this chapter.

(3) The set of colours that can be calculated by a graphics program and stored in a frame memory. For a 24-bit system (16 million colours) this will generally be a subset of (1) but a superset of (2). That is unless we take special precautions we may generate colours that are outside the display gamut or range.

The hierarchy is illustrated (Figure 15.1) in a cross-section of a three-dimensional colour space that will be explained later.

15.2 Colour and three-dimensional space

Why is colour a three-component vector? Again we have to bear in mind that colour is a human sensation. Traditionally we describe colours in words, usually by allusion to common objects 'apple green' or 'blood red' etc. More precisely, colour is communicated in the painting and dyeing industry by the production of charts of sample colours. The numerical specification of colour has a long history that began with Isaac Newton, but it was only in the twentieth century that numerical systems became important industrially.

The answer to the question 'why is colour specified by three numerical labels?' is that we have three different types of cone in our retinas which have different sensitivities to different wavelengths (Figure 15.7(a)). Light can be specified physically as a spectral power distribution or SPD – the objective measurement of light energy as a function of wavelength – and we should be able to categorize the effect of any SPD on a human observer by three weights – the relative response of the three different types of cone. And so it happens that we can visually match a sample colour by additively mixing three coloured lights. We can, for example, match a sample or target colour by controlling the three intensities of a red, green and a blue light. However, note the important point that in matching with primary colours red, green and blue we are not basing the labelling of an SPD on the cone spectral sensitivity curves, but are using the human vision system to match colours with a mix of primaries. To do this for all colours on a wavelength-by-wavelength basis leads to spectral sensitivity curves that our retinas would have if the cones responded maximally to these colours. The reason for this somewhat convoluted approach is that we can derive these functions easily from colour matching experiments; precise knowledge of the actual spectral sensitivity curves of the retina was harder to come by.

Thus numerical specification of colour is by a triple of primary colours. Most, but not all, perceivable colours can be produced by additively mixing appropriate amounts of three primary colours (red, green and blue, for example). If we denote a colour by $\mathbf{C}$, we have:

$$\mathbf{C} = r\mathbf{R} + g\mathbf{G} + b\mathbf{B}$$

where r, g and b are the relative weights of each primary required to match the colour to be specified. The important point here is that this system, even though it is not specifying information related directly to the SPD of the colour, is saying that a colour $\mathbf{C}$ can be specified by a numerical triple because if a matching experiment was performed an observer would choose the components r, g, b to match or simulate the colour $\mathbf{C}$.

In a computer graphics monitor a colour is produced by exciting triples of adjacent dots made of red, green and blue phosphors. The dots are small and the eye perceives the triples as a single dot of colour. Thus we specify or label colours in reality using three primaries and the production of colours on a monitor is also specified in a similar way. However, note the important distinction that colour on a monitor is not produced by mixing the radiation from three light sources but by placing the light sources in close proximity to each other.

Unfortunately in computer graphics this three-component specification of colour together with the need to produce a three-component RGB signal for a monitor has led to a widely held assumption that light–object interaction need only be evaluated at three points in the spectrum. This is the 'standard' RGB paradigm that tends to be used in Phong shading, ray tracing and radiosity. If it is intended to simulate accurately the interaction of light with objects in a scene, then it is necessary to evaluate this interaction at more than three wavelengths; otherwise aliasing will result in the colour domain because of undersampling of the light distribution and object reflectivity functions. Of course, aliasing in the colour domain simply consists of a shift in colour away from a desired effect and in this sense it is invisible. (This is in direct contrast to spatial domain aliasing which produces annoying and disturbing visual artefacts.) Colours in most computer graphics applications are to a great extent arbitrary and shifts due to inaccurate simulation in the colour domain are generally not important. It is only in applications where colour is a subtle part of the simulation, say, for example, in interior design, that these effects have to be taken into account.

Given that we can represent or describe the sensation of colour, as far as colour matching experiments are concerned, with numeric labels, we now face the question: which numbers shall we use? This heralds the concept of different colour spaces or domains.

It may be as we suggested in the previous section, that a calculation or rendering domain be a wavelength or spectral space. Eventually, however, we need to produce an image in RGB$_{monitor}$ space to drive a particular monitor. What about the storage and communication of images? Here we need a universal standard. RGB$_{monitor}$ spaces, as we shall see, are particular to devices. These devices have different gamuts or colour ranges all of which are subsets of the set of perceivable colours. A universal space will be device independent and will embrace all perceivable colours. Such a space exists and is known as the CIE XYZ standard. A CIE triple is a unique numeric label associated with any perceivable colour.

Another requirement in computer graphics is a facility that allows a user to manipulate and design using colour. It is generally thought that an interface that allows a user to mix primary colours is anti-intuitive and spaces that are inclined to perceptual sensations such as hue, saturation and lightness are preferred in this context.

We now list the main colour spaces used in computer imagery.

(1) CIE XYZ space: the dominant international standard for colour specification. A colour is specified as a set of three tri-stimulus values or artificial primaries XYZ.

(2) Variations or transformations of CIE XYZ space (such as CIE xyY space) that have evolved over the years for different contexts. These are transforms of CIE XYZ that better reflect some detail in the perception of colour, for example, perceptual linearity.

(3) Spectral space: in image synthesis light sources are defined in this space as n wavelength samples of an intensity distribution. Object reflectivity is similarly defined. A colour specified on a wavelength-by-wavelength basis is how we measure colour with a device such as a spectrophotometer. As we have pointed out, this does not necessarily relate to our perception of an SPD as one colour or another. We synthesize an image at n wavelengths and then need to 'reduce' this to three components for display.

(4) RGB space: the 'standard' computer graphics paradigm for Phong shading. This is just a three-sample version of spectral space, light sources and object reflectivity are specified as three wavelengths: Red, Green and Blue. We understand the primaries R, G and B to be pure or saturated colours.

(5) RGB$_{monitor}$ space: a triple in this space produces a particular colour on a particular display. In other words it is the space of a display. The same triple may not necessarily produce the same colour sensation on different monitors because monitors are not calibrated to a single standard. Monitor RGBs are not pure or saturated primaries because the emission of light from an excited phosphor exhibits a spectral power distribution over a band of frequencies. If the usual three-sample approach is used in rendering then usually whatever values are calculated in RGB space are assumed to be weights in RGB$_{monitor}$ space. If an n sample calculation has been performed then a device-dependent transformation is used to produce a point in RGB$_{monitor}$ space.

(6) HSV space: a non-linear transformation of RGB space enabling colour to be specified as Hue, Saturation and Value.

(7) YIQ space: a non-linear transformation of RGB space used in analogue TV.

We will now deal with the issues surrounding these colour spaces. We will start with RGB space because it is the most familiar and easiest to use. We will then look at certain problems that lead us on to consideration of CIE space.

⟨15.2.1⟩ ## RGB space

Given the subtle distinction between (4) and (5) above we now describe RGB space as a general concept. This model is the traditional form of colour specification in computer imagery. It enables, for example, diffuse reflection coefficients in shading equations to be given a value as a triple (R, G, B). In this system (0, 0, 0) is black and (1, 1, 1) is white. Colour is labelled as relative weights of three primary colours in an additive system using the primaries Red, Green and Blue. The space of all colour available in this system is represented by the RGB cube (Figure 15.2 and Figure 15.3 (Colour Plate)). Important points concerning RGB space are:

(1) It is perceptually non-linear. Equal distances in the space do not in general correspond to perceptually equal sensations. A step between two points in one region of the space may produce no perceivable difference; the same increment in another region may result in a noticeable colour change. In other words, the same colour sensation may result from a multiplicity of RGB triples. For example, if each of RGB can vary between 0 and 255, then over 16 million unique RGB codes are available.

(2) Because of the non-linear relationship between RGB values and the intensity produced at each phosphor dot (see Section 15.5), low RGB values produce

Figure 15.2
The RGB colour solid. See
also Figure 15.3 (Colour
Plate).

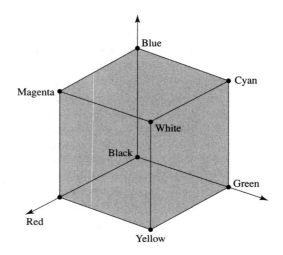

small changes in response on the screen. As many as 20 steps may be necessary to produce a 'just noticeable difference' at low intensities; whereas a single step may produce a perceivable difference at high intensities.

(3) The set of all colours produced on a computer graphics monitor, the RGB space, is always a subset of the colours that can be perceived by humans. This is not peculiar to RGB space. Any set of three visible primaries can only produce through additive mixing of a subset of the perceivable colour set.

(4) It is not a good colour description system. Without considerable experience, users find it difficult to give RGB values to colours known by label. What is the RGB value of 'medium brown'? Once a colour has been chosen it may not be obvious how to make subtle changes to the nature of the colour. For example, changing the 'vividness' of a chosen colour will require unequal changes in the RGB components.

15.2.2

The HSV single hexcone model

The H(ue) S(aturation V(alue) or single hexcone model was proposed by A.R. Smith in 1978 (Smith 1978). Its purpose is to facilitate a more intuitive interface for colour than the selection of three primary colours. The colour space has the shape of a hexagonal cone or hexcone. The HSV cone is a non-linear transformation of the RGB cube and although it tends to be referred to as a perceptual model, it is still just a way of labelling colours in the monitor gamut space. Perceptual in this context means the attributes that are used to represent the colour are more akin to the way in which we think of colour; it does not mean that the space is perceptually linear. The perceptual non-linearity of RGB space is carried over into HSV space; in particular, perceptual changes in hue are distinctly non-linear in angle.

It can be employed in any context where a user requires control or selection of a colour or colours on an aesthetic or similar basis. It enables control over the range or gamut of an RGB monitor using the perceptually based variables Hue, Saturation and Value. This means that a user interface can be constructed where the effect of varying one of the three qualities is easily predictable. A task such as make a colour brighter, paler or more yellow is far easier when these perceptual variables are employed, than having to decide on what combinations of RGB changes are required.

The HSV model is based on polar coordinates rather than Cartesian and H is specified in degrees in the range 0 to 360. One of the first colour systems based on polar coordinates and perceptual parameters was that due to Munsell. His colour notation system was first published in 1905 and is still in use today. Munsell called his perceptual variables Hue, Chroma and Value and we can do no better than reproduce his definition for these. Chroma is related to saturation – the term that appears to be preferred in computer graphics.

Munsell's definitions are:

- Hue: 'It is that quality by which we distinguish one colour family from another, as red from yellow, or green from blue or purple.'

- Chroma: 'It is that quality of colour by which we distinguish a strong colour from a weak one; the degree of departure of a colour sensation from that of a white or grey; the intensity of a distinctive hue; colour intensity.'

- Value: 'It is that quality by which we distinguish a light colour from a dark one.'

The Munsell system is used by referring to a set of samples – the Munsell Book of Colour. These samples are in 'just discriminable' steps in the colour space.

The HSV model relates to the way in which artists mix colours. Referring to the difficulty of mentally imagining the relative amounts of R, G and B required to produce a single colour, Smith says:

Try this mixing technique by mentally varying RGB to obtain pink or brown. It is not unusual to have difficulty. . . . the following [HSV] model mimics the way an artist mixes paint on his palette: he chooses a pure hue, or pigment and lightens it to a tint of that hue by adding white, or darkens it to a shade of that hue by adding black, or in general obtains a tone of that hue by adding some mixture of white and black or grey.

In the HSV model, varying H corresponds to selecting a colour. Decreasing S (desaturating the colour) corresponds to adding white. Decreasing V (devaluing the colour) corresponds to adding black. The derivation of the transform between RGB and HSV space is easily understood by considering a geometric interpretation of the hexcone. If the RGB cube is projected along its main diagonal onto a plane normal to that diagonal, then a hexagonal disc results.

The following correspondence is then established between the six RGB vertices and the six points of the hexcone in the HSV model:

RGB		HSV
(100)	red	(0, 1, 1)
(110)	yellow	(60, 1, 1)
(010)	green	(120, 1, 1)
(011)	cyan	(180, 1, 1)
(001)	blue	(240, 1, 1)
(101)	magenta	(300, 1, 1)

where H is measured in degrees. This hexagonal disc is the plane containing V = 1 in the hexcone model. For each value along the main diagonal in the RGB cube (increasing blackness) a contained sub-cube is defined. Each sub-cube defines a hexagonal disc. The stack of all hexagonal discs makes up the HSV colour solid.

Figure 15.4 shows the HSV single hexcone colour solid and Figure 15.5 (Colour Plate) is a further aid to its interpretation showing slices through the achromatic axis. The right-hand half of each slice is the plane of constant H and the left-hand half that of H + 180.

Apart from perceptual non-linearity another subtle problem implicit in the HSV system is that the attributes are not themselves perceptually independent. This means that it is possible to detect an apparent change in Hue, for example, when it is the parameter Value that is actually being changed.

Finally, perhaps the most serious departure from perceptual reality resides in the geometry of the model. The colour space labels all those colours reproducible on a computer graphics monitor and implies that all colours on planes of constant V are of equal brightness. Such is not the case. For example, maximum intensity blue has a lower perceived brightness than maximum intensity yellow. We conclude from this that because of the problems of perceptual non-linearity and the fact that different hues at maximum V exhibit different perceptual values, representing a monitor gamut with any 'regular' geometric solid such as a cube or a hexcone is only an approximation to the sensation of colour and this fact means that we have to consider perceptually based colour spaces.

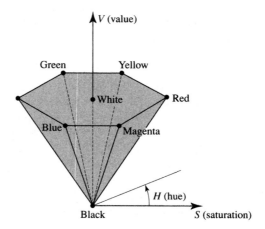

Figure 15.4
HSV single hexcone colour solid. See also Figure 15.5 (Colour Plate).

A simpler way of expressing this fact is to reiterate that colour is a perceptual sensation and cannot be accurately labelled by dividing up the RGB voltage levels of a monitor and using this scale as a colour label. This is essentially what we are doing with both the RGB and the HSV model and the association of the word 'perceptual' with the HSV model is unfortunate and confusing.

(15.2.3)   **YIQ space**

YIQ space is a linear transformation of RGB space that is the basis for analogue TV. Its purpose is efficiency in terms of bandwidth usage (compared with the RGB form) and to maintain compatibility for black and white TV (all the information required for black and white reception is contained in the Y component).

$$\begin{bmatrix} Y \\ I \\ Q \end{bmatrix} = \begin{bmatrix} 0.299 & 0.587 & 0.144 \\ 0.596 & -0.275 & -0.321 \\ 0.212 & -0.523 & 0.311 \end{bmatrix} \begin{bmatrix} R \\ G \\ B \end{bmatrix}$$

Note that the constant matrix coefficients mean that the transformation assumes that the RGB components are themselves defined with respect to a standard (in this case an NTSC definition). The Y component is the same as the CIE Y primary (see Section 15.3.1) and is called luminance. Colour information is 'isolated' in the I and Q components (equal RGB components will result in zero I and Q values). The bandwidth optimization comes about because human beings are more sensitive to changes in luminance than to changes in colour in this sense. We can discriminate spatial detail more finely in grey scale changes than in colour changes. Thus, a lower bandwidth can be tolerated for the I and Q components resulting in a bandwidth saving over using RGB components.

Colour representations where the colour and luminance information are separated are important in image processing where we may want to operate on image structure without affecting the colour of the image.

(15.3)   **Colour, information and perceptual spaces**

We now come to consider the use of perceptual spaces in computer imagery. In particular we shall look at the CIE XYZ space – an international numerically based colour labelling system first introduced in 1931 and derived from colour matching experiments.

To deal with colour reality we need to manipulate colours in a space that bears some relationship to perceptual experience. We have already alluded to applications where such considerations may be important. For example, in CAAD for interiors, the design of fabrics or the finish on such expensive consumer durables as cars, it will be necessary for computer graphics to move out of the arbitrary RGB domain into a space where colour is accurately simulated. Of course, in attempting to transmit an illusion of reality in a computer graphics simulation there are many other factors involved – surface texture, the macroscopic nature of the colour (metallic paint or ordinary gloss paint, for example) and geometrical accuracy, but at the moment in computer graphics it is the case that the RGB triple is the *de facto* standard for rendering.

Colour is used much in visualization applications to communicate numerical information. This has a long history. Possibly the most familiar manifestation is a coloured terrain map. Here colours are chosen to represent height. Traditionally colours are chosen with green representing low heights. Heights from 0 to 100 m may be represented by lightening shades of green through to yellow. Darkening shades of brown may represent the range 1000 to 3000 m. Above 3000 m there are usually two shades of purple, and white is reserved for 6000 m and above.

This technique has been used in image processing and computer graphics where it is called pseudo-colour enhancement. It is used most commonly to display a function of two variables, $f(x, y)$, in two space where before such a function would have been displayed using 'iso-f'contours. In pseudo-colour enhancement a deliberately restricted colour list (of, say, 10 colours) is chosen and the value of f is mapped into the nearest colour. The function appears like a terrain map with islands of one colour against a background of another.

In computer graphics and image processing the most popular mapping of $f(x, y)$ into colour has been some variation of the rainbow colours with red used to represent high or hot and blue used for low intensity or cold – in other words a path around the outer edge of HSV space. One of the problems with this mapping is that depending on the number of colour steps used, transitions between different colours appear as false contours. Violent colour discontinuities appear in the image where the function f is continuous. There is a contradiction here: we need these apparent discontinuities to highlight the shape of the function but they can easily be interpreted as transitions in the function where no transition exists. This is particularly true in non-mathematical images which are not everywhere continuous to start with. Natural discontinuities may exist in the function anyway, say in a medical image made up of the response of a device to different tissue. The appearance of false contours in such an image may be undesirable.

Thus, whether the contours add to or subtract from the perception of the nature and shape of f depends in the end on the image context. The effect of false contours is easily diminished by adding more colours to the mapping but this may have the effect of making the function more difficult to interpret.

The use of perceptual colour spaces in the context of numerical information is extremely important. If an accurate association between colours and numeric information is required, then a perceptually linear colour scale should be used. We discussed in Section 15.2.1 the perceptual non-linearity of RGB space and it is apparent that unless this factor is dealt with, it will interfere with the association of a colour with a numeric value. There is no good reason, apart from cultural associations like the example of the terrain map coding in cartography, why a hue circle should be used as a pseudo-colour scale.

The use of pseudo-colour in two space to display functions of two spatial variables has been around for many years. The last ten years have seen an increasing application of three-dimensional computer graphics techniques in the visualization of scientific results and simulations (an area that has been awarded the acronym ViSC). The graphics techniques used are mainly animation, volume rendering (both dealt with elsewhere in this text) and the use of pseudo-colour in three space, which we will now examine.

Figure 13.1 (Colour Plate) illustrates an application. It shows an isosurface extracted from a Navier–Stokes simulation of a reverse flow pipe combustor. In this simulation the primary gas flow is from left to right. Air is forced into the chamber under compression at the left, and dispersed by two fans. Eight fuel jets, situated radially approximately halfway along the combustor, are directed in such a way as to send the fuel mixture in a spiralling path towards the front of the chamber. Combustible mixing takes place in the central region and thrust is created at the exhaust outlet on the right. The isosurfaces shown connect all points where the net flow along the long axis is zero – a zero velocity surface.

Such an isosurface can be displayed by using conventional three-dimensional rendering techniques as the illustration demonstrates. In the second illustration we have sought to superimpose a pseudo-colour that represents temperature. A spectral colour path, from blue to magenta, around the circumference of the HSV cone is used.

Thus, in the same three-dimensional image we are trying to represent two functions simultaneously. First, the shape of an isosurface and, second, the temperature at every point on the isosurface. Perceptual problems arise in this case because we are using colour to represent both shape and temperature, whereas normally the colour is experienced as an association with a single phenomenon. For example, it tends to be difficult in such representations, to interpret the shape of the isosurface in regions of rapidly varying hue or temperature. Nevertheless representational schemes like this are becoming commonplace in visualization techniques. They represent a kind of summary of complex data that, prior to the use of three-dimensional computer graphics, could only be examined one part at a time. For example, the simulation in the illustration may have been investigated by using a rotating cross-section. This leaves the difficult task of building up a three-dimensional picture of the data to the brain of the viewer.

(15.3.1)

CIE XYZ space

We have discussed in previous sections that we need spectral space to try to simulate reality. This implies that we need a way of 'reducing' or converting spectral space calculations for a monitor display. Also, we saw that we need perceptual colour spaces for choosing mappings for pseudo-colour enhancement. Another *raison d'être* for perceptual colour spaces in computer graphics is for the storage and the communication of files within the computer graphics community and for communication between computer graphicists and industries that use colour.

The CIE standard allows a colour to be specified as a numeric triple (X, Y, Z). CIE XYZ space embraces all colours perceivable by human beings and it is based on experimentally determined colour matching functions. Thus, unlike the three previous colour spaces, it is not a monitor gamut space.

The basis of the standard, adopted in 1931, was colour matching experiments where a user controls or weights three primary light sources to match a target monochromatic light source. The sources used were almost monochromatic and were **R** = 700 nm, **G** = 546.1 nm and **B** = 435.8 nm. In other words the weights in:

$$\mathbf{C} = r\mathbf{R} + g\mathbf{G} + b\mathbf{B}$$

are determined experimentally.

The result of such experiments can be summarized by colour matching functions. These are shown in Figure 15.6(b) and show the amounts of red, green and blue light which when additively mixed will produce in a standard observer a monochromatic colour whose wavelength is given by λ. That is:

$$\mathbf{C}_\lambda = r(\lambda) + g(\lambda) + b(\lambda)$$

For any colour sensation **C** which exhibits an SPD $P(\lambda)$, r, g and b are given by:

$$r = k \int_\lambda P(\lambda)r(\lambda)d(\lambda)$$

$$g = k \int_\lambda P(\lambda)g(\lambda)d(\lambda)$$

$$b = k \int_\lambda P(\lambda)b(\lambda)d(\lambda)$$

Thus, we see that colour matching functions reduce a colour **C**, with any shape of spectral energy distribution to a triple rgb. At this stage we should make the extremely important point that the triple rgb bears no relationship whatever to a triple RGB specified in the aforementioned (computer graphics) system. As we discussed in Section 15.2, computer graphicists understand the triple RGB to be three samples of the SPD of an illuminant or three samples of the reflectivity function of the object which are linearly combined in rendering models to produce a calculated RGB for reflected light. In other words, we can render by working with three samples or we can extend our approach to working with *n* samples. In contrast the triple rgb is *not* three samples of an SPD but the values obtained by integrating the product of the SPD and each matching function. In other words, it is a specification of the SPD as humans see it (in terms of colour matching) rather than as a spectrophotometer would see it.

There is, however, a problem in representing colours with an additive primary system which is that with positive weights, only a subset of perceivable colours can be described by the weights (r, g, b). The problem arises out of the fact that when two colours are mixed the result is a less saturated colour. It is impossible

Figure 15.6
The 'evolution' of the CIE
colour matching functions.

Spectral sensitivity curves
of the ρ, δ and β cones in the
retina and their relationship
to the monochromatic colours:
red = 700 nm
green = 546.1 nm
blue = 435.8 nm

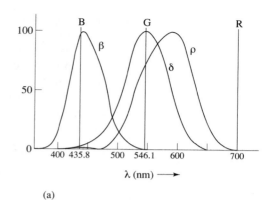

(a)

RGB colour matching
functions for the CIE 1931
Standard Colourimetric
Observer

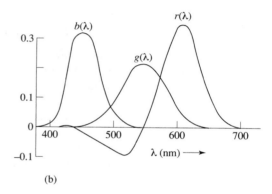

(b)

CIE matching functions
for the CIE 1931 Standard
Colourimetric Observer

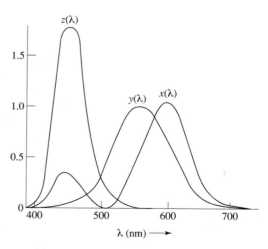

(c)

to form a highly saturated colour by superimposing colours. Any set of three primaries forms a bounded space outside of which certain perceivable highly saturated colours exist. In such colours a negative weight is required.

To avoid negative weights the CIE devised a standard of three supersaturated (or non-realizable) primaries X, Y and Z, which, when additively mixed, will produce all perceivable colours using positive weights. The three corresponding matching functions $x(\lambda)$, $y(\lambda)$ and $z(\lambda)$ shown in Figure 15.6(c) are always positive. Thus we have:

$$X = k \int_{\lambda} P(\lambda)x(\lambda)d(\lambda)$$

$$Y = k \int_{\lambda} P(\lambda)y(\lambda)d(\lambda)$$

$$Z = k \int_{\lambda} P(\lambda)z(\lambda)d(\lambda)$$

where:

$k = 680$ for self-luminous objects

The space formed by the XYZ values for all perceivable colours is CIE XYZ space. The matching functions are transformations of the experimental results. In addition the $y(\lambda)$ matching function was defined to have a colour matching function that corresponded to the luminous efficiency characteristic of the human eye, a function that peaks at 550 nm (yellow-green).

The shape of the CIE XYZ colour solid is basically conical with the apex of the cone at the origin (Figure 15.7). Also shown in this space is a monitor gamut which appears as a parallelepiped. If we compare this space to HSV space we can

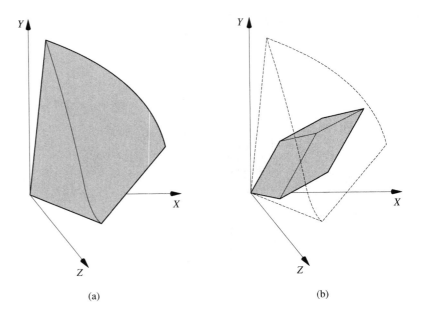

Figure 15.7
(a) CIE XYZ solid.
(b) A typical monitor gamut in CIE XYZ space.

(a)

(b)

view the solid as distorted HSV space. The black point is at the origins and the HSV space is deformed to embrace all colours and to encompass the fact that the space is based on perceptual measurements. If we consider, for example, the outer surface of the deformed cone, this is made of rays that emanate from the origin terminating on the edge of the cone. Along any ray is the set of colours of identical chromaticity (see the next section). If a ray is moved in towards the white point, situated on the base of the deformed cone then we desaturate the set of colours specified by the ray. Within this space, the monitor gamut is a deformed (sheared and scaled) cube, forming a subset of the volume of perceivable colours.

CIE xyY space

An alternative way of specifying the (X, Y, Z) triple is (x, y, Y) where (x, y) are known as chromaticity coordinates:

$$x = \frac{X}{X + Y + Z}$$

$$y = \frac{Y}{X + Y + Z}$$

Plotting x against y for all visible colours yields a two-dimensional (x, y) space known as the CIE chromaticity diagram.

The wing-shaped CIE chromaticity diagram (Figure 15.8) is extensively used in colour science. It encompasses all the perceivable colours in two-dimensional space by ignoring the luminance Y. The locus of the pure saturated or spectral colours is formed by the curved line from blue (400 nm) to red (700 nm). The straight line between the end points is known as the purple or magenta line. Along this line is located the purples or magentas. These are colours whose perceivable sensation cannot be produced by any single monochromatic stimulus, and which cannot be isolated from daylight.

Also shown in Figure 15.8 is the gamut of colours reproducible on a computer graphics monitor from three phosphors. The monitor gamut is a triangle formed by drawing straight lines between three RGB points. The RGB points are contained within the outermost curve of monochromatic or saturated colours. Examination of the emission characteristics of the phosphors will reveal a spread about the dominant wavelength which means that the colour contains white light and is not saturated. When, say, the blue and green phosphors are fully excited their emission characteristics add together into a broader band meaning that the resultant colour will be less saturated than blue or green.

The triangular monitor gamut in CIE xy space is to be found in most texts dealing with colour science in computer graphics, but it is somewhat misleading. The triangle is actually the projection out of CIE xyY space of the monitor gamut, with the vertices formed from phosphor vertices that each have a different luminance. Figure 15.9 shows the general shape of monitor gamut in CIE

Figure 15.8
CIE chromaticity diagram
showing typical gamuts for
colour film, colour monitor
and printing inks.

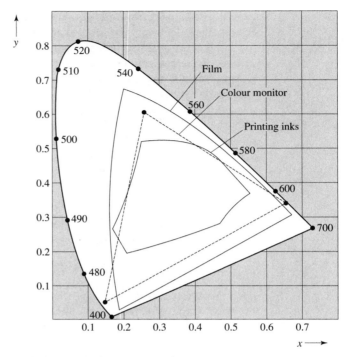

Figure 15.8
CIE chromaticity diagram
showing typical gamuts for
colour film, colour monitor
and printing inks.

xyY space and Figure 15.10 (Colour Plate) shows three slices through the space. The geometric or shape transformation from the scaled and sheared cube in XYZ space to the curvilinear solid (with six faces) in xyY space is difficult to interpret. For example, one edge of the cube maps to a single point.

There are a number of important uses of the CIE chromaticity diagram. We give one important example. It can be used to compare the gamut of various display devices. This is important in computer graphics when an image is eventually to be reproduced on a number of different devices. Figure 15.8 shows a CIE chromaticity diagram with the gamut of a typical computer graphics monitor together with the gamut for modern printing inks. The printing ink gamut is enclosed within the monitor gamut, which is itself enclosed by the gamut for

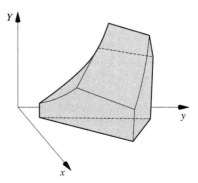

Figure 15.9
Monitor gamut in CIE xyY
space (see also Figure 15.10
(Colour Plate)).

colour film. This means that some colours attainable on film are not reproducible on a computer graphics monitor, and certain colours on a monitor cannot be reproduced by printing. The gamut of display devices and reproduction techniques is always contained by the gamut of perceivable colours – the saturated or spectral colours being the most difficult to reproduce. However, this is not generally a problem because spectral and near spectral colours do not tend to occur naturally. It is the relative spread of device gamuts that is important rather than the size of any gamut with respect to the visual gamut.

15.4 Rendering and colour spaces

We have discussed reasons for the lack of accurate colours in computer graphics and now look at one of these reasons in more detail – colour aliasing is invisible.

Physics tells us that the light reflected from a surface, as a function of wavelength, is the product of the wavelength-dependent surface reflectance function and the spectral energy distribution function of the light source. If we simply evaluate this product at three wavelengths (the RGB Phong shading model discussed in Chapter 6) then clearly, because of the gross undersampling, we will not produce a result that simulates the real characteristic. What happens is that the three-sample approach will produce a colour shift away from the real colour. However, this shift is in most contexts completely invisible because we have no expectations of what particular colour should emerge from a computer graphics model anyway. A wrong colour does not necessarily look wrong.

To try to simulate real colour interaction numerically we can simply expand our three-sample rendering approach to n samples and work in spectral space, sampling the light source distribution function and the reflectivity of the object at appropriate wavelength intervals.

We look at three approaches which are summarized in Figure 15.11. The first – the *de facto* standard approach to rendering – takes no account of colour except in the most approximate way. The illuminant SPD is sampled at three wavelengths, or more usually arbitrarily specified as 1, 1, 1 for white light. Similarly the reflectivity of the object is specified at each of the R, G and B wavelengths. Three rendering equations/models are applied and the calculated RGB intensities are fed directly to the monitor without further alteration. This method produces works with input values that are arbitrary in the sense that a user may want to render a dark red object, but may not be concerned with specifying the colour of the object and illuminant to any degree of accuracy. Only three rendering equations are used.

The second approach applies the rendering equations in spectral space for a set of wavelengths ($n = 9$ appears to be a good compromise). Here the rendering cost is at least a factor of three greater than the 'arbitrary' colour method. The output from the renderer is a sampled intensity function and this must be transformed into (three-sample) $RGB_{monitor}$ space for display. The implication here is that if we have gone to the trouble to render at n wavelengths then we wish to display the

Figure 15.11
Rendering strategies and colours. (a) 'Standard' rendering for 'arbitrary' colour applications. (b) Spectral space rendering for colour-sensitive applications. (c) CIE space rendering for colour-sensitive applications.

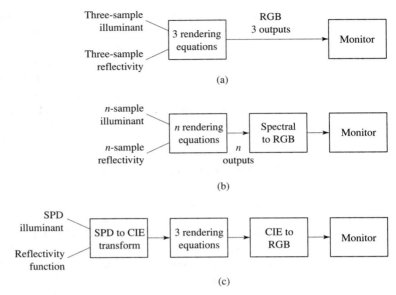

result as accurately as possible and we need certain monitor parameters to be able to derive the spectral-to-RGB$_{monitor}$ transformation (see Section 15.5.2).

In the final approach we render in CIE space. This means specifying the SPD illuminant as CIE XYZ values using the matching functions. However, we have the problem of the surface reflectivity. What values do we use for this? This is a subtle point and the reader is referred to the paper by Borges (1991) which addresses exactly this issue. Here, we can note that we can simply express the reflectivity function as a CIE XYZ triple and use this in a three equation rendering approach. The output from the renderer is a CIE XYZ triple and we then require a CIE-to-RGB$_{monitor}$ transform to display the result.

The difference between an image produced by 'spectral rendering' and 'RGB rendering' is shown (to within the limits of the reproduction process) in Figure 15.12 (Colour Plate) for a ray tracer.

We must remember that we are only attending to a single aspect in the simulation of reality – which is the prevention of erroneous colour shifts due to undersampling in spectral space. Colour is also determined by the local reflection model itself. Defects in the accuracy with which the reflection model simulates reality still exist. We cannot overcome these simply by extending the number of samples in spectral space.

15.5 Monitor considerations

15.5.1 RGB$_{monitor}$ space and other monitor considerations

Serious use of colour in computer imagery needs careful attention to certain aspects of the display monitor. Computer graphics monitors are not standardized and the application of the same RGB triple to different monitors will produce different colours on the screen. The most important factors are:

(1) Colour on a monitor is not produced by the superposition mixing of three lights, but relies on the eye to spatially mix the tiny light sources produced by three phosphor dots. There is nothing that we can do about this. One of the consequences is that saturated colours are not displayed at their full brightness – an area of pure red is only one-third red and two-thirds black. This means that, for example, even as we as human beings seem to compensate for this effect, taking photographs directly from the screen produces poor results.

(2) Different monitors are manufactured with phosphors that have different spectral energy distributions. For example, different phosphors are used to achieve different persistences (the length of time a phosphor glows after being activated). This can be corrected by a linear transformation as we demonstrate in the next section.

(3) The relationship between the RGB values applied to the monitor and the intensity of light produced on the screen is non-linear. The cure for this, gamma correction – a non-linear transformation – is described in the next section.

(4) In image synthesis, shading equations can produce colours that are outside the gamut of the monitor – undisplayable colours. We have somehow to clip these colours or bring them back into the monitor gamut. This is also a non-linear operation.

(15.5.2)

Monitor considerations – different monitors and the same colour

Contexts in which real colours are produced in computer imagery are, for example, rendering in spectral space and using perceptual space mapping. With spectral space we can produce a CIE XYZ triple from our final set of results. CIE XYZ space is used as a final standard and we need a device-specific transformation to go from CIE XYZ space to the particular $\text{RGB}_{\text{monitor}}$ space.

We can write:

$$\begin{bmatrix} X \\ Y \\ Z \end{bmatrix} = \begin{bmatrix} X_r & X_g & X_b \\ Y_r & Y_g & Y_b \\ Z_r & Z_g & Z_b \end{bmatrix} \begin{bmatrix} R_m \\ G_m \\ B_m \end{bmatrix}$$

$$= T \begin{bmatrix} R_m \\ G_m \\ B_m \end{bmatrix}$$

where T is particular to a monitor and a linear relationship is assumed between the outputs from the phosphors and the RGB values. If T_1 is the transformation for monitor 1 and T_2 the transformation for monitor 2, then $T_2^{-1} T_1$ converts the

RGB values of monitor 1 to those for monitor 2. T can be calculated in the following way. We define:

$$D_r = X_r + Y_r + Z_r$$
$$D_g = X_g + Y_g + Z_g$$
$$D_b = X_b + Y_b + Z_b$$

giving:

$$\begin{bmatrix} X \\ Y \\ Z \end{bmatrix} = \begin{bmatrix} D_r x_r & D_g x_g & D_b x_b \\ D_r y_r & D_g y_g & D_b y_b \\ D_r z_r & D_g z_g & D_b z_b \end{bmatrix} \begin{bmatrix} R_m \\ G_m \\ B_m \end{bmatrix}$$

where:

$$x_r = X_r/D_r \quad Y_r = Y_r/D_r \quad z_r = Z_r/D_r \text{ etc.}$$

Writing the coefficients as a product of two matrices we have:

$$\begin{bmatrix} X \\ Y \\ Z \end{bmatrix} = \begin{bmatrix} x_r & x_g & x_b \\ y_r & y_g & y_b \\ z_r & z_g & z_b \end{bmatrix} \begin{bmatrix} D_r & 0 & 0 \\ 0 & D_g & 0 \\ 0 & 0 & D_b \end{bmatrix} \begin{bmatrix} R_m \\ G_m \\ B_m \end{bmatrix}$$

where the first matrix is the chromaticity coordinates of the monitor phosphor. We now specify that equal RGB voltages of (1, 1, 1) should produce the alignment white:

$$\begin{bmatrix} X_w \\ Y_w \\ Z_w \end{bmatrix} = \begin{bmatrix} x_r & x_g & x_b \\ y_r & y_g & y_b \\ z_r & z_g & z_b \end{bmatrix} \begin{bmatrix} D_r \\ D_g \\ D_b \end{bmatrix}$$

For example, with standard white D_{65} we have:

$$x_w = 0.313 \quad y_w = 0.329 \quad z_w = 0.358$$

and scaling the white point to give unity luminance yields:

$$X_w = 0.951 \quad Y_w = 1.0 \quad Z_w = 1.089$$

Example chromaticity coordinates for an interlaced monitor (long persistence phosphors) are:

	x	y
red	0.620	0.330
green	0.210	0.685
blue	0.150	0.063

Using these we have:

$$\begin{bmatrix} X \\ Y \\ Z \end{bmatrix} = \begin{bmatrix} 0.584 & 0.188 & 0.179 \\ 0.311 & 0.614 & 0.075 \\ 0.047 & 0.103 & 0.939 \end{bmatrix} \begin{bmatrix} R_m \\ G_m \\ B_m \end{bmatrix}$$

Inverting the coefficient matrix gives:

$$\begin{bmatrix} R_m \\ G_m \\ B_m \end{bmatrix} = \begin{bmatrix} 2.043 & -0.568 & -0.344 \\ -1.036 & 1.939 & 0.043 \\ 0.011 & -0.184 & 1.078 \end{bmatrix} \begin{bmatrix} X \\ Y \\ Z \end{bmatrix}$$

The significance of the negative components is that RGB space is a subset of XYZ space, and XYZ colours that lie outside the monitor gamut will produce negative RGB values.

15.5.3 Monitor considerations – colour gamut mapping

Monitor gamuts generally overlap and colours that are available on one monitor may not be reproducible on another. This is manifested by RGB values that are less than zero, or greater than one, after the transformation $T_2^{-1}T_1$ has been applied. This problem may also arise in rendering. In accurate colour simulation, using real colour values, it is likely that colour triples produced by the calculation may lie outside the monitor gamut. In other words the image gamut may be, in general, greater than the monitor gamut. This problem is even greater in the case of hard copy devices such as printers which have smaller gamuts than monitors.

The goal of the process is to compress the image gamut until it just fits in the device gamut in such a way that the image quality is maintained. This will generally depend on the content of the image and the whole subject area is still a research topic. There are, however, a number of simple strategies that we can adopt. The process of producing a displayable colour from one that is outside the gamut of the monitor is called 'colour clipping'.

Clearly we could adopt a simple clamping approach and limit out of range values. Better strategies are suggested by Hall (1989). Undisplayable colours fall into one of two categories:

(1) Colours that have chromaticities outside the monitor gamut (negative RGB values).

(2) Colours that have displayable chromaticities, but intensities outside the monitor gamut (RGB values greater than one).

Any correction results in a shift or change from the calculated colour and we can select a method depending on whether we wish to tolerate a shift in hue, saturation and/or value.

For the first category the best approach is to add white to the colour or to desaturate it until it is displayable. This maintains the hue or dominant wavelength and lightness at the cost of saturation. In the second case there are a number of possibilities. The entire image can be scaled until the highest intensity is in range; this has an effect similar to reducing the aperture in a camera. Alternatively the chromaticity can be maintained and the intensity scaled. Finally, the dominant hue and intensity can be maintained and the colour desaturated by adding white.

Monitor considerations – gamma correction

All of the foregoing discussion has implicitly assumed that there is a linear relationship between the actual RGB values input to a monitor and the intensity produced on the screen. This is not the case. That we need to maintain linearity comes from the fact that as far as possible we require a person viewing, say, a TV image of a scene on a monitor, to see the colour relationships as he perceives them from the scene. This implies that the end-to-end response of the TV system should be linear (Figure 15.13(a)). In a TV system gamma correction is applied at the camera (for reasons that also have to do with coding the signal optimally for noise) to pre-compensate for the monitor non-linearity. This is shown in Figure 15.13(b) which shows gamma correction introduced in the camera compensating for the non-linear relationship at the monitor. A computer graphics system (Figure 15.13(c)) is analogous to a TV camera with a linear intensity characteristic because the rendering calculations are linear. Because of this gamma correction is required after the calculation and this is usually implemented in the form of a look-up table.

Now consider the details. The red intensity, for example, produced on a monitor screen by an input value of R'_i is:

$$R_m = K(R'_i)^{\gamma_r}$$

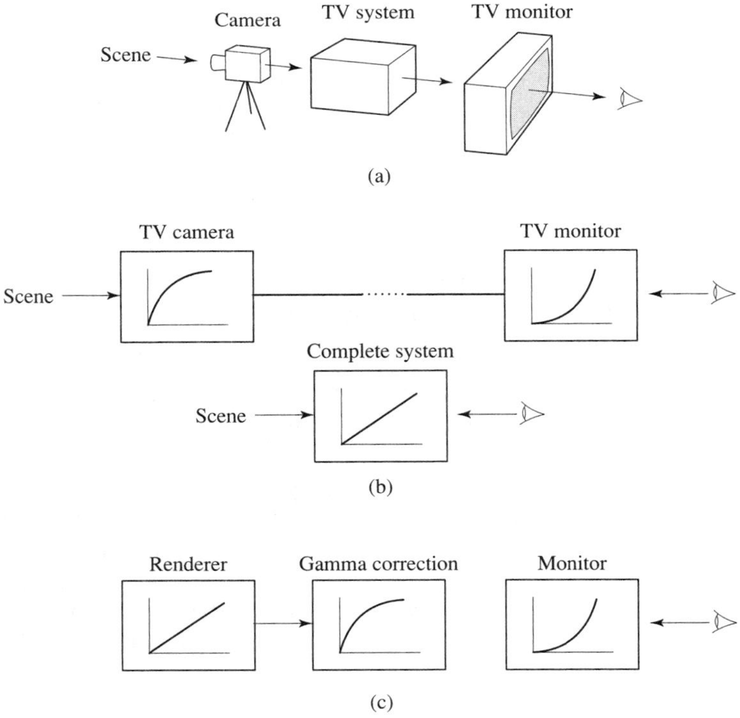

Figure 15.13
Gamma correction.
(a) A viewer should ideally see the same colours on a TV monitor as if he or she were viewing the scene.
(b) Gamma correction is applied in a TV camera.
(c) Computer graphics system.

where γ_r is normally in the range 2.3 to 2.8. The goal of the process is to linearize the relationship between the RGB values produced by the program and if γ_r, γ_g and γ_b are known then so-called gamma correction can be applied to convert the program value R_i to the value that when plugged into the above equation will result in a linear relationship. That is:

$$R'_i = k(R_i)^{1/\gamma_r}$$

An inexpensive method for determining γ is given in a paper by Cowan (1983). The two relationships are shown in Figure 15.14. The second graph is easily incorporated in a video look-up table. Note that the price paid for gamma correction is a reduction in the dynamic range. For example, if k is chosen such that 0 maps to 0 and 255 to 255 then 256 intensity levels are reduced to 167. This can cause banding and it is better to perform the correction in floating point and then to round.

Using a monitor with uncorrected gamma results in both intensity and chromaticity shifts away from the colour calculated by the program. Consider, for example, the triple (0, 255, 127). If this is not gamma corrected the

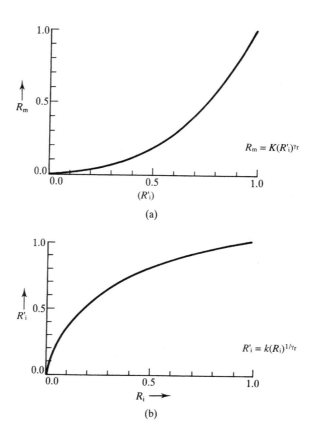

Figure 15.14
Gamma correction.
(a) Intensity as a function of applied voltage values.
(b) Corrected values as a function of applied ones.

display will decrease the blue component, leaving the red and green components unchanged.

Gamma correction leaves zero and maximum intensities unchanged and alters the intensity in mid-range. A 'wrong' gamma that occurs either because gamma correction has not been applied or because an inaccurate value of gamma has been used in the correction will always result in a wrong image with respect to the calculated colour.

Image-based rendering and photo-modelling

Introduction

A new field with many diverse approaches, image-based rendering (IBR) is difficult to categorize. The motivation for the name is that most of the techniques are based on two-dimensional imagery, but this is not always the case and the way in which the imagery is used varies widely amongst methods. A more accurate common thread that runs through all the methods is pre-calculation. All methods make cost gains by pre-calculating a representation of the scene from which images are derived at run-time. IBR has mostly been studied for the common case of static scenes and a moving view point, but applications for dynamic scenes have been developed.

There is, however, no debate concerning the goal of IBR which is to decouple rendering time from scene complexity so that the quality of imagery, for a given frame time constraint, in applications like computer games and virtual reality can be improved over conventionally rendered scenes where all the geometry is reinserted into the graphics pipeline whenever a change is made to the view point. It has emerged, simultaneously with LOD approaches (see Chapter 2) and scene management techniques, as an effective means of tackling the dependency of rendering time on scene complexity.

We will also deal with photo-modelling in this chapter. This is related to image-based rendering because many image-based rendering schemes were designed to operate with photo-modelling. The idea of photo-modelling is to capture the real-world complexity and at the same time retain the flexibility advantages of three-dimensional graphics.

16.1 Reuse of previously rendered imagery – two-dimensional techniques

We begin by considering methods that rely on the concept of frame coherence and reuse of already rendered imagery in some way. Also, as the title of the section implies, we are going to consider techniques that are essentially two-dimensional. Although the general topic of image-based rendering, of course, itself implies two-dimensional techniques there has be some use of the depth information associated with the image, as we shall see in future sections. The distinction is that with techniques which we categorize as two-dimensional we do not operate with detailed depth values, for example, a value per pixel. We may only have a single depth value associated with the image entity as is implied by visibility ordering in image layers (see Section 16.2.2).

A useful model of an image-based renderer is to consider a required image being generated from a source or reference image – rendered in the normal way – by warping the reference image in image space (Figure 16.1). In this section we shall consider simple techniques based on texture mapping that can exploit the hardware facilities available on current 3D graphics cards. The novel approach here is that we consider rendered objects in the scene as texture maps, consider a texture map as a three-dimensional entity and pass it through the graphics pipeline. The common application of such techniques is in systems where a viewer moves through a static environment.

To a greater or lesser extent all such techniques involve some approximation compared with the projections that are computed using conventional techniques and an important part of such methods is determining when it is valid to reuse previously generated imagery and when new images must be generated.

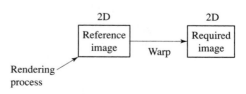

Figure 16.1
Planar imposters and image warping.

IBR as a process that produces an image by warping a reference image

16.1.1　Planar impostors or sprites

Impostor is the name usually given to an image of an object that is used in the form of a texture map – an entity we called a billboard in Chapter 8. In Chapter 8 the billboard was an object in its own right – it was a two-dimensional entity inserted into the scene. Impostors are generalizations of this idea. The idea is that because of the inherent coherence in consecutive frames in a moving view point sequence, the same impostor can be reused over a number of frames until an error measure exceeds some threshold. Such impostors are sometimes qualified by the adjective dynamic to distinguish them from pre-calculated object images that are not updated. A planar sprite is used as a texture map in a normal rendering engine. We use the adjective planar to indicate that no depth information is associated with the sprite – just as there is no depth associated with a texture map (although we retain depth information at the vertices of the rectangle that contains the sprite). The normal (perspective) texture mapping in the renderer takes care of warping the sprite as the view point changes.

There are many different possible ways in which sprites can be incorporated into a rendering sequence. Schaufler's method (Schaufler and Sturzlinger 1996) is typical and for generating an impostor from an object model it proceeds as follows. The object is enclosed in a bounding box which is projected onto the image plane resulting in the determination of the object's rectangular extent in screen space – for that particular view. The plane of the impostor is chosen to be that which is normal to the view plane normal and passes through the centre of the bounding box. The rectangular extent in screen space is initialized to transparent and the object rendered into it. This is then treated as a texture map and placed in the texture memory. When the scene is rendered the object is treated as a transparent polygon and texture mapped. Note that texture mapping takes into account the current view transformation and thus the impostor is warped slightly from frame to frame. Those pixels covered by the transparent pixels are unaffected in value or z depth. For the opaque pixels the impostor is treated as a normal polygon and the Z-buffer updated with its depth.

In Maciel and Shirley (1995) 'view-dependent impostors' are pre-calculated – one for each face of the object's bounding box. Space around the object is then divided into view point regions by frustums formed by the bounding box faces and its centre. If an impostor is elected as an appropriate representation then whatever region the current view point is in determines the impostor used.

16.1.2　Calculating the validity of planar impostors

As we have implied, the use of impostors requires an error metric to be calculated to quantify the validity of the impostor. Impostors become invalid because we do not use depth information. At some view point away from the view point from which the impostor was generated the impostor is perceived for what it is – a flat image embedded in three-dimensional space – the illusion is destroyed.

The magnitude of the error depends on the depth variation in the region of the scene represented by the impostor, the distance of the region from the view point and the movement of the view point away from the reference position from which the impostor was rendered. (The distance factor can be gainfully exploited by using lower resolution impostors for distant objects and grouping more than one object into clusters.) For changing view point applications the validity has to be dynamically evaluated and new impostors generated as required.

Shade *et al.* (1996) use a simple metric based on angular discrepancy. Figure 16.2 shows a two-dimensional view of an object bounding box with the plane of the impostor shown in bold. v_0 is the view point for the impostor rendering and v_1 is the current view point. x is a point or object vertex which coincides with x' in the impostor view. Whenever the view point changes from v_0, x and x' subtend an angle θ and Shade *et al.* calculate an error metric which is the maximum angle over all points x.

Schaufler and Sturzlinger's (1996) error metric is based on angular discrepancy related to pixel size and the consideration of two worst cases. First, consider the angular discrepancy due to translation of the view point parallel to the impostor plane (Figure 16.3(a)). This is at a maximum when the view point moves normal to a diagonal of a cube enclosing the bounding box with the impostor plane coincident with the other diagonal. When the view point moves to v_1 the points x', x_1 and x_2 should be seen as separate points. The angular discrepancy due to this component of view point movement is then given by the angle θ_{trans} between the vectors v_1x_1 and v_1x_2. As long as this is less that the angle subtended by a pixel at the view point this error can be tolerated. For a view point moving towards the object we consider the construction in Figure 16.3(b). Here the worst case is the corner of the front face of the cube. When the view point moves in to v_1 the points x_1 and x_2 should be seen as separate and the angular discrepancy is given as θ_{size}. An impostor can then be used as:

use_imposter := $(\theta_{trans} < \theta_{screen})$ or $(\theta_{size} < \theta_{screen})$

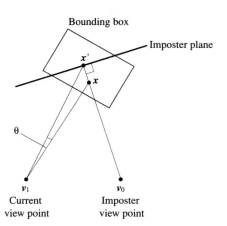

Figure 16.2
Angular discrepancy of an impostor image (after Shade *et al.* (1996)).

Figure 16.3
Schaufler's worst case
angular discrepancy metric
(after Shaufler (1996)).
(a) Translation of view point
parallel to an impostor.
(b) Translation of view point
towards an impostor plane.

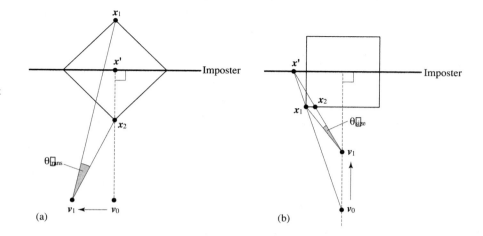

where:

$$\theta_{screen} = \frac{\text{field of view}}{\text{screen resolution}}$$

The simplest way to use impostors is to incorporate them as texture maps in a normal rendering scheme exploiting texture mapping hardware.

So far we have said nothing about what makes up an impostor and the assumption has been that we generate an image from an object model. Shade *et al.* (1996) generalize this concept in a scheme called Hierarchical Image Caching and generate impostors from the entire contents of nodes in a BSP tree of the scene combining the benefits of this powerful scene partitioning method with the use of pre-rendered imagery. Thus, for example, distant objects that require infrequent updates can be grouped into clusters and a single impostor generated for the cluster. The algorithm thus operates on and exploits the hierarchy of the scene representation. Objects may be split over different leaf nodes and this leads to the situation of a single objects possessing more than one impostor. This causes visual artefacts and Shade *et al.* (1996) minimize this by ensuring that the BSP partitioning strategy splits as few objects as possible and by 'inflating' the geometry slightly in leaf regions so that the impostors overlap to eliminate gaps in the final image that may otherwise appear.

16.2   Varying rendering resources

16.2.1   Priority rendering

An important technique that has been used in conjunction with 2D imagery is the allocation of different amounts of rendering resources to different parts of the image. An influential (hardware) approach is due to Regan and Pose (1994).

They allocated different frame rates to objects in the scene as a function of their distance from the view point. This was called priority rendering because it combined the environment map approach with updating the scene at different rates. They use a six-view cubic environment map as the basic pre-computed solution. In addition, a multiple display memory is used for image composition and on the fly alterations to the scene are combined with pre-rendered imagery.

The method is a hybrid of a conventional graphics pipeline approach with an image-based approach. It depends on dividing the scene into a priority hierarchy. Objects are allocated a priority depending on their closeness to the current position of the viewer and their allocation of rendering resources and update time are determined accordingly. The scene is pre-rendered as environment maps and, if the viewer remains stationary, no changes are made to the environment map. As the viewer changes position the new environment map from the new view point is rendered according to the priority scheme.

Regan and Pose (1994) utilize multiple display memories to implement priority rendering where each display memory is updated at a different rate according to the information it contains. If a memory contains part of the scene that is being approached by a user then it has to be updated, whereas a memory that contains information far away from the current user position can remain as it is. Thus overall different parts of the scene are updated at different rates – hence priority rendering. Regan and Pose (1994) use memories operating at 60, 30, 15, 7.5 and 3.75 frames per second. Rendering power is directed to those parts of the scene that need it most. At any instant the objects in a scene would be organized into display memories according to their current distance from the user. Simplistically the occupancy of the memories might be arranged as concentric circles emanating from the current position of the user. Dynamically assigning each object to an appropriate display memory involves a calculation which is carried out with respect to a bounding sphere. In the end this factor must impose an upper bound on scene complexity and Regan and Pose (1994) report a test experiment with a test scene of only 1000 objects. Alternatively objects have to be grouped into a hierarchy and dealt with through a secondary data structure as is done in some speed-up approaches to conventional ray tracing.

(16.2.2) Image layering

Lengyel and Snyder (1997) generalized the concept of impostors and variable application of rendering resources calling their technique 'coherent image layers'. Here the idea is again to devote rendering resources to different parts of the image according to need expressed as different spatial and/or temporal sampling rates. The technique also deals with objects moving with respect to each other. This is done by dividing the image into layers. (This is, of course, an old idea; since the 1930s cartoon production has been optimized by dividing the image into layers which are worked on independently and composed into a final film.) Thus fast-moving foreground objects can be allocated more resources than slow-moving background objects.

Another key idea of Lengyel and Snyder's work is that any layer can itself be decomposed into a number of components. The layer approach is taken into the shading itself and different resources given to different components in the shading. A moving object may consist of a diffuse layer plus a highlight layer plus a shadow layer. Each component produces an image stream and a stream of two-dimensional transformations representing its translation and warping in image space. Sprites may be represented at different resolutions to the screen resolution and may be updated at different rates. Thus sprites have different resolution in *both* space and time.

A sprite in the context of this work is now an 'independent' entity rather than being a texture map tied to an object by the normal vertex/texture coordinate association. It is also a pure two-dimensional object – not a two-dimensional part (a texture map) of a three-dimensional object. Thus as a sprite moves the appropriate warping has to be calculated.

In effect the traditional rendering pipeline is split into 'parallel' segments each representing a different part of the image (Figure 16.4). Different quality settings can be applied to each layer which manifests in different frame rates and different resolutions for each layer. The layers are then combined in the compositor with transparency or alpha in depth order.

A sprite is created as a rectangular entity by establishing a sprite rendering transform A such that the projection of the object in the sprite domain fits tightly in a bounding box. This is so that points within the sprite do not sample non-object space. The transform A is an affine transform that maps the sprite onto the screen and is determined as follows. If we consider a point in screen space p_s then we have:

$$p_s = Tp$$

where p is the equivalent object point in world space and T is the concatenation of the modelling, viewing and projection transformations.

We require an A such that (Figure 16.5):

$$p_s = A^{-1}ATp = Aq$$

Figure 16.4
The layer approach of Lengyel and Snyder (after Lengyel and Snyder (1997)). Rendering resources are allocated to perceptually important parts of the scene (layers). Slowly changing layers are updated at a lower frame rate and at lower resolution.

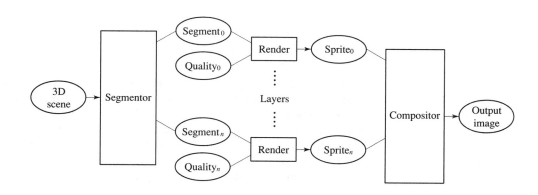

Figure 16.5
The sprite rendering transform A.

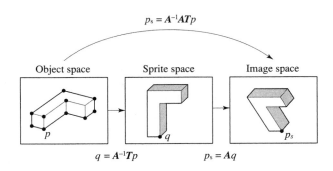

$$p_s = A^{-1}ATp$$

Object space Sprite space Image space

$$q = A^{-1}Tp \qquad p_s = Aq$$

where q is a point in sprite coordinates and:

$$A = \begin{bmatrix} a & b & t_x \\ c & d & t_y \end{bmatrix}$$

Thus, an affine transformation is used to achieve an equivalent warp that would occur due to a conventional transformation T.

The transform A – a 2×3 matrix – is updated as an object undergoes rigid motion and provides the warp necessary to change the shape of the sprite in screen space due to the object motion. This is achieved by transforming the points of a characteristic polyhedron (Figure 16.6) representing the object into screen space for two consecutive time intervals using T_{n-1} and T_n and finding the six unknown coefficients for A. Full details of this procedure are given in Lengyel and Snyder (1997).

Calculating the validity of layers

As any sequence proceeds, the reusability of the layers needs to be monitored. In Section 16.1.2 we described a simple geometric measure for the validity of sprites. With image layers Lengyel and Snyder (1997) develop more elaborate criteria based upon geometric, photometric and sampling considerations. The geometric and photometric tests measure the difference between the image due to the layer or sprite and what the image should be if it were conventionally rendered.

A geometric error metric (Lengyel and Snyder call the metrics fiducials) is calculated from:

$$F_{\text{Geometric}} = \max_i \lVert P_i - A p'_i \rVert$$

where $A p'_i$ is a set of characteristic points in the layer in the current frame warped into their position from the previous frame and p_i the position the points actually occupy. (These are always transformed by T, the modelling, viewing and perspective transform in order to calculate the warp. This sounds like a circular argument but finding A (previous section) involves a best fit procedure. Remember that the warp is being used to approximate the transformation T.) Thus a threshold can be set and the layer considered for re-rendering if this is exceeded.

Figure 16.6
The effect of the rigid motion of the points in the bounding polyhedron in screen space is expressed as a change in the affine transform **A** (after Lengyel and Snyder (1997)).

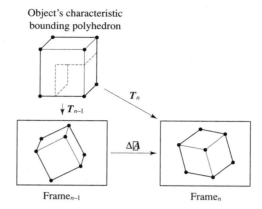

For changes due to relative motion between the light source and the object represented by the layer, the angular change in **L**, the light direction vector from the object, can be computed.

Finally, a metric associated with the magnification/minification of the layer has to be computed. If the relative movement between a viewer and object is such that layer samples are stretched or compressed then the layer may need to be re-rendered. This operation is similar to determining the depth parameter in mip-mapping and in this case can be computed from the 2×2 sub-matrix of the affine transform.

After a frame is complete a regulator considers resource allocation for the next frame. This can be done either on a 'budget-filling' basis where the scene quality is maximized or on a threshold basis where the error thresholds are set to the highest level the user can tolerate (freeing rendering resources for other tasks). The allocation is made by evaluating the error criteria and estimating the rendering cost per layer based on the fraction of the rendering budget consumed by a particular layer. Layers can then be sorted in a benefit/cost order and re-rendered or warped by the regulator.

Ordering layers in depth

So far nothing has been said about the depth of layers – the compositor requires depth information to be able to generate a final image from the separate layers. Because the method is designed to handle moving objects the depth order of layers can change and the approach is to maintain a sorted list of layers which is dynamically updated. The renderer produces hidden surface eliminated images within a layer and a special algorithm deals with the relative visibility of the layers as indivisible entities. A Kd tree is used in conjunction with convex polyhedra that bound the geometry of the layer and an incremental algorithm (fully described in Snyder (1998)) is employed to deal with occlusion without splitting.

Using depth information

Three-dimensional warping

As we have already mentioned, the main disadvantage of planar sprites is that they cannot produce motion parallax and they produce a warp that is constrained by a threshold beyond which their planar nature is perceived.

We now come to consider the use of depth information which is, of course, readily available in synthetic imagery. Although the techniques are now going to use the third dimension we still regard them as image-based techniques in the sense that we are still going to use, as source or reference, rendered images albeit augmented with depth information.

Consider, first, what depth information we might employ. The three commonest forms in order of their storage requirements are: using layers or sprites with depth information (previous section), using a complete (unsegmented) image with the associated Z-buffer (in other words one depth value per pixel) and a layered depth image or LDI. An LDI is a single view of a scene with multiple pixels along each line of sight. The amount of storage that LDIs require is a function of the depth complexity of the average number of surfaces that project onto a pixel.

We begin by considering images complete with depth information per pixel – the normal state of affairs for conventionally synthesized imagery. It is intuitively obvious that we should be able to generate or extrapolate an image at a new view point from the reference image providing that the new view point is close to the reference view point. We can define the pixel motion in image space as the warp:

$$I(x, y) \rightarrow I'(x', y')$$

which implies a reference pixel will move to a new destination. (This is a simple statement of the problem which ignores important practical problems that we shall address later.) If we assume that the change in the view point is specified by a rotation $\boldsymbol{R} = [r_{ij}]$ followed by a translation $\boldsymbol{T} = (\Delta x, \Delta y, \Delta z)^{\mathrm{T}}$ of the view coordinate system (in world coordinate space) and that the internal parameters of the viewing system/camera do not change – the focal length is set to unity – then the warp is specified by:

$$x' = \frac{(r_{11}x + r_{12}y + r_{13})Z(x, y) + \Delta x}{(r_{31}x + r_{32}y + r_{33})Z(x, y) + \Delta z}$$

$$y' = \frac{(r_{21}x + r_{22}y + r_{23})Z(x, y) + \Delta y}{(r_{31}x + r_{32}y + r_{33})Z(x, y) + \Delta z}$$

[16.1]

where:

$Z(x, y)$ is the depth of the point $\boldsymbol{P}$ of which (x, y) is the projection.

This follows from:

$$x' = \frac{x_{v'}}{z_{v'}} \qquad y' = \frac{y_{v'}}{z_{v'}}$$

where $(x_{v'}, y_{v'}, z_{v'})$ are the coordinates of the point $\textbf{\textit{P}}$ in the new viewing system. A visualization of this process is shown in Figure 16.7.

We now consider the problems that occur with this process. The first is called image folding or topological folding and occurs when more than one pixel in the reference image maps into position (x', y') in the extrapolated image (Figure 16.8(a)). The straightforward way to resolve this problem is to calculate $Z(x', y')$ from $Z(x, y)$ but this requires an additional rational expression and an extra Z-buffer to store the results.

McMillan (1995) has developed an algorithm that specifies a unique evaluation order for computing the warp function such that surfaces are drawn in a back-to-front order thus enabling a simple painter's algorithm to resolve this visibility problem. The intuitive justification for this algorithm can be seen by considering a simple special case shown in Figure 16.9. In this case the view point has moved to the left so that its projection in the image plane of the reference view coordinate system is outside and to the left of the reference view window. This fact tells us that the order in which we need to access pixels in the reference is from right to left. This then resolves the problem of the leftmost pixel in the reference image overwriting the right pixel in the warped image. McMillan shows that the accessing or enumeration order of the reference image can be reduced to nine cases depending on the position of the projection of the new view point in the reference coordinate system. These are shown in Figure 16.10. The general case, where the new view point stays within the reference view window divides the image into quadrants. An algorithm structure that utilizes this method to resolve depth problems in the many-to-one case is thus:

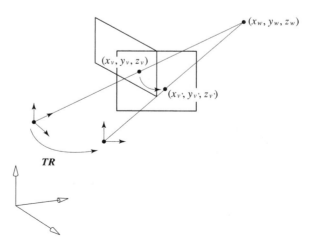

Figure 16.7
A three-dimensional warp is calculated from rotation $\textbf{\textit{R}}$ and translation $\textbf{\textit{T}}$ applied to the view coordinate system.

Figure 16.8
Problems in image warping.
(a) Image folding: more
than one pixel in the
reference view maps
into a single pixel in the
extrapolated view. (b) Holes:
information occluded in the
reference view is required
in the extrapolated view.
(c) Holes: the projected area
of a surface increases in the
extrapolated view because
its normal rotates towards
the viewing direction.
(d) See Colour Plate section.

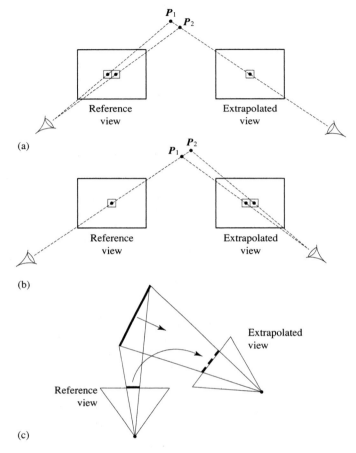

(1) Calculate the projection of the new view point in the reference coordinate system.

(2) Determine the enumeration order (one out of the nine cases shown in Figure 16.10) depending on the projected point.

(3) Warp the reference image by applying Equation 16.1 and writing the result into the frame buffer.

The second problem produced by image warping is caused when occluded areas in the reference image 'need' to become visible in the extrapolated image (Figure 16.8(b)) producing holes in the extrapolated image. As the figure demonstrates, holes and folds are in a sense the inverse of each other, but where a deterministic solution exists for folds no theoretical solution exists for holes and a heuristic needs to be adopted – we cannot recover information that was not there in the first place. However, it is easy to detect where holes occur. They are simply unassigned pixels in the extrapolated image and this enables the problem to be localized and the most common solution is to fill them in with colours from

Figure 16.9
The view point translates to the left so that the projection of the new view point in the image plane of the reference view coordinate system is to the left of the reference view window. The correct processing order of the reference pixels is from right to left.

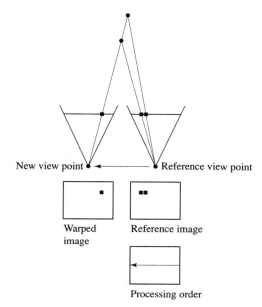

neighbouring pixels. The extent of the holes problem depends on the difference between the reference and extrapolated view points and it can be ameliorated by considering more than one reference image, calculating an extrapolated image from each and compositing the result. Clearly if a sufficient number of reference images are used then the hole problem will be eliminated and there is no need for a local solution which may insert erroneous information.

A more subtle reason for unassigned pixels in the extrapolated image is apparent if we consider surfaces whose normal rotates towards the view direction in

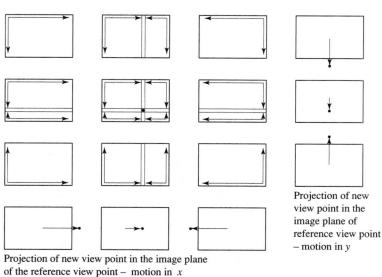

Figure 16.10
A visualization of McMillan's priority algorithm indicating the correct processing order as a function of view point motion for nine cases (after McMillan (1995)).

the new view system (Figure 16.8(c)). The projected area of such a surface into the extrapolated image plane will be greater than its projection in the reference image plane and for a one-to-one forward mapping holes will be produced. This suggests that we must take a rigorous approach to reconstruction in the interpolated image. Mark *et al.* (1997) suggest calculating the appropriate dimension of a reconstruction kernel, for each reference pixel as a function of the view point motion but they point out that this leads to a cost per pixel that is greater than the warp cost. This metric is commonly known as splat size (Chapter 13) and its calculation is not straightforward for a single reference image with Z depth only for visible pixels. (A method that stores multiple depth values for a pixel is dealt with in the next section.)

The effects of these problems on an image are shown in Figure 16.8(d) (Colour Plate). The first two images show a simple scene and the corresponding Z-buffer image. The next image shows the artefacts due to translation (only). In this case these are holes caused by missing information and image folding. The next image shows artefacts due to rotation (only) – holes caused by increasing the projected area of surfaces. Note how these form coherent patterns. The final image shows artefacts caused by both rotation and translation.

Finally, we note that view-dependent illumination effects will not in general be handled correctly with this simple approach. This, however, is a problem that is more serious in image-based modelling methods (Section 16.6). As we have already noted in image warping we must have reference images whose view point is close to the required view point.

(16.3.2) Layered depth images (LDIs)

Many of the problems encountered in the previous section disappear if our source imagery is in the form of an LDI (Shade *et al.* 1998). In particular we can resolve the problem of holes where we require information in the extrapolated image in areas occluded in the source or reference image. An LDI is a three-dimensional data structure that relates to a particular view point and which samples, for each pixel, all the surfaces and their depth values intersected by the ray through that pixel (Figure 16.11). (In practice, we require a number of LDIs to represent a scene and so can consider a scene representation to be four-dimensional – or the same dimensionality as the light field in Section 16.5.) Thus, each pixel is associated with an array of information with a number of elements or layers that is determined by the number of surfaces intersected. Each element contains a colour, surface normal and depth for surface. Clearly this representation requires much more storage than an image plus Z-buffer but this requirement grows only linearly with depth complexity.

In their work Shade *et al.* (1998) suggest two methods for pre-calculating LDIs for synthetic imagery. First, they suggest warping n images rendered from different view points into a single view point. During the warping process if more than one pixel maps into a single LDI pixel then the depth values associated

Figure 16.11
A representation of a
layered depth image (LDI).

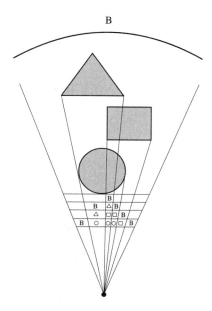

with each source view are compared and enable the layers to be sorted in depth order.

An alternative approach which facilitates a more rigorous sampling of the scene is to use a modified ray tracer. This can be done simplistically by initiating a ray for each pixel from the LDI view point and allowing the rays to penetrate the object (rather than being reflected or refracted). Each hit is then recorded as a new depth pixel in the LDI. All of the scene can be considered by precalculating six LDIs each of which consists of a 90° frustum centred on the reference view point. Shade *et al.* (1998) point out that this sampling scheme is not uniform with respect to a hemisphere of directions centred on the view point. Neighbouring pixel rays project a smaller area onto the image plane as a function of the angle between the image plane normal and the ray direction and they weight the ray direction by the cosine of that angle. Thus, each ray has four coordinates: two pixel coordinates and two angles for the ray direction. The algorithm structure to calculate the LDIs is then:

(1) For each pixel, modify the direction and cast the ray into the scene.

(2) For each hit: if the intersected objects lies within the LDI frustum it is re-projected through the LDI view point.

(3) If the new hit is within a tolerance of an existing depth pixel the colour of the new sample is averaged with the existing one; otherwise a new depth pixel is created.

During the rendering phase, an incremental warp is applied to each layer in back to front order and images are alpha blended into the frame buffer without the need for *Z* sorting. McMillan's algorithm (see Section 16.3.1) is used to ensure

Figure 16.12
Parameters used in splat size
computation (after Shade *et
al.* (1998)).

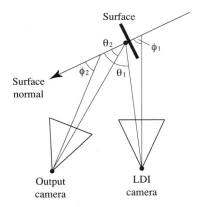

that the pixels are selected for warping in the correct order according to the projection of the output camera in the LDI's system.

To enable splat size computation Shade *et al.* (1998) use the following formula (Figure 16.12):

$$\text{size} = \frac{d_1^2 \cos \theta_2 \, \text{res}_2 \tan \dfrac{\text{fov}_1}{2}}{d_2^2 \cos \theta_1 \, \text{res}_1 \tan \dfrac{\text{fov}_2}{2}}$$

where:

size is the dimension of a square kernel (in practice this is rounded to 1, 3, 5 or 7)
the angles θ are approximated as the angles ϕ, where ϕ is the angle between the surface normal and the z axis of the camera system
fov is the field of view of a camera
res = $w*h$ (the width and height of the LDI)

16.4 View interpolation

View interpolation techniques can be regarded as a subset of 3D warping methods. Instead of extrapolating an image from a reference image, they interpolate a pair of reference images. However, to do this three-dimensional calculations are necessary. In the light of our earlier two-dimensional/three-dimensional categorization they could be considered a two-dimensional technique but we have decided to emphasize the interpolation aspect and categorize them separately.

Williams and Chen (1993) were the first to implement view interpolation for a walkthrough application. This was achieved by pre-computing a set of reference images representing an interior – in this case a virtual museum. Frames required in a walkthrough were interpolated at run time from these reference frames. The interpolation was achieved by storing a 'warp script' that specifies the pixel motion between reference frames. This is a dense set of motion vectors that relates a pixel in the source image to a pixel in the destination image. The simplest example of a motion field is that due to a camera translating parallel to its image plane. In that case the motion field is a set of parallel vectors – one for each pixel – with a direction opposite to the camera motion and having a magnitude proportional to the depth of the pixel. This pixel-by-pixel correspondence can be determined for each pair of images since the three-dimensional (image space) coordinates of each pixel is known, as is the camera or view point motion. The determination of warp scripts is a pre-processing step and an interior is finally represented by a set of reference images together with a warp script relating every adjacent pair. For a large scene that requires a number of varied walkthroughs the total storage requirement may be very large; however, any derived or interpolated view only requires the appropriate pair of reference images and the warp script.

At run time a view or set of views between two reference images is then reduced to linear interpolation. Each pixel in both the source and destination images is moved along its motion vector by the amount given by linearly interpolating the image coordinates (Figure 16.13). This gives a pair of interpolated images. These can be composited and using a pair of images in this way reduces the hole problem. Chen and Williams (1993) fill in remaining holes with a procedure that uses the colour local to the hole. Overlaps are resolved by using a Z-buffer to determine the nearest surface, the z values being linearly interpolated along with the (x, y) coordinates. Finally, note that linear interpolation of the motion vectors produces a warp which will not be exactly the same as that produced if the camera was moved into the desired position. The method is only exact from the special case of a camera translating parallel to its image plane. Williams and Chen (1993) point out that a better approximation can be obtained by quadratic or cubic interpolation in the image plane.

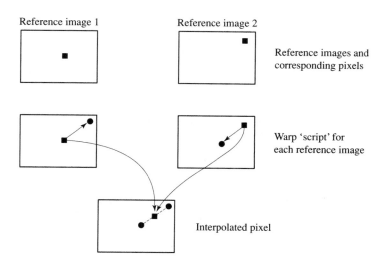

Reference image 1   Reference image 2

Reference images and corresponding pixels

Warp 'script' for each reference image

Interpolated pixel

Figure 16.13
Simple view interpretation: a single pair of corresponding pixels define a path in image space from which an interpolated view can be constructed.

View morphing

Up to now we have considered techniques that deal with a moving view point and static scenes. In a development that they call view morphing Seitz and Dyer (1996) address the problem of generating in-between images where non-rigid transformations have occurred. They do this by addressing the approximation implicit in the previous section and distinguish between 'valid' and 'non-valid' in-between views.

View interpolation by warping a reference image into an extrapolated image proceeds in two-dimensional image plane space. A warping operation is just that – it changes the shape of the two-dimensional projection of objects. Clearly the interpolation should proceed so that the projected shape of the objects in the reference projection is consistent with their real three-dimensional shape. In other words, the interpolated view must be equivalent to a view that would be generated in the normal way (either using a camera or a conventional graphics pipeline) by changing the view point from the reference view point to that of the interpolated view. A 'non-valid' view means that the interpolated view does not preserve the object shape. If this condition does not hold then the interpolated views will correspond to an object whose shape is distorting in real three-dimensional space. This is exactly what happens in conventional image morphing between two shapes. 'Impossible', non-existent or arbitrary shapes occur as in-between images because the motivation here is to appear to change one object into an entirely different one. The distinction between valid and invalid view interpolation is shown in Figure 16.14.

An example where linear interpolation of images produces valid interpolated views is the case where the image planes remain parallel (Figure 16.15). Physically, this situation would occur if a camera was allowed to move parallel to its image plane (and optionally zoom in and out). If we let the combined viewing and perspective transformations (see Chapter 5) be V_0 and V_1 for the two reference images then the transformation for an in-between image can be obtained by linear interpolation:

$$V_i = (1 - s) \, V_0 + s V_1$$

If we consider a pair of corresponding points in the reference images P_0 and P_1 which are projections of world space point P, then it is easily shown (see Seitz and Dyer (1996)) that the projection of point P from the intermediate (interpolated) view point is given by linear interpolation:

$$\begin{aligned} P_i &= P_0(1 - s) + P_1 s \\ &= V_i P \end{aligned}$$

In other words linear interpolation of pixels along a path determined by pixel correspondence in two reference images is exactly equivalent to projecting the scene point that resulted in these pixels through a viewing and projective transformation given by an intermediate camera position, provided parallel views are maintained, in other words using the transformation V_i, which would

Figure 16.14
Distinguishing between
valid and invalid view
interpolation. In (a), using
a standard (morphing)
approach of linear
interpolation produces
gross shape deformation
(this does not matter if we
are morphing between
two different objects – it
becomes part of the effect).
(b) The interpolated (or
morphed view) is consistent
with object shape.
(Courtesy of Steven Seitz.)

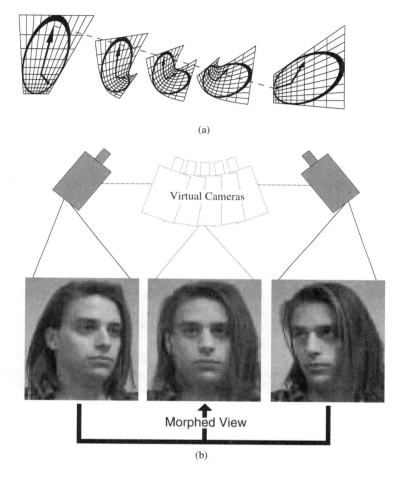

(a)

Virtual Cameras

Morphed View

(b)

be obtained if V_0 and V_1 were linearly interpolated. Note also that we are interpolating views that would correspond to those obtained if we had moved the
camera in a straight line from C_0 to C_1. In other words the interpolated view
corresponds to the camera position:

$$C_i = (sC_x, sC_y, 0)$$

If we have reference views that are not related in this way then the interpolation
has to be preceded (and followed) by an extra transformation. This is the general
situation where the image planes of the reference views and the image plane of
the required or interpolated view have no parallel relationship. The first transformation, which Seitz and Dyer call a 'prewarp', warps the reference images so
that they appear to have been taken by a camera moving in a plane parallel to
its image plane. The pixel interpolation, or morphing, can the be performed as
in the previous paragraph and the result of this is postwarped to form the final
interpolated view, which is the view required from the virtual camera position.

Figure 16.15
Moving the camera from C_0 to C_1 (and zooming) means that the image planes remain parallel and P_i can be linearly interpolated from P_0 and P_1 (after Seitz and Dyer (1996)).

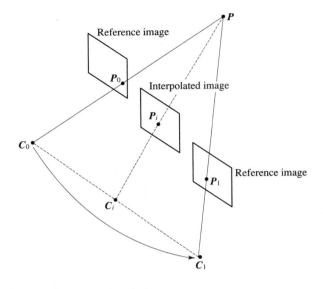

A simple geometric illustration of the process is shown in Figure 16.16. Here R_0 and R_1 are the references images. Prewarping these to R_0' and R_1' respectively means that we can now linearly interpolate these rectified images to produce R_i'. This is then postwarped to produce the required R_i. An important consequence of this method is that although the warp operation is image based we require knowledge of the view points involved to effect the pre- and post-warp transformations. Again this has ramifications for the context in which the method is

Figure 16.16
Prewarping reference images, interpolating and postwarping in view interpolation (after Seitz and Dyer (1996)).

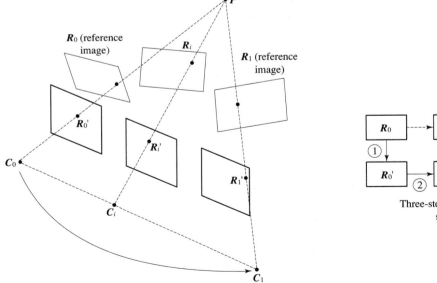

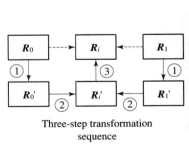

Three-step transformation
sequence

used, implying that in the case of photographic imagery we have to record or recover the camera view points.

The prewarping and postwarping transformations are derived as follows. First, it can be shown that any two perspective views that share the same centre of projection are related by a planar projective transformation – a 3 × 3 matrix obtained from the combined viewing perspective transformation V. Thus R_0 and R_1 are related to R_0' and R_1' by two such matrices T_0 and T_1. The procedure is thus as follows:

(1) Prewarp R_0 and R_1 using T_0^{-1} and T_1^{-1} to produce R_0' and R_1'.

(2) Interpolate to calculate R_i', C_i and T_i.

(3) Apply T_i to R_i' to give image R_i.

16.5   Four-dimensional techniques – the Lumigraph or light field rendering approach

Up to now we have considered systems that have used a single image or a small number of reference images from which a required image is generated. We have looked at two-dimensional techniques and methods where depth information has been used – three-dimensional warping. Some of these methods involve precalculation of a special form of rendered imagery (LDIs) others post-process a conventionally rendered image. We now come to a method that is an almost total pre-calculation technique. It is an approach that bears some relationship to environment mapping. An environment map caches all the light rays that arrive at a single point in the scene – the source or reference point for the environment map. By placing an object at that point we can (approximately) determine those light rays that arrive at the surface of the object by indexing into the map. This scheme can be extended so that we store in effect an environment map for every sampled point in the scene. That is, for each point in the scene we have knowledge of all light rays arriving at that point. We can now place an object at any point in the scene and calculate the reflected light. The advantage of this approach is that we now minimize most of the problems related to three-dimensional warping at the cost of storing a vast amount of data.

A light field is a similar approach. For each and every point of a region in the scene in which we wish to reconstruct a view we pre-calculate and store or cache the radiance in every direction at that point. This representation is called a light field or Lumigraph (Levoy and Hanrahan 1996; Gortler *et al.* 1996) and we construct for a region of free space by which is meant a region free of occluders. The importance of free space is that it reduces the light field from a five-dimensional to a four-dimensional function. In general, for every point (x, y, z) in scene space we have light rays travelling in every direction (parametrized by two angles) giving a five-dimensional function. In occluder free space we can assume (unless there is atmospheric interaction) that the radiance along a ray is constant. The two 'free space scenes' of interest to us are: viewing an object from anywhere outside its convex hull and viewing an environment such as a room from somewhere within its (empty) interior.

The set of rays in any region in space can be parametrized by their intersection with two parallel planes and this is the most convenient representation for a light field (Figure 16.17(a)). The planes can be positioned anywhere. For example, we can position a pair of planes parallel to each face of a cube enclosing an object and capture all the radiance information due to the object (Figure 16.7(b)). Reconstruction of any view of the object then consists of each pixel in the view plane casting a ray through the plane pair and assigning $L(s, t, u, v)$ to that pixel (Figure 16.7(c)). The reconstruction is essentially a resampling process and unlike the methods described in previous sections it is a linear operation.

Light fields are easily constructed from rendered imagery. A light field for a single pair of parallel planes placed near an object can be created by moving the camera in equal increments in the (s, t) plane to generate a series of sheared perspective projections. Each camera point (s, t) then specifies a bundle of rays arriving from every direction in the frustum bounded by the (u, v) extent. It could be argued that we are simply pre-calculating every view of the object that we require at run time; however, two factors mitigate this brute-force approach. First, the resolution in the (s, t) plane can be substantially lower than the resolution in the (u, v) plane. If we consider a point on the surface of the object coincidence, say, with the (u, v) plane, then the (s, t) plane contains the reflected

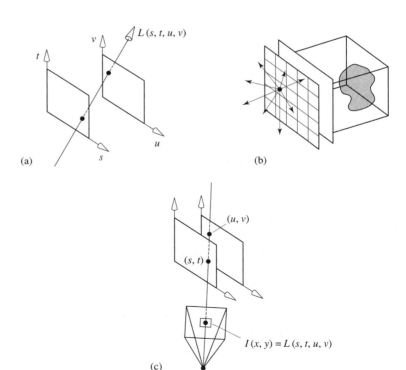

Figure 16.17
Light field rendering using parallel plane representation for rays. (a) Parametrization of a ray using parallel planes. (b) Pairs of planes positioned on the face of a bounding cube can represent all the radiance information due to an object. (c) Reconstruction for a single pixel $I(x,y)$.

light in every direction (constrained by the (s, t) plane extent). By definition, the radiance at a single point on the surface of an object varies slowly with direction and a low sampling frequency in the (s, t) plane will capture this variation. A higher sampling frequency is required to calculate the variation as a function of position on the surface of the object. Second, there is substantial coherence exhibited by a light field. Levoy and Hanrahan (1996) report a compression ratio of 118:1 for a 402 Mb light field and conclude that given this magnitude of compression the simple (linear) re-sampling scheme together with simplicity advantages over other IBR methods make light fields a viable proposition.

16.6 Photo-modelling and IBR

Another distinguishing factor in IBR approaches is whether they work only with computer graphics imagery (where depth information is available) or whether they use photographs as the source imagery. Photography has the potential to solve the other major problem with scene complexity – the modelling cost. Real world detail, whose richness and complexity eludes even the most elaborate photo-realistic renderers, is easily captured by conventional photographic means. The idea is to use IBR techniques to manipulate the photographs so that they can be used to generate an image from a view point different from the camera view point.

Photographs have always been used in texture mapping and this classical tool is still finding new applications in areas which demand an impression of realism that would be unobtainable from conventional modelling techniques, except at great expense. A good example is facial animation where a photograph of a face is wrapped onto a computer graphics model or structure. The photo-map provides the fine level of detail, necessary for convincing and realistic expressions, and the underlying three-dimensional model is used as a basis for controlling the animation.

In building geometric representations from photographs, many of the problems that are encountered are traditionally part of the computer vision area but the goals are different. Geometric information recovered from a scene in a computer vision context usually has some single goal, such as collision avoidance in robot navigation or object recognition, and we are usually concerned in some way with reducing the information that impinges on the low-level sensor. We are generally interested in recovering the shape of an object without regard to such irrelevant information as texture; although we may use such information as a device for extracting the required geometry, we are not interested in it *per se*. In modelling a scene in detail, it is precisely the details such as texture that we are interested in, as well as the pure geometry.

Consider first the device of using photography to assist in modelling. Currently available commercial photo-modelling software concentrates on extracting pure geometry using a high degree of manual intervention. Common approaches use a pre-calibrated camera, knowledge of the position of the camera for each shot and a sufficient number of shots to capture the structure of the building, say, that is being modelled. Extracting the edges from the shots of the building enables a wireframe model to be constructed. This is usually done semi-automatically with an operator matching corresponding edges in the different projections. It is exactly equivalent to the shape from stereo problem using feature correspondence except that now we use a human being instead of a correspondence-establishing algorithm. We may end up performing a large amount of manual work on the projections, as much work as would be entailed in using a conventional CAD package to construct the building. The obvious potential advantage is that photo-modelling offers the possibility of automatically extracting the rich visual detail of the scene, as well as the geometry.

It is interesting to note that in modelling from photographs approaches, the computer graphics community has side-stepped the most difficult problems that are researched in computer vision by embracing some degree of manual intervention. For example, the classical problem of correspondence between images projected from different view points is solved by having an operator manually establish a degree of correspondence between frames which can enable the success of algorithms that establish detailed pixel-by-pixel correspondence. In computer vision such approaches do not seem to be considered. Perhaps this is due to well-established traditional attitudes in computer vision which has tended to see the imitation of human capabilities as an ultimate goal, as well as constraints from applications.

Using photo-modelling to capture detail has some problems. One is that the information we obtain may contain light source and view-dependent phenomena such as shadows and specular reflections. These would have to be removed before the imagery could be used generate the simulated environment from any view point. Another problem of significance is that we may need to warp detail in a photograph to fit the geometric model. This may involve expanding a very small area of an image. Consider, for example, a photograph – taken from the ground – of high building with a detailed facade. Important detail information near the top of the building may be mapped into a small area due to the projective distortion. In fact, this problem is identical to view interpolation.

Let us now consider the use of photo-modelling without attempting to extract the geometry. We simply keep the collected images as two-dimensional projections and use these to calculate new two-dimensional projections. We never attempt to recover three-dimensional geometry of the scene (although it is necessary to consider the three-dimensional information concerning the projections). This is a form of image-based rendering and it has something of a history.

Consider a virtual walk through an art gallery or museum. The quality requirements are obvious. The user needs to experience the subtle lighting conditions designed to best view the exhibits. These must be reproduced and sufficient detail must be visible in the paintings. A standard computer graphics approach may result in using a (view-independent) radiosity solution for the rendering together with (photographic) texture maps for the paintings. The radiosity approach, where the expensive rendering calculations are performed once only to give a view-independent solution may suffice in many contexts in virtual reality, but it is not a general solution for scenes that contain complex geometrical detail. As we know, a radiosity rendered scene has to be divided up into as large elements as possible to facilitate a solution and there is always a high cost for detailed scene geometry.

This kind of application – virtual tours around buildings and the like – has already emerged with the bulk storage freedom offered by videodisk and CD-ROM. The inherent disadvantage of most approaches is that they do not offer continuous movement or walkthrough but discrete views selected by a user's position as he (interactively) navigates around the building. They are akin to an interactive catalogue and require the user to navigate in discrete steps from one position to the other as determined by the points from which the photographic images were taken. The user 'hops' from view point to view point.

An early example of a videodisk implementation is the 'Movie Map' developed in 1980 (Lippman 1980). In this early example the streets of Aspen were filmed at 10-foot intervals. To invoke a walkthrough, a viewer retrieved selected views from two videodisk players. To record the environment four cameras were used at every view point – thus enabling the viewer to pan to the left and right. The example demonstrates the trade-off implicit in this approach – because all reconstructed views are pre-stored the recording is limited to discrete view points.

An obvious computer graphics approach is to use environment maps – originally developed in rendering to enable a surrounding environment to be reflected in a shiny object (see Chapter 8). In image-based rendering we simply replace the shiny object with a virtual viewer. Consider a user positioned at a point from which a six-view (cubic) environment map has been constructed (either photographically or synthetically). If we make the approximation that the user's eyes are always positioned exactly at the environment map's view point then we can compose any view direction-dependent projection demanded by the user changing his direction of gaze by sampling the appropriate environment maps. This idea is shown schematically in Figure 16.18. Thus we have, for a stationary viewer, coincidentally positioned at the environment map view point, achieved our goal of a view-independent solution. We have decoupled the viewing direction from the rendering pipeline. Composing a new view now consists of sampling environment maps and the scene complexity problem has been bound by the resolution of the pre-computed or photographed maps.

The highest demand on an image generator used in immersive virtual reality comes from head movements (we need to compute at 60 frames per second to avoid the head latency effect) and if we can devise a method where the rendering cost is almost independent of head movement this would be a great step forward. However, the environment map suggestion only works for a stationary viewer. We would need a set of maps for each position that the viewer could be in. Can we extend the environment map approach to cope with complete walkthroughs? Using the constraint that in a walkthrough the eyes of the user are always at a constant height, we could construct a number of environment maps

Figure 16.18
Compositing a user
projection from an
environment map.

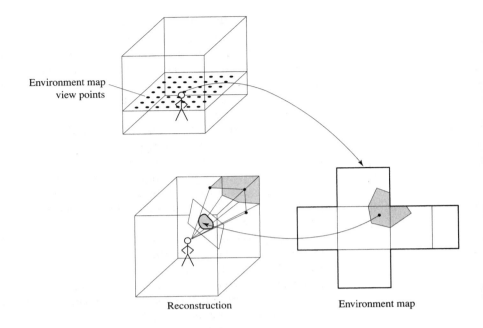

Environment map
view points

Reconstruction

Environment map

whose view points were situated at the lattice points of a coarse grid in a plane, parallel to the ground plane and positioned at eye height. For any user position could we compose, to some degree of accuracy, a user projection by using information from the environment maps at the four adjacent lattice points? The quality of the final projections are going to depend on the resolution of the maps and the number of maps taken in a room – the resolution of the eye plane lattice. The map resolution will determine the detailed quality of the projection and the number of maps its geometric accuracy.

To be able to emulate the flexibility of using a traditional graphics pipeline approach, by using photographs (or pre-rendered environment maps), we either have to use a brute-force approach and collect sufficient views compatible with the required 'resolution' of our walkthrough, or we have to try to obtain new views from the existing ones.

Currently, viewing from cylindrical panoramas is being established as a popular facility on PC-based equipment (see Section 16.5.1). This involves collecting the component images by moving a camera in a semi-constrained manner – rotating it in a horizontal plane. The computer is used merely to 'stitch' the component images into a continuous panorama – no attempt is made to recover depth information.

This system can be seen as the beginning of development that may eventually result in being able to capture all the information in a scene by walking around with a video camera resulting in a three-dimensional photograph of the scene. We could see such a development as merging the separate stages of modelling and rendering, there is now no distinction between them. The virtual viewer can then be immersed in a photographic-quality environment and have the freedom to move around in it without having his movement restricted to the excursions of the camera.

Image-based rendering using photographic panoramas

Developed in 1994, Apple's QuickTime® VR is a classic example of using a photographic panorama as a pre-stored virtual environment. A cylindrical panorama is chosen for this system because it does not require any special equipment beyond a standard camera and a tripod with some accessories. As for re-projection – a cylindrical map has the advantage that it only curves in one direction thus making the necessary warping to produce the desired planar projection fast. The basic disadvantage of the cylindrical map – the restricted vertical field of view – can be overcome by using an alternative cubic or spherical map but both of these involve a more difficult photographic collection process and the sphere is more difficult to warp. The inherent viewing disadvantage of the cylinder depends on the application. For example, in architectural visualization it may be a serious drawback.

Figure 16.19 (Colour Plate) is an illustration of the system. A user takes a series of normal photographs, using a camera rotating on a tripod, which are then 'stitched' together to form a cylindrical panoramic image. A viewer positions himself at the view point and looks at a portion of the cylindrical surface. The re-projection of selected part of the cylinder onto a (planar) view surface involves a simple image warping operation which, in conjunction with other speed-up strategies, operates in real time on a standard PC. A viewer can continuously pan in the horizontal direction and the vertical direction to within the vertical field of view limit.

Currently restricted to monocular imagery, it is interesting to note that one of the most lauded aspects of virtual reality – three-dimensionality and immersion – has been for the moment ignored. It may be that in the immediate future monocular non-immersive imagery, which does not require expensive stereo viewing facilities and which concentrates on reproducing a visually complex environment, will predominate in the popularization of virtual reality facilities.

Compositing panoramas

Compositing environment maps with synthetic imagery is straightforward. For example, to construct a cylindrical panorama we map view space coordinates (x, y, z) onto a cylindrical viewing surface (θ, h) as:

$$\theta = \tan^{-1}(x/z) \qquad h = y/(x^2 + z^2)^{1/2}$$

Constructing a cylindrical panorama from photographs involves a number of practical points. Instead of having three-dimensional coordinates we now have photographs. The above equations can still be used substituting the focal length of the lens for z and calculating x and y from the coordinates in the photograph plane and the lens parameters. This is equivalent to considering the scene as a picture of itself – all objects in the scene are considered to be at the same depth.

Another inherent advantage of a cylindrical panorama is that after the overlapping planar photographs are mapped into cylindrical coordinates (just as if we had a cylindrical film plane in the camera) the construction of the complete panorama can be achieved by translation only – implying that it is straightforward to automate the process. The separate images are moved over one another until a match is achieved – a process sometimes called 'stitching'. As well as translating the component images, the photographs may have to be processed to correct for exposure differences that would otherwise leave a visible vertical boundary in the panorama.

The overall process can now be seen as a warping of the scene onto a cylindrical viewing surface followed by the inverse warping to re-obtain a planar projection from the panorama. From the user's point of view the cylinder enables both an easy image collection model and a natural model for viewing in the sense that we normally view an environment from a fixed height – eye level – look around and up and down.

16.6.3 Photo-modelling for image-based rendering

In one of the first comprehensive studies of photo-modelling for image-based rendering, Debevec *et al.* (1996) describe an approach with a number of interesting and potentially important features. Their basic approach is to derive sufficient information from sparse views of a scene to facilitate image-based rendering (although the derived model can also be used in a conventional rendering system). The emphasis of their work is architectural scenes and is based on three innovations:

(1) **Photogrammetric modelling** in which they recover a three-dimensional geometric model of a building based on simple volumetric primitives together with the camera view points from a set of sparse views.

(2) **View-dependent texture mapping** which is used to render the recovered model.

(3) **Model-based stereo** which is used to solve the correspondence problem (and thus enable view interpolation) and the recovery of detail not modelled in (1).

Debevec *et al.* (1996) state that their approach is successful because:

it splits the task of modelling from images into tasks that are easily accomplished by a person (but not by a computer algorithm), and tasks which are easily performed by a computer algorithm (but not by a person).

The photogrammetric modelling process involves the user viewing a set of photographs of a building and associating a set of volumetric primitives with the photographic views to define an approximate geometric model. This is done by invoking a component of the model, such as a rectangular solid and interactively associating edges in the model with edges in the scene. In this way a box, say, can be fitted semi-automatically to a view or views that contain a box as a structural element. This manual intervention enables a complete geometric model to be derived from the photographs even though only parts of the model may be visible in the scene. The accuracy of the geometric model – that is the difference between the model and the reality – depends on how much detail the user invokes, the nature of the volumetric primitives and the nature of the scene. The idea is to obtain a geometric model that reflects the structure of the building and which can be used in subsequent processing to derive camera positions and facilitate a correspondence algorithm. Thus a modern tower block may be represented by a single box, and depth variations, which occur over a face due to windows that are contained in a plane parallel to the wall plane, are at this stage of the process ignored.

Once a complete geometric model has been defined, a reconstruction algorithm is invoked, for each photographic view. The purpose of this process is to recover the camera view points, which is necessary for view interpolation, together with the world coordinates of the model, which are necessary if the model is going to be used in a conventional rendering system. This is done by projecting the geometric model, using a hypothesized view point, onto the photographic views and comparing the position of the image edges with the position of the projected model edges. The algorithm works by minimizing an objective function which operates on the error between observed image edges and the projected model edges. Correspondence between model edges and image edges having already been established, the algorithm has to proceed towards the solution without getting stuck at a local minimum.

These two processes – photogrammetric modelling and reconstruction – extract sufficient information to enable a conventional rendering process that Debevec calls 'view-dependent texture mapping'. Here a new view of a building is generated by projecting the geometric model from the required view point, treating the reference views as texture maps and reprojecting these from the new view point onto the geometric model. The implication here is that the building is 'oversampled' and any one point will appear in two or more photographic views. Thus when a new or virtual view is generated there will, for each pixel in the new view, be a choice of texture maps with (perhaps) different values for the same point on the building due to specularities and unmodelled geometric detail. This problem is approached by mixing the contributions in inverse proportion to the angles that the new view makes with the reference view directions as shown in Figure 16.20. Hence the term 'view-dependent texture mapping' – the contributions are selected and mixed according to the position of the virtual view point with respect to the reference views.

The accuracy of this rendering is limited to the detail captured by the geometric model and there is a difference between the real geometry and that of the

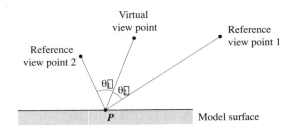

model. The extent of this difference depends on the labour that the user has put into the interactive modelling phase and the assumption is that the geometric model will be missing such detail as window recesses and so on. For example, a facade modelled as a plane may receive a texture that contains such depth information as shading differences and this can lead to images that do not look correct. The extent of this depends on the difference between the required viewing angle and the angle of the view from which the texture map was selected. Debevec *et al.* (1996) go on to extend their method by using the geometric model to facilitate a correspondence algorithm that enables a depth map to be calculated and the geometric detail missing from the original model to be extracted. Establishing correspondence also enables view interpolation.

This process is called 'model-based' stereo and it uses the geometric model as *a priori* information which enables the algorithm to cope with views that have been taken from relatively far apart – one of the practical motivations of the work is that it operates with a sparse set of views. (The main problem with traditional stereo correspondence algorithms is that they try to operate without prior knowledge of scene structure. Here the extent of the correspondence problem predominantly depends on how close the two views are to each other.)

Computer animation

Computer animation is a huge subject and deserves a complete textbook in its own right. This chapter concentrates on foundation topics that have become established in the field and serves as an introduction to the subject, rather than comprehensive coverage. The aim of the material is to give the reader a good grounding in the concepts on which most modern systems are based.

Introduction

Leaving aside some toys of the nineteenth century, it is interesting to consider that we have only had the ability to create and disseminate moving imagery for a very short period – since the advent of film. In this time it seems that animation has not developed as a mainstream art form. Outside the world of Disney and his imitators there is little film animation that reaches the eyes of the common man. It is curious that we do not seem to be interested in art that represents movement and mostly consign animation to the world of children's entertainment. Perhaps we can thank Disney for raising film animation to an art form and at the same time condemning it to a strange world of cute animals who are imbued with a set of human emotions.

With the advent of computer animation, will this situation change? Perhaps it is too early to say. Computer animation has for many years been locked into its own 'artistic' domain and its most common manifestations are for TV title sequences and TV commercials. These productions, known derisively as 'flying logos' move rigid bodies around in three-dimensional space and have been the mainstream form of computer animation for around two decades. Their novelty having palled a long time ago, the productions exhibit a strange ambivalence: the characters have to retain their traditional function and at the same time have an 'animation personality'.

Computer animation is becoming increasingly used in the cinema, more, however, as a special effects tool than as a medium in its own right. (And indeed one of the most ubiquitous tools used by recent productions – morphing – is strictly not computer animation at all, but the two-dimensional pixel-by-pixel post-processing of filmed imagery.) The late 1990s, have seen the emergence of full-length computer animation productions, but it is still too early to judge whether this medium will develop and endure.

At first there was much optimism for computer animation. In a 1971 edition of the classic *The Techniques of Film Animation* (Hallas and Manvell 1971) the authors commenting on early scientific computer animation state:

The position at present is that the scientist and the animator can now create drawings that move in three or four dimensions, drawings that can rotate in space, and drawings involving great mathematical precision representing a complex mathematical factor or scientific principle. The process takes a fraction of the time for a production of a conventional cartoon, a condition every animator has wished for ever since the invention of cinematography. What may now be needed is an artist of Klee's talent who could invent a new convention for creating shapes and forms. The tools are there and the next ten years will surely lead to the development of exciting visual discoveries.

In fact, the next 20 years saw little development of computer animation beyond its utilitarian aspects, but perhaps in the 1990s we are beginning to see evidence of this early prediction.

What can computer animation offer to an animation artist? Two major tools certainly. First, the substantial shortening of routine workload over conventional cel animation. Second, the ability to make three-dimensional animation which means that we can 'film' the movement and interaction of three-dimensional objects. Film animation has been firmly locked into two-dimensional space with most effort being spent on movement and characterization with only a nod here and there to three-dimensional considerations such as shading and shadows. It would seem that animators still want to use manual techniques in the main, and indeed some of the most popular commercial productions in the 1990s have used stop-motion animation of characters made from modelling clay.

Leaving aside the issue of art, the main practical problem that is central to all computer animation is motion specification or control. Beyond the obvious labour involved in building complex models of objects or characters that are going to make up a computer animation (which are the same problems faced by static rendering), there is the scripting or control of realistic movement, which is after all the basis of the art of animation. This becomes more and more difficult as models become more and more complex. Animating a single rigid body that possesses a single reference point is reasonably straightforward; animating a complex object such as an animal which may have many parts moving, albeit in a constrained manner, relative to each other, is extremely difficult. Certainly at the moment the most complex computer animations are being produced in Hollywood and to highlight the difficult problem of movement control we will start the chapter by examining a contemporary example.

Steven Speilberg's film *Jurassic Park* is reckoned to be the most life-like computer animation accomplished to date. It has an interesting history, and recognizing that it is a pinnacle of achievement in realistic animation we will look briefly at the techniques that were used to produce it (in Section 17.3). The role of computer animation in this case was to bring to life creatures that could not be filmed and the goal was 'realism'. This, however, is not the only way in which computer animation is being used in films. In the Disney production *The Lion King* (1994), computer animation is used to imitate Disney-type animation, to give the same look and feel as the traditional animation so that it can mix seamlessly with traditional cel animation. In this production a stampede sequence was produced using techniques similar to those described in Sections 17.7 and 17.8. The sequence was perhaps more complex, in terms of the number of animal characters used and their interaction, than could have been produced manually; and this was the motivation for using computer techniques.

For *Jurassic Park*, Speilberg originally hired a stop-motion (puppet or model) animation expert to bring the creatures to life using this highly developed art form. The only computer involvement was to be the post-processing of the stop-motion animation (with motion blur) to make the sequences smoother and more realistic. This task was to be undertaken by Industrial Light and Magic (ILM) – a company already very experienced both in the use of 'traditional' special effects and the use of digital techniques such as morphing. However, at the same time ILM developed a Tyrannosaurus Rex test sequence using just computer animation techniques and when Speilberg was shown this sequence, so the story goes, he immediately decided that all the animation should be produced by ILM's computers. *Jurassic Park* is viewed as a turning point in the film industry and many people see this film as finally establishing computer graphics as the preferred tool in the special effects industry and as a technique (given the commercial success of *Jurassic Park*) that Hollywood will make much of in the years to come.

The advance in realism that emerged from this animation was the convincing movements of the characters. Although great attention was paid to modelling and detail such as the skin texture, it is in the end the motion that impresses. The realism of the motion was almost certainly due to the unique system for scripting the movements of the model. Although the computer techniques gave much freedom over stop-motion puppet animation, where the global movements of the model are restricted by the mechanical fact that it is attached to a support rig, it is the marriage of effective scripting with the visual realism of the model that produced a film that will, perhaps, be perceived in the future as *King Kong* is now.

A categorization and description of computer animation techniques

Computer animation techniques can be categorized by a somewhat unhappy mix of the type and nature of the objects that are going to be animated and the programming technique used to achieve the animation. We have chosen to describe the following types of computer animation:

- Rigid body animation.
- Articulated structure animation.
- Dynamic simulation.
- Particle animation.
- Behavioural animation.

These categories are not meant to be a complete set of computer animation techniques; for example, we have excluded the much studied area of soft body or deformable object animation. Techniques that have been used are as wide and varied as the animation productions – we have chosen these particular five because they seem to have become reasonably well established over the relatively short history of computer animation. Some animation may, of course, be produced using a mixture of the above techniques.

Rigid body animation is self-explanatory and is the easiest and most ubiquitous form. In its simplest form it means using a standard renderer and moving objects and/or the view point around.

Articulated structures are computer graphics models that simulate quadrupeds and bipeds. Such models can range from simple stick figures up to attempts that simulate animals and human beings complete with a skin and/or clothes surface representation. The difficulty of scripting the motion of articulated structures is a function of the complexity of the object and the complexity of the required movements. Usually we are interested in very complex articulated structures, humans or animals, and this implies, as we shall see, that motion control is difficult.

Dynamic simulation means using physical laws to simulate the motion. The motivation here is that these laws should produce more realistic motion than that which can be achieved manually. The disadvantage of dynamic simulation is that it tends to remove artistic control from the animator.

Particle animation means individually animating large populations of particles to simulate some phenomenon viewed as the overall movement of the particle 'cloud' such as a fireworks display. Particles, as the name implies, are small bodies each of which normally has its own animation script.

Behavioural animation means modelling the behaviour of objects. What we mean by 'behaviour' is something more complex than basic movement, and may depend on certain behavioural rules which are a function of object attributes and the evolving spatial relationship of an object to neighbouring objects. Behavioural animation is like particle animation with the important extension that particle scripts are not independent. A collection of entities in behavioural animation evolve according to the behaviour of neighbours in the population. The stampeding animals in *The Lion King*, for example, moved individually and also according to their position in the stampeding herd. Another example is the way in which birds move in a flock and fishes move in a shoal. Each individual entity has both autocratic movement and also movement influenced by its continually changing spatial relationship with other entities in the scene. The goal of the behavioural rules in this context is to have a convincing depiction of the herd as an entity.

17.2 Rigid body animation

Rigid body animation is the oldest and most familiar form of computer animation. Its most common manifestation is the ubiquitous 'flying logo' on our TV screens and it appears to have established itself as a mandatory technique for titles at the beginning of TV programmes. Rigid body animation could be described as the fundamental animation requirement and is likely to be used in some form by all of the other categories. It is the simplest form of computer animation to implement and is the most widely used. It is mainly used by people who do not have a formal computer or programming background, consequently the interface issue is critically important. This type of animation was an obvious extension of programs that could render three-dimensional scenes. We can produce animated sequences by rendering a scene with an object in different positions, or by moving the view point (the virtual camera) around, recording the resulting single frames on video tape or film.

The problem is: how do we specify and control the movement of objects in a scene. Either the objects can move, or the virtual camera can move or we can make both move at the same time. We will describe how to move a single object but the technique extends in an obvious way to the other cases.

There are two established approaches to 'routine' rigid body animation – keyframing or interpolation systems and explicit scripting systems.

17.2.1 Interpolation or keyframing

Keyframing systems are based on a well-known production technique in film or cel animation. To cope with the prodigious workload in developing an animation sequence of any length, animation companies developed a hierarchical system wherein talented animators specify a sequence by drawing keyframes at certain intervals. These are passed to 'inbetweeners' who draw the intermediate frames which are then coloured by 'inkers'. (This hierarchy was reflected in the rewards received by the members of the team. In Disney's *Snow White and the Seven Dwarfs* the four chief animators were paid $100 a week, the inbetweeners $35 and the inkers $20.)

It was natural that this process be extended to three-dimensional computer animation – the spatial juxtaposition of objects in a scene can be defined by keyframes and the computer can interpolate the inbetween frames. However, many problems arise and these are mainly due to the fact that simple interpolation strategies cannot replace the intelligence of a human inbetweeners. In general, we need to specify more keyframes in a computer system than would be required in traditional animation.

Consider the simple problem of a bouncing ball. If we use three key frames – the start position, the end position and the zenith together with linear interpolation, then the resulting trajectory will be unrealistic (Figure 17.1). Linear interpolation is generally inadequate in most contexts.

We can improve on this by allowing the animator to specify more information about the motion characteristics between the key frames. For example, a curved path could be defined. This, however, would say nothing about how the velocity varied along the path. A ball moving with uniform velocity along, say, a parabola would again look unrealistic. Thus to control motion correctly when we are moving objects around we must explicitly define both the positional variation as a function of time and the dynamic behaviour along the specified path.

We can give such information in a number of ways. We could, for example, work with a set of points – key frame points – defining where an object is to be at certain points in time and fit a cubic, say, through these points.

If we use B-splines for the interpolation – as described in Section 3.6.3 – then the key positions become knot points. Generally, we require a curve that is C^2 continuous to simulate the motion of a rigid body. If we restrict ourselves to considering position then we emplace an object as a function of time in the scene using a 4×4 modelling transformation M of the form:

$$M(t) = \begin{bmatrix} 0 & 0 & 0 & t_x(t) \\ 0 & 0 & 0 & t_y(t) \\ 0 & 0 & 0 & t_z(t) \\ 0 & 0 & 0 & 1 \end{bmatrix}$$

Figure 17.1
Linear interpolation will produce an unrealistic trajectory for a bouncing ball specified at three key positions.

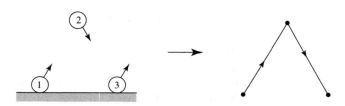

Newton's law gives us that:

$$\frac{\boldsymbol{F}}{m} = \boldsymbol{a} = \frac{d^2\boldsymbol{M}(t)}{dt^2}$$

Thus, to imitate the effect of a moving object in space – to make the motion look 'natural' – the elements of the transformation matrix must have continuous second derivatives. So it seems that interpolation from keys is straightforward, and indeed it is for simple cases. However, there are a number of problems. Usually we want to animate an object that exhibits a some rotation as it translates along a path. We cannot apply the same interpolation scheme to:

$$\boldsymbol{M}(t) = \begin{bmatrix} a_{11}(t) & a_{12}(t) & a_{13}(t) & t_x(t) \\ a_{21}(t) & a_{22}(t) & a_{23}(t) & t_y(t) \\ a_{31}(t) & a_{32}(t) & a_{33}(t) & t_z(t) \\ 0 & 0 & 0 & 1 \end{bmatrix}$$

because the matrix elements $a_{11}, \ldots, a_{33}$ are not independent. We do not want the body to change shape and so the sub-matrix $\boldsymbol{A}$ must remain orthonormal at all times – the column vectors must be unit vectors and form a perpendicular triple. Thus, positional elements can be interpolated independently but rotational elements cannot. If we attempt to linearly interpolate between nine pairs of elements $a_{11}, \ldots, a_{33}$ then the in-between matrices $\boldsymbol{A}_i$ will not be orthonormal and the object will change shape. (The subject of interpolation of rotation is dealt with separately in Section 17.2.3.)

Another problem arises from the fact that the kinematics of the motion (the velocity and acceleration) of the body and the geometry of the path are specified by the same entity – the transformation matrix $\boldsymbol{M}(t)$. In general an animator will require control so that that the kinematics of the body along the path can be modified.

Yet another problem emerges from the specifics of the interpolation scheme. It may be that the nature of the path between keys is not what the animator requires, in particular depending on the number of keys specified, unwanted excursion may occur. Also, there is the problem of the locality of influence of the keys which are the knot points in the B-spline curve. It may be that the animator requires to change the path in a way that is not possible by changing the position of a single key and requires the insertion of new keys. These disadvantages suggest an alternative approach where the animator explicitly specifies the curves for path and motion along a path rather than presenting a set of keys to an interpolation scheme whose behaviour is 'mysterious'.

(17.2.2)   ## Explicit scripting

We are thus led the idea of an explicit script and some kind of interface that enables a person to write the script. The best approach is to use a graphical interface. This will suffer from the usual problem of trying to perceive the threedimesionality of a scene or scene representation from a two-dimensional projection, but if we can produce the sequences, or a wireframe version of the finished sequence, in real time then this difficulty is ameliorated.

An obvious idea is to use cubic parametric curves as a script form (Chapter 3). Such a curve can be used as a path over which the reference point or origin of the object is to move. These can be easily edited and stored for possible future use. The best approach, called the double interpolant method, is to use two curves, one for the path of the object through space and one for its motion characteristic along the path. Then a developer can alter one characteristic independently of the other.

An interface possibility is shown in Figure 17.2. The path characteristic is visualized and altered in three windows that are the projections of the curve in the xy, yz and xz planes. The path itself can be shown embedded in the scene with three-dimensional interpretative clues coming from the position of other objects in the scene and vertical lines drawn from the curve to the xy plane. The animator sets up the path curve $Q(u)$, applies a velocity curve $V(u)$ and views the resulting animation, editing either or both characteristics if necessary.

Generating the animation from these characteristics means deriving the position of the object at equal intervals in time along the path characteristic. This is shown in principle in Figure 17.3. The steps are:

(1) For a frame at time t find the distance s corresponding to the frame time t from $V(u)$.

(2) Measure s units along the path characteristic $Q(u)$ to find the corresponding value for u.

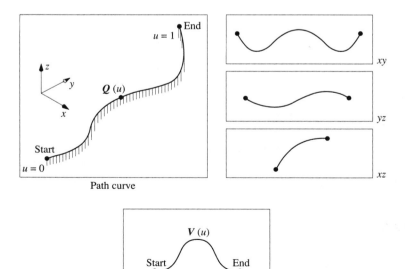

Figure 17.2
Motion specification for rigid body animation – an interface specification.

Figure 17.3
Finding the object position
(x, y, z) at time t.

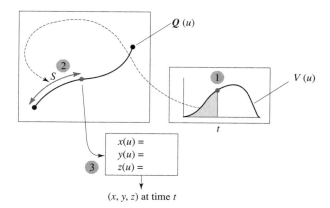

(x, y, z) at time t

(3) Substitute this value of u into the equations for $\mathbf{Q}(u)$ to find the position of the object (x, y, z).

(4) Render the object in this position.

This simple process hides a subsidiary problem called reparametrization. $\mathbf{V}$ is parametrized in terms of u, that is:

$$\mathbf{V}(u) = (t, s)$$

where $t = T(u)$ and $s = S(u)$

Given the frame time t_f we have to find the value of u such that $t_f = T(u)$. We then substitute this value of u into $s = S(u)$ and 'plot' this distance on the path characteristic $\mathbf{Q}(u)$. Here we have exactly the same problem. The path characteristic is parametrized in terms of u not s. The significance of this problem is demonstrated graphically in Figure 17.4 which compares equal (arclength) intervals with equal intervals in the curve parameter.

The general problem of reparametrization in both cases involves inverting the two equations:

$$u = T^{-1}(t) \quad \text{and} \quad u = \mathbf{Q}^{-1}(s)$$

An approximate method that given t or s finds a close value of u, is accumulated chord length. Shown in principle in Figure 17.5 the algorithm is:

(1) Construct a table of accumulated chord lengths by taking some small interval in u and calculating the distances $l_1, l_2, l_3, \ldots$ and inserting in the table $l_1, (l_1+l_2), (l_1+l_2+l_3), \ldots$ the accumulated lengths.

(2) To find the value of u corresponding to s, say, to within the accuracy of this method, we take the nearest entry in the table to s.

This simple approach does not address many of the requirements of a practical system, but it is a good basic method from which context-dependent enhancements can be grown. In particular it can form the basis for both a scripting system and an interactive interface. We briefly describe some of the more important omissions.

Figure 17.4
Intervals of equal parametric length (outline arrowheads) do not correspond to equal intervals of arclength (black arrowheads)

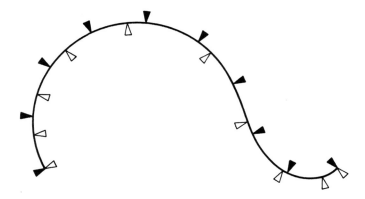

The first is that if we freely change $\boldsymbol{V}(u)$, then the total time taken for the object to travel along the curve will in general change. We may, for example, make the object accelerate more quickly from rest shortening the time taken to travel along the path. Many animations, however, have to fit into an exact time slot and a more normal situation would involve changing $\boldsymbol{V}(u)$ under the constraint that the travel time remains fixed.

Another more obvious problem is: what attitude does the object take as it moves along a path? The method as it stands is only suitable for single particles or, equivalently, a single reference point in an object which would just translate 'upright' along the path. Usually we want the object to rotate as it translates. Simplistically we can introduce another three script curves to represent the attitude of the object as it moves along the path. The easiest way to do this is to parametrize the rotation by using three angles specifying the rotation about each of three coordinate axes rigidly attached to the object. These are known as Euler angles and are called roll, pitch and yaw.

If we are producing an animation with many objects moving in the scene and if these objects are animated, one at a time, independently, then what do we do about collisions? If we use a standard rendering pipeline (with a Z-buffer) then colliding objects will simply move through each other, unless we explicitly detect this event and signal it through the design interface. Collision detection is a distinctly non-trivial problem. Objects that we normally want to deal with in computer animation can be extremely complex – their spatial extent specified by a geometric description that in most cases will not be amenable to collision

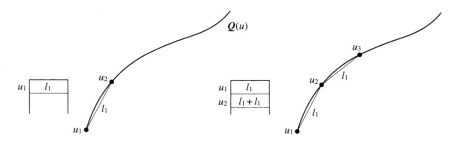

Figure 17.5
Accumulated chord-length approximation.

detection. Consider two polygon mesh objects that each contain a large number of polygons. It is not obvious how to detect the situation that a vertex from one object has moved inside the space of another. A straightforward approach would involve a comparison between each vertex in one object against every polygon in the other – an extremely time consuming problem. And the detection of a collision is only part of the problem; how do we model the reaction of objects, their deformation and movement after a collision? (Collision detection is described in more detail in Section 17.5.)

(17.2.3)

Interpolation of rotation

In rigid body animation we usually want to be able to deal with both translation and rotation. An object moves through space and changes its orientation in the process. To do this we need to parametrize rotation. (We distinguish between rotation and orientation as: orientation is specified by a normal vector embedded in an object; rotation is specified by an axis and an angle.) The traditional method is to use Euler angles where rotation is represented by using angles with respect to three mutually perpendicular axes. In many engineering applications – aeronautics, for example – these are known as roll, pitch and yaw angles. We can thus write down a rotation as:

$R(\theta_1, \theta_2, \theta_3)$

Euler angles are implemented by using a transformation matrix – one matrix for each Euler angle – as introduced in Chapter 1. A general rotation is thus effected by the product of the three matrices. As we saw in Chapter 1, to effect a rotation we specify three rotation matrices noting that rotation matrices are not commutative and the nature of the rotation depends on the order in which they are applied. However, leaving that problem aside we will now see that more significant difficulties for an animator occur if rotation is parametrized in this way.

We now consider a simple example. Figure 17.6 shows a letter **R** moving from an initial to a final position. In both cases the start and final positions are the same but the path between these is substantially different. In the first case a single rotation about the x axis of 180° has been applied. In the second case two rotations of 180°, about the y and z axes are applied simultaneously. The single rotation results in the character moving in a two-dimensional plane without 'twisting' while in the latter case the character follows a completely different path through space twisting about an axis through the character as it translates. What are we to conclude from this? There are two important implications. If an animator requires a certain path from one position and orientation to another then, in general, all three Euler angles must be controlled in a manner that will give the desired effect. Return to Figure 17.6. The examples here were generated by the following two sequences:

$R(0, 0, 0), \ldots, R(\pi t, 0, 0), \ldots, R(\pi, 0, 0)$ \qquad $t \in [0, 1]$

for the first route, and

Figure 17.6
Euler angle parametrization.
(a) A single *x*-roll of π.
(b) A *y*-roll of π followed by
a *z*-roll of π.

$$R(0, 0, 0), \ldots, R(0, \pi t, \pi t), \ldots, R(0, \pi, \pi)$$

for the second route. Examining in particular the second case we could conclude that it would be practically unworkable to expect an animator to translate an idea involving an object twisting through space into a particular movement specified by Euler angles.

The same consideration applies to interpolation: if an animator specifies keys, how is the interpolation to proceed? In fact there exists an infinity of ways of getting from one key to another in the parameter space of Euler angles. Clearly there is a need for an understood rotation from one key to the other. This single rotation may not be what the animator desires, but it is better than the alternative situation where no unique rotation is available.

Euler's theorem tells us that it is possible to get from one orientation to another by a single steady rotation. In particular it states that for two orientations O and O' there exists an axis l and an angle θ such that O undergoes rotation to O' when rotated θ about l. And we can interpret Figure 17.6 in the light of this – the first example being the single-axis rotation that takes us from the start to the stop position. But that was a special case and easy to visualize; in general for two orientations O and O' how do we find or specify this motion? This problem is solved by using quaternions.

There is another potentially important consideration in the above interpolation scheme of Euler angles. We separated motion and path in the explicitly scripted animation method because we considered that an animator would, in general, require control of the motion an object exhibited along a path separate to the specification of the path in space. The same consideration is likely to apply in specifying rotation – it may be that the motion (angular velocity) that results from linearly interpolating Euler angles is not what the animator requires.

17.2.4

Using quaternions to represent rotation

A useful introductory notion concerning quaternions is to consider them as an operator, like a matrix, that changes one vector into another, but where the infinite choice of matrix elements is removed. Instead of specifying the nine elements of a rotation matrix we define four real numbers. We begin by looking at angular displacement of a vector, rotating a vector by θ about an axis $\boldsymbol{n}$.

We define rotation as an angular displacement given by $(\theta, \boldsymbol{n})$ of an amount θ about an axis $\boldsymbol{n}$. That is, instead of specifying rotation as $R(\theta_1, \theta_2, \theta_3)$ we write $R(\theta, \boldsymbol{n})$. Consider the angular displacement acting on a vector $\boldsymbol{r}$ taking it to position $R\boldsymbol{r}$ as shown in Figure 17.7.

The problem can be decomposed by resolving $\boldsymbol{r}$ into components parallel to $\boldsymbol{n}$, $\boldsymbol{r}_{\parallel}$, which by definition remains unchanged after rotation, and perpendicular to $\boldsymbol{n}$, $\boldsymbol{r}_{\perp}$ in the plane passing through $\boldsymbol{r}$ and $R\boldsymbol{r}$.

$$\boldsymbol{r}_{\parallel} = (\boldsymbol{n} \cdot \boldsymbol{r})\boldsymbol{n}$$

$$\boldsymbol{r}_{\perp} = \boldsymbol{r} - (\boldsymbol{n} \cdot \boldsymbol{r})\boldsymbol{n}$$

$\boldsymbol{r}_{\perp}$ is rotated into position $R\boldsymbol{r}_{\perp}$. We construct a vector perpendicular to $\boldsymbol{r}_{\perp}$ and lying in the plane orthogonal to $\boldsymbol{n}$. In order to evaluate this rotation, we write:

$$\boldsymbol{V} = \boldsymbol{n} \times \boldsymbol{r}_{\perp} = \boldsymbol{n} \times \boldsymbol{r}$$

where × specifies the cross-product. So:

$$R\boldsymbol{r}_{\perp} = (\cos \theta)\,\boldsymbol{r}_{\perp} + (\sin \theta)\boldsymbol{V}$$

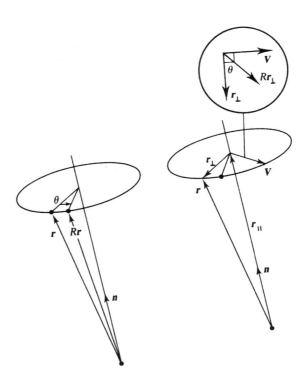

Figure 17.7
Angular displacement $(\theta, \boldsymbol{n})$ of $\boldsymbol{r}$.

hence:

$$\begin{aligned}
R\mathbf{r} &= R\mathbf{r}_\| + R\mathbf{r}_\perp \\
&= R\mathbf{r}_\| + (\cos\theta)\,\mathbf{r}_\perp + (\sin\theta)\mathbf{V} \\
&= (\mathbf{n}\cdot\mathbf{r})\mathbf{n} + \cos\theta(\mathbf{r} - (\mathbf{n}\cdot\mathbf{r})\mathbf{n}) + (\sin\theta)\mathbf{n}\times\mathbf{r} \\
&= (\cos\theta)\mathbf{r} + (1 - \cos\theta)\mathbf{n}(\mathbf{n}\cdot\mathbf{r}) + (\sin\theta)\,\mathbf{n}\times\mathbf{r}
\end{aligned}$$

[17.1]

We will now show that rotating the vector $\mathbf{r}$ by the angular displacement can be achieved by a quaternion transformation. That is, we apply a quaternion like a matrix to change a vector.

We begin by noting that to effect such an operation we only need four real numbers (this compares with the nine elements in a matrix). We require:

- The change of length of the vector.
- The plane of the rotation (which can be defined by two angles from two axes).
- The angle of the rotation.

In other words, we need a representation that only possesses the four degrees of freedom required according to Euler's theorem. For this we will use unit quaternions. As the name implies, quaternions are 'four-vectors' and can be considered as a generalization of complex numbers with s as the real or scalar part and x, y, z as the imaginary part:

$$\begin{aligned}
q &= s + x\mathbf{i} + y\mathbf{j} + z\mathbf{k} \\
&= (s, \mathbf{v})
\end{aligned}$$

Here we can note their similarity to a two-dimensional complex number that can be used to specify a point or vector in two-dimensional space. A quaternion can specify a point in four-dimensional space and, if $s = 0$, a point or vector in three-dimensional space. In this context they are used to represent a vector plus rotation. $\mathbf{i}$, $\mathbf{j}$, and $\mathbf{k}$ are unit quaternions and are equivalent to unit vectors in a vector system; however, they obey different combination rules:

$$\mathbf{i}^2 = \mathbf{j}^2 = \mathbf{k}^2 = \mathbf{ijk} = -1, \quad \mathbf{ij} = \mathbf{k}, \quad \mathbf{ji} = -\mathbf{k}$$

Using these we can derive addition and multiplication rules each of which yields a quaternion:

Addition $\qquad q + q' = (s + s', \mathbf{v} + \mathbf{v}')$

Multiplication $\quad qq' \quad = (ss' - \mathbf{v}\cdot\mathbf{v}', \mathbf{v}\times\mathbf{v}' + s\mathbf{v}' + s'\mathbf{v})$

The conjugate of the quaternion:

$$q = (s, \mathbf{v})$$

is:

$$\bar{q} = (s, -\mathbf{v})$$

and the product of the quaternion with its conjugate defines its magnitude:

$$q\bar{q} = s^2 + |\mathbf{v}^2| = q^2$$

If:

$$|q| = 1$$

then q is called a unit quaternion. The set of all unit quaternions forms a unit sphere in four-dimensional space and unit quaternions play an important part in specifying general rotations.

It can be shown that if:

$$q = (s, \boldsymbol{v})$$

then there exists a $\boldsymbol{v}'$ and a $\theta \in [-\pi, \pi]$ such that:

$$q = (\cos \theta, \boldsymbol{v}' \sin \theta)$$

and if q is a unit quaternion then:

$$q = (\cos \theta, \sin \theta \, \boldsymbol{n}) \qquad\qquad \text{[Proposition 17.1]}$$

where $|\boldsymbol{n}| = 1$.

We now consider operating on a vector $\boldsymbol{r}$ in Figure 17.7 by using quaternions. $\boldsymbol{r}$ is defined as the quaternion $p = (0, \boldsymbol{r})$ and we define the operation as:

$$R_p(p) = qpq^{-1}$$

That is, it is proposed to rotate the vector $\boldsymbol{r}$ by expressing it as a quaternion multiplying it on the left by q and on the right by q^{-1}. This guarantees that the result will be a quaternion of the form $(0, \boldsymbol{v})$, in other words a vector. q is defined to be a unit quaternion $(s, \boldsymbol{v})$. It is easily shown that:

$$R_p(p) = (0, (s^2 - \boldsymbol{v}\cdot\boldsymbol{v})\boldsymbol{r} + 2\boldsymbol{v}(\boldsymbol{v}\cdot\boldsymbol{r}) + 2s(\boldsymbol{v} \times \boldsymbol{r}))$$

Using Proposition 17.1 and substituting gives:

$$Rq(p) = (0, (\cos^2\theta - \sin^2\theta)\boldsymbol{r} + 2\sin^2\theta \, \boldsymbol{n}(\boldsymbol{n}\cdot\boldsymbol{r}) + 2\cos\theta\sin\theta \, (\boldsymbol{n} \times \boldsymbol{r}))$$
$$= (0, \boldsymbol{r}\cos2\theta + (1 - \cos2\theta) \, \boldsymbol{n}(\boldsymbol{n}\cdot\boldsymbol{r}) + \sin2\theta \, (\boldsymbol{n} \times \boldsymbol{r}))$$

Now compare this with Equation 17.1. You will notice that aside from a factor of 2 appearing in the angle they are identical in form. What can we conclude from this? The act of rotating a vector $\boldsymbol{r}$ by an angular displacement $(\theta, \boldsymbol{n})$ is the same as taking this angular displacement, 'lifting' it into quaternion space, by representing it as the unit quaternion:

$$(\cos(\theta/2), \sin(\theta/2) \, \boldsymbol{n})$$

and performing the operation $q()q^{-1}$ on the quaternion $(0, \boldsymbol{r})$. We could therefore parametrize orientation in terms of the four parameters:

$$\cos(\theta/2), \quad \sin(\theta/2) \, \boldsymbol{n}_x, \quad \sin(\theta/2) \, \boldsymbol{n}_y, \quad \sin(\theta/2) \, \boldsymbol{n}_z$$

using quaternion algebra to manipulate the components.

Let us now return to our example of Figure 17.6 to see how this works in practice. The first single x-roll of π is represented by the quaternion:

$$(\cos(\pi/2), \sin(\pi/2) \, (1, 0, 0)) = (0, (1, 0, 0))$$

Similarly a y-roll of π and a z-roll of π are given by $(0, (0, 1, 0))$ and $(0, (0, 0, 1))$ respectively. Now the effect of a y-roll of π followed by a z-roll of π can be represented by the single quaternion formed by multiplying these two quaternions together:

$$(0, (0, 1, 0)) \, (0, (0, 0, 1)) = (0, (0, 1, 0) \times (0, 0, 1))$$
$$= (0, (1, 0, 0))$$

which is identically the single x-roll of π.

We conclude this section by noting that quaternions are used exclusively to represent orientation – they can be used to represent translation but combining rotation and translation into a scheme analogous to homogeneous coordinates is not straightforward.

Interpolating quaternions

Given the superiority of quaternion parametrization over Euler angle parametrization, this section covers the issue of interpolating rotation in quaternion space. Consider an animator sitting at a workstation and interactively setting up a sequence of key orientations by whatever method is appropriate. This is usually done with the principal rotation operations, but now the restrictions that were placed on the animator when using Euler angles, namely using a fixed number of principal rotations in a fixed order for each key, can be removed. In general, each key will be represented as a single rotation matrix. This sequence of matrices will then be converted into a sequence of quaternions. Interpolation between key quaternions is performed and this produces a sequence of in-between quaternions, which are then converted back into rotation matrices. The matrices are then applied to the object. The fact that a quaternion interpolation is being used is transparent to the animator.

Moving in and out of quaternion space

The implementation of such a scheme requires us to move into and out of quaternion space, that is, to go from a general rotation matrix to a quaternion and vice versa. Now to rotate a vector $\boldsymbol{p}$ with the quaternion q we use the operation:

$$q(0, \boldsymbol{p})q^{-1}$$

where q is the quaternion:

$$(\cos(\theta/2), \sin(\theta/2)\boldsymbol{n}) = (s, (x, y, z))$$

It can be shown that this is exactly equivalent to applying the following rotation matrix to the vector:

$$M = \begin{bmatrix} 1 - 2(y^2 + z^2) & 2xy - 2sz & 2sy + 2xz & 0 \\ 2xy + 2sz & 1 - 2(x^2 + z^2) & -2sx + 2yz & 0 \\ -2sy + 2xz & 2sx + 2yz & 1 - 2(x^2 + y^2) & 0 \\ 0 & 0 & 0 & 1 \end{bmatrix}$$

By these means then, we can move from quaternion space to rotation matrices.

The inverse mapping, from a rotation matrix to a quaternion is as follows. All that is required is to convert a general rotation matrix:

$$\begin{bmatrix} M_{00} & M_{01} & M_{02} & M_{03} \\ M_{10} & M_{11} & M_{12} & M_{13} \\ M_{20} & M_{21} & M_{22} & M_{23} \\ M_{30} & M_{31} & M_{32} & M_{33} \end{bmatrix}$$

where $M_{03} = M_{13} = M_{23} = M_{30} = M_{31} = M_{32} = 0$ and $M_{33} = 1$, into the matrix format directly above. Given a general rotation matrix the first thing to do is to examine the sum of its diagonal components M_{ii} which is:

$$4 - 4(x^2 + y^2 + z^2)$$

Since the quaternion corresponding to the rotation matrix is of unit magnitude we have:

$$s^2 + x^2 + y^2 + z^2 = 1$$

and:

$$4 - 4(x^2 + y^2 + z^2) = 4 - 4(1 - s^2) = 4s^2$$

Thus, for a 4 × 4 homogeneous matrix we have:

$$s = \pm \frac{1}{2} \sqrt{M_{00} + M_{11} + M_{22} + M_{33}}$$

and:

$$x = \frac{M_{21} - M_{12}}{4s}$$

$$y = \frac{M_{02} - M_{20}}{4s}$$

$$z = \frac{M_{10} - M_{01}}{4s}$$

Spherical linear interpolation (slerp)

Having outlined our scheme we now discuss how to interpolate in quaternion space. Since a rotation maps onto a quaternion of unit magnitude, the entire group of rotations maps onto the surface of the four-dimensional unit hypersphere in quaternion space. Curves interpolating through key orientations should therefore lie on the surface of this sphere. Consider the simplest case of interpolating between just two key quaternions. A naive, straightforward linear interpolation

Figure 17.8
A two-dimensional analogy showing the difference between simple linear interpolation and simple spherical linear interpolation (slerp).

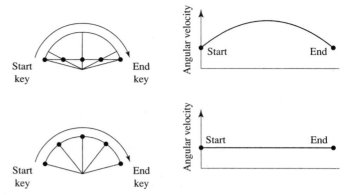

between the two keys results in a motion that speeds up in the middle. An analogy of this process in a two-dimensional plane is shown in Figure 17.8 which shows that the path on the surface of the sphere yielded by linear interpolation gives unequal angles and causes a speed-up in angular velocity.

This is because we are not moving along the surface of the hypersphere but cutting across it. In order to ensure a steady rotation we must employ spherical linear interpolation (or *slerp*), where we move along an arc of the geodesic that passes through the two keys.

The formula for spherical linear interpolation is easy to derive geometrically. Consider the two-dimensional case of two vectors A and B separated by angle Ω and vector P which makes an angle θ with A as shown in Figure 17.9. P is derived from spherical interpolation between A and B and we write:

$$P = \alpha A + \beta B$$

Trivially we can solve for α and β given:

$$|P| = 1$$
$$A \cdot B = \cos \Omega$$
$$A \cdot P = \cos \theta$$

to give:

$$P = A \, \frac{\sin (\Omega - \theta)}{\sin \Omega} + B \, \frac{\sin \theta}{\sin \Omega}$$

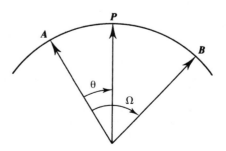

Figure 17.9
Spherical linear interpolation

Spherical linear interpolation between two unit quaternions q_1 and q_2, where:

$$q_1 \cdot q_2 = \cos \Omega$$

is obtained by generalizing the above to four dimensions and replacing θ by Ωu where $u \in [0, 1]$. We write:

$$\text{slerp } (q_1, q_2, u) = q_1 \frac{\sin (1 - u)\Omega}{\sin \Omega} + q_2 \frac{\sin \Omega u}{\sin \Omega}$$

Now given any two key quaternions, p and q, there exist two possible arcs along which one can move, corresponding to alternative starting directions on the geodesic that connects them. One of them goes around the long way and this is the one that we wish to avoid. Naively one might assume that this reduces to either spherically interpolating between p and q by the angle Ω, where:

$$p \cdot q = \cos \Omega$$

or interpolating in the opposite direction by the angle $2\pi - \Omega$. This, however, will not produce the desired effect. The reason for this is that the topology of the hypersphere of orientation is not just a straightforward extension of the three-dimensional Euclidean sphere. To appreciate this, it is sufficient to consider the fact that every rotation has two representations in quaternion space, namely q and $-q$, that is, the effect of q and $-q$ is the same. That this is so is due to the fact that algebraically the operator $q()q^{-1}$ has exactly the same effect as $(-q)()(-q)^{-1}$. Thus, points diametrically opposed represent the same rotation. Because of this topological oddity care must be taken when determining the shortest arc. A strategy that works is to choose interpolating between either the quaternion pair p and q or the pair p and $-q$. Given two key orientations p and q find the magnitude of their difference, that is $(p-q) \cdot (p-q)$, and compare this to the magnitude of the difference when the second key is negated, that is $(p+q) \cdot (p+q)$. If the former is smaller then we are already moving along the smallest arc and nothing needs to be done. If, however, the second is smallest, then we replace q by $-q$ and proceed. These considerations are shown schematically in Figure 17.10.

So far we have described the spherical equivalent of linear interpolation between two key orientations, and, just as was the case for linear interpolation, spherical linear interpolation between more than two key orientations will produce jerky, sharply changing motion across the keys. The situation is summarized in Figure 17.11 as a three-dimensional analogy which shows that the curve

Figure 17.10
Shortest arc determination
on quaternion hypersphere.

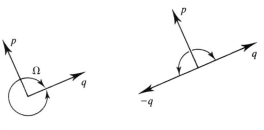

Incorrect   Correct

Figure 17.11
A three-dimensional analogy of using slerp to interpolate between four keys.

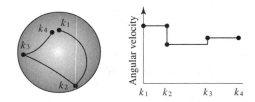

on the surface of the sphere is not continuous through the keys. Also shown in this figure is the angular velocity which is not constant and which is discontinuous at the keys. The angular velocity can be made constant across all frames by assigning to each interval between keys a number of frames proportional to the magnitude of the interval. That is, we calculate the magnitude of the angle θ between a pair of keys q_t and q_{t+1} as:

$$\cos\theta = q_i \cdot q_{i+1}$$

where the inner product of two quaternions $q = (s, \boldsymbol{v})$ and $q' = (s', \boldsymbol{v}')$ is defined as:

$$q \cdot q' = ss' + \boldsymbol{v} \cdot \boldsymbol{v}'$$

Curing the path continuity is more difficult. What is required for higher order continuity is the spherical equivalent of the cubic spline. Unfortunately because we are now working on the surface of a four-dimensional hypersphere, the problem is far more complex than constructing splines in three-dimensional Euclidean space. Duff (1986) and Shoemake (1985) have all tackled this problem.

Finally, we mention a potential difficulty when applying quaternions. Quaternion interpolation is indiscriminate in that it does not prefer any one direction to any other. Interpolating between two keys produces a move that depends on the orientations of the keys and nothing else. This is inconvenient when choreographing the virtual camera. Normally when moving a camera the film plane is always required to be upright – this is usually specified by an 'up' vector. By its very nature, the notion of a preferred direction cannot easily be built into the quaternion representation and if it is used in this context the camera-up vector may have to be reset or some other fix employed. (Roll of the camera is, of course, used in certain contexts.)

17.2.6 The camera as an animated object

Any or all of the external camera parameters can be animated but the most common type of camera animation is surely that employed in first person computer games and similar applications where a camera flies through a mostly static environment under user interface control – the so-called 'walkthrough' or 'flyby'. Here, the user is controlling the view point, and usually a (two degrees of freedom) viewing direction. Interpolation is usually required between consecutive interface samples that form the keys and the most important constraint is to keep the camera-up vector up; normally no orientation about the view direction vector is tolerated. (The only time the camera rolls about the view direction in first person games is when you die.)

Another common application is where the view point is under user control but the camera always points to an object of interest which can be static or itself moving. A common example of this is the (confusingly called) third person computer games where the camera is tied to (say) the head of the character via an 'invisible' rigid link. Instead of seeing the environment through the eyes of the character the user sees over the character's shoulder. In this case the view direction vector is derived from the character. The view point effectively moves over a part of the surface of a sphere centred on the character. If quaternion interpolation is used in this application then the up vector has to be reset after an interpolation.

⟨17.3⟩ Linked structures and hierarchical motion

Scripting of movement of quadruped or biped models in computer animation has, for some time, been an energetically pursued research topic. The computer models are known as articulated or linked structures and most approaches for movement control in animation have attempted to extend techniques developed in the industrial robotics field. Just as interpolation was the first idea to be applied to rigid body animation, parametrizing the movement of links or limbs in an articulated structure using robotic methodology seemed the way to proceed. Although this is perhaps an obvious approach it has not proved very fruitful. One problem is that robot control is itself a research area – by no means have all the problems been solved in that field. Probably a more important reason is that the techniques required to control the precise mechanical movements of an industrial robot do not make a comfortable and creative environment in which an animator can script the freer, more complex and subtler movements of a human or an animal.

Yet another reason is that animal structures are not rigid and the links themselves deform as illustrated in Figure 17.12. In fact, the most successful articulated structure animation to date, *Jurassic Park*, used an ad hoc technique to represent or to derive the motion of the links in complicated (dinosaur) models. Let us look briefly at these techniques. This will give an appreciation of the difficulty of the problem faced by the animators in *Jurassic Park* and the efficacy of their solution.

First, what is an articulated structure? It is simply a set of rigid objects, or links, connected to each other by joints which enable the various parts of the structure to move, in some way, with respect to each other. For animal animation the links form a simplified skeleton, a stick figure, and only exist to facilitate control of the structure. They are an abstraction which is not rendered. Instead, the link is 'covered' with the external surface of the animal object and

Figure 17.12
Spine flexion in a horse and a cheetah (after Gray (1968)).

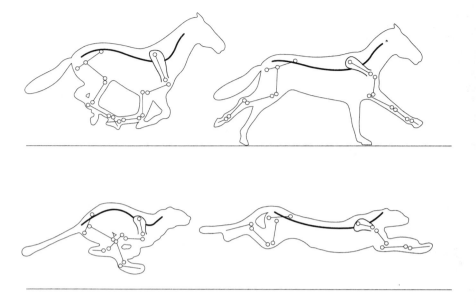

this is rendered. (This is no different in principle from a rigid object represented by a polygon mesh. Here, we are effectively controlling the position and orientation of a vector representing the object.)

Consider a simple example – a single human leg. We might model this as represented in Figure 17.13(a) using two links connecting three joints – the hip joint, the knee joint and the ankle joint. Simplistically, we could constrain movement to the plane containing the joints and allow the link between the hip and the knee to rotate, between certain limits, about the hip joint and allow the link between the ankle and the knee to rotate about the knee joint (and, of course, we know that this link can only rotate in one direction). The rotation of the foot about the ankle joint is more complicated since the foot itself is an articulated structure. Given such a structure how do we begin to specify a script for, say, the way the leg structure is to behave to execute a walk action? It is fairly obvious that the motion of the structure is constrained by the overall connectivity – the structure comprises some chain of links and one link causes its neighbour to move, and constraints that the links themselves possess, like the rotational limits in human animal skeletal joints. The practical effect of this is that we cannot easily use a key frame system because these constraints must function across all interpolated positions. Thus, a system is adopted where the links have their relative motion specified. That is, the motion of link i is specified relative to that of link j to which it is connected. Such systems are thus animated by separately animating each link. They also, by definition, must possess a hierarchy – every link has one above it, unless it is the top link, and one below it, unless it is the bottom link or end effector. A link inherits the transformations of all links above it.

Figure 17.13
A simple articulated
structure and its hierarchical
representation.

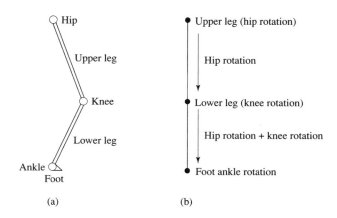

(a)   (b)

There are two major approaches to this problem both of which come out of robotics – forward kinematics and inverse kinematics.

Forward kinematics is a somewhat tedious low-level approach where the animator has to specify explicitly all the motions of every part of the articulated structure. Like any low-level approach the amount of work that has to be done by the animator is a function of the complexity of the structure. The articulated structure is considered as a hierarchy of nodes (Figure 17.13(b)) with an associated transformation which moves the link connected to the node in some way. Each node represents a body part such as an upper or lower arm. We could animate such a structure by using explicit scripting curves to specify the transformation values as a function of time. Instead of having just a single path characteristic which moves a reference point for a rigid body, we may now have many characteristics each moving one part of the structure. Consider the inheritance in this structure. The hip rotation in the example causes the lower leg as well as the upper leg to rotate. The following considerations are apparent:

● **Hip joint**   This is the 'top' joint in the structure and needs to be given global movement. In a simple walk this is just translation in a plane parallel to the ground plane. In a more realistic simulation we would have to take into account the fact that the hip rises and falls during the walk cycle due to the lifting action of the feet.

● **Hip–knee link rotation about the hip joint**   We can specify the rotation as an angular function of time. If we leave everything below this link fixed then we have a stiff-legged walk (politely known as a compass gait but possibly more familiar as the 'goose step').

● **Knee–ankle link rotation about the knee joint**   To relax the goose step into a natural walk we specify rotation about the knee joint.

And so on. To achieve the desired movement the animator starts at the top of the hierarchy and works downwards explicitly applying a script at every point. The evolution of a script is shown in Figure 17.14. Applying the top script would result in a goose step. The second script – knee rotation – allows the lower leg to

Figure 17.14
Evolution of a script for a
leg.

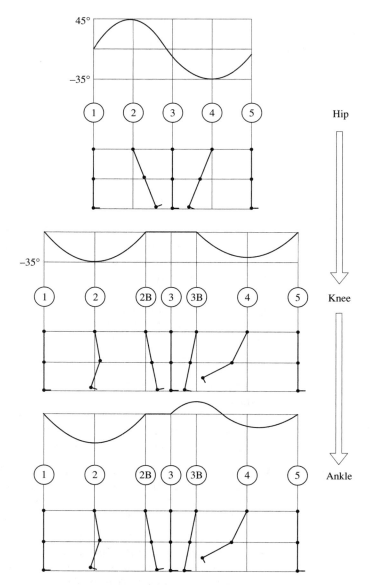

bend. Applying both these scripts would result in a walk where the foot was always at right angles to the lower leg. This leads us into the ankle script.

Even in this simple example problems begin to accrue. It is not too difficult to see that when we come to script the foot, we cannot tolerate the hip joint moving in a straight line parallel to the floor. This would cause the foot to penetrate the floor. We have to apply some vertical displacement to the hip as a function of time and so on. And we are considering a very simple example – a walk action. How do we extend this technique for a complex articulated structure that has to execute a fight sequence rather than make a repetitive walk cycle?

Inverse kinematics, on the other hand, is a more high-level approach. Here an animator might specify something like: walk slowly from point A to point B. And the inverse kinematics technique works out a precise script for all the parts of the structure so that the whole body will perform the desired action. More precisely inverse kinematics means that only the required position of the end (or ends) of the structure are specified. The animator does not indicate how each separate part of the articulated structure is to move only that the ends of it move in the desired way. The idea comes from robotics where we mostly want the end effector of a robot arm to take up precise positions and to perform certain actions. The inverse kinematics then works out the attitude that all the other joints in the structure have to take up so that the end effector is positioned as required. However, herein lurks the problem. As the articulated structure becomes more and more complex the inverse kinematics solution becomes more and more difficult to work out. Also inverse kinematics does not, generally, leave much scope for the animator to inject 'character' into the movements, which is after all the art of animation. The inverse kinematics functions as a black box into which is input the desired movement of the ends of the structure and the detailed movement of the entire structure is controlled by the inverse kinematics method. An animator makes character with movement. Forward kinematics is more flexible in this respect, but if we are dealing with a complex model there is much expense. Figure 17.15 (also a Colour Plate) shows a simple character executing a somewhat flamboyant gait that was animated using forward kinematics.

Thus, we have two 'formal' approaches to scripting an articulated structure. Inverse kinematics enables us to specify a script by listing the consecutive positions of the end points of the hierarchy – the position of the hands or feet as a function of time. But the way in which the complete structure behaves is a function of the method used to solve the inverse kinematic equations and the animator has no control over the 'global' behaviour of the structure. Alternatively, if the structure is complex it may be impossible to implement an inverse kinematics solution anyway. On the other hand, forward kinematics enables the complete structure to be explicitly scripted but at the expense of inordinate labour, except for very simple structures. Any refinements have to be made by starting at the top of the hierarchy again and working downwards.

Figure 17.15
Simple characterization using an articulated structure – the flamboyant gait was animated using forward kinematics. (See also Colour Plate version.)

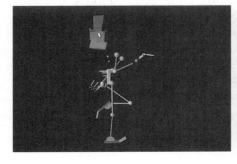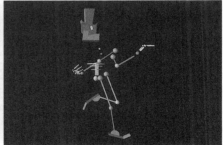

We now illustrate the distinction between forward and inverse kinematics more formally using as an example the simplest articulated structure possible – a two-link machine where one link is fixed and each link moves in the plane of the paper (Figure 17.16). In forward kinematics we explicitly specify the motion of all the joints. All the joints are linked and the motion of the end effector (hands or feet in the case of an animal figure) is determined by the accumulation of all transformations that lead to the end effector. We say that:

$$X = f(\Theta)$$

where X is the motion of the end effector and Θ is a state vector specifying the position, orientation and rotation of all joints in the system. In the case of the simple two-link mechanism we have:

$$X = (l_1 \cos \theta_1 + l_2 \cos (\theta_1 + \theta_2), l_1 \sin \theta_1 + l_2 \sin (\theta_1 + \theta_2)) \qquad [17.2]$$

but this expression is irrelevant in the sense that to control or animate such an arm using forward kinematics we would simply specify:

$$\Theta = (\theta_1, \theta_2)$$

and the model would have applied to it the two angles which would result in the movement X.

In inverse kinematics we specify the position of the end effector and the algorithm has to evaluate the required Θ given X. We have:

$$\Theta = f^{-1}(X)$$

and in our simple example we can obtain from trigonometry:

$$\theta_2 = \frac{\cos^{-1}(x^2 + y^2 - l_1^2 - l_2^2)}{2l_1l_2}$$

$$\theta_1 = \tan^{-1}\left(\frac{-(l_2 \sin \theta_2)x + (l_1 + l_2 \cos \theta_2)y}{(l_2 \sin \theta_2)y + (l_1 + l_2 \cos \theta_2)x} \right)$$

Now, as the complexity of the structure increases the inverse kinematics solution becomes more and more difficult. Quickly the situation develops where many configurations satisfy the required end effector movement. In the simple two-link mechanism, for example, it is easy to see that there are two link configurations possible for each position X, one with the inter-link joint above

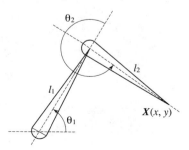

Figure 17.16
A two-link structure.

the end effector the other with it below. The attitude or state of this mechanism is specified by two angles (degrees of freedom) and we can easily foresee from this that as a structure becomes more complex it becomes increasingly difficult to derive an expression of the form $\Theta = f^{-1}(X)$. Thus, with forward kinematics the animator has to handle more and more transformations while in inverse kinematics a solution may not be possible except for reasonably simple mechanisms. A human body possesses more than 200 degrees of freedom. An inverse kinematics solution for this is practically impossible and a forward kinematics script is inordinately complicated. A way forward is to invest such models with pre-written forward kinematic scripts for common gestures such as walking, running, grasping etc. An animator then creates a script by putting together a sequence from pre-written parts.

In animating the dinosaurs in *Jurassic Park*, ILM used neither of these approaches, and in the time-honoured tradition of efficacious innovations, came up with a much simpler solution than those offered by the literature of articulated computer graphics animation. Their approach was to drive the models with a low-level forward kinematics script but they by-passed the script complexity problem by creating a script semi-automatically. They effectively enabled stop-motion animators to input their expertise directly into the computer. The stop-motion animators moved their models in the normal way and the computer sampled the motion producing a script for the computer models. ILM describe their technique in the following way:

The system is precise, fast, compact, and easy to use. It lets traditional stop-motion animators produce animation on a computer without requiring them to learn complex software. The working environment is very similar to the traditional environment but without the nuisances of lights, a camera and delicate foam-latex skin. The resulting animation lacks the artefacts of stop-motion animation, the stops and jerkiness, and yet retains the intentional subtleties and hard stops that computer animation often lacks.

The general idea is not original. For many years it has been possible to train industrial robots by having a human operator hold the robot's hand, taking it through the actions that the robot is eventually going to perform in the stead of the human operator. Spot welding and paint spraying in the car industry is a good example of the application of this technique. Movements of all the joints in the robot's articulated structure are then read from sensors and from these a script to control the robot is produced. Future invocations of the motion sequence involved in a task can then be endlessly and perfectly repeated – indeed the robot will go on reproducing the sequence perfectly even if something else has gone wrong and the car is not present.

In *Jurassic Park* robots were already available because the stop-motion animators had already built 'animatronic' models in anticipation of the film being produced by stop-motion techniques. These were then used, in reverse as it were, by the stop-motion animators, to produce a script for the computer models. Figure 17.17 shows a stop-motion animator working out the movements for the dinosaur wrestling with the car scene. The models now, instead of being clothed

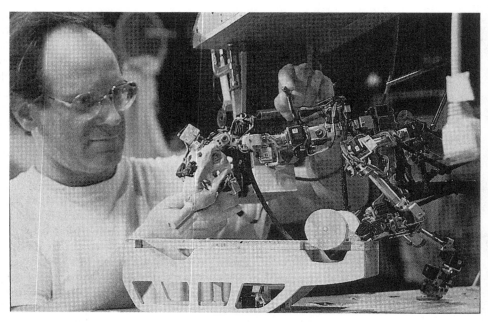

Figure 17.17
A stop-motion animator using a (real) model fitted with transducers from which a script is derived for a (virtual) computer model. (*Source*: Magid, R. 'After Jurassic Park', *American Cinematographer*, December 1993.)

and filmed one frame at a time, are turned into an input device from which a script is derived.

A similar approach, known as 'motion capture', is to use human actors from which to derive a motion script for a computer model. This involves fixing motion tracking devices to the appropriate positions of the actor's body and deriving a kinematic script in this way from the real movements of the actor. This approach is particularly popular in the video games industry which in recent years has made a transition from two-dimensional to three-dimensional animation. In this type of interactive computer animation the pre-recorded motion sequences are replayed in response to user interaction events. It is natural and economic to use motion capture in this context to record the original motion scripts for the computer models, although implicit in the approach is the limitation that the animation seen by the user can only be combinations of pre-calculated sequences.

Thus, we see from these examples that we are only at the beginning of this difficult problem of specifying motion for complex articulated structures and that many solutions to the problem have involved going outside the computer and deriving a script from the real world (reminiscent somewhat of early photographs of Disney animators who were to be seen building up facial animations by using their own image in a mirror as a guide).

(17.3.1) Solving the inverse kinematics problem

In this section we look at an important notion that forms the basis for inverse kinematics algorithms. We will deal with the topic enough to give an appreciation of the difficulties involved. A full treatment of an inverse kinematics engine is given in Watt and Watt (1992). Most approaches to this problem involve iteration towards a desired goal. That is we compute a small change $\partial\Theta$ in the joint angles that will cause the end effector to move towards the goal. This is given by:

$$d\boldsymbol{x} \,/\, d\Theta \;=\; J(\Theta)$$

J is the so-called Jacobian – a multi-dimensional extension to differentiation of a single variable. In this case it relates differential changes in Θ to those in $\boldsymbol{x}$, the position of the end effector. Note that J is a function of the current state of the structure Θ. We recall that the general problem encountered in inverse kinematics systems stems from the fact that in:

$$\Theta = f^{-1}(\boldsymbol{x})$$

the function $f()$ is non-linear and becomes more and more complex as the number of links increases. The inversion of this function soon becomes impossible analytically. The problem can be made linear by inverting the Jacobian and localizing the behaviour of the structure to small movements about the current operating point:

$$d\Theta = J^{-1}(\Theta)\,(d\boldsymbol{x})$$

The goal is known and so the iteration consists of calculating a $d\boldsymbol{x}$ by subtracting the current position and the goal and substituting into the above equation to get $d\Theta$ and proceeds as:

repeat

        $d\boldsymbol{x} :=$ *small movement in the direction of* $\boldsymbol{x}$

        $d\Theta := J^{-1}(\Theta)\,(d\boldsymbol{x})$

        $\boldsymbol{x} := f(\Theta + d\Theta)$

        $J := d\boldsymbol{x}/d\Theta$

        invert J

        $\boldsymbol{x} := \boldsymbol{x} + d\boldsymbol{x}$

until *goal is reached*

An iteration for the three-link arm is shown in Figure 17.18.

Using the chain rule to differentiate Equation 17.2, the Jacobian for the two-link arm is given as:

$$J = \left[\begin{array}{cc} -l_1\sin\theta_1 - l_2\sin(\theta_1 + \theta_2) & -l_2\sin(\theta_1 + \theta_2) \\ l_1\cos\theta_1 + l_2\cos(\theta_1 + \theta_2) & l_2\cos(\theta_1 + \theta_2) \end{array} \right]$$

We are now in a position to discuss the problems engendered by this approach. First, the complexity of the expression for $\boldsymbol{x}$ makes differentiation extremely difficult to perform and a geometric approach to determining the Jacobian is desirable (Watt and Watt 1992). Second, the Jacobian is not invertible unless it is a

Figure 17.18
One iteration step towards
the goal.

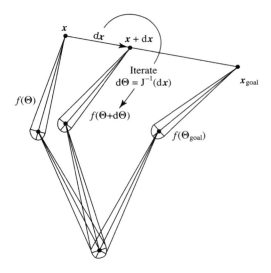

square matrix and in most (skeletal) structures that we would want to use in computer graphics applications this is not the case. Approximate solutions to this problem introduce difficulties in the iteration. In particular, tracking errors where the desired change in x is different from the actual change. Tracking error is given by:

$$\|J(d\Theta) - d\mathbf{x}\|$$

A more intelligent iteration than the one given by the pseudo-code above must be employed. This involves starting with a $d\mathbf{x}$ evaluating the tracking error and subdividing $d\mathbf{x}$ until the error falls below a threshold. Yet another problem arises from singularities that exist in any system. In the two-link arm when both links line up ($\theta_2 = 0$) changes in either θ_1 or θ_2 produce motion in the end effector in exactly the same direction – perpendicular to the (common) link axis. There is now no motion possible towards the base – one degree of freedom has been lost. Another singularity occurs in this case when $\theta_2 = \pi$ when the outer link folds back to line up with the inner one. These singularities are called workspace boundary singularities in robotics because that is where they occur. The work space – the region that can be reached by the end effector – of the two-link arm is a hollow disc (providing $l_1 \neq l_2$) and the circumference of the inner and outer boundaries form the loci of all points in the two-dimensional space at which singularities occur.

Of course, we have only discussed a very simple mechanical structure. Animal skeletons are as we know far more complicated. In particular, they contain branching links. Figure 17.19 shows a simple structure used in typical human animation. In this case the root of the structure is the joint located between the hips (which has six degrees of freedom). Also shown is a categorization of the nodes from the perspective of an inverse kinematics solution. There is a single root node – the remainder of the nodes being children of the root. The base

Figure 17.19
A 'minimum' stick figure for
a human-type articulated
structure.

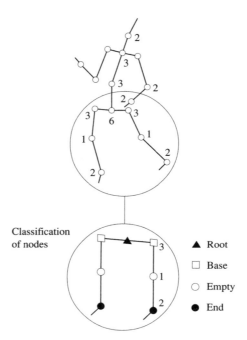

Classification
of nodes

▲ Root

□ Base

○ Empty

● End

nodes and the end nodes define a chain for which we may invoke an inverse kinematics solution. We can apply inverse kinematics between any two nodes in the skeleton; the only rule to be observed is that the end node is lower down the chain than the base node. The inverse kinematics solution specifies the position and orientation of all nodes between the end and base nodes – called empty nodes.

Other arrangements are possible; Philips and Badler (1991), for example, positioned the root at one foot, making the other an end node, in order to animate such motions of a standing figure as shifting the weight from one foot to another and turning.

However, there are other major differences between robot systems and animals involving the constraints. In robotics, the predominant constraints are determined by the degrees of freedom and joint angle constraints which determine the workspace of the machine. A simple example is the links in a human finger which, because of the tendon that runs through the finger do not tend to move independently. Another consideration is whether energy constraints should be taken into account to influence an inverse kinematics approach into producing a visually convincing solution for the motion of the structure. This means that both the geometric constraints and the muscle constraints are satisfied – we could presume that animals effect a change in the geometric state of their structure by minimizing the energy needed for the change. Satisfying only the geometric constraints may produce an animation that does not 'look right'.

Dynamics in computer animation

The approaches to computer animation that we have described so far have been kinematic, that is they involve the specification of motion without consideration of the masses and forces involved in the physical environment that we are trying to simulate. In this section we will look at how we can in principle write programs that simulate the forces in a scene and through Newtonian mechanics produce the desired motion 'automatically'. Such an approach is known as dynamic simulation or physically based animation.

Luxo Jr. (Figure 17.20 Colour Plate), an animated short produced by John Lasseter of Pixar in 1987, was possibly the first computer graphics animation that was perceived to have motion and appeal comparable in quality to that of traditional animators. The skills of John Lasseter imbued a desk lamp with some of the anthropomorphic behaviour reminiscent of Disney-type cartoons. The motion in *Luxo Jr.* was produced by keyframing where the animator specifies the state of the articulated structure as a key and the global motion of the structure as a spline curve. Although it is not 100% explicit control, where the animator specifies the entire state of every frame, he has a high degree of control. And, in fact, the title of Lasseter's presentation to SIGGRAPH '87, 'Principles of Traditional Animation Applied to 3D Computer Animation', reinforces this observation.

In 1988, Witkin and Kass presented a paper (Witkin and Kass 1988) in which they demonstrated that a higher-level motion control technique, based on dynamic simulation, could be used to animate *Luxo Jr.* and commented on their motivation as follows:

Although *Luxo Jr.* showed us that the team of animator, keyframe system, and renderer can be a powerful one, the responsibility defining the motion remains almost entirely with the animator. Some aspects of animation – personality and appeal, for example – will surely be left to the animator's artistry and skill for a long time to come. However, many of the principles of animation are concerned with making the character's motion look *real* at a basic mechanical level that ought to admit to formal physical treatment . . .. Moreover, simple changes to the goals of the motion or to the physical model give rise to interesting variations on the basic motion. For example, doubling (or quadrupling) the mass of *Luxo Jr.* creates amusingly exaggerated motion in which the base *looks* heavy.

In other words, they are saying that this type of computer animation can benefit by higher-level motion control. Beyond performing rudimentary interpolation for in-between frames, a program can be set up to interpret scripts such as 'jump from A to B'. The dynamic simulation will then produce motion that is accurate and therefore realistic. Thus, we see that the motivation for using dynamics in computer animation is that in certain contexts it is easier to write the differential equations that control the motion than it is to specify the motion directly or by using keyframing. We also assume that if the physical simulation is set up correctly the subsequent motion will be more 'natural' than that produced by a kinematics system. Set against these apparent advantages the disadvantages of using dynamics is that the environments that are easy to set up – particle systems – are too simple for most animation environments of interest and complex interacting environments are far more difficult to specify. Another problem is that the solution for such systems is computationally intensive.

Dynamic simulation may not provide a complete solution to many animation applications – there is still the problem of overall artistic control. In comparing dynamic simulation with computer methods that imitate traditional animation techniques, Cohen (1992) puts it this way:

Traditional animation methods provide great *control* to the artist, but do not provide any tools for *automatically* creating realistic motion. Dynamic simulations on the other hand, generate physically correct motion (within limits) but it does not provide sufficient control for an artist or scientist to create desired motion.

17.4.1 Basic theory for a rigid body – particles

The basic familiar law of motion – Newton's Second Law is:

$$\boldsymbol{F} = m\,\boldsymbol{a}$$

and this is easiest to consider in the context of a particle or a point mass. $\boldsymbol{F}$ is a three-dimensional vector as is $\boldsymbol{a}$, the acceleration that the point undergoes. A point mass is a simple abstraction that can be used to model simple behaviour – we can assume that a rigid body that has extent behaves like a particle because we consider its mass concentrated at a single point – the centre of mass. A point mass can only undergo translation under the application of a force.

Newton's Second Law can also be written as:

$$\boldsymbol{F} = m\,\frac{\mathrm{d}\boldsymbol{v}}{\mathrm{d}t} = m\,\frac{\mathrm{d}^2\boldsymbol{x}}{\mathrm{d}t^2}$$

where $\boldsymbol{v}$ is the velocity and $\boldsymbol{x}$ the position of the particle. This leads to a method that finds, by integration, the position of the particle at time $t+\mathrm{d}t$ giving its position at time t as:

$$\boldsymbol{v}(t + \mathrm{d}t) = \boldsymbol{v}(t) + \frac{\boldsymbol{F}}{m}\,\mathrm{d}t$$

$$\boldsymbol{x}(t + \mathrm{d}t) = \boldsymbol{x}(t) + \boldsymbol{v}(t)\mathrm{d}t + \frac{1}{2}\,\frac{\boldsymbol{F}}{m}\,\mathrm{d}t^2$$

$\boldsymbol{F}$ can itself be a function of time and we may have more than one force acting on the body and in that case we simply calculate the net force using vector addition. If the mass of the body changes as it travels, the case of a vehicle burning fuel, for example, then the Second Law is expressed as:

$$\boldsymbol{F} = \frac{\mathrm{d}(m\cdot\boldsymbol{v})}{\mathrm{d}t}$$

As a simple example, consider a cannonball being fired from the mouth of a cannon. This could be modelled using the above equations. The cannonball is acted on by two forces – the constant acceleration due to gravity and an air resistance force that acts opposite to the velocity and is a function (quadratic) of the velocity and the square of the cross-sectional area. A simulation would be provided with the initial (muzzle) velocity and the inclination of the barrel and Newton's Second Law used to compute the arc of the missile. What we have achieved here is a simulation where at each time step the program computes continuous behaviour as a function of time.

This basic theory can only be applied directly to initial value problems where the course of the simulation is completely determined by the start conditions. We may fire a cannonball out of a cannon and its parabolic track is then completely determined by the muzzle velocity, its mass and gravity. However, an animator may rather require a system where he specifies that a cannon situated at point A is to eject a missile which is to hit the castle wall at point B.

In simulations of the initial value type the animator has no control once the start conditions have been specified. In other words we need to supply constraints to the problem. It is through those constraints that the animator is able to design a desired motion. Any potentially useful system has to be both a valid physical model, that can provide realistic motion, and at the same time admit constraints that enable the animator to achieve the desired overall motion. These have been called space–time constraints and, along with such other problems as collision response, comprise a much more difficult aspect of dynamic simulation than the application of the physical laws. We shall return to these problems later.

17.4.2 The nature of forces

Only in very simple cases can we proceed by considering an object as a point mass or equivalently as a lumped mass undergoing acceleration upon application of a force. The way in which an object moves in the modelled environment depends on the model itself, its constraints and the nature of the force. Common examples of the different types of forces used in physically based animation are:

- Acceleration due to gravity (which we have already discussed): is a constant downwards force on a body proportional to its mass and acting on the centre of mass.

- A damping force: this is opposite and proportional to the body's velocity and resists its motion. Damping forces remove energy from the body dissipating it as heat. A viscous damping force is linearly proportional to velocity and a quadratic force is proportional to the square of speed. Air resistance is approximately quadratic if we ignore effects due to the disturbance of the air.

- Elastic springs: these can connect two bodies with a force proportional to the displacement of the string from its rest length (Hooke's law).

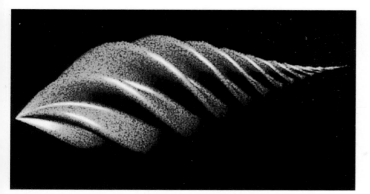

Figure 1.5
Global transformations on a polygon mesh model – a corrugated cylinder, twisted and tapered. (Courtesy of Steve Maddock.)

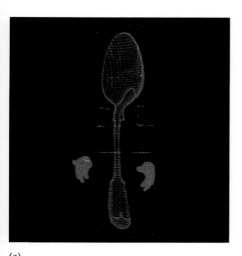

(a)

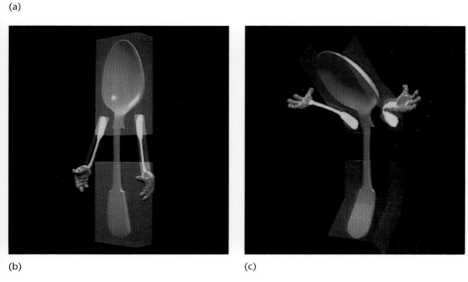

(b)

(c)

Figure 3.42
FFD applied to a polygon mesh object. (a) Wireframe of the object. (b) The object rendered with the trivariate patch grid shown as semi-transparent grey boxes. (c) Moving the control points in the patch causes the object model to deform in an appropriate manner.

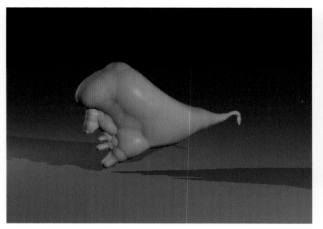
An object (based on a famous Salvador Dali painting)

Point generators – the radius of each sphere is the influence of each generator

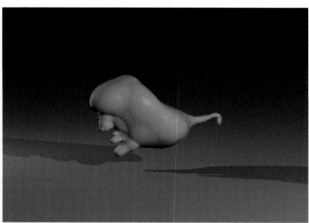

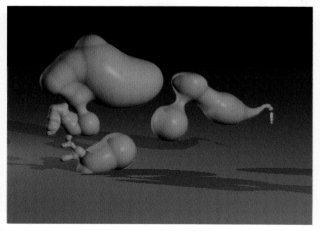
Unwanted blending as the generators are moved

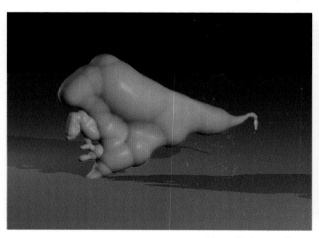

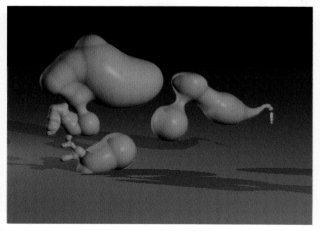
Unwanted separation as the generators are moved

Figure 2.20
An example of an implicit function modelling system. (Courtesy of Agata Opalach.)

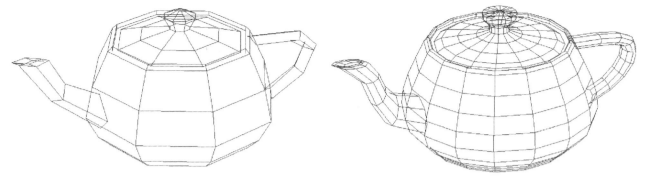

Polygons for the 128 and 512 rendered images.

Figure 4.9
Parametric patch rendering at different levels of uniform subdivision (128, 512, 2048 and 8192 polygons). (Courtesy of Steve Maddock.)

Figure 7.8
A selection of materials simulated using
the model described in Section 7.6.
The differences between some of the
materials (for example, polished brass
and gold) would be difficult to obtain
by fine-tuning the parameters in Phong
shading. In these images the reflection
model was used as the local component
in a ray tracer.

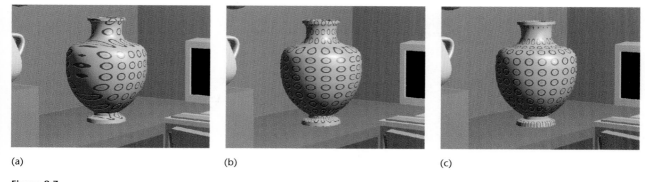

(a)   (b)   (c)

Figure 8.7
Examples of two-part texture mapping with a solid of revolution. The intermediate surfaces are: (a) a plane (or no surface); (b) a cylinder; and (c) a sphere.

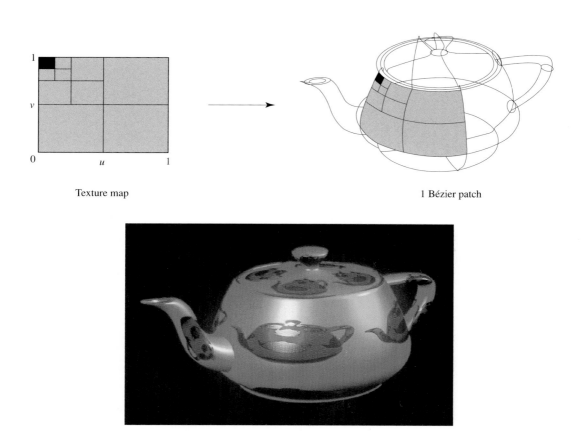

Texture map   1 Bézier patch

Figure 8.8   (Left) Texture map. (Right) One Bézier patch on the object. (Below) Recursive teapot. (Courtesy of Steve Maddock.)

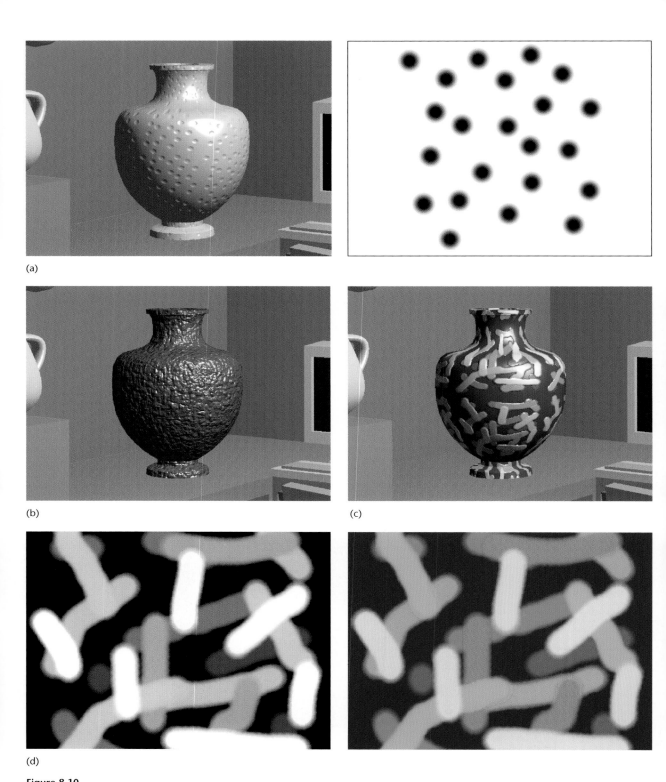

(a)

(b)

(c)

(d)

Figure 8.10
Bump mapping. (a) A bump mapped object together with the bump map. (b) A bump mapped object from a procedurally generated height field. (c) Combining bump and colour mapping. (d) The bump and colour map for (c).

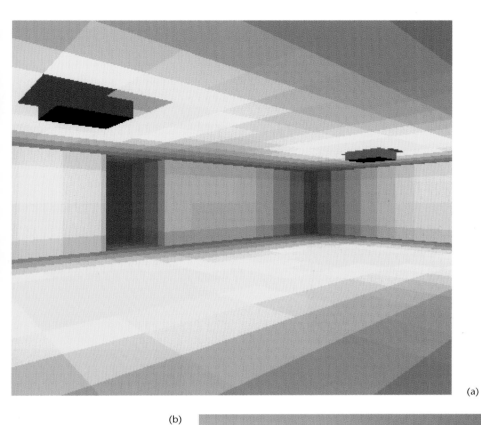

(a)

(b)

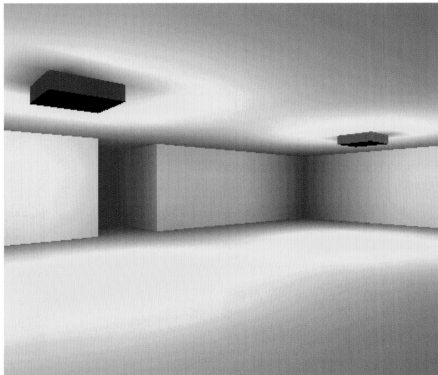

Figure 8.14
A simple scene lit using light maps.
(a) In this image the size of the
lumels in the scene is shown.
(b) In this image a bilinear
interpolation technique – known
as texture interpolation – has been
used to diminish the visibility of the
lumels in (a).

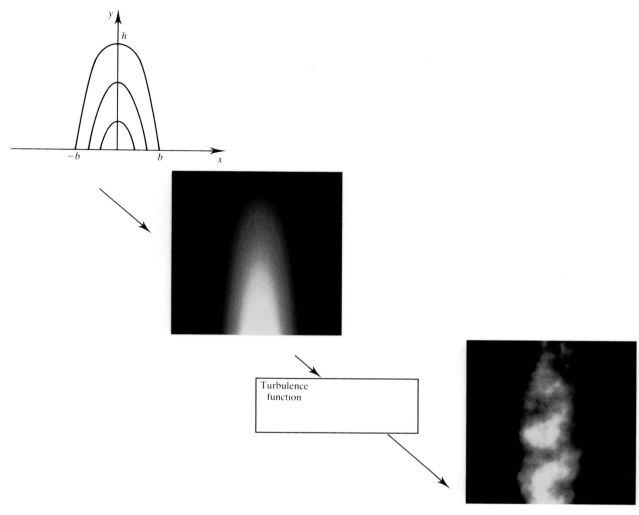

Turbulence
function

Figure 8.22 Modelling and simulating flame using a turbulence function. (Above) Unturbulated flame. (Right) Turbulated flame.

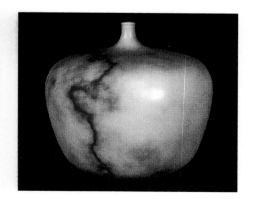

Figure 8.21 Imitating marble – the classic example of three-dimensional procedural texture.

Figure 8.26 Mip-map used in Figure 8.8. (Courtesy of Steve Maddock.)

Figure 10.4 (a)
An image generated using RADIANCE.

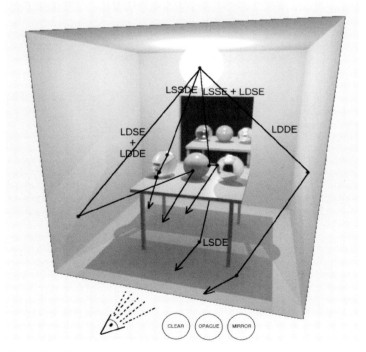

Figure 10.4 (b)
A selection of global illuminations paths in (a).

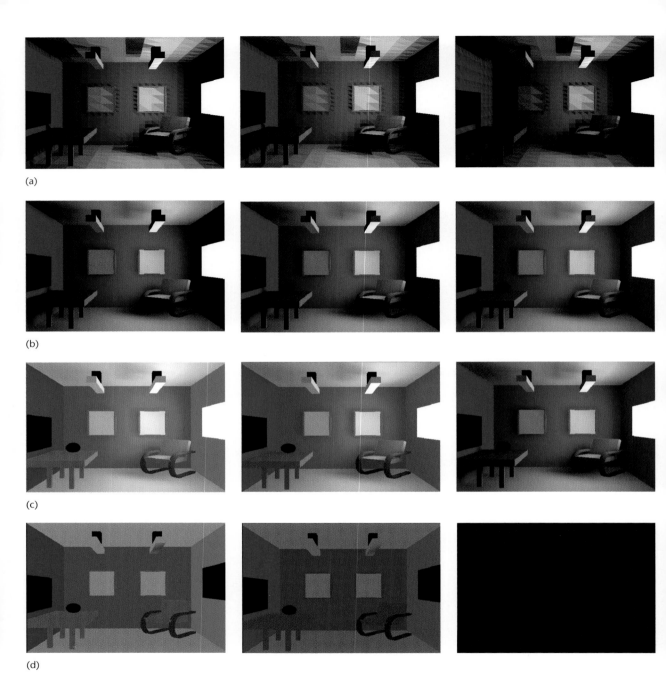

(a)

(b)

(c)

(d)

Figure 10.7
A radiosity image after 20, 250, and 5000 iterations of the progressive refinement method. From top to bottom for each column: (a) The radiosity solution as output from the iteration process. Each patch is allocated a constant radiosity. (b) The previous solution after it has been subjected to the interpolation process. (c) The same solution with the addition of the ambient term. (d) The difference between the previous two images. This gives a visual indication of the energy that had to be added to account for the unshot radiosity.

Figure 10.14
Depth of field effect rendered using a distributed ray tracer.

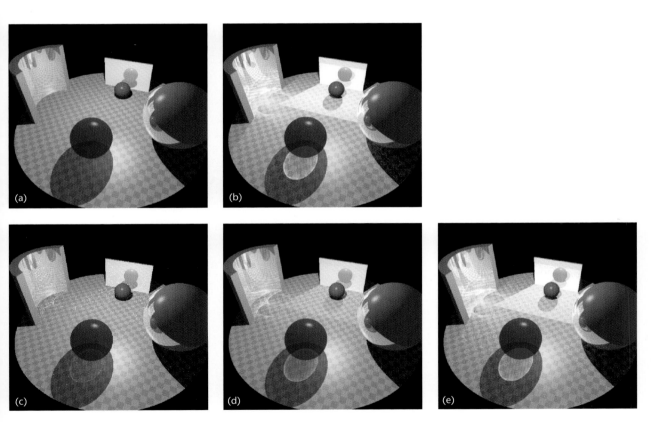

Figure 10.20
Two pass ray tracing example. (a) and (b) show a scene rendered using both a Whitted and two-pass ray tracer. In this scene there are three LSD paths:
- two caustics from the red sphere – one directly from the light and one from the light reflected from the curved mirror
- one (cusp) reflected caustic from the cylindrical mirror
- secondary illumination from the planar mirror (a non-caustic LSDE path).

(c) to (e) were produced by shooting an increasing number of light rays and show the effect of the light sprinkled on the diffuse surface. As the number of rays in the light pass increases, the rays can eventually be merged to form well defined LSD paths in the image. The number of rays shot in the light pass was 200, 400, and 800 respectively.

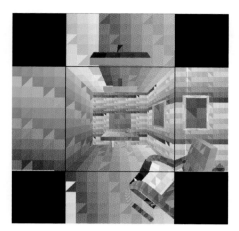

Figure 11.5
Shows the state of a hemicube placed on the window after all other patches in the scene have been projected onto it. A colour identifies each patch in the scene (and every partial patch) that can be seen by this hemicube. The algorithm then simply sums all the hemicube element form factors associated with each patch. (The scene for this figure is shown in Figure 10.7.)

The Whitted scene simple recursive ray tracing.

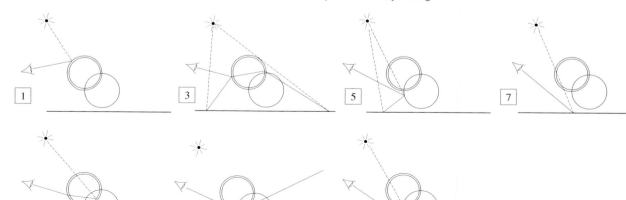

Figure 12.4
The Whitted scene.

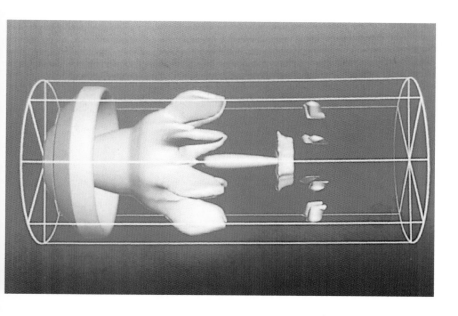

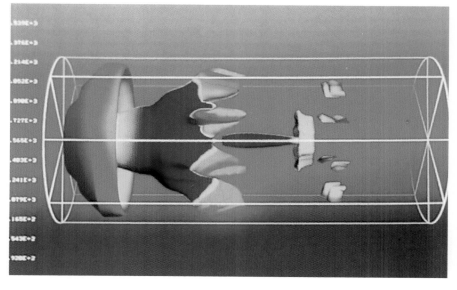

Figure 13.1
Marching cubes and CFD data. (top) A Navier–Stokes CFD simulation of a reverse flow pipe combuster. Flow occurs from left to right and from right to left. The interface between these flows defines a zero velocity isosurface. The marching cubes algorithm is used to extract this surface which is then conventionally rendered. (bottom) A texture-mapped zero velocity surface. A pseudo-colour scale that represents field temperature is combined with the colour used for shading in the illustration above. (Courtesy of Mark Fuller.)

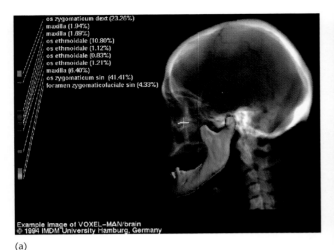

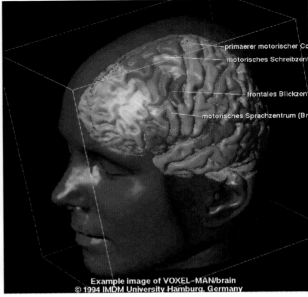

Figure 13.3

(a) and (b) show extracted objects embedded in a transparent surround of the skull. The extracted structures have been turned into computer graphics objects and rendered normally. They are then effectively re-embedded in the three-dimensional data volume which is displayed with the surrounding voxels set to some semi-transparent value. (c) and (d) are examples of cutting away a rendered version of the skin to show internal organs as a cross-section positioned within a three-dimensional model. Here the organs are assigned an appropriate pseudo-colour simply to highlight their shape. (Courtesy IMDM University, Hamburg.)

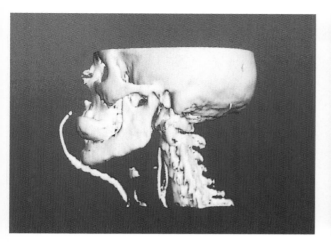

Figure 13.10
The marching cubes algorithm applied to X-ray CT data.
(Courtesy of Klaus de Geuss.)

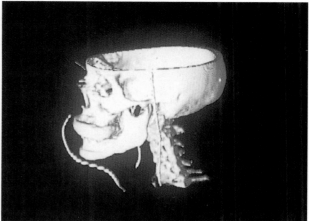

Figure 13.11
The same data using volume rendering with the bone voxels set
to unity opacity and others set to zero. (Courtesy of Klaus de
Geuss.)

Figure 15.3
The RGB cube.

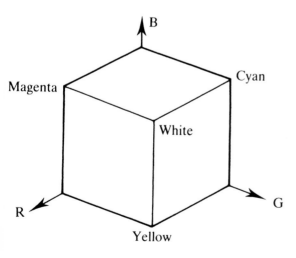

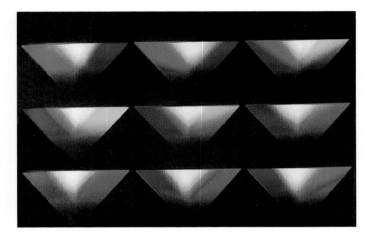

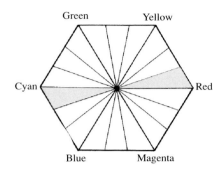

Figure 15.5
HSV colour model: slices through the value axis at 20° intervals.

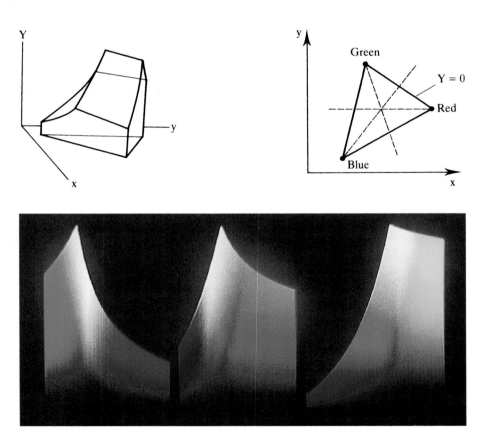

Figure 15.10
(Top left) Monitor gamut solid in CIE xyY space; (above) three cross-sections through the solid CIE xyY space; (top right) the position of the cross-sections on the plane Y=0.

Figure 15.12
Rendering in spectral space compared with RGB space for a ray traced image.

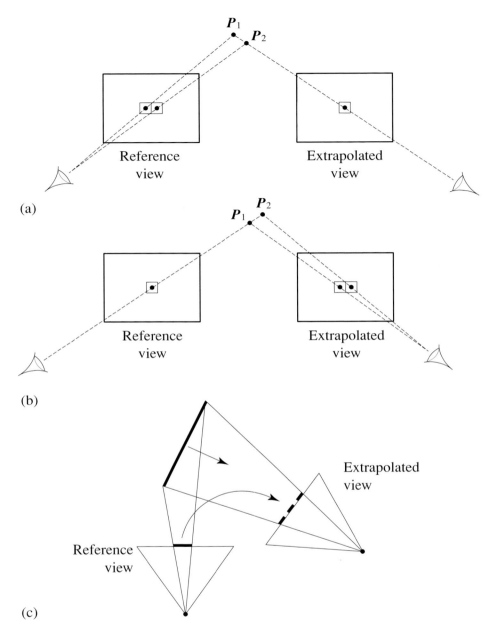

Figure 16.8
Problems in image warping. (a) Image folding: more than one pixel in the reference view maps into a single pixel in the extrapolated view. (b) Holes: information occluded in the reference view is required in the extrapolated view. (c) Holes: the projected area of a surface increases in the extrapolated view because its normal rotates towards the viewing direction. (d) See opposite page.

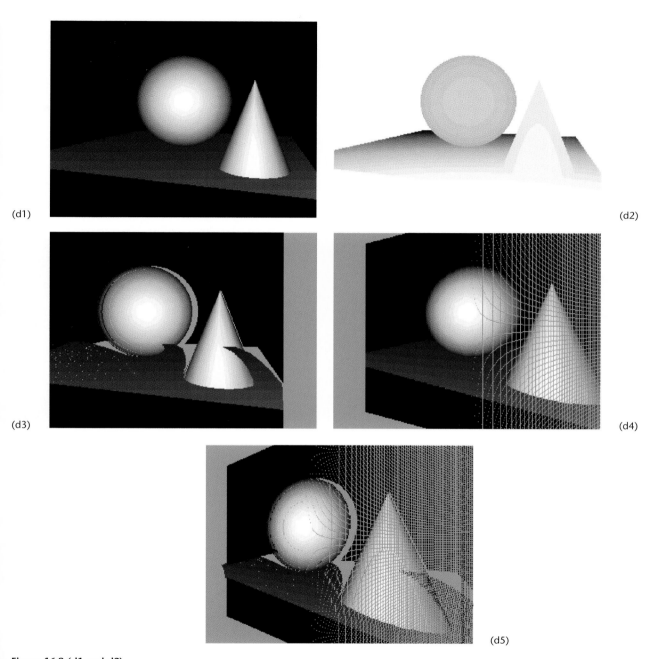

Figure 16.8 (d1 and d2)
A simple scene and the corresponding Z-buffer image.

Figure 16.8 (d3)
Artefacts due to translation (only) in this case are holes (cyan) caused by missing information and image folding.

Figure 16.8 (d4)
Artefacts due to rotation (only) are holes caused by increasing the projected area of surfaces. Note how these form coherent patterns.

Figure 16.8 (d5)
Artefacts caused by both rotation and translation.

1 Overlapping frames from a rotating camera

2 'Stitched' into a cylindrical panoramic image

3 A section of which is warped into a planar polygon

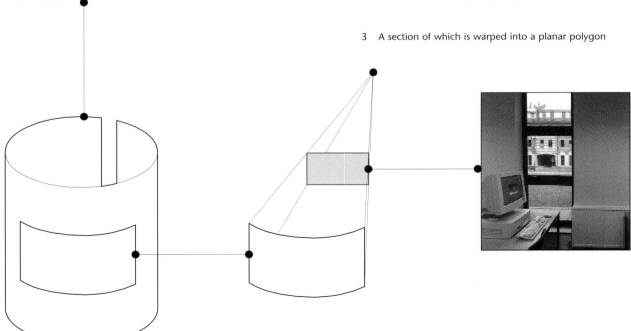

Figure 16.19 QuickTime® VR system. (Courtesy of Guy Brown.)

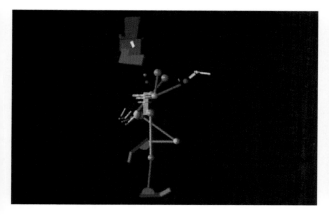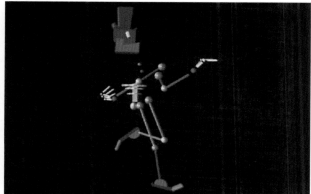

Figure 17.15

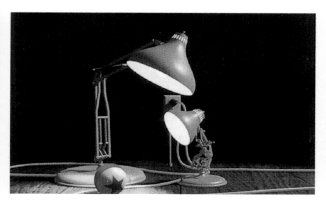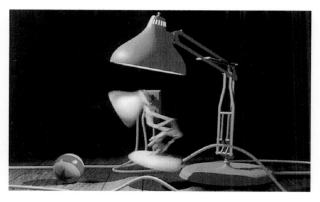

Figure 17.20
(Left) A frame from *Luxo Jr.* produced by John Lasseter, Bill Reeves, Eben Ostby and Sam Leffler; 1986 Pixar; Luxo is a trademark of Jak Jacobson Industries. The film was animated by a keyframe animation system with procedural animation assistance, and frames were rendered with multiple light sources and procedural texturing techniques. (Right) This frame from *Luxo Jr.* exhibits motion blur as described in Chapter 10.

Figure 18.1
An office scene, together with a wireframe visualization, that has been shaded using the constant ambient term only.

Figure 18.2
The same scene using flat shading. Flat shading shows the
polygonal nature of the surfaces due to discontinuities in intensity.

(a)

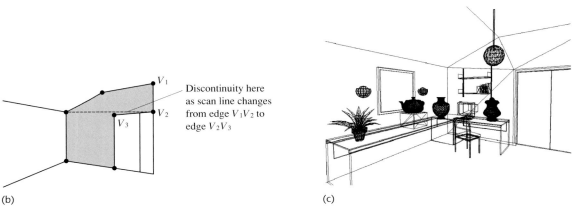

V_1
V_2
V_3

Discontinuity here
as scan line changes
from edge V_1V_2 to
edge V_2V_3

(b)

(c)

Figure 18.3
Main defects in Gouraud interpolation. (a) Colour image. The two defects in this image (described in detail in the text) are: Mach banding
(may not be visible in the reproduction) and the interpolation artefact on the back wall. (b). Dotted line shows the position of the
discontinuity. (c) New wireframe triangulation necessary to eliminate the interpolation artefact.

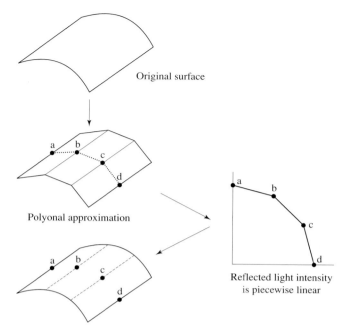

Original surface

Polyonal approximation

Reflected light intensity
is piecewise linear

This produces Mach bands in the image

Figure 18.4
Mach bands in Gouraud shading.

Figure 18.5
The same scene using Phong shading. A glaring defect in Phong interpolation is demonstrated in this figure. Here the reflected light from the wall light and the image of the light have become separated due to the nature of the interpolation.

Figure 18.6
Zoom on one of the wall lights. The top row compares Gouraud and Phong shading. If the polygon mesh shading is sufficiently high the difference between Gouraud and Phong shading can be quite subtle. (Bottom row) Polygon resolution is reduced and the Gouraud highlight disappears.

Figure 18.7
The office scene with 'traditional' two-dimensional texture.

Figure 18.8
The same scene with shadow and environment mapping
(the teapot) added.

Shadow map

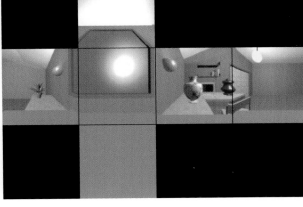

Environment map

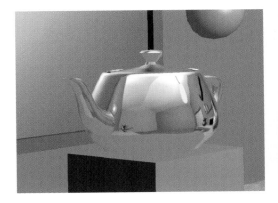

Figure 18.9
This is a comparison between generating reflections using environment mapping (left) and ray tracing (right).

Figure 18.10
The scene ray traced using a Whitted-type ray tracer.

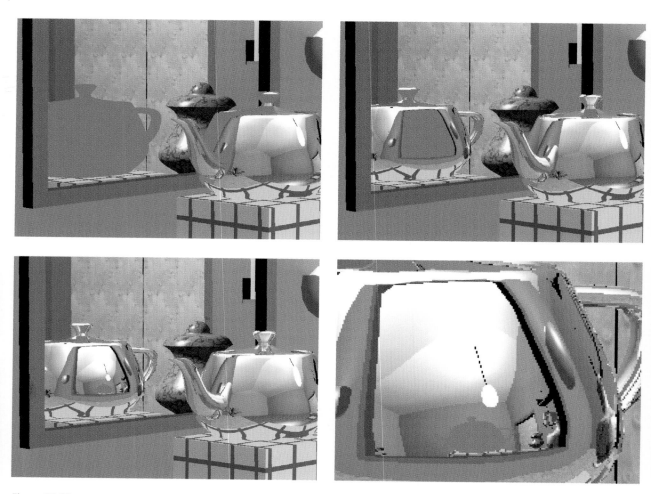

Figure 18.11
A recursive depth demonstration. The trace terminates at depth 2, 3, 4 and 5 (zoom image) respectively. 'Unassigned' pixels are coloured grey. Bad aliasing as a function of recursive depth (the light cable) is apparent.

Figure 18.12

These images demonstrate the mutual exclusivity of standard ray tracing and radiosity as far as the nature of the global interaction that each attends to is concerned. (a) is a ray traced image of the scene with the main light turned off, emphasizing that ray tracing omits all light paths except LDE and LDS*E. (b) is the previous scene with an 'ambient lift'. The value of the ambient component is the same as that used to render the scene with the main light on (Figure 18.10), and is supposed to be a substitute for the illumination which would be present if diffuse–diffuse interaction had been considered. (c) is a radiosity rendered image, with ray tracing for the specular objects, and the main light turned off. (The ray traced component has been included to facilitate a comparison with the next illustration.) The rest of the room is now visible since radiosity methods account for diffuse interreflections.

(a)

(b)

(c)

Anti-aliasing

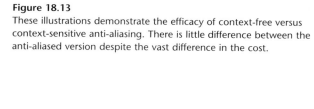

Figure 18.13
These illustrations demonstrate the efficacy of context-free versus context-sensitive anti-aliasing. There is little difference between the anti-aliased version despite the vast difference in the cost.

Supersampling (x3)

Non-uniform sampling

Figure 18.14
This illustration shows a radiosity version of the scene.

Figure 18.15
(a) A photograph of the Museu de Arte Contemporânea (Museum of Contemporary Art), Niteroi, Rio de Janeiro (designed by Oscar Niemeyer), taken in the bright light of the midday sun. The colour bleeding is vividly apparent and fixed in the photograph. Do you experience it to this extent in reality? (b) Exaggerated colour bleeding in a radiosity solution.

(a)

(b)

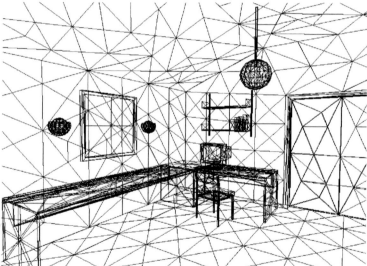

Figure 18.16
This image, suffering from significant shadow and light leakage, was computed
using a 'minimum' specification – a triangulated version of the representation
shown in Figure 18.1.

Figure 18.17
The three pairs of images in this illustration show the effect of a subdivision strategy operating within a progressive refinement framework. The relationship between increasing subdivision and image quality is obvious.

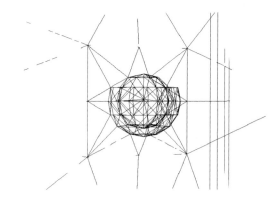

Figure 18.18
The result of meshing the area around a wall light after considering the interpenetrating geometry. Now the wall patch boundaries coincide with the light patch boundaries. The result of this mesh completely eliminates the leakage around the wall lights.

Figure 18.19
The scene rendered using the RADIANCE renderer.

- Bodies can possess geometric constraints which can be considered as a (constraint) force. A simple pendulum exhibits a 'point to nail' constraint. These forces adapt to maintain the geometric constraints regardless of the force applied to the body. Points on a clock pendulum can only move along the circumference of a circle irrespective of where the impulse force, that the pendulum receives to keep it in motion, is applied.

17.4.3   Rigid bodies – extended masses

When a motive force is applied to bodies with extent, the movement induced can consist of both translation and rotation. It is obvious that an unconstrained long thin cylinder will tumble through space if a force is applied to it other than at the centre of mass. We describe such a force as a torque τ. We now consider any motive as a force F (or a number of forces which combine to produce F) which acts on the centre of mass and induces motion as if it were a particle, and a torque τ which induces rotation about a particular axis. The body translates and rotates through space.

Consider applying two equal forces to a symmetric body at equal distances from its centre of mass. In the absence of any geometric constraints the body undergoes translation. If we now move the points of application of the forces, the body both translates and rotates. An important point that emerges from this example is that although the same net force is applied in both cases, in the rotating case the body has acquired a higher kinetic energy at time $t+dt$ because it has acquired both a linear and an angular velocity.

To incorporate this intuitive motion into physical laws we need first to specify how the mass of a body is distributed about its centre of mass. For symmetrical bodies this is done by specifying three moments of inertia – one about each axis. Considering a rigid body as an infinity of particles, a moment of inertia is just the sum of the masses of each particle weighted by the square of the perpendicular distance to each axis:

$$I_x = \int (y^2 + z^2)\mathrm{d}m$$
$$I_y = \int (x^2 + z^2)\mathrm{d}m$$
$$I_z = \int (x^2 + y^2)\mathrm{d}m$$

Examples of moment of inertia for symmetrical homogeneous rigid bodies are:

- A sphere of radius R and mass m:

$$I_x = I_y = I_z = \frac{2}{5}\ mR^2$$

- A cylinder of radius R and height h where the z axis is coincident with the long axis of the cylinder:

$$I_x = I_y = \frac{1}{4}\ m(R^2 + \frac{1}{3}\ h^2)$$

$$I_z = \frac{1}{2} mR^2$$

● A rectangular box of sides *a*, *b* and *c* where the axes *x*, *y* and *z* are along sides *a*, *b* and *c* respectively:

$$I_x = \frac{1}{12} m(a^2 + b^2)$$

$$I_y = \frac{1}{12} m(a^2 + c^2)$$

$$I_z = \frac{1}{12} m(b^2 + c^2)$$

The box formulation is useful because a common approximation to an object is its bounding box. The mass *m* is given by some default density multiplied by the volume and the centre of mass is the centre of the box. If we calculate moments of inertia of a polyhedron using a bounding volume then the degree of approximation depends on how tightly the volume fits the object.

If the body is not symmetrical then the products of inertia are also required for a complete specification of the mass distribution for a dynamic model. These are:

$$I_{xy} = \int xy \, dm$$
$$I_{xz} = \int xz \, dm$$
$$I_{yz} = \int yz \, dm$$

All of these are arranged into a 3 × 3 matrix known as the inertial tensor:

$$\boldsymbol{I} = \begin{bmatrix} I_x & -I_{xy} & -I_{xz} \\ -I_{xy} & I_y & -I_{yz} \\ -I_{xz} & -I_{yz} & I_z \end{bmatrix}$$

$\boldsymbol{I}$ is constant providing the integrations are performed in a 'body' coordinate system that is rigidly attached to the object and moves with it. This makes $\boldsymbol{I}$ an invariant description of the object which is calculated once only. There is, for any arbitrarily shaped object, a special coordinate system for which $\boldsymbol{I}$ is diagonalized (the products of inertia are zero). This is known as the principal axis and the diagonal elements of $\boldsymbol{I}$ as the principal moments of inertia. It makes sense then to choose this as a body coordinate system. To find the principal axis we rotationally transform the inertia tensor to a frame in which it is diagonalized. This is done by finding the eigenvectors $\boldsymbol{E}$ and the associated eigenvalues.

The motion of rigid bodies can be represented by the sum of two motions. Recall that we consider two coordinate systems: a fixed system and a moving system embedded in the body and participating in its motion. This is conveniently positioned at the centre of mass of the body. The car example below is a good demonstration of this requirement. Most forces such as yaw – the force due to the angular acceleration of a turning motion – are dealt with in a coordinate system fixed to the car. At the same time we need a coordinate system for the ground through which the car moves to deal with, for example, the kinematics of steering.

An infinitesimal displacement used in an integral model can then be described as a translation of the body from its position at time t to its position at time $t + dt$ together with a rotation about its centre of mass which orientates the body about the final position of its centre of mass. This makes a rigid body a system with six degrees of freedom.

The Euler method can be used to describe the motion and this results in six equations. Three are the translational equations of motion for the translational component:

$$\boldsymbol{F} = m\boldsymbol{a}$$

as before, and three are the rotational equations of motion relating angular acceleration and mass to torque (the rotational analogue of the above equation). The rotational dynamics of an object that possesses a diagonal inertia tensor is given by:

$$\tau = \frac{d\boldsymbol{H}}{dt}$$

$$\boldsymbol{H} = \boldsymbol{I}\omega$$

where $\boldsymbol{H}$ is the angular momentum of the body, τ is the applied torque and ω is the angular velocity. These two equations lead to a set of simplified Euler equations, assuming that the products of inertia are zero:

$$\tau_x = I_x \frac{d\omega_x}{dt} + (I_z - I_y)\,\omega_z\omega_y$$

$$\tau_y = I_y \frac{d\omega_y}{dt} + (I_x - I_z)\,\omega_x\omega_z$$

$$\tau_z = I_z \frac{d\omega_z}{dt} + (I_y - I_x)\,\omega_y\omega_x$$

where ω, the angular velocity, is with respect to the local frame of reference.

These equations can be numerically integrated as before.

A complete simulation can now be set up and consists of calculating the invariant physical characteristics of the body – centre of mass, inertia tensor and principal axes. Applied torque and applied forces are summed. Forces are specified by a three-dimensional vector and a position vector for the point of application. The net force is given by summing the force vectors (irrespective of points of application). The net torque is found by summing the torques produced by the force components at their point of application. This gives six equations (three for the torque and three for the force). The dynamic state of an object – linear and angular velocities and position and orientation at time $t+dt$ – is calculated from its state at time t where in most applications dt will be equal to the frame interval. If there is more than one object in the scene then collisions are possible – a topic dealt with in Section 17.5.

Using dynamics in computer animation

The previous two sections cover material that can be found in a physics or dynamics textbook and forms the absolute basics of any computer simulation. How do we use dynamics in a practical situation? One of the easiest ways of extending the above material is to set up systems consisting of (say) thousands of particles and using these to model phenomena such as the behaviour of water in a fountain, or fireworks. Although each single particle obeys the simple laws of motion described above, the effect of total population is to model types of 'fluid' objects. This simulation method is called particle systems and is dealt with in Section 17.7.

More generally, animation environments that can usefully exploit dynamic simulation have a much more complex framework. We can consider the basic simulation that incorporates the motion of a rigid body as a black box. The inputs to this engine are the forces and torques that drive the motion. But how are these to be calculated or derived. The simple initial value problem introduced above is generally insufficient for most practical animation. An animator is concerned not only with the start position but where the object finishes its motion and the path it follows getting there. The problem might be stated as: find the necessary forces and torques that will cause the object to move from a start position to a stop position along a certain path and additionally be subject to other constraints such as using the minimum energy in executing the motion or the time needed to reach the goal. This is a difficult, much studied problem for objects of any complexity. For example, the motion of animals or humans is a popular application and in this case both complex geometric constraints of the body structure and dynamic constraints of the muscles must be satisfied. Energy constraints also exist because changes in the pose of a body usually occur in a way that minimizes the energy required for the change. (This contrasts with the kinematics approach to such structures – itself a difficult problem.)

A simple example of the need to determine an appropriate path might be a football game where a higher-level process decides that the next shot at goal is to strike the top of the goal – the crossbar – at (say) the highest point of the ball's trajectory. This means that the initial velocity and angle of the kick have to be determined so that the desired outcome occurs. We may do this by using inverse dynamics rather than forward dynamics. In forward dynamics we input forces and torques into the simulator which outputs position. With inverse dynamics the input/output is reversed – we input position and output forces and torques.

All of this means that the approaches are extremely varied and most are also mathematically demanding. They vary in the ways in which constraints are specified and the way in which a solution is calculated. Many systems that we would want to simulate are multi-body systems and although the Newtonian dynamics outlined above underlies all behaviour, the difficulty of the task for the animator is to determine the kinematic and dynamic equations for the system of interest. The variety and complexity of modern engineering systems is such that whole textbooks may be devoted to each system. Consider, for example, vehicle simulation. Car simulation requires a widely different set of equations from aircraft simulation.

We will thus restrict ourselves to considering two examples that demonstrate some of the principles and the nature of the difficulties involved. These will be treated only in sufficient depth to give an appreciation of the topic.

Although techniques vary widely according to application and the nature of the simulation there is a major distinction between off-line animation currently seen as full-length productions in the cinema and interactive real-time animation whose common manifestation is computer games. With computer games most processing resources per frame are allocated to producing visual complexity in the image and this implies that the dynamic simulation has to be fairly simple.

Simulating the dynamics of a lumped mass

We will begin by looking at a simple approach to a vehicle simulator or car racing game. We will consider three aspects of this popular type of animation: an overall view showing how the dynamics simulation is embedded in the complete program, a basic simulation and the extensions that this would require to make it more accurate and thus realistic. This example will demonstrate another important point which is that the granularity of the simulation depends strongly on the application. A vehicle simulator required for car design will, of necessity, be far more detailed than that required for a recreational driving simulator found in a computer game and in our treatment here we consider the vehicle initially as a single lumped mass with a single centre of gravity. The whole car is then treated as one rigid body.

Interactive computer animation of this form admits a simple branching structure where for each frame input devices are sampled and the program may enter a new state depending on the parameters of the current state and the new input. State variables control the graphics and are associated with all parts of the car that are modelled. State variables simply contain the current values for all the parameters involved in the simulation. For a particle these would be mass, acceleration and position. Simple catastrophic states can also be introduced. For example, if the car is driven too fast around a bend it may turn over. An overall structure is shown in Figure 17.21. A control module will sample the input devices and provide a current acceleration or engine torque as input to the dynamic simulator. A simple but effective scheme is proportional control:

$$a_c = k_1(v_t - v_i)$$

where:

v_t is the target speed given by the position of the accelerator pedal, or set to zero if the brakes are applied

v_i is the current speed

k_1 is a vehicle-dependent constant (or variable) for acceleration and braking

Figure 17.21
Functional components in
an interactive dynamic
simulation.

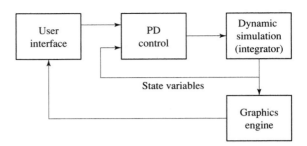

This basic control has to be enhanced by a limit factor, since as a first-order approximation, the acceleration available is a function of engine HP and is inversely proportional to v_i. That is:

$$0 \le a_c \le \frac{k_2}{v_i} \qquad k_2 = \frac{550\ \text{HP}}{m}$$

where HP is the engine horse power and m is the mass of the vehicle. A similar control can be set up for steering.

The program states are, for example, the current position which gives the current road condition (flat, incline, decline or banked), the current attitude of the car: travelling ahead in a straight line, turning or (catastrophically) overturned.

An approximate dynamic simulation can be very simple and consist of a vehicle which has the axles rigidly attached to the car body, in other words no suspension. This gives us a simulation of just three equations which control the car's behaviour and whether or not it is about to overturn. These are:

$$\sum \boldsymbol{F}_f = ma_c$$
$$\sum \boldsymbol{F}_p = 0$$
$$\sum M = 0$$

where:

$\boldsymbol{F}_f$ is the tractive force applied at the surface on which the car travels in the direction of the linear acceleration
$\boldsymbol{F}_p$ is the force perpendicular to the tractive force
M represents the moments of all forces about the mass centre

Note that the car moves forward or slows down by the tractive force which acts as a frictional force between the road surface and the tyres. The engine or the brakes only supplies power to the wheels. Thus for a car accelerating in a straight line on a flat surface we have (Figure 17.22(b)):

$$\boldsymbol{F}_t = ma_c$$
$$mg = R_r + R_f$$
$$\boldsymbol{F}_t h + R_f l_1 = R_r l_2$$

The last equation implies an anti-clockwise moment which tends to lift the front wheels off the ground. For a normal car we assume that the weight is sufficient to keep it on the road (although the front end will rise for a real car with suspension). In a drag racing car, however, because of the position of the centre of gravity, it is easy to cause the front wheels to lift off the ground ($R_f = 0$).

An important point that should be mentioned here is that we have in this trivial simulation implicitly implemented a constraint by *not* implementing any wheel slip whatever the magnitude of the tractive force – we assume that the coefficient of friction between the tyres and the road surface is such that slippage will not occur.

We now consider the forces of the car travelling around a bend on a surface (Figure 17.22(c)). In a steady state turn the vehicle will now be subject to a

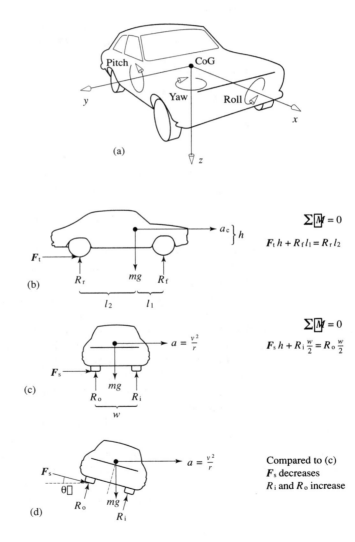

$$\sum \boxed{M} = 0$$

$$F_t h + R_f l_1 = R_r l_2$$

$$\sum \boxed{M} = 0$$

$$F_s h + R_i \frac{w}{2} = R_o \frac{w}{2}$$

Compared to (c)
F_s decreases
R_i and R_o increase

Figure 17.22
Forces for quasi-static calculations for a vehicle. (a) Vehicle coordinate system (Society of Automotive Engineers Inc.). (b) Forward motion in a straight line. (c) Steady state turning. (d) Steady state banked turning compared to (c) F_s decreases, R_i and R_o increase.

centripetal acceleration of v^2/r directed towards the centre of a circle whose circumference forms the bend. This is manifested in a sideways frictional force $\mathbf{F}_s$ between the tyres and the road and using the same three equations as before we have:

$$\mathbf{F}_s = m \frac{v^2}{r}$$

$$mg = R_o + R_i$$

$$\mathbf{F}_s h + R_i \frac{w}{2} = R_o \frac{w}{2}$$

This implies that R_o is greater than R_i and if v and r are such that R_i goes to zero then the car overturns.

A banked road, of course, ameliorates the situation – indeed, that is its *raison d'être* and we now have (Figure 17.22(d)):

$$\mathbf{F}_s \cos \theta = m \frac{v^2}{r}$$

$$mg + \mathbf{F}_s \sin \theta = (R_o + R_i)\cos \theta$$

$$\mathbf{F}_s h + R_i \frac{w}{2} = R_o \frac{w}{2}$$

The effect of banking is to decrease $\mathbf{F}_s$ and to increase both wheel reaction forces thus reducing the roll-over tendency. The reaction forces now have a horizontal component which assists in producing the required acceleration reducing the friction force.

Now, to return to an earlier point which is that the granularity and thus the accuracy of the simulation depends on its application. In this context it is instructive to examine the deficiencies in the above simulation.

Consider the roll-over calculation. In practice, a car would have suspension and in a turn this causes lateral shift in the centre of gravity of the suspended mass. In this case the suspension characteristics and the roll rate (the angular velocity about the x axis) have to be considered. Furthermore, even if these factors are taken into account the calculations are 'quasi-static': they assume the car is executing a steady turn and there is no angular acceleration (yaw) about the vertical z axis through the centre of gravity. Quasi-static calculations cannot, for example, model the transient behaviour of the inner wheels lifting off the ground and returning because of interactions between suspension components. They simply determine, for the current condition, a roll-over threshold. Thus, in such a simulation once the threshold had been reached by the driver there is no possibility of recovery – the car rolls. In practice, this kind of roll-over rarely occurs for family cars because a driver will not steer the car into a steady state turn that will cause roll-over. The driver makes transient adjustments to the steering all the time and roll-over in a family car usually occurs when a car slides and strikes an obstruction – a so-called tripped roll over. This occurrence is far more difficult to model.

Apart from the non-implementation of suspension another critical factor is the physics of the tyres and the tyre–road surface interaction. The entire behaviour of the car is determined by the contact forces between the four tyres and the road surface. If the vehicle is not travelling in a straight line then the lateral forces developed can cause the tyres to slip or skid. The characteristics of tyres, temperature, wear and inflation pressure change as the car is driven and are, of course, critically important in F1 car racing.

Aerodynamic effects, although easily modelled at low speeds as a simple braking function proportional to the square of the speed, become increasingly complex at high speeds where the shape of the car needs to be taken into account.

Thus, this simple example demonstrates that accurate dynamic simulations can be extremely complex and are properly a part of mechanical engineering design rather than computer graphics. A would-be animator usually resorts to a simplified simulation, both in terms of those aspects modelled and of the accuracy of the modelling.

(17.4.6) Space–time constraints

In the previous section we gave a simple example of dynamic simulation. This type of simulation is known as an initial value problem or forward simulation. The user inputs initial value(s) – albeit continuously in the case of computer games – and the motion is then completely determined by the equations used to perform the simulation. This is adequate for the application exemplified above, but certainly for most types of off-line animation greater control by the animator is required. Animators are more likely to specify motion for a dynamic simulation and that makes it a two-point boundary value problem. Such problems are far more difficult to solve. In such animation the animator wants to specify that the ball is to be kicked by the player, execute physically based motion in flight, and land at a particular point. Because of the computational requirements such simulations are currently constrained to be off-line.

The success of the early classic computer animations, such as the aforementioned *Luxo Jr.*, was due to the artistry of the animator who specified and tuned the motion. The role of the computer in such productions was to interpolate and render, the animator retaining complete control over the motion. In this section we will describe the basis of important developments whose aim is to enable the animator to exploit the realistic motion that results from dynamic simulation without the loss of control that the use of initial value systems implies.

In 1988 Witkin and Kass (Witkin and Kass 1988) introduced the concept of space–time constraints, using as an example a (planar) model of *Luxo Jr.* parametrized by four joint angles and translation (Figure 17.23). These parameters, and only these, would be controlled by an animator using a conventional animation system. The aim of the study was to enable a physically based animation together with high-level control by allowing the animator to specify:

- *What* the character has to do, for instance 'jump from here to there'.
- *How* the motion should be performed, for instance 'don't waste energy' or 'come down hard enough to spatter whatever you land upon'.
- What the character's *physical structure* is – what the pieces are shaped like, what they weigh, how they are connected etc.
- What *physical resources* are available to the character to accomplish the desired motion, for instance the character's muscles . . . a floor to push off from etc.

Commenting on the success of their approach, Witkins and Kass (1988) state:

making a Luxo lamp execute a convincing jump just by telling it where to start and end. The results . . . show that such properties as anticipation, follow-through, squash and stretch, and timing indeed emerge from a bare description of the motion's purpose and the physical context in which it occurs.

Such motion subtleties, developed as part of the animator's art by Disney animators in the 1930s, are precisely the effects that John Lasseter manually built into the original animation. The potential of the approach is not only to give the animator control over a physically based animation but to engender a higher-level motion control leaving the physical model to take care of its own detailed movements.

The solution to such a problem is then a set of five motion curves – one for translation and four for the joint angles. These are a function both of time and the positional constraints given by the animator or which emerge from some higher-level scripting control – hence the term 'space–time constraints'.

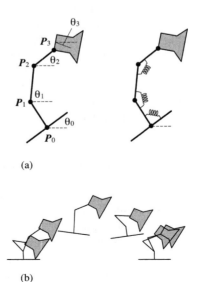

(a)

(b)

Figure 17.23
Witkin and Kass's simulation of *Luxo Jr.* (Based on an illustration in Witkin and Kass (1988).) (a) A planar model constructed of rigid links and frictionless joints. (b) The simulation of a jump.

A solution is enabled by introducing an objective function which is minimized together with the constraints, which in this case comprise the initial and final pose and position. The framework of the solution algorithm is then: find the set of joint angle motion curves that minimizes the objective function subject to the constraints. The forces in the system are 'muscle' forces, the contact force between the floor and the base and gravity. Muscles are simulated by three angular springs joining the links at each joint, where the spring force is given by:

$$\mathbf{F}_i = k_i(\varphi_i - \rho_i)$$

where:

k_i is the spring stiffness
φ_i is the joint angle
ρ_i is the rest angle

Both the stiffness and rest angle are allowed to vary. The springs are used to build the objective function which optimizes the motion's mechanical efficiency by ensuring that minimum power is consumed by the muscles at each time step, where muscle power is the product of the muscle force and the joint's angular velocity.

This example demonstrates both the potential of the approach and its limitations. Essentially this is a simple model. The complexity growth of the problem is severe for 'creatures' that we would like to animate and more recent research on space–time constraints has concentrated on addressing this problem (see, for example Liu *et al.* (1994)).

17.5 Collision detection

A mandatory part of any animation system that admits more than a single moving object is collision detection. Collision detection is a much studied problem whose expense is a quadratic function of the number of moving objects in the scene and their complexity (average number of faces per object). This is easy to see for the standard approach to collision detection which is a 'broad phase' followed by a 'narrow phase'. The broad phase finds those pairs of objects that may collide and the narrow phase determines the exact collision point (if any). A naive broad phase algorithm has complexity $O(n^2)$. Within this process an exact collision calculation for polyhedra will typically have complexity $O(m^2)$ where m is the number of faces per object.

We can compare this with a ray tracing intersection test – a much simpler collision detection problem. Here, the equivalent broad phase checks for intersection between a known object – the current ray – and object bounding volumes and has complexity $O(n)$. The narrow phase in ray tracing – finding the ray–polygon intersection – has complexity $O(m)$. The other association that collision detection has with ray tracing is the extensive use of bounding volumes. When checking for collision between a pair of bounded objects we first invoke a (fast) intersection test between the objects' bounding volumes. If the bounding volumes do not collide then the objects cannot. Bounding volume checks are possibly the most popular approach to the broad phase of two-phase algorithms (described in the next section).

Another source of computational expense is what Hubbard (1993) refers to as the 'fixed-timestep weakness' which combines with the above 'all pairs weakness'. The fixed-timestep weakness is simply the application of an all pairs algorithm at equal intervals in time – a wasteful approach unless the environment is going to produce a collision for each time interval. What is required is a sampling interval that is inversely proportional to the likelihood of collision.

Apart from the expense there are other difficulties associated with collision detection to do with time sampling. If the simulated velocity of objects is high with respect to the sampling rate for collision detection then objects can pass through each other without a collision being detected. In general, a collision will not be detected at the instant an impact occurs but at some time later when the colliding objects have moved into each other's space. Some strategy is then necessary to detemine the impact point, say, moving one of the objects back along its path.

(17.5.1) Broad phase/narrow phase algorithms

This is the most common approach at the moment. This structure tries to cull away pairs of moving objects that cannot possibly collide, leaving exact collision detection to be applied to the remaining pairs that survive the culling process. An important advantage of this strategy is that the choice of algorithm for each phase can be made independently. In this section we will look briefly at broad phase strategies.

Many broad phase strategies exist – the use of temporal coherence, spatial coherence and bounding volumes with the most common (possibly) being bounding volumes or hierarchies of bounding volumes.

A direct method of exploiting time coherence is given by Hubbard (1993) where four-dimensional space–time bounding volumes are associated with an object. Hubbard shows that the four-dimensional object swept out by a three-dimensional moving object, moving with any motion from a start point, is a 'parabolic horn'. To simplify the intersection check he bounds this with a four-dimensional trapezoid. The broad phase is based on calculating the earliest time that a collision can occur between any pair of objects and doing no further collision detection checking until that time has been reached. (The motivation of the work was collision detection for VR which must function in real time.) If two objects are to collide at some future time t then their space–time bounds must intersect at some time $t' \leq t$ because the space–time bounds are conservative in four-dimensional space just as bounding volumes are in three-dimensional space. The detection algorithm computes the earliest t' over all pairs of objects. This approach, by definition, ameliorates the constant timestep weakness and

Hubbard also addresses the all pairs weakness in the intersection test. If the path of the object(s) is known then a simpler bounding volume can be used to bound the space that the object occupies over a time interval. Prior knowledge of object paths is unlikely to be a feature of interactive computer animation and this approach is only suitable for off-line animation.

Spatial coherency is most easily exploited by dividing the scene space up into unit cells. For interactive computer animation where the moving objects remain on the ground then the cells become a two-dimensional grid. Collisions are checked by examining a cell to see if it contains more than one object. The problem with this simple approach is the optimal choice for the size of a cell and the algorithm is only really suitable for an environment where all the objects are more or less the same size.

The obvious enhancement to uniform spatial subdivision is to use an octree partitioning (Chapters 1 and 12). To check for potential colliding pairs the tree is descended and only those regions that contain more than one object are examined. In effect, the octree eliminates testing pairs of objects which are distant from each other. However, unlike the application in Chapter 12, because objects are moving the octree must be updated at each timestep. This can result in significant extra computation.

Another possible approach is to maintain, for each object, a list of nearest neighbours based on some distance threshold. This strategy can also admit an adaptive timestep. Cohen *et al.* (1995) maintain potential collision pairs that are in close proximity by sorting axis aligned bounding boxes (AABBs).

The use of bounding boxes in broad phase collision detection is extremely common and three types of volumes are used – spheres, AABBs (bounding boxes aligned with the coordinate axis) and OBBs (bounding boxes whose orientation 'best suits' the object they are bounding). OBBs are set up for a particular object by considering the vertices as a set of points and applying a multivariate statistical technique known as principal component analysis (full details are given in Gottschalk *et al.* (1996)).

17.5.2 Broad phase collision detection with OBBs

Although overlap checking with AABBs involves straightforward one-dimensional limit checks, checking OBBs for overlap is reportedly faster (Gottschalk *et al.* (1996)) and we will now describe how this works.

A naive algorithm for checking for interference between two OBBs would require an edge–face test from each resulting in $12 \times 6 \times 2 = 144$ edge–face tests. Gottschalk *et al.* develop the following strategy. First consider Figure 17.24 which shows two OBBs projected onto an (arbitrary) axis. It is clear from this that if the intervals of the projected vertices do not overlap then the boxes cannot overlap. The axis is then a separating axis because it is oriented in such a way as to produce disjoint intervals from disjoint OBBs. If the intervals do overlap then the OBBs may or may not be disjoint and a further test is necessary.

Figure 17.24
Projecting OBBs onto an
axis. If the intervals are
disjoint, the axis is a
separating axis. Checking
for disjoint OBBs involves
searching for a separating
axis.

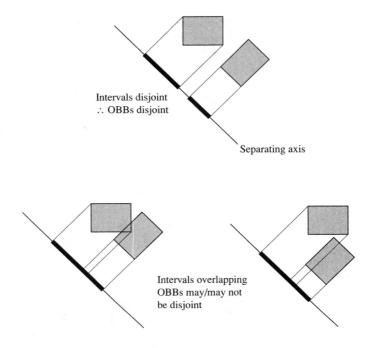

Intervals disjoint
∴ OBBs disjoint

Separating axis

Intervals overlapping
OBBs may/may not
be disjoint

Now consider that if the OBBs are disjoint they can be (possibly) separated by a plane that contains one of their faces. It is less obvious that if they are disjoint but cannot be separated by a face plane, they can be separated by a plane parallel to an edge from each box. This means that the OBBs are disjoint if there exists a separating axis orthogonal to a face from either OBB or orthogonal to an edge from each. Thus to test for separation it is sufficient to test 15 potential axes. (Three face orientations from each box plus nine pairwise edge combinations.) Positive interference will thus require 15 tests and if the OBBs do not intersect, determining this will take on average 7.5 tests.

Testing for the existence of a separating axis proceeds as follows. Refer to Figure 17.25 and note that the placement (but not the orientation) of the axis is immaterial and we assume that it passes through the centre of the box A, although for clarity it is shown outside the box. Up to 15 Ls are chosen according to the geometry of the boxes involved in the comparison as we have explained. If the axes of box A are the unit vectors A_1 A_2, and A_3 and the half dimensions of A are a_1, a_2 and a_3, then we have the projected length of the 'radius' of the box:

$$r_A = a_1 A_1 \cdot L + a_2 A_2 \cdot L + a_3 A_3 \cdot L$$

$$= \sum_{i=1}^{3} |a_i A_i \cdot L$$

Figure 17.25
L is an axis being tested to see if it is a separating axis. The 'radius' of each OBB is projected onto **L**. For separaton: $\boldsymbol{D} \cdot \boldsymbol{L} > r_A + r_B$.

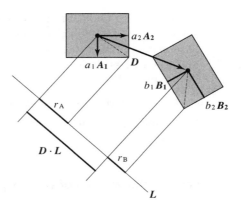

A similar expression exists for $\boldsymbol{r}_B$ of box B. If $\boldsymbol{D}$ is the translation of B relative to A, then we find that the intervals are disjoint if:

$$\boldsymbol{D} \cdot \boldsymbol{L} > \sum_{i=1}^{3} |a_i \boldsymbol{A}_i \cdot \boldsymbol{L}| + \sum_{i=1}^{3} |b_i \boldsymbol{B}_i \cdot \boldsymbol{L}|$$

or:

$$\boldsymbol{D} \cdot \boldsymbol{L} > r_A + r_B$$

Since the 15 potential separating axes are defined with respect to one of the objects they move with the object and the intervals themselves have a velocity associated with them. If we assume, for simplicity, that the object moves in a straight line with constant velocity between frames the velocity of the interval corresponding to that object is easily calculated and we can find out if, for any time between the frames, the moving object is likely to collide with a static one that it is currently being compared to.

Gottschalk *et al.* (1996) measure the effectiveness of OBBs by employing a cost function first proposed by Weghorst *et al.* (1984) to analyze the effectiveness of hierarchical methods in ray tracing. This is:

$$T = N_v C_v + N_p C_p$$

where:

T is the total cost of testing for interference between two large objects represented by OBB trees
N_v is the number of bounding volume pair overlap tests
C_v is the cost of the bounding volume tests
N_p is the number of primitive pair tests
C_p is the cost of primitive pair tests

The idea of a tight bounding volume is to lower N_p as far as possible but this is usually at the expense of C_v. C_v for spheres and AABBs is much faster than that for OBBs. Also collision detection differs from ray tracing in that we are in general, comparing two complex objects. (In ray tracing one object is always a ray.) Gottschalk *et al.* (1996) point out that the overall cost depends on the relative placements of the models; when they are far apart, sphere trees and AABB trees tend to cost less than OBB trees. They conclude that for large models in close proximity:

- C_v is one order higher than that for sphere trees and AABB trees.

- N_v and N_p for OBB trees are asymptotically lower than those for sphere and OBB trees.

17.5.3 Narrow phase: pairs of convex polyhedra – exact collision detection

In this section we will describe common 'straightforward' exact collision detection algorithms using the constraint that the objects must be convex polyhedra. (In principle, concave polyhedra can be decomposed into collections of convex ones.) The algorithm is due to Moore and Wilhelms (1988).

Three tests are applied and the success of any of these implies that a collision has occurred. Consider two polyhedra P and Q. First, all the vertices of Q are checked to see if they are contained by P and vice versa (Figure 17.26(a)). Second, the edges of Q are tested for penetration against the faces of P and vice versa (Figure 17.26(b)). Finally, the infrequent case of two (identical) polyhedra moving through each other with faces perfectly aligned is tested for. This is done by considering the centroid of each face of Q and using the same test as for vertex inclusion.

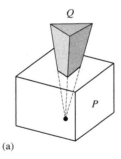

(a)

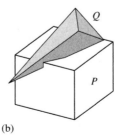

Figure 17.26
Collision detection tests for convex polyhedra. (a) Any vertex of Q contained in P. (b) Any edge of Q penetrates a face of P.

(b)

Consider the first test: each vertex of Q has to be checked against every face of P and a collision is detected if any vertex is on the inward side of all the faces of P. Thus for each vertex $\boldsymbol{v}_i$ of Q and for each face j of P the dot product:

$$(\boldsymbol{v}_i - \boldsymbol{u}_j)\cdot\boldsymbol{n}_j$$

is evaluated, where $\boldsymbol{u}_j$ is any vertex of face j and $\boldsymbol{n}_j$ is its (outwards) normal (Figure 17.27(a)). If this dot product is negative then the vertex $\boldsymbol{v}_i$ is on the inward side of face j.

The second test proceeds by first calculating for an edge $(\boldsymbol{v}_i, \boldsymbol{v}_j)$ of Q the intersections of the edge with the (infinite) planes containing the faces of P. For any plane k of P an edge intersects it if the perpendicular distance from each vertex to the plane changes sign (see Chapter 1). The intersection point $\boldsymbol{x}$ can then be calculated as:

$$d_i = (\boldsymbol{v}_i - \boldsymbol{u}_k)\cdot\boldsymbol{n}_k$$
$$d_j = (\boldsymbol{v}_j - \boldsymbol{u}_k)\cdot\boldsymbol{n}_k$$
$$t = \frac{|d_i|}{|d_i| + |d_j|}$$
$$\boldsymbol{x} = \boldsymbol{v}_i + t(\boldsymbol{v}_j - \boldsymbol{v}_i)$$

This gives, in general, a number of intersection points along the edge. Those for which $t \notin [0,1]$ are discarded and the remainder are sorted into order of their t values. These form a sequence of potential intersections from one vertex to the other (Figure 17.27(b)). Each pair of points is formed by the planes containing adjacent faces. Finally, to check for intersection Moore and Wilhelms (1988) use the midpoint of each pair substituting this value into the first test.

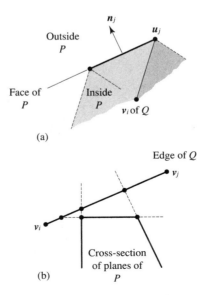

(a)

(b)

Figure 17.27
Notation for collison detection tests for convex polyhedra. (a) Notation for a vertex of Q contained by P test. (b) Notation for an edge of Q cutting a face of P.

A more elaborately structured algorithm based on finding and tracking the closest points between two polyhedra was introduced by Cohen *et al.* (1995). The interesting feature of this algorithm is that it utilizes pre-processing of the objects to facilitate an execution time that is independent of the complexity of the objects. In other words it uses off-line computation within the exact collision detection phase rather than in an inexact pre-process.

Single phase algorithms – object hierarchies

Hierarchies are used in two distinct ways in collision detection algorithms. They can be used to represent the entire space of the environment – using octrees for example – or each object can have a hierarchy associated with it. The potential advantage of an object hierarchy is that it enables a unified approach – we can build a single phase algorithm that detects collisions to an accuracy that depends on how far we have descended the hierarchy. This enables what Hubbard (1996) calls time-critical collision detection where in interactive computer animation the accuracy is determined by the time available for the calculation. This approach – a hierarchical representation of an object surface – is, of course, the same as the level of detail approach we describe in Chapter 2. However, in this context an LoD hierarchy comprising polygons is not convenient for collision detection and Hubbard (1996) uses a sphere tree for fast determination of intersection. The topmost level of a sphere hierarchy is the bounding sphere from the object and, as we descend, smaller and smaller spheres 'shrink' onto the surface as is evident in Figure 17.28. Hubbard (1996) states that two important requirements of the sphere tree are that the (off-line) building process should be automatic and each level in the hierarchy must fit the object as tightly as possible.

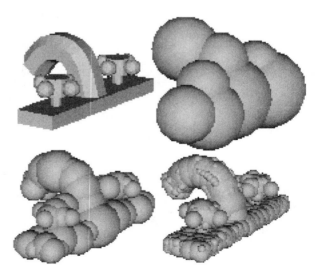

Figure 17.28
An example of three levels in the construction of a sphere tree. *Source*: Hubbard, P.M., *ACM Transactions on Graphics*, 15:3, July 1996, reprinted with permission from ACM Publications.

(Note that the requirements of the process are somewhat different from using a hierarchical bounding volume in ray tracing. Ray tracing, by definition, is a two-phase process – we must have a narrow phase which evaluates exactly the intersection between a ray and a polygon. It may be sufficient in ray tracing to build hierarchies that simply enclose parts of the object. For example, a table may be represented by just five bounding volumes. In collision detection we need to compare spheres at any level in the hierarchy for intersection and the spheres must intersect and range over the surface of an object as Figure 17.28 clearly shows.)

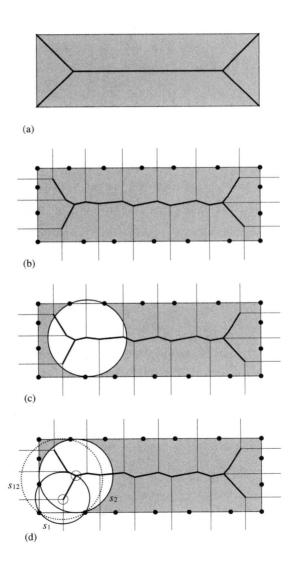

Figure 17.29
A two-dimensional analogy of Hubbard's scheme for building sphere trees (based on illustrations in Hubbard (1996). (a) Medial axis of a polygon (bold lines). (b) Deriving an approximation of the medial axis by 'populating' the edges with points and finding the associated Voronoi regions. (c) Each Voronoi vertex is the centre of a circle that passes through three points. (d) Merging the two circles s_1 and s_2.

To obtain such a tree is not straightforward and we will simply overview the process using a two-dimensional analogy – full details of the algorithm are given in Hubbard (1996). Hubbard first derives a medial axis surface from the object and then uses this surface to place the spheres. A medial axis for a two-dimensional object is shown in Figure 17.29(a)). Sometimes called a skeleton, a medial axis is the locus of points equidistant from two sides of the object. In the case of an object it would be a surface. The medial axis is approximated by building a Voronoi diagram for a set of points P that are assigned to the surface of the object. Figure 17.29(b)) shows a set of points on the shape and their associated Voronoi regions. A Voronoi region for a point is defined as that region of space closer to that point than to any other of the points, and so, for a set of points on the surface of the object, the Voronoi cells must have faces lying approximately on the medial axis. More specifically, the vertices of the Voronoi cells interior to the object lie on the medial axis. As shown in Figure 17.29(c) each such vertex by definition is the centre of a circle (sphere in three dimensions) which passes through three of the points (four points in three dimensions) and these circles (spheres) are the basis of the building of the hierarchy.

The complete set of such spheres tightly enclose the surface of the object and form the leaves of the hierarchy which is now built by reducing the number of spheres occupying each level using a merging operation. The process is shown as a two-dimensional analogy again in Figure 17.29(d). Two spheres, s_1 and s_2 are merged into a sphere s_{12} using an algorithm that ensures s_{12} either passes through or contains the forming points for s_1 and s_2. Hubbard (1996) treats this operation as a minimization problem by choosing the minimum cost merger – the candidate pair whose merger most preserves the level's tightness.

17.6 Collision response

Collision response is strictly application dependent. The application may not admit collisions, for example in path planning, an object may have to move a source to a destination without colliding. When objects are allowed to collide the reaction depends on the nature of the objects and the calculations involved are properly part of dynamic simulation.

The clear distinction is between elastic collisions where the bodies do not permanently deform and where there is no loss of kinetic energy and non-elastic collisions where they do. Non-elastic collisions and the deformations caused by them are more difficult to deal with and in this case energy is dissipated in the collision. Classical dynamics treats the problem by considering a large impulsive force or reaction acting for a very short period of time – the duration of the collision. Consider Figure 17.30 which shows two spheres moving along a line joining their centres. We have:

$$m_1 \left(v_1^{\text{after}} - v_1 \right) = -P$$
$$m_2 \left(v_2^{\text{after}} - v_2 \right) = P$$

Figure 17.30
Two spheres colliding.

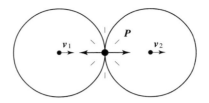

where:

P is the impulse force
v_1 and v_2 are the velocities of the spheres before impact
v_1^{after} and v_2^{after} are the velocities of the spheres after impact

thus:

$$m_1 v_1^{after} + m_2 v_2^{after} = m_1 v_1 + m_2 v_2$$

which we may have deduced anyway since there is no internal force acting on the system.

We define:

$$v_{rel}^{before} = v_1 - v_2$$

as the speed of approach, and:

$$v_{rel}^{after} = v_1^{after} - v_2^{after}$$

as the speed of separation and hypothesize that these are connected by a coefficient of restitution e:

$$v_{rel}^{after} = -e v_{rel}^{before}$$

where:

If $e = 0$ then $v_1^{after} = v_2^{after}$ there is no rebound – an inelastic collision
If $e = 1$ then $v_1^{after} = v_2$ and $v_2^{after} = v_1$ the spheres exchange velocities – a perfectly elastic collision

Thus the coefficient of restitution determines how much kinetic energy is lost in the collision. In practice, of course, this loss of energy would be manifested as a deformation of one or both of the bodies, which by definition is a redistribution of mass. This then invalidates the analysis and so we assume that any deformation does not result in a change in the centre of gravity.

Now consider polyhedra colliding. For simplicity we will only consider one mode of contact – a vertex colliding with a face. (In practice, we can, of course, have two faces or two vertices colliding.) In this case the surface of contact is the face of one of the colliding bodies and we can define a normal N to this surface of contact. We then consider what happens to the component of the relative velocity in the direction of N. If $e = 1$ (Figure 17.31(b)) then the component in the direction of N is reversed and the relative velocity perpendicular to N remains unchanged. For the case $0 \le e \le 1$ the relative velocity in the direction of N is reduced.

Figure 17.31
Vertex face collision for
polyhedra. (a) A vertex face
contact. (b) $e = 1$. The
relative velocity in the
direction of $\boldsymbol{N}$ is reversed.
The relative velocity
perpendicular to $\boldsymbol{N}$ remains
the same.

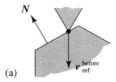

(a)

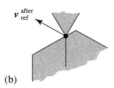

(b)

The collision detection procedure is responsible for determining that a collision has occurred and the point of impact. The normal assumption is that there is no interpenetration, and if a collision detection routine detects interpenetration it 'moves the simulation back' until the point of contact is determined.

In general, we must consider that rigid bodies in motion are both translating and rotating and we can define the velocity of the point of contact $\boldsymbol{Q}$ immediately after the time of the collision as:

$$\boldsymbol{v}_A^{\text{after}} = \boldsymbol{v}_A^{\text{after}} + (\omega_A^{\text{after}} \times \boldsymbol{r}_A)$$

where ω_A^{after} is the angular velocity of body A after impact and $\boldsymbol{r}_A$ the distance from the point of contact to the centre of gravity of A.

We now return to consider the nature of the impulse force $\boldsymbol{P}$ in more detail. As we have already mentioned, $\boldsymbol{P}$ is an entity that acts over a very short time interval:

$$\boldsymbol{P} = \int_{\Delta t} \boldsymbol{F} \mathrm{d}t$$

The effect of $\boldsymbol{P}$ is to produce an instantaneous change in velocity and it has the units of momentum. If we denote the magnitude of $\boldsymbol{P}$ as p we can write:

$$\boldsymbol{v}_A^{\text{after}} = \boldsymbol{v}_A^{\text{before}} + \frac{p\boldsymbol{N}}{m_A}$$

where m_A is the mass of body A, and

$$\omega_A^{\text{after}} = \omega_A^{\text{before}} + \boldsymbol{I}_A^{-1} (\boldsymbol{r}_A \times p\boldsymbol{N})$$

Similar expressions can be obtained for body B. Deriving the relative velocities as a function of p and the equations for the velocity and angular velocity of A and B, and using the previous equation yields:

$$p = \frac{-(1-e)\boldsymbol{V}_{\text{rel}}^{\text{before}}}{\dfrac{1}{m_A} + \dfrac{1}{m_B} + \boldsymbol{N} \cdot (\boldsymbol{I}_A^{-1}(\boldsymbol{r}_A \times \boldsymbol{N})) \times \boldsymbol{r}_A + \boldsymbol{N} \cdot (\boldsymbol{I}_B^{-1}(\boldsymbol{r}_B \times \boldsymbol{N})) \times \boldsymbol{r}_B}$$

If a moving body collides with a large mass static body, which we can assume does not move at all, then $1/m$ can be set to zero and I is a zero matrix.

Particle animation

Particle animation is a classic technique that was invented more than a decade ago. It has found wide acceptance and is still a popular tool. The basic idea is that certain (natural) phenomena can be simulated by scripting the movement of and rendering a large population of individual particles. A particle is usually a primitive whose geometrical extent is small or zero – that is, many particles can project into a single pixel extent – but which possesses certain fixed attributes such as colour. Each particle is scripted and the idea is that rendering a population of particles from frame to frame produces a sort of cloud object that can grow, shrink, move, change shape etc. An animation may involve literally tens or hundreds of thousands of particles and supplying an individual script for each one is out of the question. Rather, a general script is provided for each particle with in-built random behaviour which produces the requisite differences for each particle as the position, say, of the particle evolves over time. Different phenomena are modelled by using general particle scripts and varying the attribute of the particle, such as colour. For example, in simulating a firework the basic particle script may be a parabola. Parameters that would be varied for each particle may include the start point of the parabola, its shape parameters, the colour of the particle as a function of its position along its parabolic path and its lifetime (extinction) along the path.

Thus the dynamic behaviour of the particles and their appearance, as a function of time, can be merged into the same script. Stochastic processes can be used to control both these aspects of particle behaviour. The overall result is an animated object such as a cloud which changes shape as the scripts for the thousands of particles that make up its overall shape are obeyed. The pioneer in this field is Reeves, who published a paper in 1983 that used particle sets to model 'fuzzy' objects such as fire and clouds. Other people have used his idea to model, for example, the behaviour of water in fountains, in waterfalls and in the spray of breaking waves.

Reeves (1983) describes the generation of a frame in an animation sequence as a process of five steps:

(1) New particles are generated and injected into the current system.

(2) Each new particle is assigned its individual attributes.

(3) Any particles that have exceeded their lifetime are extinguished.

(4) The current particles are moved according to their scripts.

(5) The current particles are rendered.

The instantaneous population of a particle cloud is controlled or scripted by an application-dependent stochastic process. For example, the number of particles generated at a particular time t can be derived from:

$$N(t) = M(t) + \text{rand}(r)V(t)$$

where $M(t)$ is the mean number of particles perturbed by a random variable of variance V. The time dependency of this equation can be used to control the overall growth (or contraction) in cloud size.

Reeves (1983) used a linear time dependency with constant variance in the examples given, but he points out that the control can incorporate quadratic, cubic or even stochastic variations. The number of particles can also be related to the screen size of the object – a mechanism that allows the amount of computation undertaken to relate to the final size of the object.

Although this mechanism will clearly contribute something to shape evolution of the cloud; this is also determined by individual particle scripts. The combination of these two scripting mechanisms was used to animate phenomena such as an expanding wall of fire used in the motion picture *Star Trek II: The Wrath of Khan*, and has been used to simulate multicoloured fireworks. Individual particle scripting is based on the following attributes:

(1) Initial position.

(2) Initial velocity and direction.

(3) Initial size.

(4) Initial transparency.

(5) Shape.

(6) Lifetime.

Velocity and lifetime scripts can be based on dynamic constraints. An explosion, for example, may cause a particle to be ejected upwards and then pulled down under the influence of gravity. Associated with both the attribute script and the population script is a 'generation shape' – a geometric region about the origin of the particle cloud into which 'newly born' particles are placed. For example, an exploding firework might have a spherical generation shape. Figure 17.32 is an example of part of an animation sequence produced using these techniques.

Although the applications Reeves (1983) described are generally growing phenomena, where the population of the particle cloud tends to increase, the method is general enough to model phenomena where, say, the population remains constant, while the shape of the cloud perturbs or where the population decreases or implodes. As we have already pointed out, the final object appearance is determined from the net effect of individually rendering all the particles. Rendering is carried out by simply treating each particle as a single light source and using the final value of the appearance parameters.

In a later paper Reeves and Blau (1985) further develop particle systems. Moving away from using particles to model amorphous and continually changing shapes, they use them as 'volume filling' primitives to generate solid shapes whose form then remains generally constant, but which have the ability to change shape in such situations as blades of grass moving in the wind. These

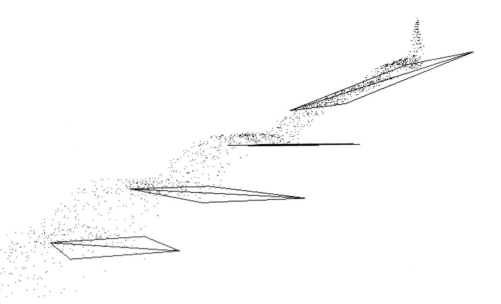

Figure 17.32
An example of physically based particle animation. A stream of particles is released at the top of the space and falls under gravity, bouncing off each step.

techniques were used in the film *The Adventures of André and Wally B* to generate the three-dimensional background images of a forest and grass.

The primary significance of particle systems in this context is not their ability to model shape-changing objects, but rather the property of 'database amplification' – the ability of a simple database to describe the general characteristics of an object that can then be modelled to the required level of detail. Objects are modelled with a resulting complexity that is far higher than that obtainable by conventional techniques. For example, in a forest scene, Reeves (1983) states that, typically, well over a million particles will be generated from basic tree descriptions.

17.8 Behavioural animation

Behavioural animation is, in many of its manifestations, an elaboration of particle animation. Usually we set up a kind of rudimentary 'sociological' model involving the behaviour of a population of entities (or a single entity). The significant difference between behavioural and particle animation is that in behavioural animation each entity is allocated a set of rules that govern its behaviour as a function of its relationship (usually spatial) to neighbouring entities.

An early and influential example of a behavioural model was developed by Reynolds (1987) to simulate the flocking phenomenon in birds and fishes. Here, each bird or fish possessed a set of rules that governed its behaviour with respect to neighbouring members of the group which was controlled by supplying global direction vectors. This basic idea was used to great effect in the Disney production *The Lion King* (1994) where a stampede sequence was controlled in this way.

Reynolds (1987) points out that flocking behaviour consists of two opposing factors – a desire to stay close to the flock and a desire to avoid collision within the flock. He simulated this behaviour as three rules which in order of decreasing precedence are:

(1) Collision avoidance: avoid collisions with nearby flock mates.

(2) Velocity matching: attempt to match the velocity of nearby flock mates.

(3) Flock centring: attempt to stay close to nearby flock mates.

The behaviour of the model is summarized by Reynolds (1987) as follows:

The flocking model described gives birds an eagerness to participate in an acceptable approximation of flock-like motion. Birds released near one another begin to flock together cavorting and jostling for position. The birds stay near one another (flock centring) but always maintain prudent separation from their neighbours (collision avoidance), and the flock becomes quickly 'polarized' – its members heading in approximately the same direction at approximately the same speed (velocity matching); when they change direction they do it in synchronization. Solitary birds and smaller flocks join to become larger flocks, and in the presence of external obstacles, larger flocks can be split into smaller flocks.

From the pioneering work of Reynolds we now look at a recent ambitious system of behavioural animation. This work by Tu and Terzopoulos (1994), simulating the behaviour of fish, is a self-animating system where the models are equipped with rudimentary vision, a physics-based locomotion capacity that reacts with hydrodynamic forces to simulate swimming behaviour and a set of behavioural rules. This appears to be the first attempt in computer animation to integrate all these aspects into one system.

The autonomous model that makes up each fish is made up of different levels of abstraction. Internal to the fish body is an 'animate spring–mass system'. This is a set of 23 nodes interconnected by 91 springs – some of the springs also serving as contractile muscles. The position of the nodes control the shape of the fish. The fish swims as a real fish by contracting its muscles – decreasing the rest length of a muscle spring. The characteristic swinging of the tail, for example, is set up by contracting muscles on one side of the body while simultaneously relaxing muscles on the other side. An equation is set up for each node relating the mass and acceleration of the node together with the forces exerted, through the springs, from all other nodes to the external hydrodynamic force. These equations are solved at each timestep to give the overall movement of the nodes. Thus the basis of this part of the model is a cloud of nodal points moving forwards through the water and at the same time moving with respect to each other. Motion is initiated by motion controllers which translate a desired action such as swimming ahead or turning into detailed muscle actions.

To these nodes is coupled the control points of a parametric surface which models the skin of the fish. This results in a deformable body whose deformation is controlled by the underlying physical model. Additionally, controlling the orientation of fins gives pitch, yaw and roll control to the basic motion. To this model, which successfully imitates fish locomotion to a high level of fidelity, is added a behaviour system to which is input information from a rudimentary visual perception and a temperature sensor. The visual sensor extracts such information as the colour, size, distance and identity of objects that enter its field of view.

The behavioural aspect is implemented by as a set of routines that generates the appropriate actions to control the muscles. These are selected by an intention generator which selects a behaviour based on the sensory information, the fish's current mental state and its habits. Habits are represented as parameters and the mental state by variables. A state such as hunger is incremented by time and decremented when a fish eats a food particle. The behavioural routines simulate such activities as avoid-static-obstacle, avoid-fish, eat-food, mate, escape, school etc. A representation of information flow in a fish model is shown in Figure 17.33.

The developers claim that their system yields 'some astonishing behaviours' and indeed their production 'Go Fish' is extremely impressive. The visual success of their animations, however, begs some questions. Again, we see problems with artistic freedom. If all the animation is to emerge from the model, how can animators use the tool? What are the potential applications of complete self-animation? – As an experimental testbed on which behavioural scientists can test or simulate their theories? As a virtual environment? The authors make this

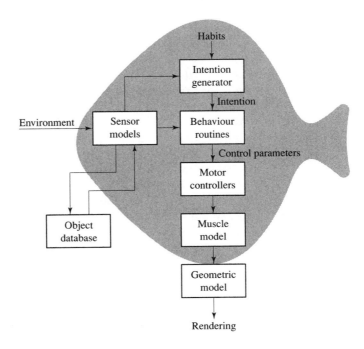

Figure 17.33
Information flow in the artificial fish (after Tu and Terzopoulos (1994)).

exotic claim: 'We may be within reach of computational models that imitate the spawning behaviour of the female and the male, hence the evolution of new varieties of artificial fishes through simulated sexual reproduction.'

(17.9) Summary

A good way of comparing animation approaches is through the level of motion control implemented in the system, in other words the crucial issue of high-level versus low-level motion control. It is a crucial issue because for animation to pass from the hands of programmers into the artistic community requires the development of high-level scripting tools. There is an analogy here with the development of high-level languages and APIs. Originally using a computer was exclusively in the hands of machine code programs. Development of high-level program languages enabled a vast expansion of computer usage. Nowadays the almost universal use of computers is by running programs through APIs. It could be said that at the moment the ease of using computer animation is roughly equivalent to the relative ease by which people could program in the late 1960s and early 1970s with the emergence of high-level languages.

How do the terms high level and low level relate to computer animation? Consider rigid body animation by explicit scripting. In this method the animator has total control over the motion at every point in the animation sequence. This is low-level motion specification. As far as the animator is concerned there is complete artistic control over the motion – the animator has complete freedom to choose whatever motion is appropriate for the application. The price paid for this freedom is the labour involved in the specification albeit that the use of curves as a scripting form cuts the workload down to an acceptable level.

In the case of articulated structures there is a choice – at least in theory. If a forward kinematics system is used then this is a low-level motion specification – every joint has to be separately scripted. The workload depends on the complexity of the system but again the animator has complete freedom. However, even using a curve script for each link the workload is prodigious. Generally, articulated structures are ordered into a hierarchy. For example, with a leg, the structure can be represented as a tree with the hip joint as the topmost node, the knee joint as the next node down, the ankle as the node below the knee etc. An animator will script such a model by starting at the top node and working downwards. Every node 'inherits' the transformation of the node above it and so on and a problem occurs if the movement of the end effector is wrong. The animator has to start again at the topmost node and work downwards. The alternative is to use an inverse kinematics system – a high-level system. Here the animator may simply specify that a character is to walk from point A to point B. There is no control over the nature of the walk – this is evaluated by the inverse kinematics algorithm. The work is less but there is no detailed artistic control possible.

Dynamic simulation is, in most of its manifestations, a high-level specification. Some control may be invested in the variation of the parameters that have been built into the model, but usually you simply set the simulation going and the animation is calculated without any further intervention. The efficacy of the animation depends on how well the movement is simulated by the procedure(s).

Behavioural animation, as we have seen, can be totally autonomous. The system is self-animating after it is set up. All the design freedom is incorporated in designing the system. If no alterations are made to the design of the system then it only has the ability in the end to produce a very large number of animations. The artistic freedom is invested in the design of the society and the members, although an animator could have access to the system through an interface and alter, for example, the behavioural routines. The system that we discussed is impressive in the motion realism that it produces, but the technique suffers from the disadvantage that it involves highly detailed modelling strategies that are in the end restricted to one species – in this case, fish. This problem of specificity occurs often in image synthesis. It means that we design a modelling strategy, which, although it suits a particular physical reality well, does not have general applications. Classic examples here are the use of fractal strategies to model mountainous terrain and the use of L systems in the modelling of plants.

So we can conclude that, in general, the current techniques in computer animation carry a trade-off which results in a contradiction. Low-level motion specification can be inordinately tedious, especially if the animated object has many degrees of freedom, but it leaves an opportunity for the animator to invent his own motion at the cost of much work. High-level specification is easier for an artist to use but generally results in less artistic freedom. Perhaps it is the existence of this contradiction that has prevented the dissemination of computer animation, which its attendant advantages, into the artistic community, and the continuance of animation as a manual art form.

18 Comparative image study

18.1 Local reflection models

18.2 Texture and shadow mapping

18.3 Whitted ray tracing

18.4 Radiosity

18.5 RADIANCE

18.6 Summary

Introduction

This section takes the form of a comparative image study that attempts to illustrate the visual differences between the mainstream rendering techniques that have been described in the text. The images should be viewed on a monitor rather than looking at the colour plates; some of the defects produced by renderers are difficult to reproduce but are nevertheless visible on the screen. This study comprises a small part of a 400-image study on the CD-ROM.

The treatment is based on an old idea of using the same scene (as far as possible) as input to different renderers. This enables a good comparison of the wide differences between the methods, visual differences that are not too apparent when one views individual scenes 'tuned' for a particular renderer. The imagery is used to illustrate both the advantages and defects of the different methods. The original scene used contains around 10 000 polygons. This is too many for a naive intersection test ray tracer and far too many for a radiosity renderer where one polygon equals one patch. The ray tracing problem can be solved by using spatial partitioning. In the radiosity case the relationship between the representation and the rendering method is far more difficult and we will demonstrate some possibilities with an example.

Detail in the scene has been changed slightly between the examples according to the point that is being illustrated and the rendering method. The small (specular) objects have been removed for the radiosity examples.

The material deals with the following topics:

- Local reflection models and interpolative shading.
- Texture and shadow mapping.
- Whitted (light backwards or eye) ray tracing.
- Radiosity using scene subdivision.
- RADIANCE renderer.

18.1 Local reflection models

This first series of illustrations is the standard cost–image quality used in mainstream polygon mesh rendering. Low quality images are used to preview and tune work.

Figure 18.1 (Colour Plate)
An office scene, together with a wireframe visualization, that has been shaded using the constant ambient term only.

Figure 18.2 (Colour Plate)
The same scene using flat shading. Flat shading shows the polygonal nature of the surfaces due to discontinuities in intensity.

Figure 18.3 (Colour Plate)
The office scene with Gouraud shading.

There are three highly visible defects in shaded imagery that uses interpolative techniques. The first always occurs in Gouraud shaded imagery and is called Mach banding. This is almost impossible to reproduce in a text (but is usually visible on a monitor) and we will restrict ourselves to a description. If we consider the light intensity profile across the surface of a polygon mesh object then this will be piecewise linear as shown in Figure 18.4 (Colour Section). When the surface is viewed on the screen the human visual system sees bands or lines on the surface that correspond to the polygon edges. These do not physically exist but are the response of low-level processing in the retina to the piecewise linear changes in the light intensity. They appear as faint but still discernible bands that appear to exhibit a lighter intensity than the surrounding surface. (They also appear in radiosity images that use Gouraud style interpolation to calculate the final projected image.)

Interpolation defects in Gouraud shading manifest as unwanted changes in light intensity across a surface. This problem is clearly visible in Figure 18.3 on the wall adjacent to the door. Here the discontinuities occur on scan lines as the edges that are being used in the interpolation switch (see Section 1.5 for the interpolation equations used to produce this illustration). This can be solved by subdividing the large polygon into triangles – in other words, we have to sample the geometry more accurately; we cannot necessarily map large flat areas into single polygons without considering the consequences in the renderer.

Figure 18.5 (Colour Plate)
This is the same scene using Phong shading.

A glaring defect in Phong interpolation is demonstrated in this figure. Here the reflected light from the wall light and the image of the light have become separated due to the nature of the interpolation. In this case, to calculate the reflection we have interpolated using equal steps along a scan line in screen space. However, the image of the light appears in a different position because this has been mapped from world space using a perspective projection. In other words, the screen space projection uses equal pixel units along the wall but these do not correspond to equal length units in world space. This problem, and others that occur when we try to include a light source as part of the scene, is a motivation for excluding lights from rendered scenes. Consider the spherical light. Treating it as a shaded object does not quite work. In this case the point light source is inside the surrounding sphere and cannot by definition illuminate it. The light object can only get illumination from the wall light and we can turn up the ambient component for the point light to make it look more like a source.

Figure 18.6 (Colour Plate)
This is a zoom on one of the wall lights. The top row compares Gouraud and Phong shading. If the polygon mesh resolution is sufficiently high the difference between Gouraud and Phong shading can be quite subtle. As the size of the polygons approaches single pixels in screen space, Gouraud shading approaches Phong shading. In the bottom row the polygonal resolution has been reduced. Here the Gouraud highlight disappears because none of the mesh vertices is close to it.

18.2 Texture and shadow mapping

We continue down the cost–image quality hierarchy with the standard 'add-on' effects of texture mapping and shadow mapping.

Figure 18.7 (Colour Plate)
The office scene with 'traditional' two-dimensional texture maps. The addition of apparent complexity/'reality'/visual interest of simple textures to a Phong shaded scene is the reason for its enduring popularity. If anything, the addition of textures makes a scene look less real in the sense that its obvious computer signature is increased.

Figure 18.8 (Colour Plate)
The same scene with shadow and environment mapping (the teapot) added. The resolution on the shadow maps are 256 × 256 and this causes geometric aliasing – as is apparent in the leaf shadow on the wall which has actually broken up. Note that there is 'interaction' between shadow mapping and environment mapping; the order of operations is important. In this image the environment map was computed before the shadow map and hence the shadow of the teapot does not appear in the reflections of the teapot.

Alternatively, we can generate the shadow map for the whole scene including the teapot then remove it and compute the environment map. The teapot is then reinserted in the scene for the rendering and environment mapping will now include its shadow.

Note also the shadow edge definition. The inadequacies are due to the spatial resolution of the shadow map which here is 256 × 256 for each component.

Figure 18.9 (Colour Plate)
This is a comparison between generating reflections using environment mapping and ray tracing. The demonstration illustrates the extent of geometric distortion introduced by environment mapping. The 'incorrectness' is a function of the size of the object in the environment – as the object approaches a point the reflections become correct. Another defect of environment mapping is that it does not implement self-reflections – the teapot does not contain a reflection of its spout. When the environment map is generated the object is 'removed' from the scene.

A point worth noting is that in ray tracing it is easy to assign a global specular reflectivity coefficient to as many objects as we require. With environment mapping we have to create a separate map for each object.

18.3 Whitted ray tracing

The next three illustrations are demonstrations of certain aspects of the mainstream ray tracing technique – Whitted or recursive ray tracing using infinitesimally thin beams traced through a subdivided object space.

Figure 18.10 (Colour Plate)
The scene ray traced using a Whitted-type ray tracer. In this scene there are around 10 000 polygons and a naive or brute force intersection test, where each spawned ray is tested against every polygon in the scene, would result in a very long execution time. The scene was thus ray traced using an octree representation. Although the differences between this and the Phong shaded scene are obvious, a few points are worth observing. The shadows are hard edged which is the normal option in ray tracing. (At each intersection point a light ray is shot to the point source.) These look wrong and it is far more difficult to implement or approximate soft shadows in a ray tracer compared with building such a facility into a shadow mapper (see the previous figure).

Another effect that looks 'wrong' is the blue glass vase by the door. Here the sharp reflection of the shadow on the wall makes the vase look as if it possesses a black band rather than reflecting detail.

In ray tracing we generate a set of initial rays that sample the scene geometry. In the simple case of an orthographic projection, this bundle would emerge from the image plane parallel. After the first hit all this parallel bundle will diverge and converge depending on the nature of the surfaces that the initial rays hit. In general this will mean that all the second hit surfaces will be sampled with a lower density of rays and so on down through the recursion. This means that reflected images become poorer as a function of the recursive depth (see next figure). At the same time the defects become less noticeable as the reflections within reflections become smaller and smaller.

Figure 18.11 (Colour Plate)
A recursive depth demonstration. Shown is the teapot–mirror interaction for a depth of 2, 3, 4 and 5 respectively. Both objects are perfect reflectors and have no local component. All colour has to come from the global specular component. Terminating the recursion results in an unknown component which is rendered as grey. A grey 'shadow' of the teapot recurses into the mirror. The interesting point here is shown in the zoom images which show the light cord breaking up as a function of recursive depth.

Figure 18.12 (Colour Plate)
These three images demonstrate the mutual exclusivity of standard ray tracing and radiosity as far as the nature of the global interaction that each attends to is concerned.

Figure 18.12(a) is a ray traced image of the scene with the main light turned off emphasizing that ray tracing omits all light paths except LDE and LDS*E. In this scene, which is not untypical of interiors, most of the global interaction is diffuse–diffuse (that is, indirect lighting from the upward facing lights on the wall) and ray tracing is thus wholly inappropriate. Figure 18.12(b) is the previous scene with an 'ambient lift'. The value of the ambient component is the same as that used to render the scene with the main light on (Figure 18.10), and is supposed to be a substitute for the illumination which would be present if diffuse–diffuse interaction had been considered. Figure 18.12(c) is a radiosity rendered image, with ray tracing for the specular objects, and the main light turned off. (The ray traced component has been included to facilitate a comparison with the next illustration.) The rest of the room is now visible since radiosity methods account for diffuse interreflections.

Figure 18.13 (Colour Plate)
Ray tracing is particularly appropriate for the incorporation of a non-uniform sampling approach (Figure 18.13 Colour Plate) because it allows us to generate initial rays anywhere in the image plane. (This contrasts with polygon mesh

rendering, where the most commonly used rendering strategy dictates that calculation intervals are equally spaced in the image plane.)

Non-uniform sampling appears in Whitted's original paper where he uses a classic adaptive refinement scheme. Initial rays are generated at the rate of one per pixel – the standard first approximation. The calculated intensity values at four pixel corners are then compared and if they differ by more than a pre-specified threshold then the pixel is recursively subdivided until the threshold limit is achieved or the resolution limit is reached. To reconstruct a final value for a pixel the contribution of each sub-pixel area is weighted by its area. The process is represented in Figure 14.12 which details the numerical weighting of the samples when a pixel is subdivided. Embedded in this algorithm is a refinement test and a method of combining (or reconstructing and filtering) the intensities returned from the new rays into a single value. The refinement test uses intensity values on a weighted area basis. These are particular solutions and since Whitted published his classic paper many other approaches to the refinement strategy and reconstruction problem have been published.

These illustrations demonstrate the efficacy of context-free versus context sensitive anti-aliasing. The images are respectively, no anti-aliasing, supersampling at 3× the screen resolution and the context-sensitive scheme just described. Note that there is no apparent difference between the two anti-aliased versions. The normal scheme involves 9× the work of the anti-aliased version whereas the context sensitive scheme is just over 1.5×.

18.4 Radiosity

The radiosity illustrations were produced using a progressive refinement hemicube based method.

Figure 18.14 (Colour Plate)
This illustration shows a radiosity version of the scene. One of the noticeable differences between this image and previous ones is the effect of so-called colour bleeding – the image colours are different. Because of diffuse–diffuse interaction the colour from a diffuse surface is transmitted to adjacent patches. This is particularly noticeable on the ceiling. The 'apparentness' of colour bleeding in real life is debatable. In other words we may not perceive much colour bleeding – which can be measured instrumentally – because of the perceptual predominance of colour constancy. This means that we, as human beings, tend to see the colour of an object as a constant attribute of the object irrespective of the colour of the light illuminating it. Thus the question arises: should we include this effect in image synthesis or not. Certainly, colour bleeding is 'fixed' in photographs and seems to be more apparent in a photograph of a scene than is experienced by actually viewing the scene from the camera point. Figure 18.15(a) (Colour Plate) is a photograph taken at midday in the bright light of Rio de Janeiro. The colour bleeding is vividly apparent even at a distance.

Figure 18.15(b) (Colour Plate) is a radiosity image showing colour bleeding from a coloured light source onto the walls and the colour bleeding that results from window light reflecting from a coloured object. These have been taken from near convergence and the effect, although correct as far as the algorithm is concerned, somehow looks wrong. This may be due in part to the different way in which our colour constancy works in a real environment compared with viewing a photograph. The reflectivity of the cylinder was set at 0.85. It may also be a consequence of the fact that a solution is only computed at three wavelengths.

Figure 18.16 (Colour Plate)

Most serious defects in the radiosity method are due to inadequate meshing. Although there are other visual defects produced by the radiosity method – notably problems due to the finite size of the hemicube cells and Mach banding due to the interpolation – those that result from inadequate meshing or subdivision are usually the most visible. The most common results of inadequate meshing are blocky shadows, shadow leakage and light leakage. Unless the scene is extremely simple or constructed to take these artefacts into account, they will always occur.

As we know, the radiosity method calculates a view-independent solution from a scene database that has been subdivided into elements called patches. The solution assigns a constant radiosity to each patch and Gouraud-type interpolation is then used to provide a linearly varying light intensity across the patches. The radiosity method can only be made to work in a reasonable time by making these patches fairly large and this implies that a basic radiosity algorithm that uses arbitrary subdivision will always produce image defects.

This image was computed using a 'minimum' representation. The wireframe is a triangulated version of the representation shown in Figure 18.1 and is the most basic subdivision that we could try a radiosity solution with. Despite the fact that there are many more polygons than in the original scene the quality is unacceptably low due to shadow and light leakage.

Figure 18.17 (Colour Plate)

The three pairs of images in this illustration show the effect of a subdivision strategy (as described in Section 11.7.1) operating within a progressive refinement framework. The relationship between increasing subdivision and image quality is obvious. Examination of the image and the mesh for the final image pair illustrates a problem with the subdivision. This is that the mesh exhibits subdivided areas which appear not to be required. Look at 'streaks' near the door. Bear in mind that subdivisions occur after every patch is shot and areas that are subdivided because of this may subsequently be illuminated by energy shot from other patches.

Figure 18.18 (Colour Plate)
Despite the high level of subdivision exhibited by the last pair of images in Figure 18.17, light leakage is still apparent around the wall lights. This can be completely eliminated, as this illustration shows, by meshing the area around a wall light after considering the interpenetrating geometry. Now the wall patch boundaries coincide with the light patch boundaries.

18.5 RADIANCE

The RADIANCE renderer is a global illumination renderer that deals with scenes that contain both specular and diffuse objects.

Figure 18.19 (Colour Plate)
The scene is rendered using the RADIANCE renderer. This has a slight grainy appearance compared with the other images which is due to the way in which the diffuse interreflection is sampled (see Section 10.9).

18.6 Summary

Comparing the various images it is apparent that they exhibit many differences. Possibly the more noticeable of these concern light levels and colour shifts. Only a cursory attempt was made to match object properties and light levels through each interface – apart from the obvious algorithmic attributes (hard-edged versus soft-edged shadows, for example). It is difficult to deduce what differences are due to the different models and methodology of the algorithms and which are due to inadequate tuning through the renderers' interfaces. This is an enduring practical problem encountered when using renderers.

References

Abram A. G., Westover L. and Whitted T. (1985). Efficient alias-free rendering using bit-masks and lookup tables. *Computer Graphics*, **19** (3), 53–9

Appel A. (1968). Some techniques for machine rendering of solids. *AFIPS Conference Proc*, **32**, 37–45

Arvo J. (1986), Backwards ray tracing, developments in ray tracing. *SIGGRAPH Course Notes*, **12**

Arvo J. and Kirk D. (1987). Fast ray tracing by ray classification. *Computer Graphics*, **21**(4), 55–64. (*Proc. SIGGRAPH '87*)

Atherton P., Weiler K. and Greenberg D. (1978). Polygon shadow generation. *Computer Graphics*, **12** (3), 275–81

Balakrishnan A. V. (1962). On the problem of time jitter in sampling. *IRE Trans. on Information Theory* (April 1962), pp. 226–36

Barr A. H. (1984). Global and local deformations of solid primitives. *Computer Graphics*, **18** (3), 21–30

Bartels R., Beatty J. and Barsky B. (1987). *An Introduction to Splines for use in Computer Graphics and Geometric Modelling*. Los Altos CA: Morgan Kaufmann

Bartels R. H., Beatty J. C. and Barsky B. A. (1988). *Splines for Use in Computer Graphics and Geometric Modeling*. Los Altos CA: Morgan Kaufmann

Baum D. R., Rushmeier H. E. and Winget J. M. (1989). Improving radiosity solutions through the use of analytically determined form factors. *Proc. SIGGRAPH '89*, pp. 325–34

Bergeron P. (1986). Une version générale de l'algorithme des ombres projetées de Crow basée sur le concept de volumes d'ombre. MSc Thesis. University of Montreal

Bier E. A. and Sloan K. R. (1986). Two-part texture mapping. *IEEE Computer Graphics and Applications*, **6** (9), 40–53

Blinn J. F. (1977). Models of light reflection for computer synthesized pictures. *Computer Graphics*, **11** (2), 192–8

Blinn J. F. (1978). Simulation of wrinkled surfaces. *Computer Graphics*, **12** (3), 286–92

Blinn J. F. (1988). Me and my (fake) shadow. *IEEE Computer Graphics and Applications*, **8** (1), 82–6

Blinn J. F. and Newell M. E. (1976). Texture and reflection in computer generated images. *Comm. ACM*, **19** (10), 362–7

Borges C. F. (1991). Trichromatic approximation for computer graphics illumination models. *Computer Graphics*, **25** (4), 101–4 (*Proc. SIGGRAPH '91*)

Bouknight W. J. and Kelly K. (1970) An algorithm for producing half-tone computer graphics presentations with shadows and moveable light sources. *Proc. AFIPS, Spring Joint Computer Conf.*, **36**, 1–10

Bresenham J. E. (1965). Algorithm for computer control of a digital plotter. *IBM Systems J.*, January, 25–30

Brotman L. S. and Badler N. I. (1984). Generating soft shadows with a depth buffer algorithm. *IEEE Computer Graphics and Applications*, **4** (10), 5–12

Cabral B., Max N. and Springmeyer R. (1987). Bidirectional reflection functions from surface bump maps. *Computer Graphics*, **21** (4), 273–81. (*Proc. SIGGRAPH '87*)

Carpenter L. C. (1984). The A-buffer, an anti-aliased hidden surface method. *Computer Graphics*, **18** (3), 103–8

Catmull E. (1974). Subdivision algorithm for the display of curved surfaces. PhD Thesis, University of Utah

Catmull E. (1975). Computer display of curved surfaces. In *Proc. IEEE Conf. on Computer Graphics, Pattern Recognition and Data Structures*, May 1975 (Reprinted in Freeman H. (ed.) (1980). *Tutorial and Selected Readings in Interactive Computer Graphics*. New York (IEEE), pp. 309–15)

Catmull E. (1978). A hidden surface algorithm with anti-aliasing. *Computer Graphics*, **12** (3), 6–10

Clark J. H. (1979). A fast scan line algorithm for rendering parametric surfaces. *Computer Graphics*, **13** (2), 289–99

Cohen J. D., Lin M. C., Manocha D. and Pongami M. K. (1995). I-COLLIDE: An interactive and exact collision detection system for large scale environments. *Proc. 1995 Symp. on Interactive 3D Graphics* (Monterey CA) pp. 291–302

Cohen M. F. (1992). Interactive spacetime control for animation. *Proc. SIGGRAPH '92*, pp. 293–302

Cohen M. F. and Greenberg D. P. (1985). A radiosity solution for complex environments. *Computer Graphics*, **19** (3), 31–40

Cohen M. F. and Wallace J. R. (1993). *Radiosity and Realistic Image Synthesis*. Boston MA: Academic Press Professional, Harcourt Brace and Co.

Cohen M. F., Greenberg D. P. and Immel D. S. (1986). An efficient radiosity approach for realistic image synthesis. *IEEE Computer Graphics and Applications*, **6** (2), 26–35

Cohen M. F., Chen S. E., Wallace J. R. and Greenberg D. P. (1988). A progressive refinement approach to fast radiosity image generation. *Computer Graphics*, **22** (4), 75–84

Cook R. L. (1986) Stochastic sampling in computer graphics. *ACM Trans. on Computer Graphics*, **5** (1), 51–72

Cook R. L. and Torrance K. E. (1982). A reflectance model for computer graphics. *Computer Graphics*, **15** (3), 307–16

Cook R. L., Porter T. and Carpenter L. (1984). Distributed ray tracing. *Computer Graphics*, **18** (3), 137–45

Cook R. L., Carpenter L. and Catmull E. (1987). The REYES images rendering architecture. *Computer Graphics*, **21** (4), 95–102

Cowan W. B. (1983). An inexpensive scheme for the calibration of a colour monitor in terms of CIE standard coordinates. *Computer Graphics*, **17**, 315–21

Cox M. G. (1972). The numerical evalutation of B-splines. *J. Inst. Maths. Applics.*, **10**, 134–49

Crow F. C. (1977). Shadow algorithms for computer graphics. *Computer Graphics*, **13** (2), 242–8

Crow F. C. (1981). A comparison of anti-aliasing techniques. *IEEE Computer Graphics and Applications*, **1** (1), 40–8

Crow F. C. (1987). The origins of the teapot. *IEEE Computer Graphics and Applications*, **7** (1), 8–19

Debevec P. E., Taylor C. J. and Malik J. (1996). Modelling and rendering architecture from photographs: a hybrid geometry and image based approach. *Proc. SIGGRAPH '96*, pp. 11–20

De Boor C. (1972). On calculating with B-splines. *J. Approx. Th.*, **6**, 50–62

Drebin R. A., Carpenter L. and Hanrahan P. (1988). Volume rendering. *Computer Graphics*, **22** (4), 65–74

Duff T. (1985). Compositing 3-D rendered images. *Computer Graphics*, **19** (3), 41–4

Duff T. (1986). Splines in animation and modelling. *SIGGRAPH Course Notes*, **15**

Farin G. (1990). *Curves and Surfaces for Computer Aided Design*. 2nd edn. Boston: Academic Press

Faux I. D. and Pratt M. J. (1979). *Computational Geometry for Design and Manufacture*. Chichester: Ellis Horwood

Fiume E., Fournier A. and Rudolph L. (1983). A parallel scan conversion algorithm with anti-aliasing for a general-purpose ultracomputer. *Computer Graphics*, **17** (3), 141–50

Foley J. D., Van Dam A., Feiner S. K. and Hughes J. F. (1989). *Computer Graphics: Principles and Practice*. Reading MA: Addison-Wesley

Forsey D. R. and Bartels R. H. (1988). Hierarchical B-spline refinement. *Computer Graphics*, **22** (4), 205–12

Fournier A., Fussell D. and Carpenter L. (1982). Computer rendering of stochastic models. *Comm. ACM*, **25** (6), 371–84

Fuchs H. (1980). On visible surface generation by *a priori* tree structures. *Computer Graphics*, **14**, 124–33

Fujimoto A., Tanaka T. and Iwata K. (1986). ARTS: Accelerated ray tracing system. *IEEE Computer Graphics and Applications*, **6** (4), 16–26

Glassner A. S. (1984). Space subdivision for fast ray tracing. *IEEE Computer Graphics and Applications*, **4** (10), 15–22

Glassner A. S. (1995). *Principles of Digital Image Synthesis*. San Francisco CA: Morgan Kaufmann Pubs Inc.

Goral C., Torrance K. E., Greenberg D. P. and Battaile B. (1984). Modelling the interaction of light between diffuse surfaces. *Computer Graphics*, **18** (3), 212–22

Gortler S., Grzeszczuk R., Szeliski R. and Cohen M. F. (1996). The lumigraph. *Proc. SIGGRAPH '96*, pp. 43–52

Gottschalk S., Lin M. C. and Manocha D. (1996). OBB trees: A hierarchical structure for rapid interference detection. *Proc. SIGGRAPH '96*, pp. 171–80

Gouraud H. (1971). Illumination for computer generated pictures. *Comm. ACM*, **18** (60), 311–17

Gray J. (1968). *Animal Locomotion*. London: Weidenfeld and Nicolson

Greene N. (1986). Environment Mapping and Other Applications of World Projections. *IEEE Computer Graphics and Applications*, **6** (11), 21–9

Greene N., Kass M. and Miller G. (1993). Hierarchical Z-buffer visibility. *Proc. SIGGRAPH '93*, 231–8

Greger G., Shirley P., Hubbard P. M. and Greenberg D. (1998). The irradiance volume. *IEEE Computer Graphics and Applications*, March/April, pp. 32–43

Griffiths J. G. (1984). A depth-coherence scan line algorithm for displaying curved surfaces. *Computer Aided Design*, **16** (2), 91–101

Haeberli P. E. and Akeley K. (1990). The accumulation buffer: hardware support for high-quality rendering. *Computer Graphics (Proc. SIGGRAPH '90)* **24**, August, pp. 309–318

Haeberli P. and Segal M. (1993). Texture Mapping as a Fundamental Drawing Primitive. From: http://www.sgi.com/grafica/texmap/index.html

Haines E. (1991). Essential ray–convex polyhedron intersection. In *Graphics Gems II*, Arvo. J. (ed.) pp. 247–50. Boston: Harcourt Brace Jovanovich

Haines E. A. and Greenberg D. P. (1986). The light buffer: a shadow-testing accelerator. *IEEE Computer Graphics and Applications*, **6** (9), 6–16

Hall R. A. (1989). *Illumination and Color in Computer Generated Imagery*. New York: Springer-Verlag

Hall R. A. and Greenberg D. P. (1983). A testbed for realistic image synthesis. *IEEE Computer Graphics and Applications*, **3** (8), 10–19

Hallas J. and Manvell R. (1971). *The Techniques of Film Animation*. 3rd edn. London: Focal Press

Hanrahan P. and Haeberli P. (1990). Direct WYSIWYG painting and texturing on 3D shapes. *Proc. SIGGRAPH '90*, pp. 287–96

Hanrahan P. and Kreuger W. (1993). Reflection from layered surfaces due to sub-surface scattering. *Proc. SIGGRAPH '93*, pp. 165–74

Hanrahan P., Salzman D. and Aupeperle L. (1991). A rapid hierarchical radiosity algorithm. *Proc. SIGGRAPH '91*, pp. 197–206

He X. D., Torrance K. E., Sillion F. X. and Greenberg D. P. (1991). A comprehensive physical model for light reflection. *Computer Graphics*, **25** (4), 175–86

Heckbert P. S. (1986). Survey of texture mapping. *IEEE Computer Graphics and Applications*, **6** (11), 56–67

Heckbert P. S. (1990) Adaptive radiosity textures for bi-directional ray tracing. *Proc. SIGGRAPH '90*, pp. 145–54

Heckbert P. S. and Hanrahan P. (1984). Beam tracing polygonal objects. *Computer Graphics*, **18** (3), 119–27

Hoppe H. (1996). Progressive meshes. *Proc. SIGGRAPH '96*, pp. 99–108

Hubbard P. M. (1993). Interactive collision detection. *Proc. IEEE Symp. on Res. Frontiers in Virtual Reality*, pp. 24–31

Hubbard P. M. (1996). *ACM Transactions on Graphics*, **15** (3), July, 179–210

Kajiya J. T. (1986). The rendering equation. *Proc. SIGGRAPH '80*, pp. 143–50

Kaplan M. R. (1985). Space Tracing, a constant time ray tracer. *SIGGRAPH '85 Course Notes*, San Francisco CA, July

Lafortune E. P. and Williams Y. D. (1995). A 5D tree to reduce the variance of Monte Carlo ray tracing. *Proc. 6th Eurographics Workshop on Rendering*, Dublin, Ireland, June, pp. 11–20

Lane J. M. and Riesenfeld R. F. (1980). A theoretical development for the computer generation and display of piecewise polynomial surfaces. *IEEE Trans. on Pattern Analysis and Machine Intelligence*, **2** (1), 35–46

Lane J. M., Carpenter L. C., Whitted T. and Blinn J. T. (1980). Scan line methods for displaying parametrically defined surfaces. *Comm. ACM*, **23** (1), 23–34

Lengyel J. and Snyder J. (1997). Rendering with coherent layers. *Proc. SIGGRAPH '97*, pp. 233–42

Levoy M. (1990). Efficient ray tracing of volume data. *ACM Trans. on Graphics*, **9** (3), 245–61

Levoy M. and Hanrahan P. (1996). Light field rendering. *Proc. SIGGRAPH '96*, pp. 31–42

Lewis J. P. (1989). Algorithms for solid noise synthesis. *Computer Graphics*, **23** (3), 263–70

Lippman A. (1980). Movie maps: an application of the optical videodisc to computer graphics. *Proc. SIGGRAPH '80*, pp. 32–43

Lischinski D., Tampieri F. and Greenberg D. (1992). Discontinuity meshing for accurate radiosity. *IEEE Computer Graphics and Applications*, November, pp. 25–39

Liu Z., Gortler S. and Cohen M. (1994). Hierarchical spacetime control. *Proc. SIGGRAPH '94*, pp. 35–42

Lorensen W. E. and Cline H. E. (1987), Marching cubes: a high resolution 3D surface construction algorithm. *Computer Graphics*, **21** (4), 163–9

Maciel P. W. and Shirley P. (1995). Visual navigation of a large environment using textured clusters. *Symposium on Interactive 3D Graphics*, April, pp. 95–102

Mandelbrot B. (1977). *Fractals: Form, Chance and Dimension*. San Francisco CA: Freeman

Mandelbrot B. (1982). *The Fractal Geometry of Nature*. San Francisco CA: Freeman

Mantyla M. (1988). *Introduction to Solid Modelling*. Rockville MD: Computer Science Press

Mark W. R., McMillan L. and Bishop G. (1997). Post-rendering 3D warping. *Proc. 1997 Symposium on Interactive 3D Graphics*, pp. 7–16, Providence RI, April

Max N. and Troutman R. (1993). Optimal hemi-cube sampling. *4th Eurographics Workshop on Rendering* (June), pp. 185–200

McMillan L. (1995). *A List-priority Rendering Algorithm for Redisplaying Projected Surfaces.* UNC Technical Report 95-005, University of North Carolina

McReynolds T. and Blythe D. (1997). Programming with OpenGL: Advanced Rendering. From: http://www.sgi.com/software/opengl/advanced97/notes/

Miller G., Halstead M. and Clifton M. (1998). On-the-fly texture computation for real-time surface shading. *IEEE Computer Graphics and Applications*, March/April, pp. 44–58

Miller G. S. and Hoffman C. R. (1984). Illumination and reflection maps: simulated objects in simulated and real environments. *SIGGRAPH '84 Course Notes*, July

Moore M. and Wilhelms J. (1988). Collision detection and response for computer animation. *Computer Graphics*, **22** (4), 289–98

Munsell A. H. (1946). *A Color Notation.* Baltimore MD: Munsell Color Co.

Nakamae E., Harada K., Ishizaki T. and Nishita T. (1986). A montage method: the overlaying of computer generated images onto a background photograph. *Computer Graphics*, **20** (4), 207–14

Newell M. E., Newell R. G. and Sancha T. L. (1972). A new approach to the shaded picture problem. *Proc. ACM National Conf.*, pp. 443–50

Newman W. and Sproull R. (1973). *Principles of Interactive Computer Graphics.* New York: McGraw-Hill

Ney D. N., Fishman E. K., Magid D. and Drebin R. A. (1990). Volumetric rendering of computed tomography data: principles and techniques. *IEEE Computer Graphics and Applications*, **10** (2) pp. 33–40

Nishita T. and Nakamae E. (1985). Continuous tone representation of three-dimensional objects taking account of shadows and interreflection. *Computer Graphics*, **19** (3), 23–30

Novins K. L., Sillion F. X. and Greenberg D. P. (1990). An efficient method for volume rendering using perspective projection. *Computer Graphics*, **24** (5), 95–102

Oppenheim A. V. and Shafer R. W. (1975). *Digital Signal Processing.* Englewood Cliffs NJ: Prentice-Hall

Oppenheimer P. E. (1986). Real-time design and animation of plants and trees. *Proc. SIGGRAPH '86*, pp. 55–64

Peachey D. R. (1985). Solid texturing of complex surfaces. *Computer Graphics*, **19** (3), 279–86

Peercy M., Airey J. and Cabral B. (1997). Efficient bump mapping hardware. *Proc. SIGGRAPH '97*

Perlin K. (1985). An image synthesizer. *Computer Graphics*, **19** (3), 287–96

Perlin K. (1989). Hypertexture. *Computer Graphics*, **23** (3), 253–62. (*Proc. SIGGRAPH '98*)

Philips C. B. and Badler N. I. (1991). Interactive behaviour for bipedal articulated figures. *Computer Graphics*, **25** (4), 359–62. (*Proc. SIGGRAPH '91*)

Phong B. (1975). Illumination for computer-generated pictures. *Comm. ACM*, **18** (6), 311–17

Piegl L. (1993). *Fundamental Developments of Computer-Aided Geometric Modelling.* New York: Academic Press

Porter T. and Duff T. (1984). Composing digital images. *Computer Graphics*, **18** (3), 253–9

Reeves W. T. (1983). Particle systems – a technique for modelling a class of fuzzy objects. *Computer Graphics*, **17** (3), 359–76

Reeves W. T. and Blau R. (1985). Approximate and probabilistic algorithms for shading and rendering structured particle systems. *Computer Graphics*, **19** (3), 313–22

Reeves, W., Salesin, D. and Cook, R. (1987). Rendering antialiased shadows with depth maps. *Computer Graphics*, **21** (4), 283–91. (*Proc. SIGGRAPH '87*)

Regan M. and Pose R. (1994). Priority rendering with a virtual reality address re-calculation engine. *Proc. SIGGRAPH '94*, pp. 155–62

Reynolds C. W. (1987). Flocks, herds, and schools: a distributed behavioural model. *Computer Graphics*, **21** (4), 25–34

Rossignac J. R. and Requicha A. A. G. (1986). Depth buffering display techniques for constructive solid geometry. *IEEE Computer Graphics and Applications*, **6** (9), 29–39

Rubin S. M. and Whitted T. (1980). A three-dimensional representation for fast rendering of complex schemes. *Computer Graphics*, **14**, 110–16

Schaufler G. and Sturzlinger W. (1996). A 3D image cache for virtual reality. *Proc. Eurographics '96*, August, pp. 227–36

Schlick C. (1993). A customizable reflectance model for everyday rendering. *4th Eurographics Workshop on Rendering*, Puech C. and Sillion F. (eds), Amsterdam: Elsevier, pp. 73–89

Schroeder W. J., Zarge J. A. and Lorenson W. E. (1992). Decimation of triangular meshes. *Proc. SIGGRAPH '92*, 65–70

Schumaker R. A., Brand B., Guilliland M. and Sharp W. (1969). *Applying Computer Generated Images to Visual Simulation.* Technical Report AFHRL-Tr-69, US Airforce Human Resources Lab.

Schweitzer D. and Cobb E. S. (1982). Scan line rendering of parametric surfaces. *Computer Graphics*, **16** (3), 265–71

Sederburg T. W. and Parry S. R. (1986). Free-form deformation of solid geometric models. *Computer Graphics*, **20** (4), 151–60

Seitz S. M. and Dyer C. R. (1996). View morphing. *Proc. SIGGRAPH '96*, pp. 21–30

Shade J., Gortler S., He L. and Szeliski R. (1998). Layered depth images. *Proc. SIGGRAPH '98*

Shade J., Lischinski D., Salesin D., DeRose T. and Snyder J. (1996). Hierarchical image caching for accelerated walkthroughs of complex environments. *Proc. SIGGRAPH '96*, pp. 75–82

Shinya M., Takahashi T. and Naito S. (1987). Principles and applications of pencil tracing. *Computer Graphics*, **21** (4), 45–54. (*Proc. SIGGRAPH '87*).

Shoemake K. (1985). Animating rotation with quaternion curves. *Computer Graphics*, **19** (3), 245–54. (*Proc. SIGGRAPH '85*)

Shoemake K. (1987). Quarternion Calculus and Fast Animation. *SIGGRAPH Course Notes*, **10**, 101–21

Siegel R. and Howell J. R. (1984). *Thermal Radiation Heat Transfer*. Washington DC: Hemisphere Publishing

Smith A. R. (1978). Color gamut transformation pairs. *Computer Graphics*, **12**, 12–19

Speer L. R., DeRose T. D. and Barsky B. A. (1986). A theoretical and empirical analysis of coherent ray tracing. *Computer Generated Images*, **27** (31), 11–25

Snyder J. M. (1992). *Generative Modelling for Computer Graphics*. New York: Academic Press

Snyder J. M. (1998). Visibility sorting and compositing without splitting for image layer decomposition. *Proc. SIGGRAPH '98*, pp. 219–30

Sutherland I. E. and Hodgman G. W. (1974). Reentrant polygon clipping. *Comm. ACM*, **17** (1), 32–42

Sutherland I. E., Sproull R. F. and Schumacker R. (1974). A characterization of ten hidden-surface algorithms. *Computer Surveys*, **6** (1), 1–55

Swanson R. W. and Thayer L. J. (1986). A fast shaded-polygon renderer. *Computer Graphics*, **20** (4), 107–16

Tu S. and Terzopoulos D. (1994). Perceptual modelling for the behavioural animation of fishes. *Proc. Second Pacific Conf. on Computer Graphics* (PG '94), Beijing, China

The Visible Human Project, National Library of Medicine (1998). From: http://www.nlm.nih.gov/pubs/factsheets/visible_human.htn

Wallace J. R., Cohen M. F. and Greenberg D. P. (1987). A two-pass solution to the rendering equation: a synthesis of ray tracing and radiosity methods. *Computer Graphics*, **21** (4), 311–20

Wallace J. R., Kells A. E. and Haines E. (1989). A ray tracing algorithm for progressive radiosity. *Computer Graphics*, **23** (3), 315–24. (*Proc. SIGGRAPH '89*)

Walter B., Hubbard P. M., Shirley P. and Greenberg D. P. (1997). Global Illumination using local linear density estimation. *ACM Trans. on Graphics*, **16** (3) July, pp. 217–59

Ward G. J. (1994). The RADIANCE lighting simulation and rendering system. *Proc. SIGGRAPH '94*, pp. 459–71

Warn D. R. (1983). Lighting controls for synthetic images. *Computer Graphics*, **17** (3), 13–21

Warnock J. (1969). *A Hidden-Surface Algorithm for Computer Generated Half-Tone Pictures*. Technical Report 4–15; NTIS AD-753 671, University of Utah Computer Science Department

Watt A. and Policarpo F. (1998). *The Computer Image*. Harlow: Addison-Wesley

Watt A. and Watt M. (1992). *Advanced Animation and Rendering Techniques*. Wokingham, England: Addison-Wesley

Weghorst H., Hooper G. and Greenberg D. P. (1984). Improved computational methods for ray tracing. *ACM Trans. on Graphics*, **3** (1), 52–69

Weiler K. and Atherton P. (1977). Hidden surface removal using polygon area sorting. *Computer Graphics*, **11** (2), 214–22

Westover L. (1990). Footprint evaluation for volume rendering. *Computer Graphics*, **24** (4), 367–76. (*Proc. SIGGRAPH '90*)

Whitted J. T. (1978). A scan line algorithm for the computer display of curved surfaces. *Proc. 5th Conf. on Computer Graphics and Interactive Techniques*, Atlanta GA, p. 26

Whitted J. T. (1980). An improved illumination model for shaded display. *Comm. ACM*, **23** (6), 342–9

Williams L. (1978). Casting curved shadows on curved surfaces. *Computer Graphics*, **12** (3), 270–4

Williams L. (1983). Pyramidal parametrics. *Computer Graphics*, **17** (3), 1–11

Williams L. and Chen S. E. (1993). View interpolatrioin for image synthgesis. *Proc. SIGGRAPH '93*, pp. 279–88

Witkin A. and Kass M. (1988). Spacetime constraints. *Proc. SIGGRAPH '88*, pp. 159–68

Wolberg G. (1990). *Digital Image Warping*. Los Alamitos CA: IEEE Computer Society Press

Yagel R., Cohen D. and Kaufman A. (1992). Discrete ray tracing. *IEEE Computer Graphics and Applications*, **12** (5), 19–28

Yellott I. (1982). Spectral analysis of spatial sampling by photoreceptors: topological disorder prevents aliasing. *Vision Research*, **22**, 1205–10

Zhukov S., Iones A. and Kronin G. (1998). Using light maps to create realistic lighting in real-time applications. *Proc. WSCG '98*. (Central European Conf. on Computer Graphics and Visualisation 1998)

Index

IMPORTANT: READ CAREFULLY

WARNING: BY OPENING THE PACKAGE YOU AGREE TO BE BOUND BY THE TERMS OF THI LICENCE AGREEMENT BELOW.

This is a legally binding agreement between You (the user or purchaser) and Pearson Education Limited. By retaining this licence, any software media or accompanying written materials or carrying out any of the permitted activities You agree to be bound by the terms of the licence agreement below.

If You do not agree to these terms then prompt return the entire publication (this licence and software, written materials, packaging and any ot components received with it) with Your sales rece to Your supplier for a full refund.

SINGLE USER LICENCE AGREEMENT

☐ YOU ARE PERMITTED TO:

- Use (load into temporary memory or permanent storage) a single copy of the software on only one computer at a time. If this computer is linked to a network then the software may only be installed in a manner such that it is not accessible to other machines on the network.

- Make one copy of the software solely for backup purposes or copy it to a single hard disk, provided you keep the original solely for back up purposes.

- Transfer the software from one computer to another provided that you only use it on one computer at a time.

☐ YOU MAY NOT:

- Rent or lease the software or any part of the publication.

- Copy any part of the documentation, except where specifically indicated otherwise.

- Make copies of the software, other than for backup purposes.

- Reverse engineer, decompile or disassemble the software.

- Use the software on more than one computer a time.

- Install the software on any networked compute in a way that could allow access to it from mor than one machine on the network.

- Use the software in any way not specified abov without the prior written consent of Pearson Education Limited.

ONE COPY ONLY

This licence is for a single user copy of the software

PEARSON EDUCATION LIMITED RESERVES THE RIGHT TO TERMINATE THIS LICENCE BY WRITTEN NOTICE AND TO TAKE ACTION TO RECOVER ANY DAMAGES SUFFERED BY PEARSON EDUCATION LIMITED IF YOU BREACH ANY PROVISION OF THIS AGREEMENT.

Pearson Education Limited owns the software; You only own the disk on which the software is supplie

LIMITED WARRANTY

Pearson Education Limited warrants that the diskette or CD rom on which the software is supplied are free from defects in materials and workmanship under normal use for ninety (90) days from the date You receive them. This warranty is limited to You and is not transferable. Pearson Education Limited does not warrant that the functions of the software meet Your requirements or that the media is compatible with any computer system on which it is used or that the operation of the software will be unlimited or error free.

You assume responsibility for selecting the software to achieve Your intended results and for the installation of, the use of and the results obtained from the software. The entire liability of Pearson Education Limited and its suppliers and your only remedy shall be replacement of the components that do not meet this warranty free of charge.

This limited warranty is void if any damage has res from accident, abuse, misapplication, servic modification by someone other than Pe Education Limited. In no event shall Pearson Educ Limited or its suppliers be liable for any dar whatsoever arising out of installation of the sof even if advised of the possibility of such dar Pearson Education Limited will not be liable fc loss or damage of any nature suffered by any par result of reliance upon or reproduction of or any in the content of the publication.

Pearson Education Limited does not limit its for death or personal injury caused by its negligence.

This licence agreement shall be governed by and interpreted and construed in accordance with English law.